DOCUMENTING GLOBAL LEADERSHIP

Also by George Modelski

EXPLORING LONG CYCLES (*editor*)
LONG CYCLES IN WORLD POLITICS
SEAPOWER IN GLOBAL POLITICS, 1494–1993
(*with William R. Thompson*)

Also by Sylvia Modelski

THE WAY OF THE MASKS by CLAUDE LÉVI-STRAUSS (*translator*)

Documenting Global Leadership

Edited by

George Modelski

and

Sylvia Modelski

[redacted]

University of Washington Press
Seattle and London

Printed in Hong Kong

Library of Congress Cataloging-in-Publication Data
Documenting global leadership.
Edited by George Modelski and Sylvia Modelski.
Bibliography: p.
Includes index.
1. World politics—Sources. I. Modelski, George.
II. Modelski, Sylvia.
D105.D63 1988 909.82–dc19 87–34029
ISBN 0–295–96635–1

Contents

List of Documents

Maps, Tables and Illustrations

MAPS

TABLES

ILLUSTRATIONS

Acknowledgements

The documents in this book have taken a number of years and a good deal of preparation to bring together in a form suitable for publication. We are grateful for the co-operation of others in this enterprise.

Special thanks are due to the University of Washington's Suzallo Library, in particular to Eleanor Chase of the Government Publications Division and the staff of the Interlibrary Borrowing Service, and to the Law Library. The University's Department of Political Science has provided limited but essential logistic support, as has the Netherlands Institute for Advanced Study in the Humanities and Social Sciences, Wassenaar, in the closing stages of the project.

Materials were consulted at the Public Record Office, London, The Library of Congress, Washington, DC, the Archives Diplomatiques, Ministère des Relations Extérieures, Quai d'Orsay, Paris, the Algemeen Rijksarchief, The Hague, the British Library of Political and Economic Science, London, the Rockefeller Foundation Study and Conference Center at Bellagio, Italy, the University of California at Los Angeles Library, the University of California at Irvine Library, the University of Oregon Library, Eugene, and the California State University at Long Beach Library.

Additional information was sought and obtained through correspondence with Francesca Tiepolo, Archivio di Stato, Venice, the Library and Records Department of the Foreign and Commonwealth Office, London, the India Office Library, London, the British Library, London, the Biblioteca Nazionale Marciana, Venice, and the University of Chicago Library.

We wish to give our thanks for their help to Henk Nellen and Arthur Eyffinger of the Grotius Instituut, The Hague, to Kelly Osborne of the University of Washington, Robert Ross of the Centre for the History of European Expansion, University of Leiden, and Jean-Luc Vellut of Louvain University. Elsa Possolo kindly reviewed parts of Document 9.

We thank the following for permission to quote extracts from copyright works: the University of Minnesota Press (Doc. 4), the Council of the Hakluyt Society (Doc. 7), Herbert Rowen and the Princeton University Press (Doc. 11), and the Royal Institute of International Affairs (Doc. 51).

Illustrations are by permission of the British Library and the United States National Archives and Records Administration.

George Modelski
Sylvia Modelski

Introduction

> this great nation – if it is to remain
> worthy of global leadership – cannot
> manage its foreign relations as an amateur.
>
> *Cyrus Vance, former US Secretary of State*
> *(14 January 1987, addressing the*
> *Senate Foreign Relations Committee)*

The present work documents landmarks in the evolution of the foreign relations of leading states, from the start of the modern era until the mid-twentieth century. It is meant as a contribution to the professionalisation of the practice of leadership at the global level. For the responsibilities, dangers and opportunities of global leadership merit much more explicit (yet also well informed) treatment than they have received so far. And a most important need is for a memory (or genealogy) of the problems experienced by those who dared to launch great global initiatives, and of the solutions that did (or did not) serve them well.

AIMS

In this volume, we attempt to show states in the act of exercising global leadership. Not any states, but a specific set of 'lead' states or world powers, one at a time, the most recent being the United States. And, obviously, not the act itself but the traces of it left in records still extant that tell the story directly to us.

First of all, we wish to demonstrate that the goals and activities of these world powers fit their description as acts of global leadership: acts whose impact, objectively, extends beyond the national or regional sphere and carry a wider significance. It is by tackling global problems that such states have structured the situation for the world as a whole.

Secondly, we aim to show not only that these were acts of leadership as they might be understood by observers, but also that those initiating them were aware of their global role. This is the subjective side of global leadership.

Finally, by concentrating on the highlights, we offer a narrative of a half millennium of world politics. We learn from the past by hearing stories: this is a story of the modern age, told through old records, many of them long forgotten and now hard to trace. The subject of the story is simultaneously the *substance* of the process – that is, the problems that were encountered along the way – and also its *form* – the instruments used in the conduct of war and diplomacy, such as conferences, alliances, balances of power, and their development over a course of more than five centuries.

'Global leadership' is a fairly new concept in the literature of world politics (Rapkin, 1987) where, for the past generation, 'power' in its various more or less crude forms has held centre stage. We do not ignore 'power' (and seapower in particular) but we do believe that a more rounded view of politics must also consider 'purpose' and 'meaning'. Definitions, explanations and justifications of goals, motives and objectives, all general statements of policy, belong equally with 'power' in the study of world politics. The analysis of leadership accomplishes this function nicely, allowing us to translate past experience into lessons for the future.

The emphasis on the communication of purpose makes it possible to get away from the all-too-close (and unjustified) identification of leadership with hegemony, dominion, or domination. The essence of leadership is the capacity to set an agenda, organise coalitions, and to achieve a decision on implementing global problems. Such is the picture of leadership this volume attempts to capture.

THE LONG CYCLE

The question of global leadership merits attention in its own right, but it is also related to the study of the long cycles that are the rhythm of the global political system. As shown in two earlier books, the waxing and waning of leadership is a necessary element of that rhythm. Modelski (1988) examined this element theoretically and analytically; Modelski and Thompson (1987) gave it empirical and quantitative backing. The present volume rounds off the picture in a qualitative sense.

The long cycle is the ordered movement of global politics through time: each cycle comprises a succession of four 'phases': global war, world power, delegitimation, and deconcentration (see Table A), that is repeated regularly. The global war has been the strong beat of the cycle, and we hardly need reminding that the two world wars gave shape to the twentieth century, or that the wars of the French Revolution and of Napoleon lent form and structure to the nineteenth. The global war serves as the decision mechanism generating new leadership – and, by the same token, new policies – for the global system. That is why each global war (that 'inaugurates' each systematic long cycle) is followed by a 'world power' phase in which the exercise of global leadership assumes its clearest form. A global war tends 'normally' to be followed by a lengthy interval of general peace at the global level, even though at the regional and national levels wars are far from absent once the system enters the phases of delegitimation and deconcentration.

As the 'product' of global wars, then, we observe an orderly procession of 'world powers' (that is, states exercising leadership at the global level): Portugal, the Netherlands, Great Britain (twice), and the United States. The world powers have not 'ruled' the world but may perhaps be said, each in their own time, to have ruled the 'oceanic waves'. Each world power had to contend with rivals, competitors and challengers: Spain, France, Germany, and more recently the Soviet Union; the story of the resulting tensions and conflicts (in periods of delegitimation and deconcentration) forms much of the stuff of world politics. But in this volume we single out for special emphasis the world powers and make them the centrepiece of our presentation.

The attribution of special traits of leadership to states such as the United States – and, earlier, Britain or the Netherlands – has recently become a common currency of writings on international political economy.

Table A Long cycles in global politics (systemic mode)

CYCLE	Phases			
	Global war (Major warfare)	*World power (Lead state)*	*Delegitimation*	*Deconcentration (Challenger)*
PORT.	**1494** Italian and Indian Ocean wars	**1516** Portugal	**1540**	**1560** Spain
NETH.	**1580** Spanish–Dutch wars	**1609** Netherlands	**1640**	**1660** France
BRIT.	**1688** Wars of Grand Alliance	**1713** Britain – I	**1740**	**1763** France
BRIT.	**1792** Wars of Revolution and Napoleon	**1815** Britain – II	**1850**	**1873** Germany
USA	**1914** First and Second World Wars	**1945** United States	**1873**	**2000** Soviet Union

The distinctive characteristic of long cycle theory is its emphasis on periodicity; it argues a regularity of the process by which leadership has been assumed and exercised at the global level, and the centrality of global wars to that process.

Long cycle theory raises two sets of questions of our sources:

(1) Do the documents offer evidence for the 'existence' of global leadership? Do they support the prediction that states labelled here the 'world powers' assumed that role, and exercised it in a regular and potentially predictable pattern?

(2) We know from the study of seapower when each lead state attained a condition of absolute naval superiority over all rivals: Portugal in 1502, the Netherlands in 1608, Great Britain in 1713, and then again in 1809, and the United States in 1944. Do the regular peaks of seapower concentration correspond with verbal or behavioural expressions of principles and commitments by the world powers, as proposed in Table B? Do we have evidence that statesmanship found the words to match the deeds of seapower?

Table B The correlation between oceanic supremacy and acts of leadership[1]

Oceanic supremacy[2]	*Occasion for global leadership*
(1502–44) (Portugal)	(1494) Treaty of Tordesillas (1499) Manuel assumes title of 'Lord of Conquest, Navigation and Commerce'
(1608–42[3]) (Netherlands)	(1602) Dutch East Indies Company founded
(1719–23) (Britain – I)	(1701) William III to Parliament: 'hold the balance of Europe'
(1809–90[3]) (Britain – II)	(1793) William Pitt the Younger leads coalition against France
(1944–) (United States)	(1941) Atlantic Charter (1947) Marshall Aid offered

1. Cf. Modelski (1987) Table 2.2.
2. *Source*: Modelski and Thompson (1988), Table 5.3 gives years in which the world power's naval concentration ratio equalled or surpassed 0.5 (that is, the world power, in that year, held one-half or more of the world's total of capital warships).
3. Intermittent, for better than one-half to two-thirds of that period.

CRITERIA OF SELECTION

In the light of the questions just asked, we have chosen our documents according to the following principles:

(1) The emphasis is on the world powers: Portugal, the Netherlands, Great Britain and the United States, with separate chapters allotted to each (including two for Britain). For reasons of economy and priority we give little space to the challengers. We feature one substantial fifteenth-century contribution from Venice to form a base line and a background for what is to follow. We do this because this Italian city-state served as a prototype for the modern world powers: several of the key themes that we find throughout this collection – alliance, diplomacy, trade, and naval power – make their first appearance there.

(2) Our main interest lies in the forms the idea of global leadership assumed in international practice, in the way the representatives of the lead powers expressed their concept of their role and place in the world, and in actions they took that might be held to amount to taking the lead. The utterances might assume a broad formulation, as in Doge Mocenigo's description of Venice as 'supplying the whole world' or William III's call to England to 'hold the balance of Europe'; or they might be more narrowly and operationally framed as in King Manuel's instructions to Francisco de Almeida on how to organise the trade in spices and to build the fortresses needed to support it. The Atlantic Charter of 1941 is an articulation of the war aims of the retiring and the ascending world powers at the moment the torch was being passed to the United States. Sometimes leadership needs to be inferred from behaviour – as in the Dutch decision to create a United East Indies Company and thereby challenge directly the basis of the Iberian world system.

(3) Coalitions and alliances – especially the arrangements between the lead state, its predecessor, and its ultimate heir – have been critical elements in the succession of world powers; they constitute one basic dimension of global politics. These are the 'core alliances' of the global system, and yet most of them seem to have been forgotten or ignored. We reproduce the essential documents bearing on the Portuguese–Venetian, Portuguese–Spanish, Spanish–Dutch, Anglo–Dutch, and Anglo–American relationships, and the power transitions they stand for.

(4) Given the centrality of global wars to the emergence of leadership, the beginnings and endings of these events deserve especial attention: the beginnings because they help to shed light on the causes of these most extensive, expensive, and protracted of modern wars; the endings because global war settlements registered the systemic decision process and defined the framework within which world politics unfolded in the subsequent period of general peace. The more indirect antecedents of the global wars must be sought in the emergence of rivals and challengers to the established order, and we pay some attention to the way in which, e.g., the French and the English questioned Dutch supremacy in the seventeenth century, or the Germans acted at the turn of the twentieth. It is one of the purposes of this collection to further the understanding of

global war as a macro-decision process of the entire global political system. We give at least some attention to all the peace settlements that terminated periods of global warfare; we bypass the Treaties of Westphalia (1648) because they ended a regional war, the Thirty Years' War, and embodied, in the main, the settlement of German affairs, that is of regional European problems.[1]

(5) Last but not least, given our interest in seapower, and whenever appropriate, we include documents illuminating some aspects of the framework of maritime and naval problems animating the world powers (but no accounts of naval battles or other sea operations). Among the more interesting ones are the instructions (the *Regimento*) given to the first Portuguese viceroy to India, the Charter of the Dutch East India Company, the naval understandings between Western Europe's two 'maritime powers' (England and the Netherlands), and examples of correspondence between the two former 'naval persons' (Roosevelt and Churchill). These documents underscore the importance of naval affairs at the global level, and the continuity of the salience of that problem.

In addition, we have applied the following procedural criteria:

(6) All documents chosen for inclusion are 'official', in the sense that they are statements or instructions issued by authorities in public office – in the vast majority of cases holding the position of chief executive of the world power (or its close equivalent) or, in the case of treaties, the formal expressions of the position of two or more governments. There are no commentaries or analyses; the only (partial) exception is Hugo Grotius's Brief on the freedom of the seas (Doc. 14) that he prepared for the Dutch East Indies Company, and even that may be regarded as an official document.

(7) All are contemporary statements, policy pronouncements or expressions of agreed positions (as in treaties) made at the time the relevant decisions were made. They are not *ex post* explanations or late rationalisations of bygone stands. As often as possible, they have been chosen from primary sources, with emphasis on freshness and originality, including material not previously translated from the Italian, Portuguese, Latin, Dutch, and French. The preference throughout, in the interest of fairness to authors and readers, has been to reproduce the entire document; but in a number of cases, given the limitations of space, excerpting was unavoidable.

(8) With the exception of the first two items and the last address, the documents are confined to the period 1494–1945 – that is, in effect, to the European era of modern world politics. The basic cut-off date is 1945. Events since that year are reasonably familiar to all and the sources more readily accessible; they need either less or more documentation than we

are prepared to supply at this stage. But it is also arguable that the structure erected in 1945 is still intact in its essentials, and that little has happened so far to alter it.

Finally, a word on how the documents fit into the phases of the long cycle. A glance at Table C shows that the bulk of the documents (some two out of three) illuminate the global war phases of world politics (those that start in 1494, 1580, 1688, 1789, 1914). That is no surprise, for it is there that leadership is formed and binding decisions made on basic programmes for the future. But some mark significant other phase-transitions, and most phases have at least one item to give them character. In the seventeenth century, for example, Docs 17–19 stand for the several stages in the transformations of the Dutch system, and in the nineteenth century, Docs 45–48 illustrate successive changes in the character of the second British system. In that way, the documents reflect and reinforce the idea of periodicity and regularity.

Table C Where the documents fit in the phases of the long cycle (learning mode)

Phases beginning in years			
1420 1, 2[1]	**1450**	**1494** 3, 4, 5, 6, 7, 8, 9	**1516**
1540 10	**1560**	**1580** 11, 12, 13, 14	**1609** 15, 16
1640 17	**1660** 18, 19	**1688** 20, 21, 22, 23, 24, 25, 26, 27, 28	**1713** 29
1740	**1763** 30	**1792** 31, 32, 33, 34, 35, 36, 37, 38	**1815** 39, 40, 41, 42, 43
1850 44	**1873** 45, 46, 47, 48	**1914** 49, 50, 51, 52, 53, 54, 55, 56, 57, 58, 59	**1945** 60, 61, 62, 63

1. Document no.

1 Venetian Prologue

We open this collection with four speeches given between 1420 and 1423 by Tomaso Mocenigo, Doge of Venice.

WHY VENICE, AND WHY THESE TEXTS?

In the fifteenth century, its golden *quattrocento*, Venice was a widely admired, populous, well-governed, and stable Italian city-state, at the peak of its power. Venice had defeated Genoa in 1382, and all her other rivals, actual or potential, were distracted by endemic warfare.

Mocenigo became Doge in 1414. His previous long and distinguished career in the naval, diplomatic and colonial services (Captain General of the Seas, Procurator of St Mark, many times ambassador, Duke of Crete) had given him a special interest in the defence of Venice's distant overseas dominions in the East. To this end, he greatly expanded the republic's nearby territory in the Friule and in Dalmatia during his dogeship.

Venice's activities thus extended well beyond her immediate vicinity. From her special position in the Mediterranean–European region, she reached outward and organised the life of a substantial area. 'We supply the whole world' claims Doge Mocenigo in the speech of early 1423, and his boast was only a slight exaggeration. In fact, Venice was a regional lead power, in structure and function akin, albeit on a smaller scale to the global powers we shall study in the following centuries. From a long cycle perspective, then, Venice was a prototypical world power.

Mocenigo's 'Political Testament' (Doc. 1) may have been inspired, in idea, if not in content, by Caesar Augustus's *Res Gestae Divi Augusti* (Acts of the Divine Augustus), part of the Roman Emperor's Will which, according to Tacitus and Suetonius, he deposited with the Vestal Virgins shortly before his death in AD 14. There is no text of this Will extant, although it was meant to be made public.

A possible precedent for the 'Farewell Address' (Doc. 2), the compilers of *Bilanci Generali* (Reale Commissione . . ., 1912, p. 97n.) also suggest, may have been another part of Caesar Augustus's Will, the *Breviarium Imperii*, a summary of the military and financial resources of the Roman Empire. Just before his death, Augustus gave instructions for a list of the national resources to be produced and read posthumously. The document gave the numbers of regular and auxiliary troops serving in the army; the strength of the navy; statistics concerning the provinces and dependent kingdoms; direct and indirect taxation; recurrent expenditures and gifts. Tacitus reports that 'Augustus [wrote] all this out of his own hand.

Furthermore, he . . . added a clause advising that the Empire should not be extended beyond its present frontiers. Either he feared dangers ahead, or he was jealous' (Tacitus, 1971, pp. 39–40).

Whether Mocenigo was following Augustus's example is not known for certain. Be that as it may, his account of Venice's naval power and financial resources remains impressive to this day and, *inter alia*, bears out Fernand Braudel's argument (1984, p. 120) that the city's budget at the time was by far the largest in Europe. The Doge also gives a detailed picture of Venetian trade with Lombardy, Florence, and the mainland possessions, showing, *inter alia*, the important role spices (such as pepper and ginger) played in it; indeed, he proudly reports the wealth that was built on this foundation. The statistics cited are unique, for their time, and in their detail. Braudel (1984, p. 119) has also used these figures to reconstruct Venice's gross product in those years and puts it at between 7.5 and 15 million ducats, or 50–100 ducats *per capita*. If we remember that the ducat was a gold coin weighing 1/8th of an ounce, and if we factor in the 1987 price of gold $440 per ounce), we reach amazing figures of a *per capita* income of $US 2750–5500, comparing favourably with the United States' figure of some $US 15 000 *per capita* today. The maritime strength of Venice was notable too: 45 galleys in permanent service, as compared with, say, the 20 galleys that Portugal could mobilise for a major expedition against Ceuta a few years earlier. The size of land armies, though, strikes one as small by our standards: a total of 3000 soldiers defending the frontiers against powerful Milan.

It is the statistics that give a contemporary air to the speeches. Other passages, on the other hand, such as those reaching out for historical analogies – as in the speech of July 1421 – exude a distinctly pre-modern aura. All in all, these documents seem to provide a base-line by which subsequent development may be judged. They show us how evolved in some ways Venice was, and yet make it possible to say how much more complex the world has become since, especially in its political aspects.

Furthermore, the addresses shed light on a critical policy choice for a lead power: what to do next? what to do once the zenith of power has been attained? In the 1420s, broadly speaking, Venice faced two choices: *either* to continue enjoying the status quo, in peace (at least in Italy), *or else* to do something new, by reordering its priorities and going after important new problems. The crisis of what to do next gathered around the succession to Mocenigo and the Florentine proposal for an alliance against Milan. We see the constitutional bodies of the Republic in the process of taking a fundamental decision.

The documents give us only one side of the debate: the Doge's arguments in favour of keeping the peace of the status quo. Mocenigo's earlier record as fleet commander and as Chief Executive of Venice hardly bears him out as a life-long pacifist. But arguing against armed intervention in a dispute he sees as a local quarrel, he depicts Northern Italy as Venice's own *garden* that should be *cultivated* in peace and protected against military adventures that would surely devastate it.

Mocenigo's often reiterated horticultural metaphor for Venice brings to mind Candide's admonition in the conclusion of Voltaire's eponymous philosophical tale of 1759: 'we must cultivate our garden'. Voltaire had an Italian secretary at the time who may have been familiar with the Sanudo version of the speech, published by Muratori in 1733.

The Doge's reasoning is based, among other things, on an explicit and rational 'calculus of conquest': the expense and trouble of military operations is larger than any benefits that might accrue from it. He warns, in utterly modern terms, of the dangers of 'territoriality', of confusing landed acquisitions with the substance of political power. We might infer that his arguments did not go altogether unchallenged (cf. the question his council asked about the revenue derived from the recently annexed *terra ferma*) but in the main he carries the core of his argument strongly: Venice must stick to the proven formula of her regional functions, defined by him as long-distance trade and defence against the East, and avoidance of the 'strategic trap of territorial commitments' (cf. Thompson and Zuk, 1986).

The alternative to the status quo policy is some new policy initiative or innovation that responds to the requirements of this age. For Mocenigo's nemesis, the 'young procurator' Foscari, the alliance with Florence, a fellow Republic, was apparently an opportunity for additional territorial gains in Italy (even though, or maybe because, some notable acquisitions in the *terra ferma* had just been accomplished).

Both substantively and procedurally, this turned out to be, as we know, a fateful decision. Substantively, the Venice–Florence alliance was to become the axis around which Italian politics would keep revolving for the next generation. More significantly, perhaps, it became the phenomenon around which the idea of a 'balance of power' would soon crystallise: Venice's weight in Italy became so great that by the 1440s Florence would justify abandoning that alliance in favour of Milan by the need for 'balance'. Procedurally, the alliance became the occasion on which an entirely new form of diplomacy – that of the resident embassy – would take shape. The documents illustrate how the comings and goings of the various travelling missions were obviously inefficient (as in the case of the Florentine embassy to Milan). Within just a few years, the exigencies of alliance politics produced the first exchange of resident missions (between Milan and King Sigismund of Hungary against Venice, in 1425), and the first permanent embassy (by Venice, in Rome, by 1435) (see Mattingly, 1955, Chapter VII).

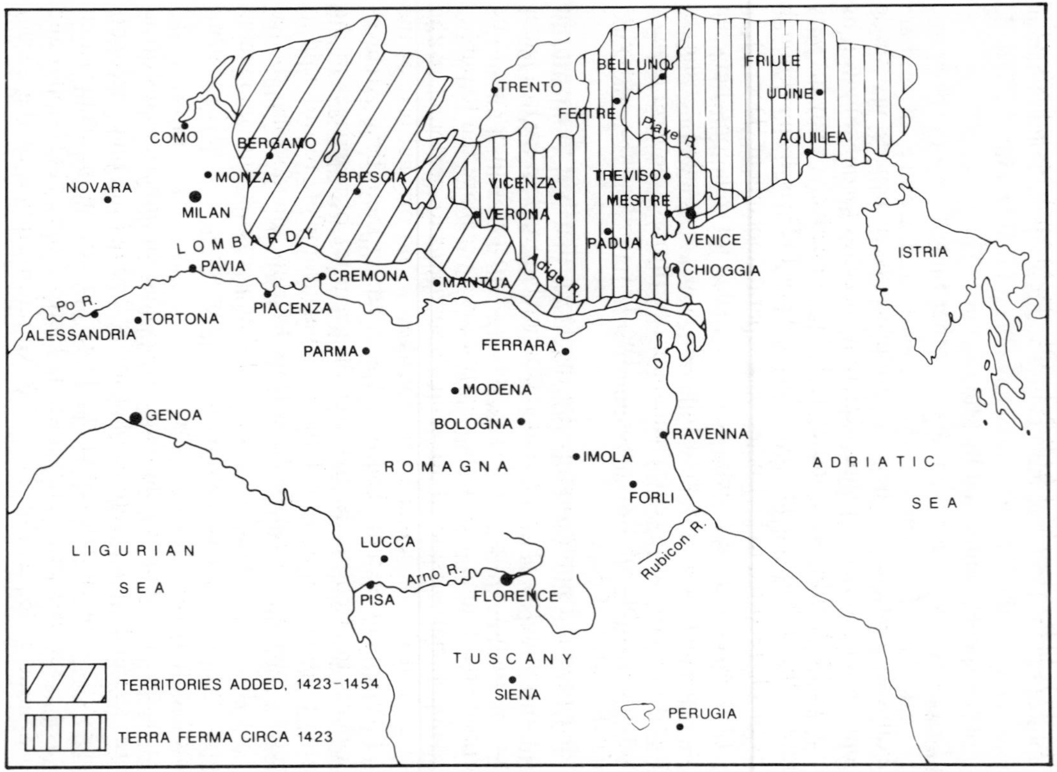

Map 1.1 Venice and the *terra ferma* in the first half of the fifteenth century

Documents

1 THE 'POLITICAL TESTAMENT' OF TOMASO MOCENIGO[1]

Introduction

The 'Political Testament', here reproduced as a continuous single document, in fact consists of three different speeches (*arringhe*) given by Mocenigo in 1420, July 1421, and early 1423, respectively. Only his very last address, the '*Ultima Arringa*' of March–April 1423, is distinct enough in the available records, to be treated as a separate document (Doc. 2).

The 1420 *arringa* is an analysis of the state of relations between Florence and Milan. The speech of July 1421 contains detailed statistics of trade with Lombardy and Venice's mainland territories (the *terra ferma*), and uses the parable of the 'garden'. The last of the three speeches reaffirms the value of peace.

An *arringa* was a public address by the Doge that had to have prior approval by a majority of the Venetian Council before delivery to a wider audience (Romanin, 1913, Vol. IV, p. 66n.). But because they were to be given outside the boundaries of the constitutional organs of the Republic, there is no official version of Mocenigo's *arringhe* to be found in the relevant files of the Venetian Chancery; there is no original text of the 'Political Testament' extant. The only traces left in the official Archives are fragments inserted on the flyleaves of a register of marriages in the *Avogaria di Comun* (State Law Offices). This incomplete record, said to have been copied by Pietro Barbaro from Marino Sanudo (also spelled Marin Sanuto), is in places careless in dating events and in naming personages (see *Bilanci Generali*, Reale Commissione . . ., 1912, p. 97n.; Cessi and Sambin (eds), 1943, p. xxiv).

Nevertheless, the 'Political Testament' became an important historical source for succeeding generations of scholars through the fuller accounts that appeared, some decades after the Doge's death, in the handwritten histories of respected chroniclers such as Pietro Dolfin (1427–1506) and Marino Sanudo (1466–1536). The 1733 Muratori edition of the earlier

1. Doge of Venice 1414–23.

speeches used here, and attributed to Sanudo, contains the same mistakes as the informal inscription by Barbaro mentioned above.[2]

It would not be surprising if, after an interval of more than half a century, some historical facts were added or distorted to suit political interests. Norwich (1983, p. 198) considers the speeches 'too riddled with anachronisms to be anything but apocryphal'. *Bilanci Generali* (Reale Commissione . . . , 1912, pp. 577–8n.) questions and corrects some of the data. Romanin (1913, p. 92) regards them as true in the substance but cautions that the 'Testament' contains errors in chronology that Mocenigo himself could not have made.

For example, it is stated in the speech of 1420 that a Florentine delegation came to Milan in 1412 to congratulate the young Duke, Filippo Maria, on his having regained the lands that had been usurped during his minority; Romanin remarks that 1412 was the year in which Filippo Maria became Duke, and that it took him some years to win back his inheritance, the last part of it (Genoa) not having been secured until 1420.

Another unlikely date is 1414 for the Milan take-over of Forli after its Lord's death which the annals place in 1422 – that is, after the speech of 1420 that refers to it. Thus, apart from containing minor flaws, such as misnaming historical characters, the 'Testament' antedates at least one event that took place after Mocenigo is supposed to have mentioned it.

Most non-Italian historians (Braudel, Hazlitt, Lane, Norwich), while steering clear of the rhetoric, have availed themselves of the hard facts and figures that Mocenigo gives on Venetian wealth and trade. For the sake of completeness, the 'Testament', literally as reported in Muratori, is here given in its entirety in English for the first time. Some of the historical inaccuracies are pointed out in footnotes by the editors. Within the text, editorial intervention was limited to reformatting (sub-headings, paragraphs and punctuation) and clarifications in square brackets.

Source: L. A. Muratori (ed.), *Rerum Italicarum Scriptores*, Vol. 22: "Vite de' Dogi di Marino Sanuto", cols 946–58 (Milan: Typographia Societatis Palatinae, 1733). Reproduces the Sanudo MS in the Biblioteca Marciana, *Italiani*, Classe VII, Codice 800. Translated from the Italian by Sylvia Modelski.

2. It is said that while writing his *Vite dei Dogi*, Sanudo consulted the Dolfin Annals (up to the year 1422) at the house of the Loredan family (see Cessi and Sambin (eds), 1943, p. xxvi). Pietro Loredan had been Mocenigo's favorite to succeed him. Could it be that the uncertainty surrounding the authenticity of the *Political Testament* may thus be due, in part, to the fact that Francesco Foscari, who became Doge, may have discouraged its inclusion in the official record, because of the unflattering portrait of him it contains, while the Loredans salvaged it as part of their on-going feud against the Foscaris? (See p. 29 below.)

Texts

Speech of 1420

Most illustrious Signori: the origins of the scandalous war between Florence and the Lord of Milan are known to you. Nonetheless, I will briefly recapitulate them. When the Duke of Milan, dubbed 'the Virtuous'[3] died in 1402, he left two young sons, and the Duchess ruled that state with the help of the said Duke's Council. Then the Duchess died. The sons were little boys. Facino Cane became their guardian. And so, Gabrino Fondolo assumed the lordship of Cremona, Pandolfo Malatesta made himself master of Brescia, Piermaria de' Rossi took over Parma, Jacopo dal Verme and many others did the same, helping themselves to whatever suited them. The Florentines set up camp in Pisa, which had been lorded over by a bastard son of the old Duke, the so-called 'Count of Virtue'. They approved of all these gentlemen's usurpations. So that in less than a year the considerable estate which the Duke had left to his sons was reduced to nothing; the children were now the servants of their former servants. It was God's justice that allowed this to happen, because their father had acquired a large part of his vast domains unjustly.

When Facino Cane died, Filippo Maria[4] married Cane's wife,[5] and with her wealth and her late husband's soldiers, and above all thanks to the talents of Francesco Carmagnole whom he had put at the head of his army, and with popular support, little by little, he retrieved the major part of his ancestral lands from the hands of the usurpers.

Then, in 1412,[6] the Florentines sent an embassy to Filippo Maria, ostensibly to express joy at his success, adding that, in the interest of peace and security, they had some proposals to make that were fair and advantageous to his state, namely, that the Duke of Milan promise not to acquire land either beyond Trento or beyond the Rubicon. And that the Florentines would then also promise not to acquire land on his side of either Trento or the Rubicon. And the Duke was satisfied with this and agreed. With due process, he sent them his ambassador with the signed treaty. And so the matter was sealed.

In 1414, Ordelaffo,[7] the Lord of Forli died, and because he did not trust his relative, the Lord of Imola, he had stipulated in his Will that the Duke of Milan should become the guardian of his two daughters and the administrator of his land until the minors reached the age of twenty. In accordance with this testament, Filippo Maria despatched a force of 1000 cavaliers and infantrymen to Forli, under Cecco de Montagnana.

3. Gian Galeazzo Visconti (1351–1402), also known as 'The Valorous' and 'The Cruel'.
4. Gian Galeazzo's younger son (1392–1447) who survived his murdered sadistic older brother Giovanni Maria to become Duke.
5. Beatrice Tenda, Cane's widow, was 40 and a woman of substance in her own right; her dower included Tortona, Novara, Alessandria, Vercelli, and Como, plus 100 000 florins. But soon after marrying her, Filippo Maria had her beheaded on a trumped-up charge of infidelity (Napier, 1847, Vol. 3, pp. 58–9).
6. Romanin (1913, p. 92n.) corrects several inaccuracies here.
7. Giorgio degli Ordilaffi died in 1422. His sister Catarina, as head of the Forli Ghibellines, wanted her husband Bartolomeo da Campo Fregoso to become Lord of Forli. Ordilaffi's widow, Lucrezia degli Alidosi of Imola, opposed this scheme. Filippo Maria played one sister-in-law against the other (Napier, 1847, Vol. 3, p. 61; this might explain the erroneous attribution of two daughters to Ordilaffi who left only one infant son, Tebaldo.

The Lord of Imola could not suffer that his kinsman had had such a low opinion of him. So he went to Florence, and there he presented himself to those who govern Florence explaining that the terms of the agreement between them and Filippo Maria had not been respected and that Filippo Maria had violated the pact by bringing his army beyond the agreed limit. He argued that if they let this breach of the agreement pass in silence now, it would set a precedent and they would then have to remain tacit on future occasions that might not be so convenient to ignore. And he convinced a few who were greedy and wanted to enrich themselves through war.

A general Council was convened the same year, consisting of the Patriciate [i Gentiluomini], the Merchants' Council,[8] the Council of the Fine Arts, and the Council of the Applied Arts, that is of the Artisans. It was put to the meeting that the Duke of Milan had broken the treaty because he had crossed the Rubicon. Niccolo da Uzzano, the most distinguished intellect among those present, who were all *savii* [high-ranking committeemen] said that it did not seem to him that the Duke had broken his word (which would have been the case only if he had made himself Lord of Forli, but as Commissioner he was only the guardian of Ordelaffo's two children), and added: 'Our treaty was not at all concerned with such matters'. The 300 *savii* debated whether to send an ambassador to the Duke of Milan to remind him of the pacts he had made with the Florentines, which he had violated. It does not seem that they sent the said ambassador. Instead, they sent Bartolomeo Valori, a Jewish banker who had, it must be said, a quite proud bearing,[9] and he was given the same instructions. But Filippo Maria, who whenever he wants to dissimulate something feigns illness,[10] never met the ambassador. Instead, he sent Secretaries to hear what he had to say.

But the ambassador had been commissioned to stay no longer than fifteen days, not counting the days of arrival and departure, and moreover had orders that if offered to negotiate with the Duke's Secretaries he should insist that the Republic of Florence rejects this, and warn them of the number of days the deputation could stay there, at the end of which he would return to Florence. The Duke continued to avoid seeing him, pretexting illness; he asked the ambassador to deliver his message to his Council, namely Guido Torello, Uguccione, Piermaria de'Rossi, Giovanni da Lampugnano, and Messer Cato. The said ambassador, following his instructions from the Republic of Florence, refused to talk to any of them, and the time having expired, he left, and arrived in Florence and explained everything that had happened.

The Governors of Florence felt they had been insulted. They called the Council and described the way things had gone, concluding from it that Florence had been slighted. (That Duke always leads and provokes other states into war, just as his

8. Councils were committees representing the powerful guilds.
9. Bartolomeo Valori (1355–1427) was a member of a prominent Florentine family that originated in Fiesole. His father had been ambassador to Hungary. At the time of his mission to Milan, he was a member of the inner core that ruled Florence, and of 'i Dieci della Balia'.
10. After the cruel treatment he dealt his wife, Filippo Maria devoted himself to his life-long mistress, and settled down as a neurotic recluse, more bent on political manipulation than violence. Romanin (1913, p. 97n.) suggests that he refused to let the deputation headed by Valori enter Milan because of rumours of pestilence in Florence.

father did with King Ladislas).[11] Niccolo d' Uzzano, that wise man, contradicted them, saying that they should not go to war; he described the harm done by wars, how houses, monasteries, and hospitals would be destroyed, and how it would increase the burden of taxes on the citizenry, the patricians, and country people, to meet the expense of the fighting. That a growing number of rough folk would enter the patrician class whom it is important to be able to trust. That it would swallow up the gold. He reminded the assembly of the bad times with the old Duke and with King Ladislas.

But they proposed to pledge themselves to war, under threat of death; and whoever engaged in further peace talks, within the next ten years, would have his property confiscated. The motion was put to the ballot and carried by 300 votes, with 200 abstentions [*non balotte*]. And this decision was upheld.

The Duke of Milan, hearing this, sent two emissaries to Florence, Guido Torello, and Uguccione, to express regret that the ambassador had not been able to carry out his mission because of the Duke's illness, having left Milan without seeing him.

They said that the Duke personally had sent them to explain the reason. And they added, that if there was any discord, he was ready to settle the differences.

The Florentines summoned their Council and replied to the Duke's emissaries, who participated in the debates, that whoever talked peace would be decapitated, and his property confiscated. They said that the war was caused by the question of Forli. The ambassadors replied to the Florentines that the Duke had not violated his agreement with them, and that he wanted to place his case in the judgement of whoever they wished; he stood by his rights but would be satisfied with whatever verdict was rendered. The Florentines did not want to accept any judgement, having already made up their minds in favour of war.

In 1415, Florence set up '*i Dieci della Balia*',[12] The Ten, who decided to punish the city of Florence with a tax, and at 1 per cent they managed to extract 50 000 ducats from the population; and then they paid the Marquis of Ferrara 2000 per month and gave him 1500 cavaliers and 1500 infantrymen. The said Marquis accepted the command and provisions and entered Forli to rule it in the name of Florence. Whereupon Cecco da Montagnana left the place and wrote to the Duke of Milan. The Duke wrote to the Marquis in such a way as to cause him to go back to Florence and renounce his governance of Forli, and Cecco da Montagnana reentered that city and reassumed his position there.

The Ten then took the Lord of Imola and put him in Forli, and Cecco da Montagnana again departed, sending the news to the Duke of Milan. The latter despatched Guido Torrello with 1000 horses and 1000 infantry to join forces with Cecco da Montagnana and enter Forli. The Ten called up 8000 horses and 6000 infantry and summoned Captain Ser Carlo de'Malatesti of Rimini. The Duke despatched Uguccione with 1000 horses and some infantry to meet up with Guido Torello and Cecco. They came to hand to hand combat, so that the Duke's cavalry destroyed the Florentines' cavalry and inflicted great damage upon them.

Again The Ten undertook to refurbish their camp which was decimated many times, and always the Florentines renewed their army. And the Duke of Milan

11. Ladislas of Durazzo, King of Naples in 1386, contributed to the already existing political strife in Italy by expanding his domains. He made himself King of Hungary and sold Dalmatia to Venice in exchange for her acquiescence to his deeds. But he was ousted by Sigismund, the rightful King of Hungary, who then waged war against Venice to reclaim Dalmatia. Ladislas died in 1414.
12. 'The Ten Bailees', 'Decemvirate of War' or 'War Board'.

always came back against them, seconded by the Luccans, the Siennese, the Bolognese and the Perugians. And this was possible because, before this business of Forli, the Florentines had behaved poorly; they used to rove all over these places at the time of the wheat and grape harvests, laying them to waste and scouring the countryside. And so, those were the origins of this war. Signori, I beseech you to reply to the Florentine ambassadors that if they want peace, they should write to Florence and ask for full powers.

[In July 1421, the ambassadors had received a reply from Florence which said that they must obey the law if they did not want to lose their heads. A meeting of the Senate was called to formulate Venice's reaction, and it was decided by vote to ask the ambassadors to leave soon, since they wanted war not peace.]

Speech of July 1421

We have explained to our young Procurator[13] Ser Francesco Foscari, one of the *savii* of the Council, all that the Florentines have argued in the Collegio[14] and which we have put before the Signoria, and in reply he tells us that we should go to the aid of the Florentines, because what is good for them is good for us, and consequently their misfortune is our misfortune. We shall reply to this in due course.

Young Procurator, when God created and made the world of the angels, which was the most noble thing ever created, he endowed them with a certain balance; they could discern between the good way and the evil way. The angels chose the bad way of evil. God punished them; he threw them out of Paradise and into Hell, and from good they became bad. The same thing can be said of the Florentines who go in search of evil. This is what will happen to us, if we agree to help them, which is what our young Procurator Ser Foscari has suggested. We urge you to remain at peace. Should the Duke of Milan ever wage an unjust war against us, we will have God, who sees everything, on our side. He will do what is necessary to ensure our victory. We live in peace because God is peace; and let those who want war go to Hell.

Young Procurator: God made Adam wise, good, and perfect, and He gave him the earthly Paradise, where peace reigned, together with two commandments, namely: 'enjoy the peace with all that is here in Paradise; but do not eat the fruit of that tree'. And he disobeyed and sinned in pride, refusing to accept that he was just a creature. And God deprived him of and banished him from Paradise, where peace prevailed, and gave him war, which is this world, and cursed him as well as the whole of humanity. And brother killed brother, and things went from bad to worse. The same fate awaits the Florentines who seek war; the same will befall them and all theirs. And if you do as our young Procurator says we should, the same thing will happen to us.

Young Procurator: after the sin of Cain who ignored the will of God, God's punishment was the Deluge, except for Noah, whom He wanted to preserve. The same will happen to the Florentines for wishing to gratify their own desires; God will destroy their land and their property, and they will come to live here, just as His Family with the women and children went to live in the city of Noah, who wished to obey God and put his trust in him. Conversely, if our young Procurator has his way, we shall see our kin abandoning this city to go and live in foreign lands.

Young Procurator: Noah was a godly man, chosen by the Lord, and Cam [?Ham] deserted God; he killed Japheth and God punished him; and from him issued the race of Giants, who were tyrants, and they did everything they wanted without fear of God. God made 66 languages out of one, and in the end they destroyed each other, so that the seed of the Giants disappeared. The same will happen to the Florentines for doing as they please without fear of God. Their language will divide into 66 idioms. That is why they travel every day to France,

13. Foscari was 50 years old. As a Procurator of San Marco he administered the church's trust funds, to which post of honour he was elected for life by the Great Council which consisted of all the nobles of Venice (Lane, 1973, pp. 95–8).
14. The Collegio was a joint meeting of the chief ministers and the Signoria composed of the Doge, six Ducal Councillors, and three Heads of the Forty (the Quarantia), roughly comparable to the modern cabinet (Norwich, 1982, p. 283; Lane, 1973, p. 255).

Germany, Languedoc, Catalonia, Hungary and Italy; and they will disperse themselves until they will no longer describe themselves as Florentines. This will be our fate if we do as the young Procurator says. Instead, fear God, and put your faith in Him.

Young Procurator: of all the descendants of Noah, God elected Abraham as the most perfect man that existed in those days, and He ordered him to circumcise himself so as to be distinguished from the others. And among all those who were to be conceived and born from men and women tainted by original sin, God chose and saved from the taint our Lady, because only through her would be born the Lord Jesus Christ, our Redeemer, God and man, whose flesh did not issue from any man, but from the pure blood and milk of our Lady governed by the Holy Spirit, who created that most holy body, and most holy soul, the noblest that ever was, and whose perfection will never be surpassed. Thus the Word was incarnated in his Flesh, although one should not compare God with creature.

But among all the things that God created, was Attila who descended upon the West, plundering the people and bringing them ruin and devastation. And God inspired a few princes, who came, for the sake of security, to live in these lagoons; and so they were saved, because they were elected by God. Praise be to God that in this land great monasteries and hospitals were built, and great charities established. If we do as our young Procurator proposes, God will no longer regard us as elect, and we can expect the same as has befallen other lands that were ruined and sacked, with their population killed and many misfortunes. Since the Florentines go looking for evil, leave them to it; we are the city chosen above all others. Therefore, keep the peace.

'*We must seek peace*'

Young Procurator: in His Gospel Christ says: 'I give you peace'. And so I say that we must seek peace. If we do as our young Procurator suggests, and disobey His commandments, what can you expect but evil and destruction? If you want to protect yourselves, do not stray from the Gospel and Scriptures. The Florentines strayed. But see what waste and injuries God has sent them. Let us continue to respect the Old Testament, and the New. See how many great cities have been reduced to ruin by war! And it is through peace that they became great, with thriving populations, palaces, gold, silver, jewels, crafts, lords, barons and knights. But as soon as they turned their attention to warmongering, which is the work of the Devil, God abandoned them, and they crumbled. The men were killed in battle, gold and silver reserves were exhausted. Power vanished. And they destroyed themselves as they destroyed the other lands, and they became the slaves of others. This land that has reigned for 1008 years, God will destroy in no time. Do not follow the advice of our young Procurator.

Young Procurator: Troy achieved greatness because it was peaceful: the generations proliferated, and so did the houses, palaces, gold, silver, trades, Lords, barons and knights. As soon as she entered war, her men were killed in battle. The women were left widowed. No more gold and silver, but poverty thrived. They destroyed themselves, so that not much power was needed to destroy them. The City was ruined and the Trojans became the slaves of others. This is what will happen to Florence, who loves to cut up the land of others and to despoil them. And already she has begun to meet with disasters. Her countryside has been ravaged. Her citizens are fleeing to save themselves. This can happen to us too, if we do as our young Procurator proposes. Instead, let us live in peace, so that our city will be made wealthy in gold and silver, in crafts, navigation, trade, nobility, in houses, wealthy citizens, in population growth while other countries are at war. In war, this land would be destroyed. But if you will it, you can remain in peace, and put your trust in God.

Jerusalem grew in houses, palaces, lords, knights, gold, silver, because she remained in peace. Then Solomon built a Temple and worshipped false gods . . . and his son Rehoboam rebelled against God, coveting the lands, cities, and property of others. God destroyed and ruined him; the people, unable to bear any more burdens, asked for relief . . . and Jeroboam left the kingdom with ten major tribes. And the same thing is happening to the Florentines today, because they wanted to aggrandise themselves with other people's property. The lands and castles that were once theirs gave their allegiance to the Duke. And it is true what they say in the Psalm: 'And another shall take his crown. His children will be made orphans; his wife a widow' [109.9]. This is what will befall us if we do as the young Procurator advises.

Rome became so mighty and rich through good government and peace that she did not envy what belonged to others. Brave and rich men thrived there. But when Rome launched herself in the first Punic war, there followed great destruction of the men of the country of gold and silver; many widows were created, to the detriment of the multiplication of the generations; and then Scipio Africanus arrived and saved her, winning gold, silver, and much wealth for her. But in the end, because the long wars had so much exhausted the lands, the citizens demanded a new state, Caesar made himself its master, and things deteriorated even more. Exactly the same thing is occuring to Florence. The men-at-arms[15] are despoiling them of their money and are their lords, while they obey those who were their servants, rough people, cursed people, men-at-arms. Such will be our fate if we do as the young Procurator says.

Pisa became great, rich and prosperous, because of its peaceful and good government. Then she eyed the property of others and impoverished herself, a prey to the factions fomented among the citizenry by the Duke of Milan. Each aspired to be master; they killed each other until they ended up as subjects of the most wicked republic in Italy, which is Florence. The same degradation awaits the Florentines themselves with their schemes for getting rich. And already one can see that they are getting poorer and divided. One tyrant succeeds another. And as one tyrant overthrows the other, another has this one murdered. Just as the Pisans ended up in the hands of their enemies, the same will happen to us if we follow the young Procurator. And what I have said of this city can be said of any other.

Therefore, you Ser Francesco Foscari, our young Procurator, before ever again making speeches such as you have given, you must first acquire good understanding and good experience. Take notice, young Procurator, that Florence is not the port of Venice, either by sea or by land, because its port is five days' journey from our borders. Our opening is through Verona. The Duke of Milan is our neighbour, it is he with whom we must maintain good relations, because his great city of Brescia, which borders on Verona and Cremona, is less than a day away from here, and that other city[16] of his which is a mere day's journey by land. Genoa could harm us; she is redoubtable on the sea under the Duke. And with those too we should remain on good terms. And if the Genoese did anything, we would

15. *uomini d'arme*: medieval term for bands led by the second sons of the lower nobility who, at an early age, were trained for the military life by their social superiors (Ranke, 1915, pp. 24–5).
16. Possibly Piacenza.

have justice on our side. We can defend ourselves against the Genoese, against the Duke, and do so righteously. The mountains of the Veronese are our rampart against the Duke. This province has an inbuilt defence: the marshes that keep the Duke at bay. The Adige river protects us; and the Duke with his 3000 horses and 3000 infantry and with 1000 crossbows defends our whole territory. Our population is more than enough to raise a force of 3000 able to resist all the Duke's might, should he become our enemy. But I repeat, enjoy the peace that you have. If the Duke takes Florence, the Florentines, who are accustomed to republican ways, will leave Florence and come to settle in Venice, and they will produce their silk and woollen fabrics here, so that Florence will lose its manufacturers while our prosperity will grow, as happened with Lucca when that citizen[17] became its master. Lucca's industry and wealth came to Venice, and Lucca became poor. So, I repeat, stay in peace.

Ser Francesco Foscari, young Procurator, if you are able to counter the following arguments, we shall encourage the Council to follow your advice.

'Suppose you had a garden'

Suppose you got yourself a garden in Venice that produced, every year, enough wheat to make a living for 500 people, and besides, there was much left over to sell; suppose this garden yielded enough wine to make a living for 500 people and there was also a good surplus to trade at a good price; and if this garden gave you all sorts of grains and vegetables worth a lot of money; and if this garden also brought forth many kinds of fruits, enough to make a living for 500 people every year, with some to spare for sale; and suppose that same garden produced, yearly, so many oxen, lambs, goats, and birds of all sorts, that it made a living for 500 people, and there would be some saved for trade; and if this garden gave you so much cheese and eggs that it made a living for 500, and there would be some left over to sell; and suppose that the said garden gave you enough fish of all kinds to make a living for 500 people, and some were left over to market very profitably; it can reasonably be said that this is a most noble garden, giving so much and in addition to providing a living for 500 people, yielding a revenue of 500 ducats, which means that it does not entail any extra expense for its upkeep.

Now suppose that one morning some one came up to you and said: 'Ser Francesco, your enemies have come to the Piazza and they have hired 500 mariners and ordered them to enter this garden of yours; they have given them 500 bill hooks with which to slash trees and vineyards; they have also hired 100 rustics and given them 100 pairs of oxen and 100 harrows to uproot the plants that are in the garden and to kill all the animals, big and small, that are in this garden'. If you are competent, you will not tolerate that your garden be destroyed. You will go to your cash box and take enough gold to enlist 1000 men to march against those who want to ruin that garden. But, Ser Francesco, what if it were you who hired the 500 men armed with bill hooks and the 100 rustics to plough up your garden? You would rightly be thought to have gone mad. Yet this hypothetical situation could become ours.

17. Castruccio Castracani degli Antelminelli. He was an exiled Luccan 'White' who, after helping Ghibelline Pisa take over the previously 'Black' Lucca in 1314, made himself its Duke (1316–28). The city did not recover its independence until 1369.

Trade with Lombardy

We have made an inventory of all the trade done by Venice today, and with whom, as far as we can ascertain. According to the Milanese merchants, and also the bank records, we receive:

From	*Weekly (thousand ducats)*	*Annually (thousand ducats)*
Milan	17 or 18	900
Monza	1	56
Como	2	104
Alessandria dalla Paglia	1	56
Tortona and Novara	2	104
Pavia	2	104
Cremona	2	104
Bergamo	1.5	78
Parma	2	104
Piacenza	1	52

These figures are verified by the testimony of all the banks which estimate that every year the Milanese must settle 1 612 000 gold ducats[18] on us. Don't you think this is a most beautiful and noble garden that Venice owns at no cost? Furthermore:

City *Buys*	*Thousand bolts (per year)*	*Price per bolt (ducats)*	*Total (thousand ducats)*
Alessandria dalla Paglia, Tortona and Novara	6	15	90
Pavia	3	15	45
Milan (broadcloth)	4	30	120
Como	12	15	180
Monza	6	15	90
Brescia	5	15	75
Bergamo	10	7	70
Cremona (fustian)	40	4.25	170
Parma	4	15	60

In all, 90 000 bolts of cloth bringing in a total of 900 000 ducats. Entrance and exit fees, at only 1 ducat per bolt, give us 200 000 ducats. The revenue from our trade with Lombardy is estimated to amount to 28 000 000[19] ducats. Don't you agree that Venice has a most beautiful garden? And you must also add the hemp for cordage for the sum of 100 000 ducats.

18. The ducat (first minted in Venice in 1284) contained 3.55 grammes (=1/8 ounce) of pure gold (Lane, 1973, p. 149). At the current (1987) price of gold (1 ounce = $440.00), 1 ducat would be worth $55.00.
19. *Bilanci Generali* (Reale Commissione . . . , 1912, p. 578n.) corrects this unlikely figure to 2 800 000 ducats, see also the tabulation of exports to Lombardy on p. 24.

The Lombards buy from you every year:

Product	*Quantity*	*Price (ducats)*	*Total (thousand ducats)*
Cotton	5000[1]		250
Thread	20 000[1]	15 or 20[5]	30
Catalonian wool	4000[1]	60[6]	120
French wool	40[1]	300[6]	120
Gold and silk cloth			250
Pepper	3000[2]	100[7]	300
Cinnamon	400[3]	100[8]	64
Ginger	200[1]	40[6]	8
Sugars [3 grades]		up to 15[5]	95
Green ginger (worth many thousand ducats)			
Miscellaneous merchandise (for sewing and embroidering)			30
Brazilwood[4]	4000[1]	30[6]	120
Indigo and cochineal			50
Soaps			250
Slaves			30

1. Thousandweight.
2. Measures.
3. Bales.
4. *verzino*, a red dyewood that later gave its name to Brazil.
5. Per cwt.
6. Per thousandweight.
7. Per measure.
8. Per bale.

The aggregate should come to 2 800 000 ducats. This is indeed a very nice garden we have here, that costs us nothing. And I have not counted the salt[20] which brings in considerable revenue every year. And this commerce with Lombardy is beneficial to our land. Consider how many ships the movement of these goods keeps active, either to take them to Lombardy or to bring them from Syria, Romania, Catalonia, Flanders, Cyprus, Sicily, and other parts of the world. Venice earns 2½ to 3 per cent of this trade through provisioning and freighting: brokers, dyers, freight for vessels and galleys, fishermen, couriers, boats, seamen, galley captains, and merchants' agents; altogether the revenue to Venice is about 60[0] 000 ducats, and this without incurring any costs to the city. From this profit, many thousand of persons make a fat living. And is this a garden you would want to destroy? Of course not. But you must be on guard against those who wish to do just that.

If we went to war against the Duke of Milan, as our young Procurator suggests, it would be the same as if we armed men with bill hooks to cut down the trees that bear so many good and profitable fruits for Venice; as if we gave harrows to rustics with which to plough up the plants that are so fertile and profitable, whose produce the Lombards come every year to purchase from us. It would be like

20. Lane (1973, p. 237) estimates the proceeds from salt sales ca 1500 at 100 000 ducats.

hiring soldiers to come to this land to destroy trees and vegetation, to set fire to houses and villages, to kill the animals, to bring down the city and castle walls, and to spread desolation among the population, both those who live in the city and those in the country; we would be taxing our houses, our goods, our ships and galleys.

Trade with the terra ferma

God can see what we intend to do to the Duke of Milan's country. It could happen that the Duke of Milan will find a remedy for each injury we did to him, and we would have ruined our territory needlessly. What would then be the use of so much spice, gold and silk cloth? No one will take them because they will not have the means to do so. And, Signori, in case you do not already have this information, the yearly purchase of gold, silver, and silk cloth is as follows:

City	*Bolts*
Verona	200
Vicenza	120
Padua	200
Treviso	120
The Friule	50
Feltro and Belluno	12

And we supply them[21] annually with the following spices:

Spice	*Quantity*
Pepper	400[1]
Cinnamon	120[2]
Sugar	100[3]
Wax	200[4]
Gingers of all kinds (and many other spices)	100[3]

1. Measures.
2. Bales.
3. Thousandweight.
4. Loaves.

If we ruined their harvests, how would they be able to afford all the goods with which Venice abounds? So don't believe what our young Procurator says. To defend himself, the Duke of Milan would also have to incur expenses to hire the military; and he would tax the peasants, countryfolk and citizenry, and their having no more money to spend would bankrupt our own city and citizenry. And so, Signori, rest assured. Let us reply to the Florentine ambassadors that they should write to the Republic of Florence asking for full powers for themselves, so that they may negotiate about peace, and that they should forget their pledge so that they may have peace.

[This proposal was adopted unanimously, and the embassy was sent back to Florence.]

21. These are mainland territories (*terra ferma*) then controlled by Venice.

Speech of 1423

And so, we have seen in our own days [Gian Galeazzo], Duke of Milan, conquer the whole of Lombardy, Romagna, the Roman Campagna, and all of Tuscany except Florence; and he assumed so many expenses that he could not keep up with them; he was forced to make peace as he could no longer pay his servants. The same thing happens to all. If you remain in peace, you will amass so much gold that the whole world will fear you, and in everything you do, you will have God on your side. We repeat here, once more, what we have been saying for a year now. Let us hope God will grant you peace, if you want to have it. God, the master of all, together with our Lady, and with the Lord St Mark will grant us peace, which is ours now.

In January 1422, the Florentines again sent their embassy to this land. They explained the same things that were first explained in July 1421. In the end they concluded that if you don't become their allies, they will use force, and follow the example of Samson, who brought down the column that killed him together with his enemies. Having themselves been subjugated, they wish to see the whole of Italy subjected to one King of Italy; that is why we have called this Council and notified it of all the things I have just said.

I will continue.

Signori, every year you see how, because of the new products of Italy, the agricultural bounty, and other things available in Venice, many families, with their women, children and property, come to settle here, to the great advantage of our city. In the same way, from Verona, Vicenza, Padua and Treviso, every year from all parts, citizens come here with their families with much benefit to our city. Similarly, from all parts, we see country folk and good families moving to our land, because they want to live peacefully while practising their trades and raising their children. If you decide for war, these people will leave, and ruin your city, as well as others, and they will desert us. Instead of this, cherish peace. If the Florentines have given themselves to the Duke, so much the worse for them, who cares? Justice is on our side. They have squandered and consumed, and are now in debt. We are rich, and we have an invested capital of about ten million ducats, which earns us four million ducats.[22] We urge you to live in peace, fear nothing, and do not trust the Florentines.

Remember how they once dragged us into war against the House of della Scala, and asked us for a loan of half a million ducats; and when we agreed to give it to them, they allied themselves with those of Scala against us. This was in 1333.[23]

In 1412, Pippo Fiorentino,[24] Captain of the Hungarians, came down to fight us; we inflicted great damage upon him. We urge you to send the ambassadors back the same way we did before.

Signori, do not let yourselves be charmed by our young Procurator. His benevolence towards these Florentines ignores the righteousness and integrity of Filippo Maria; the war was caused by the iniquity of the Florentines who could have peace if they wanted it, but don't. Their plan is to incite us to war, and then

22. See note (5) in the 'Farewell Address' (Doc. 2), p. 30.
23. Fearful of an economic blockade, Venice countered the threat of expansion by the della Scala of Verona by an alliance with Florence. In the peace treaty ending that war (1339), Venice acquired Treviso, her first important mainland possession, briefly lost between 1380 and 1389 (Norwich, 1982, pp. 204–8; 262–4).
24. Filippo degli Scolari, better known as Pippo Speno, was a brilliant young Florentine *condottiere* whom Sigismund hired to lead his army into the Friule (Norwich, 1982, pp. 204–8; 262–4).

leave us standing alone after taking our money, to make us look ridiculous; and with our money they want to aggrandise themselves, as they did in 1333. Signori, don't be swayed by our young Procurator and his goodwill towards these Florentines, for there is much more at stake here, as I have tried to show.

The Collegio has asked us to ascertain the amount of revenues from Verona to Mestre,[25] it is 464 000 ducats. You also want to know the expenditures. With the majority of the countries of the world, the revenues cover the expenses. If there is war, you must expect to have to subsidise the factions with our money. If we take our troops beyond Verona, we shall have to bear even heavier costs: a burden that will ruin our patricians, citizens, artisans, and the Loan Office. And so, it is better to keep what we have, and to remain at peace.

'*You supply the whole world*'

Signori, we do not say this to glorify ourselves, but only to extol the truth and goodness of peace in our speech. Listen to the captains returning from Aigues Mortes [France] and Flanders, to our ambassadors, our consuls and merchants who unanimously say: 'Venetian Lords, yours is a virtuous and good Prince; he has secured peace for you, and has given you a life of harmony; you are the only Lords who navigate both across the sea and the land, you are the source of all the goods; you supply the whole world, and all the world loves you, and welcomes you. All the gold in the world comes to your land. You will be blessed as long as that Prince lives and continues his policy. All of Italy is at war; all France, Spain, Catalonia, England, Burgundy, Persia, Russia and Hungary. Your only war is with the Infidels, who are the Turks, and this war is to your great credit and honour'. And so, Signori, as long as we live, we shall follow the same way. Therefore, I advise you to choose peace and reply to the Florentines in the same fashion we did a year ago, with the full backing of the Council.

[After the departure of the Florentine embassy, the young Procurator presented his case to the Collegio.]

Ser Francesco Foscari, if an estate agent came to you and said: 'I can sell you a beautiful property in *terra ferma*, which can be bought for 20 000 ducats and yields annually 10 000 ducats' you would think this a good deal, no? Concealing your excitement, you will try everything to acquire the property, because it is very profitable. As you were talking to this agent, another one accosts you and says: 'Ser Francesco, I have a property, valued at 5000 ducats, that earns 200 ducats a year'. Reason tells you not to listen to the second agent but to pay attention to the first one with the 20 000 ducats property. And so you ask him where the revenue from the land comes from. He will answer that it comes from wheat, wine, and all sorts of grain and pasture. Then you will ask this agent if the maintenance of that property involves any expense. He will reply yes, that the 10 000 ducats revenue from the property is not enough to cover the expenses; and that you can expect to spend 1000 of your own ducats every year. And again, you ask where the 1000 ducats expenses go. He will reply: this property is in the middle of horrible woods inhabited by wolves, bears, lions, and other most ferocious beasts. In order to control these beasts, one has to keep 500 field spaniels to guard the grazing animals; and for each dog, you need, annually, six bushels of flour, amounting to 3000 ducats; and 100 men are necessary to look after the dogs, at 20 ducats per man, which comes to 2000 ducats. If those were not hired, it would be impossible for the animals to graze in the pastures. The

25. I.e., from Venice's new mainland possessions or *terra ferma*.

second expense in the maintenance of this property is made necessary by the fact that it is surrounded by four great rivers; and when it rains in summer and winter, the waters from these rivers rise so high that they can carry away the whole estate. As a defence against this, one must retain 300 men to watch over the land so that the floods do not wash away the property. These 300 men want 26 ducats each every year, which comes to 7800 ducats. Whoever tries to cut down this expense will be unable to sow, nor have vineyards and fruits.

I am certain that your reply to the agent will be: 'This property is not for me, because I don't want to pay 20 000 ducats damage for your and your children's benefit; a man who invests 20 000 ducats in anything could earn annually 5 per cent interest on it, which would amount to 1000 ducats. And you will immediately go to the second agent to close the deal on that 5000 ducats property in order to make 200 ducats a year net, that would yield 4 per cent a year for you and your children.

Do you see what I am getting at? Remember how, in order to get Padua, Verona, Vicenza, and the Friule, we spent a total of 900 000 ducats. That is not counting the destruction of the houses of our citizens and their heirs, and the taxing of their goods, savings and jewels that sent them roaming about with their children; and after we had secured these places, this Republic did not send for those who had been abandoned and ruined, nor for their impoverished heirs, nor did it repay them for the damages the new acquisitions had cost them. And the reason for this is that the 464 000 ducats earned by these territories are swallowed up by the 1000 lances, 3000 infantry, and 100 crossbows needed to maintain ownership of the lands. If they did not cost so much, the revenue would go to Venice. And it would be much worse if there were to be troubles, which would entail the hiring of military men; we would have to mortgage our houses and goods; and things would go from bad to worse. Moreover, if we cross over beyond Verona, into open country, all the income of the Republic and of its citizens on land and sea would not be sufficient to pay for the military. Why should we want to bring suffering and ruin upon our heads? Just as you would relinquish the 20 000 ducat property for being a drain, you should lead this country along profitable and benign paths rather than favour wicked and impoverishing ones. And this I say to you for your instruction.

2 DOGE TOMASO MOCENIGO'S 'FAREWELL ADDRESS' TO A FEW SENATORS GATHERED AROUND HIS DEATHBED (MARCH–APRIL 1423)

Introduction

The sources for these last words are basically the same as for the 'Political Testament', yet the veracity of the 'Farewell Address' or 'Ultima Arringa' is more generally accepted by modern historians. The speech has been mined for its detailed information on the Venetian budget and navy. Norwich (1982, p. 298) says of this address: 'in so far as we can judge, [it] is authentic'.

The immediate context for the 'Farewell Address' may be inferred from the mention, at the beginning, of Antonio della Massa, who had been sent by Pope Martin V to find out what were Venice's intentions for the defence of Constantinople, besieged by the Turks. On 21 March 1423, the Senate replied to Friar della Massa that Venice was ready to contribute three fully equipped galleys, provided the other Christian states supplied their own contingents. This was, in fact, the other side of the problem of the Florentine alliance: a serious involvement against Milan would preclude a strong defence against the Ottomans.

Doge Mocenigo died on 4 April 1423, soon after giving this address; he was 80. Francesco Foscari was immediately elected to succeed him. The new Doge proceeded to enter into an alliance with Florence and started a war against the Duke of Milan. Foscari did show some interest in the problems of the East. In 1424, he dispatched a fleet to defend Salonika (today's Thessaloniki) against the Turks; the commander of that fleet was Pietro Loredan, who had earlier been the likeliest choice for the dogeship in opposition to Foscari. Loredan had defeated the Ottomans at the battle of Gallipoli in 1416 and was a popular hero. Not surprisingly, relations between the houses of Loredan and Foscari gradually 'reached a stage not far short of open vendetta' (Norwich, 1982, p. 335) and were a factor in forcing the resignation of Foscari in 1457, a week before his demise at the age of 84.

Under Foscari, Venice fought 30 years of Milanese wars and devoted fewer men and less money to the defence of her maritime empire; she was soon sending a bigger navy up the Po river than she was to the Aegean sea; Salonika was lost in 1430, and Constantinople fell in 1453.

At the end of the century, Italian wars were still absorbing Venetian resources and the Ottoman Turks were reaching for naval supremacy in the Mediterranean. It would become the destiny of another Loredan, Leonardo (elected Doge on 2 October 1501), to face the greater challenge of the Iberians who, with the help of the Genoese, were opening up the world ocean in the West.

Text

Signori, we have sent for you all because God has willed to give us this illness that will terminate our pilgrimage on this earth. We praise above all the omnipotence of the Father, the Son, and the Holy Ghost, who are one God in three persons, that assumed carnal human form, who was the Son according to the doctrine of our preacher, messer Friar Antonio della Massa.[1] We are obligated to that God, who is a Trinity, for many reasons. As is expected of us by this said God, we must give the Forty-One[2] who will elect the head of this our City, great admonitions to defend the Christian religion, to love our neighbours, administer justice, love and defend peace. We are obligated to practice all these things. Praise be to God, the Creator of all things.

Let me inform you that, during the time of our administration, we have reduced the government debt by 4 million ducats. This debt was incurred in the war against Padua, Vicenza and Verona. Our burden amounts to 6[3] million ducats and we have taken measures that enable us to make two half-yearly disbursements: one for repayment of the loans, and the other to meet the payroll of all public offices and the army, all the outlays of the Arsenal; and everything we had to do, we did.

Moreover, to ensure our peace, the City of Venice sends 10 million ducats[4] in capital annually to all the world, by ships, galleys and other small ships, so that the income from interest amounts to 2 million ducats, and the profits from trade to Venice are 2 million ducats, and between interest and trade it comes to 4 million[5] in total.

Source: *Reale Commissione per la publicazione dei documenti financiari della Republica di Venezia* (Venice, 1912), 2nd series, *Bilanci Generali*, Vol. I, Tome 1, Document 85, pp. 94–7; this is stated to be a reproduction of the speech in the Pietro Dolfin Annals, in the Biblioteca Nazionale Marciana (*Italiani*, cl.VII, cod. 794, c.24), judged to be the most consistent and fullest account extant. It is interesting to note that the Dolfin Annals were purchased in 1763 by the British Consul in Venice, Joseph Smith, on behalf of King George III who was starting the second Royal Library. They are now in the British Library (King's 149). However, the last pages of this MS, that carry the present text, remained in Venice. A practically identical version is found in Sanudo's *Vite* (Muratori (ed.), 1733) cols 958–60. Formatting and footnotes by the editors. Translated from the Italian by Sylvia Modelski.

1. Antonio della Massa is described by Sanudo as 'Generale de'Frati Minori' and by Thiriet as a 'frère mineur', i.e., a Dominican priest; in this text, Mocenigo calls him 'our preacher' (*nostro Predicatore*), which would indicate a member of the Franciscan order. His mission, however, was diplomatic.
2. A 41-member committee, selected from the Great Council by a complicated procedure, to nominate a new Doge for approval by the Assembly (Lane, 1973, p. 111).
3. *Bilanci Generali* (Reale Commissione . . ., 1912, doc. 80, p. 577n.), questions this and a few other figures. It seems that the Roman numeral I in the original text was wrongly copied as V in several places, and the correct amount for the debt should be 2, not 6, million.
4. The equivalent of $US 550 000 000 today (1987).
5. These figures were once challenged, but have now been accepted (Braudel, 1984, p. 121).

We have 3000 vessels of from 10 to 200 *anforas*[6] with 17 000 seamen, navigating the seas. We also have 300 round ships [nave] with 8000 seamen. We keep 45 light and heavy galleys with 11 000 seamen in active duty, yearly.[7] We have 3000 ship carpenters and 3000 caulkers. As you know, we have 16 000 weavers of silk cloth and fustian. The estimated value of the houses is 7 050 000[8] ducats, and the rent from these houses is 500 000 ducats. We have 1000 patricians with annual incomes of between 700 and 4000 ducats, in all 490 000. As you have seen, the revenue from Venice is 774 000 ducats, from the *terra ferma*, 464 000, from overseas 376 000. You know the life style of our patricians and citizens. So, we urge you to ask the Divine omnipotence to inspire you to pursue peace, as we have done, and thus abide by Him and show Him gratitude. If you follow my advice, you will become the masters of all the gold in Christendom; the whole world will fear and respect you. Beware of setting fire among what belongs to others, and of waging unjust wars, because God will destroy you.

And in order to be informed about who you will elect to be Doge, I will ask you to secretly whisper the name in my ear so that I may be able to advise you on who is the best in our city.

Signori, I see that many of you would choose among the following: Messer Marino Caravello who is a worthy man of merit, well liked on account of both his intellect and his goodness. The same is true of Messer Francesco Bembo and Messers Pietro Loredano, Iacomo Trivisan, Antonio Contarini, Fantino Michiel, and Albano Badoer. All these men are wise, eligible and deserving. But I can't understand those who say they want Messer Francesco Foscari because Francesco Foscari tells lies and also spreads many unfounded rumours; he flies and soars worse than a hawk. And God does not want this. If you make him Doge, in no time you will be at war. He who now has 10 000 ducats will be left with only 1000. He who has 10 houses will have only one. And he who owns 10 overcoats will be reduced to one, and who has 10 doublets, shoes or shirts, will have trouble finding one. And so on with everything, so that your gold and silver will be destroyed, as will your honour and reputation. And where now you are the masters you will become the servants and vassals of the soldiery, the plunderers, the gangs. That is why I have sent for you. May God let you govern and protect you.

Let me advise you that in the war between us and the Turks many valorous men, experts at sea, were tested in all kinds of interventions, both in administration and in battle. For your information: you have six admirals [*capitani*] who can command 60 galleys and more. And on your ships, among the crossbow men, you have patricians qualified to be masters of galleys and to lead them. You have 100 practised commanders, adept at taking charge of war galleys, who know how to execute missions; and enough knowledgeable and wise officers for 100 galleys; of experienced galley hands, we have enough for 100 galleys. And it is with these that we waged the war against the Turks, so that the world said: the Venetians are masters when it comes to captains, officers and galley crews. You have 10 men with great deeds to their credit in positions of trust, in embassies, where they have shown good reasoning in their discourses. You have many doctors who are learned in science. You have numerous experts employed in the offices of the

6. 1 *anfora* = 600 litres (Sottas, 1938, p. 39).
7. Sottas (1938, p. 39) categorises the 45 galleys roughly thus: 25 large merchant, 15 light, 2–3 pilgrim, 2 passenger and mail.
8. This figure should be corrected to 3 050 000 (see note 3, p. 30).

Palace.[9] See how many foreigners remain content in their own lands under the jurisdiction of our judges at the Palace. Continue along the same path you are on; may you and your children be blessed.

Annually, our Mint strikes 1 200 000 ducats in gold; and in silver, 800 000 ducats' worth of *grosseti* and *mezzanini*, and *soldi*;[10] of these, 5000 ?marks [*marche*] are sent to Syria and Egypt annually; to the surrounding districts of the *terra ferma* go 100 000 ducats in *mezzanini* and *soldi*. Your maritime places[11] receive 50 000 ducats in *mezzanini* and *soldi* every year. England gets 100 000 ducats' worth of *soldi* every year. The rest remains in Venice.

You see how the Florentines send us every year, 16 000 bolts of the finest, fine, and medium cloth; we export these to Apulia, the Kingdom of Sicily, Barbary, Syria, Cyprus, Rhodes, Egypt, Romania, Candia, Morea, Lisbon.[12] And the said Florentines bring in 7000[13] ducats weekly in all kinds of money, worth a total of 150 000 ducats a year. They buy French and Catalonian woollens, crimson, grains, silk, gold and silver threads, wax, sugars, Greek silver, big and small coins, rock crystal, indigo, leathers, jewels, to the great advantage of our country. And the same thing was done by every generation, in the same way.

If you strive to preserve the conditions you are in now, you will be superior to all. May God help you prosper, rule, and govern well. Amen.

9. The Doge's Palace which Mocenigo (after paying a fine because such ducal ostentation was not allowed) had had remodelled during his time in office; he also was responsible for starting the Library of San Marco.
10. *grosseti* and *mezzanini* were medieval silver coins of small value; the mostly copper *soldi* were worth about a pre-1971 English half-penny each.
11. Such as, presumably, Corfu, Crete, Negroponte, or Modon.
12. In Marino Sanudo's account, this list ends with Istria instead of Lisbon.
13. *Bilanci Generali* (Reale Commissione . . . , 1912, p. 577n.) suggests 3000 as the more likely figure, see note 3, p. 30.

Source: W. de G. Birch, *The Commentaries of the Great Afonso Dalbuquerque* (1877)

Figure 2.1 Francisco de Almeida

2 Portugal Starts a Global System

At about the time that Venice pondered the merits of deeper involvement in the affairs of Northern Italy, the economic centre of gravity of what Braudel (1984, p. 486) has called the 'super-world-economy' consisting of Islam, India and China, became 'stabilised' in the East Indies (around such ports as Malacca). Meanwhile, Islam was threatening Europe with conquest and cutting off its contacts with the East. Both Portugal and China embarked upon great oceanic voyages aimed at that region.

The leader of Ming China's expeditionary fleets was Cheng Ho, a navigator of Moslem origin. Just before setting off on the seventh and last of their voyages across the 'Western Ocean', he and his companions erected a stone (dated 5 December 1431–2 January 1432) at Chang-lo, in the province of Fukien; the inscription on the monument reads in part:

> The Imperial Ming Dynasty, in unifying seas and continents, surpassing the three dynasties even goes beyond the Han and T'ang Dynasties. The countries beyond the horizon and at the ends of the earth have all become subjects and to the most western of the western or the most northern of the northern countries, however far they may be, the distances and routes may be calculated. Thus the barbarians from beyond the seas, though their countries are truly distant, with double translation have come to audience bearing precious objects and presents.[1]
>
> The Emperor, approving of their loyalty and sincerity, has ordered us (Cheng Ho) and others at the head of several tens of thousands of officers and flagtroops to ascend more than a hundred large ships to go and confer presents on them in order to make manifest the transforming power of the (imperial) virtue and to treat distant people with kindness. From the third year of Yung-lo (1405) till now we have several times received the commission of ambassadors to the countries of the Western Ocean. The barbarian countries which we have visited are: by way of Chan-ch'eng (Champa), Chao-wa (Java), San-fo-ch'i (Palembang) and Hsien-lo (Siam), crossing straight over to Hsi-lan-shan (Ceylon) in South India, Ku-li (Calicut) and K'o-chih (Cochin), we have gone to the western regions Hu-lo-mo-ssu (Hormuz), A-tan (Aden), Mu-ku-tu-shu (Mogadishu, in Africa), all together more than thirty countries large and small. We have traversed more than one hundred thousand *li*[2] of immense waterspaces and have beheld in the ocean huge waves like mountains rising sky-high, and we have set eyes on barbarian regions far away hidden in a blue transparency of light vapours, while our sails, loftily unfurled like clouds, day and night continued their course (rapid like that) of a star, traversing those savage waves as if we were treading a public thoroughfare. Truly this was due to the majesty and the good fortune of the Court and moreover we owe it to the protective virtue of the Celestial Spouse (Duyvendak, 1949, pp. 28–9).

For reasons that are still not fully explained however, China abandoned her world-spanning ambitions soon after this seventh expedition by Cheng Ho.

Portugal proved to be a far more determined traveller as she embarked upon a grand collective design for overseas and oceanic enterprise; Ceuta was taken in 1415; the Madeira Islands were explored and settled between 1418 and 1425, and the Azores were discovered in 1427 (Diffie and Winius, 1977, pp. 57–61). Daniel Boorstin (1983, p. 157) regards this activity as a 'grand prototype of modern exploration' because it was a 'product of clear purpose' and because it called for a 'progressive, step-by-step national program for advances through the unknown . . . As an organized, long-term enterprise of discovery the Portuguese achievement was more modern, more revolutionary than the more widely celebrated exploits of Columbus'.

In the century that followed, this 'organized discovery' (the detailed account of which need not detain us here) set up the prerequisites for the global system and laid the foundation of Portugal's claim to leadership at the global level. The country's role in that process cannot be adequately portrayed in a few documents, but it is well known in general outline, if contested in some details. The grounds for asserting a special position for Portugal have been sketched out in Modelski (1987). The extensive maritime activities deployed, and the impressive naval capabilities available especially after 1500 have been documented in Modelski and Thompson (1988, especially Chapter 7). All that can (and needs) to be done at this point is to marshall evidence for the purpose of answering the question: did the Portuguese see themselves, at the time, in a role of such leadership, and did others see them likewise?

Let us, first of all, deal briefly with two objections commonly heard regarding a possible global role for Portugal: was not Portugal much too small to have undertaken such a task, and was not Spain, in any event, more important?

Even if we grant, in general terms, that this was a relatively small country to serve as the base for global operations, we would point out that its not insubstantial territory was superbly located and equipped for maritime enterprise. The population, though some ten times that of the city of Venice, was not large. Estimated at $1\frac{1}{2}$ million, it may have been only one-fifth that of Castile. But while the latter kingdom experienced, in the fifteenth century, severe problems of internal strife and disorganisation, and was only just entering upon the union with Aragon and the absorption of Granada, Portugal had already attained national unity. Its leadership was well-organised for collective enterprise, and capable of decisive action – not just activity that could be sustained over a period of generations, as had been shown in the explorations, but also action that could be mobilised at short notice for urgent political purposes, as it was in the months leading up to the settlement of Tordesillas. When Isabella and Ferdinand proposed to define their rights in the discoveries of Columbus without consulting him, John II, the King of Portugal, threatened war, and mobilised his fleet.[3] An even higher degree of organisation and determination was shown in the planning of the establishment of a monopoly of trade in the Indian Ocean, as is evidenced by the instructions issued to Viceroy Francisco de Almeida in 1505 (Doc. 9), at a time when knowledge of this region in Lisbon was minimal (no King of Portugal ever visited the East in person).

Portugal's complex relationship with Spain had elements of both conflict and cooperation, of rivalry and competition tempered by an awareness of a convergence of interests. In the century preceding Tordesillas the two countries had fought a couple of major wars (both conflicts having strong elements of internal dispute): first, the long war (whose principal issue was the independence of Portugal from Castile) that ended only in 1411, and secondly, the one that concluded with the peace of Alcaçovas (1479). That last conflict was primarily internal, involving the Portuguese king's claims to the throne of Spain, but it also brought to the fore a strong drive on the part of Spanish interests (especially from Seville, and the small port of Palos) to enter the trade with gold-rich Guinea, on which the Portuguese had established a firm grip in the preceding decades. It was from Palos that Christopher Columbus sailed on his first voyage to the west, whose results produced another crisis in Spanish–Portuguese relations. As for Guinea, Alcaçovas engaged the Spaniards not to disturb 'the King of Portugal . . . in [his] possessions . . . in all the trade, lands and barter in Guinea or in any other islands, coasts or lands . . . from the Canary Islands down toward Guinea' (Davenport, 1917, p. 44).

But there were also strong currents conducive to an accommodation. The outcome of both wars produced something like a balance between the countries; Portugal clearly held its own against the larger Castile, even Castile united with Aragon. In the end, as the latter conceded Portuguese independence, Portugal all but abandoned its designs on Spain, and, as just mentioned, she acquired a monopoly of the trade with Guinea in the settlement of 1479. A series of marriages consolidated the relations between the two nations at a time when Portugal's traditional allies – in Burgundy (i.e., the Netherlands) and in England – were going through periods of internal uncertainty. For a few years in the 1490s a union of the two countries under one monarch appeared imminent and was frustrated only by a series of accidents and deaths in the two royal families. But when Isabella and Ferdinand finally established a dynastic link between their own house and the Hapsburgs (newly established in Burgundy) this also helped stabilise relations with Portugal. The treaty of Tordesillas of 1494 (Doc. 3), brought about an enduring settlement of Spanish–Portuguese competing claims overseas, at the same time as it stabilised the emerging global political regime of which it became the charter.

Because of its importance, and as an early instance of diplomatic procedures still in use today, we reproduce the treaty in its entirety, together with the full powers of the delegations that negotiated it. This agreement brought a solution to the problem of allocating roles in the discoveries. Furthermore, it brilliantly resolved another disagreement by transforming it into a platform of mutual cooperation. It gave Portugal what it wanted, and what mattered most at the time: control over the trade with the Indian Ocean, as well as a claim on what was to become Brazil; but it also granted Spain safe access to the newly discovered lands in the west, whose organisation kept Seville occupied for the next three centuries. The need, from time to time, to defend that newly created oceanic regime against interlopers produced an added community of interests between the two countries, the naval convention of 1552 being a case in point (Doc. 10). The closeness of these ties is also evident in the two letters Manuel wrote reporting the successful outcome of the voyages of da Gama and of Cabral to his parents-in-law (Docs 4; 7).

To simplify somewhat, the relationship between Portugal and Spain congealed into a pattern set by the outcome of the war of 1476–79 'in which the Castilians were victorious on land and the Portuguese at sea' (Diffie and Winius, 1977, p. 152). Spain continued to dominate on land, contended for empire in Europe,[4] went to the Americas and built another large empire there. Portugal, on the other hand, stayed on the ocean, captured the trade of the East, and, in the process, built a global system; that is why it needs to be called the world power.

We are drawing this distinction between the land power of Spain, and the sea power of Portugal, a question of relative emphasis between two west European powers. But in a wider sense, the way it looked to the Ottomans – perhaps to excuse their own neglect of naval (hence global) affairs – 'God has given the earth to the Mussulmans, and the sea to the Christians' as Sir William Temple (1754, Vol. III, p. 381), writing in the late 1600s, explained.

GROUNDS FOR LEADERSHIP

The Portuguese saw themselves assuming a position of global leadership by:

(1) pursuing the enterprise of discovery;
(2) deliberately supplanting the system managed, so far, by Venice; and
(3) purposely putting in place a global network.

First, we need to draw a distinction between 'exploration' (or 'discovery' – terms used interchangeably by Portugal to describe its activities and characterising this age to this day) and 'territorial conquest' in the traditional, or imperial, mode. The Spanish title of the treaty of Tordesillas: *Capitulacion per la Particion del mar Oceano* (Agreement for the Division of the Ocean Sea) makes it plain that it concerned maritime and not territorial affairs. It is in this sense that it can be regarded as instituting the first global political regime, because the global system emerged as soon as the concept of the ocean surfaced as a sphere of activities distinct from those of a regional (e.g., European) or national (e.g., Portuguese or Spanish) nature.

Discoveries (*descobrimentos*) is a term that today describes that entire epoch. But as the documents show it was also current at the time; it recurs in the treaty of Tordesillas (Doc. 3), and it is discovery that is reported to the world (Docs 4; 7) and is acknowledged by the Venetians (Doc. 8) as the major achievement. Portugal made of discovery a distinct kind of global activity, established that it rebounded to the general interest, and on that basis proceeded to claim special rights and privileges.

The rights claimed were summarised most succintly in the titles assumed by King Manuel. According to the chronicle of Damião de Gois, the King added to his existing titles in the same year in which he married for the second time a daughter of Isabella and Ferdinand, Maria (August 1500). This could have been the first occasion on which the new titles were publicly proclaimed. But the first use in correspondence occurs in Manuel's letter to a Portuguese cardinal in Rome, dated 28 August 1499 (Ravenstein (ed.), 1898, pp. 114–16), within weeks of Vasco de Gama's return from India.

An immediate precedent for changing the royal title was the 1486 addition by John II (Manuel's predecessor) of the phrase 'Lord of Guinea' to his own description (as it appears, for instance, in the Treaty of Tordesillas (1494) Doc. 3). This was done soon after John II gained acknowledgment from Spain of his exclusive rights and erected a fortress at El Mina (in today's Ghana). The new title was a claim to the monopoly of trade and control of sea traffic, but signified no intention to conquer West Africa.

Similar reasoning was implied when Manuel made himself 'Lord of Guinea and of the Conquest, the Navigation and Commerce of Ethiopia, Arabia, Persia and India' (Doc. 5). It signified the intention to establish a trading and maritime monopoly but no desire to conquer Ethiopia, or India, etc. – and no such design appeared later. From the language used in the *Regimento* (Doc. 9, see Items 45, 48, 52, 95, for instance), 'Lord of Conquest' might be taken to infer 'feudal lordship'. Writing in 1566, Manuel's biographer, Damião de Gois, thought that the title assumed by the King in 1500 of *Lord of the Conquest, Navigation etc.*, was 'as honorable as the conquest itself' ['*titulo tam honroso quanto ho he ha mesma conquista*'] (Gois, 1949, Part I, p. 114). According to Godinho (1982, Vol. II, p. 174), when he made this decision the King was not interested in any territorial conquest as such but instead resolved to assume from then on 'the effective lordship of the sea and trade'. 80 years later, the Low Countries would rebel against Spain precisely because the latter treated them 'as if they had been conquered' (Doc. 11) and Hugo Grotius, in his famous legal Brief *Mare Liberum*, based the Dutch East India Company's case against Portugal on the distinction between title to Lordship and actual possession (see Doc. 14).

The second proof of Portuguese leadership was their clear intention to supplant the Venetian system, and in particular its hold on the profitable spice trade flowing along the central artery of the pre-modern world system, linking China with India and Europe via the Near East. That Egypt at that time and in the following decades was in a state of chaos over the Mamluk succession, and its trade disrupted, created additional opportunities for the Portuguese. By sailing around Africa they outflanked and destroyed the monopoly held by Venice, and Cairo. The concern with spices, as with gold, is evident in all the reports on the voyages, and just as much in the Venetian reactions. True, the oration of the Republic's ambassador's in Lisbon (Doc. 8) makes light of it, but it is the very substance of his full report to the home government (Doc. 6). In Venice itself, according to Priuli, the effect was electric:

> if this voyage should continue, the King of Portugal could call himself the King of Money because all would convene to that country to obtain spices, and the money would accumulate greatly in Portugal . . . When this news was truly learned in Venice, the whole city was much stirred by it and every one was stupefied that in this our time there should have been found a new voyage which was never heard of or seen in the times of the ancients and of our ancestors. And this news was held by the learned to be the worst news which the Venetian republic could have had, to lose the liberty abroad . . . there is no doubt at all that the city of Venice came to such a great reputation and fame, as it now enjoys, only through the sea (Greenlee, 1938, pp. 132–3).

The Venetians had rested on their laurels, had stopped innovating at sea and in trade, and were taken by surprise; but Portugal's design was instantly, if belatedly, recognised by them (and soon by others) as a creative effort at a higher level of global organisation.

Thirdly, Portugal's goals were not merely a matter of aspirations or intentions. They were promptly backed by action. King Manuel told the Venetian envoy (Doc. 6) that it was his intention to put 40 ships on the route to India and Table 2.1 makes it plain that this was no mere boast. Considering that Venice at that time employed fewer than 20 trading galleys on all of its regular shipping routes, this represented a tremendous commitment. The *armada* of 30 ships that the King sent that year to the Eastern Mediterranean in response to Venetian pleas for help against the Ottomans (Docs 5; 8) was a practical demonstration that these were not empty words (although not really sincere, since he was simultaneously busy ruining her trade with the East at its source). Portugal's shipbuilding programme took off that year (cf. Modelski and Thompson, 1988, Table 7.2).

But the initial period of necessarily scattered efforts ended in 1505 when it was clearly realised that an ambition for global control must be treated in a global way. The *armada* commanded by Francisco de Almeida that sailed in March of that year was only one of the annual fleets that the King of Portugal was sending to India but it was the largest ever (see Table 2.1) and it was armed with instructions for the establishment of a permanent system. The *Regimento* for that enterprise, presented here at some length (Doc. 9), outlines in great detail the practical steps that had to be taken to create a nucleus of what turned out to be a global system, consisting of fleets, fortresses, trading posts, and alliances. Almeida started on the implementation of this design, and Afonso de Albuquerque, his successor, completed it by 1515. The design was amazing in the boldness of its conception. It was indeed modelled on Venice's *oltre-mar*, composed of the same elements, but it was projected on the scale of a global, and not a regional, system. For where Venice coped, in a familiar environment, with distances of 1000 or 2000 miles, Portugal launched into a totally unfamiliar millieu, over distances of 10 000 miles, and more.

The documents thus show that the King of Portugal and his advisors knew exactly what they were doing when they assumed control of the ocean space won at Tordesillas; in one stroke, they acted to displace both Venice and Cairo in the spice trade, and constructed a global network. This was something so entirely new that it merits being called the nucleus of the global system.

Table 2.1 *Armadas* sailing from Lisbon for the East, 1497–1515

Departure	*Commandant*	*Naus*	*Caravels*
1497			
(July 8)	Vasco da Gama (4, 7)[1]	3 (1 *navio*)	1
1500			
(March 9)	Pedro Alvares Cabral (6, 7)	13	
1501			
(March 15)	João da Nova (9)	4	
1502			
(February 10)	Vasco da Gama (9)	15	
(March 25)	Estevão da Gama	5	
1503			
(April 6)	Afonso de Albuquerque (9)	3	
(April 14)	Francisco de Albuquerque (9)	3 (sail)	
(May)	Antonio de Saldanha	3 (sail)	
1504			
(April 22)	Lopo Soares (9)	13	
1505			
(March 25)	Francisco de Almeida (9)	14	6
(May 18)	Pedro de Añaya	6	
1506			
(March 6)	Tristão da Cunha and Afonso de Albuquerque	11	
1507			
(April 12, 15, 20)	Jorge de Melo Pereira	12	
1508			
(April 5)	Diogo Lopes de Sequeira (Malacca)	4 (*navios*)	
(April 9)	Jorge de Aguiar	13 (sail)	
1509			
(March 12)	Dom Fernando Coutinho	15	
1510			
(March 12)	Diogo Mendes (for Malacca)	4	
	João Serrão		3
(March 16)	Gonzale de Sequeria	7	
1511			
(March 25)	D. Garcia de Noronha	6	
1512			
(March 25)	Jorge de Melo Pereira	8	
	Garcia de Sousa	4	
1513			
(March 20)	João de Sousa de Lima	4	
1514			
(March 27)	Cristovão de Brito	5	
(June 2)	Sebastião de Sousa	3 (*navios*)	
1515			
(April 7)	Lopo Soares (third Viceroy)	15	

1. Doc. no.

Sources: Almeida (1929) pp. 433n.–434n.; *Armadas da India*, *passim*.

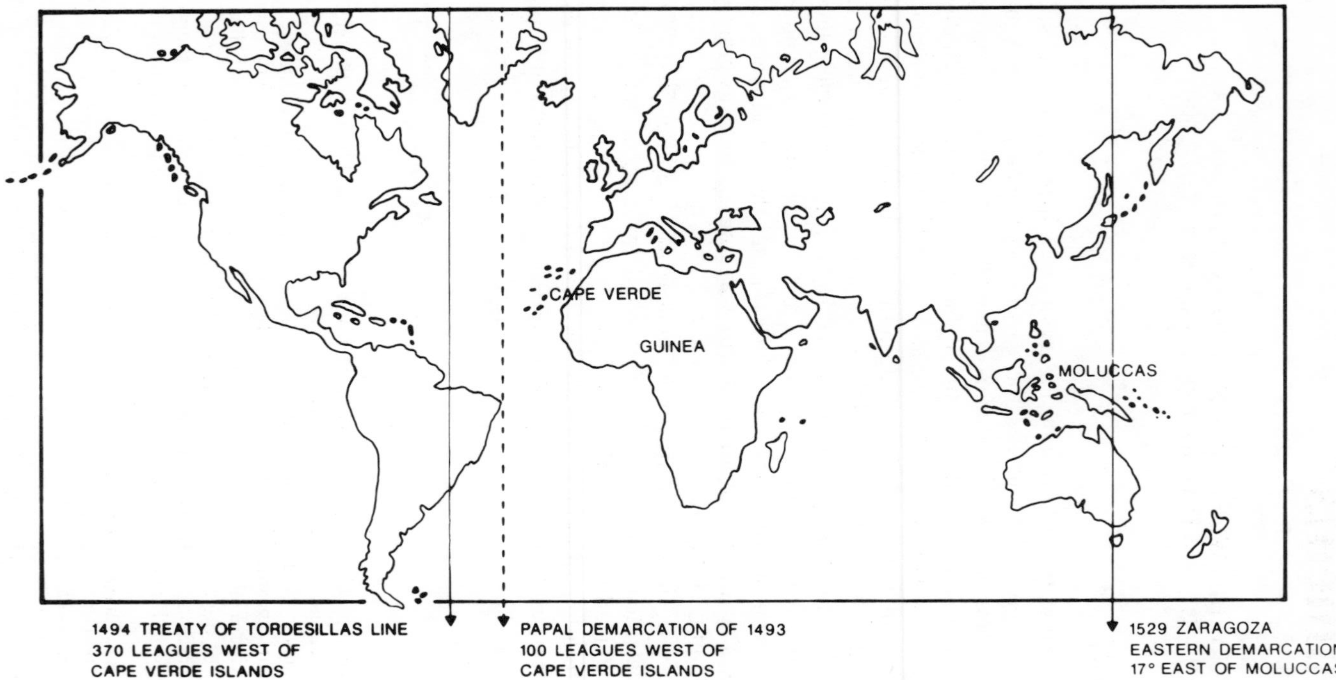

Map 2.1 The Tordesillas regime

Documents

3 TREATY BETWEEN SPAIN AND PORTUGAL, CONCLUDED AT TORDESILLAS ON 7 JUNE 1494

Introduction

The main clause (item 1) of this Treaty draws a spectacular line 'straight from pole to pole' that divides the earth's ocean space unambiguously between the two parties. The idea of demarcating the zones of Portuguese and Spanish influence on the oceans by means of a North–South division first occurred (possibly at the suggestion of Christopher Columbus) in 1493, in a bull issued by Pope Alexander VI at the request of King Ferdinand, a fellow Aragonian. But a year later, during the negotiations at Tordesillas, the Portuguese succeeded in moving the dividing line 270 leagues to the West (see Fig. 2.2). The Treaty clearly states that no Papal declaration can absolve the signatories from the observance of its provisions. Papal approval for the treaty was sought, and was granted by the next Pontiff, Julius II.

Item 3, with detailed instructions for a joint expedition in 1495, was not implemented. But the rules established by items 2 and 3 became operative immediately, and they worked.

An eastern line of demarcation for the world ocean, 17 degrees east of the Moluccas, was assumed and later confirmed by the Treaty of Zaragoza in 1529.

Text

Full powers of the Portuguese delegation

Don Juan, by the Grace of God, King of Portugal and of Algarve, this side and beyond the sea in Africa, and Lord of Guinea:

To whomever shall see this letter of authority and procuration, we make known: That, inasmuch as by order of the very exalted and very excellent powerful Princes, the King Don Ferdinand and the Queen, Doña Isabella, King and Queen of Castile, of Leon, of Aragon, of Sicily, of Granada, etc., our much loved and precious brothers, some islands were discovered and newly found, and other islands and lands may be hereafter discovered and found, in regard to both

Sources: Blair, Emma Helen, and James Alexander Robertson, *The Philippine Islands* (1903–09) Vol. I, pp. 122–8; Thatcher, John Boyd, *Christopher Columbus* (New York and London, 1903) Vol. 2, pp. 175–86; Davenport, Frances Gardiner, *European Treaties bearing on the History of the United States* . . . (Washington, D.C., 1917) Vol. 1, pp. 95–9. Headings added. Slight inconsistencies in spelling and style are due to varying renditions from the Portuguese and Spanish by different translators.

of which, found and to be found, by the right and consideration which we have therein, there might occur between us and our Realms and Dominions, subjects and natives thereof, debates and differences, which may our Lord forbid, and it pleases us by the great love and friendship which there is between us, and for the seeking, procuring and preserving of greater peace and firmer concord and tranquillity, that the sea in which the said islands are and shall be found, be divided and marked between us in some good, sure and restricted manner. And as we, at present, cannot participate in the matter personally, confiding in you, Ruy de Sousa, Lord of Sagres and Berenguel, and Don Juan de Sousa, our Chief Steward, and Arias de Almadana, Corrector of the Civil Acts in our Court and of our Desembargo, all of our Council, by this present letter we give you all our full power and authority and special command, and we make and constitute you all, jointly and each one of you *in solidum*, in any manner, if the others shall be prevented, our Ambassadors and Representatives in the most ample form possible, and which in such case shall be generally and specially required: and in such manner that the generality may not derogate from the specialty, nor the specialty from the generality, in order that for us and in our name and the names of our heirs and successors, and of all our Realms and Dominions, subjects and natives thereof, you can treat, agree and adjust, – and make treaties and agreements, with the said King and Queen of Castile, our brothers, or with whomever holds their authority for that purpose, – any agreement and adjustment and limitation, demarcation and compact, in regard to the Ocean-sea, the islands and mainland which shall be therein, by those boundaries of winds and degrees from north and south and by those parts, divisions and places on dry land and sea and of the earth, which shall appear well to you. And thus we give you the said authority in order that you can leave and do leave to the said King and Queen and to their Realms and successors, all the seas, islands, and lands which shall be and might be within any boundary and demarcation which shall remain to the said King and Queen: and in the same manner we give you the said authority in order that in our name and the names of our successors and the heirs of all our Realms and Dominions, the subjects and natives thereof, you can, with the said King and Queen, or with their Representatives, accord, agree and receive and determine, that all the seas, islands and lands which shall be and might be within the limits and demarcation of coasts, seas, islands and lands, which shall remain for us and for our successors, shall be ours and for our dominion and conquest, and thus for our Realms and successors in them, with those limitations and exceptions of our islands, and with all the other clauses and declarations which shall appear well to you. Which said authority we give to you, the said Ruy de Sousa and Don Juan de Sousa and the Licentiate Almadana, in order that in regard to all that is said and in regard to each one thing and part of it, and in regard to what relates to it and depends upon it and is united to and connected with it, in any manner, you can act, execute, agree, treat and undo, receive and accept, in our name, and the names of the said our heirs and successors and of all our Realms and Dominions, the subjects and vassals thereof, any capitulations and contracts and writings with any charges, compacts, forms, conditions and renunciations which you wish and which you approve, and in regard to it you can act and execute, and do act and execute all the things and each one of them of whatever nature and quality, gravity and importance they may be or can be, although they may be such as by their condition would require another, – our singular and especial command, – and of which there should be made, actually and rightfully, singular and express mention, and which we, being present, would be able to do and execute and receive. And likewise, we give you full power, in order that you can swear and do swear in our place, that we and our heirs and successors and subjects and natives and vassals acquired and to be acquired, will hold, observe and fulfil, and there will be held, observed and fulfilled, actually and in effect, all which you here arrange and capitulate and swear and execute and affirm, renouncing all precaution, fraud and deception and pretence, and thus you can in our name capitulate, assure and promise, that we in person will assure, swear, promise and confirm all which you in the aforesaid name, in regard to what is said, do assure, promise and capitulate, within that term and time which appears well to you, and that we will observe and fulfil it actually and in effect, under the conditions, penalties and obligations contained in the contract of the treaties of peace made and concluded between us, and under all the others which you promise and arrange in the aforesaid our name, which from the present we promise to pay and will pay actually and in effect, if we shall incur them. For which, all and each thing and part of it, we give you the said authority with free and general administration, and we promise and assure by our Royal faith to hold and observe and fulfil, and in the same manner our heirs and successors, all that which by you, in regard to what is said in any form and manner, shall be done, capitulated and sworn and promised, and we promise to consider it as sure, firm and acceptable, stable and valid from now for all time, and that we will not oppose or dispute it, and that it will not be opposed or disputed, or any part of it, at any time, nor in any manner, by us, neither in person nor by persons interposed, directly or indirectly, under any pretence or cause, in justice or out of justice, under the express obligation which we make for it, of the said our Realms and Dominions, and of all our property, patrimonial and fiscal, and any other property whatever of our vassals and subjects and natives, movable and landed property, possessed and to be possessed. In testimony and certification of which we order this our letter given, signed by us and sealed with our seal. Given in our city of Lisbon, March 8. Done by Ruy de Piña in the year of the birth of our Lord Jesus Christ 1494. THE KING.

Full powers of the Spanish delegates

Don Ferdinand and Doña Isabella, by the Grace of God, King and Queen of Castile, of Leon, of Aragon, of Sicily, of Granada, of Toledo, of Valencia, of Galicia, of Mallorca, of Seville, of Cerdeña, of Cordova, of Córcega, of Murcia, of Jaen, of Algarve, of Algeciras, of Gibraltar, of the Islands of the Canaries: Count and Countess of Barcelona and Lords of Vizcaya and of Molina: Dukes of Atenas and of Neopatria: Counts of Rosellon and Cerdania: Marquises of Oristan and of Gociano, etc.: Inasmuch as the Most Serene King of Portugal, our very dear and much loved brother, sent to us by his Ambassadors and Representatives, Ruy de Sousa, to whom belong the towns of Sagres and Berenguel, and Don Juan de Sousa, his Chief Steward, and Arias de Almadana, his Corrector of the Civil Acts in his Court and of his Desembargo, all of his Council, to discuss and make a treaty and agreement with us and with our Ambassadors and persons in our name, in regard to the difference which exists between us and the said Lord, the King of Portugal, our brother, as to what part belongs to us and what part belongs to him of that which up to the present is to be discovered in the Ocean-sea: Therefore, confiding in you, Don Henrique Henriquez, our Chief Majordomo, and Don Gutierre de Cárdenas, Commander-in-Chief of Leon, our Chief Auditor, and the Doctor Rodrigo Maldonado, all of our Council, that you are persons who will be observant of our service, and that you will well and faithfully do that which you were sent for, and charged by us to do: by this present letter we give you our authority, made out in manner and form as we are able and as is required in such case, especially in order that, for us and in our names and the names of our heirs, subjects and the natives of our realms, you can treat, agree and adjust, – and make treaty and agreement with the Ambassadors of the Most Serene King of Portugal, our brother, in his name, – any arrangement and limitation of the Ocean-sea, or agreement in regard to that which is said, by the winds and degrees from North and South, and by those parts, divisions and places on dry land and on sea, and of the earth, which to you shall seem well, and thus we give you the said authority in order that you can leave to the said King of Portugal and to his Realms and successors, all the seas, islands and lands which shall be and might be within any boundary and demarcation of coasts, seas, islands and lands, which shall be fixed and established. And moreover, we give you the said authority in order that in our name and the names of our heirs, and the successors in our realms and dominions, subjects and natives thereof, you can agree and adjust and receive and determine with the said King of Portugal, and with the said his Ambassadors and Representatives in his name, that all the seas, islands and lands that shall be or might be within the boundary and demarcation of the coasts, seas, islands and lands which shall remain for us and for our successors and for our dominion and conquest, shall belong to our Realms and our successors therein, with those limitations and exemptions, and with all the other clauses and declarations which you shall approve: and in order that, in regard to what is said, and in regard to each thing and part of it, and in regard to what relates to it and depends upon it, and is united to and connected with it in any manner, you can act and execute, agree and treat, and receive and accept, – in our name and the names of the said our heirs and successors, and of all our Realms and Dominions, subjects and natives thereof, – any capitulations, contracts and writings, with any charges, acts, forms, conditions and obligations and stipulations, penalties, submissions and renunciations which you desire, and which you approve: and in regard to it, you can act and execute, and do act and execute all the things and each one of them, of whatever nature and quality, gravity and importance they may be or can be, although they may be such as by their condition require another, – our singular and especial command, and of which there should be made, actually and rightfully, singular and express mention, and which, We, being present, would make and execute and receive. And moreover, we give you full power in order that you may swear and do swear in our place, that we and our heirs and successors and subjects and natives and vassals, acquired and to be acquired, will hold and observe and fulfil, and that there shall be held, observed and fulfilled, actually and in effect, all that you shall thus adjust, capitulate and swear and execute and affirm, renouncing all precaution, fraud, deception, fiction and simulation: and thus you can in our name capitulate, assure and promise that we in person will assure, swear, promise and execute and confirm all that which you in our name in regard to what is said, to secure, promise and capitulate, within any term and time which shall appear well to you: and that we will observe and fulfil it, actually and in effect, and under the conditions and penalties and obligations contained in the contract of the parties, between us and the said Most Serene King, our brother, made and agreed, and under all the other things which you shall promise, which from the present time we promise to pay, if we shall incur the said penalties. For which, all and each one thing and part of it, we give you the said authority with free and general administration, and we promise and assure by our faith and Royal word, that we will hold and observe and fulfil, we and our heirs and successors, all that which by you, in regard to what is said, shall be in any form and manner made and capitulated and sworn and promised, and we promise to hold it as established, firm and acceptable, stable and valid, now and in all time and ever after, and that we will not oppose or dispute it, or any part of it, we, nor our heirs and successors, in person or by persons interposed, directly or indirectly, under any pretence or for any cause, in justice or out of justice, under the express obligations which we make for it, of all our property, patrimonial and fiscal, and any other property belonging to our vassals, and subjects and natives, movable property and landed property, possessed and to be possessed: for confirmation of which we order given, this, our letter of authority, which we sign with our names and order sealed with our seal. Given in the city of Tordesillas, the 5th day of the month of June, 1494. I, THE KING. I, THE QUEEN. I, Fernando Alvarez, of Toledo, Secretary of the King and of the Queen, our Lords, caused it to be written by their command.

Full text of the Treaty of Tordesillas

Thereupon[1] it was declared by the above-mentioned representatives of the aforesaid King and Queen of Castile, Leon, Aragon, Sicily, Granada, etc., and of the aforesaid King of Portugal and the Algarves, etc.:

[1.] That, whereas a certain controversy exists between the said lords, their constituents, as to what lands, of all those discovered in the ocean sea up to the present day, the date of this treaty, pertain to each one of the said parts respectively; therefore, for the sake of peace and concord, and for the preservation of the relationship and love of the said King of Portugal for the said King and Queen of Castile, Aragon, etc., it being the pleasure of their Highnesses, they, their said representatives, acting in their name and by virtue of their powers herein described, covenanted and agreed that a boundary or straight line be determined and drawn north and south, from pole to pole, on the said ocean sea, from the Arctic to the Antarctic pole. This boundary or line shall be drawn straight, as aforesaid, at a distance of three hundred and seventy leagues west of the Cape Verde Islands, being calculated by degrees, or by any other manner as may be considered the best and readiest, provided the distance shall be no greater than abovesaid. And all lands, both islands and mainlands, found and discovered already, or to be found and discovered hereafter, by the said King of Portugal and by his vessels on this side of the said line and bound determined as above, toward the east, in either north or south latitude, on the eastern side of the said bound, provided the said bound is not crossed, shall belong to, and remain in the possession of, and pertain forever to, the said King of Portugal and his successors. And all other lands, both islands and mainlands, found or to be found hereafter, discovered or to be discovered hereafter, which have been discovered or shall be discovered by the said King and Queen of Castile, Aragon, etc., and by their vessels, on the western side of the said bound, determined as above, after having passed the said bound toward the west, in either its north or south latitude, shall belong to, and remain in the possession of, and pertain forever to, the said King and Queen of Castile, Leon, etc., and to their successors.

[2.] Item, the said representatives promise and affirm by virtue of the powers aforesaid, that from this date no ships shall be despatched – namely as follows: the said King and Queen of Castile, Leon, Aragon, etc., for this part of the bound, and its eastern side, on this side the said bound, which pertains to the said King of Portugal and the Algarves, etc.; nor the said King of Portugal to the other part of the said bound which pertains to the said King and Queen of Castile, Aragon, etc. – for the purpose of discovering and seeking any mainlands or islands, or for the purpose of trade, barter, or conquest of any kind. But should it come to pass that the said ships of the said King and Queen of Castile, Leon, Aragon, etc., on sailing thus on this side of the said bound, should discover any mainlands or islands in the region pertaining, as abovesaid, to the said King of Portugal, such mainlands or islands shall pertain to and belong forever to the said King of Portugal and his heirs, and their Highnesses shall order them to be surrendered to him immediately. And if the said ships of the said King of Portugal discover any islands and mainlands in the regions of the said King and Queen of Castile, Leon, Aragon, etc., all such lands shall belong to and remain forever in the possession of the said King and Queen of Castile, Leon, Aragon, etc., and

1. From the beginning of the treaty proper, as far as to 'The said Don Enrique Enriques', on p. 52, the translation is taken from Blair and Robertson (1903–9) *The Philippine Islands*.

their heirs, and the said King of Portugal shall cause such lands to be surrendered immediately.

[3.] Item, in order that the said line or bound of the said division may be made straight and as nearly as possible the said distance of three hundred and seventy leagues west of the Cape Verde Islands, as hereinbefore stated, the said representatives of both the said parties agree and assent that within the ten months immediately following the date of this treaty their said constituent lords shall despatch two or four caravels, namely, one or two by each one of them, a greater or less number, as they may mutually consider necessary. These vessels shall meet at the Grand Canary Island during this time, and each one of the said parties shall send certain persons in them, to wit, pilots, astrologers, sailors, and any others they may deem desirable. But there must be as many on one side as on the other, and certain of the said pilots, astrologers, sailors, and others of those sent by the said King and Queen of Castile, Aragon, etc., and who are experienced, shall embark in the ships of the said King of Portugal and the Algarves; in like manner certain of the said persons sent by the said King of Portugal shall embark in the ship or ships of the said King and Queen of Castile, Aragon, etc.; a like number in each case, so that they may jointly study and examine to better advantage the sea, courses, winds, and the degrees of the sun or of north latitude, and lay out the leagues aforesaid, in order that, in determining the line and boundary, all sent and empowered by both the said parties in the said vessels, shall jointly concur. These said vessels shall continue their course together to the said Cape Verde Islands, from whence they shall lay a direct course to the west, to the distance of the said three hundred and seventy degrees, measured as the said persons shall agree, and measured without prejudice to the said parties. When this point is reached, such point will constitute the place and mark for measuring degrees of the sun or of north latitude either by daily runs measured in leagues, or in any other manner that shall mutually be deemed better. This said line shall be drawn north and south as aforesaid, from the said Arctic pole to the said Antarctic pole. And when this line has been determined as abovesaid, those sent by each of the aforesaid parties, to whom each one of the said parties must delegate his own authority and power, to determine the said mark and bound, shall draw up a writing concerning it and affix thereto their signatures. And when determined by the mutual consent of all of them, this line shall be considered as a perpetual mark and bound, in such wise that the said parties, or either of them, or their future successors, shall be unable to deny it, or erase or remove it, at any time or in any manner whatsoever. And should, perchance, the said line and bound from pole to pole, as aforesaid, intersect any island or mainland, at the first point of such intersection of such islands or mainland by the said line, some kind of mark or tower shall be erected, and a succession of similar marks shall be erected in a straight line from such mark or tower, in a line identical with the above-mentioned bound. These marks shall separate those portions of such land belonging to each one of the said parties; and the subjects of the said parties shall not dare, on either side, to enter the territory of the other, by crossing the said mark or bound in such island or mainland.

[4.] Item, inasmuch as the said ships of the said King and Queen of Castile, Leon, Aragon, etc., sailing as before declared, from their kingdoms and seigniories to their said possessions on the other side of the said line, must cross the seas on this side of the line, pertaining to the said King of Portugal, it is therefore concerted and agreed that the said ships of the said King and Queen of Castile, Leon, Aragon, etc., shall, at any time and without any hindrance, sail in either direction, freely, securely, and peacefully, over the said seas of the said King of

Portugal, and within the said line. And whenever their Highnesses and their successors wish to do so, and deem it expedient, their said ships may take their courses and routes direct from their kingdoms to any region within their line and bound to which they desire to despatch expeditions of discovery, conquest, and trade. They shall take their courses direct to the desired region and for any purpose desired therein, and shall not leave their course, unless compelled to do so by contrary weather. They shall do this provided that, before crossing the said line, they shall not seize or take possession of anything discovered in his said region by the said King of Portugal; and should their said ships find anything before crossing the said line, as aforesaid, it shall belong to the said King of Portugal, and their Highnesses shall order it surrendered immediately. And since it is possible that the ships and subjects of the said King and Queen of Castile, Leon, etc., or those acting in their name, may discover before the twentieth day of this present month of June, following the date of this treaty, some islands and mainlands within the said line, drawn straight from pole to pole, that is to say, inside the said three hundred and seventy leagues west of the Cape Verde Islands, as aforesaid, it is hereby agreed and determined, in order to remove all doubt, that all such islands and mainlands found and discovered in any manner whatsoever up to the said twentieth day of this said month of June, although found by ships and subjects of the said King and Queen of Castile, Aragon, etc., shall pertain to and remain forever in the possession of the said King of Portugal and the Algarves, and of his successors and kingdoms, provided that they lie within the first two hundred and fifty leagues of the said three hundred and seventy leagues reckoned west of the Cape Verde Islands to the above-mentioned line – in whatsoever part, even to the said poles, of the said two hundred and fifty leagues they may be found, determining a boundary or straight line from pole to pole, where the said two hundred and fifty leagues end. Likewise all the islands and mainlands found and discovered up to the said twentieth day of this present month of June by the ships and subjects of the said King and Queen of Castile, Aragon, etc., or in any other manner, within the other one hundred and twenty leagues that still remain of the said three hundred and seventy leagues where the said bound that is to be drawn from pole to pole, as aforesaid, must be determined, and in whatever part of the said one hundred and twenty leagues, even to the said poles, – they that are found up to the said day shall pertain to and remain forever in the possession of the said King and Queen of Castile, Aragon, etc., and of their successors and kingdoms; just as whatever is or shall be found on the other side of the said three hundred and seventy leagues pertaining to their Highnesses, as aforesaid, is and must be theirs, although the said one hundred and twenty leagues are within the said bound of the said three hundred and seventy leagues pertaining to the said King of Portugal, the Algarves, etc., as aforesaid.

And if, up to the said twentieth day of this said month of June, no lands are discovered by the said ships of their Highnesses within the said one hundred and twenty leagues, and are discovered after the expiration of that time, then they shall pertain to the said King of Portugal as is set forth in the above.

The said Don Enrique Enriques, chief steward, Don Gutierre de Cardenas, chief auditor, and Doctor Rodrigo Maldonado, representatives of the said very exalted and very mighty princes, the lord and lady, the king and queen of Castile, Leon, Aragon, Sicily, Granada, etc., by virtue of their said power, which is incorporated above, and the said Ruy de Sousa, Dom João de Sousa, his son, and Arias de Almadana, representatives and ambassadors of the said very exalted and very excellent prince, the lord king of Portugal and of the Algarves on this side and beyond the sea in Africa, lord of Guinea, by virtue of their said power, which is incorporated above, promised, and affirmed, in the name of their said constituents, [saying] that they and their successors and kingdoms and lordships, forever and ever, would keep, observe, and fulfil, really and effectively, renouncing all fraud, evasion, deceit, falsehood, and pretense, everything set forth in this treaty, and each part and parcel of it; and they desired and authorized that everything set forth in this said agreement and every part and parcel of it be observed, fulfilled, and performed as everything which is set forth in the treaty of peace concluded and ratified between the said lord and lady, the king and queen of Castile, Aragon, etc., and the lord Dom Alfonso, King of Portugal (may he rest in glory) and the said king, the present ruler of Portugal, his son, then prince in the former year of 1479, must be observed, fulfilled, and performed, and under those same penalties, bonds, securities, and obligations, in accordance with and in the manner set forth in the said treaty of peace. Also they bound themselves [by the promise] that neither the said parties nor any of them nor their successors forever should violate or oppose that which is abovesaid and specified, nor any part or parcel of it, directly or indirectly, or in any other manner at any time, or in any manner whatsoever, premeditated or not premeditated, or that may or can be, under the penalties set forth in the said agreement of the said peace; and whether the fine be paid or not paid, or graciously remitted, that this obligation, agreement, and treaty shall continue in force and remain firm, stable, and valid forever and ever. That thus they[2] will keep, observe, perform, and pay everything, the said representatives, acting in the name of their said constituents, pledged the property, movable and real, patrimonial and fiscal, of each of their respective parties, and of their subjects and vassals, possessed and to be possessed. They renounced all laws and rights of which the said parties or either of them might take advantage to violate or oppose the foregoing or any part of it; and for the greater security and stability of the aforesaid, they swore before God and the Blessed Mary and upon the sign of the Cross, on which they placed their right hands, and upon the words of the Holy Gospels, wheresoever they are written at greatest length, and on the consciences of their said constituents, that they, jointly and severally, will keep, observe, and fulfil all the aforesaid and each part and parcel of it, really and effectively, renouncing all fraud, evasion, deceit, falsehood, and pretense, and that they will not contradict it at any time or in any manner. And under the same oath they swore not to seek absolution or release from it from our most Holy Father or from any other legate or prelate who could give it to them. And even though, *proprio motu*, it should be given to them, they will not make use of it; rather, by this present agreement, they, acting in the said name, entreat our most Holy Father that his Holiness be pleased to confirm and approve this said agreement, according to what is set forth therein; and that he order his bulls in regard to it to be issued to the parties or to whichever of the parties may solicit them, with the tenor of this agreement incorporated therein; and that he lay his censures upon those who shall violate or oppose it at any time whatsoever. Likewise, the said representatives, acting in the said names, bound themselves under the same penalty and oath, that within the one hundred days next following, reckoned from the day of the date of this agreement, the parties would mutually exchange the approbation and ratification of this said agreement, written on parchment, signed with the names of the said lords, their constituents, and sealed with their hanging leaden seals; and that the instrument which the said lords, the king and queen of Castile, Aragon, etc., should have to issue, must be

2. I.e., the constituents.

signed, agreed to, and sanctioned by the very noble and most illustrious lord, Prince Don Juan, their son. Of all the foregoing they authorized two copies, both of the same tenor exactly, which they signed with their names and executed before the undersigned secretaries and notaries public, one for each party. And whichever copy is produced, it shall be as valid as if both the copies which were made and executed in the said town of Tordesillas, on the said day, month, and year aforesaid, should be produced. The chief deputy, Don Enrique, Ruy de Sousa, Dom Juan de Sousa, Doctor Rodrigo Maldonado, Licentiate Ayres. Witnesses who were present and who saw the said representatives and ambassadors sign their names here and execute the aforesaid, and take the said oath: The deputy Pedro de Leon and the deputy Fernando de Torres, residents of the town of Valladolid, the deputy Fernando de Gamarra, deputy of Zagra and Cenete, *contino* of the house of the said king and queen, our lords, and João Suares de Sequeira, Ruy Leme, and Duarte Pacheco, *continos* of the house of the said King of Portugal, summoned for that purpose. And I, Fernando Alvarez de Toledo, secretary of the king and queen, our lords, member of their council, and their scrivener of the high court of justice, and notary public in their court and throughout their realms and lordships, witnessed all the aforesaid, together with the said witnesses and with Estevan Vaez, secretary of the said King of Portugal, who by the authority given him by the said king and queen, our lords, to certify to this act in their kingdoms, also witnessed the abovesaid; and at the request and with the authorization of all the said representatives and ambassadors, who in my presence and his here signed their names, I caused this public instrument of agreement to be written. It is written on these six leaves of paper, in entire sheets, written on both sides, together with this leaf, which contains the names of the aforesaid persons and my sign; and the bottom of every page is marked with the notarial mark of my name and that of the said Estevan Vaez. And in witness I here make my sign, which is thus. In testimony of truth: Fernando Alvarez. And I, the said Estevan Vaez (who by the authority given me by the said lords, the king and queen of Castile, and of Leon, to make it public throughout their kingdoms and lordships, together with the said Fernando Alvarez, at the request and summons of the said ambassadors and representatives witnessed everything), in testimony and assurance thereof signed it here with my public sign, which is thus.

Ratification by the King of Portugal

Which said draft of treaties and capitulation and agreement above incorporated, being seen and understood by us, we approve, praise, confirm, execute and ratify it, and promise to hold, observe and fulfil all the aforesaid, therein contained, and each one thing and part of it, actually and in effect, renouncing all fraud, precaution, fiction and simulation, and not opposing or disputing it, or any part of it, at any time or in any manner which may be or can be possible: and for greater certainty, we swear to God and to St Mary and by the words of the Holy Evangels, wherever they are written more at length, and by the sign of the Cross ✠ on which we corporally place our right hand in the presence of Fernan, Duke of Estrada, First Gentleman of the most Illustrious Prince, Don Juan, our very dear and precious nephew, whom the said King and Queen of Castile, of Leon, of Aragon, etc., our brothers, sent to us for that purpose, to thus hold, observe and fulfil it, and each one thing and part of it, which is really and in effect incumbent upon us, as is said, for ourselves, and for our heirs and successors, and for the said our Realms and Dominions, subjects and natives of them, under the penalties, obligations, charges and renunciations in the said Contract of Capitulation, written and contained above. In certification and corroboration of which, we sign this, our letter, with our sign, and we order it sealed with our official seal, hanging on threads of coloured silk. Given in the City of Setubal the 5th day of the month of September. Done by Joan Ruiz the said year of the birth of our Lord Jesus Christ, 1494. THE KING.

Capitulation of the division of the Ocean-sea.

4 KING MANUEL OF PORTUGAL'S LETTER TO KING FERDINAND AND QUEEN ISABELLA OF SPAIN, DATED JULY 1499

Introduction

In 1495, Manuel the Fortunate (1469–1521) succeeded his cousin and brother-in-law John II on the Portuguese throne. John's own son and heir had died in 1491 leaving his wife Isabel a widow. Isabel was the daughter of the King and Queen of Spain. Manuel married Isabel in 1496 and came within sight of becoming the heir to the throne of Castile; but Isabel herself soon died in childbirth. At the time when he wrote the present letter, Manuel had been a widower for almost two years. In 1500 he married for the second time into the Spanish royal family: Isabel's sister Maria by whom he had nine children.

By all accounts on his personality, King Manuel was a cautious young man of average ability and character who reaped the benefits of the bold policies carried out by his predecessors (Romanin, 1913, Vol. IV, pp. 465–6).

Text

Most high and excellent Prince and Princess, most potent Lord and Lady!

Your highnesses already know that we had ordered *Vasco da Gama, a nobleman of our household, and his brother Paulo da Gama, with* four vessels to make discoveries by sea, and that two years have now elapsed since their departure. And as the principal motive of this enterprise has been, with our predecessors, the service of God our Lord, and our own advantage,[1] it pleased Him in His mercy to speed them on their route. From a message which has now been brought to this city by one of the captains, we learn that they did reach and discover India and other kingdoms *and lordships* bordering upon it; that they entered and navigated its sea, finding large cities, large edifices and rivers, and great populations, among whom is carried on all the trade in spices and precious stones, which are forwarded in ships (which these same explorers saw and met with in good numbers and of great size) to Mecca, and thence to Cairo, whence they are dispersed throughout the world. Of these [spices, etc.] they have brought a quantity, including cinnamon, cloves, ginger, nutmeg, *and pepper*, as well as other kinds, together with boughs and leaves of the same; also many fine stones of all sorts, such as rubies and others. And they also came to a country in which there are mines of gold, of which [gold], as of spices and precious stones, they did

Source: Ravenstein, E. G. (ed.) *A Journal of the First Voyage of Vasco da Gama, 1497–99* (New York: Burt Franklin Publications, 1898) pp. 113–14; originally published by Hakluyt Society, no. 99. Translated from the Portuguese by E. G. Ravenstein.

1. *e proveito nosso*, Ravenstein comments in a footnote: 'This, in *Alguns Documentos*, is rendered *e principalemente nosso*. It is just possible that the King meant to say that the service of God was his principal object, as it had been that of his predecessors'.

not bring as much as they could have done, for they took no merchandise with them.

As we are aware that Your Highnesses will hear of these things with much pleasure and satisfaction, we thought well to give this information. And your Highnesses may believe, in accordance with what we have learnt concerning the Christian[2] people whom these explorers reached, that it will be possible, notwithstanding that they are not as yet strong in the faith or possessed of a thorough knowledge of it, to do much in the service of God and the exaltation of the Holy Faith, once they shall have been converted and fully fortified [confirmed] in it. And when *they shall have thus been fortified in the faith there will be an opportunity for destroying the Moors of those parts. Moreover, we hope, with the help of God, that* the great trade which now enriches the Moors of those parts through whose lands it passes without intervention of other persons or peoples, shall, in consequence of our regulations [*ordenanças*] be diverted *to the natives and ships of our own kingdom*, so that henceforth all Christendom, *in this part of Europe*, shall be able, *in large measure*, to provide itself with these spices and precious stones. This, with the help of God, who in His mercy thus ordained it, will cause our designs and intentions to be pushed with more ardour [especially as respects] the war upon the Moors of *the territories conquered by us in these parts*, which your Highnesses are so firmly resolved upon, and in which we are equally zealous.

And we pray your Highnesses, in consideration of this great favour, which, with much gratitude, we received from Our Lord, to cause to be addressed to Him those praises which are His due.

Most high *and excellent Prince and Princess, most potent Lord and Lady, may the Lord our God ever hold your persons and kingdoms in His holy keeping.*

Written at Lisbon, July 1499.

2. Vasco da Gama mistook the first Hindus he met for Christians or Gentiles.

5 TEXT OF A LETTER SENT BY THE KING OF PORTUGAL TO THE DOGE OF VENICE, IN ANSWER TO THE LATTER'S APPEAL TO HIM FOR HELP IN THE WAR AGAINST THE TURKS, DATED 22 FEBRUARY 1501

Note on Moslem Nomenclature in Portuguese Documents

Portuguese activities at this time impinged on a number of power centres in the Moslem world: (1) Morocco, 'the infidels of Africa' mentioned in the present letter; (2) the Ottomans or 'Turks' who did not worry the Portuguese as much as they did the Venetians to whose formal request for assistance this letter is the answer; (3) Egypt, the Mamluks and their dependent 'Moors of Mecca' referred to in Docs 6 and 9; (4) the Sultan of Gujerat who was a Moslem, though merchants in his state were mostly Hindu; in addition, there were Moslem traders in India and the Persian Gulf.

Text

Emmanuel, King of Portugal and of the Algarves on this side and the far side of the sea of Africa, Lord of Guinea and of the conquest [*conquestae*], navigation and trade in Ethiopia, Arabia, Persia and India, to our dearest friend, and most illustrious and powerful Agostino Barbarigo, Doge of Venice, [may you have] the greatest health and increasing prosperity.

We saw and listened with the greatest pleasure to your distinguished spokesman, Domenico Pisani, in our opinion an outstanding man and one who is most worthily honoured everywhere.

If only we had been able to rejoice! For he deplored, in a most excellent speech, as sorrowful as it was accomplished, your troubles and those of Christendom.

In the end, in your name, he earnestly sought from us, and urged us to be willing to take charge of a most pious and holy war against the Turks; a matter not opposed to our wishes, but inconvenient by reason of the timing and our [other] involvements.

For, at the beginning of this spring, with the mobilisation of our announced and thoroughly equipped expedition, we were going to cross over into Africa against the infidels with larger forces of infantry and cavalry, and with a more expensive preparation of everything than has hitherto been sent over to those lands from our kingdom, lest the perfidious Turks and other infidels think that Christian force of arms is growing numb and failing everywhere.

Wherefore many things seemed to stand in the way of your request at present; especially because the Most High would be served to the greatest extent by an African war; and also since the defence of His faith which, through His omnipotence he possesses elsewhere, [should] not be lacking anywhere.

Source: Sanudo, Marino, *Diarii* (Bologna, 1969) Vol. III, cols 1593–5. Translated from the Latin by Kelly Osborne with the assistance of Professor Paul Pascal of the University of Washington.

Indeed, of those things which most seemed to be a hindrance, the first was that an additional preparation had to be made for a maritime war against the Turks while another kind of war had to be undertaken by us.

Also, that the war must be waged for a longer time on account of the distance of the lands from our kingdoms, partly at our own cost and effort and partly at the much greater expense and effort of our men.

Most of all, that the use and expenditure would be lost for the war to be waged in Africa.

And finally, our recent marriage, since no offspring has issued for the comfort of ourselves and our subjects, [with regard] to the inheritance of the kingdom.

However, with such divergent concerns in mind, the needs of Christendom and our friends gained the upper hand, since we do not seek our own things, but rather the things which are of Christ, and since we consider all the losses for His sake to be the greatest gain.

So, with the care of the African expedition laid aside, we decreed at once by reason of the shortness of time, to send you some help in the meantime: not mercenary soldiers hired from elsewhere, but mostly our own nobles and courtiers.

We also made up our mind and decreed with the agreement of all, if God grant it, to set out to that place in our own person (if, as is only right, the other Christian princes will allow it) for such a pious war, both for the common cause of Christendom, and also for your sake whose losses, like our own, we endure with the greatest of sorrow.

And these things that we are doing should be welcomed all the more since we fear nothing at present from the Turks and, up to this point, we have not been urged by any exhortations, either from the Apostolic See or from anyone else; nor have we been helped by any money, as it is the proper custom for the Apostolic See to do in such matters.

On the contrary, when the difficulties of your affairs became known in recent days, we did not cease to lay before our most holy lord the things which seemed to pertain most to the defence of Christians and the attack on the Turks, adding that our own mind was most thoroughly prepared for such an undertaking.

Since this is the way things are, it behoves your Excellency to strive, in the meantime, as much as is in your power, and as the situation demands, to encourage and arouse the Christian princes so that they, with one accord and to the best of their ability, may be willing to apply themselves to a war so sacred and useful, either with land or naval forces, as is more appropriate for each; and also to support our decision and decree.

We ourselves will also send them encouragement; putting our greatest hope in the Lord that the minds of Christians will be illumined at last by their unending piety toward Him; and hoping that because, exalted by His holy faith, we are appealing and knocking at the door of His mercy, it will at last be opened to Christendom.

From our city of Lisbon, 22nd February 1501.

THE KING

6 LETTER SENT TO THE DOGE OF VENICE BY HIS AMBASSADOR TO PORTUGAL, PIETRO PASQUALIGO, DATED: LISBON, 27 JUNE 1501

Introduction

Up until 1501, the Venetian ambassador to Madrid, Domenico Pisani, had doubled as ambassador to Lisbon. Now the Venetians wanted to know more about the Portuguese and appointed a separate ambassador to King Manuel's court, Pietro Pasqualigo. Pisani, and his able secretary Il Cretico, spent some time with Pasqualigo at the beginning of his mission in Lisbon to help him settle in.

The present letter is a representative sample of the numerous colourful accounts of Cabral's famous voyage extant (see Greenlee, 1938). Its point of view is of particular interest for our study. The letter sounds the alarm for the future of Venetian trade, its tone a far cry from the reverential oration addressed to King Manuel (Doc. 8). This 'letter home' concludes with a brief but vivid description of the jubilation in Lisbon, after the fleet's return, and of the conversation held by Manuel and the Venetian ambassador on that occasion: a celebration of what may be seen, in retrospect, as the birth of the modern world system. A different perspective on the voyage is offered in Doc. 8, Manuel's own version of events, sent to the Spanish King and Queen.

Text

Most Serene Prince, etc.

I believe that Your Serenity has learned through letters of your magnificent ambassador[1] that this Most Serene King of Portugal has sent ships in the direction of India, which have now returned, but of the thirteen vessels that went, seven were lost during the voyage.

They began their journey, Most Serene Prince, along the coast of Mauretania and Getulia[2] where the south wind took them as far as Cape Verde, which in ancient times was called Experveras, where the Hesperides islands[3] are. Here

Source: Priuli, Girolamo, *Diarii*, L. A. Muratori (ed.) (Bologna, 1934) Tome XXIV, Part III, pp. 154–5. Translated from the Italian by Sylvia Modelski.

1. Pisani's letters as well as the present one by Pasqualigo are believed to have been drafted by Il Cretico, their secretary and translator, a reader of Greek rhetoric at Padua University, 'a person of great learning in Latin and Greek' (according to Sanudo), who had spent some time in Crete, hence his nickname. (See Greenlee, 1938, pp. 114–18.)
2. Mauretania and Getulia: region of ancient North Africa bordered by the Mediterranean in the North, the Atlantic in the West, the Sahara in the South and Libya in the East.
3. Legendary Isles which the ancients placed in the Atlantic, at the outer limits, the edge, of the world in the West; on them grew the famed golden apples stolen by Hercules.

begins Ethiopia[4] and from there onwards was unknown to the ancients. From this point, the coast of Ethiopia runs towards the east, until it corresponds by direct line to Sicily. This said coast is five or six degrees from the equinoctal line, and in the middle of it is the Mina[5] of this Most Serene King, and then a cape extends to the south, exceeding the Tropic of Capricorn by nine degrees. This cape is called of Good Hope, and the breadth from Barbary[6] to this place and along the shores that turn in towards us is more than five thousand miles. Next, they came upon another cape called the Prassim Promontory[7] by the ancients, which territory, up to that point, was known in antiquity. On the other side of this Cape, then, they ran almost due east, to the land of the Troglodytes,[8] where they found another gold mine which is called Sofala [Zeffala] where the ancients claimed there was a greater abundance of gold than anywhere else. From here they entered the Barbaric Sea and then that of India and arrived at Calicut; this is their voyage, which is more than fifteen thousand miles, but, by crossing the seas, they will shorten the passage considerably.

Before the Cape of Good Hope, towards the southwest, they discovered a new land,[9] which they named 'Land of the Parrots' [Pappagalli] because of the birds found there that are one and a half arm long and multi-coloured, of which we saw two specimens. They think that this is a mainland because they sailed along the coast for more than two thousand miles, but never saw the end. It is inhabited by naked and well-formed people.

On the voyage out they lost four ships; and two, which were sent to the new mine, are also believed to have been lost. The seven went to Calicut where they were at first well received and given a house[10] by that Lord,[11] and some of the vessels remained there, while others stayed at nearby places. Then the Sultan's *zerme*[12] arrived, and they were angry because [the Portuguese] might interfere with their consignment and they wanted to load their ships first. The factor[13] of that King complained to the Lord of Calicut who, they suspect, must have had an understanding with the Moors, and who told him that if they loaded the vessels, he would seize the spices; from this they came to blows and all the natives favoured the Moors, and they ran to the house that had been assigned to the Portuguese, and tore to pieces all those who were in them and on land, in all forty people, among them the factor, who had jumped in the water to escape. After which, the other vessels came and burned the Sultan's *zerme* who numbered ten, and with their artillery they inflicted great damage to the land and they set many of the straw-covered houses on fire.

And in the midst of all this tumult, they left Calicut, and were led by their

4. A vague region of Africa south of a line drawn from the Red Sea to the Atlantic.
5. São Jorge da Mina, El Mina, Portuguese fort and factory on the river Volta in the Gold Coast (today's Ghana), established in 1482 to defend the monopoly of the gold trade.
6. Ancient designation for Arabia.
7. Cape Delgado in modern Mozambique. (To be in correct geographic sequence, this sentence in the narrative should follow the next one instead of preceding it.)
8. Cave-dwellers who lived along the shores of South Eastern Egypt and the Gulf of Arabia.
9. Brazil; this 'discovery' preceded the rounding of the Cape.
10. This 'house' was meant for a factory, which they started.
11. The Hindu Zamorin (or Prince) of Calicut.
12. The Moslem merchants, 'Moors of Mecca', agents of the Sultan of Egypt. Later in this paragraph, *zerme* refers to the merchants themselves as well as to their ships.
13. The chief factor was Ayres Correia, a rich Portuguese merchant who had been acting as King Manuel's agent.

guide, who is a baptised Jew, to another land some forty miles away, called Cochin [Chucim], that belongs to a different king, enemy of that in Calicut. He gave them a good welcome and a great quantity of spices, which they did not have in Calicut. They loaded the seven vessels and stowed them with spices at a price I am afraid to tell you, because they say they obtained one canter[14] of cinnamon for one ducat or less. This Lord of Cochin sent his ambassadors with these ships to that Most Serene King and also hostages [?to ensure] their safe return.[15] On the journey back, the Moors and those of Calicut made preparations to capture them and they armed more than one hundred and fifty ships with more than fifteen thousand men; but since the Portuguese were laden with cargo, they did not want to fight, and neither could the others take the offensive, because the Portuguese had set their sails to the north wind which the others did not know how to use.

Next, they arrived at an island, on which is the body of Saint Thomas, the Apostle[16]: the Lord of the island showed them great affection and gave them relics of the said Saint; he asked them to take spices on credit until the return journey. But they were already fully laden and could take no more.

They were altogether fourteen months on the voyage, but only four months on the way back, and they say that in the future they will make the trip in eight to ten months at the most. On the return voyage, of the seven vessels, six came in safely, the other one is said to have hit a shoal all aboard were rescued: this was a six hundred botte[17] ship and still richly laden; only one three hundred botte vessel has arrived here to date, the others are not far behind, according to what they say.

That ship came in on the evening of Saint John's Day. I was with the Most Serene King, who called for me and said I should congratulate him because his Indian fleet had arrived loaded with spices and so I joined him in celebration as was appropriate. He summoned a feast to be held at the palace that night and merry bell ringing throughout the city. The next day he called for solemn processions to be held across the land. Some time later, as I happened to be with His Majesty, he again brought up the subject of his ships, and said that I should write to Your Serenity that, before long, you should send your galleys to get spices from here, that he would welcome them and they should consider yourselves as guests in his house, and that he will prevent the Sultan from getting them, and he wants to commit forty vessels to this route, some for the journey out, and the others for the return. He deems to have India at his command.

The ship that came to port belongs to Bartolomeo [Marchioni] the Florentine, its cargo consists of about three hundred cantera of pepper, one hundred and twenty cantera of cinnamon, fifty to sixty cantera of lac, fifteen cantera of benzoin; of cloves there are none, because the Moors took them; nor any ginger, because they didn't have it where they took the cargo, but they grow it in Calicut; of minor spices there aren't any at all. They say that a great deal of jewelry was

14. A canter = one quintal or hundredweight.
15. It was Portuguese practice to detain Indian hostages on board to ensure the safe return to the ships of their compatriots who were on land. It seems that on account of the fleet's quick departure from Cochin, two Indian hostages became unexpected passengers on the voyage home to Europe (see Greenlee, 1938, p. xxviii).
16. Legend has it that St Thomas established a number of Christian (Syrian) churches on the Malabar Coast and was martyred in Mylapore, Madras, about 500 miles from Cochin.
17. According to Greenlee (1938, p. 65n.), a botte was about one-third of a Portuguese ton; according to Lane (1973, pp. 479–80) the botte used by the Venetians to indicate the size of ships was about 0.6 metric ton.

lost in the troubles at Calicut. I must not omit to mention the visit here of the ambassadors of that King of Ethiopia called King of Ubenam, who sent the King here as presents slaves and ivory tusks, although such things have been known here for a long time.[18] They also grow pepper there, but not of as fine quality as the other. Moreover, this ship on its return trip met two large vessels that had sailed from the new mine[19] and were heading towards India, and were carrying great quantities of gold, and, because they were afraid that [the Portuguese] might want to take it, they offered them, to start with, fifteen thousand doble[20]; each ship was worth more than five hundred thousand ducats. But the Portuguese refused to take anything, instead, they offered them presents and good will, for they hope to be able to navigate those seas.

18. This sentence is a digression from the main stream of the letter; it could start 'By the way, I mustn't forget to tell you . . .', and probably refers to one of the embassies sent to Lisbon, on another occasion, by Ozolua, King of Benin. The narrative of Cabral's voyage continues after this informational detour.
19. Probably Sofala.
20. The doble (dobra in Portuguese) was an old Almohadian gold coin weighing about 4.6 grammes.

7 LETTER FROM KING MANUEL TO FERDINAND AND ISABELLA, 29 JULY 1501

Introduction

Manuel was now married to Maria, the Spanish monarch's daughter (see Introduction to Doc. 4, p. 56) and is addressing his father- and mother-in-law. He boasts about his fleet's successes in India and glosses over the many setbacks that ambassador Pasqualigo was glad to report at length in his letter to Venice (Doc. 6).

Text

Most high and most excellent and most powerful Sovereigns, Father and Mother:[1]

During these past days, after the first news arrived from India, I did not write at once to Your Majesties concerning the matters there because Pedro Alvarez Cabral, my chief captain of the fleet, which I had sent there, had not yet returned. And after his arrival I also delayed in doing so because two ships of his company had not yet come.[2] One of these he had sent to Çofalla, a gold-mine which was discovered recently, not to establish trade, but only to have true information of what was there; because of the two ships which went there for this purpose, one was lost at sea, and the other was separated from the fleet in stormy weather and did not go there. And after the aforesaid ships had arrived, and I was on the point of notifying Your Majesties, Pero Lopes de Padilha told me that you would be glad to have news of what had happened there. The following is briefly everything which took place. My aforesaid captain with thirteen ships departed from Lisbon the 9th of March of last year, and during the octave of Easter he reached a land which he newly discovered, to which he gave the name of Santa Cruz. In it he found the people nude as in the first innocence, gentle, and peaceable. It seemed that Our Lord miraculously wished it to be found, because it is very convenient and necessary for the voyage to India, because he repaired his ships and took water there. And on account of the long voyage which he had to make, he did not stop to obtain information about the said land; he only sent me a ship from there to notify me how he found it; and he pursued his route by way of the Cape of Good Hope. In that gulf, before arriving at it, he encountered great storms, in

Source: Greenlee, William Brooks, *The Voyage of Pedro Alvares Cabral to Brazil and India* (London: the Hakluyt Society) 2nd series, no. 81 (1938) pp. 43–52; notes by Greenlee, reprinted by permission.

1. Queen Isabella of Castile was half Portuguese on her mother's side, and her grandfather was the Infante John, one of the sons of John I. It would not be strange, therefore, when listening to the story of Columbus and of his hopes for new discoveries for Spain that she would be fired with some of the spirit of adventure shown by her great uncle, Prince Henry. Queen Isabella was a first cousin of Dom Manuel, and through his marriage to her daughter, Isabel, and, after Isabel's death, to Maria, was still more closely related to him. Ferdinand, in addition to being the father-in-law of Dom Manuel, was also related to the House of Aviz.
2. Those of Sancho de Tovar and Pedro de Ataíde. Sancho de Tovar had gone to Sofala. From this letter it would appear that Cabral and Simão de Miranda arrived on 21 July 1501, Sancho de Tovar and Pedro de Ataíde on 25 July, and Diogo Dias on 27 July.

which, during one single day, four ships foundered together before his eyes, of which not a single person escaped. At this time, also, another of his ships disappeared, of which no news has been received up to this time.[3] And that in which he went, with the others which remained, passed through great danger. And thus he went his way to make port at the kingdom of Quiloa, which belongs to the Moors, under whose sovereignty is the said mine of Çofalla, because he carried my letters and messages for its king, to establish peace with him, and a treaty concerning purchases and trade at the said mine. And before reaching the aforesaid kingdom, he found two ships with a great quantity of gold, which he took possession of, and because they belonged to the said King of Quiloa, after doing them much honour, he let them go. He was very well received by that king, who came in person to converse with my said captain on the sea, and entered with him in his boat, and he sent him presents; and after receiving my letters and messages, he agreed to the treaty. And since the ships which were destined for that mine were among those which were lost, no trade was begun there at that time, because the merchandise which the other ships carried was not suitable for what was needed for that land.[4] And he departed from there and went to another kingdom, Melinde, for which he also was carrying my letters and messages, because its king, who likewise is a Moor, had done good deeds to Dom Vasco, who first went there to discover it. This king likewise visited him on the sea and also sent him presents, and confirmed and established peace and friendship with him, and gave him the pilots whom he needed for his voyage.[5] These kingdoms extend from the Red Sea in this direction, and in the interior they border on Gentiles, and these Gentiles border on the land of Prester John, whom they call the *abechy*.[6] In their language this means 'branded with iron', because, as a matter of fact, they do this, and they are branded with iron as a sign that they are baptized in water.[7] From there he departed for Calecut, which is seven hundred leagues beyond. This city, as I believe you must already know, is of the Gentiles who worship many things and believe that there is only one God. And it is very populous, and there are in it many Moors who, until now, always traded there in spices, because it is thus like Bruges in Flanders,[8] the principal trading place for the things of India, which come to it from outside; and in it there are only cassiafistula and ginger. He arrived at this city five months after having departed from Lisbon. And he was very honourably received by the king, who came to a house beside the sea to speak to him, with all his lords and many other people. And there he gave him my messages and established with him my peace and concord. Concerning this agreement the aforesaid king ordered a letter written on a sheet of silver with his seal inlaid in gold, for this is the custom in his land in

3. At the end of this letter the king states that he has just heard that the ship of Diogo Dias was not lost.
4. That is, trinkets, beads, copper, etc.
5. The ports of Malindi and Mombasa were the rendezvous for the pilots for India and the East African coast.
6. *Coavixi* in the Spanish version.
7. Branding in the form of a cross was practised at an early date by the Jacobites and Syrians. The Abyssinians also so branded, but not necessarily as a fire baptism. Father Álvares, who visited Abyssinia in 1520 and witnessed several baptisms, does not mention this custom in that connexion. He describes, however, branding on the forehead as a preventive from colds.
8. Bruges, which had been the northern counterpart of Venice in the fourteenth century, while still retaining a position as a financial centre, was losing much of its commerce to Antwerp because of the gradual silting up of the river Zwyn. This could not be navigated by 1490.

matters of great importance, and other letters written on leaves of trees which resemble palms, on which they ordinarily write. And from these trees and their fruit are made the following things: sugar, honey, oil, wine, water, vinegar, charcoal, and cordage for ships, and for everything else, and matting of which they make some sails for ships, and it serves them for everything which they need. And the aforesaid fruit, in addition to what is thus made of it, is their chief food, particularly at sea. After the agreement had thus been made with the said king, my factor sent on shore the entire establishment which I had ordered for the above-mentioned factory, and at once he began to trade with his merchandise and to load the ships with spices. In the meantime, the King of Calecut sent word to my captain that a very large and well-armed ship which had annoyed him on previous occasions, belonging to another king, his enemy, had sent word to him that it was passing before his port, without any fear of him, and he begged him to order it to be captured, enlarging on the matter, as it greatly concerned his estate and honour.

And the said captain, in view of the good treatment which he and also my factor were beginning to receive, and in order to confirm further peace and friendship, agreed to do it. And in order to show him the strength of our people in ships and artillery, he sent against it only the smallest ship which he had, with a large bombard.[9] And it overtook them within the harbour of another king,[10] his neighbour, and before his eyes and those of all his people he captured it, and brought it to Calecut with 400 bowmen and some artillery and with seven elephants, trained in warfare, on board (there these would be worth thirty thousand cruzados,[11] for they gave five thousand for only one of them), and with other merchandise of spices. This ship my captain ordered to be presented to him, and he gave it to him with everything which came in it, and he came to the shore with all his state and pomp to see it, since it was to them a very great surprise that so small a ship with so few men should take so large a ship with so many people, and to receive the message which the said captain was sending him concerning it. And the Moors, especially those of Mecca, who were there, seeing that they were in this concord and friendship, and that two ships were already loaded with spices, and seeing also the great loss which they were suffering, sought all the means that they could to put discord between my factor and the king. And they stirred up a tumult on land to hinder them; and because all the merchandise was in the hands of the Moors they hid it, and secretly sent it elsewhere. When he learned this, the aforesaid captain sent word to the King of Calecut, complaining to him and asking him to fulfil what he had agreed, which was that in twenty days he would give him merchandise with which to load the said ships, and that until they were loaded, he would not give authority to load to any others. And the king answered him that he would at once order all the merchandise which there was in the land to be given to him, and that if any ship should be loaded in his harbour without the knowledge of his officials, he gave him the authority and power to detain it until he sent his said officials, so that they might arrange to turn it over to him. As soon as the Moors learned of this, they agreed to load a ship publicly with great diligence, using still greater care in hiding the merchandise than they had previously done, and this, in order to give an excuse for an outbreak to begin, for they are powerful. And the city is of many nationalities and of extensive

9. This was the caravel *S. Pedro* of Pedro de Ataíde. The use of bombards on caravels was the invention of John II.
10. The King of Cananore.
11. The cruzado was approximately equivalent to the Venetian ducat.

population, in which the king can, with difficulty, attend to the tumults of the populace. And when my factor saw that the ship was being loaded, he asked the said captain to detain it, as the king had agreed. And the said captain, fearing an outbreak, hesitated to do it; and the said factor again asked him to detain it, telling him that the chief Moors and also some Gentiles told him that if the said ship were not held they could in no way load their ships. According to what followed it appears that they were doing it in order to give rise to the said outbreak. And my captain, after hesitating many times, fearing what followed, ordered the people of that ship to be told that, because of the authority which he had for this, it should not leave; but they were not willing to agree to this. And then it was necessary to order it to be held. And he commanded his boats to bring it inside the harbour, where it surely could not leave without his permission. And as soon as the Moors saw this, since it was the end which they desired, at that very moment they came quickly with all the rest of the population, whom they had already stirred up, to attack the said factor and his house, and fought with him. And he with those few whom he had with him, defended themselves for some time, and leaving the house, rallied at the sea. And my captain, who was then ill,[12] as soon as he was told of the uprising on land, ordered all his boats to aid him, and although the sea was very rough he nevertheless gathered up some of the people. They killed the factor and with him fifty people were lost, either dead or captives. After this was done, when my captain saw that the king had not come to help and that he sent no message and was providing himself with some equipment implying war, and also had taken possession of my property which had remained on shore, he waited one day to see if he would make amends for the said matter. When he saw that he was sending him no message, fearing that he was arming himself effectively, as he afterwards did, to prevent him from taking the vengeance he could take at that time, he decided to act at once, and he took ten large ships which were in the harbour, and ordered all the people who were on them to be put to the sword, with the exception of a few who, concealing themselves, escaped death, and whom afterwards he did not wish to kill, but brought captive to me. And he ordered the said ships to be burned in front of the port, which caused great horror to the king and to the people of the land. On the ships there were three elephants which died there. In this manner he spent the entire day; and as soon as it was night, he went with all the ships, and placed himself as near land as he could in front of the city; and as soon as it was dawn, he began to fire with artillery, and bombarded it until night, especially the houses of the king. In this he did much damage, and killed many of his people, as he learned afterwards, and he killed one of the chief men who was near the king. On account of this, the king immediately departed from the city, for it seemed to him that he was not safe anywhere. And he sailed from there to another port of his, which was called Fandarene [Pandarani], which he also damaged with artillery, and killed people. And from there he sailed to the kingdom of Cochim, which is the region from which spices come, 30 leagues beyond Calecut, and on the way, he found two other ships of Calecut, which he also captured and ordered to be burned. And when he reached Cochim, after having informed the king of what had happened in Calecut, he was very well received by him, and made an agreement with him in the same manner which he had done in Calecut. Then he immediately sent my factor and certain men with him on shore, for whom they gave him honourable men as hostages, whom he brought to me; and they loaded

12. At this time Cabral was suffering from fever and ague, and was being bled by the ship's barber.

his ships in 16 days; and the merchandise they brought to him in their boats was brought with so much greater friendliness and security that it appeared that Our Lord permitted the outbreak at Calecut in order that this other agreement might take place, which is of greater profit and security, because the harbour is much better and of much more extensive trade, since, of almost all the merchandise which goes to Calecut, most of it is to be found in that land, and because others go there first without going to Calecut. In this city of Cochim there are many ships, and he learned that two merchants alone had as many as 50 ships. In that kingdom there are many true Christians of the conversion of Saint Thomas, and their priests follow the manner of life of the apostles with much strictness, having nothing of their own except what is given them as alms. And they practise celibacy, and have churches in which they say mass, and they consecrate unleavened bread, and wine which they make from dried fruit with water, for they cannot make other. In their churches they have no images save the cross, and all the Christians wear the apostolic garments, and never cut their beards and hair. And there he found definite information concerning where the body of Saint Thomas lies, which is 150 leagues from there, on the sea coast, in a city which is called Maliapor [Mailapur], of a small population; and he brought me earth from his tomb.[13] And all the Christians and also the Moors and Gentiles, on account of the great miracles which are performed, go to his house on pilgrimage. He also brought us two Christians who came of their own accord and with the permission of their prelate, so that we might send them to Rome and to Jerusalem, to see the things of the Church there, and to be informed about them, for they consider that they are better ruled by being ordained by Saint Peter, who, they believe, was the chief of the apostles. And he also learned certain news of great Christian nations which are on the other side of that kingdom, who come on pilgrimage to the aforesaid house of Saint Thomas, and have very great kings who obey One only. They are white men of fair hair, and are considered strong. The land is called Malchima,[14] and from it come porcelain, and musk and amber, and aloe-wood, which they bring from the river Ganges, which is on this side of them. And there are such fine vases of porcelain there, that a single one of them is worth a hundred cruzados. And while he was in the kingdom of Cochim, when the treaty had been agreed to and the ships loaded, there came to him messages from the King of Cananor, and from the King of Colum [Quilon] who are near by, requesting him to come to them because they would make more profitable trade with him, but, because he had already made the treaty, he declined to go. At this time, as he was about to depart from Cochim, the same king sent word to him that a large fleet from Calecut was coming against him, and that as many as 15 000 men were in it. It did not seem well to my captain to fight with it, because he had his ships loaded, and had few men, and it did not seem to him that there was time or necessity for taking the risk, since he feared that they might kill or disable some of them, and on account of the length of the journey which he had to go, which was 4000 leagues from here. But he set sail, with them following him, and as they did not dare to go far out to sea, they turned back, because they feared to go against him. From there he went his way, which was to the kingdom of Cananor, [ruled by] one of those kings who invited him. And as he was passing, as soon as those on land caught sight of him, they sent him another message, asking him to stop there, because the king wanted to send a messenger to me by him, whom he brought me. And in the single day that he was there, he

13. This earth was supposed to have great curative value.
14. This is probably derived from the Hindustani *Maha-Chin*, Great China.

ordered so much spicery to be brought to the ships that he might have entirely filled them, had they been empty; and they gave what they might carry free, as a present to win my friendship. And all his chief men came also to my captain, telling him on behalf of the king that they would see to it that he was treated there in a different manner than in Calecut, assuring him that if he wanted to make war on Calecut they would help him, and that he in person would go on land, and all his fleet on the sea. And after thanking him greatly in my name, he took leave of him, saying to him that in the other fleet which I was to send soon, I would send him my answer regarding everything. He went his way, and in the middle of that crossing he took a very large ship loaded with merchandise. It appeared to him that it was a ship of Mecca which was just coming from Calecut. And finding that the aforesaid ship belonged to the King of Cambaia [Cambay], he abandoned it, sending word by it to the said king that he had released it because he did not intend to make war with any one; he had made it only on those who had broken the word which they had given to him in my name. Continuing farther on his way, he lost one of the ships which was laden, for it ran aground during the night. Its people were saved, and he ordered the ship to be burned because it could not be dislodged safely. From this place he sent a ship to obtain news of the mine of Çofalla which I have mentioned before. This has just arrived, and brought me definite information of it and also concerning the trade and the merchandise of the country and of the great quantity of gold which is there; and there he found news, that among the men who carry gold from there to the coasts, they saw many who have four eyes, namely, two in front and two behind. The men are small of body and strong, and it is said that they are cruel, and that they eat the men with whom they have war, and that the cows of the king wear collars of heavy gold around their necks. Near this mine there are two islands on which they gather much pearl and amber. My aforesaid captain departed from there, and reached Lisbon 16 months from the day he had left it, and, blessed be Our Lord, in all this voyage he lost only three men from sickness, and all the others are healthy and of good spirits.[15] And now a certain message comes to me saying that one of the ships that was going to Çofalla which he believed lost, is coming, and will be here shortly. They say that it entered the Red Sea, and that it is bringing from there some silver and also some information concerning matters there, although I am already informed in detail concerning the said Red Sea, having been informed thereof by my above-mentioned captain, who had information concerning it in many ways. I leave the other details of this matter to Pero Lopes, who was present at everything.[16] Very exalted and very excellent and very puissant Sovereigns, Father and Mother, may Our Lord have your life and royal estate in His holy care.

Written in Santarem the 29th of July.

EL REY.

15. This is a mistake, since many had died of scurvy.
16. There were thus at least three Spaniards with the fleet: Master John, Sancho de Tovar, and Pedro Lopez de Padilla. Pedro Lopez may have been the bearer of this letter to the Spanish sovereigns.

8 THE ADDRESS OF PIETRO PASQUALIGO, VENETIAN AMBASSADOR TO MANUEL, KING OF PORTUGAL, 20 AUGUST 1501

Introduction

Venice most urgently needed help against the Turks in the eastern Mediterranean. It invited the Holy Roman Emperor, the pope, the King of Spain and other christian rulers to join in a holy league. It slyly called on King Manuel for help, hoping to divert his ships away from India. To its surprise, Manuel offered to send 35 stout ships against the common enemy. But the promised armada arrived too late and with ambiguous orders that made it ineffective. In his oration, the ambassador pretends to be grateful. Manuel continued to profess cordiality towards Venice, knighting Pasqualigo and making the Signoria the godfather of his baby son. In the spring of 1502, Venice had had enough, it recalled the ambassador and broke diplomatic relations with Portugal (see Diffie and Winius, 1977, pp. 208, 230).

Text

AS SOON as we learned that you had come into possession of this realm the ancient cordiality and desire for mutual friendship that prevails with your Majesty on behalf of Venice, deriving as it does from your forefathers, brought great hope, Most Serene King, to our Doge Agostino[1] and to our entire Senate. We knew that you would wish not only to be known as but also to be a friend of the Venetian Republic as always, and to be as close to her in every kind of endeavour as any of the kings who have been her greatest allies and friends in the present or the past.

We are confirmed in this opinion not only by the old friendship of the ancient Portuguese kings, a friendship still preserved between us most sacredly right down to the present day, but primarily by your own high character which has already long been known and reported far and wide throughout the world. And this excited great hope even beyond the city of Venice in all the peoples, realms, and nations of Europe. For everyone has been convinced by those assiduously circulated reports of your virtues that, as the Christian religion teaches, the good and great God will soon give them a king who in his virtue, wisdom, and felicity will not only protect the weary and tottering Christian Commonwealth but even extend it far and wide. Indeed, this common opinion of your character and wisdom has been more and more confirmed, and men have been most impressed, oh illustrious King, by the authority and judgment of the most powerful and

Source: Weinstein, Donald, *Ambassador from Venice: Pietro Pasqualigo in Lisbon 1501* (Minneapolis: University of Minnesota Press, 1960) pp. 43–51. Translated from the Latin by Donald Weinstein. Reprinted by permission.

1. Agostino Barbarigo, Doge of Venice (1486–1501), died within days of this speech and was succeeded by Leonardo Loredan.

invincible Catholic sovereigns of Castile, the parents of your wife. I can hardly believe that they of their own accord would have sought you as their son-in-law unless you were all that you are said to be, for nature is so disposed that every noble man strongly desires his fellow. Thus it is not surprising if, on such evidence, men expect so much from you and from your most happy reign, if they cherish this hope and imagine such felicitous results.

And indeed, oh renowned King, from the very beginning of your reign you have proven and strengthened this judgment of men about you. For, passing over your domestic achievements, which are such as to exhaust eloquence no matter how great before it could finish the description, what could you have done for the sake of immortal God that would have contributed more to the strength of the realm? Even though still a youth you have gained the good will of many princes by your moderation as well as by your wonderful generosity. You have allied with some by treaty and with others through marriage. You have not surrendered to easy living or idleness. When you are free from affairs of war you keep yourself and your followers so busy, either in hunting or in military exercises, that you are never less at leisure than when you are thought to have plenty of leisure. Yet at the same time you have wisely fostered the arts of peace with no less zeal than the shrewdness and force with which you have fostered the duties of war. For as to your clemency, probity, piety, kindness, magnanimity, and the rest of the virtues with which you shine, it is better that I pass over them than say too little, lest I reveal in the very middle of my discourse the slightness of my talent by comparison with the greatness of your virtues and your glory.

But, although they are so great and wonderful as to discourage the orator and leave envy far behind, Your Majesty's virtues seem less significant if they are compared to just one of your deeds, with which not even those of the most illustrious ancient kings and peoples can be compared. What kingdom is there on earth, what nation so remote and so far removed from commerce with all men, that has not been reached by your fame? In this brief time a world of other lands entirely unknown to Ptolemy and to Strabo and to the rest of the world's writers has been discovered and made known to men through your diligence and under your direction. This is indeed a wonderful and brilliant accomplishment, hitherto unheard of, worthy of being commemorated in history, a matter which all scholars ought to study and exercise their talents upon. That which neither the Carthaginians of old achieved, nor the Romans who held the power after the overthrow of Carthage, nor Alexander, that great world explorer, nor all of Greece in the days when she flourished, nor the Egyptian and Assyrian kings, your excellence and good fortune have achieved. At your command the whole coastline of outer Libya, from the Atlantic Ocean as far as the Barbarian Gulf which is joined to the Red Sea, has been navigated. Peoples, islands, and shores unknown until now have either surrendered to your military might or, overawed by it, have voluntarily begged for your friendship. The greatest kings and unconquered nations of the past used to boast justifiably that they had extended their power to the ocean, but you, invincible King are entitled to take pride in having advanced your power to the lower hemisphere and to the Antipodes. What is greatest and most memorable of all, you have brought together under your command peoples whom nature divides, and with your commerce you have joined two different worlds.

Now that I have started on the subject of commerce I can hardly say enough. It should be understood how much benefit and utility the whole world gains from the cane sugar and the many other products which are then transported in great abundance in all directions for the use of mankind, and how much even posterity will benefit from the spices of every sort recently found by your ships.

Can we doubt that your name has already been made immortal? Believe me, most excellent King, every age will commemorate your deeds; posterity will be amazed at them and nations will celebrate them. Every man, if he does not want to be ungrateful, will affirm that he owes more to you alone than to any of the ancient or modern kings. Truly your fame will be as great as your deeds. Yet, oh most glorious King, in nothing do your piety and greatness appear more admirable, in nothing do you seem more deserving of heaven, than in the fact that when Cavalier Domenico Pisani, our ambassador, sent by the Catholic sovereigns of Castile and by our Senate to visit and honor you, had declared to Your Highness how great is the peril threatening not only our Republic but also the Christian religion from the most fierce and powerful King of the Turks, and how his power has now grown beyond all bounds, and how many Christians he has slaughtered, and finally, how many dreadful new weapons of every kind he may be preparing against Christendom, you threw yourself freely, with such dedication, devotion, and zeal into the war against this most ferocious monster, the war that for the third year we are supporting at incredible cost.

In order to help with your forces you put aside your Mauritanian project, and the whole of the very powerful navy you had prepared at such expense for use against Mauritania you assigned instead against this godless enemy. And not only for this year, for you have given assurance that if necessary you will send a much larger and stronger force in the future; in short, that you will leave nothing untried that might bring victory over the cruel enemy, nothing that might appear necessary and useful for ending the war altogether. This is what Your Majesty's letters and our ambassador's dispatches to our Senate declare. When I reflect on this, most reverend King, I do not know of anything you could do or conceive that is finer, braver, or more lofty, of anything, in short, more worthy of your godlike character and brilliant abilities. Your forefathers have always taken up arms for the recovery of Jerusalem with a wonderful sense of duty, and we read that they have performed great deeds in Syria. But far greater and more important to the Christian Commonwealth is that which Your Majesty is doing now. For as the Turks are more powerful than were the kings of Syria, this war must be considered graver and more dangerous. Besides, if we think it is a fine thing to attack an enemy who is far off it seems much more important and necessary to drive out one who has got into our very vitals. And so, although you always deserved it in the past, now our Doge, our Senate, and the entire city have special cause for regarding and venerating you as an outstanding man, a celebrated prince, and devout king, and therefore they admit owing so much to Your Highness that there is nothing they have which they do not feel to be also yours.

Not content to express by letter to Your Sublimity their joy at your taking up the cause of the Christian faith as a most devout king and our cause as a great friend of Venice, they immediately chose me by senatorial decree as the new ambassador to Your Serenity to thank you in person in the measure you deserve. You have accepted fully your responsibility for helping in this war which is so difficult and so dangerous for the Christian religion, and such is your good faith and trustworthiness that having accepted it you will see it through. It was especially gratifying that you chose to join in friendship with the Venetians against the common enemy of Christendom. This adds to your glory, for you are joined to them by laws of public friendship and ancient good will passed down by our forefathers, laws the more binding as they are hereditary. Renewing and strengthening and increasing your old ties with the city of Venice will be no less an honor to Your Sublimity in this affair than if you were to smash the enemy first and tell us about the victory afterwards.

And so this deed will bring Your Excellency double praise. First, because when you have helped Venice in this wearisome and difficult war you will have bound her to you more closely in eternal gratitude. Second, because you will be looked upon as the most Christian king who, together with his most Christian people has defended the Christian commonwealth. As for that which pertains to the Venetians, never was there a better time or occasion for laying our Republic under an obligation than now, when our city, no more concerned for its own affairs than for those of all Christianity, has to deal with the raging of this most ferocious people. Further, this will be a greater thing to have bestowed upon Venice than the hereditary service one of your ancestors is said to have left as a charge upon his descendants in memory of his reception as a guest of our city. It will be greater, I say, than the time when our rowers and helmsmen, half-naked and wounded, were received on these shores humanely and kindly, and were helped with shelter, clothing, and provisions after our transport triremes had been attacked on the seas by pirates. That was a matter of private, this of public, welfare. Surely more glory and fame are to be expected for defending our religion, and for this reason there are more who work out of a sense of public duty, for the good of all, which is highest, than there are who work for the good of single states. A fair thing it is, to be sure, and splendid for your fame, to have crossed a great part of the ocean by ship, to have explored new shores and lands, and to have gained unknown people and islands for the commerce of our men. But a far fairer thing it is, far more splendid and more promising for the immortality of your name, to defend the most noble part of the world from the fury of the infidels, to fight to protect the common faith, repel the danger that threatens Christendom, and extinguish the flame that threatens us all. It goes without saying that other people will be grateful, but especially Venice, which so freely supported the first part of this war, so much the more is she concerned for its outcome as she is closer to the danger.

As soon as Your Majesty's letter was read in council our Doge and the Venetian Senate, prompted by this concern, ordered me to rush to Your Highness without sparing myself, not however, to thank you for having decided of your own accord to help the Venetian state and indeed Christendom with your ships in this war, but since you have done so, to urge Your Majesty in the public name, out of your kindness and sense of duty, to take up the holy, supreme, and glorious cause of guarding the faith, and after Your Majesty has taken it up, not to abandon it, but to cherish and support it with your aid and guard it always with might and main.

May Your Highness be an example to the other princes of the Christian religion of their duty to protect the community. May they desire, following your example, to earn the gratitude of Christendom like those who are now seen to desire it after having heard how you, oh invincible King, are eager to fight for the Christian religion, and, inspired by your magnificent act, wish to add their ships to meet the onslaught of the enemy, as soon as you and the Venetians have joined forces. The Most Christian King of the French is sending his very powerful fleet to help in this war. The Catholic rulers of Castile, as Your Highness knows, again hold theirs in readiness for it in Sicily. The Most Serene King of Hungary, with whom the Pope and our Senate, by the guidance of the good and great God, have just made an alliance for the duration of this war, is about to mount a land attack against this pernicious destroyer of the Christian people. At this moment he is hurrying to battle and arming himself as quickly as he can lest the troops raised be too late in rushing there where that barbarian stained with Christian blood is every day burning and overturning everything with impunity, while his forces are allowed to grow too powerful. The King is making war as much because of necessity as out of confidence in his own forces. His brother, the renowned and most fearless King of Poland, and the two Dukes of the Wallachians have not failed to come forward to His Majesty with their troops in order to strike a more powerful blow against the common enemy. Thus, if you, Magnanimous King, also cleave to this holy, religious alliance of Christian princes so that the other kings follow your virtuous and pious example, there is no doubt that they will straightway send the troops they have already raised for the war now, no doubt that they will keep them there after they have been sent, or that even they themselves will take arms. In this way the Christian commonwealth will soon be restored to unity.

For this the best and greatest God will grant Your Majesty eternal praise, incomparable glory, a famous victory, and an immortal name, and, at last, that state of blessedness which is so much to be desired.

If on the contrary, the danger threatening the Christian religion is neglected – would that I were a false prophet – it is greatly to be feared that this fire that has already ravaged Greece and now torments the Venetian Republic will soon consume all Europe.

I have had my say.

Pronounced on August 20, 1501, in Lisbon. Printed in Venice by Bernardino de' Vitali the year of Our Lord 1501 on the 22nd day of December.

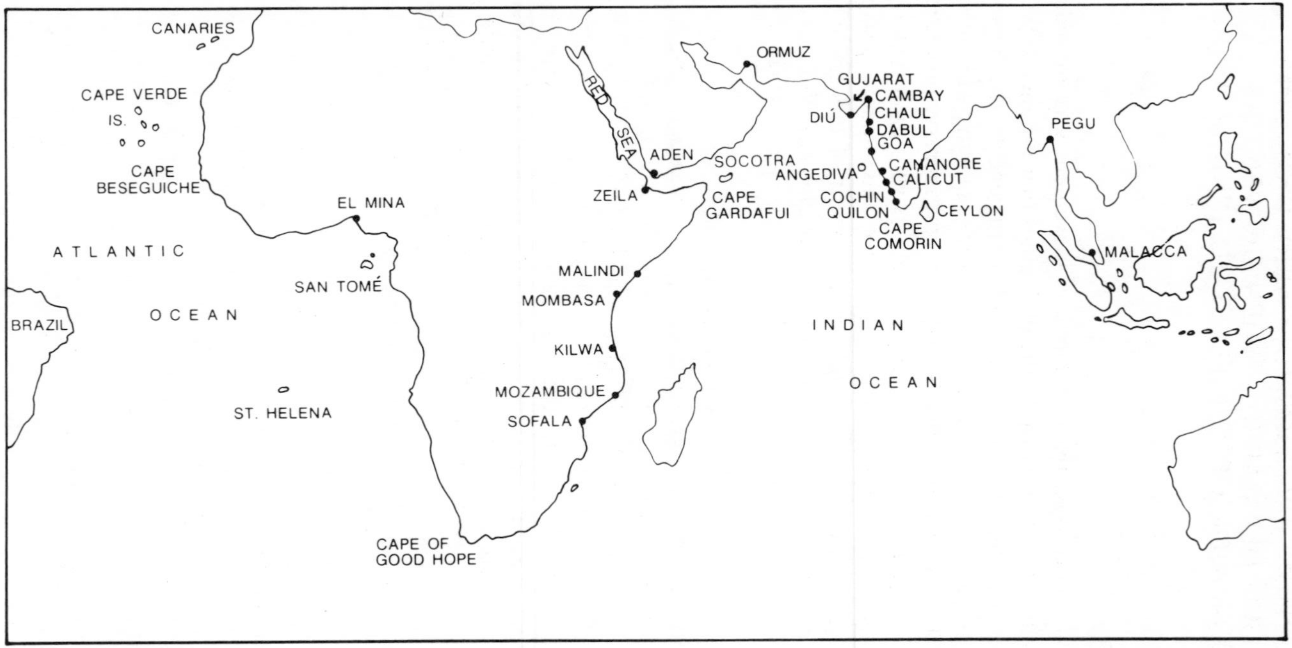

Map 2.2 The route to India

9 INSTRUCTIONS [*REGIMENTO*] CARRIED BY DOM FRANCISCO DE ALMEIDA WHEN HE WENT AS CAPTAIN-MAJOR OF THE FLEET TO INDIA, 5 MARCH 1505

Introduction

Like all great enterprises, the Portuguese achievement was grounded on enthusiasm allied to a firm grasp of the difficulties that lay ahead. With its meticulous instructions that try to meet all contingencies, the *Regimento* is a good example of the careful and imaginative planning without which even the best ideas will flounder: a step-by-step itinerary, protection of the fleet and its men, building fortresses, relations with local populations and chiefs, care of vessels, handling of spices and money, discipline, control of weapons, division of spoils, management of officers, etc.; all these problems are dealt with in detail by the *Regimento*. We reproduce this document at some length because it is not available in English elsewhere.

Almeida was 55 at the time of his appointment; a veteran of the wars against the Moors. According to a contemporary account, King Manuel reneged on a promise to give him the title of *Viceroy* of India 'which in my days no other person will hold' (Diffie and Winius, 1977, p. 239). As can be seen above, the word *Viceroy* does not appear in the title, nor is it to be found anywhere else in the *Regimento*. When his sailing orders came, Almeida read that his rank was that of Captain-major (sometimes rendered as Chief-Captain, Captain-general, Supreme Commander, etc. by writers in English), and for three years only. Nevertheless, he was later commonly acknowledged as the first Viceroy or Governor of India, and Albuquerque as the second; but neither of them was officially appointed as such.

Fourteen *náus*, six caravels, and 1500 fighting men left Lisbon with Almeida in March 1505. Among those accompanying him was his son Lourenço who acted as his father's lieutenant and scout. Lourenço was to lead the first Portuguese expedition to Ceylon and established a settlement in Malacca. In 1508, while on patrol off the coast of Chaul and Dabul (see Instruction 99), he was met by a combined Egyptian–Gujerati fleet (indirectly supported by Venice) under the Mameluk admiral Emir Hussain. The small Portuguese squadron was defeated and Lourenço killed (aged 21). It was Almeida's need to avenge his son's death that led him to capture and burn Dabul and to fight the decisive naval battle of Diu against the Mamluks. This was the greatest triumph of his career since it established once and for all Portugal's supremacy in the Indian ocean. Only then did Almeida yield his post to Albuquerque whom he had kept under house arrest in Cannanore meanwhile. On his way back

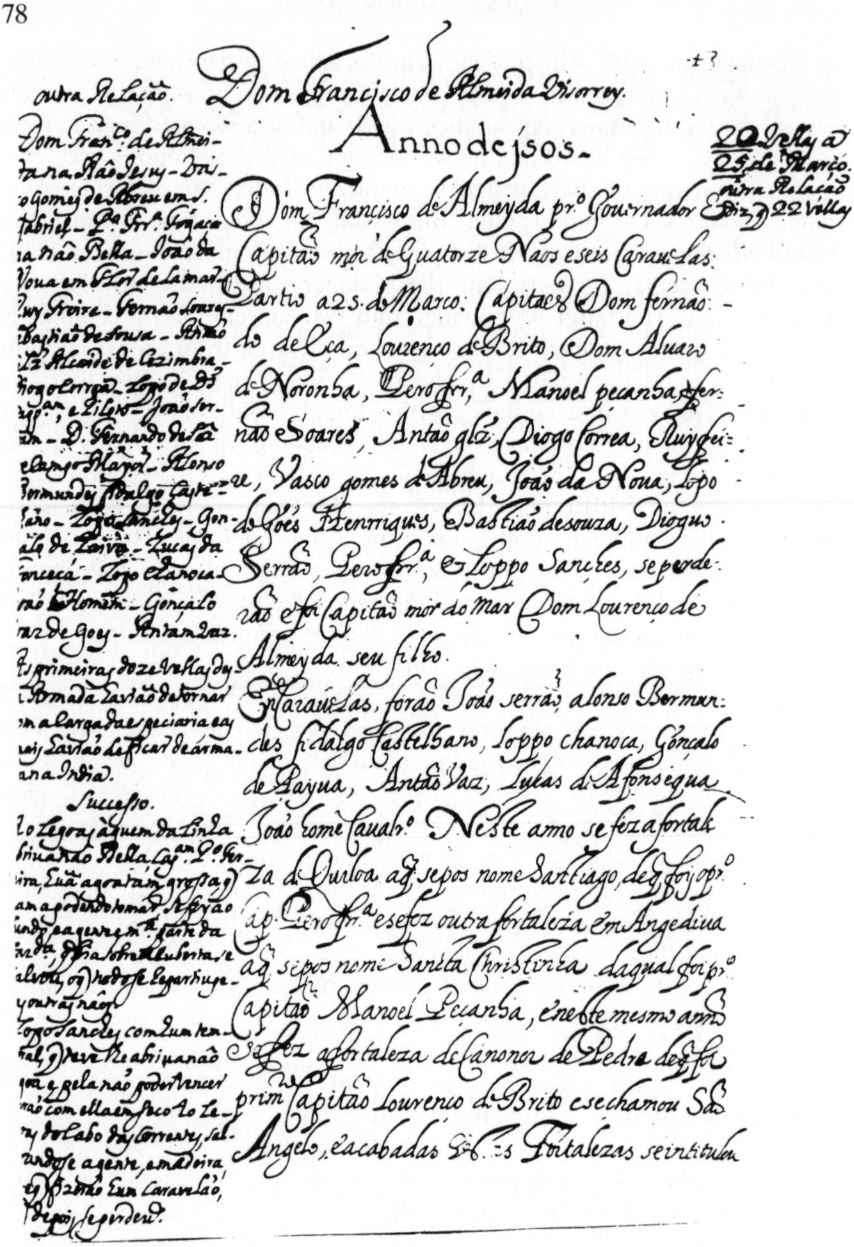
outra Relação. Dom Francisco de Almeida Visorrey.

Anno de 1505.

22 de Mayo a 25 de Março. outra Relação 22 vellas

Dom Francisco de Almeyda pr.º Gouvernador e Viz. Capitão mór de Quatorze Naos e seis Carauelas: Partio a 25 de Março: Capitaes Dom fernão de Eça, Lourenço de Brito, Dom Aluaro de Noronha, Pero fr.ª Manoel peçanha, fernão Soares, Antão glz, Diogo Correa, Ruy freire, Vasco gomes de Abreu, João da Noua, Lopo de Goes Henriques, Bastião de souza, Diogo Serrão, Pero fr.ª, e Loppo Sanches, se perderão e foi Capitão mór do mar Dom Lourenço de Almeyda seu filho.

Carauelas, forão João serrão, alonso Bermudes fidalgo castelhano, Loppo chanoca, Gonçalo de Payua, Antão Vaz, Lucas de Afonsequa, João homem Caualr.º Neste anno se fez a fortaleza de Quiloa a q se pos nome Santiago, de q foy o pr.º Cap. Pero fr.ª e se fez outra fortaleza em Angediua a q se pos nome Sancta Christinea da qual foi pr.º Capitão Manoel Peçanha, e neste mesmo anno se fez a fortaleza de Canonor de Pedra de q foi prim Capitão Lourenço de Brito e se chamou São Angelo, e acabadas [illegible] Fortalezas se intitulou

From an old catalogue of all the armadas sent to India, compiled some time after their return to Portugal by (an) anonymous chronicler(s). It lists departure dates, numbers of ships, names of captains, and achievements (especially in the construction of fortresses).

Source: British Library, MS: Additionals 20902

Figure 2.2 Report on the armada of Francisco de Almeida 1505

to Portugal, in 1510, Almeida himself was killed by Hottentots at Table Bay (today's Capetown in South Africa) where he went ashore to take on water. As for Albuquerque, he died a sick and disappointed man in Goa in 1515, having just heard that he was being replaced by Lopo Soares.

When thinking of the Portuguese empire in India, the enduring place name that comes to mind is Goa. But during Almeida's time in India, the island of Angediva, strategically placed about 50 miles south of Goa, became the centre for patrolling the Malabar coast and controlling the Indian ocean. The latter was divided into two supreme naval commands [*capitanias-mores do mar*]: the first covered the area from Cape Gardafui to Cambay, and the second defended the seas from Cambay to Cape Camorin. This was in accordance with Almeida's belief in the priority of maintaining naval supremacy over the building of too many forts. Angediva declined in importance when neighbouring Goa (captured by Albuquerque in 1510) replaced Cochin as the premier city in Portuguese India. Cochin had been another enduring achievement of Almeida. Item 52 of the *Regimento* erroneously refers to a fortress already in existence there. But in 1505 there was nothing but a factory or trade post that Vasco da Gama had started there (as well as at Cannanore) in 1503.

Stirring thoughts on Portuguese ambitions are scarce in the *Regimento.* On the other hand, there are numerous instructions emphasising detailed clerical procedures, as opposed to grand designs, as if King Manuel suspected Almeida of disdaining the minutiae of trade. The *Casa da India e Guiné* was created in 1501 out of the *Casa da Guiné e da Mina* (which traced its origins to the *Casa da Ceuta* of ca 1430). The Casa, located in Lisbon, combined the functions of government office with those of trade post; it received and registered all letters from overseas; it equipped and dispatched the fleets of India; headed by a factor [*feitor*] assisted by a treasurer and three scribes (the staff was expanded in 1509), it controlled all sales on behalf of the King. Godinho remarks that once the initial complicated bureaucratic pattern was set, it continued to be followed through sheer force of habit (Godinho, 1982, Vol. III, p. 61).

Spices were of two kinds, *major* (pepper, cinnamon and ginger) and *minor* (all the others). Traffic in the major spices, plus coral and coinage metals (gold, silver, copper) was a royal monopoly. But private individuals, through purchase and manipulation of special licences (*quintaladas*) and cargo space could participate in the importation of major spices, provided this was done through the intermediary of the *Casa da India* at prices fixed by it, and in the outwardbound shipment of metals and coral, provided this was done, also at fixed prices, through the intermediary of the factors, i.e. agents directly responsible to the King (see Godinho, 1982, Vol. III, p. 60). According to Cortesão, the basic pay of land and sea officers and soldiers of India was in *quintaladas*, an annual share of the pepper trade that varied with each individual and rank and was measured in quintals (hundredweights). This obviously gave the men a stake in maintaining the royal monopoly.

Because of their intrinsic interest, Instructions 21–32 (dealing with Pedro de Añaya's installation in Sofala) are included in this document although they were countermanded by the King in a later Item (145) of the *Regimento.* In actual fact, Añaya, a Spaniard in Manuel's service, left Lisbon with his own armada of six sailing ships in May 1505. Easily reaching a peaceful understanding with the local chief, he completed the fortress in November 1505. In September 1505 an elephant from Sofala was sent as a gift to King Manuel who had never seen one (Almeida, 1929, p. 434n.).

Text

We, the King, inform you, Dom Francisco de Almeida, member of our Council, that these are the instructions we have agreed upon; we order you to follow and respect them during this voyage on which we send you to India as captain-major [*capitam moor*] of the fleet you have raised. And they will remain in force for the three years we order you to stay there.

1. *The roll-call at departure time*: First of all, we order and command that as soon as full advance payment of the salaries of captains and all other individuals and crew who will be going with you is completed at the *Casa da Guiné e India*, the scribes [*spryvaes*] of all the *náos* and *navios*[1] copy, from the said Casa, each in his own record book, with separate entries for each and all the persons, the names of all those who have received the said salary and who will be going in the vessel of which he is the scribe; and before setting sail to leave, having assembled all the people in the *Restelo* [Lisbon dockside] you in your *náo* and each captain in his, will take a roll-call, off the lists in the said books, of all the persons in each *náo*; and in the entry for each person, besides his name and any surname or sobriquet he is known by, he will state whether he was married and where, the name of his father or mother, or whatever additional information so that, before long he can be better known. And if, in the said *náos*, there are some other persons who are there by our licence, besides those mentioned above who have received the said salary, upon showing our warrants, they too shall have their names entered in our said books – without them [the warrants] they shall not go, they shall be invited to disembark immediately with whatever things they may have carried aboard with

Source: Torre do Tombo (National Archive) C.Chron., P.1.a, Mac. 7, D.56, fol. 22 v.e; reproduced in Raimundo de Bulhão Pato (ed.), *Cartas de Affonso de Albuquerque seguidas de documentos que as elucidam*, Vol. 2 (of 7) (Lisboa: Academia das Sciencias, 1898) pp. 272–334. In this Portuguese edition, the 'Chapters' of Instructions (or Items) are not numbered. We list them here serially from 1 to 148 for the sake of convenience and, due to lack of space, have summarised most, with selected Chapters translated in full by Sylvia Modelski. Square brackets indicate abridged Items or editorial interpolations. Punctuation is modernised.

1. *náo* is the old form of *nau*, meaning *great ship*, *navio* is the generic term for any vessel.

them, otherwise they will forfeit their property. And once that roll-call has been made, should all the persons who have received the said salary not be present, their captains will immediately communicate to you the list of all those who are absent, which you will send with your signature, before your departure, to the factor and scribes of the *Casa da India e Guiné*, so that the latter will know that these are not going and the payment they have received must be returned by the missing ones or their bondsmen [*fiadores*]; and if their presence it is not an obvious necessity, they shall be given the penalty they thereby deserve.

[2. A continuous, day and night, fire watch to be maintained.]

[3–5. Provisions and wine to be carefully rationed to avoid waste and shortgages. Stores to be kept under lock and key. Captain and steward of every ship to have a key to stores each.]

[6. First call in the itinerary is on Cape Verde Islands, to replenish supplies and take advice of pilots as to best route to the Cape of Good Hope.]

[7. A brief stop to take on water and supplies may be made along the coast of Beseguiche.]

[8. Should the route agreed on pass Cruz Island [*Ilha da Cruz],*[2] you can stop there for water and wood. But whether to go there or not will be your decision.]

[9–11. Rules concerning fire signals from and to the captain major to synchronise the fleet's movements and keep it together throughout the voyage.]

[12. Vessels that are blown off course and become separated before reaching the Canary Islands should return to Lisbon, Setubal, or other such home port and await orders from the *Casa da India*.]

[13. If the fleet misses a vessel after passing the Canaries, you will go to Beseguiche and while getting water there you will erect, as a sign of your passage, at the edge of the forest where those who follow will disembark, a cross made of a tree, white because it will have been stripped of its bark; you will mark this cross with an X, to distinguish it from a similar cross left there by Lopo Soares on a previous voyage. In addition, you will leave, with some natives, three or four written messages, saying you have been there and left and that they should proceed to the Cape of Good Hope directly. On no account are captains of separated vessels to stop anywhere else along the coast. The natives should be rewarded with three to four bracelets [*manilhas*] each, to be paid by the *Casa da India*, if they deliver the notes to the captains.]

[14. Keep close communications between ships to avoid tragedies.]

[15. If a ship arrives at the watering stop of Beseguiche before you and the main body of the fleet, it should take whatever supplies it needs there and wait for you eight days. If you don't rejoin it by then, it should go on to double the Cape of Good Hope, leaving behind the same cross and messages described above, to let you know what happened.]

[16. After the Cape crossing, a separated ship should . . . [blank] and wait ten days there; it will then depart leaving five stakes well dug into the ground as a signal to you, in addition to letters as described above, and then proceed to Malindi where, not finding you, it will depart immediately without waiting, but leaving behind the same messages for you. Copies of these instructions to be conveyed to all captains.]

[17–19. Further instructions if the fleet arrives separately at Angediva and Cochin. Factors on the spot to take charge of unloading and loading.]

[20. If the fleet meets ships of the not yet returned armadas of either Lopo

2. Probably one of the Canary Islands, although it could conceivably refer to Brazil.

Soares or Francisco de Albuquerque,[3] it should try to get as much information as possible about what they have seen in India and offer assistance in case of need. Stops for repairs to vessels may be made at either Mozambique or Malindi.]

21. In this voyage, as you know, we wish, with the help of our Lord, to build the fort at Sofala, of which Captain Pedro De Añaya is to assume command with all the required naval artillery, personnel and other necessities. You and the entire fleet that you will have collected will land in . . . (blank). And here, the more securely to make a landing, the entire fleet will emerge suddenly, and will tie up and stay in the best possible haven to meet any contingency, and choose the site with the utmost care so that its sheltered position and good vantage point will provide a strong base from which to surmount anything that may befall it, be it a storm or whatever, which our Lord forbid.

22. And after having thus come into view all at once and having moored, you will transfer to one of two of the smaller vessels that seem most suitable to you for entering the [Buzi] river of Sofala, taking with you Pedro De Añaya, and in the other small vessel his son or any one else he will decide; and you will take along with you in these vessels, the men who you think are necessary and who can go, men who must be able to work as a team to accomplish what is to be done, as well as the artillery and all other arms that seem to you to be needed. And two caravels or as many more as you will order shall escort these two vessels. And, with your small boats leading the way, towing buoys to place at the entrance to Sofala, you will advance towards the said town in such a peaceful fashion and so relaxed that you will seem to be cargo and merchant vessels such as others that have already been there;[4] and the best way to suggest this would be to begin to pull out and show the merchandise; and thanks to this subterfuge you should be able to jump on land from your boats, and with the utmost caution and secrecy possible you shall immediately capture all the merchant Moors who are there, whatever their origin, and all the gold and tradegoods that you will find; and for this stratagem to best serve our interest, you will seize the said Moors, while to the natives of the land you shall inflict no damage to their persons or to their possessions because we want them to be protected. We order that the said Moors be captured and despoiled because they are enemies of our sacred catholic faith, and we have had continuous war with them; however, with the others we always had happy relations and dealings at all times; they should not be scandalised by anything but rather receive favor and good treatment. As far as the rights of the King are concerned, to wit, his powers on land over the place, do not quarrel with those and leave them alone as they were before our intervention, until instructed otherwise, let the said King and the inhabitants be well treated and favored with all good words.

23. Upon leaving the main body of the fleet behind, in such a convenient spot that no damage whatever could be inflicted upon it from any quarters, you will have appointed as captain-major [*capitam moor*] to take your place such a person in whom the said responsibility may safely rest.

And, similarly, you will order some ships of the same smaller kind as you will be sailing on to follow you soon after in such a way that when you set foot on land they too will be in a position to come to your rescue and help in your enterprise,

3. Lopo Soares left Lisbon on 22 April 1504 with thirteen vessels; Francisco de Albuquerque, Afonso's cousin, left Lisbon on 14 April 1503.
4. Sancho de Tovar visited Sofala (near present-day Beira in Mozambique) in 1501. In 1502, Tomé Lopes visited Sofala and Mozambique and established informal trade links with local merchants in both cities (see Godinho, 1982, Vol. I, p. 204).

and these arrangements you will leave in such good order and state of preparedness as you will see fit, and also, as I have recommended to you, with all the discretion and secrecy possible because if the fact that they are warships can be hidden before the deed is done it will be to our great advantage.

24. And once the said place has been seized, and all the Moors that are there captured, as well as their gold and merchandise, you will come back with everything to the ships and all the said gold and merchandise that was seized shall be loaded without missing anything, taking care that nothing can be taken away; and all this you will immediately cause to be delivered to the factor Manuel Fernandes who will have a receipt drawn by his scribes. And as for the Moors whom you have captured, you will select 10 or 12 among the most important to accompany you in the first voyage, if so pleases our Lord, and the others shall stay there to serve in the fortress that is to be built, and also to take to the other posts in India, if there are enough taken. But if this procedure we are decreeing here seems unsuitable to you, and another way appears to be preferable or more appropriate to our objectives, you will, with the counsel of Pedro de Añaya and of the other captains, do whatever seems best and to our greatest advantage.

But in whatever way you and your vessels make your entrance I remind and recommend to you that you use great caution because this place and port is very dangerous according to the information we have, and therefore it is appropriate that you be extremely vigilant.

25. Once, hopefully with the help of our Lord, this first stage of the enterprise has been accomplished, you with the said Pedro De Añaya and two other captains of your choosing and whatever other persons that in your opinion shall get on well together, shall at once look over the site where you think the fort should be built, taking into account all the things that in such a case must be observed, to wit, a very strong situation that should be protected from both the ocean and the land sides, because we are informed that the sea there is very treacherous and the river is also prone to powerful floods; thus your vessels must be able to drop anchor besides the said fortress, and it should have water inside it, or water should be available as near to it as possible and this should never be a problem; and there should also be security of all other necessary services such as timber and everything else; and take a good look at the spot that you shall agree upon, and you will immediately order work to begin on the said fort by the officers and crew who will be ordered to remain there as well as all other men of the fleet, the work being apportioned to teams by the captains and each team remaining the responsibility of its captain. And give it as much dispatch and haste as possible, so as to ensure, at least, the housing of the artillery and whatever else will herewith be ordained. And as soon as possible, as a further security, have a cave or hideaway dug in such a way that one could hole-in safely in the said fortress and sustain whatever may happen. You need not stay there until everything is done because of the journey still ahead of you, and the limited time you have for the passage across to India. With great dispatch in all there is to do, work should proceed day and night.

26. And when the work is sufficiently advanced that it seems to you that it can safely be left to the said Pedro de Añaya, you shall leave him the vessels that are to remain with him, and their officers and crews, and depart at a propitious hour and make your journey as shall be ordained below, and should it be the case that it seems a good idea to leave to the said Pedro de Añaya things that you are carrying that are intended for other forts in India, let him have as many of these as you think fit, because as far as possible we shall be happy to provide him with everything, because our ships shall not be able to visit him as soon as they will the other fortresses.

27. If in the spoils you will have taken here the gold amounts to as much as 50 000 dobra,[5] we expect you to send us at once, through the fastest vessel in the fleet, 20 000 of them, with discretion in everything you do, and up to 30 000 of what you carry will be added to the capital in India; it will be handed over to the factor from your *náo*, and delivered by your ship's scribe to the factors of the *Casa da India* in exchange for a receipt stating that it was sent by you, with the relevant information recorded by your scribes and signed and countersigned as to how they were brought in; and if the gold is more than the said 30 000, whatever more you shall send to us.

[28. If Pedro De Añaya is missing when you arrive in Sofala, you should proceed to do what has to be done, without him, if you think it can be done.]

[29. If Pedro De Añaya fails to appear before your departure from Sofala, you will leave a couple of caravels to protect the fortress.]

[30. If Pedro De Añaya arrives in Sofala before you, after a wait of [blank] days, he should proceed with building the fortress.]

[31. If, though the whole fleet arrives in Sofala, for any reason the fort is not established, and the project abandoned after consultations with Pedro De Añaya, Manuel Pecanha and other captains, Pedro De Añaya can travel on to Kilwa with all the ships.]

[32. If neither the Sofala nor the Kilwa fort is established, Pedro De Añaya is to proceed with you on the crossing to India and remain at the fortress you are to build at the mouth of the Red Sea, replacing Manuel Pecanha who, in this case, will accompany you to help fortify Angediva, as instructed below.]

33. You will leave Sofala at a propitious hour with all your fleet and make your way towards Kilwa. If, on this journey, you should come upon any vessels and booty of the Moors, or hear of reliable sightings of them, and if you can look for them where they are without losing your way or wasting too much time, go forward to intercept and then seize them. As for the vessels you are certain belong to the King of Malindi, Cannanore, or Cochin, who are our friends, do not touch them in any way; we recommend and order that they receive from you the most favourable treatment, and also ordain the same attitude be shown by all the captains of the fleet. If, with the help of our Lord, you should take any booty and find some individuals and principal merchants, you will take them along with you, and in the vessels that belong to those kings, you will in good time send us ten to twelve of the most important for service in the forts of India, like those from Sofala, and also to receive ransom from them and benefit our cause as much as possible; and with their vessels you do what seems best to you. And thus if there is any *náo* or *náos* that while on their own have found any booty, they can go ahead and take it, always making sure that they do not touch vessels belonging to the kings of Malindi, Cannanore and Cochin who are our friends.

34. And since in such matters and at such times there is bound to be confusion due to the way the goods are taken if they are not collected with care, we recommend and order you to choose certain trustworthy individuals whom you shall deem useful for the task of helping our factors and ship scribes, to ensure that the prizes taken are gathered in an orderly fashion and left in charge of our factor who will be travelling in your *náo*, entered and recorded as having been received in the ledger of your scribe; and if among the said things there are any gems, pearls, seed-pearls and other such like, besides being surrendered to the said factor to be weighed, counted or measured, they should, in your presence, be put in a box or coffer of which you will have the key; and the said factor and

5. A gold coin weighing about 4.6 grammes.

scribes should sign them as having been secured away there and received; thus they shall be beyond all suspicion. And if any vessel or vessels take booty you have ordered them to take while outside your vicinity, and, not being there, you cannot check it, you will have informed all captains in your fleet that each must follow the same procedure in his own ship, so that all that is taken is properly delivered to be recorded by the factors on the said ships until it is added to your booty and put in the charge of our factor on your ship, or left under the control of the others as seems best to you.

35. And if you should hear rumour that some things are being concealed and hidden away, you will have a public announcement posted in all the *náos* that either they must be returned and delivered to our said factor to be recorded within the days that seem necessary to you, or else you will call for an inquisition aboard all the said vessels; and if, in this way, you will make them surrender them; and those who did not initially declare the goods will lose all their salary for the round trip, their *quintaladas*, and whatever else besides is their due by our ordinance; and they may receive any additional penalty we may deem they deserve.

[36. Seized goods that would be more valuable and profitable for trading in Portugal to be reported to Vasquo Queymado, Receiver of India, by the factors of the vessels where they were loaded, duly recorded, etc.]

[37. Great care to be taken of all spoils while crossing to India. Everything acquired in those parts should be stowed and accounted for in detail and in an orderly fashion as expected.]

[38. Arrival in Kilwa of all the fleet; entrance through its river; careful choice of mooring place; safety of all vessels a primary consideration.]

[39. Having dropped anchor and moored at Kilwa, all men to disembark under command of their captains, leaving ships well guarded. Proceed with caution and avoid all setbacks.]

40. And as you endeavour to take Kilwa, and the Moors defend themselves, you will exercise that good judgement we are confident you possess to accomplish your mission without the loss of a single man if possible, which we trust our Lord will be the case; whether taking it by force or it being abandoned by the Moors, you will try to capture and seize as many as you can, and of the most important; as for the others who remain in the place without resorting to force, which may it please our Lord will be the case, you will allow them to come and go without inflicting any further damage to their persons; your only work should consist of taking all the wealth of the village, to wit, gold and merchandise; because we are assured that the king as well as the traders of this place possess very great riches, and this will require all the fine judgement which we trust you to have; and all that is seized shall be surrendered to our factor on your *náo* as we have ordered to be done in Sofala.

41. And in case you find the King disposed to serve us, and he has paid the money and tribute we have obligated him to give each year to any of the captains who are there, then you will do him no harm at all, and tell him that we need, to serve our mission, to have a fort for housing ourselves and our goods, and that with or without his consent, we shall build it; and you will go ahead and build it without wasting travel time that should go to loading the vessels; and the site and fashion and mode of execution we leave to your own good discretion, with the advice of the captains and the people you will care to consult; and doing it without the chief's agreement, if he wants to obstruct you, you will inflict as much damage upon him as possible as has already been your instruction; and as for the people of the place, allow whoever you wish to remain and take the others [*e a outra se tyrara*]. As for the said fort, we recommend that you make it as strong as

possible, because, it being so far away, and having no other recourse on land apart from itself, it is necessary to build it with the utmost security.

42. And if you take the place by force, you must be sure to capture the local chief and his sons if he has any, and any other important Moors you should send back to us by the first ship that stops there; and of the others you seize, choose those who seem most suitable for serving in the forts of India, and the others you should exchange for ransom and make as much profit out of it as possible.

43. And let me remind you, in case you want to do damage to them, that we have information here that they have great wealth in gold, and that they have run the Sofala trade for a long time, and we are told that the King is very rich and that there are very wealthy merchants; and that a great deal of very profitable goods go to Sofala. Therefore, you must watch out for this and do what I have entrusted you to do with such care that nothing is lost.

44. If perchance the king, seeing your determinaiton and equipment to injure him, surrenders and peacefully yields the place to you, and puts everything at your disposal and is completely defenceless, accept this and freely let go of him and his; but all his properties [*suas fazendas*] shall become ours and you shall order that they be secured as stated above.

45. If it seems to you, while looking at the place, that the Moors are preparing to defend themselves, and you see that your exit by land cannot be accomplished safely, then you will do as the captains advise you is the best way out. But having agreed not to retreat, use the ships' artillery to make them leave the site; and whatever the means you use to take the place, either by force or by [peaceful] surrender, always say that we have ordered the said place taken because the king being our tributary and vassal, and as such obligated to serve us, he did not subsequently receive our *náos*, *navios* and men who went there with that good treatment and understanding that is our due and that he was obliged to accord us, and that having experienced their disloyalty we order that he thus be punished as it should be done and as was done in all other cases; and we must reward the true ones and those who deal with us in good faith, peace, and friendship; they should be well treated by our captains and men, and protected as well as their possessions. And so, to those who act contrary to this we order that they be punished as their crime deserves, because this justice must be applied to all equally, to wit, recompense for those who are friendly and true in exchange for their good work and loyalty, and damage to those who are bad and deceitful in exchange for their crimes.[6]

46. Having thus taken the said place and all the spoils secured to our advantage in the stated fashion, you shall leave Pedro Ferreira there as captain, and with him men [?who have been commissioned for India] and who seem to you needed for the effective defence of and watch over the said garrison, and also the artillery, arms, and all other things needed. This artillery and things you can take from what is ear-marked for the fort, as well as those that are on the ships. And also whatever provisions appear necessary to you. And with the said Pedro Ferreira, it would be good that Duarte de Melho, son of Pedro de Melho, remain as commander [*alcayde*], and you shall appoint officers to stay on land among those that seem to you most suitable; and the people who are to stay on as military men should have the same liberties accorded to them as were given to the men in Sofala. And you will leave a caravel there, manned by a captain with everything on it; and also a brigantine of the kind that goes to India. And we

6. As it happened, the sheikh of Kilwa, after unsuccessful attempts at diplomatic evasion failed, abdicated and fled without a fight.

recommend to you especially that this be made with the greatest care, the building of the fort as well as everything else that is to be settled there; we remind you, however, that this not be done to the detriment of the loading of the ships, because the loading of the ships of India is our whole purpose.

47. In all the places where you will call, where there are Moors and infidels, we strongly advise you to give stern warning on your ship and have the same posted on all ships, that under no circumstances are weapons and other military equipment to be sold, except for use in the defence of the Holy Father and ourselves; and whoever does sell, in addition to the penalties already announced, they shall receive further punishment as we shall see fit, and we will be most displeased if arms are passed.

48. Having accomplished your objective in Kilwa, in the manner stated above, your fleet shall weigh anchor at a propitious hour for the crossing to India. And if in Kilwa or on your way you should find a native vessel that is going to Malindi, in which you can safely send one of your captives [*degradados*] that you have seized, send a message to the King of Malindi[7] saying you carry our greetings to him, and that we regard him with great good will, and how we always treat him and his possessions with the utmost respect and favour, and that we have instructed you and all our captains that all his things be as well treated as our own, and we have done this because he has deserved it; and that because you are in a hurry, and cannot afford to lose time on the way ahead of you to India, you regret not being able to visit him. And you will give the letter to whoever is going, and if he [the King of Malindi] asks questions of you, give him an account of why we are there with our weapons and armadas; and also the events in Sofala and Kilwa, if they did occur, how everything happened and that we punished the King of Kilwa because he did not recognise our Lord's mercy in putting him under our patronage; as our vassal in exchange for our protection and favour, and although obliged, as such, to serve us, he did not extend a welcome to our ships and men who went there; they did not find there what it was his duty to offer in good will; instead, he acted as if he was not obligated as he was, and for this reason he was punished; because just as it always gives us pleasure to supply all good treatment, favour and respect to our friends and servants, the reverse is also the case, with whatever further account of the facts he will request from you, showing him that he will always have our trust, and we hope that this will always be so, always giving much respect, favour and mercy, as stated.

49. After Kilwa,[8] we think it a good plan for you to send a pair of [?barinels] [*barynes*][9] that seem most suitable to you, to sail along the coast up to Cape Guardafui without entering the strait, and you will caution them not to be detained there. They should report to you all they have seen and found, and if they come upon any booty which they want to take from the Moors, they can do so provided it can be done safely, in all security, but they should not touch anything belonging to Malindi, Cannanore and Cochin. However, they must not otherwise waste any time, but rather strive to rejoin you in India as soon as possible.

7. This Moslem ruler was friendly to Vasco da Gama when the latter called on Malindi (now in Kenya) in 1498, and he subsequently became a firm ally of Portugal.
8. Almeida's powers of destruction, unused in Kilwa (in today's Tanzania), were soon fully deployed against a resisting town north of it, not mentioned in the *Regimento*: Mombasa (now in Kenya), which he pillaged and brought to ruins in August 1505.
9. Barinel: sailing vessel of relatively humble size, used in the early voyages of discovery along the West African coast, later abandoned in favour of the sturdier India ships.

50. Having left that area, you shall continue, with your assembled fleet, your journey on the route to India, following the advice of the pilots as to how best to get there. And you shall travel directly to Angediva where we want a fort built. Here you will moor in the most secure spot available so that our ships will be sheltered from any inconvenience, and protected from both the land and ocean sides. And after dropping anchor, you will step ashore with Manuel Pecanha and Dom Alvaro and Lourenço de Brito, and other captains and members of the fleet, whoever seem to you to get on well together. And you will look over the island and places for the best site on which to build the said fort, bearing in mind the need to have water, within its walls if possible, or at least near enough never to be a problem; and also that the landing site should be as near the fortress as can be, and all other things thought to be convenient for that kind of construction. And after agreeing on the spot where it is to be built, which you should do as expeditiously as possible, you will immediately get all the artillery out as well as the other things herewith detailed, and also officers, masons and carpenters, and the men here stated, and with all the fleet you shall order for work to start on the said fortress; and also to do any other repairs, in order to establish, in all security, Manuel Pecanha who is hereby named captain; so that during your stay of a few days great work will be done. And you will also order the wood for the galleys to be unloaded on that site and the manpower to build them; and to be put in charge of this task, you will appoint João Serrão who will be sufficient for this work, because we want Lopo Sanches to continue with you until Cochin to serve there in the completion of as many galleys as are being built. And with the said João Serrão will stay the men who are to go on the said galleys and all their officers and crew, with whom, when you depart from there, you will leave a record of what they are to do: how the galleys are to be finished and launched to sea. Still, it seems to us that to have your message about what they are to do they must wait, because according to what you find in Cochin you will know better what is to be done. However, whatever you decide, you will leave it to Manuel Pecanha to do it. And we recommend to you that all that has to be done here must be done with the greatest dispatch possible; you should remain there at most as few days as possible because the charge you are taking on will keep you so busy to ensure the departure of the fleet in short time, and because the loading of the ships is so important for our objective, as you know, we recommend and caution you about these things. And the said João Serrão, and all the individuals of the galleys' detail who are to remain there with him, come under the jurisdiction of the said Manuel Pecanha, as are all the other people manning the fortress.

51. When a fort is established in Angediva, on such a spot where you think Manuel Pecanha can remain in all security, and also when all the other things that are to stay there have been set on land, which should be done with the greatest dispatch, as it has been stated, you shall leave one pair of caravels of those you have, also for his further protection, since he can, through them, send you any message or warning he wants; and if it seems to you fitting to leave behind, with them, any other vessels, leave as many as appears necessary for his safety, for in such things, it is very advantageous to our service that they should not suffer any reverse in the initial period. And when all these things are done, you will weigh anchor with all the rest of the fleet, taking with you Lopo Sanches, and his brigantine, and the other will remain waiting near the said galleys; and you will make your way in good time to Cochin, coasting along the shore as closely as possible without risk to the ships; and in such a way that if you find any *náos* or *navios* from Calicut, you can seize them and their cargo; and to the said Calicut you will do all the harm and damage that you can, without however incurring any delay thereby, nor touching anything belonging to the King of Cannanore. Before

coming to Cannanore, you will send him a letter from us and you will communicate to him that you are passing by and cannot see him, but that he should be assured that we hold him in very good esteem; and because of his goodness and trustworthiness, we wish his things to be well treated, and that when you have settled down there will be time to talk, and that when, in due course, you return to approvision Angediva, you will visit him.

52. And you will proceed directly to Cochin where, we pray our Lord, the fort has been built and the people there are well, the land is all right and the king remains our servant as before. You will speak to our factor and the other officers of the factory, and through them you will inform your self about how things are and how they have been so far, and how things are in Calicut,[10] and what preparations have been made for loading. And taking in all this information you can see the king with the confidence which you know is advantageous to our purpose; and you will give him the letter that you are carrying, as well as the present which we are sending him through you. And besides our letter, you shall tell him on our behalf that he has earned much honour because he has trust in the things of our service, and we are grateful as is due, and that we put our hope in our Lord that, because of his honesty and virtue much good and many benefits and honours shall befall him; and that for the little we have done to him he has given us the most; he should have faith that his possessions will always be as well looked after, protected and treated, as our own, because his virtue deserves it. And all such good words in order to thank him for his good will. And in the fortress of Cochin you shall appoint Dom Alvaro whom we are sending with you as captain; and you will give him all the assistance he may need in artillery as well as the other things required for his greater safety. Landing with him in the said fortress will be . . . [blank] who will be chief commander [*alcaide moor*], as well as all the officers and men who are to remain there, and all that is here ordained.

53. About the fort in Angediva, we think it a good idea to remove all the artillery and arms that were meant for the fortress at Cochin and take it there, as well as what was to go to the fortress at Quilon. Because Angediva seems to us to provide better protection and security, from which it will be possible to extract weapons for use wherever needed; and we order that, having done this, you do not take more than is necessary for the forts at Cochin and Quilon. And place the remainder in the fortress of Angediva, as stated, because the said fort of Quilon will not be done until later, as will be instructed in a following Item.

[54. The loading of a convoy of vessels to start after consultations with the local king and factor Alvaro. Appointment of a chief captain [*capitam principall*] to be obeyed by all the other ships' captains. Dom Alvaro to receive all that he requests for the welfare and defence of the fortress.]

55. Should it happen, which God forbid, that you find things at the fort of Cochin are in a bad way, and also the King, you shall hurry in and furnish it so as best to serve our purpose, as you must do any time the fort suffers any damage; and you will supply the King of Cochin with what he needs, because we are obligated to furnish him with all his necessities, without, however, forgetting to arrange for the loading that has to be done there.

56. After leaving orders in Cochin for loading to proceed, as has been stated, you will travel to Quilon where Afonso de Albuquerque took his consignment,

10. King Manuel had good reasons to be anxious about what Almeida might find in the wake of da Gama's vengeful bombardment and savagery in Calicut two years previously. But the Raja of Cochin proved to be a steadfast friend though himself imperilled by their presence; he protected the Portuguese (but see Panikkar, 1929, pp. 55–71).

and where we are assured many spices are to be found. And besides that, you will have sought information in Cochin in order to be aware of what you have to do. You will also inquire from our factor on the spot about the deals he has arranged, and about the lie of the land, and whatever other thing you think you ought to be warned about to succeed in what you have to do. And if there is a king of this land, and if you can safely see him, give him our letter which you are carrying, and tell him that we remember when our captain came to his city he was well received and treated by its governors, and he was given a consignment; and that he was able to buy and sell in all honesty and security, and that we heard this with much pleasure because where there is justice and truth, as we are assured there is in his land, there must be all goodness. And with our message, we have the pleasure of sending our vessels with our merchandise to his harbour in order to take on cargo; and that it would please us if he would receive from us nothing but benefit for his land; and in order to have friendship and relations with him more abundantly than with any other king of India, we beg him to agree to receive us with the same good will as we extend to him. And other such good words. And should there be no king, while you are there, you will still give our letter, that you are carrying, to the governors of the city, and tell them we remember how the said Afonso de Albuquerque, our captain, how he was treated and his ships loaded in all security; and because he spoke to us about their honesty and goodness, we have sent our vessels and a letter to the king; and that we would very much like to have an agreement, and our merchandise in greater abundance there than in other parts, because of the trust and fairness that our captain said he met. And you will devote all your efforts to start right away to load as speedily as possible the ships that you are taking with you for that purpose. And you will leave there our factor who is hereby appointed, and also the officers of the factory, making sure that the land is safe, and also the friars and ?vallenciano, and all the church things, assuming that all can be settled safely. And also, you will leave that part of the merchandise that seems suitable to you; however, we think there shouldn't be much before the fort is built, and the bulk of the merchandise shall be in Cochin; because we now assume it to be understood that the first concern is to have good friendship in the land and safety for our ships. And the building of the fort shall not start before you order it.

And once the said consignment is aboard, you will go to Cochin, and you will send another shipment from there, if it has not already left; and you will also see to what needs to be done there, and then you will travel to Angediva where you will also do the same, as is necessary.

[57–59. Storage and protection of cargo and victuals on ships. Economic use of space: previous consignments were stowed at rate of two quintals per ton of ship. Vessels to make the return trip three at a time, with a chief captain to lead the three; fast succession of convoys urged. Departure time: end of January at the latest.]

[60. Goods loaded in Lisbon are to be weighed, assessed, signed for and entered in the register of each ship's scribe, in the presence of the factor.]

[61. Factors to keep careful record of prices paid for spices and other goods in India, as well as the value of the goods shipped from Portugal to India. *Casa da India* to be notified of same.]

[62. Our goods not to be sold for less than what was paid to Lopo Soares for same; Indian goods not to be bought for a higher price than he settled for. Dom Martinho, our Overseer, to keep register.]

[63. If pepper is unavailable in the desirable quantity or quality, buy more of the other spices, as much as double the agreed amount of fine cinnamon and ginger, available funds permitting. Watch out for cheating in the weighing which accounted for many losses in past voyages.]

[64. If not enough spices can be found to fill all the vessels, the ships that are with cargo should return home while the others will remain in India for the new winter crop, at our expense and that of the other merchants; the spices that do arrive will be paid by the pound and divided between us and them, and we shall have first choice; those with money in the *Casa* shall first draw half their *quintaladas*, and the second half shall be shared with us and paid for by the pound.]

65. For the better benefit of our service and for greater profits, we command that all spices bought in India be purchased through our factors and officers who are there, and not in any other way; and to them should be delivered our money and that for the shares of the pepper due; and because the completion of records and distributions might cause too much delay at the other end, particularly when all the pepper that was hoped for could not be acquired or was not available, that is, our own consignment and the said shares, then everything will be agreed upon for the best to give each one his due on the return journey, which may it please God to make possible. And you have our agreement and command that, before leaving here, the captain and men of each *náo* to whom we have granted a licence to carry cargo in excess of their usual *quintaladas*, and also, for the duration of the voyage, the captains, commandants, factors and officers, and all others who are manning the fortresses shall directly surrender to the factor of the ships on which they sail, all the money they are carrying to buy pepper, for the *quintaladas* as well as for anything more for which they have our licence. And their money, as well as that addressed to our own shipment shall be put under the control and protection of the captain of each ship in a coffer or chest with two keys, one of which he will keep and the said factor will take the other. And it will be entered by the ship's scribe in his book, what each person puts in. All the money will then go to Vasquo Queymado, Receiver of the *Casa da India*, who will keep a separate book for this purpose, stating what each captain and persons of each ship has brought, naming all, and how much money from each, and that they assume the risk; everything duly declared and signed for by Vasquo Queymado and entrusted to his keeping; and he will ensure their payment on the return journey in the manner stated above. And the master pilots and sailors and crews of the said ships shall keep the money for their *quintaladas* in their own possession, or in the most convenient way, because Vasquo Queymado need not receive those.

[66. Sailors to surrender their *quintaladas* money to the factor of each vessel, in the same manner.]

[67. How the money and merchandise will be transferred from the ships to the factors in India, duly acknowledged as received by Vasquo Queymado.]

[68. Pepper to be purchased by factors in India, in one joint amount, half of which goes to King Manuel by right. Should some loss be incurred through faulty weighing, the loss will be shared equally by all.]

[69. If a ship or its consignment gets lost at sea, we and the rest of the fleet shall share the loss with the captain, crew and others on that ship; remainder of the profits to be shared equally among all.]

[70. All the spices carried on every vessel to be carefully registered separately; this is in addition to the general record of all the goods on the said vessel.]

[71. Captains, crews, etc. can carry as much money as they like, to spend on things other than pepper.]

[72. Each vessel to carry six shipments of good pepper: 2 shipments of 4 quintal each, 2 shipments of seamen's *quintaladas*, 2 shipments of cabin-boy *quintaladas*; weighing and registration to be in presence of captain, master and scribe, any surplus weight, above what was licensed, to be for the King.]

[73. Pepper cargos to be well packaged, recorded and stored, marked and counter-marked, with weight declared, whether it is in *old* or *new* quintals; weighing of spices to be in old, not new, quintals.]

74. No captain or any other person aboard will be allowed to go ashore, only the factors and their scribes can do that on the days on which they must load or unload money or goods they are delivering or receiving and must be there personally. Also, any one else whose going ashore, in your opinion, is necessary for the benefit of our service and cannot be avoided, must return to the ships for the night under penalty; if inevitable, with your permission, they are to sleep in the factor's house. And whoever disobeys this, having rank of captain, we shall confiscate all his salary, plus any other penalty we may ordain. All other ranks, including master pilots, will forfeit their salary and *quintaladas* and any other property they will own, and they will be banished to the island of St Helena on the way back, for as long as will be our wish. If they don't pass by the island because they return by a different route from the one they sailed out, they will be sent to the island of St Tomé for ever. And, if they pillage [*se for piam*], besides their banishment and loss of *quintaladas*, they will be flogged in public. Their punishment is to be announced in advance by public proclamation. This warning is to be posted in all vessels.

75. The said captains, individuals and crew members, besides the *quintaladas* we have licensed them to purchase in pepper, and also whatever else they can fetch with our licence, will be able to buy and bring back all sorts of drugs and retail goods [*cousas de botica*], linen, benzoin, and also all kinds of precious stones, pearls, seed pearls, scents, cloth, caps [*toucas*], and whatever else is to be found in these parts. We give them all the storage space and permission to trade freely for their own account; and they shall pay a quarter part [*quarto e vymtena*] of these as duty. However, this does not apply to the factors and officers in our factories, and the captains of those places, because these will buy only the *quintaladas* of pepper we have allowed, as stated in the instructions in Lopo Soares' *regimento*; they cannot carry or bring back anything else, under penalty of losing it all as well as what they were contracted to receive from us and that we had granted.

[76. How these goods are to be purchased: a person to be entrusted with the task of going around with a scribe asking each one what he wants to buy; those two are then to go ashore but not to sleep there. Upon their return each person who placed a written order is to be given his goods. Storing of merchandise. Gems and valuables to be kept in a coffer with 4 keys (1 for the captain, 1 for the representative, 1 for the factor, 1 for the scribe); everything to be carefully weighed, counted and registered to avoid confusion.]

[77–78. Purchasing factor and his scribe are under oath to buy only the said goods and only for the said person. No one to carry merchandise without royal licence. Penalties.]

[79. No slaves to be bought during the voyage. He who does shall forfeit his salary. In case of shortage of sailors at departure time [from India], it is permissible to hire able-bodied hands or servants.]

[80. If it can be managed without creating a scandal or damage to ourselves or the natives, when loading at a port, do not allow any other vessels to leave the place with a shipment of spices, victuals or anything else.]

[81. Once the loading of the *náos* is completed, and the vessels on their way home, go to Cochin and see whatever needs to be done there. Then proceed to Angediva with the same mission.]

82. And it appears to us that nothing could be more important to our service than to have a fort at the mouth of the Red Sea,[11] or close to it, situated inside or outside the mouth, so that no more spices will ever again be able to pass to the land of the Sultan. Then all those who are in India will cease imagining that they can trade with any one but us. Furthermore, this is very near the land of Prester John, from which great benefit might accrue, primarily to Christianity, and also to expand our enterprise, and also in case of war, if we want to wage it. It seems that our interest would be better served from there than from anywhere else. It would please us that, as soon as you have accomplished in Angediva all that is needed for its security, and once the things we have ordered above have been done, you should assemble all the fleet around you, except for those that seem to you needed in Angediva and Cochin, and those vessels that appear not fit for the crossing.

83. You will also collect the ships that carried all that was sent for the fortress at Quilon, and also the officers, masons, carpenters, and all else that is required for the building of a fortress, and also all the artillery and arms that can be spared from Angediva and Cochin.

84. And with this whole fleet assembled, it would please us that you cross to the mouth of the Red Sea with Manuel Pecanha, and also Lourenço de Brito. You will proceed to the vicinity of the mouth, inside it or outside, or whatever place that seems convenient to you to control the entrance of the Strait and the traffic through it; finding such a situation as seems to you suitable for building a fortress, as strong as is necessary for the location, looking for all the qualities that were aimed at in the past for the forts at Sofala and Angediva. As for the choice of the site as well as all the other things, let us remind you that you shall be near the Sultan from where many people could have access to it; and also that any assistance to you will be very far away. Given all these conditions, and others besides that you can think of as obstacles to this venture, if you still manage to bring it about that you can secure such a place, you will make a landing and build the said fortress, taking advice from Manuel Pecanha and Lourenço de Brito, as well as the captains and other persons going with you. And if you agree to go ahead and the fortress is built, you have our consent that Capt. Manuel Pecanha should stay there – assuming that Pedro de Añaya is not with you, as instructed above; because, if he is with you, that is in case neither the fort at Sofala nor that at Kilwa was established, he should be the one who remains here as Captain as stated above – and you shall give him the men and artillery and weapons that seem justified for the place and for the defence of our interest; and each thing must be supplied with a good back-up.

85. You will leave there the vessels that seem to you to be needed to defend the building as well as to inflict damage on the passing ships belonging to the Moors, and also to trade, because we are informed that much profit and gold is to be got in Zeila.

86. To this fort, you will appoint the officers who seem to you most suitable, namely, one factor, two scribes and, as chief commander [*alcaide moor*], Fernam Sanches, barring Pedro de Añaya, because all those who were assigned to Sofala should otherwise serve here.

87. While Manuel Pecanha is on this journey with you, you have our consent that his son João Rodrigues should remain in Angediva: and we agree that Joham Peegas and Sancho Sanches, and any other person you wish, should remain with him so that the fort will be safe. But, once the Red Sea fortress is established, you

11. Almeida ignored this Instruction. It was Albuquerque, on his way (with Tristão da Cunha) to India to succeed Almeida, who captured Socotra in 1506.

will send for the son of Manuel Pecanha to be with his father if he is to be stationed there, and whoever else you wish. And as captain in Angediva you will appoint Lourenço de Brito; if the latter is later assigned to Quilon but would rather stay where he is, he will remain wherever he prefers; should Lourenço de Brito go to Quilon, then we advise that Vasco Dabreu shall go to Angediva; and if Lourenço de Brito doesn't want to transfer to Quilon, you will appoint Lourenço Gomes there, and whoever seems suitable to you shall captain his vessel.

88. Don't forget to take all precautions so that the site chosen for the fort has harbours where our vessels can winter, and have such configuration that our galleys can be beached.

89. After the above has been accomplished, or the project abandoned because, in your judgement, it is best to not proceed with the fort, you will go to India and see to it that our interest is well served there. And after your arrival, one way or the other, you shall request of the King of Quilon and of the governors of the city, by virtue of the letter and message we have sent, that a fortress be built there; and you will proceed in the best manner possible, and once built, you will appoint Lourenço de Brito and his officers there; and it seems to us that you should not start building the fortress against the wish of the local king and city chiefs. And if at first you begin building with his consent and he seems happy about it, and he then changes his mind and withdraws his permission, if this turnabout occurs when you are already so far advanced in your work that he cannot make you stop, in this case, whether he likes it or not, you will go ahead with the building, and try with the proper words to reassure him. And if you do not succeed in assuaging him you will do what you can to make the best of the situation. And if your work has not yet advanced to the point where you can continue against his will, then you will desist, making a show of not wanting to proceed without his approval, using the best language possible, so that there will be no break between us.

[90–91. If you think that we will get good returns for this, you can spend up to 1000 *cruzados*[12] in gifts to get permission to construct the fort at Quilon. A house and church to be built to house the priests.]

92. Bear in mind that the place for the fort must be very carefully selected; it must be better than any other spot, that is, one from which the ships can cut loose promptly.

[93. The sick aboard the ships of the armada should be given good medical care. The dying are to confess and make wills that are properly recorded by the scribes. Earnings up to death to be accurately reckoned and what is due noted.]

94. You have our consent to order and forbid that in any place, whether on the coast or anywhere else in India, any one should ever be on land except where we have forts, barring places that are deserted, and where you have complete security, and can do so with the utmost confidence, without any suspicion or doubt to the contrary. And should you see and speak to any king, it must be at sea, and with such precautions that no inconvenience whatever may befall your person, whose protection and safety we regard as of the greatest importance and necessity for our service. And should you happen to leave ship, you will warn your *náo* and all the fleet that you are doing this for our service, and transfer the responsibility to the captains and other suitable people. And if the situation arises where some individuals, captains of other vessels, must go ashore at the time of purchase, you shall then send whoever seems fit for this, but only if it cannot possibly be avoided.

12. Portuguese gold coin weighing 3.58 grammes (i.e., a Venetian ducat).

95. At the first opportunity, when you sail [from Cochin] to visit Angediva, before crossing over to the mouth of the Red Sea, you will call on the King of Cannanore, as instructed above. You will give him our letter that you are carrying, and you will excuse yourself for not visiting him when you were passing on your way to Cochin, with the best words you can; and, besides what we have written to him, show him that we consider him our good friend, and that his possessions are, in our eyes, like our possessions, and will be treated and protected as such at all times by you and our captains, and that this is by our order. Say we trust that he is such a king and so true, that the goodwill we have earned at the beginning we shall know how to preserve, and wish him and his land all goodness and peace. And that we have ordered the said forts built in the said places where they are being built or are to be built because we thought that there we would not be as safe as on his land and trading post where we feel at home without fort, with complete security and reliability; that our vessels have always traded profitably on his land; and whatever spices are to be found in his country, we have ordered you to purchase them at prices comparable to those in other parts; and that he will be favoured in everything and be well treated by you, because he deserves this treatment. Bear in mind, however, that what you find on his land does not exceed in quantity what is allotted to it in the consignment book you are carrying.

96. Should the King of Calicut behave satisfactorily and give you assurances that he wants a stable and secure peace, and thus it seems to you safe to give it to him, we agree that you should conclude peace with him. However, he should pledge that no Moors from Mecca can stay there; and if you can, make a deal to buy all the things that were agreed with Francisco de Albuquerque and all further advantages you can earn for our service. And before reaching this treaty, you should endeavour to find out if it will be favourably regarded by the kings of India, principally the King of Cochin, because without his approval and consent we should not go ahead with it. And if we do not make peace with him, we order you to wage war against him, inflicting every injury upon him by all ways and means possible, on the sea as well as on land, taking great care, however, not to put our interest in danger. And as for the fishermen and others who bring in food to the city, don't let them fish or supply any food there; and in every way, confront them, causing them as much damage as necessary. And if it should happen that you decide to make peace, write down what your commitments are; but don't concede anything as long as it seems to you that you should not yield, don't relax your determination to do him as much harm as possible, going as far as destroying everything if you can. The question of war and peace we leave to your good discretion, with two provisos: the Moors from Mecca should not remain on the land, nor should the King of Cochin be contradicted, because we do not wish anything to be done without these two conditions.

97. We recommend and order you to apply great care and aforethought in the building of the said fortresses so that, in due course, their maintenance can come from the locality when available; they should always be peaceful and not lacking necessities; and we take it as agreed that reserves of all the daily necessities for all the persons stationed in each fortress should last six months; and you can add whatever more can be obtained, because when the forts are eventually completed, the armadas too should be approvisioned from them. Take special care of this instruction.

98. All prizes taken by the said armadas, with the help of our Lord, we will agree that they be deposited in the fort nearest to the spot where the seizure was made. There they will be divided into the shares described in our *regimento*. And what belongs to us shall be delivered to our factor, according to the instructions

below governing the taking of prizes – paying special attention that all is declared and nothing hidden, as stated.

99. After returning from the mouth of the Red Sea, the fleet shall be divided as seems most suitable to you. However, along the coast of Chaul and Dabul, and between Cambay and Ormuz [Agramuz],[13] we think you should send some of the fleet's vessels which, according to the information we have, should extract profits from Moorish things from that coast; and those whom you send should seize all the Moslem ships they can. And if the kings and chiefs of the said cities wish to earn our friendship and enter our service, in exchange for becoming our vassals and acknowledging their status, each and all, by paying tribute, then we agree that an understanding be reached with them as you see fit, obligating them, for the greatest possible advantage to our interest, through the agreements, to contribute men and vessels for our fortresses; and for our money all the goods and provisions necessary for our trade and their needs, at prices to be determined; however, if we could convince them to pay in kind the tribute they owe us, in the form of goods and provisions, this would be to our best advantage. And if you could also bring about that they are obliged to carry all the said provisions and merchandise that must go to Angediva on their own ships, we shall be well served.

100. As they obligate themselves to get from our factories all the merchandise for the Levant, they will take them from our factors at the same prices as other people charge. We recommend to you that in all these things as well as others that may arise, you will decide what is convenient, according to what is available, and you will do what is best for our interest. If an agreement is reached it will be on the following conditions: that it shall wait until you have notified us, and we shall let you know if you can go ahead with what is reported to us; and assuming that our consent is given, if we have no objection to your treaty, that we have been notified two months later that you and our people, as well as your possessions, are safe. However, in this agreement, if it comes about, you must immediately stipulate that no spices destined for Mecca are to pass through their places and territories for any destination whatever; and if you find any of those spices on their vessels, you shall seize them, and consider the agreement broken.

And this applies to any treaty with any other kings of India, given that they are Moors and that they request one from you. And also, no spices from their lands should reach Aden, Ormuz, or any other places in the Strait, and with the condition stipulated above: that you must first notify us of it and received our reply in the said manner.

101. But on the question whether to have a peace treaty with any of those kings, or not to have one, and also whether to accept tribute or conclude friendship agreements, we leave the decision entirely to you, and trust you will judge each for our best advantage.

102. It would please us if the people on the territory adjacent to Angediva were favourably and well treated, because it seems to us that this would be very profitable to us and to the factory there; therefore, take great care to secure this, and pass on the message to Manuel Pecanha that he should maintain this policy also when you are not present.

[103. Christians to be honoured and favoured in everything. The same applies to those who have only recently been converted, whatever their origin; each and every one of them is to be indoctrinated and taught the faith.]

13. Albuquerque invested Ormuz in 1507, captured it in 1514, yet this city still appeared as *Agramuz* on the King Manuel's atlas of 1516. The Persian gulf area is practically ignored in the *Regimento*.

104. We order that all the people, those of the fleet as well as those in the fortresses, be well disciplined and reprimanded, and wear proper and correct dress, and that no disobedience is tolerated in any of the places where you stop; and that they shouldn't do anything they are not supposed to do; and with all those with whom they negotiate, or deal with in any other way, let them be honest; and we especially order you to look out and be vigilant in preventing meetings of the men with native women, because this would be a great disservice to our Lord; it is something which, they say, much scandalises the natives.

105. If it seems to you that, in Cochin, some oared ships [*nauyos de reemo*] can be built and you need them, and if the lumber and other materials are available there, have them built. However, let it be done in a discreet spot, with secrecy so that the local artisans cannot watch [how it's done]; and always have some wood carved in reserve against any repairs that might be needed for any ships; and have extra shrouds [ropes for rigging] set aside; because it is convenient to have those two items always easily available to meet any eventuality . . . [blank] have enough made because you don't want to waste time; better have them ready-made than start manufacturing them when they are wanted.

106. Because, according to the information we have, the merchandise from Cambay is very profitably sold in Sofala, you will try to find out how much is sent there every year, and also whether an agreement can be reached on behalf of the *Casa da India* with the King of Cambay, for him to provide the total amount of goods we wish to take to give to our factors who will make profit from them. And do the same with whatever other kings in whose land the said things are to be found, from which they will draw two benefits: our friendship, and receipt of profits from the goods. However, be sure to wait until you have notified us, and received our response, as was instructed above about treaties with other kings.

107. We expect you to take along with you from here a book that Dom Martinho, our Overseer [*veedor da fazenda*], will give you; it is a record of all the money and merchandise that was sent to our factors in India in the past and also the present; in it will be kept an account of all that is spent and will be spent, until the departure of the ships, that is to say; and of what remains in the factories, you will send us a carefully kept register, stating all the kinds of goods that were consumed, and what is left over and its estimated value; and which are the most profitable goods for trade, and what goods need to be supplied to our trading posts; and similarly what quantity of spice can be had from India, annually, in your estimation, and in what proportions; and where you can obtain reliable information; and how much merchandise from here can be absorbed there, and of what kind, and at what prices; and if you could send us an accurate balance sheet it would be of great advantage to us; and we recommend that you take special care to send it to us soon; and you shall make two or three copies of this register, each of which shall travel on a different *náo*.

108. We order that you carry a list of all the artillery and armaments and things of that sort that are on the vessels and destined for the fortresses; and this list is to be given to you by Dom Martinho, as well as a list of the ships to which they are allocated.

[109–110. Similarly, keep a record of all the *quintaladas* and provisions you carry with the fleet and their distribution among the vessels.]

111. In the matter of justice, we give you our full powers in this our enterprise from the time you leave the said parts, according to the responsibilities we have invested in you; however, with the confidence which we have in you, we strongly recommend that in everything you do for the sake of our interest, justice be preserved and dispensed equally to all. Thus besides being in charge of and

achieving the mission we are entrusting you with, you will have been of great service to us.

112. With reference to the appointment of officers to factories, forts, and other offices created therein, if the case arises that any post falls vacant you will fill the position according to the relevant rule given in the instructions of the captain of each of the said fortress, deciding for yourself if our interest might not be best served in another way; this would have to be done for valid and profitable reasons, otherwise do not contravene the said instruction.

113. As for the captains of the said forts and of the vessels that are travelling with you, as well as those who go later, and the commandants of the said fortresses, to these positions you will appoint the individuals who seem most suitable for the job and appropriate to the circumstance, for instance an appointment to replace a death or whatever; and those you have appointed to be captains or commandants shall serve until you let us know of the appointment and the reasons for it, and we shall confirm it; and you have the power to lower the salary and pay they are to receive according to your good judgement and our better service; however, there are to be no salary increases for the captains, commandants and other officers concerned, unless it is ordered by us.

114. The fleet you are taking with you is made up of different ships. In addition to the cargo vessels, and those earmarked for the *armadas*, there are some that are busy with embarcation duties; these will retain this function or be diverted to others when more profitable use for them is found; but if by the time you arrive there they are in such condition that they can make the return journey, and can be adequately manned, and can carry our spices, it will be all right for them to be loaded and sent to us, led by the captains of your choice; care should be taken, however, that they are not involved in any danger, and the merchandise arrives safely. And because we believe that they are all going to return, you must help, on your part, to load and expedite them, giving them all the provisions you can before their departure; however, should one fail to secure goods for lack of capital raised, and has empty cargo space, you may give half the space to whoever wants to use it; and this only after the needs of our own service are met; but whatever you do, now or there, use all means to meet our objective.

115. Diego Fernandes, our factor in Cochin, wrote us when Afonso de Albuquerque visited him, that it would be very profitable to us if we gave certain rewards to some native chiefs and important persons whom we can enlist in our service and who can facilitate our task; because it is customary there, and some are being bought off in this way by the King of Calicut in his war against Cochin. Hence, we order you to gather all the said information, and if it is found that it would be profitable to use the said rewards, you have our agreement that up to 3000 *cruzados* can be addressed annually to those chiefs who seem most valuable and reliable for us to deal with; you can divide the sum as seems best to you, according to each individual case, whether it be for his personal qualities or his usefulness to us; and this is to apply only if the gifts bring in good returns.

116. And you will do the same if you have information that such gifts to any parts of India would secure us a better deal on land, as long as you make sure that they are not wasted, and you give us a full account of them as well as the benefit accrued from them.

117. Let us remind you to always be very careful to send some men to make discoveries, whether in Malacca or any other quarters that are not yet too well known. And you shall send them with some merchandise on native vessels that have already been there, provided they can safely travel on them; and those you send must be competent men.

118. If two or three native Christian priests from Quilon wish to come here, it would please us if you sent them; they should be well treated and lodged on board.

119. Keep a record of all the *náos* and *navios* in the fleet: which of them are for cargo, and which are to remain with you; because although you already know this, it is better to have it in writing, and Dom Martinho shall give you the list.

120. If the King of Cochin dies, remember to work hard, but discreetly, without causing a scandal among the natives, to have us recognised as the local chief; prepare the best arguments and speeches for this, depending on the time and what conditions on the spot require; telling them that their prosperity, peace and security are our objectives; and this should be enough for you to say until the situation becomes clearer.

121. The money in the vessels of the merchants[14] you will order delivered to our factor, so that he will make the purchases himself, as agreed in the contracts, of which you will have copies handed to you by Dom Martinho. And you will do the same with the shipments they carry.

122. If it happens that it is uncertain which factors should be in charge of loading the vessels that are now going, the factors who are already there, or those who are just leaving here, in order to avoid any such uncertainty, we hereby declare that we think it right for Diego Fernandes in Cochin, and the other factors already abroad at the places from where the spices are to be loaded, to be the ones who also transfer them to the ships; because otherwise there will be too many arguments; although it may very well be that those who are going are in every way qualified, they don't as yet have much knowledge of native ways and customs, which might cause delays and slow down the dispatch of the vessels; and with the factors in charge of the loading will also be the scribes who are already there, because the factors and scribes who are on their way there should not begin their service until after the ships are on their way back.

123. From the log signed by Dom Martinho, which he will give to you, you shall take a roll-call of the factors and officers to be assigned to each factory; thus each one of them will be registered and the roll-call will give you the time of the start of their pay; and the same applies to the military men who are to stay there, to know when their salary is to begin to fall due, and also the *quintaladas* they are to be granted, and how they are to receive them. You know these things ought to be done and will not allow any misdeed or lawlessness.

[124. How the costs of maintaining the Cochin fort and the post in Quilon, up to the time of Almeida's arrival, are to be met.]

125. Although you are not supposed to get any share of the booty that, may it please God, you will seize, it being intended to go towards the payment of salaries, nevertheless it pleases us to reward you, and we stipulate that the division be done as follows:

To wit, you will draw the biggest share of the award [*joya*] according to what is extracted from the Moslem captain, but not the ransom for the Moor, nor the gold jewelry; and if there is any jewel or precious stone that, in these realms, will not fetch a price above 500 *cruzados*, you can keep it; but you cannot take any valued higher than that.

And of everything else we shall take the true fifth.

14. In the merchant fleet, two *náus* belonged to the state, and one to a Portuguese capitalist (Noronha); three others were financed by a consortium to which German merchants (Welser, Fugger, etc.) contributed 36 000, and Italians (Marchioni, etc.) 29 400 *cruzados* (Godinho, 1982, Vol. III, p. 54).

And once this fifth is subtracted, the entire residue will be divided into three equal parts, two of which will go to pay for our rigging, provisions and artillery, and the part that remains shall be distributed thus:

To wit, you shall take 25 parts
And each captain of a tall ship [*navyo dalto bordo*], 10 parts
. . . . caravel, 6 parts
. . . . master, if he is also a pilot, 4 parts
And if he is only a master, 3 parts
. . . . pilot, 3 parts
And each armed sailor, 1 and a half part
. . . . soldier, ...
. . . . ordinary seaman, 1 part
. . . . sailor, 2 and a half parts
. . . . bombardier, 2 parts
. . . . gunner, another 2 parts
. . . . crossbowman, ...
And every captain of a galley, the same as to each of the captains of the tall ships, 10 parts.

126. For Our Lady of Belém, we wish, under this our *regimento*, that some additional sum, as seems appropriate, say 6 parts from each captain of a tall ship, be donated to it.

127. As for gifts and favours that are granted to native kings and chiefs, we have learned from experience that they are harmful to our purpose; because once they are given they are expected to continue as of right; and if they are subsequently withheld, a scandal ensues. In order to avoid this, we forbid and order you not to give any presents, either on our behalf, or on your own, to any kings or chiefs, except when, in your opinion, they will assure such profitable returns and be so necessary for our service that they cannot be ignored. And when, in this case of necessity, you do make gifts, this must be done in such a way that it is clear that it is for an exceptional purpose, and we leave the modalities of this to your discretion.

128. We wish Diego Fernandes, our factor in Cochin, and with him all the scribes who were appointed in the factory there, to return, in due course, with the merchant ships on this voyage; because they are to be replaced by those who are going now to take up their posts there, the factor as well as the scribes. But we order you to assign one vessel to the said Dieguo Fernandes as captain; and it seems to us it will have to be the vessel on which you travelled, because it will be empty; and the officers of the factory will go with him; and if he will not come on that one, then they should be found good accommodations in some other vessels; because it is our pleasure that this should be done, and we strongly recommend to you, that the same be done for Gomçallo Gill and his team who are at Cannanore: in whatever *náo* he goes, he should be given the post of captain, because we want him back; and we strongly recommend that you see to it that these persons are well catered for.[15]

129. As for King Narsimha,[16] you are carrying a letter and other messages from us. According to what you understand of his lands and the products

15. Accommodations in the *náos* could be surprisingly luxurious, see Lopes de Mendonça, 1892, p. 10.
16. Of the important southern India Hindu state of Vijayanagar.

available there, you will send someone there to establish himself, if you think this useful; because if it does not seem profitable, don't send him; and if you do send someone, give to whoever you order to go there as a present, a garment of your own choice, made of silk and wool cloth such as is being shipped on your fleet . . . [blank]. And besides what we send him and what we have written, you will explain to him all that seems to you appropriate for the furtherance of our service, and we leave the details to your own good judgement.

130. We are pleased to send with this fleet, for the benefit of our interests, some horse saddles; these should be left at Angediva from whence they can be offered as gifts.

131. Because there are still so many things to be discovered in India, and the more is discovered the better for our service through profitable trading of goods from new places as well as through the right of ownership, and in other ways too, you have our consent that after the *náos* are loaded and sent on their journey back, and after everything ordained in this *regimento* has been accomplished, if you do not need all the vessels that are to remain with you, you should send a pair of caravels, or whichever you can spare, to explore Ceylon, Pegu [Burma], Malacca and whatever other places and products [*cousas*] from those parts. On the said vessels you will appoint someone who will have principal charge of them, someone who will accomplish the mission with all the care and prudence due to our service; and in the said places and in all others and whatever ports and territories they discover, they must erect stone monuments [*padroes*][17] with arms spread and Christ's cross atop; and you will order the said monuments to be built by the stone-cutters who are travelling with you.

132. On the shore, at the mouth of the Red Sea, when you get there in good time, we also recommend that you pay great attention to leaving a monument somewhere; and we very specially advise you to place a monument at Cape Gardafui.

133. In Cochin, as well as Quilon, and in the other places where our *náos* have so far taken their goods, we recommend that you should endeavour to find out through diligent inquiry if our captains, factors or any of our officers have, in the process of purchase or sale, inflicted, without provocation, any injury to any merchant or merchants,[18] and if any other wrongdoing was due to a person who is there, have it corrected and amends made as it is just that it should be done; and if the guilty one is someone who has already returned to Lisbon, and the crime is such that it can quickly be remedied by payment, have it seen to with our funds; and you shall let our factors know why you are asking them to pay such a sum and how much, and why you are charging his factory; and you shall send someone to question the native king or chief, as well as the principal traders if they have been injured or aggravated in any way; because we promise them that for anything that is done that should not have been done we shall pay full damages, because we do not want such things to happen; we only want truth and fairness and we are always displeased when it is not so. Use the best words you can to convince them that we wish to have good relations in everything, and that with honest dealings will come great peace, calm and respect for their will, and that this wrong should not alter the favourable attitude towards us they have had so far; and you could also send them word that we are making inquiries about those who have

17. These famous ornamental pillars were left as markers by the Portuguese wherever they made a landfall.

18. A common occurrence and the source of much worry to the managers of the Portuguese enterprise.

committed these misdeeds. And so as not to let any guilty party go unpunished, we order you to pursue this matter with diligence to get the facts if possible. As for dispensing justice to kings and chiefs wherever our vessels will buy goods, there too you must find out if anything was done to them that should not have been done, because we want their rights fully compensated; and I want to be fully informed of all you learn and do.

134. We have information that our officers are not using the proper weights when trading, to the detriment of our service and their conscience; we got wind of this so vaguely up to now that we can only write; you have our consent to pursue any rumours or proof of such wrongdoings for the better profit of our service; and take special care that this applies to the native merchants as well as to those who are going with you.

[135. Approvisioning of fortresses to be made locally instead of bringing in everything by sea; traffic of goods between fort and locality should benefit the natives as well as ourselves.]

[136. Vasquo Gomes Dabreu and João de Nova[19] are accompanying you to Cochin aboard great ships [*naaos grandes*]. Once their mission is accomplished they can return with any surplus vessels you don't need; each to have rank of chief captain [*capitam pryncipall*] and to head a separate convoy.]

[137. João Serrão and Lopo Sanches each to captain a galley.]

[138. *Náos* making the return journey must be very well approvisioned.]

[139. Reduce [?barnacle] [*buzano*] damage by breaming the ships, i.e. first beaching them and then having their keels thoroughly cleaned with fire; this job to be done after unloading in India and before taking on new cargo.]

[140. The sharing of prizes at sea as well as on land to be as decreed above [Item 125]; king to get one fifth plus other privileges, and the rest as stated.]

[141, Your share will be 25 parts of the prizes seized in your presence or within your sight; in your absence, the chief captain will get 20 parts.]

[142. Only the captain and crew who did the capture or were within sight of it are entitled to parts.]

[143. Choice between vessels that are to make the return journey and those that are to remain behind in India, up to you. The first must be well equipped and supplied for the trip.]

[144. Returning fleet to be manned with sailors from other ships if necessary, and also with native seamen.]

145. As for Pedro de Añaya's mission, [we have changed our mind and] we now think it best that you not go to Sofala; you should not do anything about it on this voyage as we have instructed you to do in this *regimento*. We order that, once the Cape of Good Hope is cleared, you go directly, in good time, to Kilwa, and do there all that we have ordered you to do that in this *regimento*, may it please our Lord to help you in this enterprise.

[146. Given that these instructions are set out in advance and in general terms, you may occasionally want to alter them; you can alter the rules if necessary after seeking the advice of others. But you should stick to these instructions as far as possible.]

5 March 1505, Lisbon Antonio Carneiro

[147. Take care when making arrests and imposing discipline and fines. Gambling for big money is out, but other games of chance to pass the time and relax are all right.]

19. He was the *Alcaide* (Commander) of Lisbon and the discoverer (in 1502) of the island of St Helena.

148. We strongly recommend that no time be wasted in ports where we have fortresses, except when required for our better service; because there will be more profit made in all other places than there, as was said. And the allocation of commands shall be made as ordered above; however, if you think it more appropriate that the captains have equal rank, this is up to you; because some persons will serve better if they have no one above them and thus we can avoid any discontent. And if so, you will send them your instructions, and they will obey you as Captain-in-Chief.

The King.

Regimento of the captain-major.

10 NAVAL CONVENTION, LISBON 1552

Introduction

Near the close of 1551, when Spain was reorganising the defence of her commerce, Charles V (Holy Roman Emperor, King of Spain and ruler of the Netherlands) asked his ambassador in Lisbon to negotiate a naval convention for securing Spanish, Flemish, and Portuguese shipping against France and French corsairs.

Text

Our lord, the king, and the Emperor Charles V, in view of the loss and injury which their vassals were suffering from the continual robberies and insults of the corsairs, who at all times, and in all places, kept constant watch at sea for that purpose, and since they were most Christian princes and most zealous for the good of their kingdoms, agreed together in this year of 1552, to send their fleets out to sea for the protection and defense of their coasts, and the security of the commerce of their vassals.

The agreement was that his Highness was to have twenty lateen-rigged vessels equipped, of from twenty-five to thirty tons each, which were to cruise continually in sight of land, in order to guard the coast: of which three were to be stationed at Cascaes, four in the Atouguia, four at Caminha, four at Lagos, two at Villanova, and three at Cezimbra or Sinis, as should be thought best – these being the places whither the armed vessels were wont to resort, and to which the Portuguese and Castilian vessels were forced to put in. He [i.e., his Highness] was also to send four more ships or galleons to cruise along the coast of this kingdom, further out to sea, and join with the twenty ships aforesaid whenever it should be advisable. Besides these fleets, another fleet was also to be prepared for the coast of the kingdom of the Algarve, consisting of four oared vessels, one large ship, and three caravels, which were also to unite, whenever it should be necessary, with the other lateen-rigged vessels, that were to cruise constantly along the coast of that kingdom. His Highness was to order all those ships to remain constantly at sea, summer and winter, without putting into any port, unless in case of necessity, excepting the oared vessels, which were to go in during the winter. Ten armed ships, three ships or galleons, and seven caravels were to be sent to the Islands every year in the month of April. His Highness was to order the ships bound for Arguin, Cape Verde, trade of Guinea, coast of Malagueta, Elmina, Island of St Thomas, and Brazil, to come and go during the three monsoons, [namely], the one in January, the one in March (in company with the ships from India), and the one in September. Besides the armed ships of his Highness, which were to sail during those monsoons, orders were to be given that all the other ships, or most of them, were also to be armed; and by sailing during those monsoons, it was thought that the vessels journeying to those regions might hope for security, as well as those bound for the Antilles, which might also take advantage of the monsoons. In addition to this, it would be of great advantage in helping to guard the islands of the Azores, where all these fleets had to put in.

Source: English text, translated from the Portuguese by Amalia Alberti, in Davenport, Frances Gardiner, *European Treaties bearing on the History of the United States* . . . (Washington, D.C., 1917) Vol. I, pp. 213–14.

It was thought best for the Emperor, on his side, to order the guarding of the Straits, in accordance with the news that he might have of the Turks and French, the importance of such guarding of the Straits being then clearly apparent from the trouble caused to the whole of Christendom by the channel of Flanders being blocked. It was thought best for the Emperor to send to the Islands, every year, in the months of April, the ten square-rigged ships which, it was said, were to be equipped for that purpose in Seville; and that they should be well armed, because of the importance of the safety of that region, whither it was reported that great fleets [of the corsairs] were about to sail. There was good reason to believe that such would not fail to be the case, for in no other region could they gain so much profit for themselves or do so much damage to all other parts, as indeed was their intent. [It was thought best] for this fleet to remain off the Islands until the end of the month of August, and that half of it should cruise at sea during the whole year off Cape St Vincent, since that is the region through which the ships from the Antilles and Peru must pass; that the Emperor should keep four or five armed ships off the coast of Galicia, for the protection of that coast, and the security of the ships from all the aforesaid routes, which might be driven into its ports by bad weather; that the voyages of the Castilian, Flemish, and Portuguese from these parts to Flanders should be made by their ships all together, during the two monsoons, [namely], the one in April, and the other in September, and the voyages from Flanders to those parts during the two other monsoons, [namely], the one in January, and the other in June; that for the good accomplishment of what is set forth above, the Emperor should order the armed fly-boats then retained in Flanders, and for the same reason, many other Castilian and Portuguese ships, to come at once, in the best way possible, and to come every year at the seasons above named, for by voyaging all together during the monsoons, as aforesaid, they would ensure the safety not only of the merchandise which they brought and carried themselves, but also that of others journeying within those limits from one place to another.

Besides these benefits, others, many and great, would ensue to the states of the Emperor and of our lord, the king. [It was thought best] for his Highness to order the ships of his fleets, and those of his vassals, to favor and assist those of the Emperor, and for the Emperor to do the like for those of his Highness, this to be understood only in case of necessity for the defense of each other. All of the abovesaid was approved by the Emperor and by his Highness, and the faithful observance thereof was agreed between them.

Figure 3.1 Title page of *Mare Liberum*, by Hugo Grotius, 1633 edition

3 The United Provinces Open up the Ocean

Soon after King Sebastian died on a Moroccan battle-field, Portugal lost its independence. In 1580 Philip II of Spain cashed in on a century and a half of royal intermarriages to claim the Portuguese crown for the Spanish Hapsburgs and seized the country in a decisive military and naval operation.

Was this the beginning of a world empire on which the sun would never set? Not quite. One vital part of that 'universal monarchy' in the making was already in rebellion against Philip. A jewel in the Hapsburg crown but proud of their liberties, the most active, wealthy, and urbanised part of Europe – the Low Countries – had been restive for decades. Their discontents now crystallised around the issue of religious faith and reform. The first rising (in the southern Low Countries) was suppressed fairly easily in 1566–7. But the second (in 1572) created, in the north, a new political system around the Dutch Reformed Church and not even the harsh measures of the Captain-General, the Duke of Alba (or Alva), and his Spanish troops, could suppress it. Alba was recalled, and for a while both the north and the south came together in opposition to the Spaniards. But when in 1579 the northern and southern provinces organised themselves into the Unions of Utrecht and of Arras, respectively, the fighting resumed and was to continue uninterrupted for the next 30 years. In January 1581 the States General of the United Provinces (the Union of Utrecht) renounced allegiance to the King of Spain in an action that could be regarded as a declaration of independence (Doc. 11), even though it was not independence that was being proclaimed, only a break with Philip. Drawn up by a high official of the Antwerp government, and an associate of William of Orange, the document was medieval and feudal in its reasoning, rather than Calvinist (Wilson, 1970, p. 75), but it does speak out against the Inquisition and in favour of 'some gracious and moderate freedom of religion (which principally concerns God and men's consciences)'. It clearly conveys the anti-Spanish sentiment of the rebellion, and is a full statement of contemporary grievances.

As the reading of that 'Placard of Diffidation' makes clear, the independence struggle of the Netherlands, north or south, had no global aspirations to start with. But its results did, almost immediately, have wide-ranging consequences. For the successful challenge of a power set upon world dominion pretty soon adds up to staking out a global status for oneself. Not only did the struggle that the States General (the governing organ of the new state) waged for the next generation raise them to the ranks of a major power, both on the seas (with the rapid growth of their navy) and on land (with a small but ultimately highly efficient army), it also transformed them into the focus of a general coalition against the pretensions of the Spanish rulers.

The core of that coalition was the Anglo–Dutch alliance. To begin with, the Dutch were quite plainly in the position of supplicants. Queen Elizabeth was not at all keen to aid rebels against established authority. But the rising power of Spain, buttressed by a powerful army in the heart of Europe, within striking distance of England, and growing popular and official support based on religious sympathies dictated a change in England's policy. Some volunteers were sent over in 1572; a first treaty of alliance was negotiated in 1578 (Latin text in Rymer, 1732, p. 178), but due to the break-up of the Netherlands and the renewal of the civil war in 1579, it proved abortive. When the Spanish army launched a siege of Antwerp, long a regional centre and a focus of the trade with England, the need for English aid became once more quite obvious and while the proffered sovereignty over the Provinces was declined, a comprehensive contract of mutual assistance was finally executed (Treaty of Nonsuch, 1585, Doc. 12). Antwerp fell in any case (it is argued that more timely English aid would have relieved it) and some of the provisions of Nonsuch, such as the important role for an English Governor-General, soon became redundant, but the treaty as a whole stood the test of time and served as the framework of this crucial relationship until 1609; the late Queen's financial aid was settled by the Dutch for 250 000 pounds sterling in 1616, and Flushing and Brill reverted to Dutch control.

Charles Wilson (1970, p. 83) comments that by the terms of that treaty the Queen 'took the Low Countries under her protection', but the treaty nowhere says so and is in fact a business-like arrangement between two essentially equal partners. For the assistance was indeed mutual, Article 25 being particularly significant for pledging Dutch naval aid (under English command) in case of a Spanish attack on England. Already, the 1578 treaty promised a force of 40 warships; an even stronger Dutch force (90 ships of war, with 50 merchant vessels converted for active duty) was mobilised in the months before the Great Armada sailed for England. It is now widely recognised that in that engagement (1588) 'even if the English fleet had been beaten, England could still have been defended by the Dutch' (Howarth, 1982, pp. 160–1; cf. also Motley, 1895, Vol. I(2), pp. 445–6). More generally, the Anglo–Dutch alliance signified the unity of the 'maritime powers', a matter that Johan Oldenbarnevelt recognised with especial clarity. As he told an English negotiator in 1598 'England and the Netherlands together could maintain the empire of the seas', but if the republic were to fall, the control of the seas would be lost to England (Motley, 1895, Vol. II(3), p. 496).

The other key member of the general alliance was France, both the

French monarchy, and the Huguenots (French Calvinists, many with close links to the Dutch rebellion and fighting repeated civil wars in their own country). Indeed, sovereignty over the United Provinces was first offered to Henri III of France (who declined) even before a similar approach was made to Britain (with the same result). In Dutch practice, it was often opportune to balance English with French influence; the latter was particularly strong in the southern regions of the country. This tended to make the United Provinces the linchpin of the anti-Spanish front. When Henry IV (a Huguenot) ascended the French throne, France's connection with the United Provinces became even more significant; and it also included subsidies. It was much in evidence in the prolonged negotiations leading up to the Dutch–Spanish Truce of Antwerp (1609) that terminated (for 12 years, at any rate) a major bout of warfare (Doc. 15).

MARE LIBERUM

The long war against Spain not only placed the United Provinces in the ranks of major powers – in particular, by fostering the growth of the navy – it also provided the occasion for mounting a devastating attack on the Tordesillas regime, hence for transforming the organisation of the global system. The onset was a multi-pronged one: soon after the 'fall' of Portugal a French fleet attempted to seize the Azores as a way station to Brazil and English privateers (including Hawkins and Drake) started raiding the West Indies. The first English settlement in North America was established even before the Truce of Antwerp. But it is probably fair to say that the major attack on the Iberian monopoly of the global system was undertaken by the Dutch: that assault was both naval, commercial, and intellectual.

Long the distributors (from Antwerp) of Portuguese spices in Northern Europe, the Dutch had a good understanding of the importance of the trade, and when Spanish measures put new obstacles in the way of that traffic in Lisbon, they sailed to the east on their own and so, soon afterward, did the English. After the English East India Company was founded on the last day of 1600, the Dutch, led by Oldenbarnevelt (in 1602), decided to merge the efforts of individual traders in one large state-sponsored corporation of national breadth, whose initial capital was ten times larger than that of its English counterpart. The charter of the new company known as the Vereeinigde Ostindische Compagnie (VOC, dissolved in 1799), is reproduced in translation as Doc. 13. It is the constitution of the world's first major multinational corporation. VOC placed the organisation of the trade with the East on a basis much superior to the King of Portugal's personal monopoly and for many decades, until well into the next century, it was one of the wonders of the age.

The other side of the attack on the global monopoly was intellectual and legal. When one of VOC's fleets seized a rich Portuguese merchantman in the straits of Malacca, and the fate of the ship and the cargo was being decided in the prize court in Amsterdam, a twenty year old lawyer by the name of Grotius wrote, for the Company, a Brief justifying the capture. An extract from that Brief was published anonymously as a short book under the title *Mare Liberum* in 1609. Its cogent reasoning, and its forthright, though rather unfair, onslaught on the Portuguese claims instantly gained it wide approval. The Truce of Antwerp signed the same year (Doc. 15) in fact conceded to the Dutch the right (denied in earlier negotiations with the French, and the English) to sail to the East, and to trade in places (such as Java) where the Spanish King did not exercise sovereignty. This opened the seas to navigation but it did not free the highly monopolised royal ports to generalised trade. In his tract (Doc. 14), which was in effect the start of modern International Law, Grotius won one half of his argument, freedom of the ocean, right away.

In sum therefore, the principal political achievements of the United Provinces of the Netherlands can be said to have been pruning the exclusive rights of Spain, and initiating the transformation of the global system away from closure.

THE WEBERIAN QUESTION

A notable feature of the Dutch cycle is the prominent role that religion holds within it. The sixteenth and seventeenth centuries were, of course, the time of the Reformation during which Western Christianity separated into those upholding the old religion, and the adherents of the new faith. Germany (Luther) and France (Calvin) were the principal battlefields but the Low Countries were at the very core of the struggle. Lutheranism soon established itself in large parts of Germany and in Scandinavia. But, until about 1640 and the Puritan Revolution in England, it was the Calvinist Dutch Church that assumed the leadership of the Reformation. It led the forces against Spain and erected the structure of solidarity within which the alliances in support of the revolt were formed.

One of the most fascinating and controversial questions debated by social scientists in the twentieth century has been that first posed by Max Weber in 1902 about the origins of capitalism: what explains the 'greater relative ownership of capital by Protestants' (Weber, 1958, p. 35)? Weber was the first to bring up the question prominently in the social sciences; it had earlier been noticed, for instance, by Louis XIV's Minister Colbert (Doc. 18) that in the 'great commerce' of the world, the two nations that, through their trading companies, were powerful were 'heretic'.

Weber saw this question as crucial to understanding the sources of capitalism – to identifying, in fact, the distinguishing features of the modern world. For students of long cycles the question may be rephrased as follows: what explains the predominance of Protestant states in positions of global leadership from the Dutch cycle onward? Why is it that the world powers have been predominantly Protestant?

Weber answered his question, in part (and only in part), by examining the ethics of certain Protestant 'sects', especially Calvinism. He paid particular attention to the influence upon the 'spirit of capitalism' of the doctrine of (double) Predestination, as laid down by the 'great synods of the seventeenth century, above all those of Dordrecht and Westminster' (Weber, 1958, p. 99). The Synod of the Dutch Reformed Church met at Dort (we use the short expression) in 1618–19; the Westminster Assembly (of the Church of England) sat (1643–52) during the Puritan Revolution. Weber quotes extracts from the Westminster Confession (Weber, 1958, pp. 99–101); we reproduce the chapter of the Judgement of the Synod of Dort dealing specifically with Predestination (Doc. 16).

Acknowledged by 'seasoned theologians and pastors' to be 'a mystery best not popularised too readily, since a misunderstanding (or even an understanding) of it had been found to trouble many souls' (Prestwich, 1985, p. 61) the doctrine of Predestination that evolved out of John Calvin's *Institutes of Christian Religion* asserts that, at the creation, God has chosen 'unto salvation, a set number of certain men, neither better nor more worthy than others', not for their qualities or actions but 'for his own peculiar' reasons. Of this eternal and immutable election into salvation 'the elect, in their time . . . are assured' (Doc. 16, Articles IX and X). The true elect may, on occasion, even stray from saintly ways 'but God does not wholly take away his holy spirit from them . . . in these slips he preserves in them . . . his immortal seed (by which they were borne again) that it die not, nor be lost by them' (Synod of Dort, 1619, Chap. Five, *The perseverence of true believers and saints*, Articles VI and VII).

The effect of this belief on individuals is a new level of uncertainty and complexity in the psyche. Since no one but God – who randomly 'culled' them at the creation – knows who the elect are, salvation cannot, during one's lifetime, be 'bought' through good deeds: goodness must be offered as a free gift. And, in what may be called a personal gamble, the odds are doubly in favour of the *good*: those who think of themselves as elect, and act accordingly, will at least create their own heaven on earth and, even if this happens not to be the case, there remains the rewarding possibility that, in the eyes of others, they might be seen as perhaps God's chosen ones.

But, as Weber (1958, p. 104) points out, while Predestination did remove all magical means to salvation as mere superstitions and sin, it also left the individual with the feeling of 'unprecedented inner loneliness'.

Nevertheless, it may also be argued that the doctrine developed, in those individuals who accepted it, inner strength and confidence, favourable conditions for the exercise of leadership of all kinds.

Two other features of the Synod of Dort might be mentioned in passing. First, it was the culmination of a struggle for power within the Dutch political system that brought about the end of the generation-long rule of the States Party led by Johan van Oldenbarnevelt (Modelski, 1987, Chapter 7). That party was identified, in the Dutch Reformed Church, with the Arminian tendency (which upheld a different variant of the doctrine of Predestination, one stressing faith and good works). Their opponents, the followers of the Prince of Orange, joined ranks with the Counter-Remonstrants who prevailed at the Synod and who expelled the Arminians. Oldenbarnevelt was executed within days of the Synod passing its Sentence, and for the next generation the Orangists ruled in a quasi-monarchical fashion. The Arminians lay low for some years but came back later. In some respects, therefore, the doctrinal disputes were a highly symbolic screen for a systemic process of wider ramifications and for the defeat of a political party ripe for displacement from the seats of power.

Secondly, the international context of the Synod should be noted, for it assembled not only Dutch nationals (*inlanders*) but also a significant contingent of 28 'foreigners' (*uitlanders*). This latter included a strong delegation from Great Britain, (as a gesture of the King's support for the House of Orange) and representatives from Switzerland, and Geneva, the Palatinate, Hesse, Hamburg, Bremen, and Emden. Delegates from France and from Brandenburg were prevented from attending by their rulers. The presence of the foreigners was intended to lend credence to the proceedings though as one of the English delegates observed: 'there was very little regard had to the judgement of the Foreign Divines, unless when they spoke as the Natives would have them' (Brandt, Vol. III, 1722, p. 152).

While modelled on ancient church synods, Dort was in fact an international conference that described the reach of the reformed religion (though not of Protestantism as such). It reflected the strong links already noticed between the Netherlands and England and Scotland, and outlined the boundaries of the areas of solidarity within which the nucleus of the global system would move over the next several cycles.

At this point, we have no final answer to the modified Weberian question. We know that Dutch ascent to global status occurred during a struggle over religion, with the help of alliances that had a religious infrastructure. Two variants of the doctrine of Predestination were involved, and it cannot be said that the Dort–Westminster (Presbyterian) variant was the only one that moulded the evolution of the world powers in the long cycle: the Arminians retained an important though minority position in the Netherlands; in England, they had their influence on John Wesley (the founder of Methodism in the eighteenth century), and it was the Anglican Episcopalian strand that was often in the ascendant there. In the emergence of the United States, Virginia balanced Puritan New England.

The notion of 'election' is not really confined to Calvinist doctrine. For Doge Mocenigo, Venice was 'the city chosen above all others', and he feared that if they decided wrongly, God would 'no longer regard us as elect' (Doc. 1, speech of 1421). The Portuguese, too, in their time, regarded themselves as 'the most sensitive among the nations' to questions of rank and courtesy (Prescott, 1854, p. 63, quoting Faria y Souza). So it would seem that feeling 'holier than thou' has in the past helped those aiming at leadership.

CRITIQUES

Among Dutch public documents, Grotius' Brief is an exception to the generalisation that attention given to global concerns by the Dutch is rather scant and that their overall approach is eminently practical and empirical. The world-wide impact of their actions has nevertheless been pervasive and long-lasting, and it never failed to impress those setting out to compete with them.

The Anglo–Dutch alliance concealed great rivalries, especially in matters of shipping and trade in which the Dutch position was, at that time, extremely strong. In the East, especially, the VOC virtually pushed the English India Company out of the spice trade. In Europe, Dutch shipping monopolised the carrying trade even between English ports and between England and the colonies, while Dutch herring fleets exploited what was seen as an English resource.

Oliver Cromwell, fresh from his victories in the civil war, found these conditions intolerable to England; resolved to remedy them, he used a standard 'protectionist' measure: reserving certain industries for nationals. The first Navigation Act (Doc. 17), became the storm centre of an international controversy and was a direct cause of the three Anglo–Dutch wars; in the course of time it underwent many changes, but its substance was retained until the nineteenth century. For the Dutch, it was a notice that their time was about to run out.

The 1664 policy memorandum by Jean-Baptiste Colbert (Doc. 18) is another trenchant critique of the Dutch system. It shows, in effect, that the opening of the seas carried out by the Dutch, in alliance with England, did not automatically and by its own action, redistribute sea power or the opportunities for trade. All it did was to reduce somewhat the level of monopoly that prevailed earlier.

Colbert had no trouble recognising the dominant role of the Dutch in the global system. The reforms he instituted did stimulate the French economy and French sea power generally. According to Jonathan Israel (1982, pp. 439–40), after 1659, in certain important economic fields 'the French rapidly ousted the English from second place and eventually surpassed the Dutch themselves'. Moreover, Spain's military power was breaking down and that of France expanding fast, creating a threat to the Spanish Netherlands, and therefore also to the Republic. These French gains confronted the Dutch with some intractable dilemmas and ultimately brought about a head-on clash, culminating, within less than a decade, in the (unsuccessful, but terrifying) French attack on the unprepared United Provinces in 1672.

In 1661 Pieter de la Court published a best-seller, in the preparation of which Johan de Witt, the leading Dutch politician of that era, might have had a hand. He titled it 'The True Interest of Holland', and he argued in it that that interest consisted in 'Peace'. He called 'our Fisheries, Trade, Navigations, and Manufacturers' the 'pillars on which our state is founded', and maintained that these 'will increase more by Peace than by War' (de la Court, 1702, p. 263). Hardly a very original thought, but it does remind us of what Doge Mocenigo prescribed for Venice at a similar stage of the cycle. And it did not settle the matter, either. More would be required from future world leadership.

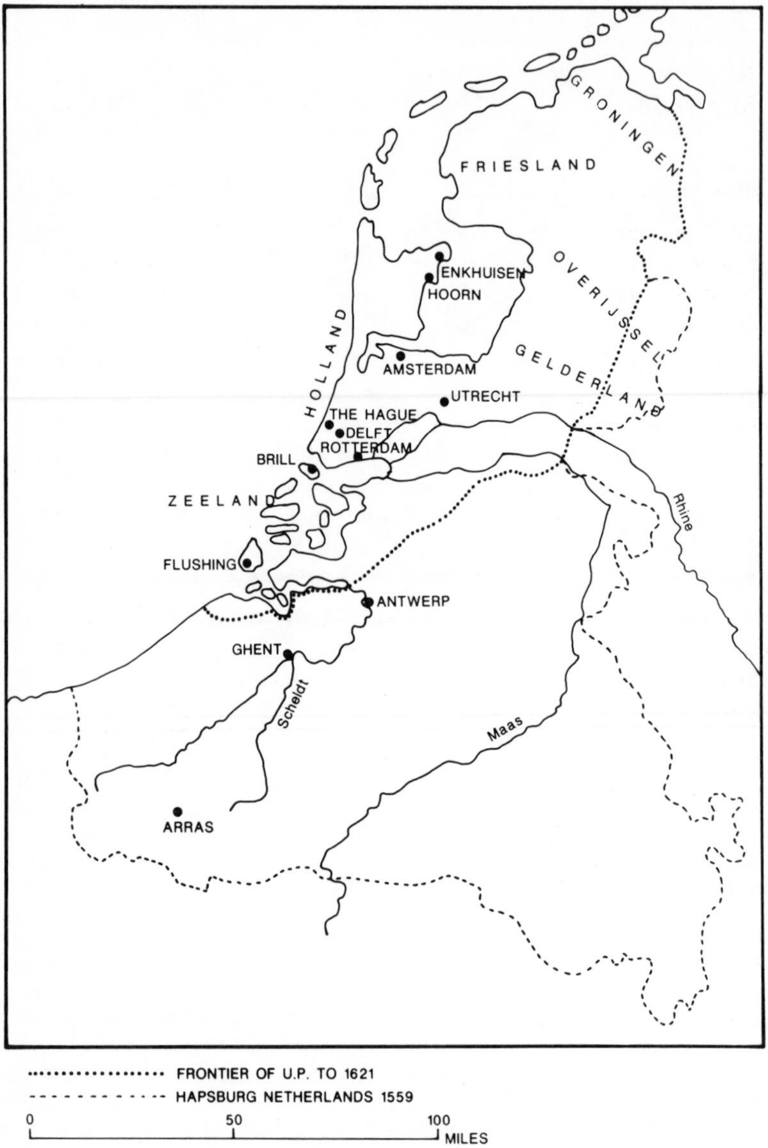

Map 3.1 United Provinces of the Netherlands

Documents

11 RENUNCIATION OF ALLEGIANCE TO THE KING OF SPAIN BY THE UNITED PROVINCES, 26 July 1581

Introduction

On 24 July 1581 William, Prince of Orange, accepted the offer of sovereignty extended to him by the 'knights, nobles, and cities' of Holland and Zealand. Two days later, the deputies of all the United Provinces issued a memorable declaration, the Act of Abjuration, that deposed Philip II of Spain but was not the proclamation of a new form of government.

'The document by which the provinces renounced their allegiance' writes James Motley (1856, p. 842) 'was not the most felicitous of their state papers. It was too prolix and technical. Its style had more of the formal phraseology of legal documents than befitted its great appeal to the whole world and to all time. Nevertheless this is but a matter of taste. The Netherlanders were so eminently a law-abiding people that, like the American patriots of the eighteenth century, they have on most occasions preferred punctilious precision to florid declaration. They chose to conduct their revolt according to law. At the same time . . . the spirit of Liberty revealed nonetheless her majestic proportions'.

Text

THE STATES GENERAL of the United Provinces of the Low Countries, to all who shall see or hear these presents, greeting. As it is common knowledge that the prince of a country is established by God as his subjects' sovereign in order to defend and protect them against all injury, force, and violence, just as a shepherd's duty is to keep his sheep safe, and that subjects are not created by God for the sake of the prince to obey all his commands, whether godly or ungodly, reasonable or unreasonable, and to serve him as slaves, but rather that the prince is established for his subjects' sake (for without them he would not be a prince), to govern them according to law and reason and to protect and love them as a father does his children and a shepherd his sheep, risking his body and life to defend and protect them; and that if he does not do this but, instead of defending his subjects, he endeavours to oppress and harass them, to deprive them of their ancient freedom and privileges and their ancient customs, and to command them

Source: 'Plakkaat van Verlatinghe', in Dumont, 1726–31, Vol. V, 1, pp. 413–14; 419–21, in the original Dutch and contemporary French translation; translated from the Dutch by Herbert H. Rowen, in H. H. Rowen (ed.), *The Low Countries in Early Modern Times* (New York: Walker, 1972) pp. 92–105; reprinted by permission. Notes by the editors.

and use them like slaves, then he must be looked upon no longer as a prince but rather as a tyrant. And therefore his subjects, according to law and reason, are not obliged to recognize him as their prince; and, without falling into error (notably when this is done by decision of the States of the country), he may be renounced and another chosen in his stead for Head and Lord to defend them. This happens mainly when subjects, by humble prayers, requests, and complaints, have at no time been able to mollify their prince nor turn him away from his tyrannical enterprises and conceptions, so that no other way remains for them to keep and defend their ancient liberty and that of their wives, children, and posterity, for which they are bound by the law of nature to expose their lives and possessions. This has happened on various similar occasions in different countries and different times, as has been seen recently in well known instances.[1] This is what should happen principally in those countries which from ancient times have been and are supposed to be governed according to the oath taken by their prince when he receives them, in conformity with their privileges and ancient customs, without any power to violate them. In addition, most of these provinces have always received and accepted their princes and lords under set conditions by sworn contracts and accords, and if the prince violated them, under the law he forfeited the sovereignty of the country. Now it has come to pass that the King of Spain, after the death of the Emperor Charles V, of exalted memory, his father from whom he received all these countries, forgot the services which both his father and he himself received from these countries and their inhabitants; which were the principal means by which he, the King of Spain,[2] won victories over his enemies of such glory and fame that his name and might were celebrated by them and held in awe by the whole world; he forgot too the admonitions which his Imperial Majesty[3] has already given him, and on the contrary he gave hearing, faith, and credit to the members of the Council of Spain who were close to him, and who had conceived a secret hatred against these countries and their liberty because they were not permitted to govern or hold office in them, as they do in the kingdoms of Naples, Sicily, Milan, in the Indies, and in other countries subject to the power of the king, and because they were tempted by the wealth and might of these countries, which was well-known to most of these counselors. This same council, or at least some of its principal members, upon various occasions remonstrated with the king that for the sake of his reputation and majesty, he should reconquer these Low Countries, so that he could command freely and absolutely in these lands according to his pleasure (that is, to tyrannize over them at his will), instead of governing them under the restrictions and conditions which he had sworn to observe when he accepted the sovereignty of these lands. Following this counsel, the King of Spain thereupon sought by every means to deprive these countries of their ancient liberty and to reduce them to servitude under the government of Spaniards. First, under the pretext of religion, he attempted to place new bishops in the principal and most powerful cities, endowing them with the wealthiest abbeys and assigning nine canons to each

1. An allusion to recent events in France and Scotland, which were the inspiration for one of the landmarks of revolutionary literature: *Vindiciae contra tyrannos*, published in 1579. This pamphlet systematised the argument for the rights of the people to rebel against royal authority.
2. Philip II (1527–98).
3. Charles V, Holy Roman Emperor from 1519 to 1556, abdicated the crowns of Spain and the Netherlands in favour of his son Philip in 1556. His imperial titles over German and other possessions to the East he bequeathed to his other son, Ferdinand.

bishop to serve as his counselors, three with special responsibility for the Inquisition. By the grant of the abbeys, the bishops, who would be the king's creatures and at his service and command, and who would be chosen from foreigners as well as from natives of these countries, would have first place and the first voice in the assemblies of the States of these countries. The assignment of the canons would bring in the Inquisition of Spain, which, as is well known, has always been held in as great horror and hatred in these countries as the worst of slavery. Thus it was that when his Imperial Majesty proposed to introduce the Inquisition in these countries at an earlier time, he received such complaints against it that he withdrew this proposal, by which action he displayed the great affection which he bore to his subjects. But, in spite of the many complaints made to the King of Spain by the individual cities and provinces as well as by several of the principal noblemen of the country – notably the Lord of Montigny and the Count of Egmont, who were in succession sent to Spain with the consent of the Duchess of Parma,[4] who was then Regent of these countries, and by the advice of the Council of State and the States General, for this purpose. Although the king gave them verbal assurances that he would satisfy the country as they requested, yet he sent orders exactly to the contrary by letter. He commanded specifically and under pain of incurring his wrath that the new bishops be accepted at once and be given possession of their bishoprics and incorporated abbeys, that the Inquisition be enforced where it had already been introduced, and that the decrees and statutes of the Council of Trent[5] (contrary in various points to the privileges of the country) be obeyed and observed. When the common people learned of this, disorders resulted among them, and the good affection which, as good subjects, they had always borne for the king and his predecessors was greatly diminished. They were justified in what they did, for what was most on their minds was that the king was trying not only to tyrannize over their persons and property but also over their consciences, for which they believed they were responsible and held accountable only to God. On this occasion, in the year 1566, out of their pity for poor common folk, the principal nobles of the country presented a remonstrance in the form of a request, in which they beseeched His Majesty, in order to pacify the commoners and to avert all rioting and sedition, to moderate these points, particularly those which concerned the rigorous Inquisition and punishments in religious matters (thereby demonstrating the love and affection which as a mild and merciful king he bore for his subjects). In order to present the remonstrance to the king in a more personal and persuasive way and to inform him how necessary it was for the good and the prosperity of the country and the preservation of its repose and tranquility to remove the aforesaid innovations and to moderate the rigor of the edicts issued in the matter of religion, the Marquis of Bergen and the Lord of Montigny, at the request of the Regent, the Council of State and the States General of the entire country, traveled to Spain as ambassadors. When they arrived there, however, the king did not give them audience or act to remedy the disorders about which they remonstrated (which disorders had in fact begun to make their appearance among the commoners almost everywhere in the country because they had not been corrected in time, as had been urgently required); instead, responding to his instincts and to the persuasions of the Council of Spain, he declared all those who had presented the said remonstrance to be rebels and guilty of the crime of high

4. Margaret of Austria, Regent of the Netherlands 1559–67. She was the illegitimate daughter of Charles V and mother of Alessandro Farnese, Prince of Parma.
5. Counter-Reformation Council held in 1545–63.

treason (*lèse majesté*), who therefore forfeited both life and property. In addition to this, believing that he had made completely sure of the Low Countries by the Duke of Alva's force and violence, and that they were under his full power and tyranny, he then had the said Lords Ambassadors imprisoned and killed and all their property confiscated, in complete violation of the law, which has always been observed inviolably even among the most barbarous and cruel nations and by the most tyrannical princes. Yet, although almost all the rioting which had occurred in the year 1566 on the occasion mentioned had been allayed by the Regent and her suite, and although most of those who had come before her on behalf of the country's freedom had fled or been driven out and the others subjugated, so that the king had no occasion to invade these countries with force of arms, nonetheless, not wishing to neglect the opportunity which the members of the Council of Spain had so long desired and awaited (as is openly admitted by the letters intercepted in the year 1566, written by the ambassador of Spain in France, Alava by name, to the Duchess of Parma), of a pretext for abolishing all the privileges of the country and putting it under tyrannical government by Spaniards as they had done in the Indies and other countries newly conquered by them, and responding to his instincts and the counsel of the said Spaniards, he sent into these countries the Duke of Alva, who was notorious for his rigor and extreme cruelty and was one of the principal enemies of these countries, accompanied by a council of persons of the same ilk and humor as he (by which the king showed how little affection he bore for his subjects in these countries, violating his obligations as their prince to be their protector and good shepherd). The Duke of Alva entered these countries with his army without any encounters or resistance and was received by the poor inhabitants with all reverence and honor, in the expectation only of kindness and clemency, for that was what the king had promised them so often in his letters, as if in good faith, as well as that he had considered coming in person to the country and settling everything there to the satisfaction of everyone. Furthermore, at the time of the departure of the Duke of Alva to these countries, the king fitted out a fleet on the coast of Spain to bring him here, and another in Zeeland to meet and receive him (as it was given out) at great cost and expense to the country, in order to deceive and delude his poor subjects and to catch them more easily in his nets. In spite of this the Duke of Alva, although he was a foreigner and not of the king's blood, immediately upon his arrival declared that he had a commission from the king as supreme captain and shortly afterward as governor-general of these countries. This was wholly contrary to the privileges and ancient usages here. Adequately revealing his purposes, the duke suddenly put garrisons into the principal cities and fortresses of the country, had castles built in the strongest and richest cities to keep them in subjugation, and by letter, or otherwise, commanded the principal noblemen of the country to appear before him, on the pretext of getting their advice and assistance for the welfare and service of the country, as the king commanded. He then imprisoned those who trusted his friendly letters, as he called them, and appeared before him, and had them taken outside the province of Brabant, where they had been seized, contrary to its privileges. He had them tried before himself and his council, although they were not their competent judges, and without investigation or hearing their full defense found them guilty of having committed the crime of treason and had them put to death publicly and ignominiously. The others, who, being more familiar with the wiles of the Spaniards, had left the country and remained away, were declared to be rebels guilty of the crime of high treason, who therefore forfeited their lives and goods, and their property in the Low Countries was confiscated. This was all done so that the poor inhabitants could not obtain their aid in the just defense of their freedom against the oppression of the Spaniards in their fortresses, nor the assistance of the said princes. In addition, the duke had a host of other noblemen and eminent burgesses put to death or driven into exile, so that he could confiscate their property, and he tormented the rest of the good inhabitants by lodging soldiers upon them, who committed outrages upon them, their wives, children and goods. He also compelled them by various exactions and taxes to contribute to the construction of new castles and fortifications in the cities, from which they could be oppressed, and to pay taxes of one, five, and ten per cent for the support of the soldiers whom he had brought with him and those whom he recruited here to be used against their fellow-countrymen and whoever risked his life to defend the liberty of the country. The subjects would be so poverty-stricken that they would retain no means to prevent his designs and he would be able to carry out more effectively the instructions given to him in Spain, to wit, to treat these countries as if they had been conquered. With this end in mind, he changed the form of government and justice in many places and the principal cities, formed new councils organized in the Spanish manner in direct violation of the privileges of the country. When finally he felt that there was nothing left to fear, he attempted to introduce by force a tax of ten per cent upon the sale of commodities and manufactures of all kinds, despite a multitude of remonstrances to the contrary submitted by each of the provinces individually as well as by all of them together, because it threatened the complete ruin of the country, whose welfare and prosperity lay chiefly in trade and manufacture. It would have been put into practice by violent means if Holland and Zeeland had not revolted against the Duke of Alva soon afterwards, with the aid of my Lord the Prince of Orange and a large number of noblemen and other natives of these countries, who had been exiled by the Duke of Alva and had followed the Prince of Orange and were for the most part in his service, as well as with the aid of other inhabitants who loved their country's freedom. Against these two provinces, which put themselves under the protection of the Prince of Orange, the Duke of Alva during the period of his governorship, and after him the Grand Commander of the Castile[6] (who was sent in his place by the king not in order to soften and relieve somewhat the tyranny of the Duke of Alva in this country, but to seek it with greater cunning and concealment than the latter had used), compelled the provinces brought under the Spanish yoke by the garrisons and the castles in their midst to employ their persons and all their power in helping to subjugate these other provinces, but gave them no relief for themselves. They were treated as enemies, and the Spanish soldiers, under the pretext of a mutiny but in the presence and view of the Grand Commander, were allowed to enter the city of Antwerp by force, to remain there for a period of six weeks living at the expense of the poor burghers who were at their mercy. Furthermore, these burghers, in order to be rid of the violence of these Spaniards, were compelled to furnish the sum of 400 000 florins for their wages. After this, these same Spanish soldiers, becoming bolder with the connivance of their chiefs, continued making armed attacks upon the country as a whole; they attempted first of all to take the city of Brussels by surprise, turning it from the ancient and ordinary seat of the princes of the country into the seat and nest of their depradations. When they failed in this design, they seized the city of Alost and then forced the city of Maastricht. They have since forced a violent entry into the city of Antwerp, sacking and pillaging, burning and slaying, doing as much harm as the most barbaric and cruel enemies of the country could have done, and causing undescribable damage not only to the poor residents but also to

6. Luis de Requesens y Zuñiga, governor-general in the Low Countries from 1573 to 1576.

almost all the nations of the world who had their goods, credit obligations, and money there.[7] Although these Spaniards were declared public enemies of the country in the presence of Hieronymo de Roda[8] himself, by ordinance of the Council of State, upon which the king had conferred the general government of the country after the recent death of the Grand Commander, this Roda, by his private authority (and, it may be presumed, by virtue of secret instructions from Spain) undertook nevertheless to act as chief of these Spaniards and their adherents. Without respecting the authority of the Council of State, he usurped the king's name and authority, counterfeited his seal, and conducted himself as Governor and King's Lieutenant in these countries. This prompted the States to make an agreement with the Lord Prince of Orange and the States of Holland and Zeeland, which was approved and found valid by the Council of State as legitimate governors, to make joint and common war upon the Spaniards as the common enemies of the fatherland and to drive them out of the country. Meanwhile, as good subjects, they endeavoured by numerous remonstrances and humble requests made with all diligence and in every proper and possible way to persuade the king to take the Spaniards out of these countries in view of the riots, disturbances, and troubles which had already occurred and apparently would continue, and to punish those who had been responsible for the sack and ruin of the principal cities of this country and innumerable other acts of force and violence against his poor subjects, as solace to those who had suffered and an example to all others. However, although the king pretended in words that what had happened was against his will and liking and that he intended to punish its chiefs and authors and wished to provide and give orders for the repose of the country with all clemency, as was proper for a kind prince, not only did he not try or punish any of the said chiefs and authors but on the contrary it became obvious that everything had been done with his consent and by prior decision of the Council of Spain. This is fully proved by some of his letters intercepted shortly afterwards in which the king wrote to Roda and the other captains who were the authors of these misdeeds that he not only did not censure what they had done but found it good and laudable and promised to recompense them, especially Roda, for their notable services; which he did for Roda and all other agents of his tyranny in this country when they returned to Spain. At the same time the king, hoping to overawe his subjects, sent Don Juan of Austria,[9] his bastard brother and therefore of his own blood, to this country as Governor-General. Pretending to the States that he approved the Pacification of Ghent[10] and giving feigned promises to send the Spaniards out of the country, to punish the authors of the violence and disorders which had occurred, and to provide for the general tranquility and re-establishment of the country's ancient freedom, he in fact sought to separate these States and to subjugate some provinces before the others. This was revealed not long after by the permission or the providence of God, who is the foe of all tyranny, when certain letters were intercepted which

7. Within a few years of the sack of Antwerp, Amsterdam had supplanted it as the chief market place of the world.
8. The only Spanish member of the Council, French-speaking, and a close adviser to Requesens. He took over the direction of the Council upon the latter's death.
9. The natural son of Holy Roman Emperor Charles V, Don John of Austria (1547–78) had led the naval victory against the Ottoman Turks at Lepanto in 1571. He died in office.
10. Declaration of union and religious truce by all the provinces of the Netherlands (1576), calling for the expulsion of Spanish troops, the restoration of local autonomy and an end to religious persecution.

made it obvious that Don Juan had instructions from the king to follow the instructions which Roda would give him when he reached the country. But, to conceal this plan more effectively, the king forbade Don Juan and Roda to meet or speak to each other, and he ordered Don Juan to behave towards the principal great nobles with every sign of kindness and good will, so as to win their affection, until, with their assistance and participation, he would be able to reduce Holland and Zeeland under his power; then he could deal with the other provinces as he wished. In accordance with these instructions, Don Juan, although he had solemnly sworn in the presence of all the States of the country to observe the Pacification made at Ghent, therefore violated its terms and sought by every means to gain to his side the German soldiers who were then in garrison and on guard in the principal cities and fortresses of the country. He used their colonels as his instruments, as they were already committed to him. In this way he tried to make himself the master of these fortresses and cities, and in many places considered himself sure he had control of them because he had already won over most of the colonels. In this way he sought to compel some to join him in waging war upon the Prince of Orange and the Hollanders and Zeelanders, and thereby hoped to arouse a civil war which would be even more cruel and bloody than it had been until then. But since things which are done secretly and by deceit will not stay hidden very long, this mad plan of Don Juan's was discovered before he could do what he intended, and he was not able to achieve what he sought. Nevertheless, he stirred up a new war which is still being waged, instead of bringing to the country the tranquility and assured peace of which he had boasted on his arrival.

These events have given us sufficient reason to forsake the King of Spain and to seek another mighty and benevolent Lord to aid in the defense of these countries and take them under his protection. This is all the truer because these countries have already suffered such oppression and outrages and have themselves been forsaken and abandoned by their king. Indeed, for the space of more than twenty years he has treated their inhabitants not as subjects but as enemies, and it was their own Prince and Lord who tried to ruin and subjugate them by force of arms. Furthermore, after the death of Don Juan, he sent here the Baron de Selles, who, under the pretext of proposing various means of reaching a settlement, declared clearly that the king would not acknowledge the Pacification of Ghent, even though Don Juan had sworn in his name to maintain it, and every day he put forward harsher conditions for agreement. In spite of this, we nevertheless did not wish to fail in the performance of our duty and sent humble remonstrances in writing and employed the favor and intercession of the principal lords and princes of Christendom, by these means seeking continually a reconciliation and accord with the king. For this purpose we kept our deputies in Cologne[11] for a long period, hoping to achieve an assured peace with some gracious and moderate freedom of religion (which principally concerns God and men's consciences), as the country then required, by the intercession of his Imperial Majesty and the Electors who had undertaken this mediation. But in the end we found by experience that we would not be able to obtain anything from the king by means of such remonstrances and meetings at Cologne, and that the only purpose and effect of this conference was to divide the provinces and sow discord among them. The king hoped that he would be able to conquer and subjugate them more easily

11. Sponsored by the Austrian Habsburgs, peace talks between Spain and the States General were held from May to November 1579. Hostilities continued throughout the months of the talks due to the intransigence of the royal delegates.

one by one. He could then execute upon them all his first purpose, which has since become publicly apparent in an edict of proscription published by the king. In it all the officials and inhabitants of these United Provinces, and those who take our side, are declared to be rebels and as such forfeit of our lives and property. Furthermore, a great sum of money is promised to anyone who kills the Prince of Orange.[12] The purpose of all of this is to render the poor inhabitants odious, to impede their trade and business, and to bring them into utter despair. Therefore, despairing utterly of any means of reconciliation and lacking any other remedy or means of relief, in accordance with the law of nature and in order to preserve and defend ourselves and our fellow-countrymen, our rights, the privileges and ancient customs and the freedom of the fatherland, and the life and honor of our wives, children, and posterity, so that we may not become the Spaniards' slaves, and foresaking the King of Spain with good right, we have been compelled to devise and practice other means which seem to provide better for the greater safety and preservation of our aforesaid rights, privileges, and liberties.

Know all men that, in consideration of the matters considered above and under the pressure of utmost necessity as has been said, we have declared and declare hereby by a common accord, decision, and consent the King of Spain, *ipso jure* [of his own right], forfeit of his lordship, principality, jurisdiction, and inheritance of these countries, and that we have determined not to recognize him hereafter in any matters concerning the principality, supremacy, jurisdiction, or domain of these Low Countries, nor to use or permit others to use his name as Sovereign Lord over them after this time. In accordance with this decision, we declare all officials, judges, individual lords, vassals, and all other inhabitants of these countries of all ranks and quality, to be henceforth discharged from any oaths to the said King of Spain as Lord of these countries, or from any other obligations which they may have to him. Since, for the aforesaid reasons, most of these United Provinces have placed themselves by a common agreement and consent of their members under the lordship and government of the Most Serene Prince, the Duke of Anjou,[13] etc., under certain conditions and articles set forth in a contract and agreement with His Highness, and since the Most Serene Archduke Matthias of Austria has resigned the post of Governor-General of these countries into our hands and we have accepted his resignation, we order and command all judges, officials, and others to whom this will appertain and whom it will affect, that henceforth they shall abandon and cease the use of the name and title, and the grand and little seals, counterseals and signets of the King of Spain, and that, for so long as My Lord the Duke of Anjou remains absent, for urgent matters concerning the welfare and prosperity of these countries, they shall use in their place for all matters concerning the provinces which have entered into a contract with His Highness the title and name of Chief and Councilors of the Country, and the other provinces shall do likewise on a provisional basis; but since the said Chief and Councilors will not in fact have been named, called, and actually established in the exercise of their posts and offices, they will use our name; except that in Holland they will continue as heretofore to use the name of My Lord the Prince of Orange and the States of these provinces until the said

12. A ban against William, Prince of Orange, was published in the Netherlands on 15 June 1580, putting the price of 25 000 crowns in gold upon his head. He was assassinated at Delft in 1584.
13. Brother of King Henri III of France. He was elected Lord of the Netherlands in 1581, a position he lost shortly before dying in 1584. Continuous feuding with the States characterised his time in office.

Council will have been effectively constituted, and then they will follow the instructions made for the Council and His Highness. In place of the seals of the king, they will henceforth use our great seal, counterseal, and signets in business concerning the General Governorship, which the Council of the Country will be authorized to conduct according to its instructions. And in business concerning the public order, the administration of justice, and other matters which belong to each province individually and separately, the Provincial Councils and others will respectively use the name and seal of the province where the case shall arise and no other name or seal, under penalty of nullification of letters, documents, or dispatches which may be so prepared or sealed. So that this may be better observed and practiced, we have ordered and commanded, and order and command by these presents, that all the seals of the King of Spain which are presently in these United Provinces be placed in the hands of the States or of such persons as shall be authorized or deputized to receive them by each of the said provinces respectively, under penalty of such punishment as they may decide. We further order and command that henceforward the arms or name of the King of Spain shall not be placed upon any monies of gold or silver which may be minted in these United Provinces, but such figure and form will be placed there as will be ordered for new coins of gold and silver, with their fractional pieces. We likewise order and command the president and lords of the Privy Council and all other chancellors, presidents, members and servants of provincial councils, and all presidents, first councilors and ordinary councilors in chambers of accounts in the various provinces, and also all other judges and officers of law, as being henceforth discharged from their oaths to the King of Spain under the terms of their commissions, that they shall be required to take a new oath to the States of the province which has jurisdiction over them, or to a person delegated for that purpose, by which they will swear to be faithful to us against the King of Spain and all his adherents, according to the formulary which we have prepared. There shall also be given to the councilors, masters of accounts, judges, and officers of law in the provinces which have made contracts with the Most Serene Duke of Anjou, an act continuing them in their offices, which will contain instead of a new commission a declaration abolishing their previous commission and granting a provisional commission until the arrival of His Highness. And there will be given to councilors, masters of accounts, judges, and officers of law under the jurisdiction of provinces which have not made contracts with His Highness, a new commission under our name and seal; provided, however, that the possessors of the original commissions shall not have been accused and convicted of having contravened the privileges of the country, of misdemeanors, or of similar abuses.

We further instruct the president and members of the Privy Council, the chancellor and members of the Council of Brabant, the governor, chancellor, and members of the Council in Gelderland, and the Count of Zutphen, the president and members of the Council in Flanders, the president and members of the Council in Holland, the governor, president, and members of the Council in Friesland, the president and members of the Council in Utrecht, the bailiff of Tournai and Tournaisis, the receivers and chief officers of law of Zeeland east and west of the Schelde, the auditor of Malines, and all other judges and officers of law to whom it appertains, their lieutenants, and to everyone to whom it will appertain, that they will immediately and without delay announce and make public this our present ordinance in all places under their jurisdiction, by the towncrier wherever it is customary or by posting, so that none may plead ignorance. And they shall have to maintain and observe this ordinance, and cause it to be maintained and observed strictly and without any violation, and to bring to trial and cause transgressors and violators thereof to be brought to trial, to be punished rigorously in the manner stated above, without any favor, escape, or dissimulation. For we have found this to be for the good of the country. We give to each and all of us full power, authority, and special instructions to do these things and what flows from them.

In witness whereof we have caused our seal to be attached hereto. Given at The Hague in our assembly, July 26, 1581.

By order of the States,
J. VAN ASSELIERS.

12 TREATY OF NONSUCH, 1585

Introduction

A treaty between Elizabeth, Queen of England, and the States General of the United Provinces of the Netherlands, by which the Queen agrees to come to the aid of the States on certain conditions. Signed on 10 (20 N.S.) August 1585 at Nonsuch, a palatial hunting lodge (now vanished) built in Surrey by Elizabeth's father Henry VIII.

This was the first formal alliance between the new republic and a foreign power. On 12 May 1585, the States General had invited Queen Elizabeth to assume the sovereignty of the Netherlands. She declined, and instead offered aid and appointed her favourite, the Earl of Leicester, as Governor-General. Lord Leicester arrived in the Netherlands in December 1585. He left on a visit to England in November 1586. During his absence, two of his commanders betrayed two fortified positions to Spain. Leicester was discredited. He returned in March 1587, but finally left in disgrace in December of that year. No other English Governor-General was sent to the Netherlands under this treaty. The treaty was revised on 16 August 1598, when the total due to be repaid for English subsidies in the previous fifteen years was agreed to be Lstg 800 000, and an annual repayment schedule of Lstg 30 000 was set up, but the provisions for mutual military and naval assistance were reaffirmed (Motley, 1895, Vol. II(3), pp. 490–95). The 'cautionary towns' were finally returned to Dutch control in 1616.

Text

I That the Queen of England shall send to the United Provinces an auxiliary army of 4000 foot, and 500 horse [but soon thereafter it was decided to send 5000 and 1000 horses], under the guidance of a Governor General of her choice, who shall be a person of quality and respect, devoted to the true religion, and under other good chiefs and captains: who shall all be paid by the Queen, for the duration of the war.

II For the restitution of the said monies the United Provinces, in the generality as well as individually, shall promise that when, by the grace of God, and of Her Majesty's assistance, they shall be restored to peace and tranquility, they shall reimburse all that Her Majesty will have spent, for levying the soldiers as well as for their transportation and for their wages, to wit, what she shall have spent during the first year, they will reimburse in the first year of peace, and the remainder in the four following years, each year a quarter: and this according to

Source: Text from Jean Dumont, *Corps Universal Diplomatique du Droit des Gens*, 1726–31, Vol. V, pp. 454–5. Translated from the French by Sylvia Modelski. Signatories from the original in the Algemeen Rijksarchief, The Hague, inv. n° 101A.

the calculation of the pay commissaries of each side, on the same basis as they were granted.

III As a further guarantee for the restitution, and within a month after the confirmation of the contract, there shall be put in the hands of such governors as will please Her Majesty to appoint: the town of Vlissingen [Flushing] and the castle of Rammekens, on the island of Walcheren, and the town of Brielle [Brill], with two fortresses, in Holland, to be held by garrisons of her subjects, until Her Majesty will have been entirely repaid in the city of London, for all the money she has disbursed. That, if the States deem it appropriate for the sake of the public peace, and to maintain the Union, that subjects of Her Majesty's in garrison be stationed in some other towns or fortresses, these shall be taken from the above mentioned 5000 men, and 1000 horses.

IV The towns and places given as surety to Her Majesty shall be kept supplied with artillery, powder, and other ammunition, in the manner that Her Majesty's Governor General shall think expedient for the defence and conservation of the said places, provided that all be inventorised, in order to be restituted later, as will be deemed appropriate.

V The States shall maintain no garrisons in the said towns and fortresses, they shall only keep a few persons of quality, and in the government of the civilian police, who shall remain there in order that Her Majesty's governors might take charge of matters touching upon the defence and protection of the places: it is well understood that they will not interfere with the police and the civil government, but be in command only of the particular garrison.

VI The chiefs and soldiers of these garrisons shall not entertain communication, intelligence, correspondence or familiarity with the Spaniards enemies of the States, and shall not suffer that others entertain such, but will show all hostility, in matters touching upon the security of the places.

VII The cautionary towns and places shall retain (as far as the police, their jurisdictions, privileges, rights and franchises are concerned, and according to their general and particular unions and covenants) their own laws, magistrates and governors, without being liable for any contribution or tax on the part of Her Majesty or of the barracks.

VIII The English garrisons shall be liable to pay the taxes, like other troops who man garrisons in the country, without the taxes being increased, unless agreed by Her Majesty's Lieutenant General.

IX And, in order that the citizens and inhabitants of the towns not be oppressed by the garrisons, Her Majesty shall see to their payment, and to their good discipline, and the above said inhabitants shall not be molested in connection with the execution of this contract, for what the States shall be required to do, provided that, in particular, they do what they are committed to do.

X When Her Majesty, or her successors, will be repaid all the expenses and disbursements of money, then the towns and places shall be given back to the States, with all their artillery and ammunition, without any difficulty or reserve, and without allowing them to fall into the hands of the King of Spain, or other enemies of the country, or under the authority of some other prince or lord, but to serve only for Her Majesty's surety and for the benefit of the above said States.

XI The chiefs and governors of Her Majesty's garrisons shall take an oath of allegiance, to Her Majesty, as well as to the States General, for the preservation of the said towns and places, and what is dependent on them; and also for the protection of the true religion, as it is at present practised in England and the United Provinces, and to uphold this treaty and have it upheld, when it concerns them. The officers, captains and soldiers of the said garrisons, shall likewise take an oath of allegiance to Her Majesty and to the States of the above said

Provinces, and also to be obedient to their chiefs and governors, as will also the inhabitants of the said towns.

XII The soldiers and troops stationed in the country shall be lodged and supplied with victuals, at a reasonable price, without their being charged any taxes on the victuals and other necessities, but shall be treated in the same way as the other military men of the States General.

XIII The governors of the above mentioned towns shall be paid every month their salaries or their garrison's wages, and Her Majesty shall make the monies available to these same towns, provided that their amount does not exceed that of the garrisons that were maintained there six months prior to the transfer of the said towns and places, on condition also that it not be grudged if the payment occasionally came eight to ten days late.

XIV The governor and the garrison shall enjoy the free exercise of religion, as in England: and, to that end, shall be assigned a church in each town.

XV These garrisons shall be treated like the others that had been there previously, with regard to lodgings as well as victuals: and the States shall decree that they may have the said victuals at the same prices as the inhabitants of these same towns and places: and shall be supplied with gun powder, tinders and cannon balls in such quantities as the garrisons of the said towns and places, that is, those of other towns and places, were accustomed to and do receive.

XVI In addition to the Governor who will be there on her behalf, Her Majesty shall be allowed to introduce two of her subjects into the Council of State, qualified persons who are practising the true Christian religion, and also, to the War Council, whenever the need arises, such persons as the Governor and the Council of State deem appropriate, to suit the business at hand. And the governors established in the towns of her garrisons may attend the Council of State whenever they think it necessary and expedient, for whatever matters touching upon Her Majesty's service, and the protection of the United Provinces, without however their being deemed to be members of the said Council.

XVII The above mentioned Governor General, together with the Council of State, shall have leave to use their authority to rectify the abuses that shall be committed in connection with taxes, and to retrench the number of officers, and to see that the monies shall be used for the greater service of the Provinces against the enemy, on water, as well as on land.

XVIII Similarly, the said Governor General, and the Council of State, shall make good the abuses that will occur with regard to the currency of the said Provinces, and shall bring them down to a stable order, and shall see to it that the money in circulation in the said Provinces, or any other, cannot be exchanged, so as to raise its value, without the consent of Her Majesty or of her Governor.

XIX Her Majesty, or the above said Governor General on her behalf, together with the Council of State, shall take care to reestablish public authority, and to maintain military discipline, which two things are now far gone into decadence, due to the equal power of the governors, and the great confusion in the councils.

XX The same Governor General, and the Council of State, shall watch over all that touches upon the preservation of the public welfare. It is well understood that they will make no change that might prejudice the true Christian religion, or the rights, advantages, privileges, customs, franchises, statutes and ordinances of the States, the Provinces, members, towns, colleges, or inhabitants, in the generality as well as individually.

XXI The States, in the generality as well as individually, shall not negotiate with the enemy without Her Majesty's seal of approval nor with any foreign prince or potentate without her approval or without the Governor General's approval.

XXII It shall also please Her Majesty not to negotiate, or have others negotiate, with the King of Spain or other enemies of the States, about any thing that touches upon the United Provinces, whether in the generality or individually, without the advice and consent of the States General, who shall legitimately be convoked on the matter.

XXIII The levying, and the payment, of the foreign force that might become necessary for the defence of the Provinces, shall be made by the Governor General and the Council of State, with the consent of the States General.

XXIV Whenever some governors of Provinces, or of frontier towns, shall die, or be replaced, the States or Provinces where this happens shall name or shall propose two or three qualified persons, of the reformed religion, from whom the Governor General and the Council of State shall choose and appoint one.

XXV Every time that Her Majesty, in the common defence, shall send ships of war to sea, to resist some of the enemy's fleet that might come to the Strait between France and England and the United Provinces, the States also shall fit out as many war vessels as Her Majesty, provided that they do not exceed the number that the Prince of Orange had offered, in the year 1584, through sire Dyer[1]: unless this is required by necessity, and the power of the States can carry the burden: the States' vessels shall join those of Her Majesty, and all together they shall come under the command of the Admiral of England: it being well understood that the booty shall be divided equally, according to the expenses incurred by each one, respectively, on both sides.

XXVI Her Majesty's vessels, when at sea, shall always have their free entrance and exit in the harbours and rivers of the United Provinces, and shall be provisioned there at a reasonable price: thus similarly, the war vessels of the United Provinces shall enjoy the same freedom and accommodation in all the rivers and harbours of England, and of other domains of Her Majesty's.

XXVII To smooth over the differences that might arise between the Provinces or some towns, and which cannot be resolved through the usual channel of law and justice, they shall be referred to Her Majesty, or the Governor General in her stead, so as to give advice and put the matter in order with the Council of State of the United Provinces.

XXVIII Her Majesty's subjects shall be permitted to transport to England horses that they are able to buy in the United Provinces, paying the normal duty, provided that they are not transported elsewhere.

XXIX The English soldiers who will want to return to England shall be allowed free passage, without any other passport than that signed and sealed by the General, as long as the number of the English troops remains complete, and the States are not constrained to incur any expense for the levy and the transportation of those that might have to be called up to replace those discharged.

1. Edward Dyer, knighted 1596, courtier, poet and diplomatist; on a mission to the Netherlands in January–February 1584, he was given a commitment by William of Orange, details of which are in the Appendix to this document, p. 132.

XXX The Governor General, the Chief, the colonels, captains, officers, and other members of Her Majesty's armed forces, shall take the usual oath, as in the States of the said Provinces, apart from the homage due by them to Her Majesty.

F. Walsingham	Rutger van Haersolte[1]
	Noel de Caron
	Jan van der Does
	Joost de Menin
	Johan van Oldenbarnevelt
	Francois Maelson
	Jacob Valcke
	Paulus Buys
	Jelger van Feytzma
	Hessel Aysma
	Lans van Yonghema

1. All Dutch signatories have affixed their personal seals, shown in some subsequent documents as (L.S.).

APPENDIX

Introduction

An account of the interview between Prince William of Orange and Edward Dyer, Queen Elizabeth's emissary, that took place at Delft in February 1584 (see Sargent, 1935, pp. 78–90). Dyer's instructions were drawn up by Sir Francis Walsingham, the Queen's chief secretary. William was assassinated in July, an event that delayed the signature of a treaty, but the commitment made by the Prince was confirmed by the States General in August, and incorporated in Article XXV of the treaty of Nonsuch, the following year.

Text

Articles presented by Mr Dyer to the Prince of Orange and the Prince's answers.

1. That her Majesty finds it necessary, in order to check the King of Spain's naval forces, to join with those of the Low Countries by sea.
2. That she [the Queen] desires his Excellency's advice as to what is most expedient to be done for their mutual defence.

Reply: The Prince of Orange, after praying Mr Dyer to thank Her Majesty humbly for the honour she does him, replied as follows:

He praises God, that he has more and more shown to her majesty the King of Spain's ill-will towards her; and as he, like herself, is informed of the King's great preparations by sea, and is convinced, however the King may proceed at first, that his real intention is to ruin these countries, and also (as shown more fully in the memoirs which the Prince sends to Mr Walsingham [a secretary of state to the Queen]) to do all the harm he can to her Majesty, he praises greatly the wise resolve contained in the two articles above, and feels sure that so laudable an enterprise cannot but bring about the advancement of God's glory and service and the common good of Christendom, and especially of these countries; he being of the same opinion, that they must unite the [sea] army of her Majesty for their mutual defence.

3. Her Majesty desires to know how many well-equipped ships of war the States can put to sea, at their own charges, if necessity require.

Reply: For the safety and defence of these countries, the Estates are obliged to arm at divers places several vessels, which they keep generally in service, and it is needful that they should have more, seeing that in summer, navigation is easier to the enemy. But besides these, which are for the guard of the channels and rivers, he can assure her Majesty that the States will arm twenty good ships; viz. ten of 400 tons, at least five of 300 to 350 tons, and five of 200 or 250 tons, which vessels will go to sea for her Majesty's service and the common defence; praying her Majesty to be satisfied therewith, considering the great burden which they have to bear on land against the King of Spain; and to rest assured that she shall have from the said States, all fidelity, service and obedience.

4. How and where can such ships most conveniently join those of her Majesty?

Reply: The Prince believes that the most convenient place would be the Isle of Wight [Wicke], to which place these ships would repair to receive the orders of

Source: Public Record Office. *Calendar of State Papers (Foreign Series): July 1583–July 1584*, Sophie L. Lomas (ed.) (London: Unwin, 1914) pp. 653–5.

her Majesty and her commanders, according to the directions which will be given to the soldiers and sailors, to obey the same; The Prince hoping that her Majesty will do him the honour to communicate to him the said instructions.

5. In what time (necessity so requiring) could these ships be ready to put to sea?

Reply: The Prince hopes that in six weeks they could be ready to put to sea.

6. What order are the States taking for their own defence and the maintenance of the war?

Reply: The Prince cannot yet reply certainly to this, as the States have taken until the 15 of March to conclude the matter, but as to the provinces of Holland, Zeeland and Utrecht, he reckons on being able to entertain 10 000 footmen, 1000 horse and 1000 pioneers, for the defence of the said countries and to aid the other provinces. And while awaiting the resolution of the States General, order has been given for recalling 1500 horse and 2000 foot, which have been hitherto in the service of the Elector [Gebhard] Truchsess [of Cologne], and which will shortly be in the country.

13 CHARTER OF THE DUTCH EAST INDIA COMPANY SIGNED ON 20 MARCH 1602

Introduction

With the great Spanish Armada defeated in 1588, and a civil war raging in France, a progressive consolidation of the United Provinces occurred in the 1590s. Dutch traders sailed to the East, to contest the monopoly of Spain and Portugal. They soon found out that to do that effectively, and to maintain prices, they needed to concentrate their forces. They consolidated their entry into the global system by forming a monopolistic organisation that was a national enterprise all their own.

Text

The States General of the United Netherlands to all those who represent them, Greetings. Let it be known. Considering the welfare of the United Provinces consists principally in navigation, trade and commerce, which has been carried out since ancient times from these lands and from time to time has most praiseworthily increased, not only with neighbouring countries and kingdoms, but also with those further from these provinces, in Europe, Asia and Africa, considering that in addition, during the last ten years, certain of the principal merchants of these provinces, lovers of navigation, trade and commerce, have, in Companies established in the City of Amsterdam, taken on the very praiseworthy navigation, trade and commerce from her to the East Indies at great cost, trouble and risk, and considering that, as these appeared good and great, certain other merchants, in Zeeland, on the Mass and in the Noorderquartier and West Friesland, have set up similar Companies and taken up the aforesaid navigation, trade and commerce, all of which having been considered and it having been maturely deliberated how much the United Provinces and their inhabitants would profit from this navigation, trade and commerce being governed, maintained and increased under a good general order, policy, correspondence and organisation, the Directors of the aforesaid Companies had agreed to describe for us and to propose what would be honest, serviceable and profitable, not just for the United Provinces, but also for all who had initiated and participated in these praiseworthy undertakings. So that these Companies may be united and the aforesaid trades be maintained, conducted and increased in common under a firm and certain unity, order and policy for all the inhabitants of the United Provinces who may wish to participate in them, which the representatives of the aforesaid Companies well

Source: The original Charter (*Octrooi*) of the Vereenigde Oost-Indische Compagnie (VOC) was written on parchment and is now in the VOC Archives in The Hague. The present English translation is of the first printing of the complete text in pp. 118–35 of J. A. van der Chys's *Geschiedenis der Stichting van de Vereenigde O.I. Compagnie en der maatregelen van de Nederlandsche regering betreffende de vaart op Oost-Indie, welke aan deze stichting voorafgingen* (Leiden, 1857). The only deviations from the original are in the numbering of articles and the punctuation, both of which are non-existent in the old document. Footnotes are van der Chys's. The translation from the Dutch is by Robert Ross.

understood and which after various communications, deliberations, discussions and reports was brought to agreement, we have, after mature deliberations, conjoined and established the aforesaid Union for the benefit and prosperity of the United Provinces and for the profit of all their inhabitants. Conjunction and establishment are determined hereby, on the basis of sovereign power and authority and in the solid knowledge, under the conditions, freedoms and advantages listed hereunder, to wit:

1. That in the division of the supply and profit from this Company, the Chamber of Directors of the City of Amsterdam shall enjoy and be liable for one half, the Chamber of Zeeland one quarter and the Chambers of the Maas, and of North Holland and West Friesland, each one eighth.

2. That, as may from time to time be necessary, a general meeting or board shall be held consisting of seventeen persons, including eight from the Chamber of Amsterdam, four from Zeeland, two from the Maas and also two from North Holland, with the seventeenth being appointed in turn from Zeeland, the Maas and North Holland. All matters concerning this United Company shall be regulated by these men, by majority vote.

3. The Board described above shall meet to resolve when expeditions will be made, with how many ships, where they shall be sent and the other matters concerning trade.

The resolutions of the aforesaid Board will be effectuated and put into practice by the respective Chambers of Amsterdam, Zeeland, the Maas, and North Holland.

4. The convocation and gathering of the aforesaid Board will be held for the first six years within the City of Amsterdam and then for two years in Zeeland, and so on throughout the life of this Company.

5. The Directors who have to journey from home on the business of the United Company, being required to do so either to meet in the aforesaid Board or for any other charge, shall receive as a daily allowance four guilders, exclusive of [passenger] barge and coach charges, with the proviso that this does not apply to those who, as Directors of the same, travel from one town to another to attend the respective Chambers. They shall receive neither allowance nor travelling expenses.

6. If it shall happen that any important matter occurs on which the Board members are unable to reach a decision, or if they consider themselves hindered from outvoting each other, then this shall be left to our decision and ordinance, and that which shall then be decided shall be followed and carried out.

7. This United Company shall be constituted and begin in the year 1602 and shall last for the period of twenty one years, consecutively, except that every ten years a general conclusion of accounts shall be made, and everyone shall be free to leave it and take his money with him, with the proviso that special accounts shall be made of the capital at the time and of the ships that may sail during those years.

8. And the expenses which shall be borne by the shareholders of the first account in the East Indies or through the Straits of Magellan, where this Company shall trade, and which shall accrue to the benefit or advantage of the shareholders of the following account, shall be borne by those of that account, for the half or such less proportion as the Board of Seventeen may consider reasonable.

9. Should any of the shareholders of these coming voyages, who may not be satisfied with this Union, wish to withdraw their money or to cancel the promised

sum, they shall be allowed to do so, provided that they be given interest on their advance of seven and a half per cent, or more as has been promised to them.

10. All inhabitants of these United Provinces shall be permitted to participate in this Company with as small or as large sums as they may wish. Then if it shall happen that larger sums are offered or presented than the voyages require, then those who have more than thirty thousand guilders in the Company shall have to reduce their capital, pro rata and in proportion, to make room for others.

11. And the inhabitants shall be warned, within the space of one month from this date, by the public posting of notices in such places as it is usual to post notices, that they may be admitted to the Company during the space of five months, beginning from the first of April next, and that they may deposit those sums which they wish to invest in three stages, namely approximately one third for the outfitting for the year 1603, one more third for the year 1604 and the last third for the expedition of the year 1605, one month after they shall be advised of this by the Directors.

Similar warnings shall be given in the month of March before the expiry of the first eleven years of the Charter, that is in the year 1612.

12. On returning from the voyages, the ships shall enter the place from which they set sail, and if, by the fortune of wind or weather, the ships which departed from one quarter return to another, for example those of Amsterdam or the Nooderquartier in Zeeland or on the Maas, or those from Zeeland in Holland, nonetheless each Chamber shall retain the control and administration over the ships and merchandise it sent out, provided that the Directors of those Chambers be required to go themselves in person to the place where the ships and merchandise have arrived, and may not be allowed to appoint factors over it, but, should they prefer not to travel, then they shall charge the Directors of the Chamber where the ships arrived with the administration.

13. If one or other Chamber receives spices or other merchandise from the Indies, and other Chambers have received none, then in such cases the Chamber which is provided for, shall at their request and as matters allow, provide the other Chambers and send the goods when they have once again sold out.

14. That the accounts of the equipment and outfitting of the ships shall be drawn up three months after the departure of the ships, and a month later copies shall be sent to the respective Chambers, and as for the return goods, the Chambers shall inform each other of the state of things as often as they are asked for it, and the accounts shall be drawn up as soon as possible, and the General account after ten years shall be rendered in public, after notices have been posted to warn whomsoever may wish to come to the rendering.[1]

15. And the Chambers shall be required to inform those Provinces or Cities whose inhabitants have invested fifty thousand guilders or more as to when a return ship arrives, the nature of the incoming cargo and the sums made by the sale of merchandise, in so far as they may be requested by the Provinces and Cities to do so.

16. And should any Provinces decide to appoint an agent who may collect the sums from the inhabitants of the respective provinces to invest them in a mass and to collect payments for the returns and dividends, then the Chamber where this agent brings the money shall allow him access to the aforesaid Chamber, in order to be informed of the state of the expenditure and income, including the debts and credits of the office, provided that the sum deposited by the aforesaid agent shall be fifty thousand guilders or above.

1. Article 1 of the 1622 Charter states that the accounts shall be rendered not only with open doors but also 'with open windows'.

17. If the returns shall be five per cent, gross, then dividends shall be payed to the shareholders.

18. The respective Chambers shall be served by the present Directors, that is, the Amsterdam Chamber by Gerrit Bycker, Reynier Pauw, Pieter Dircxz. Haselaer, Jacques de Velaer, Jehan Janssz. Carel, Bernert Berrewyns, Jehan Joppen, Hans Hunger, Heyndrick Buyck, Louys del Beque, Dirck van Os, Francois van Houve, Elbert Lucasz, Isaac le Maire, Syvert Pietersz. Sem, Gerryt Reinst, Marcus Vogelaer, Jehan Hermensen, Guert Dircxs, Huybrecht Wachtmans, Leonaert Ray, Albert Symonsz. Joncheyn and Arent ten Grootenhuys.

19. The Zeeland Chamber by Adriaen Hendricxz. ten Haeff, Jacob Boreel, Jehan Lambertsz. Coole, Jacob Pietersz. de Weert, Cornelis Meunicx, Adriaen Bommene, Laurens Bacx, Everhardt Becquer, Arnoult le Clerck, Arnoult Verhouve, Gherardt van Schoonhove, Nicolacs Pieterssz., Balthazar van Vlierden, and Balthazar de Moucheron.

20. The Delft Chamber by Jehan Janssz. Lodensteyn, Dirck Bruynssz. van der Dussen, Gerrit Dircxz. Meerman, Cornelis Adriaenssz. Bogaert, Michiel Janssz. Sasbout, Willem Joosten D'Edel, Dirck Gerritsz. Meerman, Jehan Praet, Jacob Sandersen Balbiaen, Hendrick Otte, and Jasper Moerman.

21. The Rotterdam Chamber by Fop Pietersz. van der Meyden, Willem Janssz. Frack, Gerryt Huygensen, Pieter Leonaertsz. Busch, Jehan ven der Veecken, Willem Janssz. van Loon, Jehan Jacobsz. Mus, Adriaen Spyeryng and Cornelis Matelief de Jonge.

22. The Hoorn Chamber by Claes Jacobsz. Syms, Cornilis Cornelisz. Veen, Willem Pietersz. Crap, Pieter Janssz. Liorn . . .[2]

23. And the Enkuisen Chamber by Lucas Gerrytz, Willem Cornilisz. de Jonge, Jehan Pieterssz. Schram, Hendrick Gruyter, Jehan Laurensz. van Loosen, Dirck Dircxz. Pelser, Ghysbrecht van Berensteyn, Bartholt Janssz. Steenhuysen, Jacob Jacobsz. Hynloopen, Francois de Gardyn, and Willem Brasser.

24. If any of the aforementioned directors should die or in any other way leave the service, the position shall remain unfilled and no one may be appointed in the place of the deceased or retired person, as those of that Chamber may think fit, till the Directors of the respective Chambers shall have reached the following totals.

25. The Amsterdam Chamber, twenty persons, the Zeeland Chamber, twelve, Delft, seven, Rotterdam, seven, Enkuisen, seven and Hoorn an equivalent number.

26. But should anyone of the aforesaid number die or leave the service for other reason, then the Directors of the Chamber where this occurred shall, within two or at most three months, nominate three capable and qualified persons and present them to the States of the Province in which the Chamber is situated, so that one of them may be chosen in the stead of the person who was deceased or had otherwise left the service, according to the order made for this.

27. The Directors shall solemnly swear, on their honour, oath and piety, that they shall, in their administration, act well and faithfully, that they will keep and render good and true accounts and that they will not advantage the greatest of the shareholders more than the least in the raising of the moneys necessary for the outfitting, nor in the division of the return goods.

28. And all those who hereafter shall be chosen as Directors shall have to risk at least ten thousand Flemish pounds in this Company, except for the Directors in

2. Here the full list of Directors was probably not available in time for inclusion in the Charter. These are additional names for Hoorn: Vrerich Gerritssz. Schilder, Outger Jacobssz., Pieter Janssoon Schock.

Hoorn and Enkuysen who will be allowed to risk only at least five thousand pounds.

29. [The Directors] shall enjoy a commission on the outfittings of one per cent, and a like amount on the return cargoes, divided between the Amsterdam Chamber, one half, the Zeeland Chamber one quarter and the Maas and North Holland Chambers each one eighth, irrespective of whether one Chamber brings in more or less moneys or sells more or less spices than its share.

30. With the proviso that the Directors may not charge to the Company any commission on sums raised for the Company or on goods provided for it, nor may they employ anyone else, at the Company's expense, to prepare the sailings and to buy the necessary goods.

31. And that the Bookkeeper, Cashier and servant or messenger shall be paid by the Directors or the respective Chambers, without this being charged to the shareholders.

32. Should it happen that in one Chamber one of the Directors should be in such a condition that he is unable to fulfil those tasks charged to his administration and should this result in a loss, then this will be charged against that Chamber, and not against the Company as a whole, and those sums which the Directors have in this Company shall be specifically reserved for their administration.

33. The Directors of the respective Chambers shall be responsible for their Cashiers.

34. And, so that the aspirations of this United Company may be fulfilled with greater success, for the advantage of the United Provinces, the conservation and increase of the business and the profit of the Company, we have hereby chartered and allowed the aforesaid Company that no one, of whatever condition or quality, other than those of the aforesaid Company, may during the period of twenty-one years, beginning in and including this year 1602, sail from the United Provinces to the Cape of Good Hope or through the Straits of Magellan, on pain of confiscation of their ships and goods, except that the concessions granted to certain Companies to sail through the Straits of Magellan shall be maintained, provided that they send their ships from these Provinces within the space of four years from this date, on pain of losing the benefit of the aforesaid concessions.

35. Also that the Directors of the aforesaid Company will be empowered, to the east of the Cape of Good Hope and in and through the Straits of Magellan, to conclude agreements and contracts with the Princes and Potentates in the name of the States General of the United Netherlands, or of the supreme authorities of the same, to build fortresses and strongholds there, to appoint Governors, soldiers and officers of Justice, and such other necessary positions, for the preservation of the places, the maintenance of good order, policy and justice, entirely for the furthering of trade (with the proviso that these Governors, officers of justice and soldiers shall take an oath of loyalty to the States General or the aforesaid supreme authorities, and the Company, for matters concerning business and trade)[3] and to discharge the aforesaid Governors, officers of Justice and soldiers, in so far as they consider that they have acted wrongly or untrustworthily, with the proviso that they may not prevent the aforesaid Governors, and officers of Justice from coming here to make their complaints or grievances, should they consider that they have any, known to us. And the Directors of the Company shall be required to inform the States General, by each returning ship, of the Governor and officers of Justice that they shall have appointed in the aforesaid place and fortresses, so that their commission may be agreed and confirmed.

3. This sentence within brackets is probably a later addition.

36. And should the aforesaid Company be cheated and handled badly in any place, or if they are kept from the enjoyment of any moneys or merchandise, without compensation, they shall repair the damage as is suited to the matter and to the best of their power, by whatever means is most suited to the matter, with the proviso that the ships on their return to the country shall make a report of the circumstances of the case to the Board of the Admiralty or the region in which they arrive, provided that, should they make any statements to which the Company takes exception, it may refer it to us. And the goods shall be booked, with a suitable inventory, with the Company unless anyone else but the fiscal take issue and reclaims the goods recovered, in which case the goods shall be administered as is determined by the decision of the Admiralty.

37. Should it occur that the ships of Spain, Portugal or any other enemy attack the ships of this Company, and if in the fight any of the enemy ships be captured, then these ships and their goods shall be distributed according to the law[4] of the land, namely that the state and Admiralty shall enjoy their rights. Except that any damage the Company may have sustained in the said encounter shall be deducted, and the respective Admiralties where the ships shall arrive shall take cognisance of the rights of the Prince, while the administration of the goods *pendents lite* shall remain with the Company,[5] with a proper Inventory, as mentioned above, and anyone aggrieved at any decision is free to appeal to us.

38. That the spices, Chinese silk and cotton cloths imported by this Company from the East Indies, shall, in arriving and departing, not be taxed more than they are taxed now, according to the list and the general declaration concerning the goods not specified, appended to the end of this Charter.

39. That no ships, shot or ammunition of this Company may be taken for the country's service without the said Company's consent.

40. That the spices of the Company shall be sold at no other weights than those of Amsterdam.[6]

41. That the various Chambers shall be allowed to store their spices, either on board ship or in the warehouses, without paying duties, taxes or weigh-money, provided that the spices in the aforesaid places may not be transported, but on being sold shall be weighed and the weigh-house duties paid, as is the case with other goods subject to the weigh-house, as soon as they are sold or alienated.

42. That no Directors may be restrained or hindered in their goods or persons in order that payment may be had for their administration in the aforesaid Company, nor for the wages of any Commissioners, skippers, mates, sailors or any other persons taken into the service of the Company, but that anyone who may have any claim against them shall be required to call them before the ordinary judges.

43. That the Provosts of the Company may apprehend on land the sailors who are in service with them, and may bring them to trial, no matter in what town, place or jurisdiction they may be found, provided that the aforesaid Provosts shall inform the officer and the Burgomeesters of the towns and places in advance.[7]

4. The Instruction for the Board of the Admiralty stipulated: 'the fifth penny for the commonwealth of the States and general business, and then, of the rest, the tenth penny for the Admiral'.
5. This was a privilege for the Company, as otherwise the administration was the Admiralty's affair.
6. This standardisation of weights and measures was probably determined in order to ensure credit with foreign traders, just as, a few years later, the Amsterdam bank introduced monetary uniformity.
7. There was a provost on each ship who was charged with the execution of the sentences.

44. In recognition of this Charter, and of what has gone before, the Company shall pay us the sum of twenty-five thousand Flemish pounds, each of forty groats, which we shall invest in the outfitting for the first ten years' account. The profit and the risk of this will be for the benefit of the state, and shall be equal to that enjoyed, and borne, by all other shareholders in the Company.

45. And when any ships shall return, the Generals or commanders of the fleet, ships or ship shall be required to report to us of the success of their journey and to present a written account, should it be required.

46. All of which points and advantages described above We have ordered and order hereby be maintained and complied with by each and every inhabitant and subject of the United Provinces, without them doing anything against it either within or without the United Provinces, on pain of being punished in the persons and goods as injurers of the Commonwealth of the provinces and contraveners of our Ordinances and commands. Therefore We expressly command and order all Governors, Justices, Officers, Magistrates and Inhabitants of the aforesaid United Provinces that they allow the aforesaid Directors to enjoy and use peaceably and orderly the total import of this our Charter Consent and Privilege, ceasing all contradictions and impeachments to the contrary, since We have decided that this should be so, in the interest of these Provinces. Given under our seal and signature of our recorder in The Hague on the 20th day of March Sixteen hundred and two. Alb. Joachimi v.

By order of the aforesaid States General
Aerssen[8]
1602

8. Cornelius Aerssen, Recorder of the States General, and an associate of Johan Oldenbarnevelt, Advocate of Holland.

14 HUGO GROTIUS'S *MARE LIBERIUM* (THE FREEDOM OF THE SEAS), 1609

Introduction

In 1604, the Dutch East India Company asked Hugo Grotius to justify Dutch warfare in Asia, and in particular the capture by one of its ships of the Portuguese merchantman 'Santa Catarina' in the straits of Malacca. Within a year, *De Iure Praedae* (On the Law of Prize) was written.

In 1608 Spain and Holland began the talks which resulted in the 12-year Truce of Antwerp (see Doc. 15). During the negotiations, Spain tried to secure from the United Provinces a renunciation of their right to trade in the East and West Indies. Thereupon, the Dutch East India Company requested Grotius to publish one chapter (XII) of *De Iure Praedae*, dealing with the freedom of the seas. He divided this into 13 'chapters' and, with minor adjustments, it appeared as a book under the title of *Mare Liberum.*

Text

CHAPTER I

By the Law of Nations navigation is free to all persons whatsoever

My intention is to demonstrate briefly and clearly that the Dutch – that is to say, the subjects of the United Netherlands – have the right to sail to the East Indies, as they are now doing, and to engage in trade with the people there. I shall base my argument on the following most specific and unimpeachable axiom of the Law of Nations, called a primary rule or first principle, the spirit of which is self-evident and immutable, to wit: Every nation is free to travel to every other nation, and to trade with it.

God Himself says this speaking through the voice of nature; and inasmuch as it is not His will to have Nature supply every place with all the necessities of life, He ordains that some nations excel in one art and others in another. Why is this His will, except it be that He wished human friendships to be engendered by mutual needs and resources, lest individuals deeming themselves entirely sufficient unto themselves should for that very reason be rendered unsociable? So by the decree of divine justice it was brought about that one people should supply the needs of another, in order, as Pliny the Roman writer says,[1] that in this way, whatever has been produced anywhere should seem to have been destined for all. Vergil also sings in this wise:

Not every plant on every soil will grow,[2]

Source: *The Freedom of the Seas or the Right which belongs to the Dutch to take Part in the East Indian Trade, a Dissertation by Hugo Grotius*, translated from the Latin text of 1633, and annotated, by Ralph Van Deman Magoffin (New York, 1916.) (Excerpts.)

1. *Panegyric 29*, 2.
2. *Georgics II*, 109 (Dryden's translation, II, 154).

and in another place:

Let others better mould the running mass
Of metals, etc.[3]

Those therefore who deny this law, destroy this most praiseworthy bond of human fellowship, remove the opportunities for doing mutual service, in a word do violence to Nature herself. For do not the ocean, navigable in every direction with which God has encompassed all the earth, and the regular and the occasional winds which blow now from one quarter and now from another, offer sufficient proof that Nature has given to all peoples a right of access to all other peoples? Seneca[4] thinks this is Nature's greatest service, that by the wind she united the widely scattered peoples, and yet did so distribute all her products over the earth that commercial intercourse was a necessity to mankind. Therefore this right belongs equally to all nations. Indeed the most famous jurists[5] extend its application so far as to deny that any state or any ruler can debar foreigners from having access to their subjects and trading with them. Hence is derived that law of hospitality which is of the highest sanctity; hence the complaint of the poet Vergil:

What men, what monsters, what inhuman race,
What laws, what barbarous customs of the place,
Shut up a desert shore to drowning men,
And drive us to the cruel seas again.[6]

And:

To beg what you without your want may spare –
The common water, and the common air.[7]

We know that certain wars have arisen over this very matter; such for example as the war of the Megarians against the Athenians,[8] and that of the Bolognese against the Venetians.[9] Again, Victoria[10] holds that the Spaniards could have shown just reasons for making war upon the Aztecs and the Indians in America,

3. *Aeneid VI*, 847–853 (Dryden's translation, VI, 1168–1169).
4. *Natural Questions III*, IV.
5. *Institutes II*, 1; *Digest I*, 8, 4; cf. Gentilis, *De jure belli* I, 19; cf. *Code IV*, 63, 4 (Grotius refers particularly to his famous predecessor Albericus Gentilis (1552–1608), an Italian who came to England and was appointed to the chair of Regius Professor of Civil Law at Oxford. He published his *De Jure Belli* in 1558).
6. *Aeneid I*, 539–540 (Dryden's translation, I, 760–763).
7. *Aeneid VII*, 229–230 (Dryden's translation, VII, 313–314).
8. *Diodorus Siculus XI*; Plutarch, *Pericles XXIX*, 4. (The Athenian decree prohibiting the Megarians from trading with Athens or any part of the Athenian Empire was one of the leading causes of the Peloponnesian War.)
9. Carlo Sigonio (1523–1584), an Italian humanist, in his work *On the Kingdom of Italy*.
10. Victoria, *De Indis II*, nn. 1–7; Covarruvias, in c. *Peccatum*, § 9, n. 4, *ibi Quinta* (Franciscus de Victoria (1480–1546), the famous Spanish Scholastic, a Dominican, and Professor of Theology at Salamanca from 1521 until his death. His thirteen *Relectiones* (*De Indis* is no. V) were published ('*vitiosa et corrupta*') in 1557 after his death; the 1686 Cologne edition is held to be the best.)

    Diego Covarruvias (1512–1577), styled the Bartolo of Spain. (He should probably be credited with formulating the reform decrees of the Council of Trent. The 5-vol. Antwerp 1762 edition of his works is the best.)

more plausible reasons certainly than were alleged, if they really were prevented from traveling or sojourning among those peoples, and were denied the right to share in those things which by the Law of Nations or by Custom are common to all, and finally if they were debarred from trade . . .

. . . As we read in Tacitus,[11] the Germans accused the Romans of 'preventing all intercourse between them and of closing up to them the rivers and roads, and almost the very air of heaven'. When in days gone by the Christians made crusades against the Saracens, no other pretext was so welcome or so plausible as that they were denied by the infidels free access to the Holy Land.[12]

It follows that the Portuguese, even if they had been sovereigns in those parts to which the Dutch make voyages, would nevertheless be doing them an injury if they should forbid them access to those places and from trading there.

Is it not then an incalculably greater injury for nations which desire reciprocal commercial relations to be debarred therefrom by the acts of those who are sovereigns neither of the nations interested, nor of the element over which their connecting high road runs? Is not that the very cause which for the most part prompts us to execrate robbers and pirates, namely, that they beset and infest our trade routes?

CHAPTER II *on p. 144*

11. *Histories IV*, 64 (in connection with the revolt of Civilis).
12. Andrea Alciati, *Commentaria VII*, 130; Covarruvias in c. *Peccatum*, p. 2 § 9; *Bartolus on Code I*, 11 (Alciati (1492–1550) was made Comes Palatinus by the Emperor Charles V, and offered a Cardinal's hat by Pope Paul III, which he refused, but he did become a Protonotarius Apostolicus).

CHAPTER II

The Portuguese have no right by title of discovery to sovereignty over the East Indies to which the Dutch make voyages

The Portuguese are not sovereigns of those parts of the East Indies to which the Dutch sail, that is to say, Java, Ceylon, and many of the Moluccas. This I prove by the incontrovertible argument that no one is sovereign of a thing which he himself has never possessed, and which no one else has ever held in his name. These islands of which we speak, now have and always have had their own kings, their own government, their own laws, and their own legal systems. The inhabitants allow the Portuguese to trade with them, just as they allow other nations the same privilege. Therefore, inasmuch as the Portuguese pay tolls, and obtain leave to trade from the rulers there, they thereby give sufficient proof that they do not go there as sovereigns but as foreigners. Indeed they only reside there on suffrance. And although the title to sovereignty is not sufficient, inasmuch as possession is a prerequisite – for having a thing is quite different from having the right to acquire it – nevertheless I affirm that in those places the Portuguese have no title at all to sovereignty which is [not] denied them by the opinion of learned men, even of the Spaniards.

First of all, if they say that those lands have come under their jurisdiction as the reward of discovery, they lie, both in law and in fact. For to discover a thing is not only to seize it with the eyes but to take real possession thereof, as Gordian[1] points out in one of his letters. For that reason the Grammarians[2] give the same signification to the expressions 'to find' or 'to discover' and 'to take possession of' or 'to occupy'; and all the Latin with which I am acquainted tells us that the opposite of 'to find' is 'to lose'. However, natural reason itself, the precise words of the law, and the interpretation of the more learned men[3] all show clearly that the act of discovery is sufficient to give a clear title of sovereignty only when it is accompanied by actual possession. And this only applies of course to movables or to such immovables as are actually inclosed within fixed bounds and guarded.[4] No such claim can be established in the present case, because the Portuguese maintain no garrisons in those regions. Neither can the Portuguese by any possible means claim to have discovered India, a country which was famous centuries and centuries ago! It was already known as early as the time of the emperor Augustus as the following quotation from Horace shows:

1. *Code VIII*, 40, 13 (probably Fabius Claudius Gordianus Fulgentius (468–533), a Benedictine monk, one of the Latin Fathers).
2. Nonius Marcellus, On the various significations of speech, under the word 'occupare', cf. Connan, *Commentaries on the civil law III*, 3; Donellus (Doneau), *Commentaries on the civil law IV*, 10. (François de Connan (1508–1551), a French jurisconsult, a pupil of Alciati; Hugues Doneau (1527–1591) a famous jurisconsult, who wrote many volumes of commentaries on the Digest and the Code.)
3. *Institutes II*, 1, 13.
4. *Digest XLI*, 2, 3.

That worst of evils, poverty, to shun
Dauntless through seas, and rocks, and fires you run
To furthest Ind,[5]

And have not the Romans described for us in the most exact way the greater part of Ceylon?[6] And as far as the other islands are concerned, not only the neighboring Persians and Arabs, but even Europeans, particularly the Venetians, knew them long before the Portuguese did.

But in addition to all this, discovery *per se* gives no legal rights over things unless before the alleged discovery they were *res nullius*.[7] Now these Indians of the East, on the arrival of the Portuguese, although some of them were idolators, and some Mohammedans, and therefore sunk in grievous sin, had none the less perfect public and private ownership of their goods and possessions, from which they could not be dispossessed without just cause.[8] The Spanish writer Victoria,[9] following other writers of the highest authority, has the most certain warrant for his conclusion that Christians, whether of the laity or of the clergy, cannot deprive infidels of their civil power and sovereignty merely on the ground that they are infidels, unless some other wrong has been done by them.

For religious belief, as Thomas Aquinas[10] rightly observes, does not do away with either natural or human law from which sovereignty is derived. Surely it is a heresy to believe that infidels are not masters of their own property; consequently, to take from them their possessions on account of their religious belief is no less theft and robbery than it would be in the case of Christians.

Victoria then is right in saying[11] that the Spaniards have no more legal right over the East Indians because of their religion, than the East Indians would have had over the Spaniards if they had happened to be the first foreigners to come to Spain. Nor are the East Indians stupid and unthinking; on the contrary they are intelligent and shrewd, so that a pretext for subduing them on the ground of their character could not be sustained. Such a pretext on its very face is an injustice. Plutarch said long ago that it was greed that furnished the pretext for conquering barbarous countries, and it is not unsuspected that greedy longing for the property of another often hid itself behind a pretext of civilizing barbarians. And now that well-known pretext of forcing nations into a higher state of civilization against their will, the pretext once monopolized by the Greeks and by Alexander the Great, is considered by all theologians, especially those of Spain,[12] to be unjust and unholy . . .

CHAPTER V *on p. 146*

5. *Letters I*. 1, 44–5 (Francis's translation, *English Poets XIX*, 726).
6. Pliny, *Natural History*, VI, 22.
7. *Digest XLI*, 1, 3.
8. Covarruvias in c. *Peccatum* § 10, n. 2, 4, 5.
9. *De potestate civili I*, 9.
10. *Summa II*, II, q. 10, a. 12 (Thomas Aquinas (1227–1274), one of the most famous of the Schoolmen and Theologians).
11. *De Indis I*, nn. 4–7, 19.
12. Vasquius, Preface (n. 5) to *Controversiae illustres*.

CHAPTER V

Neither the Indian Ocean nor the right of navigation thereon belongs to the Portuguese by title of occupation

If . . . the Portuguese have acquired no legal right over the nations of the East Indies, and their territory and sovereignty, let us consider whether they have been able to obtain exclusive jurisdiction over the sea and its navigation or over trade. Let us first consider the case of the sea. . . .

The question at issue . . . is not one that concerns an inner sea, one which is surrounded on all sides by the land, although it is well known that the Roman jurists cited such an inner sea in their famous opinions condemning private avarice. No! the question at issue is the outer sea, the Ocean, that expanse of water which antiquity describes as the immense, the infinite, bounded only by the heavens, parent of all things; the ocean which the ancients believed was perpetually supplied with water not only by fountains, rivers, and seas, but by the clouds, and by the very stars of heaven themselves; the ocean which, although surrounding this earth, the home of the human race, with the ebb and flow of its tides, can be neither seized nor inclosed; nay, which rather possess the earth than is by it possessed.

Further, the question at issue does not concern a gulf or a strait in this ocean, nor even all the expanse of sea which is visible from the shore. [But consider this!!] The Portuguese claim as their own the whole expanse of the sea which separates two parts of the world so far distant the one from the other, that in all the preceding centuries neither one has so much as heard of the other. Indeed, if we take into account the snare of the Spaniards, whose claim is the same as that of the Portuguese, only a little less than the whole ocean is found to be subject to two nations, while all the rest of the peoples in the world are restricted to the narrow bounds of the northern seas. Nature was greatly deceived if when she spread the sea around all peoples she believed that it would also be adequate for the use of them all. If in a thing so vast as the sea man were to reserve to himself from general use nothing more than mere sovereignty, still he would be considered a seeker after unreasonable power. If a man were to enjoin other people from fishing, he would not escape the reproach of monstrous greed. But the man who prevents navigation, a thing which means no loss to himself, what are we to say of him? . . .

CHAPTER IX *on p. 147*

CHAPTER IX

Trade with the East Indies does not belong to the Portuguese by title of occupation

Neither discovery nor occupation . . . is to be invoked on the point here under consideration, because the right of carrying on trade is not something corporal, which can be physically seized; nor would discovery or occupation help the case of the Portuguese even if they had been the very first persons to trade with the East Indies, although such a claim would be entirely untenable and false. For since in the beginning peoples set out along different paths, it was necessary that some become the first traders, nevertheless it is absolutely certain that those traders did not on that account acquire any rights. Wherefore if the Portuguese have any right by virtue of which they *alone* may trade with the East Indies, that right like other servitudes ought to arise from concession, either express or tacit, that is to say, from prescription. Otherwise no such right can exist.

CHAPTER X *on p. 148*

CHAPTER X

Trade with the East Indies does not belong to the Portuguese by virtue of title based on the Papal Donation

No one has granted it except perhaps the Pope, and he did not have the power. For no one can give away what he does not himself possess. But the Pope, unless he were the temporal master of the whole world, which sensible men deny, cannot say that the universal right in respect of trade belongs to him. Especially is this true since trade has to do only with material gains, and has no concern at all with spiritual matters, outside of which, as all admit, Papal power ceases. Besides, if the Pope wished to give that right to the Portuguese alone, and to deprive all other men of the same right, he would be doing a double injustice. In the first place, he would do an injustice to the people of the East Indies who, placed as we have said outside the Church, are in no way subjects of the Pope. Therefore, since the Pope cannot take away from them anything that is theirs, he could not take away their right of trading with whomsoever they please. In the second place, he would do an injustice to all other men both Christian and non-Christian, from whom he could not take that same right without a hearing. Besides, what are we to say of the fact that not even temporal lords in their own dominions are competent to prohibit the freedom of trade, as has been demonstrated above by reasonable and authoritative statements?

Therefore it must be acknowledged, that the authority of the Pope has absolutely no force against the eternal law of nature and of nations, from whence came that liberty which is destined to endure for ever and ever.

CHAPTER XI *on p. 149*

CHAPTER XI

Trade with the East Indies does not belong to the Portuguese by title of prescription or custom

Last of all, prescription, or if you prefer the term, custom. We have shown that according to Vasquez, neither prescription nor custom had any force as between free nations or the rulers of different peoples, or any force against those principles which were introduced by primitive law. And here as before, mere efflux of time does not bring it to pass that the right of trade, which does not partake of the nature of ownership, becomes a private possession. Now in this case neither title nor good faith can be shown, and inasmuch as good faith is clearly absent, according to legal rules prescription will not be called a right, but an injury.

Nay, the very possession involved in trading seems not to have arisen out of a private right, but out of a public right which belongs equally to all; so on the other hand, because nations perhaps neglected to trade with the East Indies, it must not be presumed that they did so as a favor to the Portuguese, but because they believed it to be to their own best interests. But nothing stands in their way, when once expediency shall have persuaded them, to prevent them from doing what they had not previously done. For the jurists have handed down as incontestable the principle that where things arbitrable or facultative are such that they produce nothing more than the facultative act *per se*, but do not create a new right, that in all such cases not even a thousand years will create a title by prescription or custom. This, as Vasquez points out, acts both affirmatively and negatively. For I am not compelled to do what I have hitherto done of my own free will, nor am I compelled to stop doing what I have never done.

What moreover could be more absurd then to deduce from the fact that we as individuals are not able always to conclude a bargain with other individuals, that there is not preserved to us for the future the right of bargaining with them if opportunity shall have offered? The same Vasquez has also most justly said that not even the lapse of infinite time establishes a right which seems to have arisen from necessity rather than choice.

Therefore in order to establish a prescriptive right to the trade with the East Indies the Portuguese would be compelled to prove coercion. But since in such a case as this coercion is contrary to the law of nature and obnoxious to all mankind, it cannot establish a right. Next, that coercion must needs have been in existence for so long a time that 'the memory of its beginning does not exist'; that, however, is so far from being the case that not even a hundred years had elapsed since the Venetians controlled nearly the entire trade with the East Indies, carrying it via Alexandria. Again, the coercion ought to have been such that it was not resisted; but the English and the French and other nations besides, did resist it. Finally, it is not sufficient that *some* be coerced, but it is indispensable that *all* be coerced, because the possession of freedom of trade is preserved to all by a failure to use coercion upon even one person. Moreover, the Arabians and the Chinese are at the present day still carrying on with the people of the East Indies a trade which has been uninterrupted for several centuries.

Portuguese usurpation is worthless.

15 TWELVE YEARS' TRUCE BETWEEN SPAIN AND THE UNITED NETHERLANDS, SIGNED AT ANTWERP ON 9 APRIL 1609

Introduction

The full treaty of Antwerp and its accompanying instruments may be found in the original French in Dumont, Vol. V, part 2, pp. 99–102. Only the first five (out of thirty-eight) clauses of the open treaty, and the secret treaty, pertain to the global settlement and are presented here. Misleadingly short and simple they form the tip of an iceberg that conceals more than it reveals. For this reason, we also reproduce certain auxiliary texts. The first document is in the nature of what in legal terms is called 'travaux préparatoires' or 'preliminary discussions', as reported, three weeks before the conclusion of the Truce, by Pierre Jeannin, a French delegate at Antwerp (he was also King Henri IV of France's adviser and President of the Parlement of Burgundy) to the States General of the United Provinces (the 'Lord States'); the account consists of exchanges of view with the 'Lord Archdukes' – that is, Albert and Isabella Clara Eugenia, the rulers of the southern provinces of the Low Countries (today's Belgium) who also represented the King of Spain (the 'Lord King'). The present discussion centres around Article IV of the draft, with the Spanish side trying to keep the Dutch out of Spanish 'places', i.e. the Indies, the real bone of contention. Only here do we find the word 'Indies' used. It does not even appear in the Secret Treaty, so sensitive was the issue.

The King of Spain had been petitioned by Portuguese interests to expel the Dutch from 'forbidden regions' where, thanks to the state of war, the Dutch East India Company was making serious inroads, especially in the East Indies; he was also concerned over active Dutch trade with Guiana, Brazil, etc.[1] In fact, Dutch traders were not keen for peace, because profits rose when trade was carried on armed vessels. But the Grand Pensionary Oldenbarnevelt was for a respite in the hostilities, and the Truce was signed. The Truce lasted twelve years, as stated, but some of its other stipulations had a far more permanent effect on the world.

The provisions of the open treaty are as follows:

1. In England, too, the lure of Guianian gold (Eldorado) attracted Sir Walter Raleigh who led two expeditions, in 1595 and 1616 (he was prisoner in the Tower of London in the interim). Raleigh lost a son on the second try, and his clashes with Spain, with whom James I (Elizabeth's successor) wished friendship, led to his beheading in 1618, on orders of the King.

(1) Spain implicitly acknowledges the independence of the United Provinces. (*Travaux préparatoires* for this *de facto* acknowledgement had taken the Dutch the best part of 1607 to accomplish. *De jure* recognition would have been preferable, but Spain wanted to trade it for exclusion of the Dutch from traffic in the Indies, which the States were not prepared to accept. Full recognition was not achieved until 1648).

(2) A Twelve Years' Truce is agreed upon.

(3) The two parties to enjoy the places now under their respective control.

(4) Reciprocal agreement that each party must have the other's permission to trade in places where the other has monopoly rights from a local potentate. Absolute freedom of trade is granted everywhere else, and this is the lasting achievement of the Truce.

(5) Truce to come into effect in a year's time to allow news to reach far away places.

The Secret Treaty reiterates Article IV in more detail, though it still evades the crucial word 'Indies', at Spain's request, using instead the euphemism 'beyond the limits'.

The Certificate of the ambassadors recognises the States' right to come to the aid of friends and allies in the East when the latter are molested, without this being seen as a violation of the Truce. This was one additional major consequence of the agreements: the abandonment of the Tordesillas system of closure of the oceans to all but Iberian traffic.

Sources: The following translations from the French (except Articles I and V of the Truce) are extracts from 'British Guiana Boundary, Arbitration with the United States of Venezuela: Appendix to the Counter-case on behalf of her Britannic Majesty', Foreing Office print (1898), pp. 319–24. This arbitration was based on the Treaty of Washington (February 1897) that resolved the Venezuelan dispute between the United States and Britain. The final award (October 1899) confirmed the boundary of British Guiana proper.

Articles I and V are translated by Sylvia Modelski from F. G. Davenport's *European Treaties bearing on the History of the United States and its Dependencies to 1648* (Washington, D.C.: Carnegie), 1917, Vol. 1, pp. 266–7.

Text

Brief Account of What Passed Between the Ambassadors at Antwerp Upon the Subject of the Truce; Laid Before the States General by M. Jeannin, March 18 1609, in the Name of the Kings of France and of Great Britain

[President Richardot, member of the Archdukes' delegation] . . . told us that it was sufficient that the Truce should be general in all parts, without distinction of places or persons, as is contained in . . . article [IV]. And with regard to commerce, that it should be limited and restricted, so far as concerned the kingdoms and countries of the King of Spain, to Spain and the countries which it holds in Italy. Since with regard to the localities, places, ports, and harbours, which belong to him beyond the said countries and even in the Indies, he by no means intended to allow the said trade there; and with regard to the other places which do not belong to him, he had no desire to hinder you and your subjects from trading there if you wished to do so; they offering in the name of the said Lord King to make a private treaty which should contain their consent, of which treaty, a draft whereof he had made according to his views, he then gave us a copy.

We replied that since the truce was to be general and therefore in the Indies as well as elsewhere, it was quite reasonable to also make trade free and general, without excepting any localities, places, and ports, that the said Lord King holds in the Indies or elsewhere than in Spain and Italy. But they replied that your subjects have never traded in the places and ports which they have in the Indies, and that in negotiating the Peace you had neither claimed to have done so. And that it was quite sufficient that the King of Spain consented not to obstruct in any way the trade that you might carry on everywhere else in the countries and States of the princes and peoples who will permit you to do so; a thing which he has hitherto been unwilling to grant the Kings of France and England by the treaties of peace made with them; so that if they go there, it is at the peril of themselves and their fortunes.

We thereupon told them again that you would rather go there in the same manner [any way? '*de même façon*'] and with hostility than to have your free will restrained in such a fashion as they desire: but they made answer that the hostility of the other nations was less inconvenient and harmful to them than yours, since the others do not go thither with armies and large fleets as do your merchants, but stealthily, and with only two or three ships.

We added again that neither was it reasonable to restrict commerce along the coast of Europe to the possessions of the King of Spain in the kingdoms of Spain and Italy; but that it should be extended, say, throughout Europe generally, to the Straits of Gibraltar, the Barbary Coasts, those of the Mediterranean Sea, and to the Canary Isles, especially since the subjects of the Kings and Princes who are friends and allies of the said Lord King may trade there as they please.

Having adjourned in order to see what they had written, and to give them an answer at the next meeting, we found that the draft was not worded in such a way as your security required, and we made another which was rejected by them, then a second which they would also not accept, since we made express mention of the Indies; they saying to us that the King of Spain was indeed willing to consent to this commerce in the said places, but without expressing it: so that the other kings and princes with whom he is in alliance and friendship may have no reason to make him the same demand in favour of their subjects. Also that it would be less humiliation and vexation to him to suffer and overlook the commerce, having granted it by general phrases and circumlocutions than by mention of the word

Indies. Adding also that there were other considerations concerning the interests of the King of Spain, not causing you, my Lords, any harm, which induced them to take this line of conduct, and that it should be sufficient for you that you enjoyed full security and freedom. At length, after various discussions upon this article, carried on and continued in two separate conferences, we resolved to draw up another document which seemed to us to determine and elucidate pretty clearly this commerce of the Indies, although the word was not expressed in it, on condition that it should be put into the general treaty in the place of the article concerning commerce, we being of opinion that it would be more authentic and secure than to make a separate treaty of it. We told them nevertheless that we did not intend to oblige you to approve of it, since we had neither instructions nor power, but that it was only our intention to let you see it and to refer the whole to your judgement.

We afterwards told them that since the Truce could not commence so soon in the said places as on the European side it was necessary to add to the article in question, another which serves to greatly elucidate it, and to show that the trade outside the limits there determined can only refer to that of the Indies.

* * *

This is what passed at our conferences, of which having informed the Kings our Masters, in order to have their opinion thereupon and to lay the same before you at the same time as we make you this report, they sent us word that they did not expect that it would obtain the consent of the King of Spain, who has caused it to be published everywhere that he would never agree to the article of freedom as it stands in our draft, nor to the commerce of the Indies; that they also did not think that the Archdukes, whose subjects are greatly interested in the trade of the country, would be willing to agree to the article concerning commerce precisely as it is set down in our draft: but that, since they have agreed to it and signed it, as well as all the other articles, except that of the contributions, and since they seem also to be willing to agree to a term of twelve years for the duration of the Truce, their Majesties regard matters as being, at present, in such a good condition that you may conclude and pass this Treaty with safety and great profit.

Although the article relating to the Indies, as it is inserted in the treaty of which they have seen a copy, is in their opinion so well and intelligently expressed that it can give rise to no ambiguity nor wrong interpretation to your disadvantage, if there be taken in conjunction therewith the following article, in which it is said that the Truce shall not commence outside Europe and the other limits determined in the preceding one, until one year after the Treaty, in order to afford time to warn the forces which are now there not to commit any act of hostility, which article can only be understood to refer to the Indies, and for which reason they made difficulties for a very long time about agreeing to it, and we obtained it only at the moment of our departure, as has been said above. Yet our Kings have nevertheless still further charged us to inform you that in order to content and reassure those who might raise any difficulty, they offer to bind themselves by the Treaty which shall contain the guarantee of the Truce, that in case you are molested and obstructed in the said commerce with the Indies, they will regard the Truce as violated and will render you such assistance as shall be obligatory upon them, in the same way as if it were violated and broken in all the other articles of the Treaty.

We therefore beg and exhort you in their name not to indulge further in vain disputes and replies which only lead to a useless waste of time: you have already lost too much of the latter. Delay and hesitation is very harmful to you; it causes you to distrust each other and might finally divide your State and cause it to be broken up into factions: instead of which a prompt resolution will unite you all and make known to everyone that, although you have been divided in your opinions, your intentions have always been the same and that you have all had only one aim and design, to wit, that of preserving your country.

You will never meet with such a combination of circumstances to aid you in obtaining an advantageous treaty as at present. The Archdukes are lovers of peace. The King of Spain submits to conditions which he would undoubtedly reject were it not out of consideration to them. Two great Kings, whose friendship endeavours have been made to alienate from you, have remained firm and constant in their first affection, and have had between them but one opinion in the conduct of this affair, and have moreover clearly shown that they in no way desire to abandon the care of your preservation; and all these considerations together have been those which have induced or rather constrained the Princes who are treating with you to consent to this agreement. The greatest prudence in affairs of importance is to take advantage of opportunity and to remember that within a short time such changes may take place in the instability of human things and of men's wills as may render impossible what was easy before.

Twelve Years' Truce Between Spain and the United Netherlands Signed at Antwerp, on April 9 1609

I. Firstly, the said Lords Archdukes declare in their own names as well as in that of the said Lord King, that they are happy to negotiate with the said Lords of the States General of the United Provinces by virtue of their capacity as representatives of countries, provinces, and free states, over which they lay no claim whatsoever, and to achieve with them . . . a truce, on the following written and declared conditions.

II. To wit: that the said Truce shall be good, valid, loyal, and inviolable and for the period of twelve years, during which there shall be a cessation of all acts of hostility of what kind soever between the said Lords King and Archdukes, and States General, as well by sea and other waters as by land in all their realms, countries, lands, and lordships, and in respect of all their subjects and inhabitants of whatever quality and condition they may be without exception of places or of persons.

III. Each party shall remain seised of and shall enjoy effectually the countries, towns, places, lands, and lordships which he holds and possesses at present, without being troubled or disquieted therein in any manner whatever during the said Truce, in which are understood to be included the market towns, villages, hamlets, and country lands appertaining thereto.

IV. The subjects and inhabitants of the countries of the Said King, Archdukes, and States shall have entire good correspondence and friendship together during the said Truce, without bearing in mind the offences and losses they have suffered in the past; they may also frequent and stay in each others territory, and there carry on their trade and commerce in all security, as well as by sea and other waters as by land; but this always the aforesaid King understands to be restricted and limited to the realms, countries, lands, and lordships which he holds and possesses in Europe and other places and seas where the subjects of Kings and Princes who are his friends and allies allow the said traffic by mutual agreement – and with regard to places, towns, ports, and havens which he holds outside the limits above mentioned – that the said States and their subjects cannot carry on any trade there without the express permission of the said King. – However, they can carry on the said trade if they think fit to do so, in countries of all other Princes, Potentates, and peoples who may be willing to allow it, even outside the said limits, without the said King, his officers and subjects dependent on him, offering any hindrance on that account to the said Princes, Potentates, and peoples who have allowed, or shall allow, it to them; or similarly to those or to private persons with whom they have carried on, and shall carry on, the said trade.

V. And since a fairly long time is needed to notify those who are outside the said limits and have arms and ships that they should desist from all hostile acts, it has been agreed that the truce will only begin a year from today. Of course, should the news of the said truce arrive sooner, then hostilities will cease immediately, but if after the said space of one year some hostility is committed therein, damages will be paid without fail.

Private and Secret Treaty, Which the Deputies of the States Demanded of the King of Spain, and Which has Been Granted Them in the Following Form

Whereas by the fourth article of the Treaty of the Truce made this same day between His Majesty the Catholic King and the Most Serene Archdukes of Austria on the one hand, and the Lords, the States General of the United Provinces on the other, the commerce accorded to the said Lords States and to their subjects has been restricted and limited to the kingdoms, countries, lands, and lordships which the said Lord King has in Europe and elsewhere, in which it is permissible for the subjects of the Kings and Princes who are his friends and allies to carry on the said commerce at their pleasure; and whereas the said Lord King has moreover declared that he had no intention of obstructing in any way the trade and commerce which the said Lords States and their subjects may carry on hereafter in whatever country and place it may be, either by sea or by land, with the potentates, peoples and private individuals who may permit them to do so, or likewise those who shall carry on the said trade with them, which however has not been couched in writing in the said Treaty; now therefore, on this ninth day of April, one thousand six hundred and nine, which is that on which the said truce was agreed to, their lordships the Marquess Spinola, President Richardot, Mancidor, Friar Jean de Neyen and Verreiken, in the name and as deputies of the said Lord King and Archdukes, by virtue of the same power granted them and under the same promise to have this present document ratified in due and proper form together with and at the same time as the General Treaty, have promised, and do promise, in the name of the said Lord King and of his successors during the time that the said truce shall last, that His Majesty will not obstruct in any way, either by sea or by land, the said Lords States or their subjects in the trade which they may carry on hereafter in the countries of all princes, potentates, and peoples who may permit them to do so, in whatever place it may be, *even beyond the limits*[1] determined above and anywhere else, or likewise those who shall carry out all the above in good faith, so that the said trade may be free and secured to them, consenting even, in order that the present document may be more authentic, that it be regarded as inserted and forming part of the principal Treaty. To which the said Lords Deputies of the States have agreed.

1. I.e., in the Indies; those were the crucial words worked so hard to secure in these negotiations.

Certificate of the Ambassadors of France and England Concerning the Matter of the Limits and the Commerce of the Indies

We, the undersigned Ambassadors of His Most Christian Majesty and the King of Great Britain hereby declare to all whom it may concern, that by the third article of the Treaty made this day between the Deputies of the Lords, Archdukes, and States General of the United Provinces, it has been agreed on both sides, and has been so understood by us, that what the said Lords States have in Brabant and in Flanders, as well as in the other provinces which they enjoy, shall remain theirs in full right of superiority, including the marquisate of Bergen-op-zoom, the baronies of Breda, Graves, and all that is bound up and united with the boroughs, villages, and lands dependent therefrom. We also declare that the Deputies of the said Lords Archdukes have likewise consented and agreed that the said Lords States and their subjects shall not be able to trade at the ports, localities and places held by the Catholic King in the Indies, if he do not permit it; that it shall neither be lawful for his subjects to trade at the ports, localities, and places which the said Lords hold in the said Indies, except by their permission; and moreover that the Deputies of the said Lords have several times declared in our presence and in that of the Deputies of the Archdukes that if any attack be made upon their friends and allies in the said countries they intend to succour and assist them without allowing such a step to be claimed as an infraction and violation of the Truce.

Done at Antwerp this 9th day of April, 1609.

[Signed:]
P. Jeannin
Elie de la Place
Russy
Ri. Spencer
Rodolphe Winwood

16 THE JUDGEMENT OF THE SYNOD OF DORT

Text

Published by reading in Latin in the Great Church at Dort, 6 May 1619 (NS)

In attendance: the Reformed Belgique Churches, and many divines of note from Great Britain, county Palatine of Rhene, Hesse, Helvetia, correspondence of Weterav, Geneva, Breme, and Embden. Representatives of King James of Great Britain, Princes, Lantgraves, Commonwealths.)

First Chapter or Head Doctrine [Tenet]: Predestination

IV

Whosoever beleeve not these glad tydings, the wrath of God remaines upon them: but they which receive them, and embrace our Saviour Jesus with a true and lively faith, they are delivered by him from the wrath of God, and destruction, and eternal life is given them.

V

The cause, or fault of this unbeliefe, as of all other sinnes, is no wise in God, but in man. But faith in Jesus Christ, and salvation through him is the free gift of God, as it is written [Ephes. 2.8] . . . [Phil. 1.29] . . .

VI

But whereas in processe of time, God beastoweth faith on some, and not on others, this proceedes from his eternall decree. For 'from the beginning of the world God knoweth all his workes' [Acts 15.18. Ephes. 1.11]. According to which decree, he graciously softens the hearts of the elect, however otherwise hard, and as for those that are not elect, he in just judgement leaveth them to their malice and hardnesse.

And heere especially is discovered unto us the deepe, and both mercifull and just difference put between men, equally lost; that is to say, the decree of Election, and Reprobation, revealed in Gods Word. Which as perverse, impure, and wavering men doe wrest unto their owne destruction, so it affords unspeakable comfort to godly, and religious soules.

Sources: The First Chapter, or 'Doctrine of Predestination', is taken from an Englished version of the Latin text, printed in London by John Bill (1619) pp. 4–11. The 'Sentence' is reproduced from *The History of the Reformation and other Ecclesiastical Transactions in and about the Low-Countries*, by Rev. Gerard Brandt (London: Timothy Childe, 1721) Vol. II, pp. 301–3. Old spelling retained. (Excerpts.)

VII

Now Election is the unchangeable purpose of God, by which, before the foundation of the world, according to the most free pleasure of his will, and of his meere grace, out of all mankinde, fallen, through their owne fault, from their first integrity into sinne and destruction, he hath chosen in Christ unto salvation a set number of certaine men, neither better, nor more worthy than others, but lying in the common misery with others: which Christ also from all eternity he appointed the Mediator, and Head of all the Elect, and foundation of salvation; and so he decreed to give them to him to bee saved, and by his Word, and Spirit, effectually to call, and draw them to communion with him: that is, to give them a true faith in him, to justifie, sanctifie, and finally glorifie them, beeing mightily kept in the communion of his Sonne, to the demonstration of his mercy, and praise of the riches of his glorious grace, as it is written [Ephes. 1, 4, 5, 6] . . .

VIII

This election is not manifold, but one and the same all, which are to be saved, both under the old, & new Testament, because the Scripture speakes but of one only good pleasure, purpose, and counsell, of the will of God, by which hee hath chosen us from eternity both unto grace, and glory, both unto salvation, and the way of salvation, which he hath prepared, that we should walke therein.

IX

This sayd Election was made, not upon foresight of faith, and the obedience of faith, holinesse, or of any other good quality, or disposition (as a cause or condition before required in man to be chosen) but unto faith, and the obedience of faith, holinesse, &c. And therefore Election is the fountaine of all saving good from whence faith, holinesse, and the residue of saving gifts, lastly everlasting life itself doe flow, as the fruits, and effects thereof; according to that of the Apostle [Ephes. 1.4] . . .

X

The true cause of this free Election is the good pleasure of God, not consisting heerin, that from among all possible meanes, he chose some certaine qualities, or actions of men as a condition of salvation: but herein, that out of the common multitude of sinners he culled out to himselfe, for his owne peculiar, some certaine persons, or men, as it is written [Rom. 9.11] . . .

XI

And as God himselfe is most wise, unchangeable, omniscient, and omnipotent: so the Election made by him can neither be interrupted nor changed, revoked, or disanulled, the elect cast away, not their number diminished.

XII

Of this their eternall, and immutable election unto salvation, the elect, in their time (although by generall degrees, and in a different measure) are assured, and that, not by searching out roughly into the depths and secrets of God, but by observing themselves, with spirituall joy and holy pleasure, the infallible fruits of election, signed out unto us in Gods word, such as are, a true faith in Christ, a filliall feare of God, griefe for our sinnes according to God, hungring and thirsting after righteousnesse, &c.

XIII

Out of sense, & certainty of this election, the children of God dayly draw more and more matter of humbling themselves before God, of adoring the depth of his mercies, of purifying themselves, and of loving him fervently, who first loved them so much: so farre is this doctrine of election, & the meditation thereof, from making them carnally secure, backward in observing Gods commandements. Which abuse by Gods just judgement is wont to befall those, who either rashly presume, or vainly and malapartly prate of the grace of election, refusing withall to walke in the wayes of the elect.

XIV

And as this doctrine touching Gods election was by Gods appointment declared by the Prophets, Christ himselfe, and the Apostles, aswel under the old Testament, as the new, and afterwards commended to the records of holy Writ: so at this day in Gods Church (for which it is peculiarly ordeined) it is to bee propounded with the spirit of discretion, religiously, and holily in its place and time, without any curious searching into the wayes of the most High, and that to the glory of Gods most holy name, and lively comfort of his people.

XV

Moreover, the holy Scripture heerin chiefly manifests, and commends unto us this eternall and free grace of our election, in that it further witnesseth, that not all men are elected, but some not-elected, or passed over in Gods eternall election, whom doubtlesse God in his most free, most just, unreprooveable, and unchangeable good-pleasure hath decreed to leave in the common miserie (whereinto by their own defaults they precipitated themselves) and not to bestow saving faith, and the grace of conversion upon them, but leaving them in their own waies, and under just judgement, at last to condemne, and everlastingly punish them, not onely for their unbeleefe, but also for their owne sinnes, to the manifestation of his justice. And this is the decree of Reprobation, which in no wise makes God the author of sinne (a thing blasphemous once to conceive) but a feareful, unreproveable, and just Judge, and revenger.

XVI

Those, who as yet do not effectually perceive in themselves a lively faith, or a fine confidence of heart in Christ, the peace of conscience, an endevour of filial obedience, a glorying in God through Christ, and nevertheless use the meanes by which God hath promised, that he will work these things in us, such as these ought not be cast downe at the mention of Reprobation, nor reckon themselves amongst the reprobate, but must diligently go forward in the use of those means, & ardently desire, and humbly & reverently expect the good houure of more plentiful grace. Much lesse then ought those to be terrified with the doctrine of Reprobation, who, albeit they hartily desire to turne unto God, to please him onely, and bee delivered from this body of death, yet cannot make such progresse in the way of godlinesse, and faith, as they with. For our mercifull God hath promised that he will not quench the smoaking flaxe, nor breake the shaken reed: But to those, who forgetting God, and our Saviour Jesus Christ, have wholly enthralled themselves to the cares of the world, and pleasures of the flesh, this doctrine is not without cause terible, so long as they are not seriously converted unto God.

XVII

Seeing wee must judge of Gods will by his word, which testifies unto us that the children of the faithful are holy, not in their owne nature, but by benefit of the gracious covenant, wherein they together with their parents are comprised; godly parents ought not to doubt of the election and salvation of their children, whom God calls out of this life in their infancie.

XVIII

Whosoever murmures at this grace of free election, and severity of just Reprobation, we stop his mouth with that of the Apostle, Rom. 9.20, 'O man who are thou, that repliest against God?' . . .

Sentence

The Truth being thus far, thro' the mercy of God, explained and established, Error rejected and condemned, and all unjust Calumnies wiped off; there remains nothing more to be done by this Synod of Dort, than most seriously and conformably to that right and authority which, according to the Word of God, belongs to them over all the Members of their churches, to beseech, to warn, exhort, and charge, in the name of Christ, all and singular the Ministers of the churches throughout the United Netherlands, all Doctors, Rectors, and Governours in the Universities and Schools, and in general, all those to whom either the Care of Souls, or the Instruction of Youth is committed: That they forsake and abandon the well-known Five Articles of the Remonstrants as being false, and no other than secret magazine of Errors, and preserve this sound doctrine of saving Truth, drawn from the pure fountain of Holy Writ, unmired and inviolate to the utmost of their power, according to the duty of their office; that they faithfully and prudently instil the same into the minds of all people, both young and old; that they diligently explain the most comfortable and beneficial use thereof, both in life and death; that they gently instruct, by the bright rays of Truth, those which wander from the flock, which are of different opinions, being seduced by the Novelty of Doctrines, in hopes that God may one day give them repentance to the acknowledgement of the Truth; to the end, that they being come to a better mind, may return to the Church of God, and the Communion of the Saints, in one spirit, with one mouth, and with the same Faith and Charity; and that thus the wounds of the Church may at last be healed, and all the Members thereof become one heart and one soul in the Lord.

But whereas some, who are gone out from among us, calling themselves Remonstrants (which word, as well as that of Contraremonstrants, the Synod wills and requires to be buried in perpetual oblivion) have, out of private views and ends, unlawfully violated the discipline and government of the Church, and despised the exhortations and opinions of their Brethren, have presumed, in a violent and dangerous manner, to disturb the churches of these Provinces, which were formerly so flourishing and so strictly united in peace and love, by venting the above-mentioned doctrines; have not only trumped up old Errors, but hammered out new ones too, and have zealously promoted the same among the people both publickly and privately, both by word of mouth and in writing, have blackened and rendered odious the Established Doctrine of the Church, with impudent slanders and calumnies, without end or measure; have filled all places with scandal, discord, scruples and troubles of conscience; all which heinous offences committed against the Faith, against Charity, against Good manners, against the Unity and Peace of the Church, as they ought by no means to be endured in any persons whatever, so ought they to be restrained and punished in Clergymen with the severest censures, as has likewise been the practice of the Church in all ages: THEREFORE this National Synod, after having invoked the most holy name of God, being assured of its own authority, as grounded in his word, treading in the footsteps of all the ancient and modern lawful Synods, and lastly, being supported by the authority of the High and Mighty Lords of the States General, does hereby declare and determine, that those Ministers who have acted in the churches as Heads of Factions and Teachers of Errors, are guilty and convicted of having violated our holy Religion, of having made a rent in the Unity of the Church, and given very great scandal; and as for those who were cited before this Synod, that they are besides guilty of intolerable disobedience to the commands of the supreme Powers promulgated in this Synod, and to those of the venerable Synod itself: for all which reasons the Synod does, in the first place, discharge the aforesaid cited persons from all ecclesiastical Administration, and deprives them of their Offices; judging them likewise unworthy of any academical employment, till such time as they shall have given full satisfaction to the Church by their sincere repentance, appearing by contrary words, actions, and endeavours; as when being really and fully reconciled to the Church, they shall be re-admitted to her Communion. All which we heartily wish for their good, and for the joy of the whole Church, thro' our Lord Jesus Christ. And as for the rest of the Remonstrant Clergy, whose case has not come under the cognizance of this National Synod, they are hereby recommended to the Provincial Synods, Classes, and Consistories, conformably to the established Order; who are to take the utmost care, that the Church suffer no prejudice either now or hereafter; that the Patrons of Error be prudently discovered; that all obstinate, clamorous, and factious Disturbers of the Church under their jurisdiction be forthwith deprived of their Ecclesiastical and Academical offices; and they the said Provincial Synods, etc. are therefore exhorted, as soon as they shall have received the Sentence of this National Synod, and obtained leave from the Civil Magistrate, to meet together without delay, least the evil gather strength by missing this opportunity. They are further exhorted to endeavour to bring back to a true and entire Unity with the Church, in all meekness, gentleness, and charity, all such who doubt, and perhaps differ in small matters, and yet are men of quiet, peaceable, and unblameable lives, and ready to be better informed; yet so as to take a particular care, that they admit none into the Ministry who shall refuse to subscribe, or promise to preach the Doctrine asserted in these Synodical Decrees; and that they suffer none to continue in the Ministry, by whose publick dissent the Doctrine which has been so unanimously approved by all Members of this Synod, the Harmony of the Clergy, and the Peace of the Church, may be again disturbed. This venerable Synod does further most earnestly exhort all Ecclesiastical Assemblies diligently to watch over the flocks committed to their charge, and timely to oppose all innovations endeavoured to be introduced into the Church, and to extirpate them as tares and weeds out of the Lord's Field; to keep a watchful eye over the Schools and their Masters or Regents, to the end that the youth be not infected with strange notions and opinions, which may hereafter become dangerous and destructive to the Church and Commonwealth. Finally, this Synod returns thanks in the most respectful manner to their High Mightinesses the States General of the United Netherlands for their so seasonable and necessary assistance, graciously afforded to the Church in her deplorable and sinking condition, by the remedy of a Synod, and for taking into their protection the faithful Ministers of the Lord, and for the holy and solemn Resolutions by them taken of preserving the sacred Pledge of the Divine Presence, and all other heavenly blessings, that is to say, the Truth of God's Word in these Provinces, and for having spared no pains nor costs for promoting and perfecting so great a work; for all which favours this Synod does most heartily wish their High Mightinesses an abundant recompense from the Lord, both publick and private, both spiritual and temporal. And they most earnestly and humbly beseech the same gracious God, that their High Mightinesses may suffer and ordain this wholesome doctrine, which the Synod has faithfully expressed according to the Word of God, and the Harmony of the Reformed churches, to be maintained alone and in its purity within their Provinces; that they may oppose growing heresies, and restrain turbulent and unruly spirits; that they may henceforwards shew themselves true and beneficient Foster-fathers and Defenders of the Church; and that they may likewise put in execution the Sentence pronounced against the above-mentioned persons, conformably to the authority and rights of the Church established by the laws of the Land, and ratify and confirm the Decrees of the Synod by their authority.

17 NAVIGATION ACT, 9 OCTOBER 1651

Introduction

The Navigation Act was passed by Cromwell's Commonwealth government but reenacted in 1660 upon the restoration of the monarchy in England. In its new form, the Act introduced the practice of enumerating certain colonial products, such as sugar, indigo and tobacco, which could be shipped directly only to England or to another English colony. The enumeration was abandoned in 1822, and the Act itself repealed in 1849 and 1854.

The Navigation Act marked the start of a period of Anglo–Dutch conflict that was to last 30 years and included three major wars called the Trade Wars. The first of these wars (1652–4) was a direct result of this Act. The second Trade War (1665–7) began after the English captured New Amsterdam (New York). The war of 1672–4 formed part of the wider European war of 1672–8.

Text

For the Increase of the Shipping and the Encouragement of the Navigation of this Nation, which under the good Providence and Protection of God, is so great a means of the Welfare and Safety of this Commonwealth; Be it Enacted by this present Parliament, and the Authority thereof. That from and after the First day of December, One thousand six hundred fifty and one, and from thence forwards, no Goods or Commodities whatsoever, of the Growth, Production or Manufacture of Asia, Africa or America, or of any part thereof; or of any Islands belonging to them, or any of them, or which are described or laid down in the usual Maps or Cards of those places, as well of the English Plantations as others, shall be Imported or brought into this Commonwealth of England, or into Ireland, or any other Lands, Islands, Plantations or Territories to this Commonwealth belonging, or in their Possession, in any other Ship or Ships, Vessel or Vessels whatsoever, but onely in such as do truly and without fraud belong onely to the People of this Commonwealth, or the Plantations thereof, as the Proprietors or right Owners thereof; and whereof the Master and Mariners are also for the most part of them, of the People of this Commonwealth, under the penalty of the forfeiture and loss of all the Goods that shall be Imported contrary to this Act; as also of the Ship (with all her Tackle, Guns and Apparel) in which the said Goods or Commodities shall be so brought in and Imported; the one moyety to the use of the Commonwealth, and the other moyety to the use and behoof of any person or persons who shall seize the said Goods or Commodities, and shall prosecute the same in any Court of Record within this Commonwealth.

And it is further Enacted by the Authority aforesaid, That no Goods or Commodities of the Growth, Production or Manufacture of Europe, or of any

Source: Firth, Sir Charles Harding, and Robert Sangster Rait, *Acts and Ordinances of the Interregnum 1642–1660* (London: HMSO, 1911) Vol. II (1649–60), pp. 559–62.

part thereof, shall after the First day of December, One thousand six hundred fifty and one, be imported or brought into this Commonwealth of England, or into Ireland, or any other Lands, Islands, Plantations or Territories to this Commonwealth belonging, or in their possession, in any Ship or Ships, Vessel or Vessels whatsoever, but in such as do truly and without fraud belong onely to the people of this Commonwealth, as the true Owners and Proprietors thereof, and in no other, except onely such Forein Ships and Vessels as do truly and properly belong to the people of that Countrey or Place, of which the said Goods are the Growth, Production or Manufacture, or to such Ports where the said Goods can onely be, or most usually are first shipped for Transportation; And that under the same penalty of forfeiture and loss expressed in the former Branch of this Act, the said Forfeitures to be recovered and imployed as is therein expressed.

And it is further Enacted by the Authority aforesaid, That no Goods or Commodities that are of Forein Growth, Production or Manufacture, and which are to be brought into this Commonwealth, in Shipping belonging to the People thereof, shall be by them Shipped or brought from any other place or places, Countrey or Countreys, but onely from those of their said Growth, Production or Manufacture; or from those Ports where the said Goods and Commodities can onely, or are, or usually have been first shipped for Transportation; and from none other Places or Countreys, under the same penalty of forfeiture and loss expressed in the first Branch of this Act, the said Forfeitures to be recovered and imployed as is therein expressed.

And it is further Enacted by the Authority aforesaid, That no sort of Cod-fish, Ling, Herring, Pilchard, or any other kinds of salted Fish, usually fished for and caught by the people of this Nation; nor any Oyl made, or that shall be made of any kinde of Fish whatsoever; nor any Whale-fins, or Whale-bones, shall from henceforth be Imported into this Commonwealth, or into Ireland, or any other Lands, Islands, Plantations, or Territories thereto belonging, or in their possession, but onely such as shall be caught in Vessels that do or shall truly and properly belong to the people of this Nation, as Proprietors and Right Owners thereof: And the said Fish to be cured, and the Oyl aforesaid made by this people of this Commonwealth, under the penalty and loss expressed in the said first Branch of this present Act; the said Forfeit to be recovered and imployed as is there expressed.

And it is further Enacted by the Authority aforesaid, That no sort of Cod, Ling, Herring, Pilchard, or any other kinds of Salted Fish whatsoever, which shall be caught and cured by the people of this Commonwealth, shall be from and after the First day of February, One thousand six hundred fifty three, exported from any place or places belonging to this Commonwealth, in any other Ship or Ships, Vessel or Vessels, save onely in such as do truly and properly appertain to the people of this Commonwealth, as Right Owners; and whereof the Master and Mariners are for the most part of them English, under the penalty and loss expressed in the said first Branch of this present Act; the said Forfeit to be recovered and imployed as is there expressed.

Provided always, That this Act, nor any thing therein contained, extend not, or be meant to restrain the Importation of any of the Commodities of the Straights or Levant Seas, loaden in the Shipping of this Nation as aforesaid, at the usual Ports or places for lading of them heretofore, within the said Straights or Levant Seas, though the said Commodities be not of the very Growth of the said places.

Provided also, That this Act nor any thing therein contained, extend not, nor be meant to restrain the Importing of any East-India Commodities loaden in the Shipping of this Nation, at the usual Port or places for Lading of them heretofore in any part of those Seas, to the Southward and Eastward of Cabo Bona Esperanza, although the said Ports be not the very places of their Growth.

Provided also, That it shall and may be lawful to and for any of the People of this Commonwealth, in Vessels or Ships to them belonging, and whereof the Master and Mariners are of this Nation as aforesaid, to load and bring in from any of the Ports of Spain and Portugal, all sorts of Goods or Commodities that have come from, or any way belonged unto the Plantations or Dominions of either of them respectively.

Be it also further Enacted by the authority aforesaid, That from henceforth it shall not be lawful to any person or persons whatsoever, to load or cause to be loaden and carried in any Bottom or Bottoms, Ship or Ships, Vessel or Vessels whatsoever, whereof any Stranger or Strangers born (unless such as be Denizens or Naturalized) be Owners, part Owners, or Master, any Fish, Victual, Wares, or things of what kinds or nature soever the same shall be, from one Port or Creek of this Commonwealth, to another Port or Creek of the same, under penalty to every one that shall offend contrary to the true meaning of this Branch of this present Act, to forfeit all the Goods that shall be so laden or carried, as also the Ship upon which they shall be so laden or carried, the same Forfeit to be recovered and imployed as directed in the first Branch of this present Act.

Lastly, That this Act nor any thing therein contained, extend not to Bullion, nor yet to any Goods taken, or that shall be taken by way of Reprizal by any Ship or Ships, having Commission from this Commonwealth.

Provided, That this Act, or any thing therein contained, shall not extend, nor be construed to extend to any Silk or Silk-wares which shall be brought by Land from any parts of Italy, and there bought with the proceed of English Commodities, sold either for Money or in Barter; but that it shall and may be lawful for any of the People of this Commonwealth to ship the same in English Vessels from Ostend, Newport, Roterdam, Middleburgh, Amsterdam, or any Ports thereabouts; the Owners and Proprietors first making Oath by themselves, or other credible Witness, before the Commissioners of the Customs for the time being, or their Deputies, or one of the Barons of the Exchequer, that the Goods aforesaid were so bought for his or their own proper accompt in Italy.

18 COLBERT'S *'MEMOIRE SUR LE COMMERCE'*

Introduction

Minutes of the first meeting of the Council of Trade held by King Louis XIV at Fontainebleau, Sunday 3 August 1664.

England and France had been instrumental in bringing about the Truce of Antwerp (Doc. 15) which sanctioned Dutch free access to the ocean and to the East. The Dutch succeeded so well in supplanting the Portuguese and the Spaniards as the premier naval and trading power in the world, that they provoked the jealousy and anger of their erstwhile friends. Britain retaliated with the Navigation Act of 1651 (Doc. 17), and France decided to reconstruct her navy and economy to the point where she could challenge the United Provinces.

Jean-Baptiste Colbert (1619–83), dubbed 'the protector of merchants', was Louis XIV's Finance Minister and the architect of France's global bid. His first initiative in this direction was the creation of the Council of Trade (*Conseil de Commerce*) which remained very busy from 1665 to 1669, implementing the measures outlined in the present *mémoire.* In this document, Colbert stresses the need to establish commerce as an honourable activity in the minds of both the King and the French people and clearly sets out the main points of his trade policy in a classic exposition of the mercantilist view of economic affairs (as was England's Navigation Act).

Text

Sire, since it pleases Your Majesty to devote a few hours of your attention to the restoration, or rather, to the establishment of new commerce in your realm, given that it is a question that concerns solely the good of your subjects, and can bring no profit whatsoever to Your Majesty except in terms of future expectations and that only after having produced abundance and riches for your peoples; indeed, the enterprise will have quite the opposite effect, entailing, as it will, not only Your Majesty's repugnance to listen to frequent talk on a subject that is disagreable enough in itself, but also the diminution of your revenues in the short run; Sire, it is certain that by this noble sacrifice of two things so important and dear to a King: time that could be spent in entertainments or in other more pleasurable pursuits, and revenues; by these unprecedented marks of your love for your peoples, Your Majesty will, without doubt, immeasurably increase the veneration and respect already present in their minds as well as the admiration of foreigners.

Source: *Lettres, Instructions et Mémoires de Colbert*, Pierre Clément (ed.) (Paris: Imprimerie Impériale, 1863) Vol. II, 2, Annexes: (Industrie, Commerce) pp. cclxiii–cclxxii. Translated from the French by Sylvia Modelski.

I think it not inappropriate, Sire, to first examine very briefly whether it is to Your Majesty's advantage to pursue this kind of business; I will then proceed to examine the state of commerce in your realm, or rather, the state in which you found it when you took on the responsibilities of government, since you have already promoted a strong movement towards its reestablishment through various measures.

The state of the great commerce

It is a certain fact, Sire, that in all the histories, both ancient and modern, there are no great and mighty states such as yours ever to have devoted themselves to trade.

Such ideas were produced in the minds of men only through want.

Before the fourteenth century, the concept of trade in the Ocean, and particularly in the Atlantic, Levant and South Seas, was unknown.

Only the Mediterranean enjoyed this advantage, and the historical record shows that the earliest towns to have begun to grow rich and powerful by this means were: Phocea, Sidon and Tyre.

Before the year 1480, the Venetians and Marseillais did all the great bulk of the trade: all the precious goods from India, the peppers, the sugars, the silks, and even the gold and silver came by caravan from the great Indies and Persia to Egyptian towns where they were taken by the Venetians and then in part by the Marseillais, and brought and retailed in Europe: this is what made the city of Venice powerful, it became the emporium for all this merchandise for Europe.

With the passage of time and by dint of diligence and zeal on their part, the inhabitants of Antwerp established, in their city, the mart for all parts of the North. There they brought all the merchandise they went to Venice to get; later, under the French banner, they began to travel to Egypt themselves and to other ports of call[1] in the Levant, to obtain the goods first-hand.

Such was the great commerce of Europe when, around the middle of the fifteenth century, the Portuguese resolved to attempt sailing around the cape of Good Hope; having achieved this objective, their King began to establish colonies on this side [of Africa], in the kingdom of the Congo, in Guinea and Angola; he assumed mastership over the Canary Islands and Cape Verde, and, having passed through the Straits, he founded the settlements of Mozambique, Melinde, which assured his dominion over all the African coast on both sides; and then, pushing his conquests further ahead, he established his colonies and at the same time his domination, and penetrated the Persian Gulf, at [. . . blank space] the mouth of the Red Sea; then he pressed his establishments upon the Mogul empire, at Diu; then he conquered, in the kingdom of Bijapur, on the Malabar coast, the famous station of Goa which he made the capital city of all the Portuguese dominions in the Levant.

And then they extended their colonies and at the same time their domination in the Gulf of Bengal, on the Coromandel coast.

This settlement and these conquests were fairly easy to achieve because powerful kings such as that of Persia, the great Mogul and others, seeing strangers coming into their countries and taking away their produce and manufactures with much more facility and in greater quantity than did the caravans, received them benignly, granted them favours, dealt with them and allowed them to establish themselves in their states under such advantageous conditions that they did not have to recognise any sovereign other than their king.

1. Alexandria, Sidon, Aleppo.

Until then, the Portuguese, in their navigation, had followed the shorelines and hadn't dared venture across those great expanses of water that stretch all the way from the Cape of Good Hope to China; but when, on their first voyage, they discovered the Molucca Islands where they found a prodigious abundance of excellent spices, and cloves and nutmeg among others, they thought they had found all the riches of the new world.

Following the Portuguese example, the Castilians too began various navigations and established several colonies.

These two nations had also discovered the West Indies.

And so, to avoid possible conflicts that might arise between them, Alexander VI, whom they had chosen as their arbitrator, drew that famous line across the terrestial globe and adjudged to the king of Castile all that was on the right of it, that is all of the West, and to the king of Portugal all that was on the left, that it all the East; and this famous division inspired Magellan to have the boldest and most extraordinary thought ever to occur in the mind of man.

Until Magellan, it was never believed that there were antipodes; in our religion, this opinion was even held to be a sort of heresy.

He had served the king of Portugal in the discovery of the Moluccas, which were then all that was richest in the Indies; but he was not too satisfied with Portugal's inadequate reward as measured against such a great and considerable service. These islands belonged to the king because they happened to be on the left-hand side of the line drawn by Alexander VI. Magellan took it upon himself to circumnavigate the world, to start a journey of conquest and discovery of islands on the right of the line; he brought his proposal to the king of Castile who gave him five vessels for this celebrated project. He set off, coasting along the whole length of south America, entered a gulf he found on his way, persevered and remained there three dogged months notwithstanding the obstacles of winds and rocks; and at last, after losing two vessels, he got through to the great South Sea that had never been navigated before him; he landed in the Moluccan Islands [Philippines] [*sic*], conquered one of them, led the assault on another's fortress, but was killed there. Eventually, one of these five vessels returned after three years, having circumnavigated the whole globe. It must be mentioned here that Columbus, the Florentine [*sic*], who discovered America for the king of Castile, came to King Louis XII of France with his project; but, having been treated as a madman here, he turned to the king of Castile who gave him the ships for these voyages.

Such was the state of this great commerce of all the east and west Indies when the crown of Portugal was united to that of Castile following king Dom Sebastian's death in Africa at the battle of Alcazar-Kebir, in which three kings died sword in hand. At the time of this union, it had been forty years [*sic*] already since the Dutch had withdrawn their allegiance to the Catholic king and they had made commerce a fundamental principle of their State, since, due to the situation of their country, the industry and thrift of the people, it was their only method of survival.

They found conditions in Europe propitious for this scheme: the Spaniards had universal monarchy[2] on their minds and coveted only Europe; and the French were immersed in civil and religious wars; they had their hands full trying to survive internally, and paid no attention to what was going on outside.

At sea, the Dutch were almost everywhere superior to the Spaniards, but what set the latter back in particular was that they could not sail freely along the Dutch coast to bring the Indian goods to the North, where the biggest markets were.

2. See pp. 178–9 below, Leibniz's concept of universal monarchy.

The town of Antwerp was still paying allegiance to the king of Spain, but the Dutch, who were superior at sea, had interrupted and almost completely ruined its commerce. The town of Amsterdam had drawn profit from this, and grown considerably. Then the Dutch realised that they could no longer easily acquire the goods from the Indies due to the union between the Portuguese and Castilian crowns. Hence, in 1598, they laid the first foundations of that famous east Indies company that has grown so much since that time that it is incomparably more powerful in the Indies than, generally speaking, the States, its sovereign, are in Europe; it declares and wages war against more great kings than does its mother country, and its assets were found to amount to 800 million [*sic*] at the last inventory taken of it.[3]

The English, imitating the Dutch, have formed a company for the same Indies, so that today, in those countries, the two nations professing the Catholic, Apostolic and Roman religion are totally beaten, and the two nations that are powerful there are heretic.

After this brief presentation of the great commerce that is the only one of considerable magnitude, mention must be made of the rest of the commerce which consists of:

The West Indies that send sugars, dyes, tobacco and cotton, in which Indies the French occupy various islands but where all the traffic is handled by the Dutch.

The Levant trade, which still barely survives via Marseilles, and which is totally ruined by the poor behaviour of the Nation's consuls who were established at the Levant staging posts as a consequence of the Capitulations agreed to with the great Lords.

The Baltic and North Sea trade, under full and peaceful Dutch control.

And the internal trade of the realm, which consists of the free traffic between all of the king's subjects, the recovery of manufactures, and the transportation of our produce and merchandise from port to port.

Arguments against, and for, a commercial policy

It only remains now to examine whether or not it would be advantageous to devote our energies to this reestablishment of commerce and to new initiatives in all areas never before attempted in this realm.

The arguments against are that powerful nations (the Roman republic and emperors, the kings of Asia, France and Spain) have never been diligent in trade; it follows that such application is characteristic of weak states;

The abundance and fertility of France, which restrains and prevents industry, and even thrift.

To navigate a French vessel still requires almost twice as many men and rations as it does a Dutch vessel; this saving will always bring them profit while it will ruin the French;

The prodigious power and perseverence of the Dutch in this matter, to which first priority is always given in their state, will easily afford them the means of ruining all those who would wish to meddle in it, say by buying in Europe and in the Indies all the merchandise that might possibly be used and selling it at even a considerable loss to ruin beginners;

That even if we succeeded in our efforts, bringing about the nearly complete ruination of the Dutch – since half of their vessels subsist through trade with

3. According to prices quoted on the Amsterdam Bourse, VOC's market value was of the order of 33 million florins around 1670 (Braudel 1984: pp. 224–8).

France – it cannot be in the King's interest to destroy a republic based on his help and protection and that of his predecessors;

That since this reestablishment of commerce poses a threat of ruin to them, it may force them into alliances with jealous crowns or crowns opposed to the King's greatness;

And finally, that with regard to possessing naval power itself, it is almost a matter of indifference to the King whether he owns it personally or has it entirely at His disposal through alliances with a republic such as this.

The arguments in favour of initiating the restoration and even the establishment of new commerce are that the reasons for the country's natural bounty – which stand in the way of industry and parsimony – are deep and seem very hard to overcome.

Things that are easy produce little or no glory and profits; the opposite is true of difficult things. If the King were to unite France's natural might to that which art and diligence in commerce can yield – one need only reflect briefly on the power of towns and States that have had but a fraction of this art and industry – it will be obvious that the King's greatness and might will increase prodigiously.

The difference in maritime costs could be made good by the convenience and protection afforded to French vessels in the ports of the realm, because Dutch ships come and go in their country [France] and pay their duties. The 50 sols per barrel tax so gloriously established by the King will eventually more than compensate the French for their greater expenditure in men and rations.

As for the ruin of the Dutch, these sorts of things never go to extremities. France today has not even 200 reasonably sound vessels in her ports; the Dutch had 16 000 in 1658. What is being considered is merely that the King, by his total dedication and protection within a period of eight to 10 years, should bring the number of ships owned by his subjects up to perhaps 2000. Dutch losses on this account will amount from perhaps 1200 to 1500; the other nations' losses will make up the rest. Thus it is not a question of ruin, but only of a very inconsiderable diminution in the numbers of their vessels.[4]

While the King's power on land is superior to all others in Europe, his sea power is inferior. This is the only way of equalising it everywhere.

The Dutch will quite clearly and quickly recognise that there is always something to be gained for their commerce and their State from the French alliance, and everything to lose with the others. The difficulties their Dutch east Indies company will meet, purchasing goods in the Indies and selling them in Europe, cannot be overcome without the might and protection of the King, and,

4. Five years later, in April 1669, Colbert was to write to Arnauld de Pomponne, the French ambassador to Holland: 'The maritime trade of the whole world is carried out with 20 000 vessels or thereabouts. In the natural scheme of things, each nation ought to have its share of it, proportionate to its power, the extent of its population and of its sea coasts. Out of the 20 000, the Dutch own 15 to 16 000, and the French 5 to 600 at the most. The King employs all sorts of methods which, he believes, will help bring this number closer to the natural figure that his subjects should have. If the Dutch did the same, one would hope that the result would be as His Majesty intends, that is to say, that they too will move closer to the natural number that should be due to them . . . It would even be very beneficial to His Majesty's service, if you applied your efforts to be informed on the number of vessels that are at present owned by the States and by all their subjects' (Clément, *Lettres* . . ., pp. 463–4; Pomponne replied in May 1669 that, aside from the very numerous small and one-masted ships of the coastal trade, the figure for the whole of the United Provinces was 6000 vessels; thus Colbert's estimate of 16 000 was much exaggerated, see Braudel, 1984, p. 190, n. 89).

should it be needed, even his financial help. And, as a last argument, while upholding the treaties with the Dutch, it seems that His Majesty is obliged to give priority to the welfare of his subjects over that of his allies.

France's domestic and foreign trade

Having discussed the reasons for and against the King's application to the restoration of commerce, it is now fitting to show in detail the state to which it had been reduced when His Majesty assumed his responsibilities.

Internal and coastal trade:

The manufactures of woollens and serges and other cloths of that quality, papermills, ironmongers, the silk industry, linens and soap works, and generally speaking all other manufacturing enterprises were and still are almost entirely ruined.

The Dutch have thwarted them all. They bring us these same goods and in exchange they extract from us the commodities needed for their own consumption and commerce; whereas, if the manufactures were properly restored, not only would we have them for our own use, so that they would be forced to bring us ready money that they now keep at home, but we would even have some surplus to send abroad which would, likewise, yield revenues in cash – which, in a word, is the sole objective of trade and the only means of increasing this State's greatness and power.

With regard to maritime trade, whether from port to port or in foreign countries, we know for a fact that even in the case of coastal traffic (since in all the harbors of the realm there are in all 200 to 300 vessels at most that belong to the King's subjects) the Dutch extract from the Kingdom, annually, – according to the detailed computations that have been made of this – four million *livres* for freight; in exchange, they take our produce; these commodities being absolutely essential to them, they would be compelled to pay us this very sum in cash, if we had enough ships to ply this port-to-port traffic ourselves.

The reason for the poor state of internal trade are:

The debts incurred by towns and communities. They inhibit communication from province to province and city to city, which is the basis of all commerce by the King's subjects;

The chicaneries provoked in the cities by these debts, which consumed the inhabitants;

The number of tolls levied everywhere on lands and rivers; the ruinous condition of public highways;

The horrible proliferation of officers;

Too much taxation on all produce;

Excessive and ill-fitting tariffs in the 'five big farms' [*cinq grosses fermes*, a regional customs unit encompassing most major northern provinces].

Piracies that have destroyed an infinite number of vessels.

And, in a word, indifference to the conservation and development of the manufactures, on the part of the King and his Council – which has trickled down to all subordinate officers.

Foreign trade

It is a fact that, barring a few vessels that go to the Levant from Marseilles, the realm engages in no foreign trade. To the point that, in the islands in America inhabited by Frenchmen, there are 150 Dutch ships that take care of all the traffic. They bring produce grown in Germany and goods manufactured in Holland; they bring home sugars, tobaccos, dyestuffs, paying import duties; then they have them processed into manufactured goods, pay export taxes and bring them to us. The annual value of goods of this quality is two million *livres* which is exchanged entirely for merchandise from us which they need; whereas, if we ourselves carried this trade from our islands, they would be obliged to pay us these two million in cash.

The gains from trade

Having thus briefly described the state of domestic and foreign trade, it will not be inappropriate to say a few words on the advantages of commerce.

I think it will be readily agreed that the greatness and power of a state hinges on the abundance of money.

On this principle, it is a fact that the kingdom exports annually 12 to 18 million *livres'* worth of its own produce (wines, spirits, iron, fruits, papers, textiles, hardware, silks, haberdashery) needed for consumption in foreign countries. These are our nation's reserves. We must work carefully to conserve them.

The Dutch and other foreigners wage a perpetual war against these assets; so far, they have been so successful that instead of that sum entering the realm in the form of ready money, resulting in prodigious profit, they bring us a variety of merchandise, either of their own manufacture, or goods they extract from foreign countries. Two thirds of the total sum can be accounted for in this way, so that only four, five or six million in cash enter the country annually.

This how they do it:

Maritime freight, from port to port	3 million
Merchandise from French islands	2 million
Beautiful cloths, for which they have aroused our curiosity, Indian goods, spices, sugars, etc	3 million
Commodities from the North and naval equipment	15 million

Furthermore, they always extract some of our manufactures (such as papers, soaps, woollens, silks, which are part of our 18 million *livres* of exports mentioned above) which would bring in cash if they were sent to other countries; instead of this, they not only deprive us of this gain, but even bring them to us in lieu of money in exchange for our needed commodities [*sic*].

Their zeal and our lack of intelligence have reached such a point that by using their nation's factors and representatives they have been able to establish themselves in all the kingdom's ports; and having become the masters of all sea trade, they have set the price for all the merchandise they buy and sell.

On this premise, the obvious conclusion is that the more we succeed in cutting back the profits extracted from the King's subjects by the Dutch and the consumption of the merchandise they supply us, the greater the increase in the amount of cash due to the realm in payment for our essential commodities, and the greatness, power and wealth of the State will grow commensurately.

We can draw the same conclusion with regard to trade in bonded goods, that is, goods which we ourselves would go and get in the east and west Indies to sell in the North where we could ourselves procure the materials necessary for our own shipbuilding, another element of greatness and power for the State.

Besides the benefits accruing from an increase in the supply of money in the realm, it is certain that manufactures will supply jobs for the million people now living in depressing idleness.

Furthermore, an equal number will find employment on the ships and at seaports.

And the almost infinite proliferation of vessels will also expand the greatness and power of the State.

Methods for stimulating trade

These, in my opinion, are the objectives towards which the King's devotion, goodness and love for his people must aim.

To achieve them, the following methods are proposed:

By decree of a council attended by His Majesty, let all the peoples know of the King's resolution, through circulars.

Let all those who have the honor of serving the King talk about and publicise the benefits that will accrue to his subjects therefrom;

The merchants who might come to court should be received with special marks of protection and goodwill;

They should be assisted in all matters pertaining to trade, and be received in audience by His Majesty's council on occasions when they have important business to discuss.

They should be invited to deputise a few of their number to always be part of the King's retinue;

Order should be given to the Grand Marshal of Lodgings to always reserve for them an honest abode at Court.[5]

In the absence of deputies, a person should be appointed who will have authority to maintain a correspondence with them, to receive their dispatches, their complaints, to present all their sollicitations and to inform them of all that was decided for their good and benefit.

All police regulations in the realm affecting the restoration of all manufactures should be revised.

An examination must be made of all entry and exit duty rates; goods to be manufactured or already manufactured should be tax exempt, manufacturers should get tax relief and a reduction made of 1 200 000 or 1 500 000 *livres* a year.

Every year a considerable sum should be used for the restoration of the manufactures and for the benefit of commerce, according to the decisions that will be taken in council.

The same applies to navigation: all those who will buy or build new vessels or who will make long voyages should get rewards;

Repair public highways and continue to cancel river tolls.

Start working again on the payment of communities' debts.

Work unceasingly to make navigable those rivers inside the realm that are not navigable.

Examine carefully sea communications between Guyenne (Aquitaine) and Burgundy.

Strongly support companies of the east and west Indies;

Arouse everyone's enthusiasm for commerce;

Report personally to the King all areas where merchants are interested;

Send a general message to all [?appointed] companies [*compagnies honoraires*] of the realm, their presidents and procurators-general, to inform them of the King's resolve and to order them, on behalf of the King, to take particular care in all their affairs;

Do the same for all provincial and city governors, all the mayors and magistrates, to inform them, with the directive that they should call an assembly of merchants to read the message in their presence;

5. A House of Commerce was set up at Court, but proved of ephemeral duration (Cole, 1964, Vol. I, p. 361).

In addition to all this, each council should examine the nature of one trade in particular, namely:

The Levant trade and the disorders caused by the Consuls, with a view to applying the appropriate remedy;

All that concerns the east and west Indies company;

Trade with the North, Archangel, Moscow, the Baltic Sea and Norway;

Tolls inside the kingdom;

Payment of the communities's debts;

Public highways;

Navigation on rivers and seas;

Manufactures;

Access to the sea ports, and the difficulties therein.

4 The Cooptation of England

For decades, the Dutch prospered because France and England were weak and disunited. But when, after 1650, these two countries put their respective houses in order, the United Provinces came under severe pressure. In a space of 22 years, between 1652 and 1674, England fought the Republic in three stubborn naval contests that came to be known as the Trade Wars because commercial principles (as represented by the Navigation Acts) became important issues in them. But they were really about sea power and ascendancy. On the whole, the Dutch fought well in these combats, though they knew that they really could not win. France engaged the Dutch only once in that time but when the attack did occur (1672) it brought the French troops to the gates of Amsterdam and set off a panic that was both commercial and political, and soon enough, a reversal of alliances. Even before the war (in which, to start with, England took part on the French side) was over, English opinion became alarmed by the growth in French power and pressed the King, Charles II, to enter an alliance with the Dutch. Charles's niece, Mary, second in line to the throne, married Prince William of Orange in November 1677. The marriage was arranged by Sir William Temple, British ambassador to Holland.

An offensive and defensive alliance between Britain and the United Provinces ensued the following year (Treaty of Westminster, Doc. 19). Among the signatories of this treaty were Heneage Finch, the earls of Danby and Arlington, all leaders of the Tory party who used fear of 'popery' to arouse feelings against France and the Whigs. The marriage and the alliance were the basis on which the succession in global leadership from the Dutch Republic to the United Kingdom was effected (Fraser, 1979, pp. 347–8).

Appearances aside, the succession was in fact a cooptation: the English were selected to leadership by the Dutch. It was William of Orange who recruited Britain for that position as a way of dealing with what was, in the first place, a Dutch problem, the ambitions of Louis XIV. The medium of cooptation was the Anglo–Dutch core alliance foreshadowed in the last cycle, and the occasion was the ascension of William and Mary to the throne of England.

At the invitation of a group of Whig and Tory leaders (Danby among them), William led the Dutch fleet in a landing of Anglo–Dutch troops in Torbay (Devon) in November 1688,[1] and seized power from Roman Catholic James II. The invaders sailed under the slogan 'I shall maintain' (the House of Orange motto) to which was added 'the Protestant religion and the liberties of England'. These two values animated the Declaration of Right (Doc. 21) that accompanied the Proclamation making the Prince and Princess of Orange King and Queen of England.

They are reiterated in the two important royal addresses we have selected (Docs 22; 27). But these latter speeches are more than expressions of principles, revealing, as they do, William's broader strategic aims. Topmost among his priorities was 'the necessity of assisting our allies', especially the States General that had already invoked the Treaty of Westminster in response to Louis XIV's declaration of war in November 1688 (Doc. 20). His other priority was the fitting out, and maintenance, of a fleet such as would 'make us entirely Masters of the Sea'. William assumed his responsibilities as King of Great Britain with a clear strategic design for leading a major alliance to victory. These strategies, of course, were for fighting the global war then unfolding. But they also aimed at establishing a position of leadership for England, both on sea, in alliance with the Dutch, and on land, through a general coalition.

'ARBITER OF THE WORLD'

The condition underlying this development was what England's Lord Chancellor[2] described as early as 1678 as 'the dangerous growth of the French monarchy' (quoted in Cobbett, 1809 . . . , Vol. IV, p. 961). The ambitions of Louis XIV in the Netherlands in particular, in fact on all of his frontiers, had begun to alarm the governments of Europe. Under the command of a capable monarch France asserted a desire for predominance, justified by the country's wealth, power, and location. But as Gottfried Leibniz pointed out in a memorandum entitled *The Project for the Conquest of Egypt* (1672, in Ranum, 1972, pp. 253–8) preponderance came in two varieties: on the one hand, there was 'universal monarchy', 'the desire to conquer by military might nations that are civilised but . . . bellicose', as in Europe and, on the other hand, 'a general administration or a sort of arbitration of things'.[3] That latter kind, Leibniz advised, might be attained by France becoming the arbiter in the Levantine trade, and thereby also the 'arbiter of the world',[4] whose functions he described in the terms of one who would be:

> the judge who settles all disagreements, to attract the entire world to himself, not only by his reputation for power but also by his reputation for wisdom, to sacrifice odious details to the public peace, to make [his country] into a sort of military school of Europe from which come forth illustrious warriors, to seduce the great families and the great geniuses by furnishing them with the means to unfurl their talents, finally to be the avenger of outraged justice, the head of Christendom, the delight of Europe, and of mankind.

It is this second kind of preponderance that we saw the King of Portugal seeking in his overseas policies. The Dutch came close to attaining it, and the British would (with the help of Dutch experience) achieve it: all three were 'maritime nations' as they were called by Leibniz, and as they were known at the time.

Universal monarchy, argued Leibniz, is less than ever possible among Christians but the second object, the 'universal arbitration of affairs' is 'more desirable in the eyes of the wise men than monarchy'. Leibniz here hit upon a basic distinction of political analysis, but even as universal monarchy was already becoming impracticable and irrational, leaders of great states continued to pursue it.

The *Project for the Conquest of Egypt* did not reach Louis XIV[6] who launched his attack upon the Dutch, with consequences exactly as predicted by Leibniz: 'it is a truth of elementary experience that every power which extends its boundaries awakens the suspicions of others and unites them all against it'. The campaign against the United Provinces later that year brought to power William of Orange who devoted the rest of his life to the building of coalitions of allies against France.

Soon after his successful 'descent on England', William stirred the Anglo–Dutch alliance into life. The first act was the April 1689 agreement for a joint naval strategy (Doc. 23) in which, as foreshadowed in the Treaty of Westminster, the Dutch assumed a secondary position on the sea and in respect of naval commands but compensated for that by taking up a greater burden of land warfare. This pact is the true start of Britain's two centuries of command over the sea.

The detailed arrangements for allied operations are an early instance of careful coordination and show considerable sensitivity to problems that might have arisen in the joint operations of forces that had behind them the memory of more than a century of cooperation but also, more recently, some two decades of mutual warfare. The question of command created considerable problems in the negotiations.

The naval treaty is also notable for revealing a novel development in British strategy. For the first time, a strong squadron, including 50 great ships, was being deployed in the Mediterranean. This is the beginning of the Mediterranean strategy at which the Dutch were experienced hands due to their struggles against Spain.

The broader coalition that came to be known as the Grand Alliance was first negotiated by (Dutch) emissaries of the King in Vienna (May 1689, Doc. 24) and was then adhered to by England (December), Spain and Savoy (1690); Brandenburg, Bavaria and Mainz (1691), Braunschweig–Luneburg–Hanover and Braunschweig–Luneburg–Celle (1693), Saxony (1694) and Munster (1695). Of these, less than half were Protestant states. The Grand Alliance of 1701 was a virtual replay of the arrangements of 1689 except that Spain now was on the French side, while Portugal joined the British side. William was the effective leader of the Alliance and, after his death in 1702, this position was assumed in effect by the Earl of Marlborough.

In as much as that struggle was, for the life of a generation, a world-wide one (encompassing, *inter alia*, India, and the Americas) and soon concerned *inter alia*, the fate of the Spanish overseas empire, that leadership was global in significance.

SEMANTICS OF POWER

The bare essentials of the new global system were thus put in place in about a year in 1688–9. Within the next two years, English ascendancy was restored in Ireland, and 'mastery of the seas' was established by the victory at La Hogue. A peace was negotiated at Rijswick in 1697, but it did not last.

It was at about this time that Britain's justification of her new position came to be clothed in the phraseology of the 'balance'. Coincidentally, Isaac Newton had just published his *Principia* in 1687.

In his last speech to Parliament in 1701, shortly before his death, William alluded again to the 'common danger of Europe'. The danger stemmed from the King of France placing his grandson on the throne of Spain, while at the same time granting recognition to the Stuart pretender to the British throne. Enjoining his audience 'to lay aside parties and divisions' (the English party system was only just beginning to establish itself) he urged them to stand united 'to hold the balance of Europe and to be indeed at the head of the Protestant interest' (Doc. 27).

Queen Anne's declaration of war (Doc. 28) followed a few months later. In it the idea of balance is no longer tentative but right up front, in the clause explaining the purpose of the alliances 'for preserving the liberty and balance of Europe'. Such an assumption of wider responsibilities was by no means unanimously welcomed in England. A significant section of opinion, and in particular the Tories led by Henry St John Viscount Bolingbroke, viewed these responsibilities as unduly onerous, benefitting others, especially the Dutch. In a 1711 political tract, Jonathan Swift used terms that could be characterised as isolationist to describe the results of the war so far 'ten years of fighting to little purpose; . . . the loss of above an hundred thousand Men, and a Debt remaining of Twenty Millions', leading, he feared, to arrangements that would bring 'great advantage to the Empire and Holland, but none at all to us' (1951, p. 11).

The war was, indeed, 'both cruel and destructive', by reason of the 'frequency of battles, and the effusion of Christian blood' (preamble to the Peace of Utrecht, 1713). It was the Tories who, resentful of the continued burdens of more than a decade of war and of its entangling alliances, hastened its conclusion. Utrecht was an English rather than a general peace and contravened the express provisions of the Grand Alliance prohibiting separate arrangements. It was made worse by the British government's secret 'restraining order' to the commander in the field that told him (without informing his allies) to avoid combat with the French (Wolf, 1951, pp. 88–9). It was another year before Austria and the Empire made their own separate arrangements.

The Anglo–French Treaty (Doc. 29) is the central instrument defining the framework for the settlement of the global conflict. It resolved the principal issue (that of avoiding an union between France and Spain) in a manner that accorded with the war aims formulated by William and Anne, by enshrining the balance of power as the 'fundamental and perpetual maxim', a 'fundamental constitution' of Europe. These statements were incorporated in the treaty itself and were used as justificatory devices in the letters of renunciation (of the right to a dynastic union between France and Spain) by Louis XIV, King Philip of Spain, Charles, Duke of Berry, and Philip, Duke of Orleans. The Anglo–Spanish peace treaty (13 July 1713) declared that 'an equal balance of power (which is the best and most solid foundation of mutual friendship, and of concord which will be lasting on all sides)' was the way 'to settle and establish the peace and tranquility of Christendom'. In such manner, upon crossing the Channel, liberty and the Protestant interest of William's last speech merged with the unarguable laws of equilibrium.

A SCHOOL OF POLITICS TO THE WORLD

Britain's global significance lay not just in naval mastery, and in having prevailed against Louis XIV. It was equally significant in innovative commercial enterprises in Asia, where the VOC continued to emphasise spices and the East Indies but where the English East India Company (recently reorganised) now turned to India, and soon to China.

But it was Britain's progress in building the modern state that was probably most notable, an example and – in Leibniz's expression – a 'delight' to Europe and to the world (as it was, for instance, a learning experience for Voltaire). While elsewhere absolutism reigned triumphant, England's 'Glorious Revolution' launched an era of limited monarchy, of parliamentary government (Westminster becoming the mother of Parliaments'), of an independent judiciary, of a party system, of a free press, of religious toleration, and of new economic institutions. All these are remarkable accomplishments along the road toward the differentiation, and institutionalisation, of the separate functions of the political system, and of the successful distinction of political from economic, and religious, functions.

The Declaration of Right (Doc. 21) that accompanied the Proclamation of William and Mary, formally a restatement of grievances against the former monarch and a reassertion of traditional rights (not unlike the Act of Abjuration, Doc. 11), was the real basis of all succeeding political development. The Toleration Act (Doc. 26) was not as tolerant as its title promised but made a good beginning; the punitive laws were usually inoperative (Trevelyan, 1929, p. 474). Despite its condescension, this was an enlightened measure that, with the advantage of hindsight, we can say served Britain well in the years to come. Excluded from the political arena, the dissenters poured their energies into the economic sphere of activity. In the course of time, they became the backbone of the Industrial Revolution that propelled England forward into an unprecedented second cycle of leadership.

All the contemporary documents, including the Declaration, and William's speeches, make it clear that religion was a key element in this great transition and in the war against Louis (who expelled the Huguenots), but it gradually became a mostly inactive element in the general global situation, except at the elite level.

In this collection we can cover only the essentials of the British performance in the first cycle. The Treaty of Paris of 1763 (English text in Parry, 1969–80, Vol. 42, pp. 320–45), which ended Britain's Seven Years' War against France, Spain and Portugal, marked a peak in Britain's ascendency in that cycle. The words 'balance' and 'equilibrium', so conspicuous in the Utrecht settlement, are noticeably absent from the Paris text whose provisions would have pleased Swift a half century earlier. In exchange for the return of Cuba to Spain, a redistribution of West Indian islands with Britain, and New Orleans remaining French, France ceded Canada and Nova Scotia to England, lost fishing rights in Newfoundland, forts in India and Senegal, and relinquished Florida to Britain, as well as all the Spanish possessions in North America East and South East of the Mississippi. Article XX of the Paris treaty states: 'the Catholick King cedes and makes over the whole to the said King and to the Crown of Great Britain, and that in the most ample manner and form'. These French losses were a national humiliation.

But Britain, herself, soon ran into a period of deterioration and strain, like the other world powers before her. The low point in that decline was the conflict with the American colonies – caused, in part, by Britain's increased responsibilities in North America arising out of the Treaty of Paris, which led her to put a higher financial burden on the colonial population. The situation was aggravated by efforts to correct the inefficiencies and the corruption in the East India Company, now turning into a territorial ruler. Defeat in the war of American independence meant the end of the first British empire but it was not the end of a world role for Britain. She harboured as yet untapped resources that would bring her another spell of leadership.

One of these resources was Lord Shelburne, who led the government that negotiated the peace with America. Thanks to his breadth of vision, a generous settlement with the former colonies was made possible; this became a sound foundation for peaceful coexistence and future collaboration. For Shelburne, a disciple of Adam Smith, trade was more important than dominion (Doc. 30); he knew that for the 'general arbitration or administration of things' (in Leibniz's terms) territorial dominion of the imperial kind was not really indispensable. He was, of course, right, and the peace he negotiated was carried out, and it lasted, but for himself it meant political oblivion. Shelburne's defence of the peace settlement with America was his swansong; his government was defeated and he never held a political office again. But it was the British Prime Minister's skillful steering of the American negotiations that contributed to his country's successful transition to a second cycle of world leadership.

Documents

19 TREATY OF DEFENSIVE ALLIANCE BETWEEN GREAT BRITAIN AND THE NETHERLANDS, SIGNED AT WESTMINSTER, 3 MARCH 1678

Introduction

The high point of the delegitimation of Dutch leadership (cf. Docs 17, 18) had been the secret Treaty of Dover concluded between Charles II and Louis XIV on 22 May 1670 (French text in Parry, 1969–80, Vol. 11, pp. 297–312). Its stated purpose was the humbling of the Dutch and the reduction of their strength as a nation 'often guilty of extreme ingratitude' that dared to set itself up as 'the arbiter and judge over all other potentates' (Art.5).

The Dover pact also had the effect of placing Britain on the French side of the European conflict, in a position of dependence on French subsidies and possibly French troops; it could have made Charles II independent of Parliament and therefore an absolute ruler by divine right, like Louis XIV. (see Macaulay, 1914, Vol. 1, pp. 194 ff.) It led directly to the War of 1672.

By contrast, the present treaty was negotiated by the Parliamentary Tories (the *Cabal*) in response to public concern over Charles's Catholic leanings. Westminster put Britain firmly and openly in the Dutch (Protestant) camp and in a position of ascending leadership. It was supplemented on 26 July 1678 by another accord, bringing the joint force ratio to Great Britain 3:Netherlands 2.

Source: Public Record Office, London, State Papers 108/320; translated from the original French text of the treaty by Sylvia Modelski; Articles 4 and 5 and the first two Separate Articles are also available in English in William Cobbett, *Parliamentary History of England from the Norman Conquest in 1066 to the Year 1803* (London, 1809 . . .), Vol. V, cols 206–7.

Text

Given that the most serene King of Great Britain [Charles II], in addition to the intimate agreements he has already concluded with the States General of the United Provinces, for the preservation of the Spanish Netherlands, and for the support of common interests in this part of Europe, was strongly desirous to enter at the same time into a perpetual Defensive Alliance with the said States, for the mutual conservation of one and the other, of their subjects and states against those who would like to attempt an attack on them, or in any other way to injure or molest them.

And since the said States, being on their part equally desirous to enter into the said perpetual bond of a Defensive Treaty with His Majesty, have given Power to Messer Van Beuningen their Ambassador at His Majesty's court, to negotiate and conclude the said Alliance, His Majesty having named as Commissioners on his behalf, Messers Heneage Baron Finch Lord Chancellor of England, Thomas Earl of Danby, Lord High Treasurer of England, Henry Earl of Arlington, Lord Chamberlain of the Royal Household, Henry Coventry Esquire and Joseph Williamson Knight, first secretaries of state and commanders of His Majesty's.

The said Commissioners and the said Ambassador after several meetings and conferences, by virtue of their respective Powers, copies of which are inserted at the end of these presents, have decided and concluded the following:

1. There will be in future between the King and the successor kings of Great Britain and his kingdoms on the one side and the Lords States General of the United Provinces of the Netherlands on the other and their states and dependent territories and their subjects, reciprocally a sincere firm and perpetual friendship and good intercourse by sea as well as by land, in everything and everywhere outside as well as inside Europe.

2. Furthermore there will be between His Majesty and his successor kings of Great Britain and his kingdoms and the said Lords States General and their states and dependent territories a close alliance and faithful confederation to uphold and mutually conserve each other in tranquility, peace, friendship and neutrality by sea and by land and in the possession of all the rights, franchises and liberties that they enjoy or have the right to enjoy or that they have acquired or will acquire through treaties of peace, of friendship and of neutrality that have been concluded in the past, and that will be concluded hereafter conjointly and in common concert with other kings, republics, princes and towns, all this however within the confines of Europe only.

3. And so they promise and obligate themselves to guarantee to each other, not only all the treaties that His Majesty and the said Lords States General have already concluded with other kings, republics, princes and states which will be produced on both sides before the exchange of Ratifications, but also all those treaties that they might conclude hereafter conjointly and in common concert, and to defend each other, assist and conserve reciprocally in the possession of the territories, towns and places that presently belong and will hereafter belong to His Majesty and his successor Kings of Great Britain as well as to the said Lords States General by the said treaties, wherever the said territories, towns and places may be situated, in regard to which His Majesty and the said Lords States General happen to be disturbed or attacked by some hostility or open war by whosoever, or under whatever pretext it might be.

4. The reciprocal obligation to assist and defend each other is also understood to extend to His Majesty and the said Lords States General their countries and subjects conserved and maintained in all their rights, possessions and immunities and liberties

of navigation as well as of commerce and whatever others, by sea as well as by land, that will happen to belong to them by the law of nations, or by treaties concluded or to be concluded in the above mentioned manner towards and against all kings, princes, republics or states, so that if to the prejudice of the said present or future tranquility, peace and friendship or neutrality, His Majesty or the said Lords States General happen to be, hereafter, attacked or in any way whatever disturbed in the possession and enjoyment of the states, territories, towns, places, rights, immunities and liberties of commerce, navigation or whatever others, of which His Majesty and the said Lords States General enjoy at present or will have the right to enjoy be it by law of nations or by treaty already concluded or that might be concluded as above, His Majesty and the said Lords States General having been notified and required one by the other will conjointly do their utmost to bring about a cessation of the trouble or hostility and to repair the torts or injuries that might have been inflicted upon one of the allies.

5. In case that the said attack or disturbance is followed by an open rupture, the one of the two allies who is not attacked shall be obliged to come to a rupture two months after the first request of the one among them who is already engaged in rupture, in the course of which time he will do his dutiful best through his Ambassador or other Ministers to mediate an equitable accommodation between the aggressor or turbator and the party attacked or disturbed, notwithstanding which, he shall, in the said period, give a powerful succour to his ally, as will be agreed by the Separate Articles between His Majesty and the Lords States General, which Articles although they are not quoted in the present Article will be kept and observed as if they were inscribed and written here. And after the expiration of the said period of two months, it shall however remain up to the ally engaged in rupture whether to continue to enjoy the benefit of that seccour, in case the conjuncture of time and the state of his affairs shall cause him to prefer it [the continued assistance] to an open rupture by his ally.

6. The reciprocal guarantee having thus been established and pledged, in case one of the allies shall be attacked or disturbed, if the States of the United Provinces were to be so attacked and found themselves obliged to enter upon an open war, His Majesty shall be similarly obliged to rupture with the aggressor or turbator and to use all his power and all his forces by sea and by land, and joining them to those of the said Lords States General, when it shall be judged necessary to reduce the common Enemy to an honest, secure and equitable settlement with Great Britain and the said United Provinces.

7. And in that case, the forces of His Britanic Majesty and of the said Lords States General shall act jointly and separately according to what shall be the particular agreement at the time between His said Majesty and the said Lords States General who shall consult and resolve together as to the most appropriate means of inconveniencing the common Enemy, be it by way of diversion or otherwise, so that, as was said above, he is reduced to a settlement.

8. The same as is contained in the two immediately preceding Articles shall be done by the said Lords States General in the event of Great Britain being attacked or disturbed in the manner described above.

9. Once a state of open war occurs, with the two allies following the present Treaty, it will be possible thereafter for either of the allies to suspend hostilities with the one who will have been declared and recognised as the Enemy only conjointly and with a common agreement.

10. But should the case be that negotiations are entered upon, be it to treat of peace or of a few years' truce, these cannot be started by one of the allies without the participation of the other and without affording him at the same time, and as soon as

to himself, the ability and security required and necessary to send the ministers to the spot, where the negotiations are to be held, nor without communication subsequently and from time to time on all that will be going on at the said negotiations; and neither one nor the other will be allowed to proceed all the way to the conclusion of the said peace or truce without including his ally, and having restored to him, should he wish it, the possession of the countries, territories or places and enjoyment of the rights and immunities that he had and which he enjoyed before the war, nor without stipulating [the acknowledgement] by the common Enemy of the same rights, immunities, exemptions and prerogatives for the ally as for himself, unless the allies have agreed otherwise.

11. It will be permitted to the ally who is attacked to raise levies of all kinds of soldiers in the other ally's states to serve in the land armies, provided this is done through Capitulations such as will be mutually agreed by the Parties.

12. The Ratifications of the present Treaty shall be given in good form and exchanged on both sides, within a period of four weeks from the day of signature. In witness of all the above the said Messers Commissioners and the said Messer Ambassador have signed the present and have affixed to it the seal of their Arms. Done at Westminster the 3rd day of March 1678.

Ld Finch	H. Coventry	Ld C.V. Beuningen
Ld Danby	J. Williamson	
Ld Arlington		

SEPARATE ARTICLES

1. In the eventuality of the case envisaged in Article Five occurring, the said Lord King and his successors and the said Lords States General shall be obliged to assist each other every time they are attacked or disturbed, as is more fully expressed in the said Article, in the following manner, to wit: His Britanic Majesty to the said Lords States General ten thousand foot and the said Lords States General to His Britanic Majesty six thousand foot, well armed, under such regiments, companies, colonels and other officers as His Majesty and the said States shall think fit and deem most appropriate for such an assistance, and twenty ships of war, well equipped and provisioned; and the said seccour shall be raised and maintained at the expense of the one who shall send it to rescue the one who is attacked.

2. Whenever the force of circumstances shall lead the Parties to judge and recognise that the help promised and supplied needs to be augmented, the said Lord King and the said Lords States General shall endeavour to come to an agreement about it.

3. The assistance that is sent shall be put entirely under the command and orders of the one to whom it is sent, who shall use it and transport it to any sites he pleases by water and by land, in the country, the sieges, and to guard the places and wherever necessity and utility shall require.

In witness thereof Messers Commissioners of the King of Great Britain and Messer the Ambassador of the States General of the United Provinces have signed the present Separate Articles and have had affixed to them the seal of their Arms. Done at Westminster this 3rd day of March 1678.
[Same signatures]

20 LOUIS XIV'S DECLARATION OF WAR ON THE UNITED PROVINCES, 26 NOVEMBER 1688

Text

From the King,

After all that His Majesty has done to give peace to Europe, the important places he has restituted in order to arrive at the Treaty[1] concluded in Nijmegen in the year 1678, and the pains he has taken since then, not only to establish the truce, but also to translate it into perpetual peace, His Majesty had reason to hope that the States General of the United Provinces of the Netherlands, who had shown so much eagerness to conclude this truce, would evince no less zeal in maintaining it.

However, in the past few months, His Majesty has received several notices that the said States, allowing themselves to be swayed in accordance with the wishes of those who have no other desire than to see the resumption of war in Europe, were building up extraordinary levies and armaments, and were making agreements with princes of the Empire [the German Holy Roman Empire], in order to put all possible obstacles in the way of the installation of Cardinal von Furstenberg in the Cologne Electorate;[2] and His Majesty, finding himself forced to support the candidacy of that Cardinal, the opposition to whose election, it was declared positively and against all evidence, was due to the fact that he was believed to be tied to His Majesty's interests, he caused his Ambassador, the Count of Avaux, to urge the said States General not to use the extraordinary forces they were raising in any way that might disturb the tranquility of Europe, and had it expressly conveyed to them that he would look upon what they might attempt against Cardinal von Furstenberg as though it were aimed against his own states.

His Majesty has since learned that they have not desisted from commencing to execute their projects, and have gathered an army under the command of the Prince of Waldeck, which has now joined forces with the troops of the princes who have formed a league against Cardinal Furstenberg's interests: and so, not wanting to dissemble any longer, HIS MAJESTY has decided to declare war, as He does hereby, against the States General of the United Provinces of the Netherlands, by sea as well as by land.

To that end, His Majesty commands and calls upon all his subjects, vassals, and servants, to go after the Dutch, and has forbidden and forbids expressly their having, hereafter, any communication, commerce or intelligence with them, under penalty of death.

And to that end, His Majesty has from this moment revoked all permissions, passports, safeguards and safeconducts, that might have been granted by him or by his Lieutenants General, and other officers of his, that might conflict with the present and has declared them and declares them nul and void, forbidding whosoever it might be giving them any consideration.

Source: Printed text in the Archives des Relations Extérieures (Paris), *Correspondance de Hollande*, Tome 156, Folio 406. Translated from the French by Sylvia Modelski.

1. Peace of Nijmegen that brought the French–Dutch war of 1672–8 to a close.
2. Louis XIV and Pope Innocent XII were feuding over who should be elected Archbishop of Cologne, the King's favourite being Cardinal von Furstenberg.

His Majesty instructs and orders His Lordship the Admiral, the Field Marshals of France [*Maréchaux de France*], His Majesty's Governors, Lieutenants General in his provinces and armies, the general officers [*maréchaux de camp*] of his armies, whether horse or foot, French or foreign, and all other officers concerned, to execute, each on his own behalf, the contents of the present within the extent of their individual powers and jurisdictions.

For this is His Majesty's will; His Majesty wishes and demands that the present be published and posted up in all the towns, maritime as well as others, and in all the ports, harbours and other places in his kingdom, and territories under his authority as will be necessary, so that no one can plead ignorance.

Done at Versailles the 26th day of November 1688.

LOUIS

Colbert[3]

3. Jean-Baptiste Colbert, Secretary of the Navy 1683–9, eldest son of J.-B. Colbert (Doc. 18).

21 THE BILL OF RIGHTS: DECLARATION OF THE LORDS SPIRITUAL AND TEMPORAL, AND COMMONS ASSEMBLED AT WESTMINSTER, 12 FEBRUARY 1689

Introduction

When in February 1689 the Convention Parliament offered the throne of England jointly to Prince William of Orange and his wife Mary, it also presented them with a Declaration of Rights setting forth certain conditions. The Declaration had been shown to William in January 1689 (a misprint in the present document gives the year 1688) and was more in the nature of an informational brief, but it was understood that William and Mary were endorsing its principles when they accepted the crown (see Doc. 22). Later enacted by Parliament, and known as the Bill of Rights, these principles formed the constitutional settlement of the 'Glorious Revolution'. Together with the other settlements of the Revolution such as the religious settlement (Toleration Act, Doc. 25) and the financial settlement (Civil List, Bank of England, Doc. 26), the Bill of Rights provided the firm institutional foundations of the British political system until the reforms of the nineteenth century. Not a rigid constitutional instrument, the Bill is nevertheless regarded as the 'original contract' of England – on a par, some would say, with the Magna Carta. It was a source of inspiration for the framers of the American Constitution a hundred years later.

The result of a compromise with the Tories, the Bill was authored by a Whig politician, John Somers. It reaffirms, among other things, the supremacy of Parliament, the rights to free election and Parliamentary debate and, in the light of recent abuses by Charles II and James II, it imposes new limitations on the power of the monarchy, notably, a prohibition on the levying of taxes and on keeping a standing army without Parliamentary consent, the settlement of the future succession, and exclusion of any Catholic or spouse of a Catholic from becoming King or Queen (that remains to this day).

Source: *Journal of the House of Commons*, Vol. X (1688–93), pp. 28–9; 1803 reprint.

Text

WHEREAS the late King *James* the Second, by the Assistance of divers evil Counsellors, Judges, and Ministers, employed by him, did endeavour to subvert and extirpate the Protestant Religion, and the Laws and Liberties of this Kingdom.

By assuming and exercising a Power and dispensing with and suspending of Laws, and the Execution of Laws, without Consent of Parliament;

By committing and prosecuting divers worthy Prelates, for humbly petitioning to be excused from concurring to the said assumed Power;

By issuing and causing to be executed a Commission, under the Great Seal, for erecting a Court, called, The Court of Commissioners for Ecclesiastical Causes;

By levying Money for and to the Use of the Crown, by Pretence of Prerogative, for other Time, and in other Manner, than the same was granted by Parliament;

By raising and keeping a Standing Army within this Kingdom in Time of Peace, without Consent of Parliament; and quartering Soldiers contrary to Law;

By causing several good Subjects, being Protestants, to be disarmed, at the same time when Papists were both armed and employed contrary to Law;

By violating the Freedom of Elections of Members to serve in Parliament;

By Prosecutions in the Court of King's Bench, for Matters and Causes cognizable only in Parliament: And by divers other arbitrary and illegal Courses:

And whereas, of late Years, partial, corrupt, and unqualified, Persons have been returned, and served on Juries in Trials, and, particularly, divers Jurors in Trials for High Treason, which were not Freeholders;

And excessive Bail hath been required of Persons committed in criminal Cases, to elude the Benefit of the Laws made for the Liberty of the Subjects;

And excessive Fines have been imposed;

And illegal and cruel Punishments inflicted;

And several Grants and Promises made of Fines and Forfeitures, before any Conviction or Judgment against the Persons upon whom the same were to be levied:

All which are utterly and directly contrary to the known Laws, and Statutes, and Freedom, of this Realm:

And whereas the said late King *James* the Second having abdicated the Government; and the Throne being thereby vacant;

His Highness the Prince of *Orange* whom it hath pleased Almighty God to make the glorious Instrument of delivering this Kingdom from Popery and arbitrary Power, did, by the Advice of the Lords Spiritual and Temporal, and divers principal Persons of the Commons, cause Letters to be written to the Lords Spiritual and Temporal, being Protestants; and other Letters, to the several Counties, Cities, Universities, Boroughs, and Cinque Ports, for the Chusing of such Persons to represent them as were of right to be sent to Parliament, to meet and sit at *Westminster* upon the *22nd Day* of *January*, in this Year 1688 [*sic*], in Order to such an Establishment, as that their Religion, Laws, and Liberties, might not again be in Danger of being subverted:

Upon which Letters, Elections having been accordingly made;

And thereupon, the said Lords Spiritual and Temporal, and Commons, pursuant to their respective Letters, and Elections, being now assembled in a full and free Representative of this Nation, taking into their most serious Consideration the best Means for attaining the Ends aforesaid, do, in the First Place, (as their Ancestors, in like Case, have usually done) for the Vindication and Asserting their ancient Rights and Liberties, declare,

That the pretended Power of suspending of Laws by Regal Authority, without Consent of Parliament, is illegal:

That the pretended Power of dispensing with Laws, or the Execution of Laws, by Regal Authority, as it hath been assumed and exercised of late, is illegal:

That the Commission for erecting the late Court of Commissioners for Ecclesiastical Causes, and all other Commissions and Courts of like Nature, are illegal and pernicious:

That levying of Money for or to the Use of the Crown, by Pretence of Prerogative, without Grant of Parliament, for longer Time, or in other Manner, than the same is or shall be granted, is illegal:

That it is the Right of the Subjects to petition the King; and all Commitments and Prosecutions for such Petitioning, are illegal:

That the raising or keeping a Standing Army within the Kingdom in Time of Peace, unless it be with Consent of Parliament, is against Law:

That the Subjects, which are Protestants, may have Arms for their Defence, suitable to their Conditions, as allowed by Law:

That Election of Members of Parliament ought to be free:

That the Freedom and Debates or Proceedings in Parliament ought not to be impeached or questioned in any Court or Place out of Parliament:

That excessive Bail ought not to be required; nor excessive Fines imposed; nor cruel and unusual Punishment inflicted:

That Jurors ought to be impanelled and returned; and Jurors, which pass upon Men in Trials for High Treason, ought to be Freeholders:

That all Grants and Promises of Fines and Forfeitures of particular Persons, before Conviction, are illegal and void:

And that, for Redress of all Grievances, and for the Amending, Strengthening, and Preserving of the Laws, Parliaments ought to be held frequently.

And they do claim, demand, and insist upon, all and singular the Premises, as their undoubted Rights and Liberties; and that no Declarations, Judgments, Doings, or Proceedings, to the Prejudice of the People, in any of the said Premises, ought, in any wise, to be drawn hereafter into Consequence, or Example.

To which Demand of their Rights they are particularly encouraged by the Declaration of his Highness the Prince of *Orange*; as being the only Means for obtaining a full Redress and Remedy therein.

Having therefore an entire Confidence, that his said Highness the Prince of *Orange* will perfect a Deliverance so far advanced by him; and will still preserve them from the Violation of their Rights, which they have here asserted; and from all other Attempts upon their Religion, Rights, and Liberties;

The said Lords Spiritual and Temporal, and Commons, assembled at *Westminster*, do *Resolve*,

That *William* and *Mary*, Prince and Princess of *Orange*, be, and be declared, King and Queen of *England*, *France*,[1] and *Ireland*, and the Dominions thereunto belonging; to hold the Crown and Royal Dignity of the said Kingdoms and Dominions to them the said Prince and Princess, during their Lives, and the Life of the Survivor of them: And that the sole and full Exercise of the Regal Power be only in, and executed by, the said Prince of *Orange*, in the Names of the said Prince and Princess, during their joint Lives; and, after their Deceases, the said Crown and Royal Dignity of the said

1. This title to France (also seen in Docs 24 and 29) was originally assumed by King Edward III during the Hundred Years' War, in 1340. The description was retained by the succeeding Yorkist, Tudor, Stuart and first two Hanoverian monarchs. George III dropped it upon his accession in 1760, for by then the claim had become purely vestigial and France made light of it (Franklyn, 1969, p. 331). For instance, when, at the turn of the eighteenth century catholic James II was given sanctuary at his cousin Louis XIV's court, the Sun King took a debonair view of his guest flaunting the fleur-de-lys on his coat-of-arms (Mitford, 1966, p. 207).

Kingdoms and Dominions to be to the Heirs of the Body of the said Princess: And, for Default of such Issue, to the Princess *Ann of Denmark*, and the Heirs of her Body: And, for Default of such Issue, to the Heirs of the Body of the said Prince of *Orange*.

And the said Lords Spiritual, and Temporal, and Commons, do pray the said Prince and Princess of *Orange* to accept the same accordingly.

And that the Oaths, hereafter mentioned, be taken by all Persons of whom the Oaths of Allegiance and Supremacy might be required by Law, instead of them; and that the said Oaths of Allegiance and Supremacy be abrogated.

I, *A. B.* do sincerely promise and swear, that I will be faithful, and bear true Allegiance, to their Majesties King *William* and Queen *Mary*. So help me God.

I, *A. B.* do swear, that I do from my Heart abhor, detest, and abjure, as impious and heretical, this Damnable Doctrine and Position, That Princes excommunicated or deprived by the Pope, or any Authority of the See of *Rome*, may be deposed or murdered by their Subjects, or any other whatsoever. And I do declare, that no Foreign Prince, Person, Prelate, State, or Potentate, hath, or ought to have, any Jurisdiction, Power, Superiority, Preheminence, or Authority, Ecclesiastical or Spiritual, within this Realm. So help me God.

22 WILLIAM III'S ANSWER TO THE ADDRESS FROM PARLIAMENT, 8 MARCH 1689 (O.S.)

Introduction

At first, William saw the main purpose of his becoming King of England as an opportunity to bring a sharp reversal in Britain's then pro-French and anti-Dutch foreign policy, and to use her men and resources to aid Holland against Louis XIV's France. Although he did abide by its provisions, he never formally pledged himself to the Declaration of Rights of January 1689 preferring to base his ascension to the throne on 'mutual trust' rather than contract. In the present speech, too, given in reply to the Declaration that accompanied the proclamation of his joint sovereignty with Mary (Doc. 21), the preconditions set forth by Parliament in the Bill of Rights are acknowledged only in the most general terms: 'to preserve your Religion, Laws, and Liberties, which were the only inducements that brought me into England'. The speech gives a succinct outline of his domestic and foreign policies.

Text

My lords and gentlemen: If any thing could add to the esteem and affection I have for Parliaments, and particularly for this, they would be much increased by the kindness you shew to me, and the zeal you express for the public good in the Address you have made, which in the matter, as well as the manner, hath every thing in it that ought to recommend it to me.

I assure you I will never abuse the confidence that you shall put in me; being fully persuaded, that there is no sure foundation of a good agreement between a king and his people but mutual trust: when that is once broken, a government is half dissolved; it shall, therefore, be my chief care never to give any parliament cause to distrust me; and the best method I can use for that purpose is never to expect anything from them, but that which shall be their own interest to grant.

I came hither for the good of the kingdom, and, since it is your desire that I am in this station, I shall pursue the same ends that brought me.

God hath pleased to make me instrumental to redeem you from the ills you feared, and it is still my desire, as well as my duty, to preserve your Religion, Laws, and Liberties, which were the only inducements that brought me into England, and to these I ascribe the blessings that have attended this understanding.

When I spoke last to you, I told you of the necessity of assisting our Allies, and more especially the States of Holland, whose readiness to relieve you, at their too great hazard and expense, from the extremities you lay under, needs no further argument to move you to the consideration of it.

As I was then a witness of their zeal and affection to promote the Expedition, and second my endeavours, even with a neglect of their own safety; so I am now sensible of the inevitable ruin they have drawn upon themselves, by giving you this assistance, if you should not return it to them.

Source: Cobbett, William, *Parliamentary History of England, from the Norman Conquest in 1066 to the Year 1803* (London, 1809 . . .), Vol. V, cols 163–4.

They have already exhausted themselves to such a degree both as to Men and Money, that it is not easily to be imagined, and I am confident your generosity will have as little bounds towards them, as theirs had towards you: and that you will not only enable me to make good the Treaty with them, and repay what they have actually laid out upon this occasion, of which as Account shall be given to you; but that you will farther support them to the utmost of your ability against the power of their enemies, who must be yours too, by their interest and their religion, and do certainly design the ruin of Holland to be a step to your destruction.

I need not take pains to tell you the deplorable Condition of Ireland, which by the zeal and violence of the Popish Party there, and by the assistance and encouragement they have from France, is brought to that pass, that it is not adviseable to attempt the reducing it, otherwise than by a very considerable Force, which I think ought not to be less than 20 000 horse and foot; which by the blessing of God, will make the work shorter, and in consequence, the Charge easier, though the first Expence must, of necessity, be great.

You are to consider that, towards the more speedy and effectual Success in relation to Ireland, as well as with a regard to France, there must be such a Fleet as may, in conjunction with that of the States, make us entirely Masters of the Sea that nothing can be sent from France either to Ireland, or any where else, that may give disturbances to us, or our allies.

I must also recommend the Consideration of the Revenue to you, that it may be so settled, as that it may be collected without dispute.

My Lords and Gentlemen; These things will amount to a great sum, and must of consequence be a present weight upon the people; but, considering that neither your Religion nor your safety, can probably be secured without these means, I conclude you will think nothing can be too great a price for their preservation: and I will engage my solemn word to you, that whatever you shall give in order to these public ends shall be strictly applied to them; and that as you so freely offer to hazard all that is dear to you, so I shall as freely expose myself for the Support of the Protestant Religion and the safety and honour of the nation.

23 TREATY BETWEEN WILLIAM AND MARY, KING AND QUEEN OF GREAT BRITAIN AND THE STATES-GENERAL OF THE NETHERLANDS, CONCERNING THE FITTING OUT OF A FLEET. WHITEHALL, APRIL 29 (O.S.), 1689.

Text

The King and Queen of Great Britain, having been requested since more than two months by the Lords States General of the Netherlands, to execute without delay the Treaty of 3rd March 1678, concluded between the late King Charles the Second and the Lords States General, because the eventuality provided for by the Treaty has occurred, the Very Christian King [Louis XIV of France] has declared war on them, their Majesties wishing to publicly pledge their sincerity and the affection they have always felt and will always feel for the said Lords States General, have not only found it right to execute the said Treaty according to its tenor, but also in order to give them even greater proof of their cordial friendship and the sooner to arrive at a good peace, they have deemed it opportune to increase by greater number of vessels, the assistance stipulated by the said Treaty, to this end and the better to agree on the proper conduct at sea, their Majesties and the said Lords States General have appointed Commissioners, namely, on the side of their Majesties, Daniel Earl of Nottingham, one of the first Secretaries of State, and of their Majesties' Privy Council, John Earl of Carbery in Ireland, Baron Vaughan in England, one of the Commissioners of the Admiralty, Arthur Herbert, Esquire, first Commissioner of the Admiralty and member of their Majesties' Privy Council, and Edward Russel, Esquire, Treasurer of their Majesties' Navy and member of the Privy Council: and on the side of the said Lords States General, Messers Nicolas Witsen, Burgermaster, Councillor and Treasurer of the town of Amsterdam, William of Nassau, Baron of Cortgene, first Lord of Odyck, Seyst, Drybergen and Blickenburgh representing the Nobility on the Council and State Assembly of Zeeland; and Everhard de Weede, Lord of Weede, Dyckvelt, Rateles, founding Lord of Oudewater, President of the States Assembly of the province of Utrecht, and Deputy to the States General Assembly; the said Commissioners and Deputies, after several conferences, have decided, promised and granted in the name of their Majesties and the said Lords States General the following articles respectively.

I Their Majesties shall fit out fifty great ships of war, to wit, one of the second rate, seventeen of the third and thirty two of the fourth rate, with fifteen frigates, and eight fireships, in which shall be seventeen thousand one hundred and fifty five effective men.

II The States shall furnish thirty great ships of war, to wit, eight equipped with from seventy to eighty cannons, seven equipped with from sixty to seventy cannons, and fifteen with fifty to sixty cannons in addition to which the States shall also furnish nine frigates and four fireships, with crews totalling ten thousand five hundred and seventy two effective men.

Source: Parry, Clive: *Consolidated Treaty Series*, Vol. 18, pp. 347–52. Translated from the French by Sylvia Modelski; the translation was helped by comparison with the condensed English version found in Jenkinson's *A Collection of all the Treaties . . . etc.*, London, 1785, Vol. I, 1648–1713, pp. 279–80.

III The two fleets shall go to sea and join where the King of Great Britain will appoint, as soon as possible.

IV The said fleets shall be divided into three squadrons; the first of fifty great ships, six frigates and eight fireships for the Mediterranean; the second shall be composed of thirty great ships, eight frigates and four fireships, for the Irish Sea and Channel, unless otherwise agreed by the two parties; and the third shall have ten frigates, operating betwixt the Calais–Dover Strait to Yarmouth on the English Coast and the island of Walcheren off the coast of Zeeland, and these last two squadrons shall give each other mutual assistance on every occasion when it is needed.

V Each squadron shall consist of ships of both nations proportionably.

VI The first squadron shall be abundantly furnished with all necessaries in arms and victuals for a whole year; and what each vessel cannot carry will be held at Porto Mahon in the island of Minorca or at Portoferraio [Porto Perrara] on the island of Elba, or at such other place as the admiral and the council of war shall deem most appropriate: and the King of Spain and the Grand Duke of Tuscany, and the Republic of Genoa shall be required on the part of their Majesties and of the States General to be willing to favourably receive the said squadron, and to extend them all sorts of good welcome. And the other two squadrons shall also be furnished with provisions and other necessities for a whole year or for as long as it will be deemed appropriate for their most effective service.

VII Each of the said squadrons shall be commanded for the duration of this war by the admiral or the commanding officer in chief of the squadron of their Majesties' fleet, and this will also apply to the detachments of each squadron.

VIII Councils of war will consist of all of the officers who shall carry the flag for each side, and in equal number; but whenever the votes are equally divided, the captains of ships of both nations will join. The admiral or commander-in-chief of the English fleet or squadron will preside; and will be seated with the high officers and captains of their Majesties each according to his rank on the right side of the table.

And the admiral or commander in chief of the States' fleet or squadron will sit with the high officers and captains of the said States, on the other side of the table facing those of their Majesties.

And all questions whatever that shall be discussed in the above mentioned councils of war, or that shall be proposed for discussion there, shall be carried by plurality of votes, and all that is thus ordained or resolved shall be executed in the manner prescribed, punctually, and without any delay.

IX Disputes or proceedings involving only the officers, soldiers, seamen, and others in the service of their Majesties, shall always be settled or determined in a council of war composed only of officers of their Majesties; and similarly, disputes and proceedings concerning only the officers, soldiers or seamen or others in the service of the Lords States General, shall always be settled or determined in a council of war composed of officers of the said Lords States General.

X But if the dispute or proceeding involves the officers, soldiers, seamen or others, whatever their quality or rank may be, who are in the service of both their Majesties and the said Lords States General, or if the affair in any way concerns one side against the other, then a council of war, consisting of officers of both fleets, in the manner prescribed in article VIII, will take cognisance of the whole affair in order only to adjudicate or determine which party, or which person was guilty or whether he must be chastised or punished; after this judgement has been passed, the council of war, made up of their Majesties' officers if the criminal happens to be in their service, will have him chastised or punished according to the laws, customs and instructions established or observed in similar cases in the fleet to which the criminal belongs.

XI All prizes shall be divided between their Majesties and the said Lords States General in proportion to the number of vessels in each fleet; that is to say, that out of eight equal parts, their Majesties shall have five and the said Lords States General shall have three parts, which will always apply, even when the said prizes were taken by vessels belonging to their Majesties without assistance from those of the said Lords States General or by vessels of the said Lords States General without assistance from those of their Majesties.

XII In cases of prizes taken by ships of war, they shall be adjudged by the admiralty court of the power whose vessel made the capture, whether English or Dutch, and the proceeds shall be divided according to the rules laid in the preceding article, without the portion delivered to the admiralty that did not adjudge it being taxed with the true rights of officers on both sides, but only with the necessary expenses.

XIII And if the prizes are taken jointly by vessels of both fleets, they shall be adjudged by the admiralty court on which the ships that have most cannons do depend.

XIV Their Majesties shall ordain that in all the instructions to the captains of their ships of war assigned, or to be assigned, to convoy merchant ships everywhere, and that from time to time will also go to the West Indies, there shall be inserted an article enjoining them very explicitly to protect against insults or attacks from whomsoever it may be the merchant vessels belonging to the subjects of the said States General, that shall follow the same route as the said ships of war, and that wish to put themselves under their protection.

And that another article shall be inserted also very clearly enjoining the said captains, that in case the plantations, colonies or other states whatever, that the said Lords States General own at present, or that they will own in the future, need help to defend themselves against the attacks or insults of their enemies, they shall, as soon as they be asked, give all seccour and assistance for the defence of the said plantations, colonies or other states against the attacks and insults mentioned above, to the extent to which conditions in their Majesties' plantations, colonies or other states will allow, and the said Lords States General shall also ordain that in all instructions to captains of their vessels assigned or to be assigned to convoy merchant ships everywhere and that will also from time to time go to the West Indies, there shall be inserted similar articles, and very explicitly with regard to the protection that the said captains shall afford to the merchant ships belonging to their Majesties' subjects, and with regard to the help and assistance they will give for the defence of the plantations, colonies or other states, that their Majesties own at present, or that they will own in the future in the West Indies, everything in the manner and form prescribed above.

XV The present treaty shall be ratified by their Majesties and the said Lords States General, and the ratifications exchanged within six weeks, unless a treaty of offensive and defensive alliance between their Majesties and the said Lords States General is concluded and signed before the end of this period, in which case the present treaty shall be included and confirmed in it; however, the said commissioners and deputies agree that both parties shall not desist from carrying out all and every articles of this treaty, punctually and in good faith as if the ratifications had already been exchanged. Done at Whitehall on the 29th April 1689.

Signed by: Nottingham, Carberry, Russel, N. Witsen, W. de Nassau, De Weede.

[The treaty was in fact signed on 21 May and antedated 29 April presumably to suggest that agreement was reached before the declaration of war, see G. N. Clark, *The Dutch Alliance and the War against French Trade, 1688–1697* (Manchester, 1923).]

24 THE GRAND ALLIANCE, 1689

Introduction

An offensive and Defensive Alliance between The Holy Roman Empire and the Netherlands, signed at Vienna, 12 May 1689. This is the so-called 'Grand Alliance' to which Great Britain, Spain, and several German states later acceded.

Text

WILLIAM the third, by the grace of God, King of Great Britain, France and Ireland, Defender of the Faith, &c. To all and every one to whom these presents shall come greeting. Whereas, a certain treaty of friendship and stricter alliance between the most serene, most potent and most invincible Prince and Lord Leopold, by the Grace of God, elect Roman Emperor, always august, and of Germany, Hungary, Bohemia, Dalmatia, Croatia, Sclavonia, &c. King, &c. and the High and Mighty Lords the States General of the United Provinces, was made and concluded at Vienna, the 12th day of May last past, on the Emperor's part, by Leopold William, Count of Konigsegg, Vice-chancellor of the Empire, &c. and Theodore Althete Henry, Count of Stratman, Chancellor of the Court, his Imperial Majefty's plenipotentiaries, and counsellors of state: and on the part of the States General, by Jacob Hop, counfellor and recorder of the city of Amfterdam, and deputy for Holland and West Friezeland, in the assembly of the States General. The tenor of which treaty is as follows.

Be it known and declared, that although the treaty concluded at the Hague a few years since, between his facred and Imperial Majesty, and the High and Mighty Lords the States General of the United Provinces, for their mutual defence, does yet remain in its full vigour; nevertheless, both his Imperial Majesty, and the said States General, considering the greatness of the common danger which threatens all Christendom since the last French invasion, and the unconstant faith of the French in the observance of treaties, have judged it necessary to strengthen the conditions of the aforesaid treaty, and the former union, with stricter and firmer ties; and, at the same time, to confider of more effectual means, as well for restoring as preserving the public peace and safety: and therefore the plenipotentiaries, constituted to that purpose by both parties, viz. by his Imperial Majesty, his counsellors of ftate, Leopold William, Count of Konigsegg, Vice-chancellor of the Empire, &c. and Theodore Althete Henry, Count of Stratman, Chancellor of the Court; and by the States General, Jacob Hop, counfellor and recorder of the city of Amfterdam, and deputy for Holland and West-Friezeland, in the assembly of the States General, after the mutual exchange of their full powers, have covenanted and agreed in the manner following.

I. There shall be and remain for ever a constant, perpetual, and inviolable friendship, and good correspondence, between his Imperial Majefty and the States General; and each of them shall be obliged earnestly to promote the

Source: Parry, Clive (1969–80), *The Consolidated Treaty Series, 1648–1918*, Vol. 18, 1688–9, pp. 379–85.

other's interests, and as much as in them lies, to prevent all damages and inconveniences to them.

II. And whereas the French king has lately, without any lawful cause or pretext, attacked as well his Imperial Majesty, as the States General, by a most grievous and most unjust war, there shall be during the same not only a defensive, but also an offensive alliance between the contracting parties, by virtue whereof they shall both of them act in a hostile manner, with all their forces, by sea and land, against the said French king, and such of his allies, as upon exhortation to be used for that purpose, shall refuse to separate themselves from him; and they shall also communicate to one another, their advices for the more usefully contriving the actions of the war, either jointly or separately, for the destruction of the common enemy.

III. It shall not be lawful for either party to withdraw from this war with France, or to enter separately upon any convention, treaty of peace, or cessation of arms with France, and its adherents, upon any pretext whatsoever, without the confent and concurrence of the other party.

IV. There shall by no means any peace be concluded, before the peace of Westphalia, and thofe of Osnaburg, Munster, and the Pyreneans, have, by the help of God, and by common force, been vindicated; and that all things, both in church and state, are restored to their former condition, according to the tenor of the same.

V. In case any negotiations of peace of truth shall, by common consent, be entered into, all things that are transacted shall, on both sides, be communicated *bona fide*; nor shall one conclude any thing without the consent and satisfaction of the other.

VI. After the present war, by common consent, shall be ended, and a peace concluded, there shall remain between his sacred Imperial Majefty, his heirs and successors, and the States General of the United Provinces, a perpetual defensive alliance against the often mentioned crown of France, and its adherents; by virtue whereof, both parties shall use their utmost endeavours, that the peace to be made may remain firm and perpetual.

VII. But if it should happen, that the crown of France should again attack one or both of the confederate parties, contrary to the said peace, at what time soever this shall be done, they shall be obliged faithfully to assist each other with all their forces, and in the fame manner as now, both by sea and land, and to repel all manner of hostility and violence; and not to desist till all things are brought again into their former state, according, to the conditions of the aforesaid peace, and that satisfaction be given to the party offended.

VIII. Further, his Imperial Majesty, and the States General, shall at all times, and by all means, and with all their forces, protect and defend all the rights of each other, against the crown of France and its adherents; nor shall they themselves do any prejudice to each other in their said rights.

IX. If there are any controversies between the contracting parties, on occasion of the limits of their dominions, or that any such should arise hereafter, they shall be accommodated and composed in a friendly manner, either by a commission, or ministers deputed by both sides, without making use of any manner of force; and, in the mean time, nothing shall be innovated therein.

X. There shall be invited into the society of this present treaty, by his Imperial Majesty, the crown of Spain, and, by the States General, the crown of England; and there shall be likewise admitted into the same, all the allies and confederates of either party, who shall think fit to enter into the same.

XI. This treaty shall be ratified by both sides, within the space of four weeks, or sooner, if it may be.

In witness whereof, and for a greater confirmation of the credit and sincerity hereof, there are two instruments of the same tenor made, and signed and sealed by the plenipotentiaries of both parties, and reciprocally exchanged. Done at Vienna the 12th of May, 1689.

(L. S.) *Leopold William*, Count of *Konigsegg*.
(L.S.) *T. A. Henry*, Count of *Stratman*.
(L. S.) *F. Hop*.

Whereas the high and mighty lords, the States General of the United Provinces, have sent to us their ambassadors extraordinary, copies of the alliance lately concluded with his sacred Imperial Majesty, to the end that we should, in their name, invite the King of Great Britain to enter into this alliance; we the underwritten ambassadors extraordinary do declare, that these are true and accurate copies of those that were set us: for the confirmation whereof, we have made this declaration $\frac{10}{20}$ September, 1689.

A. Schimmelpenninck *N. Witsen,*
Vander Oge,
Arnoult Van Citters. *De Weede.*

And whereas the States General have, by their ambassadors extraordinary, invited us, by virtue of the tenth article, to enter into the alliance of the aforesaid treaty; we who desire nothing more than to lay hold of all those means which are necessary and most useful for restoring and preserving the public peace and quiet, do the more readily come into the same, that we may give this proof of our sincere affection and friendship for his Imperial Majesty, and the said States General. Know ye therefore, that we having perused, and maturely considered the said treaty, have accepted, approved, and ratified, as we do by these presents, for us, our heirs and successors, accept, approve, and ratify the fame, together with all and every article thereof; engaging, and upon the word of a king promising, that we will religiously and inviolably observe and perform the said treaty, without violating it in any article, or suffering it, to the utmost of our power, to be violated. Provided always, that his sacred Imperial Majesty, and the said States General, do admit us into the said treaty, and give and deliver to us the necessary instruments respectively drawn up in the best manner. In further witness and testimony whereof, we have caused our great seal of England to be affixed to these presents. Signed with our hand. Given at our court at Hampton-court, the 9th day of December, in the year of our Lord, as above, 1689, and of our reign the first.

WILLIAM *Rex*.

SEPARATE ARTICLES

FRANCE have openly declared, in several places and courts, that notwithstanding the most solemn renunciation, they still pretend by force of arms to assert, for the Dauphin, the succession of the Spanish monarchy, in case his Catholick Majesty should die without lawful issue, and publickly aiming to make the said Dauphin king of the Romans; the States General of the United Provinces, maturely confidering what a blow either of these pretensions would give their state, and what prejudice it would bring to the publick affairs and quiet, do promise by these feparate articles, which are as valid as if they had been inserted word for word in the principle treaty; first, That in case the present King of Spain should die without lawful issue (which God forbid) they will, with all their forces, assist his Sacred Imperial Majesty, or his heirs, in taking the succession of the Spanish monarchy, lawfully belonging to that house, together with its kingdoms, provinces, dominions and rights, and in their obtaining and fecuring the quiet possession thereof against the French and their adherents, who shall directly or indirectly oppose this succession; and with force repulse the force they bring against them.

They will likewise ufe all friendly offices and endeavours with the princes electors of the Empire, their confederates, that the most serene Joseph, king of Hungary, his Imperial Majesty's eldest fon, may be speedily chosen king of the Romans: and if France should by threats or arms hinder, oppose, or any way disturb this election, they will, in opposition thereto, assist his sacred Imperial Majesty with their utmost force.

The crown of England shall be likewise invited to enter into the agreement of these articles, made at Vienna the 12th of May, 1689. Signed,

(L. S.) *T. A. Henry Comes de Stratman*,
(L. S.) *F. Hop*.

25 THE TOLERATION ACT 1689

Introduction

What strike's today's reader of this legislation (its title notwithstanding) is the background of profound intolerance against which it was enacted. The present measure aimed at exempting non-Anglican Protestants from the penalties of the Canticle, Test and Corporation Acts which had been passed in the reigns of Elizabeth I, James I and Charles II to ensure the predominance of the established Church of England (the High Church). These laws, in effect, had made second-class citizens of English Protestants who did not conform to the doctrine and practices of the established church. Not only were dissenters (or nonconformists), as they were called, not allowed to worship freely, they were also debarred from politics through being required to receive Holy Communion according to the rites of the Church of England as a condition of acceptance to public office. At the time, dissenters (or Low Church) in England generally supported the Whigs. They included Presbyterians, Unitarians and Baptists, as well as Independents such as the Quakers and Congregationalists. They shared the view that too many 'popish' practices remained in the established church. Anglicans tended to be Tories ('the Tory Party at prayer', as they were dubbed). Influenced by Arminianism (the remonstrant defendants at the Synod of Dort) they wanted to soften Calvinism's stark emphasis on predestination and free will (see Doc. 16, also pp. 111–12 above), and favoured a visually impressive service. The full emancipation of English nonconforming Protestants as well as Catholics and Jews, was not accomplished until well into the nineteenth century, that of women not until the twentieth.

Text

An act for exempting their Majesties' protestant subjects, dissenting from the church of England, from the penalties of certain laws.

Forasmuch as some ease to scrupulous consciences in the exercise of religion may be an effectual means to unite their Majesties' protestant subjects in interest and affection:

II. Be it enacted by the King's and Queen's most excellent majesties, by and with the advice and consent of the lords spiritual and temporal, and the commons, in this present parliament assembled and by the authority of the same. That neither the statute made in the three and twentieth year of the reign of the late Queen Elizabeth, intituled, An act to retain the Queen's majesty's subjects in their due obedience; nor the statute made in the twenty ninth year of the said Queen, intituled, An act for the more speedy and due execution of certain branches of the statute made in the three

Source: *The Statutes at Large*, Danby Pickering (ed.) London, 1764) Vol. IX, 1 Will. & Mar., c. 18, pp. 19–25 (excerpts).

and twentieth year of the Queen's majesty's reign, viz. the aforesaid act; nor that branch or clause of a statute made in the first year of the reign of the said Queen, intituled, An act for the uniformity of common prayer and service in the church, and administration of the sacraments; whereby all persons having no lawful or reasonable excuse to be absent, are required to resort to their parish church or chapel, or some usual place where the common prayer shall be used, upon pain of punishment by the censures of the church, and also upon pain that every person so offending shall forfeit for every such offence twelve pence; nor the statute made in the third year of the reign of the late King James the First, intituled, An act for the better discovering and repressing popish recusants; nor that other statute made in the same year, intituled, An act to prevent or avoid dangers which may grow by popish recusants; nor any other law or statute of this realm made against papists or popish recusants, except the statute made in the five and twentieth year of King Charles the Second, intituled, An act for preventing dangers which may happen from popish recusants; and except a statute made in the thirtieth year of the said King Charles the Second, intituled, An act for the more effectual preserving the King's person and government, by disabling papists from sitting in either house of parliament; shall be construed to extend to any person or persons dissenting from the church of England that shall take the oaths mentioned in a statute made by this present parliament, intituled, An act for removing and preventing all questions and disputes concerning the assembling and sitting of this present parliament; and shall make and subscribe the declaration mentioned in a statute made in the thirtieth year of the reign of King Charles the Second, intituled, An act to prevent papists from sitting in either house of parliament; which oaths and declaration the justices of peace at the general sessions of peace, to be held for the county or place where such person shall live, are hereby required to tender and administer to such persons as shall offer themselves to take, make, and subscribe the same, and thereof to keep a register: and likewise none of the persons aforesaid shall give or pay, as any fee or reward, to any officer or officers belonging to the court aforesaid, above the sum of six pence, nor that more than once, for his or their entry of his taking the said oaths, and making and subscribing the said declaration; nor above the further sum of six pence for any certificate of the same, to be made out and signed by the officer or officers of the said court.

IV. And be it further enacted by the authority aforesaid, That all and every person and persons that shall, as aforesaid, take the said oaths, and make and subscribe the declaration aforesaid, shall not be liable to any pains, penalties, or forfeitures, mentioned in an act made in the five and thirtieth year of the reign of the late Queen Elizabeth, intituled, An act to retain the Queen's majesty's subjects in their due obedience; nor in an act made in the two and twentieth year of the reign of the late King Charles the Second, intituled, An act to prevent and suppress seditious conventicles;[1] nor shall any of the said persons be prosecuted in any ecclesiastical court, for or by reason of their non-conforming to the church of England.

V. Provided always, and be it enacted by the authority aforesaid, That if any assembly of persons dissenting from the church of England shall be had in any place for religious worship with the doors locked, barred, or bolted, during any time of such meeting together, all and every person or persons, that shall come to and be at such meeting, shall not receive any benefit from this law, but be liable to all the pains and penalties of all the aforesaid laws recited in this act, for such their meeting, notwithstanding his taking the oaths and his making and subscribing the declaration aforesaid.

1. Religious gathering of more than five persons not in conformity with the established Anglican Church.

XIII. And whereas there are certain other persons, dissenters from the church of England, who scruple the taking of any oath; be it enacted by the authority aforesaid, That every such person shall make and subscribe the aforesaid declaration, and also this declaration of fidelity following, viz.

I A.B. do sincerely promise and solemnly declare before God and the world, that I will be true and faithful to King William and Queen Mary; and I do solemnly profess and declare, that I do from my heart abhor, detest, and renounce, as impious and heretical, that damnable doctrine and position, That princes excommunicated or deprived by the pope, or any authority of the see of Rome, may be deposed or murthered by their subjects, or any other whatsoever. And I do declare, that no foreign prince, person, prelate, state, or potentate, hath or ought to have, any power, jurisdiction, superiority, pre-eminence, or authority ecclesiastical or spiritual within this realm.

And shall subscribe a profession of their christian belief in these words:

I A.B. profess faith in God the father, and in Jesus Christ his eternal son, the true God, and in the holy spirit, one God blessed for evermore, and do acknowledge the holy scriptures of the Old and New Testament to be given divine inspiration.

Which declarations and subscription shall be made and entered of record and the general quarter-sessions of the peace for the county, city, or place where every such person shall then reside. And every such person that shall make and subscribe the two declarations and profession aforesaid, being thereunto required, shall be exempted from all the pains and penalties of all and every aforementioned statutes made against popish recusants, or protestant nonconformists, and also from the penalties of an act made in the fifth year of the reign of the late Queen Elizabeth, intituled, An act for the assurance of the Queen's royal power over all estates and subjects within her dominions, for or by reason of such persons not taking or refusing to take the oath mentioned in the said act; and also from the penalties of an act made in the thirteenth and fourteenth years of the reign of King Charles the Second, intituled, An act for preventing mischief that may arise by certain persons called Quakers, refusing to take lawful oaths, and enjoy all other the benefits, privileges, and advantages under the like limitations, provisoes, and conditions, which any other dissenters shall or ought to enjoy by virtue of this act.

XIV. Provided always, and be it enacted by the authority aforesaid, That in case any person shall refuse to take the said oaths, when tendered to them, which every justice of the peace is hereby empowered to do, such person shall not be admitted to make and subscribe the two declarations aforesaid, though required thereunto either before any justice of the peace, or at the general or quarter-sessions, before or after any conviction of popish recusancy, as aforesaid, unless such person can, within thirty one days after such tender of the declarations to him produce two sufficient protestant witnesses, to testify upon oath that they believe him to be a protestant dissenter, or a certificate under the hands of four protestants, who are conformable to the church of England, or have taken the oaths and subscribed to the declaration abovementioned, and shall also produce a certificate under the hands and seals of six or more sufficient men of the congregation to which he belongs, owning him for one of them.

XV. Provided also, and be it enacted by the authority aforesaid, That until such certificate, under the hands of six of the congregation, as aforesaid, be produced, and two protestant witnesses come to attest his being a protestant dissenter, or a certificate under the hands of four protestants, as aforesaid, is produced, the justice of the peace shall and hereby is required to take a recognisance with two sureties in the penal sum of fifty pounds, to be levied of his goods and chattels, lands and tenements, to the use of the King's and Queen's majesties, their heirs and successors, for his producing the same; and if he cannot give such security, to commit him to prison, there to remain until he has produced such certificates, or two witnesses as aforesaid.

XVII. Provided always, and be it further enacted by the authority aforesaid, That neither this act, nor any clause, article, or thing therein contained, shall extend or be construed to extend to give any ease, benefit or advantage to any papist or popish recusant whatsoever, or any person that shall deny in his preaching or writing the doctrine of the blessed Trinity, as it is declared in the aforesaid articles of religion.

XVIII. Provided always, and be it enacted by the authority aforesaid, That if any person or persons, at any time or times after the tenth day of June, do and shall willingly and of purpose, maliciously or contemptuously come into any cathedral or parish church, chapel, or other congregation permitted by this act, and disquiet or disturb the same, or misuse any preacher or teacher, such person or persons, upon proof thereof before any justice of the peace, by two or more sufficient witnesses, shall find two sureties to be bound by recognisance in the penal sum of fifty pound, and in default of such sureties shall be committed to prison, there to remain till the next general or quarter-sessions; and upon conviction of the said offences at the said general or quarter-sessions, shall suffer the pain and penalty of twenty pounds, to the use of the King's and Queen's majesties, their heirs and successors.

XIX. Provided always, That no congregation or assembly for religious worship shall be permitted or allowed by this act, until the place of such meeting shall be certified to the bishop of the diocese, or to the archdeacon of that archdeaconry, or to the justices of the peace at the general or quarter sessions of the peace for the country, city, or place in which such meeting shall be held, and registered in the said bishop's or archdeacon's court respectively, or recorded at the said general or quarter sessions; the register or clerk of the peace whereof respectively is hereby required to register the same, and to give certificate thereof to such person as shall demand the same, for which there shall be no greater fee nor reward taken, than the sum of six pence.

26 THE ESTABLISHMENT OF THE BANK OF ENGLAND, AUGUST 1694

Introduction

Having finally attained a degree of internal harmony, England proceeded to put her public finances on a sound footing to meet the expenses of war. The present Act marks the beginning of the National Debt, a new system of long-term borrowing by the government based on an alliance with the financial community (or City). In the past, royal loans were repaid as soon as certain taxes had been levied. Now subscribers were incorporated into the Bank of England. Instead of demanding their capital to be paid back in the short run, they preferred to draw a good interest on it for the rest of their life, upon the security of the state. Jonathan Swift denigrated the new system as an intrusion into English life of the Dutch idea that 'it was in the public's interest to be in debt'. But though improvised in confusion and under heavy pressure of events, this Act, in fact, created an ingenious financial institution 'of amazing rectitude' (Braudel, 1984, p. 376).

(1 500 000 pounds was the estimate of funds needed to carry on with the war against France. In its earlier Articles, the Act provided for the raising of 300 000 pounds by direct taxation, and the remainder of 1 200 000 pounds was to be raised by subscriptions through the Bank of England, which it thereby established for this very purpose.)

Text

An Act for Granting Their Majesties Several Rates and Duties Upon Tonnage of Ships and Vessels, and Upon Beer, Ale and Other Liquors, for Securing Certain Recompenses and Advantages in the Said Act Mentioned to Such Persons as Shall Voluntarily Advance the Sum of Fifteen Hundred Thousand Pounds Towards the Campaigns in the War Against France

XX. And be it further enacted, that it shall and may be lawful to and for Their Majesties, by Letters Patents under the Great Seal of *England*, to limit, direct, and appoint, how and in what manner and proportions, and under what rules and directions, the said sum of 1 200 000 pounds, part of the said sum of 1 500 000 pounds, and the said yearly sum of 100 000 pounds, part of the said sum of 140 000 pounds, and every or any part or proportion thereof, may be assignable or transferrable, assigned or transferred, to such person or persons only, as shall freely and voluntarily accept of the same, and not otherwise; and to incorporate all and every such subscribers and contributors, their heirs, successors, or assigns, to be One Body Corporate and Politick, by the name of 'The Governor and Company of the Bank of *England*'; and by the same name of 'The Governor and Company of the Bank of England', to have perpetual succession, and a common seal, and that they

Source: *The Statutes at Large* (James I–William III) Printers to His Majesty (London, 1786) Vol. III, pp. 529–31 (excerpts).

and their successors, by the name aforesaid, shall be able and capable in law to have, purchase, receive, possess, enjoy, and retain to them and their successors, lands, rents, tenements, and hereditaments, of what kind, nature, or quality soever; and also to sell, grant, demise, aliene, or dispose of same, and by the same name to sue and implead, and be sued and impleaded, answer and be answered, in Courts of Record, or any other place whatsoever, and to do and execute all and singular other matters and things by the name aforesaid, that to them shall or may appertain to do; subject nevertheless to the proviso and condition or redemption hereinafter mentioned.

XXII. And, for the better and more speedy payment of the said yearly sum of 100 000 pounds, part of the said yearly sum of 140 000 pounds, in the proportions herein-before mentioned and appointed, the Commissioners of Their Majesties' Treasury, and the Under Treasurer of the Exchequer now being, and the Lord High Treasurer, and Under Treasurer, or Commissioners of the Treasury for the time being, are hereby strictly enjoined and required by virtue of this Act, and without any further or other Warrant to be sued for, had or obtained from Their Majesties, their heirs or successors, to direct their Warrants yearly for the payment of the said yearly sums of 100 000 pounds, to the contributors of the said sum of 1 200 000 pounds, in the manner and proportions as is herein before directed and appointed; and the Auditor of the Receipt of Exchequer, and all other officers of the Exchequer now and for the time being, are hereby directed and enjoined to issue the said monies so set apart for the uses before-mentioned, from time to time, without any fee or reward, in the manner and proportions before-mentioned, and under the like penalties, forfeitures, and disabilities, as are hereafter inflicted upon any officer for diverting any money appropriated or applied by this Act.

XXIII. Provided always, and be it further enacted by the Authority aforesaid, that no person or persons, bodies politick or corporate, shall, by themselves, or any other person or persons in trust for him or them, subscribe or cause to be subscribed, for and towards the raising and paying of the said sum of 1 200 000 pounds, any sum or sums of money, exceeding the sum of 20 000 pounds; and that every such subscriber shall, at the time of such subscription, pay or cause to be paid unto the Commissioners who shall be authorised and appointed for taking and receiving subscriptions as aforesaid, one full fourth part of his, her, or their respective subscriptions, and in default of such payments as aforesaid, every such subscription shall be utterly void and null: and that the residue of the said subscriptions shall be paid into the Receipt of Their Majesties' Exchequer, as Their Majesties shall direct, before the said first day of *January* next; and in default of such payments, that then the fourth part, first paid as aforesaid, shall be forfeited to and for the benefit of Their Majesties, their heirs and successors.

XXIV. Provided also, and be it enacted, that it shall not be lawful to or for any person or persons, natives or foreigners, bodies corporate or politick, at any time or times, before the first day of *July,* next ensuing, to subscribe in his, her, or their own name or names, or in any other name or names in trust for him, her, or them, for and towards the raising and paying into the Receipt of the Exchequer, the said sum of 1 200 000 pounds, part of the said sum of 1 500 000 pounds, any sum or sums, exceeding in the whole the sums of 10 000 pounds; any thing in this Act contained to the contrary in any wise notwithstanding.

XXVIII. Provided, that nothing herein contained shall any ways be construed to hinder the said Corporation from dealing in Bills of Exchange, or in buying or selling bullion, gold, or silver, or in selling any goods, wares, or merchandise whatsoever, which shall really and *bona fide* be left or deposited with the said Corporation for money lent and advanced thereon, and which shall or may be the produce of lands purchased by the said Corporation.

XXIX. Provided always, and be it enacted by the Authority aforesaid, that all and every bill or bills obligatory and of credit under the seal of the said Corporation made or given to any person or persons, shall and may, by indorsement thereon under the hand of such person or persons, be assignable and assigned to any person or persons who shall voluntarily accept the same, and so by such assignee, *toties quoties*, by indorsement thereupon; and that such assignment and assignments, so to be made, shall absolutely vest and transfer the rights and property in and unto such bill or bills obligatory and of credit, and the monies due upon the same; and the assignee or assignees shall and may sue for, and maintain an action thereupon in his own name.

XXXIII. And whereas by an Act of this present session of Parliament, intituled *An Act for granting to Their Majesties certain Rates and Duties upon Salt, and upon Beer, Ale, and other Liquors, for securing certain Recompences and Advantages, in the said Act mentioned, to such Persons as shall voluntarily advance the sum of 1 000 000 Pounds towards carrying on the War against* France, it is enacted 'That no Member of the House of Commons shall at any Time be concerned in the farming, collecting, or managing any Sum or Sums of Money, Duties or other Aids by the said Act or any other Act of Parliament granted or to be granted to Their Majesties, except the Persons in the said Act excepted; and whereas some doubts may arise, whether any Member or Members of Parliament may be concerned in the Corporation to be erected in pursuance of this Act'; be it therefore declared and enacted by the Authority aforesaid, That it shall and may be lawful to and for any Member or Members of the House of Commons, to be a Member or Members of the said Corporation for the purposes in the Act mentioned; any thing in the said recited Act contained to the contrary in anywise notwithstanding.

27 KING WILLIAM III'S LAST SPEECH IN PARLIAMENT, ADDRESSED TO BOTH HOUSES ON 31 DECEMBER 1701

Introduction

According to the deist thinker Matthew Tindal, Lord Somers, William's Whig Prime Minister and the author of the Bill of Rights (see Doc. 21), 'is supposed to have assisted in framing this Speech, which was so acceptable to the well-wishers to the Revolution, and their friends abroad, that it was printed with decorations in English, Dutch, and French, and hung up in frames in almost every house in England and Holland, as his Majesty's last legacy to his own and all Protestant people (Cobbett, 1809 . . . , Vol. V, col. 1329).

Text

My Lords and Gentlemen;

I promise myself you are met together full of that just sense of the common danger of Europe, and the resentment of the late proceedings of the French king, which has been so fully and universally expressed in the loyal and seasonable Addresses of my people. – The owning and setting up the pretended Prince of Wales for King of England, is not only the highest indignity offered to me and the nation, but does so nearly concern every man, who has a regard for the Protestant Religion, or the present and future quiet and happiness of his country, that I need not press you to lay it seriously to heart, and to consider what further effectual means may be used, for securing the Succession of the Crown in the Protestant line, and extinguishing the hopes of all Pretenders, and their open and secret abettors. – By the French King's placing his Grandson on the throne of Spain, he is in a condition to oppress the rest of Europe, unless speedy and effectual measures be taken. Under this pretence, he is become the real Master on the whole Spanish Monarchy; he has made it to be entirely depending on France, and disposes of it, as of his own dominions, and by that means he has surrounded his neighbours in such a manner, that, though the name of peace may be said to continue, yet they are put to the expence and inconveniences of war. – This must affect England in the nearest and most sensible manner, in respect to our trade, which will soon become precarious in all the variable branches of it; in respect to our peace and safety at home, which we cannot hope should long continue; and in respect to that part, which England ought to take in the preservation of the liberty of Europe. – In order to obviate the general calamity, with which the rest of Christendom is threatened by this exhorbitant power of France, I have concluded several Alliances, according to the encouragement given me by both houses of parliament, which I will direct shall be laid before you, and which, I doubt not, you will enable me to make good. – There are some other Treaties still depending, that shall be likewise communicated to you as soon as they are perfected. – It is fit I should tell you, the eyes of all Europe are upon this Parliament;

Source: Cobbett's *Parliamentary History of England from the Norman Conquest in 1066 to the Year 1803* (London 1809 . . .) Vol. V, cols. 1329–31. For the sake of clarity, the speech has been divided into three paragraphs, but spelling and punctuation have been left unchanged.

all matters are at hand, till your resolutions are known; and therefore no time ought to be lost. – You have yet an opportunity, by God's blessing, to secure to you and your posterity the quiet enjoyment of your Religion and Liberties, if you are not wanting to yourselves, but will exert the ancient vigour of the English nation; but I tell you plainly, my opinion is, if you do not lay hold on this occasion, you have no reason to hope for another – In order to do your part, it will be necessary to have a great strength at sea, and to provide for the security of our ships in harbour; and also that there be such a force at land, as is expected in proportion to the forces of our allies.

Gentlemen of the House of Commons;

I do recommend these matters to you with that concern and earnestness, which their importance requires. At the same time I cannot but press you to take care of the public credit, which cannot be preserved but by keeping sacred that maxim, that they shall never be losers, who trust to a Parliamentary security. – It is always with regret, when I do ask aids of my people; but you will observe, that I desire nothing, which relates to any personal expence of mine; I am only pressing you to do all you can for your own safety and honour, at so critical and dangerous a time; and am willing, that what is given, should be wholly appropriated to the purposes for which it is intended. – And, since I am speaking on this head, I think it proper to put you in mind, that, during the late war, I ordered the accounts to be laid yearly before the Parliament, and also gave my assent to several bills for taking the public accounts, that my subjects might have the satisfaction, how the money given for the war was applied; and I am willing that matter may be put in any further way of examination, that it may appear, whether there were any misapplications and mismanagements; or whether the debt, that remains upon us, has really arisen from the shortness of the supplies, or the deficiency of the funds. – I have already told you, how necessary dispatch will be for carrying on this great public business, whereon our safety, and all that is valuable to us depends. I hope, what time can be spared, will be employed about those other very desirable things, which I have so often recommended from the throne; I mean, the forming some good bills for employing the poor, for encouraging trade, and the further suppressing of vice.

My Lords and Gentlemen;

I hope you are come together determined to avoid all manner of disputes and differences; and resolved to act with a general and hearty concurrence for promoting the common cause, which alone can make this a happy session. – I should think it as great a blessing as could befall England, if I could observe you as much inclined to lay aside those unhappy fatal animosities, which divide and weaken you, as I am disposed to make all my subjects safe and easy as to any, even the highest offences, committed against me. – Let me conjure you to disappoint the only hopes of our enemies by your unanimity. I have shewn, and will always shew, how desirous I am to be the common father of all my people. Do you, in like manner, lay aside parties and divisions. Let there be no other distinction heard of amongst us for the future, but of those, who are of the Protestant Religion, and the present establishment, and of those, who mean a Popish Prince, and a French government. – I will only add this; if you do in good earnest desire to see England hold the balance of Europe, and to be indeed at the head of the Protestant interest, it will appear by your right improving the present opportunity.

28 QUEEN ANNE'S DECLARATION OF WAR AGAINST FRANCE AND SPAIN, 4 MAY 1702

Text

Anne R.
Whereas it hath pleased Almighty God to call us to the government of these realms, at a time when our late dear brother William 3, of glorious memory, had, in pursuance of the repeated advices of the parliament of this kingdom, entered into solemn treaties of alliance with the emperor of Germany, the States General of the United Provinces, and other princes and potentates, for preserving the liberty and balance of Europe, and for reducing the exorbitant power of France; which treaties are grounded upon the unjust usurpations and incroachments of the French King, who had taken, and still keeps possession of a great part of the Spanish dominions, exercising an absolute authority over all that monarchy, having seized Milan and the Spanish Low Countries by his armies, and made himself master of Cadiz, of the entrance into the Mediterranean, and of the ports of the Spanish West Indies by his fleets; every where designing to invade the liberties of Europe, and obstruct the freedom of navigation and commerce. And it being provided by the third and fourth article of the forementioned alliance, that if, in the space of two months (which are some time since expired) the injuries complained of were not remedied, the parties concerned should mutually assist each other with their whole strength: And whereas, instead of giving the satisfaction that ought justly to be expected, the French king has not only proceeded to farther violence, but has added thereunto a great affront and indignity to us and our kingdoms, in taking upon him to declare the pretended prince of Wales king of England, Scotland, and Ireland, and has also influenced Spain to concur in the same affront and indignity as well as in his other oppressions: We find ourselves obliged, for maintaining the public faith, for vindicating the honour of our crown, and for preventing the mischiefs which all Europe is threatened with, to declare, and we do hereby accordingly declare war against France and Spain; and placing our entire confidence in the help of Almighty God, and so just and necessary an undertaking, we will (in conjunction with our own allies) vigorously prosecute the same by sea and land, being assured of the ready concurrences and assistance of our subjects, in a cause they have so openly and heartily espoused. And we do hereby will and require our lord high-admiral of England, our general of our forces, our lieutenants of our several counties, governors of our forts and garrisons, and all other officers and soldiers under them by sea and land, to do and execute all acts of hostility in the prosecution of this war, against France and Spain, their vassals and subjects, and to oppose their attempts; willing and requiring all our subjects to take notice of the same, whom we henceforth strictly forbid to hold any correspondence or communication with France and Spain, or their subjects. But, because there are remaining in our kingdom many of the subjects of France and Spain, we do declare our royal intention to be, that all the subjects of France and Spain, who shall demean themselves dutifully towards us, shall be safe in their persons and estates. – Given at our court at St James's, the 4th day of May 1702, in the first year of our reign.

Source: Cobbett's *Parliamentary History of England from the Norman Conquest in 1066 to the Year 1802* (London 1810) Vol. VI (1702–14) cols 16–17.

29 THE TREATY OF UTRECHT, 1713

Introduction

The two wars of the Grand Alliance against Louis XIV, the latter sometimes referred to as the war of the Spanish Succession, were, from the global perspective, Balance of Power wars *par excellence*. They lasted more than two decades, and when peace came it came gradually, in stages, and in mostly bilateral negotiations. The driving forces towards a settlement were the determination of the British government, and the desire of the French, to bring the protracted and costly warfare to an end; the delaying factors were the demands of the House of Austria.

The treaty here reproduced was the cornerstone of the Peace of Utrecht, but a number of other arrangements were needed to build a global settlement. Among them was the Assiento Treaty (signed in Madrid a few weeks earlier, text in Parry, 1969–80, Vol. 27, pp. 427 ff.) by which Britain (the East India Company) supplanted the French in the privilege of selling slaves to Spanish America. The full British–Spanish peace treaty followed in July (Parry, 1969–80, Vol. 28, pp. 295 ff.). It *inter alia* handed over Gibraltar and Minorca to Britain and thus made the Royal Navy a Meditarranean power. Eight months later, Austria signed with France at Rastadt, in March 1714 (Parry, 1969–80, Vol. 31, pp. 1 ff., French text). The Great Northern War (Sweden against Russia) that had run in tandem with these conflicts since 1700 came to a close with the Treaty of Nystad on 6 March 1721 (Parry, 1969–80, Vol. 31, p. 329).

The central feature of the Franco–British treaty is the idea of balance. It is a measure of the importance attached to them that the Letters Patent of King Louis XIV of France, of his grandsons Philip V (King of Spain) and the Duke of Berry and of his nephew the Duke of Orléans (who became Regent of France in 1715) are inserted between Articles VI and VII of the Treaty, thus incorporating them in the main body of the agreement itself. Letters Patent were written instruments issued by the head of state granting rights not otherwise permitted. They were affixed with the Great Seal but left open (patent) for ready reference. In explicit reference to the 'laws' of 'political equilibrium', all Letters Patent formally acknowledge the renunciation by Philip (formerly Duke of Anjou, and the first in the Bourbon line of Spanish kings) of any claim to the French crown, and by the Dukes of Berry and Orléans to that of Spain. The main result of the treaty, namely that England alone was left 'holding' the balance, is of course not mentioned in so many words.

Source: *British and Foreign State Papers*, Vol. 35 (1846–7) pp. 815–49; (excerpts).

Text

A treaty of Peace and Friendship, between the most Serene and most Potent Princess Anne, by the Grace of God, Queen of Great Britain, France, and Ireland, and the most Serene and most Potent Prince Lewis the XIVth, the most Christian King. – Concluded at Utrecht, March 31st/April 11th 1713.

WHEREAS it has pleased Almighty God, for the glory of His name, and for the universal welfare, so to direct the minds of Kings for the healing, now in his own time, the miseries of the wasted world, that they are disposed towards one another with a mutual desire of making peace: be it therefore known to all and singular, whom it may concern, that under this divine guidance, the most Serene and most Potent Princess and Lady Anne, by the grace of God, Queen of Great Britain, France, and Ireland, and the most Serene and most Potent Prince, the Lord Lewis the XIVth, by the grace of God, the most Christian King, consulting as well the advantage of their subjects, as providing (as far as mortals are able to do) for the perpetual tranquility of the whole Christian world, have resolved at last to put an end to the war, which was unhappily kindled, and has been obstinately carried on above these 10 years, being both cruel and destructive, by reason of the frequency of battles, and the effusion of Christian blood. And for promoting this their royal purpose, of their own proper motion, and from that paternal care which they delight of use toward their own subjects, and the public weal of Christendom, have nominated and appointed . . .

Wherefore the aforesaid Ambassadors . . . have agreed

I. That there be an universal perpetual peace, and a true and sincere friendship between the most serene and most potent Princess Anne Queen of Great Britain, and the most serene and most potent Prince Lewis the XIVth the most Christian King, and their heirs and successors, as also the kingdoms, states, and subjects of both, as well without as within Europe; and that the same be so sincerely and inviolably preserved and cultivated, that the one do promote the interest, honour, and advantage of the other, and that a faithful neighbourhood on all sides, and a secure cultivating of peace and friendship do daily flourish again, and increase.

II. That all enmities, hostilities, discords, and wars, between the said Queen of Great Britain, and the said most Christian King, and their subjects, do cease and be abolished, so that on both sides they do wholly refrain and desist from all plundering, depredation, harm-doing, injuries, and annoyance whatsoever, as well by land as by sea and fresh waters, in all parts of the world, and chiefly through all tracts, dominions, and places, of what kind soever, of the kingdoms, countries, and territories of either side.

III. All offences, injuries, harms, and damages, which the aforesaid Queen of Great Britain, and her subjects, or the aforesaid most Christian King, and his subjects, have suffered the one from the other, during this war, shall be buried in oblivion, so that neither on account, or under pretence thereof, or of any other thing, shall either hereafter, or the subjects of either, do, or give, cause, or suffer to be done or given to the other any hostility, molestation, or hindrance, by themselves, or by others, secretly or openly, directly or indirectly, under colour of right, or by way of fact.

IV. Furthermore for adding greater strength to the peace which is restored and to the faithful friendship which is never to be violated, and for cutting off all occasions of distrust, which might at any time arise from the established right and order of the hereditary succession to the crown of Great Britain, and the limitations thereof by the laws of Great Britain (made and enacted in the reigns of the late King William the IIIrd, of glorious memory, and of the present Queen) to the issue of the above said Queen, and in default thereof, to the most serene Princess Sophia, Dowager of Brunswick–Hanover, and her heirs in the Protestant Line of Hanover. That therefore the said succession may remain safe and secure, the most Christian King sincerely and solemnly acknowledges the above-said limitation of the succession to the kingdom of Great Britain, and on the faith and word of a king, on the pledge of his own successor's honour, he does declare and engage, that he accepts and approves the same, and that his heirs and successors do and shall accept and approve the same for ever. And under the same obligation of the word and honour of a king, the most Christian King promises, That no one besides the Queen herself, and her successors, according to the series of the said limitation, shall ever by him, or by his heirs or successors, be acknowledged, or reputed to be King or Queen of Great Britain. And for adding more ample credit to the said acknowledgement and promises, the most Christian King does engage, that whereas the person who, in the life-time of the late King James the IInd, did take upon him the title of Prince of Wales, and since his decease, that of King of Great Britain, is lately gone, of his own accord, out of the kingdom of France, to reside in some other place, he the aforesaid most Christian King, his heirs and successors, will take all possible care, that he shall not at any time hereafter, or under any pretence whatsoever return into the kingdom of France, or any the dominions thereof.

V. Moreover the most Christian King promises, as well in his own name, as in that of his heirs and successors, that they will at no time whatever disturb or give any molestation to the Queen of Great Britain, her heirs and successors, descended from the aforesaid Protestant line, who possess the crown of Great Britain, and the dominion belonging thereunto. Neither will the aforesaid most Christian King, or any one of his heirs, give at any time any aid, succour, favour, or council, directly or indirectly, by land or by sea, in money, arms, ammunition, warlike provisions, ships, soldiers, seamen, or any other way, to any person or persons, whosoever they be, who for any cause, or under any pretext whatsoever, should hereafter endeavour to oppose the said succession, either by open war, or by fomenting seditions, and forming conspiracies against such Prince or Princes who are in possesson of the Throne of Great Britain, by virtue of the Acts of Parliament aforementioned, or against that Prince or Princess, to whom the succession to the crown of Great Britain shall be open according to the said Acts of Parliament.

VI. Whereas the most destructive flame of war, which is to be extinguished by this peace, arose chiefly from thence, that the security and liberties of Europe could by no means bear the union of the kingdoms of France and Spain under one and the same king; and whereas it has at length been brought to pass by the assistance of the Divine Power, upon the most earnest instances of Her Sacred Royal Majesty of Great Britain, and with the consent both of the most Christian, and of the Catholic King, that this evil should in all times to come be obviated, by means of renunciations drawn in the most effectual form, and executed in the most solemn manner, the tenor thereof is as follows.

[At this point, the Letters Patent, by the Kings of France and Spain, the Dukes of Berry and Orléans, admitting the Renunciation of the King of Spain to the Crown of France are inserted in the Treaty.

Each document concludes with the same paragraph beginning with 'Read and published . . .', signed by the secretary Dongois; this paragraph is omitted here after its first appearance. The Duke of Berry's Renunciation has been left out and that of the Duke of Orléans shortened. Also omitted are: King Louis XIV's Letters Patent of December 1700, the complete list of 21 witnesses to King Philip's act of renunciation, and several repetitive depositions that merely confirm the validity of the main instruments.]

LEWIS, by the grace of God, King of France and Navarre: to all people present, and to come, greeting. During the various revolutions of war, wherein we have fought only to maintain the justice of the rights of the King, our most dear, and most beloved grandson, to the monarchy of Spain, we have never ceased to desire peace. The greatest successes did not at all dazzle us, and the contrary events, which the hand of God made use of to try us, rather than to destroy us, did not give birth to that desire in us, but found it there. But the time marked out by Divine Providence for the repose of Europe was not yet come; the distant fear of seeing one day our crown and that of Spain upon the head of one and the same Prince, did always make an equal impression on the Powers which were united against us; and this fear, which had been the principle cause of the war, seemed also to lay an insuperable obstacle in the way to peace. At last, after many fruitless negotiations, God, being moved with the suffering and groans of so many people, was pleased to open a surer way to come at so difficult a peace. But the same alarms still subsisting, the first and principal condition, which was proposed to us by our most dear and most beloved sister the Queen of Great Britain, as the essential and necessary foundation of treating, was that the King of Spain, our said brother and grandson, keeping the monarchy of Spain and of the Indies, should renounce for himself and his descendants for ever, the rights which his birth might at any time give him and them to our crown; that on the other hand, our most dear and most beloved grandson the Duke of Berry, and our most dear and most beloved nephew the Duke of Orléans, should likewise renounce for themselves, and for their descendants male and female for ever, their rights to the monarchy of Spain and the Indies. Our said sister caused it to be represented to us, That without a formal and positive assurance upon this point, which alone could be the bond of peace, Europe would never be at rest: all the Powers which share the same, being equally persuaded, that it was for their general interest, and for their common security, to continue a war, whereof no one could see the end, rather than to be exposed to behold the same Prince become one day master of 2 monarchies, so powerful as those of France and Spain. But as this Princess (whose indefatigable zeal for re-establishing the general tranquillity we cannot sufficiently praise) was sensible of all the reluctancy we had to consent, that one of our children so worthy to inherit the succession of our forefathers, should necessarily be excluded from it, if the misfortunes wherewith it has pleased God to afflict us in our family, should moreover take from us, in the person of the Dauphin, our most dear and most beloved great grandson, the only remainder of those Princes which our kingdom has so justly lamented with us; she entered into our pain, and after having jointly sought out gentler means of securing the peace, we agreed with our said sister to propose to the King of Spain other dominions, inferior indeed to those which he possesses, yet the value thereof would so much the more increase under his reign, in as much as in that case he would preserve his rights, and annex to our crown a part of the said dominions, if he came one time or other to succeed us. We employed therefore the strongest reasons to persuade him to accept this alternative. We gave him to understand, that the duty of his birth was the first which he ought to consult; that he owed himself to his house, and to his country, before he was obliged to Spain; that if he were wanting to his first engagements, he would perhaps one day in vain regret his having abandoned those rights, which he would be no more able to maintain. We added to these reasons the personal motives of friendship and of tender love, which we thought likely to move him; the pleasure we should have in seeing him from time to time near us, and in passing some part of our days with him, which we might promise ourselves from the neighbourhood of the dominions that were offered him, the satisfaction of instructing him ourselves concerning the state of our affairs, and of relying upon him for the future; so that if God should preserve to us the Dauphin, we could give our kingdom, in the person of the King, our brother, and grandson, a Regent instructed in the art of Government; and that if this child so precious to us and to our subjects, were also taken from us, we should at least have the consolation of leaving to our people a virtuous king, fit to govern them, and who would likewise annex to our crown very considerable dominions. Our instances reiterated with all the force, and with all the tender affection necessary to persuade a son, who so justly deserves those efforts, which we made for preserving him to France, produced nothing but reiterated refusals on his part, ever to abandon such brave and faithful subjects, whose zeal for him had been distinguished in those conjunctures, when his throne seemed to be the most shaken. So that persisting with an invincible firmness in his resolution, asserting likewise, that it was more glorious and more advantageous for our house and for our kingdom, than that which we pressed him to take, he declared in the Meeting of the States of the kingdom of Spain, assembled at Madrid for that purpose, that for obtaining a general peace, and securing the tranquillity of Europe by a balance of power, he of his own proper motion, of his own free will, and without any constraint, renounced for himself, for his heirs and successors for ever and ever, all pretensions, rights, and titles, which he or any of his descendants, have at present, or may have at any time to come whatsoever, to the succession of our crown; that he held for excluded therefrom himself, his children, heirs, and descendants for ever; that he consented for himself and for them, that now, as well as then, his right, and that of his descendants, should pass over and be transferred to whom among the Princes, whom the law of succession, and the order of birth calls, or shall call, to inherit our crown in default of our said brother and grandson the King of Spain, and his descendants, as it is more amply specified in the Act of Renunciation, approved by the States of his kingdom; and consequently he declared, that he desisted particularly from the right which hath been added to that of his birth by our letters patent of the month of December, 1700, whereby we declared, that it was our will, that the King of Spain and his descendants should always preserve the rights of their birth and original, in the manner as if they resided actually in our kingdom; and from the registry which was made of our said letters patents, both in our Court of Parliament, and in our Chamber of Accounts at Paris, we are sensible, as king and as father, how much it were to be desired that the general peace could have been concluded without a renunciation, which makes so great a change in our royal house, and in the ancient order of succeeding to our crown, but we are yet more sensible how much it is our duty to secure speedily to our subjects a peace which is so necessary for them. We shall never forget the efforts which they made for us during the long continuance of a war which we could not have supported if their zeal had not been much more extensive than their power. The welfare of a people so faithful is to us a supreme law, which ought to be preferred to any other consideration. It is to this law that we this day sacrifice the right of a grandson, who is so dear to us, and by the price which the general peace will cost our tender love, we shall at least have the comfort of shewing our subjects, that even at the expense of our blood, they will always keep the first place in our heart.

For these causes and other important considerations us thereunto moving, after having seen in our council the said Act of Renunciation of the King of Spain, our said brother and grandson, of the 5th November last, as also the Acts of Renunciation, which our said grandson the Duke of Berry, and our said nephew the Duke of Orléans, made reciprocally of their rights to the crown of Spain, as well for themselves as for their descendants, male and female, in consequence of the renunciation of our said brother and grandson the King of Spain, the whole hereunto annexed, with a copy collated of the said letters patent of the month of December,

1700, under the counter-seal of our chancery, of our special grace, Full Power, and Royal Authority, we have declared, decreed, and ordained, and by these presents signed with our hand, we do declare, decree, and ordain, we will, and it is our pleasure, that the said Act of Renunciation of our said brother and grandson the King of Spain, and those of our said grandson the Duke of Berry, and of our said nephew the Duke of Orléans, which we have admitted, and do admit, be registered in all our Courts of Parliament, and Chambers of our Accounts in our kingdom, and other places where it shall be necessary, in order to their being executed according to their form and tenor. And consequently, we will and intend, that our said letters patent, of the month of December, 1700, be and remain null, and as if they had never been made, that they be brought back to us, and that in the margin of the registers of our said Court of Parliament, and of our said Chamber of Accounts, where the enrolment of the said letters patent is, the extract of these presents be placed and inserted, the better to signify our intention as to the revocation, and nullity of the said letters. We will that in conformity to the said Act of Renunciation of our said brother and grandson the King of Spain, he be henceforth looked upon and considered as excluded from our succession, that his heirs, successors, and descendants be likewise excluded for ever, and looked upon as incapable of enjoying the same. We understand that in failure of them, all rights to our said Crown, and succession to our dominions, which might at any time whatsoever belong and appertain to them, be and remain transferred to our most dear, and most beloved grandson the Duke of Berry, and to his children, and descendants, being males, born in lawful marriage; and successively in failure of them, to those of the Princes of our Royal House and their descendants, who in right of their birth, or by the order established since the foundation of our monarchy, ought to succeed to our crown. And so we command our beloved and trusty councillors, the members of the Court of Parliament at Paris, that they do cause these presents, together with the Acts of Renunciation made by our said brother and grandson the King of Spain, by our said grandson the Duke of Berry, and by our said nephew the Duke of Orléans, to be read, published, and registered, and the contents thereof to be kept, observed, and executed, according to their form and tenor, fully, peaceably, and perpetually, ceasing, and causing to cease all molestations and hindrances, notwithstanding any laws, statutes, usages, customs, decrees, regulations, and other matters contrary thereunto: whereto, and to the derogations of the derogations therein contained, as we have derogated and do derogate by these presents, for this purpose only, and without being brought into precedent. For such is our pleasure.

And to the end that this may be a matter firm and lasting for ever, We have caused our seal to be affixed to these presents. Given at Versailles in the month of March, in the year of our Lord, 1713, and of our reign the 70th. Signed Lewis, and underneath, by the King, Phelypeaux. Visa, Phelypeaux. And sealed with the great seal on green wax, with strings of red and green silk.

Read and published, the Court being assembled, and registered among the Rolls of the Court, the King's Attorney-General being heard, and moving for the same, to the end that they may be executed according to their form and tenor, in pursuance, and in conformity to the Acts of this day. At Paris in Parliament, the 15th of March, 1713.

DONGOIS.

* * *

THE KING

Whereas on the 5th of November in this present year 1712, before Don Manuel of Vadillo and Velasco, my Secretary of State, and Chief Notary of the Kingdoms of

Castille and Leon, and witnesses, I delivered, swore to, and signed a public instrument of the tenor following, which is word for word, as here ensues:

I Philip, by the grace of God, King of Castile, León, Aragon, the 2 Sicilies, Jerusalem, Navarre, Granada, Toledo, Valentia, Galicia, Majorca, Seville, Sardinia, Corduba, Murcia, Jaen, the Algarves, Algezira, Gibraltar, the Canary Islands, the East and West Indies, the islands and terra firma of the ocean, Archduke of Austria, Duke of Burgundy, Brabant, and Milan, Count of Hapsburg, Flanders, Tyrol, and Barcelona, Lord of Biscay and Molina, etc. By the account and information of this instrument and writing of renunciation and relinquishment, and that it may remain for a perpetual rememberance, I do make known and declare to kings, princes, potentates, commonwealths, communities, and particular persons which now are, and shall be in future ages: that it being one of the principal positions of the Treaties of Peace depending between the crowns of Spain, and of France, with that of England, for the rendering it firm and lasting, and proceeding to a general one, on the maxim of securing for ever the universal good and quiet of Europe, by an equal weight of power, so that many being united in one the balance of the equality desired might not turn to the advantage of one, and the danger and hazard of the rest; it was proposed and insisted on by England, and it was agreed to on my part, and on that of the King my grandfather, that for avoiding at any time whatever the union of this monarchy with that of France, and the possibility that it might happen in any case, reciprocal renunciations should be made by me, and for all my descendants, to the possibility of succeeding to the monarchy of France, and on the part of those princes, and of all their race, present and to come, to that of succeeding to this monarchy; by forming a proper project of abdication of all rights which may be claimed by the 2 Royal Houses of this and of that monarchy, as to their succeeding mutually to each other; by separating by the legal means of my renunciation, my branch from the royal stem of France, and all the branches of France from the stem of the blood-royal of Spain; by taking care at the same time, in pursuance of the fundamental and perpetual maxim of the balance of power in Europe, which persuades and justifies the avoiding in all cases imaginable the union of the monarchy of France with that of Spain, that the inconvenience should likewise be provided against, lest in default of my issue, the case should happen that this monarchy should devolve again to the House of Austria, whose dominions and dependencies even without the union of the Empire, would make it formidable; a motive which at other times made it justifiable to separate the hereditary dominions of the House of Austria from the body of the Spanish monarchy; It being agreed and settled to this end by England with me, and with the King my grandfather, that in failure of me, and of my issue, the Duke of Savoy and his sons and descendants, being males, born in constant lawful marriage, are to enter upon the succession of this monarchy; and in default of his male line, the Prince Amadeo of Carignan, and his sons, and descendants, being males, born in constant lawful marriage; and in default of his line, Prince Thomas, brother of the Prince of Carignan, his sons, and descendants, being males, born in constant lawful marriage, who, as descendants of the Infanta Dona Catharina, daughter of Philip II, and being expressly called, have a clear and known right, supposing the friendship and perpetual alliance, which the Duke of Savoy, and his descendants are to solicit and obtain from this crown; it being to be believed, that by this perpetual and never-ceasing hope, the needle of the balance may remain invariable, and all the Powers, wearied with the toil and uncertainty of battles, may be amicably kept in an equal poise; it not remaining in the disposal of any of the parties to alter this federal equilibrium by way of any contract of renunciation, or retrocession, since the same reason which induced its being admitted, demonstrates its permanency, a fundamental Constitution being formed, which may settle by an unalterable law the succession of what is to come. In consequence of what is above-said, and for the love I bear to the Spaniards, and from the knowledge that I have of what I owe them, and the repeated experience of their fidelity, and for making a return to Divine Providence, by this resignation to its destiny, for the great benefit of having placed and maintained me on the throne among such illustrious and well-deserving vassals, I have determined to abdicate, for myself, and all my descendants, the right of succeeding to the crown of France, desiring not to depart from living and dying with my beloved, and faithful Spaniards; leaving to all my descendants the inseparable bond of their fidelity and love. And to the end that this resolution may have its due effect, and that the matter may cease, which has been looked upon as one of the principal motives of the war, which has hitherto afflicted Europe, of my own motion, free, spontaneous, and unconstrained will, I Don Philip, by the grace of God, King of Castile, León, Aragon . . . , etc., do by this present instrument, for myself, for my heirs and successors, renounce, quit, and relinquish for ever and ever all pretensions, rights, and titles, which I have, or any descendants of mine hath at present, or may have at any time to come to the succession of the crown of France; and I declare, and hold myself for excluded and separated, me, and my sons, heirs, and descendants for ever, for excluded and disabled absolutely, and without limitation, difference, and distinction of persons, degrees, sexes, and times, from the act, and right of succeeding to the crown of France. And I will and consent, for myself, and my said descendants, that now, as well as then, it may be taken for passed over and transferred to him, who by mine and their being excluded, disabled and incapacitated, shall be found next and immediate in degree to the King, by whose death it shall become vacant; and the succession to the said crown of France, is at any time, and in any case to be settled on, and given to him, to have and to hold the same as true and lawful successor, in the same manner, as if I, and my descendants had not been born, or been in the world; since such are we to be held and esteemed, because in my person, and in that of my descendants, there is no consideration to be had, or foundation to be made of active or passive representation, beginning, or continuation of lineage effective, or contentive of substance, blood, quality, nor can the descent, or computation of degrees of those persons be derived from the most Christian King, my Lord, and grandfather, nor from the Dauphin my father, nor from the glorious kings their progenitors; nor take possession of the degree of proximity, and exclude from it the person, who, as is above-said, shall be found next in degree. I will and consent for myself, and for my descendants, that from this time, as well as then this right be looked upon and considered as passed over, and transferred to the Duke of Berry my brother, and to his sons and descendants, being males, born in constant lawful marriage; and in default of his male issue to the Duke of Orléans my uncle, and to his sons and descendants, being males, born in constant lawful marriage; and in default of his issue, to the Duke of Bourbon my cousin, and to his sons and descendants, being males, born in constant lawful marriage; and in like manner successively to all the Princes of the blood of France, their sons and descendants, being males, for ever and ever, according to the place and order in which they shall be called to the crown by right of their birth; and consequently to that person among the said Princes, who (I and all my said descendants, being, as is above said, excluded, disabled, and incapacitated) shall be found the nearest in immediate degree after that King, by whose death the vacancy of the crown of France shall happen, and to whom the succession ought to belong at any time, and in any case whatsoever, that he may possess the same as true and lawful successor, in the same manner as if I and my descendants had not been born. And for the greater strength of this Act of Abdication of all rights and titles, which appertained to me, and to all my sons and descendants, of succeeding to the aforesaid crown of France, I depart from and relinquish especially that which might moreover accrue to the rights of birth from the letters patent, of instrument, whereby the King my grandfather preserved and reserved to me, and enabled me to enjoy the right of succession to the crown of France, which instrument was dispatched at Versailles in the month of December, in the year 1700, and passed and approved, and registered by the Parliament. I will that it cannot serve me for a foundation to the purposes therein provided for, and I reject and renounce it, and hold it for null and void, and of no force, and for cancelled, and as if no such instrument had ever been executed. I promise and oblige myself, on the faith of a King's word, that as much as shall relate to my part, and that of my sons and descendants, which are and shall be, I will take care of the observation and accomplishment of this writing, without permitting or consenting that any thing be done contrary thereunto, directly or indirectly, in the whole or in part; and I relinquish and depart from all and all manner of remedies, known or unknown, ordinary or extraordinary, and which by common right, or special privilege might belong to us, to me, and to my sons and descendants, to reclaim, mention, or allege against what is abovesaid; and I renounce them all, and especially that of evident prejudice, enormous, and most enormous, which may be reckoned to have happened in this relinquishment and renunciation of the right of being able at any time to succeed to the crown afore mentioned. I will that none of the said remedies, nor others, of whatsoever name, use, importance, and quality they may be, do avail us, or can avail us. And if, in fact, or under any colour, we should endeavour to seize the said kingdom by force of arms, by making or moving war, offensive or defensive, from this time for ever, that is to be held, judged and declared, for an unlawful, unjust, and wrongly undertaken war, and for violence, invasion, and usurpation, done against reason and conscience; and on the contrary, that is to be judged and esteemed a just, lawful, and allowed war, which shall be made, or moved in behalf of him, who by the exclusion of me, and of my said sons and descendants, ought to succeed to the said crown of France, to whom the subjects and natives thereof are to apply themselves, and to obey him, to take and perform the oath and homage of fealty, and to serve him as their lawful King and Lord. And the relinquishment and renunciation, for me, and my said sons, and descendants, is to be firm, stable, valid, and irrevocable perpetually, for ever and ever. And I declare and promise that I have not made, neither will I make any protestation, or reclaiming, in public, or in secret, to the contrary, which may hinder, or diminish the force of what is contained in this writing; and that if I should make it, although it be sworn to, it is not to be valid, neither can it have any force; and for the greater strength and security of what is contained in this renunciation, and of what is said and promised on my part therein, I give again the pledge of my faith, and royal word, and I swear solemnly by the Gospels contained in this Missal, upon which I lay my right hand, that I will observe, maintain, and accomplish this Act, and instrument of renunciation, as well for myself as for all my successors, heirs, and descendants, in all the clauses therein contained, according to the most natural, literal, and plain sense and construction; and that I have not sought, neither will I seek any dispensation from this oath; and if it shall be sought for by any particular person, or shall be granted *motu proprio*, I will not use it, nor take any advantage of it. Nay, in such case as that it should be granted me, I make another the like oath, that there may always be and remain one oath above and beyond all dispensations which may be granted me. And I deliver this writing before the present Secretary, Notary of this my kingdom, and I have signed it, and commanded it to be sealed with my royal seal . . .

I, the King

PHILIP, grandson of France, Duke of Orléans, Valois, Chartres, and Nemours: to all Kings, Princes, Commonwealths, Potentates, Communities, and to all persons, as well present as to come, we make known by these presents; that the fear of the union of the crowns of France and Spain, having been the principal motive of the present war, and the other Powers of Europe having always apprehended lest these 2 crowns should come upon one head, it has been laid down as the foundation of the peace, which is treated of at present, and 'tis hoped may be cemented more and more, for the repose of such a number of countries, which have sacrificed themselves, as so many victims, to oppose the dangers wherewith they thought themselves threatened, that it was necessary to establish a kind of equality and equilibrium between the Princes who were in dispute, and to separate for ever, in an irrevocable manner, the rights which they pretend to have, and which they defended, sword in hand, with a reciprocal slaughter on each side.

That with intent to establish this equality, the Queen of Great Britain proposed, and upon her instances, it has been agreed by the King, our most honoured lord and uncle, and by the Catholic King, our most dear nephew, that for avoiding at any time whatsoever the union of the crowns of France and Spain, reciprocal renunciations should be made, that is to say, the Catholic King Philip V, our nephew, for himself and for all his descendants, of the succession to the crown of France; as also by the Duke of Berry, our most dear nephew, and by us, for ourselves, and for all our descendants to the crown of Spain; on condition likewise that neither the house of Austria, nor any of the descendants thereof, shall be able to succeed to the crown of Spain, because this house itself, without the union of the empire, would become formidable, if it should add a new power to its ancient dominions; and consequently this equilibrium, which is designed to be established for the good of the princes and states of Europe, would cease. Now it is certain that without this equilibrium, either the states suffer from the weight of their own greatness, or envy engages their neighbours to make alliances to attack them, and to reduce them to such a point, that these great Powers may inspire less fear, and may not aspire to an universal monarchy.

For attaining the end which is proposed, and by reason that His Catholic Majesty has on his part made his renunciation the 5th of this present month, we consent that, in failure of Philip V, our nephew, and of his descendants, the crown of Spain do pass over to the house of the Duke of Savoy, whose rights are clear and known, inasmuch as he descends from the Infanta Catharina, daughter of Philip II, and as he is called by the other kings his successors; so that his right to the succession of Spain is indisputable.

And we desiring on our side to concur towards the glorious end, which is proposed for re-establishing the public tranquillity, and for preventing the fears which the rights of our birth, or all others, which might appertain unto us, might occasion, have resolved to make this relinquishment, this abdication, and this renunciation of all our rights, for ourselves, and in the name of all our successors and descendants . . .

[Louis XIV's Letters Patent of December 1700 declaring that his grandson, the Duke of Anjou, now King Philip V of Spain, preserved his birth right to the crown of France 'in the same manner as if he made his actual residence in our kingdom' is also reproduced in the Treaty at this point.]

VII. That there be a free use of navigation and commerce between the subjects of both their Royal Majesties, as it was formerly in time of peace, and before the declaration of this last war, and also as it is agreed and concluded by the Treaty of Commerce[1] this day made between the 2 nations.

1. Rejected by the British Parliament, on Whig initiative (Trevelyan, 1929, p. 499).

VIII. That the ordinary distribution of justice be revived and open again through the kingdoms and dominions of each of their Royal Majesties, so that it may be free for all the subjects on both sides to sue for and obtain their rights, pretensions, and actions according to the laws, constitutions, and statutes of each kingdom.

IX. The most Christian King shall take care that all fortifications of the city of Dunkirk be razed, that the harbour be filled up, and that the sluices or moles which serve to cleanse the harbour be levelled, and that at the said King's own expense, within the space of 5 months after the conditions of peace are concluded and signed, that is to say, the fortifications towards the sea, within the space of 2 months, and those towards the land, together with the said banks, within 3 months; on this express condition also, that the said fortifications, harbours, moles, or sluices, be never repaired again. All which shall not however be begun to be ruined, till after that every thing is put into His Christian Majesty's hands, which is to be given him, instead thereof, or as an equivalent.

X. The said most Christian King shall restore to the Kingdom and Queen of Great Britain, to be possessed in full right for ever, the bay and straits, of Hudson, together with all lands, sea coasts, rivers, and places situate in the said bay and straits, and which belong thereunto, no tracts of land or of sea being excepted, which are at present possessed by the subjects of France. All which, as well as any buildings there made, in the condition they now are, and likewise all fortresses there erected, either before or since the French seized the same, shall, within 6 months from the ratification of the present Treaty, or sooner, if possible, be well and truly delivered to the British subjects having commission from the Queen of Great Britain to demand and receive the same, entire and undemolished, together with all the cannon and cannon-ball which are therein, as also with a quantity of powder, if it be there found, in proportion to the cannon-ball, and with the other provision of war usually belonging to cannon. It is however, provided that it may be entirely free for the Company of Quebec, and all other subjects of the most Christian King whatsoever, to go by land, or by sea, whithersoever they please out of the lands of the said bay, together with all their goods, merchandizes, arms, and effects, of what nature or condition soever, except such things as are above reserved in this Article. But it is agreed on both sides, to determine within a year, by commissaries to be forthwith named by each party, the limits which are to be fixed between the said Bay of Hudson, and the places appertaining to the French; which limits both the British and French subjects shall be wholly forbid to pass over, or thereby to go to each other by sea or by land. The same Commissaries shall also have orders to describe and settle in like manner the boundaries between the other British and French colonies in those parts.

XI. The above-mentioned most Christian King shall take care that satisfaction be given, according to the rule of justice and equity, to the English Company trading to the Bay of Hudson, for all damages and spoil done to their colonies, ships, persons, and goods, by the hostile incursions and depredations of the French, in time of peace, an estimate being made thereof by Commissaries to be named at the requisition of each party. The same Commissaries shall moreover inquire as well into the complaints of the British subjects concerning the ships taken by the French in time of peace, as also concerning the damages sustained last year in the island called Montserat, and others, as into those things of which the French subjects complain, relating to the capitulation in the Island of Nevis, and castle of Gambia, also to French ships, if perchance any such have been taken by British subjects in time of peace. And in like manner into all disputes of this kind which shall be found to have arisen between both nations, and which are not yet ended; and due justice shall be done on both sides without delay.

XII. The most Christian King shall take care to have delivered to the Queen of Great Britain, on the same day that the ratifications of this Treaty shall be exchanged, a solemn and authentic letter, or instruments, by virtue whereof it shall appear that the Island of St Christopher is to be possessed alone hereafter by British subjects, likewise all Nova Scotia or Accadie, with its ancient boundaries, as also the city of Port Royal, now called Annapolis Royal, and all other things in those parts, which depend on the said lands and islands, together with the dominion, propriety, and possession of the said islands, lands and places, and all rights reserved whatsoever, by Treaties, or any other way obtained, which the most Christian King, the crown of France, or any the subjects thereof, have hitherto had to the said islands, lands, and places, and the inhabitants of the same, are yielded and made over to the Queen of Great Britain, and to her crown for ever, as the most Christian King doth at present yield and Make over all the particulars abovesaid; and that in such ample manner and form, that the subjects of the most Christian King shall hereafter be excluded from all kind of fishing in the said seas, bays, and other places, on the coasts of Nova Scotia, that is to say, on those which lie towards the east, within 30 leagues, beginning from the island commonly called Sable, inclusively, and thence stretching along towards the south-west.

XIII. The island called Newfoundland, with the adjacent islands, shall from this time forward belong of right wholly to Britain; and to that end the town and fortress of Placentia and whatever other places in the said island are in the possession of the French, shall be yielded and given up, within 7 months from the exchange of ratifications of this Treaty, or sooner if possible, by the most Christian King, to those who have a commission from the Queen of Great Britain for that purpose. Nor shall the most Christian King, his heirs and successors, or any of their subjects, at any time hereafter lay claim to any right to the said island and islands, or to any part of it or them. Moreover it shall not be lawful for the subjects of France to fortify any place in the said Island of Newfoundland, or to erect any buildings there, besides stages made of boards and huts necessary and usual for drying of fish; or to resort to the said island, beyond the time necessary for fishing and drying of fish. But it shall be allowed to the subjects of France to catch fish, and to dry them on land, in that part only, and in no other besides that of the said Island of Newfoundland, which stretches from the place called Cape Bonavista to the northern point of the said island, and from thence running down by the western side, reaches as far as the place called Point Riche. But the island called Cape Breton, as also all others, both in the mouth of the River St Lawrence, and in the gulf of the same name, shall hereafter belong of right to the French; and the most Christian King shall have all manner of liberty to fortify any place or places there.

XIV. It is expressly provided, that in all the said places and colonies to be yielded and restored by the most Christian King, in pursuance of this treaty, the subjects of the said King may have liberty to remove themselves within a year to any other place, as they shall think fit, together with their moveable effects. But those who are willing to remain there, and to be subject to the kingdom of Great Britain, are to enjoy the free exercise of their religion, according to the usage of the Church of Rome, as far as the laws of Great Britain do allow the same.

XV. The subjects of France inhabiting Canada and others shall hereafter give no hindrance or molestation to the 5 nations or cantons of Indians, subject to the dominion of Great Britain, nor to the other natives of America, who are friends to the same. In like manner the subjects of Great Britain shall behave themselves peaceably towards the Americans, who are subjects or friends of France; and on both sides they shall enjoy full liberty of going and coming on account of trade. As also the natives of those countries shall, with the same liberty, resort, as they please, to the British and French colonies, for promoting trade on one side and the other, without any molestation or hindrance, either on the part of the British subjects or of the French. But it is to be exactly and distinctly settled by Commissionaries, who are and who ought to be accounted the subjects and friends of Britain and France.

XVI. That all letters, as well of reprisal as of mark and countermark,[2] which have hitherto on any account been granted on either side, be and remain null, void, and of no effect; and that no letters of this kind be hereafter granted by either of their said Royal Majesties against the subjects of the other, unless there shall have been plain proof beforehand of a denial or wrongful delay of justice, and unless the petition of him who desires the grant of letters of reprisal be exhibited and shown to the Minister who resides there in the name of that Prince, against whose subjects those letters are demanded, that he within the space of 4 months or sooner may make inquiry to the contrary, or procure that satisfaction be forthwith given to the plaintiff by the party accused. But in case no Minister be residing there from that Prince, against whose subjects reprisals are demanded, that letters of reprisal be not granted till after the space of 4 months, to be computed from the day whereon the petition was exhibited and presented to the Prince, against whose subjects reprisals are desired, or to his Privy Council.

XVII. Whereas it is expressly stipulated among the conditions of the suspension of arms, made between the above-mentioned Contracting Parties, the 11 day of August last past, and afterwards prolonged for 4 months more, in what cases ships, merchandizes, and other moveable effects, taken on either side, should either become prize to the captor, or be restored to the former proprietor; it is therefore agreed, that in those cases the conditions of the aforesaid suspension of arms shall remain in full force, and that all things relating to such captures, made either in the British and Northern Seas, or in any other place, shall be well and truly executed according to the tenor of the same.

XVIII. But in case it happened through inadvertency, or imprudence, or any other cause whatsoever, that any subject of their aforesaid Royal Majesties do, or commit anything by land, by sea, or on fresh waters, in any part of the world, whereby this present Treaty be not observed, or whereby any particular Article of the same hath not its effect, this peace and good correspondence between the Queen of Great Britain, and the most Christian King, shall not be therefore interrupted or broken, but shall remain in its former strength, force, and vigour. But that subject alone shall be answerable for his own fact, and shall suffer the punishment which is inflicted by the rules and directions of the Law of Nations.

XIX. However in case (which God Almighty forbid) the dissensions which have been laid asleep, should at any time be renewed, between their said Royal Majesties, or their successors, and break out into open war, the ships, merchandizes, and all the effects, both moveable and immoveable, on both sides, which shall be found to be and remain in the ports, and in the dominions of the adverse party, shall not be confiscated, or any wise endamaged; but the entire space of 6 months, to be reckoned from the day of the rupture, shall be allowed to the said subjects of each of their Royal Majesties, in which they may sell the aforesaid things, or any part else of their effects, or carry and remove them from thence whither they please, without any molestation, and retire from thence themselves.

XX. Just and reasonable satisfaction shall be given to all and singular the allies of the Queen of Great Britain, in those matters which they have a right to demand from France.

2. Letters of marque: a licence granted by a government to a private person to fit out an armed vessel to cruise as a privateer at sea and plunder the enemy.

XXI. The most Christian King will, in consideration of the friendship of the Queen of Great Britain, grant, that in making the Treaty with the Empire, all things concerning the state of religion in the aforesaid empire, shall be settled conformable to the tenor of the Treaties of Westphalia, so that it shall plainly appear, that the most Christian King neither will have, nor would have had any alteration made in the said treaties.

XXII. Moreover, the most Christian King engages that he will forthwith after the peace is made, cause justice to be done to the family of Hamilton, concerning the dukedom of Chatelraut, to the Duke of Richmond, concerning such requests as he has to make in France, as also to Charles Douglas, concerning certain lands to be reclaimed by him, and to others.

XXIII. By the mutual consent of the Queen of Great Britain, and of the most Christian King, the subjects of each party, who were taken prisoners during the war, shall be set at liberty, without any distinction or ransom, paying such debts, as they shall have contracted in the time of their being prisoners.

XXIV. It is mutually agreed, that all and singular the conditions of the peace made this day between his sacred Royal most Christian Majesty, and his sacred Royal Majesty of Portugal, be confirmed by this Treaty; and her sacred Royal Majesty of Great Britain takes upon herself the guaranty of the same, to the end that it may be more firmly and inviolably observed.

XXV. The Treaty of Peace made this day between his sacred Royal most Christian Majesty, and His Royal Highness the Duke of Savoy, is particularly included in this Treaty, as an essential part of it, and is confirmed by it, in the same manner as if it were word for word inserted therein; Her Royal Majesty of Great Britain declaring expressly that she will be bound by the stipulations of security and guaranty provided therein, as well as by those she has formerly taken upon herself.

XXVI. The most serene King of Sweden with his kingdoms, dominions, provinces, and rights, as also the Great Duke of Tuscany, the Republic of Genoa, and the Duke of Parma, are in the best manner included in this Treaty.

XXVII. Their Majesties have also been pleased to comprehend in this Treaty the Hanse Towns, namely Lubeck, Bremen, and Hamburg, and the city of Dantzick, with this effect, that as soon as the general peace shall be concluded, the Hanse Towns and the city of Dantzick, may for the future, as common friends, enjoy the ancient advantages which they have heretofore had in the business of trade, either by Treaties, or by old custom.

XXVIII. Those shall be comprehended in this present Treaty of Peace, who shall be named by common consent, on the one part and on the other, before the exchange of the Ratifications, or within six months after.

XXIX. Lastly, solemn Ratifications of this present Treaty, and made in due form, shall be exhibited on both sides at Utrecht, and mutually and duly exchanged within the space of 4 weeks, to be computed from the day of the signing, or sooner if possible.

XXX. In witness thereof, we the Underwritten Ambassadors Extraordinary and Plenipotentiaries of the Queen of Great Britain, and of the most Christian King, have put our seals to these present instruments, subscribed with our own hands, at Utrecht, the 31st/11th day of March/April in the year 1713.

Joh. Bristol, C.P.S.
Strafford

Huxelles
Mesnager

30 LORD SHELBURNE'S SPEECH ON THE RATIFICATION OF THE PEACE OF PARIS WITH THE UNITED STATES OF AMERICA, FRANCE, ETC. HOUSE OF LORDS, 21 FEBRUARY 1783

Introduction

The Earl of Shelburne became Prime Minister in July 1782, and helped to negotiate the Treaty of Paris that ended the war of American Independence. He resigned in February 1783, was made Marquis of Lansdowne the next year, but never returned to government.

Text

The Earl of *Shelburne* then rose. The lateness of the hour, my lords, said his lordship, will not suffer me to take the liberty of trespassing so far on your patience, as my feelings would prompt me to on the present occasion. I shall not address your passions – that candid province I will leave to those who have shewn such ability for its government to-night. As my conduct has been founded upon integrity – facts, and plain reasoning, will form its best support. I shall necessarily wave the consideration of the critical moment at which I stepped into the administration of the affairs of this country – a moment when, if there be any credit due to the solemn, public declarations of men, who seemed then, and seem now, to have the welfare of the state nearest to their hearts – every hope of renovated lustre was gone, and nothing but dreary despondency remained to the well-wishers of Great Britain. I am now speaking within memory, and consequently within proof. It is not for me to boast of my motives for standing forward at a period so alarming. My circumstances are not so obscure as to render my conduct a matter of dubiety, and my own explanation of my feelings would, I flatter myself, fall far short of that credit which sympathy would give me in the minds of men, whose patriotism is not that of words: the ambition of advancing to the service of our country in an hour when even brave men shrink from the danger, is honourable, and I shall not be catechized for entertaining such an impulse. I make no merit of my hardihood, and when I speak of mine, I wish your lordships to understand me as speaking of the generous enterprize of my noble and honourable colleagues in administration. It was our duty as good citizens, when the state was in danger, that all selfish apprehensions should be banished. I shall not, therefore, expatiate on my reasons for coming into office, but openly and candidly tell your lordships how I have conducted myself in it. A peace was the declared wish of the nation at that time. How was that to be procured best for the advantage of the country? Certainly by gaining the most accurate knowledge of the relative condition of the powers at war. Here a field of knowledge was required to be beaten, to which no one man, vast and profound as it is possible to picture human capacity, would by any means be supposed equal. Then if one man was inadequate to the whole task, the next question naturally is, what set of men are best qualified as auxiliaries in it?

Sources: Cobbett, William, *Parliamentary History of England, from the Norman Conquest in 1066 to the year 1803* (London, 1814) Vol. XXIII, pp. 407–20; Harlow, Vincent T., *The Founding of the Second British Empire 1763–1793* (London, 1952) Vol. 1, p. 436 (condensed).

What is the skill required? A knowledge of trade and commerce, with all its relations, and an intimate acquaintance with military affairs, and all its concomitants. Were men of this description consulted previous to, and during the progress of the treaty now before your lordships? I answer, they were. And with this sanction administraton need assume no false brow of bravery, in combatting the glittering expressions of that hasty opposition that had been set up to the present terms.

Let us examine them, my lords, let us take several assertions in their turn, and without wishing to intrude too much on your lordships time, I shall be pardoned for giving a distinct answer to each head of objection. Ministry, in the first place, is blamed for drawing the boundary they have done between the territories of the United States and those of our sovereign in Canada. I wish to examine every part of the treaties on the fair rule of the value of the district ceded – to examine it on the amount of the exports and imports, by which alone we could judge of its importance. The exports of this country to Canada, then, were only 140 000*l*. and the imports were no more than 50 000*l*. Suppose the entire fur trade sunk into the sea, where is the detriment to this country? Is 50 000*l*. a year imported in that article any object for Great Britain to continue a war of which the people of England, by their representatives, have declared their abhorrence? Surely it is not. But much less must this appear in our sight, when I tell parliament, and the whole kingdom, that for many years past, one year with another, the preservation of this annual import of 50 000*l*. has cost this country, on an average, 800 000*l*. I have the vouchers in my pocket, should your lordships be inclined to examine the fact. But the trade is not given up, it is only divided for our benefit. I appeal to all men conversant with the nature of that trade, whether its best resources in Canada do not lie to the northward. What, then, is the result of this part of the treaty, so wisely, and with so much sincere love on the part of England clamoured against by noble lords? Why this. You have generously given America, with whom every call under Heaven urges you to stand on the footing of brethren, a share in a trade, the monopoly of which your sordidly preserved to yourselves, at the loss of the enormous sum of 750 000*l*. Monopolies, some way or other, are ever justly punished. They forbid rivalry, and rivalry is of the very essence of the well-being of trade. This seems to be the æra of protestantism in trade. All Europe appear enlightened, and eager to throw off the vile shackles of oppressive ignorant monopoly; that unmanly and illiberal principle, which is at once ungenerous and deceitful. A few interested Canadian merchants might complain; for merchants would always love monopoly, without taking a moment's time to think whether it was for their interest or not. I avow that monopoly is always unwise; but if there is any nation under heaven, who ought to be the first to reject monopoly, it is the English. Situated as we are between the old world and the new, and between the southern and northern Europe, all that we ought to covet upon earth is free trade, and fair equality. With more industry, with more enterprize, with more capital than any trading nation upon earth, it ought to be our constant cry, let every market be open, let us meet our rivals fairly, and we ask no more. It is a principle on which we have had the wisdom to act with respect to our brethren of Ireland; and, if conciliaton be our view, why should we not reach it out also to America? Our generosity is not much, but, little as it is, let us give it with a grace. Indeed, to speak properly, it is not generosity to them, but œconomy to ourselves; and in the boundaries which are established we have saved ourselves the immense sum of 800 000*l*. a year, and shewed to the Americans our sincere love and fair intentions, in dividing the little bit of trade which nature had laid at their doors; and telling them that we desired to live with them in communion of benefits, and in the sincerity of friendship. . . . [The speaker then] turned his attention to the cognate question of the back-lands between the Ohio and the Great Lakes. While Britain governed that country she had never been able to restrain the settlers from pushing westward. Now a 'rage for new settlements' had begun; and long might it continue, for it would concentrate American energies on agriculture and away from manufacturing and navigation. So engaged, the settlers would continue to be as profitable to Britain as if they were still British subjects; and there was the additional advantage that Britain would no longer be called upon to administer an inaccessible and indefensible country. It had been proved, he declared, '*that we prefer trade to dominion*'. 'But the Indians were abandoned to their enemies!' Noble lords have taken great pains to shew the immense value of these Indians; it was not unnatural for noble lords, who had made so lavish a use of these Indians, to complain of their loss; but those who abhorred their violence would think ministry had done wisely. The Americans knew best how to tame their savage natures. The descendants of the good William Penn would manage them better than all the Mr Stuarts with all the Jewsharps, razors, trumpery, and jobs that we could contrive. 'But our treaties with them bound us to everlasting protection!' This is one of those assertions which always sounds well, and is calculated to amuse the uninformed mind: but what is the meaning of *in perpetuo* in all treaties? That they shall endure as long as the parties are able to perform the conditions. This is the meaning of perpetual alliances; and in the present treaty with America, the Indian nations were not abandoned to their enemies; they were remitted to the care of neighbours, whose interest it was as much as ours to cultivate friendship with them, and who were certainly the best qualified for softening and humanizing their hearts. But I shall dismiss this subject, though it is blended with others, and proceed to the investigation of the rest of the objections to the treaties of pacification.

'Why have you given America the freedom of fishing in all your creeks and harbours, and especially on the banks of Newfoundland', say the noble objectors to this article? Why? because, in the first place, they could from their locality have exercised a fishery in that quarter for the first season (for there are two), in spite of all our efforts to repel them. In February the first season commences, and that is entirely at their devotion; for our people can never take their stations there so soon. With regard to the other season, let us again revert to what I have said respecting the fur trade; though we have not a monopoly, we have got such superior advantages in the article of drying, curing, and preparing our fish for market, from the exclusive command of the most contiguous shores, that a rivalry can only whet our industry to reap those benefits our preferable situation in this respect presents to us. 'But why have you not stipulated a reciprocity of fishing in the American harbours and creeks?' I will tell your lordships: – because we have abundant employment in our own. Would not an American think it sordid in the extreme, nay, consider it bordering on madness, to covet the privilege of battening our cattle on some of their sterile wilds, when we had our own fertile savannahs to have recourse to? Such would be the opinion entertained of ministry, if it had childishly and avariciously made a stipulation of the nature of the objectors think they ought to have. The broad and liberal policy on which the present treaty is formed, is in my opinion much more wise and beneficial than would have been the narrow and wretched plan of bargaining for every little particle of advantage which we might have procured, perhaps, by stickling in the negociation. As to the masts, a noble lord said, we were to have in such abundance at Penobscot, I will oppose a fact to his bare assertion. I have in my pocket a certificate from one of the ablest surveyors in our service, captain Twiss, that there is not a tree there capable of being made into a mast.

I shall now advert to the preliminary Articles with France and Spain; and first to the objections respecting the cession to France on the coast of Newfoundland. This, to be sure, is not to be tried by the rule of imports and exports. But what is it? Seven degrees of latitude. These are sounding words; but they are no more. By this part of the treaty future quarrels are guarded against. The concurrent fishery formerly exercised was a source of endless strife; the French are now confined to a certain spot; it is nothing compared to the extent we possess, and it is besides situate in the least productive part of that coast. But I would not have your lordships pay greater attention to my bare assertion, than I trust you will to the assertions of those who take upon themselves to pronounce this part of the treaty wrong. I have here ready for your inspection the opinions of the ablest men on that subject. I applied to the person best qualified to point them out to me. The noble lord near me, (Keppel) then at the head of the admiralty, referred me to three officers in his Majesty's service, whose judgment and integrity he could rely on, and your lordships, on the bare naming of them, will rely on them too. Admiral Edwards's testimony must have its weight; the testimony of captain Levison Gower, whose services the nation are to enjoy in peace as well as war; and that of lieut. Lane, who took an accurate survey of the whole coast, and who was well qualified for the task, as he served under and possessed the confidence of the famous circum-navigator, captain Cook. These officers all declare, that the best fishing was to the southward, which was entirely in the possession of the English, so that we must doubt the national spirit, and the national industry of this country, before we can pronounce this so much talked of exclusive seven league fishery an injury to Great Britain.

As to the cession of St Pierre and Miquelon, where is the proof that these places can be fortified so as to annoy us? I have in my hand that which will satisfy your lordships how idle all surmises are on that head. Here are certificates from the most skilful and experienced engineers, that neither St Pierre nor Miquelon would admit the construction of a fortress, which could stand the attack of the smallest of your frigates. – With respect to the cession of the two Floridas, I must refer again to the exports and imports. The imports are not more than 100 000*l*. and the exports hardly exceeded 120 000*l*. To be sure, I would not willingly take so much from the commerce of the nation; but amidst the millions of our trade, is this an object worth contending for at the hazard of continuing the war? The navigation of the Mississippi has been reprobated as an useless acquisition. Could men seriously assert this? Was a navigation of so many hundred miles up a country, where there is a call for our manufactures, an useless thing? Surely not.

I shall now proceed to take a view of our affairs in the West Indies. All the islands there are restored to us, and in return, we cede St Lucia and Tobago. St Lucia, held in so much estimation now, may be tried more fairly by the value set upon it at the last peace. As I said before, on all hands it is allowed that that was not a humiliating, but a high and mighty peace for this country. Why, therefore, if this island was, as the objectors pretend, the key-stone that supported and connected the arch of all our power in the leeward islands, was not this island then retained? But I can produce the opinions of your most experienced seamen on this head; and I assert, that St Lucia is not of that vast consequence some noble lords would possess this House with the opinion of, in order to depreciate the merits of the treaty. With respect to Tobago, it is said, the cession of that island will ruin our cotton manufacture. Pray let me ask noble lords, was our cotton manufacture a poor one before we possessed that island? It was not poor then, why should it be poor now? We have been long in possession of that great branch of trade, consequently we can afford to give a greater price for cotton than our neighbours. Cotton, therefore, be it in the hands of friend or foe, will always find its way to our door, in preference to that of those who cannot meet it with such a purse. But I know a few over-grown monopolizers of article, or selfish proprietors, would see the nation steeped in blood, sooner than they would forfeit, by the peace, one farthing of that emolument which they used to make when

Tobago was in our hands. Let me comfort these worthy men, by telling them, that the islands restored to us, contain a vast number of acres, uncultivated, which may be applied to the growth of this so much coveted commodity. But let it be remembered, that we have kept Dominique, an island as valuable to this country, if not more so, than St Lucia, if considered as a place of observation and strength. I have it on the authority of a noble admiral, whose conquests in the West Indies have been distinguished by laurels that will bloom for ever, that Dominique is capable of being rendered all that ever St Lucia could pretend to be, and that it contains also superior advantages in respect of climate and situation.

We will now, my lords, look to Europe. I am asked, why overlook all the treaties respecting Dunkirk? Why, let me ask the question in return, why were not these treaties ever enforced during all the administrations which have passed away since the demolition of that harbour was first stipulated? This negligence is *prima facie* evidence of the little account in which the fulfilling of that treaty has hitherto been held, for were it otherwise, we had often since the power to enforce it. And I have heard that able seaman, the late lord Hawke, declare, that all the art and cost that France could bestow on the bason of Dunkirk, would not render it in any degree formidable or noxious to Great Britain. But, as was well observed by a noble friend near me, (lord Grantham) France wished to have the feathers she formerly strutted with restored to her; and, surely, no sober man would continue the war to thwart a fancy so little detrimental to us. However, if we are mistaken, let the proof be produced. Till then, I trust you lordships will suspend your judgments. The cession of Minorca has not been objected to, and therefore I do not enter into the defence of that Article; but I must take notice in this place, that it is not perfectly fair in stating the particulars of these treaties, to overlook all that we have gained. The salvation of Gibraltar, under all the circumstances of the present war, is a point of glory which would not easily be snatched from ministers. No man had ever asserted that Gibraltar might not be given up upon certain terms. Gibraltar was saved!

We will now, my lords, proceed to the examination of the objections against the part of the French treaty that respects our affairs on the coast of Africa. 'Senegal is given up, and the gum trade is therefore lost'. Is that inference just? Is not the faith of France engaged for our having a fair share of that trade? More than a share we never were in possession of. 'But what tie is this same faith?' Why, as strong a tie as all men of reflection must know every parchment tie is between rival nations: only to be observed while interest or convenience obliges. The ties of nations no man can be so wretchedly versed in history, or so miserably deficient in observation, as to place upon the parallel with those which are binding upon individuals: but on enquiry your lordships will find, that Senegal, which we have given up, is not so favourably situated for trade as Senegambia, which we have kept. The former has a bar dangerous to shipping; an inconvenience which the other is free from. In a word, by this Article of the treaty, instead of losing any thing, we secure (as much as we ever had secured) a share in the gum trade, and we are not under the necessity we formerly were of making that coast a grave for our fellow-subjects, thousands of whom were annually devoted to destruction from the unhealthiness of that climate, by means of our jealousy, which sent them there to watch an article of trade, which in vain we endeavoured to monopolize.

I must now my lords, call your attention to what concerns the part of the treaty respecting the East Indies. Here ministry are asked why they restored Pondicherry to the French? and why they gave permission to them to run a ditch round Chandernagore? Two cogent reasons can be given for this conduct: the first is unwillingness, and the inability of this country to prosecute the war; and the other is the distracted state of the British dominions in that part of the world. By the last accounts from thence, the troops were declared to be four months unpaid, and of course upon the eve of a mutiny. Nay, in such miserable situation were the affairs of the East India Company in that quarter, that they were obliged to mortgage their commodities to wealthy individuals, who would not (so reduced is the credit of the Company in that quarter of the globe) take their solemn assurance for the faithful disposal of the stock at the East India sales here, but employed agents to see the business more securely transacted. Do your lordships know that there are 1 400 000*l*. of these draughts yet unpaid; that there are 240 000*l*. more coming home? And that your lordships may form some estimate of the extravagance of the usury at which the Company were obliged to borrow from these people, I must inform your lordships, some of the very agents employed by those usurers have 20 000*l*. a-year commission for their trouble. Is it necessary, my lords, to say a word more for the necessity of conceding these matters to the French, who were at the very moment forming alliances with Hyder Aly, our most formidable and inveterate enemy, to drive us entirely out of the country? Our old foe, M. de Bussy,[1] in the decline of life, almost at the age of eighty, leaving France purposely to form alliances! And what have we to withstand their force when formed? Will unpaid troops fight, think you? But say that it was possible to expect such disinterested conduct from a common soldiery, will, or rather can famished troops fight? Our account about the same time tells us, that our forces sent out against Hyder Aly were in daily dread of being starved to death. What stand could an army of infantry (for we have no horse) make against that potent prince, and his numerous, well-appointed, formidable cavalry? None. They would be as chaff before the wind. Do your lordships know too, that all hopes of peace with the Mahrattas are frustrated; that we have been deceived by idle stories of applications being made to men of power in the Mahratta states, who promised to exert their influence, but it was found, that they had no influence upon earth? While, therefore, the French court were ignorant of the sad condition of our affairs in that quarter, while they were as yet unacquainted with the result of M. de Bussy's negociation with the Indian powers, was it not prudent in the British ministry to concede, as they did at that moment, when there was a probability that they had conceded what was no longer in their power to keep?

I have now gone, as well as my memory serves me, through the detail of all the objections which have been made to the treaties; and, I trust, your lordships see from the facts to which I have all along referred you, the necessity and the policy of our conduct in this particular. Let me, before I conclude, call to your lordships minds the general state of this country, at the period in which the pacific negociations were set on foot. Were we not at the extremity of distress? Did not the boldest of us cry out for peace? Was not the object of the war accomplished? Was not the independence of America solemnly recognized by parliament? Could that independence be afterwards made a stipulation for the restoration of tranquillity? On an entire view of our affairs at that time, is there any honest, sensible man in the kingdom that will not say the powerful confederacy with whom we had then to contend had the most decided superiority over us? Had we scarce one taxable article that was not already taxed to the utmost extent? Were we not 197 millions in debt? and had we not the enormous sum of 25 millions unfunded? Our navy bills bearing an enormous discount; our public credit beginning to totter; our resources confessedly at an end; our commerce day by day becoming worse; our army reduced, and in want of 30 000

1. As chief adviser to the Nizam of Hyderabad, de Bussy had been a powerful French influence at the centre of Muslim power in the Deccan in the 1750s. He was recalled to France in 1761 after the French challenge to Britain in India failed.

men to make up its establishments; our navy, which has been made so much the boast of some men, in such a condition, that the noble viscount, now at the head of the profession, in giving a description of it, strove to conceal its weakness by speaking low, as if he wished to keep it from going abroad into the world. But in such a day as this it must be told – your lordships must be told what were the difficulties which the King's ministers had to encounter in the course of the last campaign. Your lordships must be told how many sleepless nights I have spent – how many weary hours of watching and distress. What have been my anxieties for New York! What have I suffered from the apprehension of an attack on that garrison, which, if attacked, must have fallen! What have I suffered from the apprehension of an attack on Nova Scotia or Newfoundland! The folly, or the want of enterprize of our enemies, alone protected those places; for, had they gone there instead of Hudson's Bay, they must have fallen. What have I suffered for the West Indies, where, with all our superiority of navy, we were not able to undertake one active or offensive measure for want of troops; and where, if an attack had been made where it was meditated, – we were liable to lose our most valuable possessions! How many sleepless nights have I not suffered for our possessions in the East Indies, where our distresses were undescribable! How many sleepless nights did I not suffer on account of our campaign in Europe, where, with all our boasted navy, we had only one fleet with which to accomplish various objects! That navy, the noble viscount was fair to own, was well conducted. Its detachment to the North Seas, to intimidate the Dutch, was a happy and a seasonable stroke; but the salvation of the Baltic fleet was not at all to be ascribed to ability; accident contributed to that event; accident contributed to more than one article of our naval triumphs. How many of our ships were unclean? The noble viscount has told us the case of the fleet with which he was sent to the relief of Gibraltar. He could hardly venture to swim home in the Victory. How many of our ships were in fact undermanned? Did the House know this? Did they know that our naval stores were exhausted, that our cordage was rotten, that our magazines were in a very low condition, and that we had no prospect of our navy being much better in the next campaign than it was in the present. [The noble earl, during all these queries, directed his eyes to lord Keppel, until the noble admiral called him to order.] Do the House know all this? the noble lord is offended at my directing myself to him. I have no idea of imputing blame to the noble viscount. His abilities are unquestioned; but when the greatness of the navy is made not only a boast, but an argument, it is fain to examine the fact. Are not these things so? and are not these things to be taken into the account, before ministers are condemned for giving peace to the country? Let the man who will answer me these questions fairly, tell me how, in such circumstances, he would make a peace, before he lets his tongue loose against those treaties, the ratification of which has caused so many anxious days and sleepless nights. It is easy for any bungler to pull down the fairest fabric, but is that a reason, my lords, he should censure the skill of the architect who reared it? But I fear I trespass, my lords, on your patience too long. The subject was near my heart, and you will pardon me, if I have been earnest in laying before your lordships our embarrassments, our difficulties, our views, and our reasons for what we have done. I submit them to you with confidence, and rely on the nobleness of your natures, that in judging of men who have hazarded so much for their country, you will not be guided by prejudice, nor influenced by party.

5 Britain's Second Cycle

The transition from the first to the second British cycle is a period of considerable interest, for it harbours more fertile analogies to contemporary conditions than does the British experience of the late nineteenth and early twentieth centuries. The loss of the American colonies, (and the speech by Lord Shelburne it occasioned), in circumstances of military defeat, naval deterioration, internal disaffection, and international isolation, marked the low point of British fortunes in the eighteenth (and the nineteenth) centuries. But these setbacks proved impermanent for opportunities soon arose for beginning to validate, through victory in a global war, Britain's claim for a second 'term' of global leadership that would extend to the end of the nineteenth century.

That opportunity was the great revolutionary war that lasted from 1792 to 1815 and that we now call the period of the wars of the French Revolution and Napoleon. They were revolutionary wars that differed profoundly from the more relaxed and mannered conflicts of the age of enlightenment. They gave rise to the expression 'total war' because they were fought desperately and for large stakes, not for trade or colonies but for security and supremacy. The stakes were not just local or national – the survival of particular regimes or territorial arrangements – but in fact global and world-constitutional. They embodied a process of global macro-decision in much the same fashion that the wars of Louis XIV had done 100 years earlier, but on a larger and more intense scale. For Britain, though, they meant a repeat performance – not only as the keystone of a global conflict for the second time but facing the same principal challenger. This, we may suppose, simplified matters, and learning too.

The documents in this section highlight Britain's role in this decision process of revolutionary war and they document its place in the causation of that conflict; they illustrate the part played by her management of coalitions in the defeat of the challenger. Furthermore they show Britain at work building a stable order, in Europe and in the world at large – that is, the framework within which the nineteenth century unfolded upon its course until, in the fullness of time, another challenge surfaced and had to be confronted.

SOURCES OF THE REVOLUTIONARY–NAPOLEONIC WARS

The events we are considering here are the global wars second-nearest to our contemporary experience, and if only for that reason they repay some close attention. Their origin has been less closely scrutinised than that of the better known world wars of the twentieth century.

The 'great revolutionary war' (as the nineteenth century referred to it) was the product of the (temporary) decline of Britain, and France's renewed opposition (there was no other actual, or potential, rival in 1792, though by 1815 Russia's weight had become palpable). Britain's weakness has already been remarked upon. France's challenge had previously been fuelled by her successful intervention in the war of American independence but was most powerfully propelled by the surge of national spirit engendered by the Revolution that commenced in 1789 but soon passed (in conditions, *inter alia*, of the opening of hostilities with Austria and Prussia), to a second, more radical stage that brought the abolition of the monarchy and the proclamation of the Republic in 1792. The hostilities, in turn, led to military operations in the Austrian Netherlands (today's Belgium) a matter that immediately aroused the customary concern of the British government.

The newly fledged French Republic exuded strength and self-confidence and its spokesmen showered contempt upon the crowned heads of Europe. Little wonder then that only ten days after Louis XVI's execution, the National Convention declared war upon Britain and the Netherlands (Doc. 31), a war that with one short pause would last for 22 years. Tom Paine, author of the *Rights of Man*, participated in that debate, and so did Girondin leader Charles Jean Marie Barbaroux who, while admitting that 'naval wars are mankind's most destructive scourge', was driven by the hope of seeing 'the English people at last come out of the stupor they have been steeped by the long practice of the constitutional yoke to take revenge against the court that pushes toward their mutual destruction two peoples that ought to be united for the happiness of the world'. The rapporteur of the declaration was another Girondin leader, Jean-Pierre Brissot, a journalist of international experience (that included sojourns in Britain and the United States), a campaigner against slavery, friend of the Quakers, and author of fiery speeches proclaiming universal liberty.

Britain's reply was deliberate and decisive. In a lengthy speech William Pitt (Doc. 32) refuted in detail the matters alleged in the French Convention, including the charge of having already joined the Austro–Prussian campaign against France. Even while condemning the excesses of the Revolution, Pitt denied any intention of interfering in French internal affairs, but he did define Britain's ultimate war aim as providing for the 'security of our own country, and the general security of Europe' by means of repressing 'this French system of aggrandizement and aggression'. That aggression soon engulfed the Netherlands, a country that had been Britain's close ally for the two preceding centuries and an area whose security was seen as crucial to Britain's. The fate of the

Netherlands remained a vital British concern until the restoration of its independence in 1815.

When the war started, who could have foreseen it lasting for over 20 years? A peace of sorts was reached at Amiens in 1802 but the war was soon resumed by Britain because 'the system of violence, aggression, and aggrandizement' practiced by the French government had continued unabated, including the continued occupation of Holland by the French army, the violation of the independence of Switzerland, and of other countries, and had been added to by 'new and extraordinary pretensions'. Napoleon's reply, in a speech to the Senate, professed injured dignity ('France [is] not a province of India') and grieved 'for the fate of mankind', but avoided a detailed accounting of the British charges. The war continued until Pitt's war aims had been implemented, as formulated in his 'Memorandum' of 1805 (Doc. 33).

GLOBAL WAR LEADERSHIP

Britain's strategy in the great revolutionary war is a modern classic. It comprised four elements: (1) priority to naval, hence global predominance; (2) use of economic blockade; (3) coalition anchorage; (4) long-term vision.

Britain fought the first few years in a manner not unlike that of the several other wars of the eighteenth century, with minimal commitments in Europe, and much action over colonies and trade. Quite soon, though, the outlines of a maritime strategy emerged that quickly gave her effective control of the oceanic system and left her opponents isolated on the European mainland. Napoleon's victories in Egypt came to naught when Admiral Nelson destroyed the French fleet at Aboukir and cut off the army's lifeline to France. The decisive battle of the global war was that at Trafalgar (1805) when Nelson defeated the combined fleets of France and Spain, gained unchallenged control of the oceanic spaces, and put an end to Napoleon's design for landing in (and victory over) England. From Trafalgar onward it was only a question of when, rather than whether, Britain would prevail.

Decisive victory on the ocean meant that France was denied a 'win' at the global level but it did not mean that victory was imminent. Britain's land armies were no match for Napoleon's legions and her only immediately available weapon was economic: that is, blockade by means of control over world trade. Napoleon's response was to issue the Berlin Decrees (Doc. 35) instituting a 'continental blockade' as the only means at his disposal for inducing Britain to accept a settlement. British reaction was to tighten her own measures of control of the traffic among the ports under French control by means of 'Orders-in-Council' (Doc. 36) that proved controversial in several neutral quarters – finally inducing the United States to declare war on England, in 1812, but also ultimately quite effective. In order to enforce the Berlin Decrees Napoleon was led to decisions that proved to be his undoing: the invasion of Portugal in 1807, that embroiled Spain and led to the protracted war in the Iberian peninsula; and the Russian campaign of 1812 that finally broke the back of the French army.

A most notable feature of these great wars was the progress made in the evolution of coalition warfare. We have already had the opportunity to remark upon the role of coalitions in the wars of Louis XIV and the skill shown by William III in forging them. Under William Pitt, and later Lord Castlereagh, the Foreign Secretary, Britain had a similarly effective but even more pervasive influence in the revolutionary wars. Of all the powers, Britain had the longest continuing record of opposition to France (Table 5.1). She spent 22 years fighting these wars while Russia or Austria clocked no more than 13, and Prussia eight, thus earning a lesser claim to leadership. Napoleon kept defeating one coalition after another on land but could never reach Britain, which remained an anchor of the

Table 5.1 Coalitions, 1792–1815

	1792	*1795*	*1800*	*1805*	*1810*	*1815*	*Years of war against France*
Britain	oooooooooooooooooo			ooooooooooooooooooooooo			22
Austria	ooooooooooo		ooooo	oo	oo	oooooo	13
					xx		
Russia	oooooooooooooooo			oooo		ooooooo	13½
			xx	xxxxxxxxx			
Prussia	ooooooo			ooo		oooooo	8
			xx		xx		
Ottoman Empire			ooooo				2½
				xxxxxxxxxxx			
Portugal	ooooooo		oo	oooooooooooooooooo			13
Spain	ooooo				oooooooooooooooo		10
			xxxxxx	xxxxxxxxxxxxxxxxx			
United States			ooooo				2½
					xxxxx		
Coalitions	1st	2nd		3rd 4th	5th	6th	

oo = 1 year of war against France. xx = 1 year allied with France.

alternative system to which opponents could always rally. If Admiral Nelson was the prime symbol of the maritime strategy, the Duke of Wellington (the victor of the Peninsular War and of Waterloo) was the great star of the coalition strategy. The impressive list of his titles and foreign decorations in the preamble to the Treaty of Quadruple Alliance (Doc. 42) paraded before the world the long reach of that strategy.

In coalition warfare Britain assumed a highly specialised role that went beyond serving as the nucleus of all opposition to France. Her economic capacity, newly fortified by the first wave of the Industrial Revolution, and her hold over world trade, gave her the resources needed to finance and equip the armies of her coalition partners. The treaties constituting, and continuing, these arrangements (as the treaty with Russia, formative of the third coalition, Doc. 34) featured express provisions for subsidies 'the amount of which shall correspond to the respective forces which shall be employed'. This Russian treaty of 1805 was the first to employ the concept of a 'general League of the States of Europe' and envisage arrangements for a post-war world, on the basis of which, in treaties some coalitions later (Chaumont 1814, Doc. 38; Paris, the Quadruple Alliance, Doc. 42) a 'concert' of powers was fashioned that constituted a lasting institutional innovation in the governance of European regional affairs.

In this way, Britain's strategy also had long-range vision. It never wavered from the pursuit of its irreducible and vital interests: in Europe, the independence of the Netherlands, and maritime ascendancy elsewhere in the world (as defined again in the Cabinet instructions to Castlereagh at the end of 1813, Doc. 37). But once these vital interests were assured, flexibility was shown in all territorial arrangements, and willingness to use colonial conquests as counters for building in Europe a structure conducive to the general interest in a durable peace, founded upon a balance of power.

BUILDING THE PEACE

Macro-decisions may be defined as the struggle for establishing the rules of the game. The great revolutionary war was the struggle that defined the rules within which the game of world politics was played for the next 100 years both in Europe and in the world at large, and Britain's was the largest part in creating these rules.

The first of these rules was the distinction between the global maritime system in which Britain held undivided sway, and regional European affairs in which a balance would be maintained that would hold France in check. The maritime (global) issues were largely settled before the allied powers gathered in Vienna to decide upon the disposition of the European questions, the principles of which had already been agreed upon between the four major powers at Chaumont (Doc. 38) largely in line with what the British Cabinet laid out in their instructions to Lord Castlereagh (Doc. 37).

The second of these rules followed from the requirement, set out in the same instructions, that 'the treaty of alliance not terminate with war' but rather form the basis of continuous 'concert' in the post-war period 'at fixed periods . . . for the purpose of consulting upon the common interests . . . for the maintenance of the peace of Europe' (Quadruple alliance, Art. VI, Doc. 42). This activity was to be focused upon France and was designed to prevent a resurgence of French aggression. It served as the basis of the so-called 'Concert of Europe' and the congresses of the first post-war decade, and the more irregular meetings that discussed, for example, the Belgian question in the 1830s, or the affairs of the Near East in Berlin in 1878. In the British conception, being the one that generally prevailed, this concert (in the formulation of Castlereagh's state paper of May 1820; cf. Bourne, 1970, p. 200) 'never was intended . . . as a Union for the Government of the World, or for the Superintendance of the internal Affairs of other states' or even for the government of Europe. Yet it did express the possibility of an institutionalised search for the general public interest in these matters, and was an improvement upon the wholly unstructured arrangements of the eighteenth century.

The coalition that won the war against France did not hold together for long. Once France was no longer a danger – and we know in hindsight that Britain did not again fight a war against France – the need to rally on that particular basis disappeared too. In fact, this became apparent even before the peace was sealed at Vienna. That great assembly achieved a number of agreements of general interest, among them, the anti-slave trade declaration (Doc. 40) in which the British Parliament took a singular interest, and that could be seen as implementing, on a practical plane, the revolutionary ideas of universal liberty. Another was the agreement on diplomatic ranking (Doc. 41), another piece of institutional engineering that embodied the considerable progress accomplished in this field since the days of Mocenigo.

The principal business at Vienna, though, revolved around the territorial settlement in Europe and in that latter department the main issues of contention surged around the territories to be awarded to Prussia in 'compensation' for its 'losses' suffered earlier, Russia claiming the bulk of Poland and Prussia trying to annex Saxony. The opposition to these schemes was led by Austria that objected to them on grounds of security, and it included Britain on the basis of concern for maintaining a workable 'equilibirum'. Castlereagh had just received the news of the signing of the peace with the United States at Ghent, and so when at the end of December 1814 Prussia, supported by Russia, uttered threats of war if their demands were not met, he put together a counter-alliance of Britain,

Austria, and France (see Doc. 39). He won the day and Saxony, while reduced in size, maintained its existence, though Russia did receive the major part of Poland. Nevertheless, the Saxon–Polish crisis gave an early warning that the victorious alliance would not remain solid for long past the winning post. Russia's weight, and Prussia's aggressive posture at Vienna, foreshadowed problems that were to be encountered throughout the next 100 years, and that would culminate in the German challenge in 1914. France's entry at that point into the British alliance flagged another major realignment, in the opposite direction.

THE REST IS HISTORY

'The effect of the great revolutionary war was to place England in a position which was for the moment of surpassing splendour . . . it was the result of a desperate struggle of over twenty years in which everyone else was down in his turn, but England was ever on her feet; in which it was found that there was no ascertained limit either to her means or to her disposition to dispense them; in which, to use the language of Mr Canning, her flag was always flying a signal of rallying to the combatant and of shelter to the fallen'.

This was Prime Minister Gladstone's description, (quoted in Bourne, 1970, pp. 398–9) two generations later, of Britain's post-Napoleonic war situation. It was a position earned through global war leadership but which, at the time of writing (in 1869), had come to be seen as one of 'eminence' that was fast becoming 'perilous'.

True, since 1815 Britain had taken full advantage of the rules to shape the system, even more outside than within Europe. She presided over the establishment of independent states in Latin America; she protected, and attempted to reform, the Ottoman Empire; she opened China, and the Far East generally, to world trade, and increasingly assumed the rule over vast populations in India. Possibly the most pervasive was her influence in promoting free trade, above all through the force of her own example, when the Corn Laws (those restricting the importation of grain into Britain) were repealed in 1846, after several years of agitation by the Anti-Corn Law League, based on Manchester, the most efficient and successful of the nineteenth-century pressure groups in England. The League was organised by Richard Cobden, elected to Parliament in 1841, a leader of the Manchester School that espoused free trade and an economic system free from governmental interference, as the means toward a better and a more peaceful world. The speech that we in parts reproduce (Doc. 43) was made on the eve of the final parliamentary debate that decided the issue and it illustrates both the practical and the visionary aspects of Cobden's thought.

Throughout his career Cobden was a fierce critic of the 'balance of power' for being inimical to peace. Two years after his death, in 1867, when the phrase 'preservation of the balance of power in Europe' was abandoned as one of the objectives of the British army (part of annual legislation since 1727), Parliament in effect repealed the principle as a guide of British policy in Europe. Germany and Italy had just achieved unity, and opportunities for intervention had become fewer and riskier. It signalled a reorientation of policy, the recognition that eminence was becoming perilous. Ironically, the final swing away from the balance of power came not from the free traders, but from the opposite end of the British political spectrum.

The most eloquent spokesman of the changing mood was Benjamin Disraeli, the new leader of the Conservatives. He turned the country away from 'cosmopolitanism' (as exemplified by Cobden) toward 'national' policies and toward the Empire, not reaching after new problems and new solutions but preserving what had already been achieved (Doc. 44). Withdrawal from Europe into the Empire meant 'isolation' that at times appeared 'splendid' but soon came to be seen as dangerous (Doc. 45). For it led to clashes with other ambitious powers, not just Russia, and France (as through most of the century) but also Germany and the United States. When three large new navies – the American, the German, and the Japanese – entered into British naval planning ca. 1900 (cf. Bourne, 1970, pp. 461–2, memo by Navy Secretary) the need to rethink alliances once again became urgent.

One obvious option was the Anglo–German alliance (even possibly taking the form of a British accession to the Triple Alliance of Germany, Austria, and Italy) but constituting in effect a design for leadership succession. Joseph Chamberlain, the Colonial Secretary, discussed this possibility in some widely-noticed speeches, and Lord Salisbury, the Prime Minister, gave it serious consideration. In the end, both came out against it, Salisbury rejecting it on pragmatic grounds (set out in Doc. 47) and Chamberlain being as sensitive to the need to maintain the American connection as he was to the German link (Doc. 46). Among the principal obstacles to the German alliance were the anticipated objections from the self-governing colonies (Canada, Australia, etc.) and, as Foreign Secretary Lansdowne (a descendant of Shelburne's) put it in November 1901, 'the risk of entangling ourselves in a policy that might be hostile to America' (in Bourne, 1970, p. 470).

Within the next few years, British policy hardened in opposition to what came to be seen as a German bid for 'general political hegemony'. Authored by a member of the Foreign Office, the celebrated Crowe Memorandum (Doc. 48) is comparable in importance to George Kennan's 'Moscow Telegram' of 22 February 1946 which laid out the sources of Soviet foreign conduct (cf. Kennan, 1967, pp. 547–59). Crowe's state paper distilled a policy that returned to the old verities of the balance of power and came to recognise in Germany a potential for threatening it. Crowe was not absolutely certain that Germany was consciously aiming at such hegemony but he worried that 'semi-independent evolution, not entirely unaided by statecraft' might achieve the same situation, and he went on persuasively to prescribe a policy of firm resistance to German encroachments. The stage was set for another global macro-decision.

Documents

31 THE FRENCH NATIONAL CONVENTION'S DECLARATION OF WAR ON ENGLAND, 1 FEBRUARY 1793

Introduction

This declaration was read on behalf of the General Defence Committee by the Girondin leader Jacques-Pierre Brissot, as rapporteur. The Girondins, who were a moderate party in the assembly, had favoured war as a means of curbing the revolutionary impulse, and had been responsible for the initial declaration of war on the King of Bohemia and Hungary, in April 1792; this led to hostilities with Austria and Prussia, but, contrary to their intentions, it also contributed to radicalising the revolution. The 'second revolution' of August 1792 deposed the monarchy.

Brissot was a journalist who attracted early attention for his attacks on the British political system, his imprisonment in the Bastille, and his work for the anti-slavery movement. He visited the United States in 1788–9, but returned home to become a prominent revolutionary leader. He advocated resort to war as a means of consolidating the Revolution and inaugurating a crusade for universal liberty. But the winners of that strategy were the more radical Jacobins. The Girondins lost support after the second revolution; in June 1793 their leaders were arrested and, by October, executed on charges of treason.

Text

The National Convention, having heard the report of its general defence committee on the behaviour of the English government towards France:

Considering that, principally since the Revolution of 10 August 1792,[1] the king of England has not ceased to give the French nation proofs of his evil disposition and of his attachment to the coalition of crowned heads; that at that time he ordered his ambassador at Paris to withdraw, because he would not recognise the provisional executive council created by the Legislative Assembly;

That, at the same time, the cabinet of Saint James[2] discontinued its correspondence with the French ambassador at London, pretexting the suspension of the late king of the French;

Source: *Archives Parlementaires de 1787 à 1860* (Paris 1900) Tome 58, pp. 118–19. Translated from the French by Sylvia Modelski.

1. On that date, France became a Republic: a Paris uprising overthrew the Constitutional Monarchy created by the 1791 Constitution, and the Legislative assembly was replaced by the National Convention (elected in September 1792).
2. I.e., the British Government.

That since the inauguration of the National Convention, it has declined to resume the usual correspondence between the two states, or to acknowledge the powers of this Convention;

That it has refused to recognise the French Republic's ambassador, even though he was carrying letters of credence in its name;

That it has tried to impede the different purchases of corn, arms, and other commodities ordered in England, either by French citizens, or by agents of the French Republic; that it has ordered the interception of several boats and ships with grain destined for France, while, in contradiction of the Treaty of 1786,[3] exportation to other foreign countries continued;

That to thwart even more effectively the Republic's commercial operations in England, it obtained an act of Parliament prohibiting the circulation of assignats.[4]

That in violation of Article 4 of the Treaty of 1786,[5] it has obtained another act from the same Parliament, in the course of the month of January just passed, which subjects all French citizens, travelling to or residing in England, to most inquisitorial, vexing and dangerous procedures;

That, at the same time, and contrary to the tenor of Article 1 of the Treaty of Peace of 1783,[6] it has granted open protection, as well as monetary aid, not only to émigrés, but even to the rebel leaders who have fought against France; that it maintains with them a daily correspondence, which is obviously aimed against the French Revolution;

That, likewise, it has received the leaders of France's West-Indian colonies;

That, in the same spirit, without any provocation, and while all the maritime powers are at peace with England, the cabinet of Saint James has ordered a considerable naval armament, and an increase of its land forces;

That this armament was ordered at the moment when the English government was relentlessly persecuting those who in England supported the principles of the Revolution, and was using all means possible, both in Parliament and out of it, to defame the French Republic, and to draw upon it the hatred of the English nation and of all of Europe;

That the objective of this armament, aimed at France, was not even disguised by the English Parliament;

That although the French provisional executive council has used all means to conserve peace and fraternity with the English nation, and has responded to the calumnies and treaty violations only with objections based on the principles of justice, and expressed with the dignity of free men, the English government has persisted in its system of malevolence and hostility, continued the armament and has sent a squadron towards the Scheldt in order to upset French operations in Belgium.

That on the news of Louis's execution, it intensified its outrageous behaviour towards the French Republic to the point of ordering the French ambassador out of British territory within eight days;

That the king of England has manifested his attachment to the cause of that traitor, and his design of supporting it by various resolutions taken at the moment

3. The Eden Treaty of Commerce between France and England.
4. An assignat was a piece of paper money, secured on state lands, issued by the French revolutionary government.
5. By this treaty (revoked by the Convention later in 1793) Pitt had aimed at normalising British–French trade relations.
6. Signed at Versailles by the USA, Britain, France, and Spain in recognition of American independence.

of his death, such as nominating generals of his land army, asking the Parliament of England for a considerable increase of territorial and naval forces, and putting ships of war in commission; that his secret coalition with the enemies of France, and notably with the emperor and Prussia, has just been confirmed by a treaty concluded with the former, during this past month of January.

That he has drawn into the same coalition the Stadholder of the United Provinces; that this prince, whose servile devotion to the commands of the British and German cabinets is only too well known, has, in the course of the French Revolution, and despite the neutrality he professed, treated French agents with contempt, sheltered émigrés, harassed French patriots, obstructed their operations, set free manufacturers of counterfeit assignats, contrary to accepted usages, and in spite of the request of the French government; that in recent times, to concur with the hostile designs of the London court, he has ordered the fitting out of a fleet, nominated an admiral, sent Dutch vessels to join the English squadron, floated a loan to meet the expenditures of war, prevented exports to France while favouring the sending of goods to Prussian and Austrian stores;

Finally, considering that all these circumstances preclude any hope that the French Republic can obtain the righting of these grievances by means of friendly negotiations, and that all the acts of the British court and of the Stadholder are hostile acts amounting to a declaration of war;

The National Convention decrees as follows:

1. The National Convention decrees, in the name of the French nation, that in view of all these acts of hostility and aggression, the French Republic is at war with the king of England and the Stadholder of the United Provinces.
2. The National Convention instructs the provisional executive council to deploy the forces that will be needed to repulse their aggression and to sustain the independence, dignity, and interest of the French Republic.
3. The National Convention authorises the provisional executive council to employ the naval forces of the Republic in any way the safety of the State will seem to require, and it revokes all the special arrangements made in this respect by previous decrees.

The Convention adopts the decree unanimously.

32 BRITISH DECLARATION OF WAR ON FRANCE, SPEECH BY THE RIGHT HONOURABLE WILLIAM PITT, PRIME MINISTER, IN THE HOUSE OF COMMONS, 12 FEBRUARY 1793

Text

The question now was, not what degree of danger or insult we should find it necessary to repel, from a regard to our safety, or from a sense of honour; it was, not whether we should adopt in our measures a system of promptitude and vigour, or of tameness and procrastination; whether we should sacrifice every other consideration to the continuance of an uncertain and insecure peace; when war was declared, and the event no longer in our option, it remained only to be considered, whether we should prepare to meet it with a firm determination, and support His Majesty's government with zeal and courage against every attack. War now was not only declared, but carried on at our very doors; a war which aimed at an object no less destructive than the total ruin of the freedom and independence of this country. In this situation of affairs, he would not do so much injustice to the members of that House, whatever differences of opinion might formerly have existed, as to suppose there could be any but one decision, one fixed resolution, in this so urgent necessity, in this imminent and common danger, by the ardour and firmness of their support, to testify their loyalty to their sovereign, their attachment to the constitution, and their sense of those inestimable blessings which they had so long enjoyed under its influence. Confident, however, as he was, that such would be their unanimous decision, that such would be their determined and unalterable resolution, he should not consider it as altogether useless to take a view of the situation of the country at the time of His Majesty's last message, of the circumstances which had preceded and accompanied it, and of the situation in which we now stood, in consequence of what had occurred during that interval.

When His Majesty, by his message, informed them, that in the present situation of affairs he conceived it indispensably necessary to make a farther augmentation of his forces, they had cheerfully concurred in that object, and returned in answer, what then was the feeling of the House, the expression of their affection and zeal, and their readiness to support His Majesty in those purposes, for which he had stated an augmentation of force to be necessary. They saw the justice of the alarm which was then entertained, and the propriety of affording that support which was required. He should shortly state the grounds upon which they had then given their concurrence. They considered that whatever temptations might have existed to this country from ancient enmity and rivalship – paltry motives indeed! – or whatever opportunity might have been afforded by the tumultuous and distracted state of France, or whatever sentiments might be excited by the transactions which had taken place in that nation, His Majesty had uniformly abstained from all interference in its internal government, and had maintained, with respect to it, on every occasion, the strictest and most inviolable neutrality.

Such being his conduct towards France, he had a right to expect on their part a suitable return; more especially, as this return had been expressly conditioned for by a compact, into which they entered, and by which they engaged to respect the

Source: Cobbett, William, *Parliamentary History of England from the Norman Conquest in 1066 to the Year 1803* (London, 1817) Vol. XXX, cols 344–61.

rights of His Majesty and his allies, not to interfere in the government of any neutral country, and not to pursue any system of aggrandisement, or make any addition to their dominions, but to confine themselves, at the conclusion of the war, within their own territories. These conditions they had all grossly violated, and had adopted a system of ambitious and destructive policy, fatal to the peace and security of every government, and which, in its consequences, had shaken Europe itself to its foundation. Their decree of the 19th of November,[1] which had been so much talked of, offering fraternity and affiance to all people who wish to recover their liberty, was a decree not levelled against particular nations, but against every country where there was any form of government established; a decree not hostile to individuals, but to the human race; which was calculated every where to sow the seeds of rebellion and civil contention, and to spread war from one end of Europe to the other, from one end of the globe to the other. While they were bound to this country by the engagements which he had mentioned, they had shewed no intention to exempt it from the consequences of this decree. Nay, a directly contrary opinion might be formed, and it might be supposed that this country was more particularly aimed at by this very decree, if we were to judge from the exultation with which they had received from different societies in England every address expressive of sedition and disloyalty, and from the eager desire which they had testified to encourage and cherish the growth of such sentiments. Not only had they shewed no inclination to fulfil their engagements, but had even put it out of their own power, by taking the first opportunity to make additions to their territory in contradiction to their own express stipulations. By express resolutions for the destruction of the existing government of all invaded countries, by the means of Jacobin societies, by orders given to their generals, by the whole system adopted in this respect by the national assembly, and by the actual connection of the whole country of Savoy, they had marked their determination to add to the dominions of France, and to provide means, through the medium of every new conquest, to carry their principles over Europe. Their conduct was such, as in every instance had militated against the dearest and most valuable interests of this country.

The next consideration was, that under all the provocations which had been sustained from France, provocations which, in ordinary times, and in different circumstances, could not have failed to have been regarded as acts of hostility, and which formerly, not even a delay of twenty-four hours would have been wanting to have treated as such, by commencing an immediate war of retaliation, His Majesty's ministers had prudently and temperately advised all the means to be previously employed of obtaining reasonable satisfaction, before recourse should be had to extremities. Means had been taken to inform their agents, even though not accredited, of the grounds of jealousy and complaint on the part of this country, and an opportunity had been afforded through them of bringing forward any circumstances of explanation, or offering any terms of satisfaction. Whether the facts and explanations which these agents had brought forward were such as

1. In the name of the French nation, the national Convention offers fraternity and succour to all peoples who may want to win back their liberty, and it asks that the executive issue the necessary orders to the generals to come to their aid, and to defend the citizens who may be in distress or who may fall into distress for the cause of liberty.

The national Convention decrees that the executive shall order the generals of the French Republic to have the above decree printed and made public in different languages, in all the territories they shall traverse with the armies of the Republic (translated from *Archives Parlementaires*, 1898, p. 474).

contained any proper satisfaction for the past, or could afford any reasonable assurance with respect to the future, every member might judge from the inspection of the papers. He had already given it as his opinion, that if there was no other alternative than either to make war or depart from our principles, rather than recede from our principles a war was preferable to a peace; because a peace, purchased upon such terms, must be uncertain, precarious, and liable to be continually interrupted by the repetition of fresh injuries and insults. War was preferable to such a peace, because it was a shorter and a surer way to that end which the House had undoubtedly in view as its ultimate object – a secure and lasting peace. What sort of peace must that be in which there was no security? Peace he regarded as desirable only so far as it was secure. If, said Mr Pitt, you entertain a sense of the many blessings which you enjoy, if you value the continuance and safety of that commerce which is a source of so much opulence, if you wish to preserve and render permanent that high state of prosperity by which this country has for some years past been so eminently distinguished, you hazard all these advantages more, and are more likely to forfeit them, by submitting to a precarious and disgraceful peace, than by a timely and vigorous interposition of your arms. By tameness and delay you suffer that evil which might now be checked, to gain ground, and which, when it becomes indispensable to oppose, may perhaps be found irresistible.

It had on former debates been alleged, that by going to war we expose our commerce. Is there, he would ask, any man so blind and irrational, who does not know that the inevitable consequence of every war must be much interruption and injury to commerce? But, because our commerce was exposed to suffer, was that a reason why we should never go to war? Was there no combination of circumstances, was there no situation in the affairs of Europe, such as to render it expedient to hazard, for a time, a part of our commercial interests? Was there no evil greater, and which a war might be necessary to avoid, than the partial inconvenience to which our commerce was subjected, during the continuance of hostile operations? But he begged pardon of the House for the digression into which he had been led – while he talked as if they were debating about the expediency of a war, war was actually declared: we were at this moment engaged in a war.

He now came to state what had occurred since His Majesty's last message; and to notice those grounds which had served as a pretext for the declaration of war. When His Majesty had dismissed M. Chauvelin, what were then the hopes of peace? He was by no means sanguine in such hopes, and he had stated to the House that he then saw but little probability that a war could be avoided. Such then was his sentiment, because the explanations and conduct of the French agent were such as afforded him but little room to expect any terms which this country could, either consistently with honour or a regard to its safety, accept. Still, however, the last moment had been kept open to receive any satisfactory explanation which might be offered. But what, it might be asked, was to be the mode of receiving such explanation? When His Majesty had dismissed M. Chauvelin, as, by the melancholy catastrophe of the French monarch, the only character in which he had ever been acknowledged at the British court had entirely ceased, eight days had been allowed him for his departure, and if, during that period, he had sent any more satisfactory explanation, still it would have been received. Had any disposition been testified to comply with the requisitions of Lord Grenville, still an opportunity was afforded of intimating this disposition. Thus had our government pursued to the last a conciliatory system, and left every opening for accommodation, had the French been disposed to embrace it. Mr.

Chauvelin, however, instantly quitted the country, without making any proposition. Another agent had succeeded, (M. Maret,) who, on his arrival in this country, had notified himself as the chargé-d'affaires on the part of the French republic, but had never, during his residence in the kingdom, afforded the smallest communication.

What was the next event which had succeeded? An embargo was laid on all the vessels and persons of His Majesty's subjects who were then in France. This embargo was to be considered as not only a symptom, but as an act of hostility. It certainly had taken place without any notice being given, contrary to treaty, and against all the laws of nations. Here, perhaps, it might be said, that, on account of their stopping certain ships loaded with corn for France, the government of Great Britain might be under the same charge; to this point he should come presently. He believed if government were chargeable with any thing, it might rather be, that they were even too slow in asserting the honour and vindicating the rights of this country. If he thought that His Majesty's ministers wanted any justification, it would be for their forbearance, and not for their promptitude, since to the last moment they had testified a disposition to receive terms of accommodation, and left open the means of explanation. Notwithstanding this violent and outrageous act, such was the disposition to peace in His Majesty's ministers, that the channels of communication, even after this period, were not shut: a most singular circumstance happened, which was the arrival of intelligence from His Majesty's minister at the Hague on the very day when the embargo became known here, that he had received an intimation from General Dumouriez, that the General wished an interview, in order to see if it were yet possible to adjust the differences between the two countries, and to promote a general pacification. Instead of treating the embargo as an act of hostility, and forbearing from any communication, even after this aggression, His Majesty's ministers, on the same day on which the embargo was made known to them, gave instructions to the ambassador at the Hague, to enter into a communication with General Dumouriez; and they did this with great satisfaction, on several accounts: first, because it might be done without committing the King's dignity; for the General of an army might, even in the very midst of war, without any recognition of his authority, open any negociation of peace. But this sort of communication was desirable also, because, if successful, it would be attended with the most immediate effects, as its tendency was immediately to stop the progress of war, in the most practical, and perhaps, in the only practical way. No time was therefore lost in authorising the King's minister at the Hague to proceed in the pursuit of so desirable an object, if it could be done in a safe and honourable mode, but not otherwise. But before the answer of government could reach the ambassador, or any means be adopted for carrying the object proposed into execution, war was declared, on the part of the French, against this country. If then we were to debate at all, we were to debate whether or not we were to repel those principles, which not only were inimical to this, and to every other government, but which had been followed up in acts of hostility to this country. We were to debate whether or not we were to resist an aggression which had already been commenced. He would however refer the House, not to observations of reasoning, but to the grounds which had been assigned by the assembly themselves in their declaration of war. But first, he must again revert for a moment to the embargo. He then stated, that a detention of ships, if no ground of hostility had been given, was, in the first place, contrary to the law of nations. In the second place, there was an actual treaty between the two countries, providing for this very circumstance: and this treaty, (if not set aside by our breach of it, which he should come to presently,) expressly said, that, 'in each case of a rupture, time shall be given for the removal of persons and effects'.[2]

He should now proceed to the declaration itself. It began with declaring, 'That the King of England has not ceased, especially since the revolution of the 10th of August, 1792, to give proofs of his being evil disposed towards the French nation, and of his attachment to the coalition of crowned heads'. Notwithstanding the assertion that His Majesty had not ceased to shew his evil dispositions towards the French nation, they had not attempted to shew any acts of hostility previous to the 10th of August; nor in support of the charge of his attachment to the coalition of crowned heads, had they been able to allege any fact, except his supposed accession to the treaty between the Emperor of Germany and the King of Prussia.[3] This treaty had already, this evening, been the subject of conversation: it had then been mentioned, which he should now repeat, that the fact, thus alleged, was false, and entirely destitute of foundation; and that no accession to any such treaty had ever taken place on the part of His Majesty. And not only had he entered into no such treaty, but no step had been taken, and no engagement formed on the part of our government, to interfere in the internal affairs of France, or attempt to dictate to them any form of constitution. He declared that the whole of the interference of Great Britain had been (in consequence of French aggressions) with the general view of seeing whether it was possible, either by our own exertions, or in concert with any other powers, to repress this French system of aggrandisement and aggression, with the view of seeing whether we could not re-establish the blessings of peace, whether we could not, either separately, or jointly with other powers, provide for the security of our own country, and the general security of Europe.

The next charge brought by the national assembly was, 'That at the period aforesaid he ordered his ambassador at Paris to withdraw, because he would not acknowledge the provisional executive council, created by the legislative assembly'. It was hardly necessary for him to discuss a subject with which all were already so well acquainted. After the horrors of the 10th of August, which were paralleled but not eclipsed by those of the 2d of September, and the suspension of the French monarch, to whom alone the ambassador had been sent, it certainly became proper to recal him. He could not remain to treat with any government to whom he was not accredited; and the propriety of his being recalled would appear still more evident, when it was considered that it was probable that the banditti who had seized upon the government would not long retain their power; and, in fact, in the course of a month, they had been obliged to yield to the interest of a different party, but of a description similar to their own. It was also to be remarked, that this circumstance of recalling the ambassador had never till now been complained of as an act of hostility. When a government was overturned, it became a fair question how long an interval should intervene till that government should be acknowledged? and especially if that change of government was accompanied with all the circumstances of tumult and distraction, it certainly became a matter of extreme hardship that a war should be the consequence to the nation which should refuse to acknowledge it in the first instance. The force of this reasoning became increased in the particular application, when it was

2. Cf. the Treaty of Utrecht (Doc. 29), Art. XIX.
3. Britain signed a military convention with Prussia at Mainz on 14 July 1793, for maintaining 'the most perfect concert' and shutting 'all their ports against French ships' (Cobbett, *Parliamentary History of England from the Normal Conquest in 1066 to the Year 1803* (London, 1817) Vol. XXX, pp. 1052–3).

considered, that France had not yet established any constitution of its own; that all, hitherto, was merely provisional and temporary; and that, however the present republican system might be confirmed by force, or change of opinion, a little before, the voice of the nation, as far as its wish could be collected, had expressed itself in favour of a monarchy.

They proceeded to state, as farther grounds of their declaration of war, 'That the cabinet of St James's has ceased, since the same period, (the 10th of August,) to correspond with the French ambassador at London, on pretext of the suspension of the heretofore King of the French. That, since the opening of the national convention, it has refused to resume the usual correspondence between the two states, and to acknowledge the powers of this convention. That it has refused to acknowledge the ambassador of the French republic, although provided with letters of credit in its name'. M. Chauvelin had been received at this court as ambassador of the King, and in no other capacity or character. From the period of the suspension of the King, he, for some months, ceased to hold any communication with the government here, or to act in any capacity; nor was it till the month of December that he had received his letters of credence to act here as the ambassador of the French republic. With respect to the charge of not having acknowledged the convention, he confessed it to be true. When these letters of credence had been tendered, they were refused; but it was to be considered whether it would have been proper to have recognised them, after the repeated instances of offence, for which no compensation had been made, and of which, indeed, every fresh act presented not only a repetition, but an aggravation. Indeed, it would have been impossible at that period, without shewing a deviation from principle, and a tameness of disposition, to have recognised their authority, or accepted of the person who presented himself in the character of their ambassador. At that very moment, it was to be recollected, they were embarked in the unjust and inhuman process which had terminated in the murder of their King – an event which had every where excited sentiments of the utmost horror and indignation! Would it have been becoming in our government first to have acknowledged them at such a moment, when the power they had assumed was thus cruelly and unjustly exercised against that very authority which they usurped? But, whatever might be the feelings of abhorrence and indignation, which their conduct on this occasion could not fail to excite, he should by no means hold out these feelings as a ground for hostility, nor should he ever wish to propose a war of vengeance. The catastrophe of the French monarch, they ought all to feel deeply; and, consistently with that impression, be led more firmly to resist those principles from which an event of so black and atrocious a nature had proceeded; principles which, if not opposed, might be expected in their progress to lead to the commission of similar crimes; but, notwithstanding government had been obliged to decline all communication which tended to acknowledge the authority of the convention, still, as he had said before, they had left open the means of accommodation; nor could that line of conduct which they had pursued, be stated as affording any ground of hostility.

He should now consider, collectively, some of the subsequent grounds which they had stated in their declaration, which were expressed in the following articles:

'That the court of St. James's has attempted to impede the different purchases of corn, arms, and other commodities ordered in England, either by French citizens or the agents of the republic.

'That it has caused to be stopped several boats and ships loaded with grain for France, contrary to the treaty of 1786, while exportation to other foreign countries was free.

'That in order still more effectually to obstruct the commercial operations of the republic in England, it obtained an act of parliament prohibiting the circulation of assignats.

'That in violation of the fourth article of the treaty of 1786, it obtained another act, in the month of January last, which subjects all French citizens, residing in, or coming into England, to forms the most inquisitorial, vexatious, and dangerous.

'That at the same time, and contrary to the first article of the peace of 1783, it granted protection and pecuniary aid not only to the emigrants, but even to the chiefs of the rebels, who have already fought against France; that it has maintained with them a daily correspondence, evidently directed against the French revolution; that it has also received the chiefs of the rebels of the French West-India colonies'.

All these had been stated as provocations; but what sort of provocations? What, he would ask, was a provocation? – That we had indeed taken measures, which, if considered by themselves, and not as connected with the situation of affairs in which they were adopted, might perhaps be considered in the light of provocations, he would allow; but if these measures were justified by the necessity of circumstances – if they were called for by a regard to our own safety and interests – they could only be viewed as temperate and moderate precautions. And in this light, these grounds, assigned in the declaration, could only be regarded as frivolous and unfounded pretences. With respect to the charge of having stopped supplies of grain and other commodities, intended for France, what could be more ridiculous than such a pretext? When there was reason to apprehend that France intended an attack upon the allies of this country, and against the country itself, upon which, at the same time, it depended for the stores and ammunitions necessary for carrying on hostilities, was it natural to suppose that they should furnish, from their own bosom, supplies to be turned against themselves and their allies? Could they be such children in understanding, could they be such traitors in principle, as to furnish to their enemies the means of hostility and the instruments of offence? What was the situation of France with respect to this country? Had they not given sufficient cause for jealousy of their hostile intentions? By their decree of the 19th of November, they had declared war against all governments. They had possessed themselves of Flanders, and were there endeavouring to establish, by force, what they styled a system of freedom, while they actually menaced Holland with an invasion. Another ground which they had stated in their declaration as an act of hostility on the part of our government was, that they had not suffered assignats to be circulated in this country. Truly, they had reason to be offended that we would not receive what was worth nothing; and that, by exercising an act which came completely within our own sovereignty with respect to the circulation of any foreign paper-currency, we thus avoided a gigantic system of swindling. If such, indeed, were the pretences which they brought forward as grounds for a declaration of war, it was a matter of wonder that, instead of a sheet of paper, they did not occupy a volume, and proved that their ingenuity had been exhausted before their modesty had been at all affected. Of much the same nature was that other pretext, with respect to the passing of the alien bill; a bill absolutely necessary for the safety of the country, as it shielded us from the artifice of the seditious, perhaps the dagger of the assassin. This bill they had held out as an infringement of the treaty of commerce. It could be no infringement of their treaty, as in the treaty itself it was expressly declared, that nothing was to be considered as an infringement, unless, first, proper explanations had taken place. Secondly, it was not to be expected that any treaty could supersede the propriety of adopting new measures in a new situation of affairs. Such was the case, when an inundation of foreigners had poured into this country under circumstances entirely different from those which were provided for by the bill. But who were those who complained of the severity of the regulations adopted by the alien bill in this country? The very persons who, during the late transaction in their own country, had adopted restrictions of police ten times more severe, but of which our government, however much its subjects might be affected, had never made the smallest complaint.

The next ground, assigned in the declaration, was the armament which had taken place in this country.

'That in the same spirit, without any provocation, and when all the maritime powers are at peace with England, the cabinet of St. James's has ordered a considerable naval armament, and an augmentation of the land forces.

'That this armament was ordered at a moment when the English ministry was bitterly persecuting those who supported the principles of the French revolution in England, and was employing all possible means, both in parliament and out of it, to cover the French republic with ignominy, and to draw upon it the execration of the English nation, and of all Europe'.

And, under what circumstances had the armament complained of taken place? At the period when the French, by their conduct with regard to the treaty of the Scheldt,[4] shewed their intention to disregard the obligation of all treaties, when they had begun to propagate principles of universal war, and to discover views of unbounded conquest. Was it to be wondered that, at such a time, we should think it necessary to take measures of precaution, and to oppose, with determination, the progress of principles, not only of so mischievous a tendency, but which, in their immediate consequences, threatened to be so fatal to ourselves and our allies? Indeed they now seemed rather to despair of these principles being so generally adopted, and attended with such striking and immediate success as they had at first fondly imagined. How little progress these principles had made in this country they might be sufficiently convinced by that spirit, which had displayed itself, of attachment to the constitution, and those expressions of a firm determination to support it, which had appeared from every quarter. If, indeed, they meant to attack us, because we do not like French principles, then would this indeed be that sort of war which had so often been alleged and deprecated on the other side of the House – a war against opinions. If they meant to attack us because we love our constitution, then indeed it would be a war of extirpation; for not till the spirit of Englishmen was exterminated, would their attachment to the constitution be destroyed, and their generous efforts be slackened in its defence.

The next articles of complaint on the part of the French were,

'That the object of this armament, intended against France, was not even disguised in the English parliament.

'That although the [provisional] executive council of France has employed every measure for preserving peace and fraternity with the English nation, and has replied to calumnies and violation of treaties only by remonstrances, founded on the principles of justice, and expressed with the dignity of free men; the English minister has persevered in his system of malevolence and hostility, confirmed the armaments, and sent a squadron to the Scheldt to disturb the operations of the French in Belgium.

'That, on the news of the execution of Louis, he carried his outrages to the French republic to such a length, as to order the ambassador of France to quit the British territory within eight days.

4. The Scheldt question concerned Dutch control over the Scheldt river estuary (hence the port of Antwerp), a matter of vital interest to Britain. It was confirmed by the Treaty of Münster (1648) and by the Barrier Treaty with Austria (1715).

'That the King of England has manifested his attachment to the cause of that traitor, and his design of supporting it by different hostile resolutions adopted in his council, both by nominating generals of his land army, and by applying to parliament for a considerable addition of land and sea forces, and putting ships of war in commission'.

They clearly shewed their enmity to that constitution, by taking every opportunity to separate the King of England from the nation, and by addressing the people as distinct from the government. Upon the point of their fraternity he did not wish to say much: he had no desire for their affection. To the people they offered fraternity, while they would rob them of that constitution by which they are protected, and deprive them of the numerous blessings which they enjoy under its influence. In this case, their fraternal embraces resembled those of certain animals who embrace only to destroy.

Another ground which they had assigned was the grief which had been expressed in the British court at the fate of their unhappy monarch. Of all the reasons he ever heard for making war against another country, that of the French upon this occasion was the most extraordinary: they said they would make war on us, first, because we loved our own constitution, secondly, because we detested their proceedings; and lastly, because we presumed to grieve at the death of their murdered king. Thus would they even destroy those principles of justice, and those sentiments of compassion, which led us to reprobate their crimes, and to be afflicted at their cruelties. Thus would they deprive us of that last resource of humanity – to mourn over the misfortunes and sufferings of the victims of their injustice. If such was the case, it might be asked, in the emphatic words of the Roman writer, *Quis gemitus Populo Romano liber erit?*[5] They would not only endeavour to destroy our political existence, and to deprive us of the privileges which we enjoyed under our excellent constitution, but they would eradicate our feelings as men; they would make crimes of those sympathies which were excited by the distresses of our common nature; they would repress our sighs and restrain our tears. Thus, except the specific fact, which was alleged as a ground of their declaration of war, namely, the accession of His Majesty to the treaty between Austria and Prussia, which had turned out to be entirely false and unfounded, or the augmentation of our armament, a measure of precaution indispensably requisite for the safety of the country, and the protection of its allies, all the others were merely unjust, unfounded, absurd, and frivolous pretexts – pretexts which never could have been brought to justify a measure of which they were not previously strongly desirous, and which shewed that, instead of waiting for provocation, they only sought a pretence of aggression. The death of Louis, though it only affected the individual, was aimed against all sovereignty, and shewed their determination to carry into execution that intention, which they had so often professed, of exterminating all monarchy. As a consequence of that monstrous system of inconsistency which they pursued, even while they professed their desire to maintain a good understanding with this country, the minister of the marine had written a letter to the sea-port towns, ordering them to fit out privateers: for what purpose but the projected view of making depredations on our commerce? While they affected to complain of our armaments, they had passed a decree to fit out fifty sail of the line – an armament which, however, it was to be observed, existed only in the decree.

5. 'What lamentation will the Roman people be free to express [without fear of punishment]?' (adaptation of Cicero, *Philippic*, II, 64).

He feared that, by this long detail, he had wearied the patience of the House, and occupied more of their time than he at first intended. The pretexts, which he had been led to examine, alleged as grounds for the declaration of war, were of a nature that required no refutation. They were such as every man could see through; and in many of his remarks he doubted not he had been anticipated by that contempt with which the House would naturally regard the weak reasoning, but wicked policy, of these pretexts.

He now came to his conclusion. – We, said Mr Pitt, have, in every instance, observed the strictest neutrality with respect to the French: we have pushed, to its utmost extent, the system of temperance and moderation: we have held out the means of accommodation: we have waited to the last moment for satisfactory explanation. These means of accommodation have been slighted and abused, and all along there has appeared no disposition to give any satisfactory explanation. They have now, at last, come to an actual aggression, by seizing our vessels in our very ports, without any provocation given on our part; without any preparations having been adopted but those of necessary precaution, they have declared, and are now waging war. Such is the conduct which they have pursued; such is the situation in which we stand. It now remains to be seen whether, under Providence, the efforts of a free, brave, loyal, and happy people, aided by their allies, will not be successful in checking the progress of a system, the principles of which, if not opposed, threaten the most fatal consequences to the tranquillity of this country, the security of its allies, the good order of every European government, and the happiness of the whole of the human race!

33 WILLIAM PITT'S MEMORANDUM OF 19 JANUARY 1805 (OFFICIAL COMMUNICATION MADE TO THE RUSSIAN AMBASSADOR AT LONDON)

Introduction

The global war that began in 1792 had a brief respite when in 1802 Britain and France reached a temporary peace of exhaustion at Amiens. However, in the following year, Britain (at first alone) resumed hostilities. The encroachments of France upon her neighbours, the government explained in the declaration of war, made it impossible to create conditions that they judged 'absolutely necessary to the future tranquility of Europe'.

Britain's chief continental ally in the wars against Napoleon became Russia. The new Tsar, Alexander I, sent Count Novossilsoff, a close adviser, to London and the result of this mission was the present agreed statement of war aims by William Pitt which became the basis of the treaty of the Third Coalition (Doc. 34). In the longer perspective, the document was 'so masterly an outline for the restoration of Europe' (as Foreign Secretary Castlereagh explained to his chief envoy in Europe in 1813) that it became, in the words of historian Charles Webster (1921, p. 1) 'the text of all the British diplomacy of the period'. Not only did it deal with the essentials of the territorial settlement but it also provided for 'repressing future attempts to disturb the general tranquility'. It sowed the seeds of future international organisation and served as the blueprint of European reconstruction within the framework of British naval predominance at the global level (cf. Docs. 37–39, 42).

Text

The result of the communications which have been made by Prince Czartoriski[1] to His Majesty's Ambassador at St. Petersburgh, and of the confidential explanations which have been received from your Excellency, has been laid before the King; and His Majesty has seen with inexpressible satisfaction, the wise, dignified, and generous policy, which the Emperor of Russia is disposed to adopt, under the present calamitous situation of Europe. His Majesty is also happy to perceive, that the views and sentiments of the Emperor respecting the deliverance of Europe, and providing for its future tranquillity and safety, correspond so entirely with his own. He is therefore desirous of entering into the most explicit and unreserved explanations on every point connected with this great object, and of forming the closest union of councils, and concert of measures, with his Imperial

Source: C. K. Webster (ed.), *British Diplomacy 1813–1815*, pp. 389–94; a shorter version may be found in Hansard, Vol. XXXI, pp. 178–80.

1. Russia's adjunct Minister of Foreign Affairs.

Majesty, in order, by their joint influence and exertions, to insure the co-operation and assistance of other Powers of the Continent, on a scale adequate to the magnitude and importance of an undertaking, on the success of which the future safety of Europe must depend.

For this purpose, the first step must be, to fix as precisely as possible, the distinct objects to which such a concert is to be directed.

These, according to the explanation given of the sentiments of the Emperor, in which His Majesty entirely concurs, appear to be three:—

1. To rescue from the dominion of France those countries which it has subjugated since the beginning of the Revolution, and to reduce France within its former limits, as they stood before that time.

2. To make such an arrangement with respect to the territories recovered from France, as may provide for their security and happiness, and may at the same time constitute a more effectual barrier in future against encroachments on the part of France.

3. To form, at the restoration of peace, a general agreement and Guarantee for the mutual protection and security of different Powers, and for re-establishing a general system of public law in Europe.

The first and second objects are stated generally, and in their broadest extent; but neither of them can be properly considered in detail without reference to the nature and extent of the means by which they may be accomplished. The first is certainly that to which, without any modification or exception, his Majesty's wishes, as well as those of the Emperor, would be preferably directed, and nothing short of it can *completely* satisfy the views which both Sovereigns form for the deliverance and security of Europe. Should it be possible to unite in concert with Great Britain and Russia, the two other great military Powers of the Continent, there seems little doubt that such a union of force would enable them to accomplish all that is proposed. But if (as there is too much reason to imagine may be the case) it should be found impossible to engage Prussia in the Confederacy, it may be doubted whether such operations could be carried on in all the quarters of Europe, as would be necessary for the success of the whole of this project.

The chief points, however, to which His Majesty considers this doubt as applicable, relate to the question of the entire recovery of the Netherlands and the countries occupied by France on the left bank of the Rhine. His Majesty considers it essential even on this supposition to include nothing less than the evacuation of the North of Germany and Italy, the re-establishment of the independence of the United Provinces and of Switzerland, the Restoration of the dominions of the King of Sardinia and security of Naples; but on the side of the Netherlands it might perhaps be more prudent in this case to confine the views of the Allies to obtaining some moderate acquisitions for the United Provinces calculated (according to the principle specified under the second head) to form an additional barrier for that country. His Majesty, however, by no means intends to imply if very brilliant and decisive success should be obtained, and the power of France broken and overcome by operations in other quarters, the Allies might not in such a case, extend their views to the recovery of the whole or the greater part of these territories, but, as in the first instance it does not appear possible that they can be reconquered by the operations of the war without the aid of Prussia, His Majesty is inclined to think that this object ought in any Treaty of Concert to be described in such terms as would admit of the modifications here stated.

The second point of itself involves in it many important considerations. The views and sentiments by which His Majesty and the Emperor of Russia are equally animated in endeavouring to establish this concert, are pure and disinterested.

The insular situation and extensive resources of Great Britain, aided by its military exertions and naval superiority; and the immense power, the established Continental ascendency and remote distance of Russia already give to the territories of the two Sovereigns a security against the attacks of France – even after all her acquisitions of influence, power and dominion – which cannot be the lot of any other country. They have therefore no separate objects of their own in the arrangements which are in question, no personal interest to consult in this Concert but that which grows out of the general interest and security of Europe, and is inseparably connected with it. Their first view, therefore, with respect to any of the countries which may be recovered from France, must be to restore, as far as possible, their ancient rights, and provide for the internal happiness of their inhabitants; but in looking at this object, they must not lose sight of the general security of Europe, on which even that separate object must principally depend.

Pursuant to this principle, there can be no question that, whenever any of these countries are capable of being restored to their former independence, and of being placed in a situation in which they can protect it, such an arrangement must be most congenial to the policy and the feelings on which this system is founded: but there will be found to be other countries among those now under the dominion of France, to which these considerations cannot apply, where either the ancient relations of the country are so completely destroyed that they cannot be restored, or where independence would be merely nominal and alike inconsistent with the security for the country itself, or for Europe: happily, the larger number is of the first description. Should the arms of the Allies be successful to the full extent of expelling France from all the dominions she has acquired since the Revolution, it would certainly be the first object, as has already been stated, to re-establish the republics of the United Provinces and Switzerland, the territories of the King of Sardinia, Tuscany, Modena, (under the protection of Austria), and Naples. But the territories of Genoa, of the Italian Republic, including the three Legations, Parma, and Placentia; and on the other side of Europe, the Austrian Netherlands, and the States which have been detached from the German Empire on the left bank of the Rhine, evidently belong to the second class. With respect to the territories enumerated in Italy, experience has shown how little disposition existed in some, and how little means in any, to resist the aggression or influence of France. The King of Spain was certainly too much a party to the system of which so large a part of Europe has been a victim, to entitle the former interests of his family in Italy to any consideration; nor does the past conduct of Genoa, or any of the other States, give them any claim, either of justice or liberality. It is also obvious that these separate petty sovereignties would never again have any solid existence in themselves, and would only serve to weaken and impair the force which ought to be, as much as possible, concentrated in the hands of the chief Powers of Italy.

It is needless to dwell particularly on the state of the Netherlands. Events have put out of the question the restoration of them to the House of Austria; they are therefore necessarily open to new arrangements, and evidently can never exist separate and independent. Nearly the same considerations apply to the Ecclesiastical Electorates, and the other territories on the left bank of the Rhine, after their being once detached from the Empire, and the former possessors of them indemnified. There appears, therefore, to be no possible objection, on the strictest principles of justice and public morality, to making such a disposition with respect to any of these territories as may be most conducive to the general interests; and there is evidently no other mode of accomplishing the great and beneficent object of re-establishing (after so much misery and bloodshed) the safety and repose of Europe on a solid and permanent basis. It is fortunate too that such a plan of arrangement as is itself essential to the end proposed, is also likely to contribute, in the greatest degree, to secure the means by which that great end can best be promoted.

It is evidently of the utmost importance, if not absolutely indispensable for this purpose, to secure the vigorous and effectual co-operation both of Austria and Prussia; but there is little reason to hope that either of these Powers will be brought to embark in the common cause, without the prospect of obtaining some important acquisition to compensate for its exertions. On the grounds which have been already stated, his Majesty conceives that nothing could so much contribute to the general security as giving to Austria fresh means of resisting the views of France on the side of Italy, and placing Prussia in a similar situation with respect to the Low Countries; and the relative situations of the two Powers would naturally make those the quarters to which their views would respectively be directed.

In Italy, sound policy would require, that the power and influence of the King of Sardinia should be augmented, and that Austria should be replaced in a situation which may enable her to afford an immediate and effectual support to his dominions, in case of their being attacked. His Majesty sees with satisfaction, from the secret and confidential communications recently received through your Excellency, that the views of the Court of Vienna are perfectly conformable to this general principle, and that the extension at which she aims, might not only safely be admitted, but might even be increased, with advantage to the general interest. In other respects His Majesty entirely concurs in the outline of the arrangement which he understands the Emperor of Russia to be desirous of seeing effected in this quarter. His Majesty considers it as absolutely necessary for the general security, that Italy should be completely rescued both from the occupation and influence of France, and that no Powers should be left within it, who are not likely to enter into a general system of defence for maintaining its independence. For this purpose, it is essential that the countries now composing what is called the Italian Republic, should be transferred to other Powers. In disturbing these territories, an increase of wealth and power should undoubtedly be given to the King of Sardinia; and it seems material that his possessions, as well as the Duchy of Tuscany (which it is proposed to restore to the Grand Duke), should be brought into immediate contact, or ready communication with those of Austria. On this principle the part of the Milanese to the South West of the Adda, and the whole of the territories which now compose the Ligurian Republic, as well as perhaps Parma and Placentia, might, it is conceived, be annexed to Piedmont.

The Three Legations might in His Majesty's opinion be annexed to the territories of Austria, and the addition which may be made to the acquisitions proposed for that Power, with advantage to the common cause. And the Duchy of Modena, placed as it would be between the new acquisitions of Sardinia and the Duchy of Tuscany (which may be considered under this arrangement as virtually Austrian) might safely be restored to its former possessors.

The observations which have been stated respecting the situation of Sardinia in Italy seem, in a great measure, to apply to that of Holland and Prussia, in relation to the Low Countries; with this difference, however, that the Piedmontese dominions, affording in themselves considerable means of defence, they may be perhaps sufficiently secure in the possession of the King of Sardinia, supported by Austria, whereas the Netherlands being more open and exposed seem scarcely capable of being secured unless by annexing a considerable part of them to Prussia, and placing Holland in a second line of defence. With this view (supposing France to be reduced within its ancient limits) it might be proposed to annex to the United Provinces, as an additional Barrier, the part of Flanders lying within a military line to be drawn from Antwerp to the Meuse at Maestricht, and the remainder of the Netherlands, together with the Duchies of Luxembourg and Juliers, and the other territories between the Meuse and the Moselle to Prussia.

His Majesty indeed feels so strongly the importance both of augmenting the inducements to Prussia to take part and of rendering it a powerful and effectual Barrier for the defence not only of Holland but of the North of Germany against France, that he should even consider it as advisable in addition to what has been already proposed, to put into possession of that Power the territories which may be recovered from France on the left bank of the Rhine, eastward of the Moselle, and His Majesty entertains a strong conviction that this arrangement (if it not in other respects be thought liable to insuperable objections) would be infinitely more effective for the protection of the North of Europe than any other that can be devised.

His Majesty is, however, aware that great difficulties may arise in regulating the proportionate acquisitions of Austria and Prussia, in such a way as to prevent their being the source of mutual jealousy, and this consideration it is which, amongst others, has operated as a great additional inducement of acquisition for Austria on the side of Italy.

He thinks it also important to remark that the acquisition to be held out to Prussia ought not to be measured merely by what would be in itself desirable but by the consideration of what may be necessary to outweigh the temptations which France will not fail to offer to that Power, to secure its co-operation. These will probably be on an extensive scale, and in a quarter much more calculated to produce effects injurious to the interests of Austria and of Prussia herself while, on the other hand, if the ambition of Prussia can be gratified in the manner proposed at the expense of France, it will be diverted from the views which it will otherwise form towards the North, the accomplishment of which would tend to increase, to an alarming degree, its influence both in Germany and over the secondary Powers of the Baltic. But, if notwithstanding these powerful considerations, it should still be thought by His Imperial Majesty that the augmentation here proposed to the territories of Prussia is greater than ought to be admitted, His Majesty will, (though not without reluctance) concur in any other arrangement that may be thought preferable by which a larger portion of the Netherlands may be allotted to the United Provinces, and the acquisitions of Prussia confined within narrower limits; but he trusts that at any rate, it will not be necessary to reduce them to anything less than the territories on the left bank of the Rhine between the Meuse and the Moselle, and it will in this case, require much consideration, in what hands the territories on the left bank of the Rhine, east of the Moselle can best be placed or whether they may be safely left in the possession of France.

In the event of Prussia not being prevailed upon to enter into the concert, I have already stated His Majesty's conviction, that the views of the Allies on this side of Europe must be more limited; and in that case probably nothing more can be expected than to obtain the complete evacuation of the North of Germany, and the re-establishment of the independence of Holland, together with the

Barrier here stated within the line drawn from Antwerp to Maestricht, leaving the other territories on the left bank of the Rhine in the possession of France.

[A detailed description follows of the plan of campaign and the amount of force necessary to obtain the objects stated above. If Prussia joins the Alliance it is estimated that 500,000 men may be put into the field; if, as is more likely, she abstains, 400,000. Details of the Plan of campaign are given. Russia is urged to do her utmost to induce Prussia to co-operate and especially is asked to notify her immediately that she will not agree to the acquisition of Hanover by Prussia.]

Supposing the efforts of the Allies to have been completely successful, and the two objects already discussed to have been fully obtained, His Majesty would nevertheless consider this salutary work as still imperfect, if the restoration of peace were not accompanied by the most effectual measures for giving solidity and permanence to the system which shall thus have been established. Much will undoubtedly be effected for the future repose of Europe by these territorial arrangements, which will furnish a more effectual barrier than has before existed against the ambition of France. But in order to render this security as complete as possible, it seems necessary, at the period of a general pacification, to form a Treaty to which all the principal Powers of Europe should be parties, by which their respective rights and possessions, as they then have been established, shall be fixed and recognized; and they should all bind themselves mutually to protect and support each other, against any attempt to infringe them:—It should re-establish a general and comprehensive system of public law in Europe, and provide, as far as possible, for repressing future attempts to disturb the general tranquillity; and above all, for restraining any projects of aggrandizement and ambition similar to those which have produced all the calamities inflicted on Europe since the disastrous æra of the French Revolution.

This Treaty should be put under the special Guarantee of Great Britain and Russia, and the two Powers should by a separate engagement, bind themselves to each other jointly to take an active part in preventing its being infringed. Such a Treaty might also be accompanied by more particular and specific provisions, by which the several Powers of Italy might be united in a closer alliance for their own defence. How far any similar system could be adopted for giving additional security for the Germanic Body is well deserving of consideration. Their present state is certainly very unsatisfactory with a view either to their own immediate interests, or to the safety of Europe. At the same time it appears to His Majesty very doubtful whether from local circumstances and other causes, it would ever be possible to consolidate them into any effectual system. Should this be found to be the case, the evils to be apprehended from their weak and exposed state might (as far as relates to the danger from France) perhaps be remedied by adopting a system (but on a larger scale) similar to that formerly established by the Barrier Treaty for the protection of the Netherlands. It might not be difficult to settle some general plan for maintaining at the joint expense of the different Powers of the Empire, fortresses of sufficient strength, and properly garrisoned, along the course of the Rhine from Basle to Ehrenbreiten, commanding the principal approaches from France to the most exposed parts of Germany, and the military custody of these fortresses (without infringing in other respects on the territorial rights of the Power in whose dominions they might be placed) might be confided to the two great Powers of Germany, according to their respective means of occupying them.

It seems also desirable, in order to give further security to the United Provinces (under any of the arrangements which have already been discussed) that they should be called upon to enter into an engagement jointly with Great Britain and

Russia to maintain at all times their army on such a footing as may be thought necessary to provide for their defence against sudden attacks. In addition to this stipulation His Majesty in his Electoral capacity, might perhaps be induced to keep a considerable force (in consequence of arrangements with the British Government) ready to be employed on the first alarm for the defence of the United Provinces; and His Majesty would also be ready to enter into a Concert with other Powers for defraying the expense of maintaining at all times an adequate and effective garrison to consist of German troops for garrisoning any fortresses now existing, or hereafter to be established, on whatever may be the line ultimately fixed as the Dutch frontier.

Having thus stated what more immediately relates to the specific objects of the Concert and of the means to be employed to give effect, there still remains one great and important question for consideration, and that is how far, either now or hereafter, the views of the Allies ought to be directed towards the re-establishment of monarchy in France, and the restoration of the Bourbon Family on the throne. His Majesty agrees entirely with the Emperor of Russia in thinking that such a settlement is in itself highly desirable for the future both of France and Europe, and that no fair occasion ought to be neglected of promoting it. But he at the same time thinks, that it ought to be considered only a secondary object in the Concert now to be established and one which could in no case justify the prolongation of the war if a Peace could be obtained on the principles which have been stated. It is one with a view to which no active or decided measures can be taken, unless a series of great and signal successes shall previously have been obtained by the Allies, and a strong and prevailing disposition for the return of the Monarch, shall then manifest itself in the interior of France. In the meantime in order to afford every reasonable chance for the attainment of this object, His Majesty entirely agrees with the Emperor of Russia, that it is highly important that in the conduct of the war, and in the public declarations and language of the Allied Courts, the greatest care should be taken to prevent any apprehension in the minds of any part of the French nation of any design either to dictate to them by force any particular form of government, or to attempt to dismember the ancient territories of France.

Such are the sentiments and observations which His Majesty is desirous of offering to the consideration of the Emperor on the great outlines of the important system which they are equally anxious to establish.

His Majesty will receive with the utmost attention and satisfaction, every fresh communication of the opinion of His Imperial Majesty on all the details connected with so extensive a subject. In the meanwhile from an anxiety to lose no time in laying this foundation of this great work, His Majesty has directed a project to be prepared of a Provisional Treaty conformable to the sentiments which appear to be entertained both by the Emperor and himself: and which, if it should meet with His Imperial Majesty's concurrence, he is ready immediately to conclude.

34 TREATY BETWEEN GREAT BRITAIN AND RUSSIA (THIRD COALITION) SAINT PETERSBURG, 11 APRIL 1805

Text

In the Name of The most Holy and Undivided Trinity

His Majesty the King of the United Kingdom of Great Britain and Ireland, and His Majesty the Emperor of all the Russias, animated with the Desire of restoring to Europe the Peace, Independence, and Happiness, of which it is deprived by the unbounded Ambition of the French Government, and the immoderate Degree of Influence which it is striving to arrogate to itself, have resolved to employ every Means in their Power to obtain this salutary End, and to prevent the Renewal of similar disastrous Circumstances; and they have named in consequence, for the Purpose of fixing and agreeing upon those Measures which their magnanimous Intentions may call for, viz. His Majesty the King of the United Kingdom and Ireland, the Lord Granville Leveson Gower, Member of the Parliament of the said United Kingdom, one of His Majesty's Privy Councillors, and His Ambassador Extraordinary and Plenipotentiary to His Majesty the Emperor of all the Russias; the Sieur Adam Prince of Czartoryski, One of his Privy Councillors, Member of the Council of State, Senator, adjunct Minister for Foreign Affairs, Member of the General Direction of the Schools, Curator of the Imperial University of Wilna and of its District, Lieutenant of the Grand Prior of the Sovereign Order of St John of Jerusalem, of the Russian Catholick Priory, and Knight of the Order of St Anne, and Commander of that of St John of Jerusalem; and the Sieur Nicolas of Novossilzoff, His present Chamberlain, adjunct Minister of Justice, charged with the Examination of the Projects presented to His Majesty, and with other Commissions, President of the Academy of Sciences, Member of the General Direction of the Schools, Curator of the University of St Petersburgh and of its District, and Knight of the Order of St Vladimir, who, after having verified and exchanged their full Powers, which were found to be in good and due form, have agreed upon the following Articles:

I. As the state of suffering in which Europe is placed demands a speedy remedy, their Majesties the King of the United Kingdom of Great Britain and Ireland, and the Emperor of all the Russias, have mutually agreed to consult upon the means of putting a stop thereto, without waiting for further encroachments on the part of the French Government; they have agreed, in consequence, to employ the most speedy and most efficacious means to form a general League of the States of Europe, and to engage them to accede to the present concert; and, in order to accomplish the end proposed, to collect together a force, which, independently of the succours furnished by His Britannick Majesty, may amount to 500 000 effective men, and to employ the same with energy, in order either to induce or to compel the French Government to agree to the re-establishment of Peace, and of the equilibrium of Europe.

II. The Object of this League will be to carry into Effect what is proposed by the present Concert, namely:

Source: Treaties presented to both Houses of Parliament, 28 January 1806, *Parliamentary Papers* (1806) Vol. XIX, pp. 8–10. ('Separate Articles' omitted.)

(a) The Evacuation of the Country of Hanover and of the North of Germany.

(b) The Establishment of the Independence of the Republicks of Holland and Switzerland.

(c) The Re-establishment of the King of Sardinia in Piedmont with as large an Augmentation of Territory as Circumstances will permit.

(d) The future Security of the Kingdom of Naples, and the complete Evacuation of Italy, the Island of Elba included, by the French Forces.

(e) The Establishment of an Order of Things in Europe, which may effectively guarantee the Security and Independence of the different States, and present a solid Barrier against future Usurpations.

III. His Britannick Majesty, in order to concur efficaciously on His side to the happy effects of the present concert, engages to contribute to the common efforts, by employing His Forces, both by sea and land, as well as His Vessels adapted for transporting Troops, in such manner as shall be determined upon in the general plan of operations; His Majesty will, moreover, assist the different Powers who shall accede thereto, by subsidies, the amount of which shall correspond to the respective Forces which shall be employed; and in order that the said pecuniary succours may be proportioned in the manner most conducive to the general good, and to assist the Powers in proportion to the exertions they may make to contribute to the common success, it is agreed, that these Subsidies (barring particular arrangements) shall be furnished in the proportion of 1 250 000 pounds sterling, for each 100 000 men of regular Troops, and so in proportion for a greater or smaller number, payable according to the conditions hereinafter specified.

IV. The said Subsidies shall be payable by instalments, from month to month, in proportion to the Forces which each Power shall employ, in pursuance of its engagements, to combat the common Enemy, and according to the official report of the Armies employed at the opening of the Campaign, and of the several reinforcements which may join them. An arrangement shall be made, in conformity with the plan of operations, which shall be forthwith regulated, as to the period when these subsidies shall begin to be paid, and the mode and place of payment shall be settled so as to suit the convenience of each of the Belligerent Parties. His Britannick Majesty will likewise be prepared to advance, within the current year, a sum for putting the Troops in motion. This sum shall be settled by particular arrangements to be entered into by each Power, who shall take part in this concert; but His said Majesty understands, that the whole of the sums to be furnished to any Power within the current year, as well on account of the said advance as for the monthly Subsidies, is in no case to exceed the proportion of 1 250 000 pounds sterling for every 100 000 men.

V. The High Contracting Parties agree that the different Members of the League shall respectively be permitted to retain accredited Persons with the Commanders in chief of the different Armies, to carry on the Correspondence, and to attend to the military Operations.

VI. Their Majesties agree, that in the Event of a League being formed, such as is pointed out in the First Article, they will not make Peace with France but by common Consent of all the Powers who shall become Parties in the said League; and also that the Continental Powers shall not recall their Forces before the Peace; moreover, His Britannick Majesty engages to continue the Payment of the Subsidies during the Continuance of the War.

VII. The present Concert which is mutually acknowledged by the High Contracting Parties to be equally valid and binding as the most solemn Treaty, shall be ratified by His Majesty the Emperor of all the Russias, and the

Ratifications thereof shall be exchanged at Saint Petersburgh within the Space of Ten Weeks or sooner if possible.

In Testimony whereof the respective Plenipotentiaries have signed the same, and have thereunto affixed the Seal of their Arms. Done at Saint Petersburgh 30th March/11 April in the Year One Thousand eight hundred and five.

ADAM PRINCE CZARTORYSKI (L.S.)
NICOLAS DE NOVOSSILZOFF (L.S.)
GRANVILLE LEVESON GOWER (L.S.)

35 THE BERLIN DECREES 1806

Introduction

At war with England since 1803, France could not hope for victory unless she landed an army in the British Isles; for her part, England could not defeat France unless she brought about a continental coalition against her, which she repeatedly attempted from 1792 onward.

After 1805, France, having lost her fleet to England at Trafalgar, abandoned the thought of invading Britain. Hence, Napoleon sought to induce England's capitulation by stifling her economy with a blockade, his 'continental system'; unlike Britain's maritime blockade of one country (France), the French economic blockade aimed at closing all of Europe to British goods.

For the blockade to succeed, it had to be enforced rigorously throughout Europe. But from the start, Britain's traditional ally Portugal was reluctant to comply, seeing the blockade as her commercial ruin. Napoleon himself was later to attribute his ultimate failure to the trouble with Portugal. In 1808, he marched into Portugal through Spain which eventually led to the landing of British troops (under Wellington) in the Iberian peninsula in 1810. Soon Russia too began to ignore the blockade; the disastrous Moscow campaign of 1812 was in large part intended to enforce it at the other end of Europe; it was to prove Napoleon's undoing.

But between 1803 and 1810, Trafalgar notwithstanding, the French Emperor's star still seemed to be rising. He was proclaimed Emperor in 1804 and King of Italy in 1805. He proceeded to defeat the Third (Austria, Prussia, Sweden, Russia and Naples) and Fourth (Great Britain, Prussia and Russia) coalitions through a series of his most brilliant campaigns: 1805 Ulm, Austerlitz and Vienna; 1806 Jena–Auerstadt; 1807 Eulau. In the peace talks with Russia that followed this last battle, Napoleon even managed to get a vague promise from Tsar Alexander I that he would launch an attack against British possessions in India by land. The following documents give France's design for the defeat of England.

Source: Napoléon 1er, *Correspondance* (Paris: Plon, Dumaine, 1863) Vol. 13, pp. 552–7, translated by Sylvia Modelski.

Text

A. Decree announcing the blockade of England, issued by the Emperor Napoleon from Berlin, on 21 November 1806

Napoleon, Emperor of the French, King of Italy, etc. . . .
Considering,

1. That England does not acknowledge the law of nations which is universally followed by all civilised peoples.

2. That she deems an enemy any individual belonging to the enemy State, and therefore takes as prisoners-of-war not only the crews of armed men of war, but also the crews of commercial vessels, merchantmen, and even commercial agents and traders who travel for business purposes.

3. That she extends the right of conquest, which can only be applied to what belongs to the State, to commercial buildings and merchandise, and to the private property of individuals.

4. That she extends the right of blockade, which according to reason and the usage of all civilised nations applies only to fortified places, to non-fortified towns and commercial ports.

That she declares blockaded places where she does not even have a single warship, although a place is not deemed to be blockaded unless it is so beleaguered that one cannot attempt to approach it without imminent danger.

That she even declares as being in a state of blockade places that all her assembled forces would be incapable of blockading, whole coastlines and an entire empire.

5. That this monstrous abuse of the right of blockade has no other aim than to prevent communication between nations, and to build the commerce and industry of England upon the ruin of continental industry and trade.

6. That, this being England's obvious aim, whoever trades in English goods on the continent thereby promotes her interests and becomes her accomplice.

7. That this behaviour of England's, worthy of the very early ages of barbarism, has benefited that power to the detriment of all others.

8. Natural law allows that the same arms be used against the enemy as he uses, and that he be fought in the same manner as he fights, when he ignores all concepts of justice and all liberal sentiments, that are the products of civilisation among men:

We have decided to make use, against England, of the same practices as were sanctioned by her maritime legislation.

The provisions of the present decree shall, without delay, be considered as the fundamental principle of the Empire until England will have recognised that the law of war applies equally on land and on sea; that it cannot be extended to private properties, whatever they may be, and that the right of blockade must be limited to fortified places that are effectively beleaguered by sufficient troops.

We have therefore decreed and decree the following:

Art. 1. – The British Isles are declared to be in a state of blockade.

Art. 2. – All commerce and trade with the British Isles is forbidden.

Consequently, letters and packages addressed either to England or to an Englishman, or written in the English language, will not be allowed through the mail and will be seized.

Art. 3. – Every individual English subject, whatever his status or condition, who will be found in the countries occupied by our troops or those of our allies, will be made a prisoner-of-war.

Art. 4. – All shops, all merchandise, all property, whatever its nature might be, that belong to an English subject, shall be declared lawful prizes.

Art. 5. – Trading in English goods is prohibited and every merchandise belonging to England, or coming from her factories and colonies, is declared lawful prize.

Art. 6. – Half the yield from the confiscation of merchandise and properties that are declared lawful prizes under the preceding articles, shall be used to indemnify traders for the losses they have sustained through the capture of commercial vessels by English cruisers.

Art. 7. – No ships coming directly from England or from the English colonies, or having been there since the publication of the present decree, shall be allowed in any port.

Art. 8. – Any ship that, by making false declarations, contravenes the above rule, shall be seized; and the vessel as well as its cargo shall be confiscated as if they were English property.

Art. 9. – It will be the responsibility of the prize court in Paris to give the definitive judgement in all disputes that might arise in our Empire and in the countries occupied by the French army. Our prize court in Milan will pass the final judgement in disputes that might arise within the extent of our kingdom in Italy.

Art. 10. – The present decree shall be communicated by our minister of external affairs, to the kings of Spain, Naples, Holland and Etruria,[1] and to our other allies, whose subjects, like ours, have been the victims of the injustice and barbarity of the English maritime laws.

Art. 11. – Our ministers of external affairs, navy, finances and police, and our directors-general of the postal service, are herewith charged, each in his own area of responsibility, with the execution of the present decree.

Napoléon

1. A territorial unit in Tuscany, created by Napoleon for the House of Bourbon-Parma.

B. Message to the Senate, from Berlin, 19 November 1806

Senators, in the circumstances in which the general affairs of Europe are today, I wish to inform you and the nation of the principles we have adopted as guiding-rules of our policy.

Our extreme moderation, after each of the first three wars, was the cause of the conflict that followed them. Thus we have had to fight a fourth coalition [Great Britain, Prussia and Russia], nine months after the third had been dissolved, nine months after the brilliant victories granted us by Providence, which were supposed to ensure a long respite on the continent.

But a large number of the Cabinets of Europe are sooner or later influenced by England; and without a solid peace with that power our people will not be able to enjoy the benefits that are the first purpose of our endeavours, the sole object of our life. And so, despite our triumphant situation, we have not, in our last negotiations with England, been deterred either by the arrogance of her language or by the sacrifices she has wanted to impose on us. We had ceded the island of Malta, to which (so to speak) the honour of this war had been pinned, and which, retained by England in defiance of treaties, was the first cause of the conflict. We had agreed to England's acquisition of the Cape of Good Hope, in addition to Ceylon and the empire of Mysore.

But all our efforts were doomed when our enemies' councils abandoned the noble ambition of reconciling the wellbeing of the world with the present prosperity of their fatherland, and the prosperity of the fatherland with a durable prosperity; and there can be no durable prosperity for England, as long as it is based on an extreme and unjust policy that would rob sixty million inhabitants, their rich and brave neighbours, of all commerce and navigation.

Immediately after the death of the Prime Minister of England[1] it became easy for us to see that the continuation of talks had no other object than to cover up the web of this fourth coalition; the negotiations were smothered at birth.

In the new circumstances, we have adopted as invariable principles of our policy not to evacuate Berlin or Warsaw, or the provinces that came into our possession through force of arms until the conclusion of a general peace, the return of Spanish, Dutch and French colonies, the restoration of the foundations of the Ottoman power, and the irrevocable consecration of the absolute independence of this vast Empire [i.e., France], foremost interest of our people.

We have put the British Isles in a state of blockade, and we have ordered that necessary arrangements be made against them, which were repugnant to our heart. It has been onerous for us to tie private interests to the quarrel of kings, and to regress, after so many years of civilisation, to principles characteristic of the barbarity prevalent in the early ages of nations; but we have been forced, for the good of our people and our allies, to bring the same arms to bear against the common enemy as he was using against us. These decisions, prompted by a just feeling of reciprocity, were inspired neither by passion nor by hatred. What we proposed, after having dispersed the three coalitions which has contributed so much to the glory of our peoples, we propose it again today when we have achieved new military triumphs. We are ready to make peace with England; we are ready to make peace with Russia, and with Prussia; but it cannot be concluded on a basis such as will permit any one to arrogate to himself any right of supremacy over us; the peace must return colonies to their metropolitan countries,

1. William Pitt the Younger had died in January 1806.

and it must guarantee the prosperity to which our industry and commerce have a right to aspire.

And if the combined effect of these decisions will be to postpone somewhat longer the reestablishment of general peace, no matter how short the delay, it will seem long to our heart. But we are certain that our people will appreciate the wisdom of our motives, that, like us, they will deem a partial peace to be nothing but a truce that will waste our present advantages only to result in another war, and finally, that it is only in general peace that France can find happiness.

We are at one of those important moments for the destiny of nations; and the French people will rise to the challenge awaiting them. The *senatus-consulte*[2] which we have ordered to be proposed to you, and which will put at our disposal, in the first days of the year, the conscription of 1807 that under normal circumstances should not be called up until the month of September, will be eagerly obeyed by fathers and sons alike. And there could be no more beautiful time for young Frenchmen than when they hear the call to arms. To join their regiments, they will have to cross our enemies' capital cities, and the battlefields made famous by the victories of their elders.

2. An Act voted by the Senate, which had the force of law.

36 BRITISH ORDERS IN COUNCIL CONCERNING THE BLOCKADE OF FRENCH PORTS, 11 NOVEMBER 1807

Text

Whereas certain Orders, establishing an unprecedented system of warfare against this Kingdom, and aimed especially at the destruction of its commerce and resources, were, some time since, issued by the Government of France, by which 'The British Islands were declared to be in a state of Blockade', thereby subjecting to capture and condemnation all Vessels, with their cargoes, which should continue to trade with His Majesty's Dominions:

And whereas by the same Orders, 'all trading in English Merchandize is prohibited, and every article of Merchandize belonging to England, or coming from her Colonies, or of her manufacture, is declared lawful Prize':

And whereas the Nations in Alliance with France, and under her controul, were required to give, and have given, and do give, effect to such Orders:

And whereas His Majesty's Order of the 7th of January last has not answered the desired purpose, either of compelling the Enemy to recall those Orders, or of inducing Neutral Nations to interpose, with effect, to obtain their revocation, but, on the contrary, the same have been recently enforced with increased rigour:

And whereas His Majesty, under these circumstances finds himself compelled to take further measures for asserting and vindicating his just rights, and for supporting that Maritime Power which the exertions and valour of his People have, under the blessing of Providence, enabled him to establish and maintain; and the maintenance of which is not more essential to the safety and prosperity of His Majesty's Dominions, than it is to the protection of such States as still retain their Independence, and to the general intercourse and happiness of mankind:

His Majesty is therefore pleased, by and with the advice of his Privy Council, to order, and it is hereby ordered, that all the Ports and Places of France and her Allies, or of any other Country at war with His Majesty, and all other Ports or Places in Europe, from which, although not at war with His Majesty, the British Flag is excluded, and all Ports or Places in the Colonies belonging to His Majesty's Enemies, shall, from henceforth, be subject to the same restrictions in point of trade and navigation, with the exceptions hereinafter mentioned, as if the same were actually blockaded by His Majesty's Naval Forces, in the most strict and rigorous manner: – And it is hereby further ordered and declared, that all trade in articles which are of the produce or manufacture of the said Countries or Colonies, shall be deemed and considered to be unlawful; and that every Vessel trading from or to the said Countries or Colonies, together with all goods and merchandize on board, and all articles of the produce or manufacture of the said Countries or Colonies, shall be captured, and condemned as prize to the Captors.

But although His Majesty would be fully justified, by the circumstances and considerations above recited, in establishing such system of restrictions with respect to all the Countries and Colonies of his Enemies, without exception or qualification; yet His Majesty, being nevertheless desirous not to subject Neutrals to any greater inconvenience than is absolutely inseparable from the carrying into effect His Majesty's just determination to counteract the designs of his Enemies, and to retort upon his Enemies themselves the consequences of their own violence

Source: *British and Foreign State Papers 1820–21* (BFSP), Vol. VIII, pp. 469–72.

and injustice, and being yet willing to hope that it may be possible (consistently with that object) still to allow to Neutrals the opportunity of furnishing themselves with Colonial Produce for their own consumption and supply; and even to leave open, for the present, such trade with His Majesty's Enemies as shall be carried on directly with the Ports of His Majesty's Dominions, or of his Allies, in the manner hereinafter mentioned:

His Majesty is therefore pleased further to order, and it is hereby ordered, that nothing herein contained shall extend to subject to capture or condemnation any Vessel, or the cargo of any Vessel, belonging to any Country not declared by this Order to be subjected to the restrictions incident to a state of Blockade, which shall have cleared out with such cargo from some Port or Place of the Country to which she belongs, either in Europe or America, or from some Free Port in His Majesty's Colonies, under circumstances in which such trade from such Free Port is permitted, direct to some Port or Place in the Colonies of His Majesty's Enemies, or from those Colonies direct to the Country to which such Vessel belongs, or to some Free Port in His Majesty's Colonies, in such cases, and with such articles, as it may be lawful to import into such Free Port; – Nor to any Vessel, or the cargo of any Vessel, belonging to any Country not at war with His Majesty, which shall have cleared out from some Port or Place in this Kingdom, or from Gibraltar or Malta, under such regulations as His Majesty may think fit to prescribe, or from any Port belonging to His Majesty's Allies, and shall be proceeding direct to the Port specified in her clearance; – Nor to any Vessel, or the cargo of any Vessel, belonging to any Country not at war with His Majesty, which shall be coming from any Port or Place in Europe which is declared by this Order to be subject to the restrictions incident to a state of Blockade, destined to some Port or Place in Europe belonging to His Majesty, and which shall be on her voyage direct thereto; but these exceptions are not to be understood as exempting from capture or confiscation any Vessel or goods which shall be liable thereto in respect of having entered or departed from any Port or Place actually blockaded by His Majesty's Squadrons or Ships of War, or for being Enemies' property, or for any other cause than the contravention of this present Order.

And the Commanders of His Majesty's Ships of War and Privateers, and other Vessels acting under His Majesty's Commission, shall be, and are hereby, instructed to warn every Vessel which shall have commenced her voyage prior to any notice of this Order, and shall be destined to any Port of France, or of her Allies, or of any other Country at war with His Majesty, or to any Port or Place from which the British Flag as aforesaid is excluded, or to any Colony belonging to His Majesty's Enemies, and which shall not have cleared out as is hereinbefore allowed, to discontinue her voyage, and to proceed to some Port or Place in this Kingdom, or to Gibraltar or Malta; and any Vessel which, after having been so warned, or after a reasonable time shall have been afforded for the arrival of information of this His Majesty's Order at any Port or Place from which she sailed, or which, after having notice of this Order, shall be found in the prosecution of any voyage contrary to the restrictions contained in this Order, shall be captured, and, together with her cargo, condemned as lawful prize to the Captors:

And whereas Countries, not engaged in the War, have acquiesced in the Orders of France, prohibiting all trade in any articles the produce or manufacture of His Majesty's Dominions; and the Merchants of those Countries have given countenance and effect to those prohibitions, by accepting from Persons styling themselves Commercial Agents of the Enemy, resident at Neutral Ports, certain Documents, termed 'Certificates of Origin', being Certificates obtained at the

Ports of Shipment, declaring that the articles of the cargo are not of the produce or manufacture of His Majesty's Dominions, or to that effect.

And whereas this expedient has been directed by France, and submitted to by such Merchants, as part of the new system of warfare directed against the trade of this Kingdom, and as the most effectual instrument of accomplishing the same, and it is therefore essentially necessary to resist it:

His Majesty is therefore pleased, by and with the advice of his Privy Council, to order, and it is hereby ordered, that if any Vessel, after reasonable time shall have been afforded for receiving notice of this His Majesty's Order at the Port or Place from which such Vessel shall have cleared out, shall be found carrying any such Certificate or Document as aforesaid, or any Document referring to, or authenticating the same, such Vessel shall be adjudged lawful prize to the Captor, together with the goods laden therein, belonging to the Person or Persons by whom, or on whose behalf, any such Document was put on board.

And the Right Honourable the Lords Commissioners of His Majesty's Treasury, His Majesty's Principal Secretaries of State, the Lords Commissioners of the Admiralty, and the Judges of the High Court of Admiralty and Courts of Vice-Admiralty, are to take the necessary measures herein, as to them shall respectively appertain.

W. FAWKENER.

37 BRITISH CABINET MEMORANDUM, 26 DECEMBER 1813

Text

Present. – The Lord Chancellor, The Lord President, The Lord Privy Seal, Earl of Liverpool, Earl of Bathurst, Earl of Buckingham, Earl of Mulgrave, Viscount Sidmouth, Viscount Melville, Mr Vansittart, Mr B. Bathurst, Viscount Castlereagh.[1]

The three Allied Powers having invited the Prince Regent to send a Plenipotentiary to the Continent charged with full powers to treat both with friendly and hostile Powers on all matters which concern the general interests; and H.R.H., having previously received from the Ministers of the said Powers in London satisfactory assurances on the Maritime question, has been pleased, in compliance with the desire of the said Allies, to direct His Majesty's Secretary of State for Foreign Affairs to proceed forthwith to the headquarters of the allies in execution of this especial service.

Lord Castlereagh is charged in the first instance to enter into such preliminary explanation as may be necessary to ascertain with precision the basis on which it is proposed to negotiate. He is to endeavour to establish a clear and definite understanding with the Allies, not only on all matters of common interest but upon such points as are likely to be discussed with the enemy, so that the several Allied Powers may in their negotiations with France, and in perfect concert, and together maintain one common interest.

If called upon for an explanation of the views of his Government as to terms of peace, and the sacrifice of conquests which Great Britain is disposed to make for the general interest, he is to state that with respect to the latter, it must in a great measure be governed by the nature of the conditions with respect to the Continent, which the Allied Powers may be enabled to obtain from the enemy. If the maritime power of France shall be restricted within due bounds by the effectual establishment of Holland, the Peninsula, and Italy in security and independence, Great Britain, consistent with her own security, may then be induced to apply the greater proportion of her conquests to promote the general interests. If, on the contrary, the arrangements should be defective in any of these points, Great Britain must reserve a proportionate share of these conquests to render her secure against France.

If called on for a more detailed explanation, he may state that the objects *sine qua non* upon which Great Britain can venture to divest herself of her conquests in any material degree are: – 1. The absolute exclusion of France from any naval establishment on the Scheldt, and especially at Antwerp; and 2. The security of Holland being adequately provided for by a Barrier under the House of Orange, which shall at least include Juliers and Antwerp as well as Maestricht with a suitable arrondissement of territory in addition to Holland as it stood in 1792, it being understood that Wesel shall also be in the hands of the Allied Powers.

Source: C. K. Webster (ed.), *British Diplomacy, 1813–1815, select documents dealing with the reconstruction of Europe* (London: G. Bell & Son, 1921) pp. 123–8.

1. These instructions were drawn up for Castlereagh to take with him on the Continent so that he might decide important points without delay. They were submitted to a Cabinet meeting at which, as appears on the document, all the members were present. See an article by G. W. T. Omond in *Nineteenth Century*, March 1918.

[The Monarchies of the Peninsula must be free under their Legitimate Sovereigns, their dominions at least in Europe being guaranteed against attack by France. The Allied Powers to take engagements to this effect and to stipulate the amount of succour to be mutually furnished in each case. Great Britain is prepared to confine the *casus foederis* to the Continent. Under these circumstances Great Britain is prepared to consider her conquests as objects of negotiation. But Malta, the Mauritius and the Isle of Bourbon, Guadeloupe and the Island of Les Saintes must remain British, Mauritius being considered as necessary to protect Indian commerce, and Guadeloupe as a debt of honour to Sweden. If Guadeloupe should be made a *sine qua non*, Sweden must be compensated by Bourbon or a Dutch Colony, Holland in the latter case taking Bourbon. If Holland is secured by a Barrier, the Dutch colonies will be restored, but the Cape of Good Hope will be retained and £2 000 000 paid by Great Britain. The Danish conquests, except Heligoland, should be made instrumental to the engagements with Sweden.]

In all communications on the expediency of Peace, the same course to be pursued as heretofore, viz., to evince a desire to conform as far as possible to the general interests of the Continent; to give to the Allies the most unequivocal assurances of a firm determination to support them in contracting for an advantageous peace and to avoid everything that might countenance a suspicion that Great Britain was inclined to push them forward in the war for our purposes. The utmost exertions to be used to prevent any relaxation in the military operations, whilst negotiations are pending.

[He is also to direct force as much as possible from all quarters upon Holland and the Low Countries, but the British force cannot exceed 10 000 men and may be withdrawn. If Austria would like the Archduke Charles to be settled in the Netherlands, the proposal is to be welcomed. But the question depends on the success of the Allies afterwards in the war, i.e., whether he can have the whole of Belgium or not. The Prince of Orange is to be discouraged from attempting to extend his dominions, without the express consent of the Allies. A marriage between the Prince of Orange and the Princess Charlotte of Wales is to be suggested. If the Dutch Barrier is not obtained, then the restoration of the Dutch colonies is to be proportionately reduced.]

As the Barrier for Holland is an object most deeply interesting to all the Allies, Great Britain is willing to purchase it by a double sacrifice, by cession both to France and to Holland. If the Allies should not carry this point, so important to their own security as well as to that of Great Britain, the latter Power will, in that case, have no other alternative than to preserve her colonial conquests as a counterpoise to the dominion of the enemy, and on these grounds to withhold those cessions which she would otherwise be prepared to make to France. The cession of conquests by Great Britain being declared to be contingent upon equivalent securities to result from the continental arrangements, and especially on the side of Holland and the Low Countries, any general stipulation which does not expressly declare the principle by which it is to be regulated and connect it pointedly with these objects, appears objectionable.

[As to Italy, the military line of the Alps and the roads lately opened in the direction of Italy to be specially attended to. It is 'highly expedient' that the King of Sardinia should be restored, and he should perhaps, receive Genoa, in exchange for Savoy. If Austria connects herself with Murat, the Sicilian Family is to have Tuscany or Elba. The Pope is to be restored. The Milanese, Modena, Parma and Placentia are to be subject to discussion. Great Britain offers mediation on the internal German affairs. She is ready to sign a peace with the United States, in a general peace on the *status quo ante bellum* without involving in such

Treaty any decision on the points in dispute at the commencement of hostilities. A direct proposition to treat in London having been lately made to the American Government, this offer not to be stated unless the subject should be brought forward. Should such an offer be made to America, a time to be stated within which her acceptance or refusal must be declared. The question as to the arrangement with Denmark to be subject to discussion with Sweden. The distribution of the Command in the North to be reserved for consideration at Head Quarters. A subsidy of £5 000 000 is to be under reserve, 1. As to sending home the Russian fleet. 2. The acceptance of a proportion in credit bills. 3. The signing of engagements especially as to Holland and the Peninsula as may justify to the British Public and the Allies so great an exertion on the part of Great Britain.]

The Treaty of Alliance *not to terminate with the war*, but to contain defensive engagements with mutual obligations to support the powers attacked by France with a certain extent of stipulated succours. The *Casus Foederis* to be an attack by France on the European dominions of any one of the contracting parties. [Spain, and if possible Holland, to be included as contracting parties. Sweden being beyond the Baltick, is less interested in being included, or rather has an interest not to participate.]

Humbly submitted for your Royal Highness' Sanction.

(Signed.) GEORGE P.R.

Memorandum on the Maritime Peace[2]

Great Britain in the course of the war has conquered from her enemies the colonies and possessions according to the annexed list.[3] Great Britain has declared her disposition with certain exceptions to sacrifice these conquests for the welfare of the Continent, being desirous of providing for her own security by a common arrangement, rather than by an exclusive accumulation of strength and resources. Her object is to see a maritime as well as a military Balance of Power established amongst the Powers of Europe, and as the basis of this arrangement she desires to see the independence of Spain and Holland as maritime Powers effectually provided for. Upon the supposition that these two objects shall be obtained in the proposed arrangements, that the limits of France shall be reduced within proper bounds, and that the peace of the Continent shall be secured by an amicable understanding between the Allies, Great Britain will then be prepared also to return within corresponding limits and to throw her acquisitions into the scale of the general interests.

As nothing is yet defined with precision either as to the state of the enemy's limits nor as to that of the Allies, it is impossible to do more than state on the part of Great Britain the nature and extent of concession she would be prepared to make upon given data as to the continental arrangement. The object will best be effected by stating what the maximum of concession might be on the part of Great Britain upon assuming the reduction of France within her ancient limits, and the Allies having amicably arranged their own state of possession. In developing this subject it is desirable to state, 1st, the classes into which the conquests made by Great Britain resolve themselves, and 2ndly, the principles upon which the British Government is disposed to govern its decision with respect to their restitution.

2. This document immediately follows the Cabinet Memorandum of 26 December, and may be considered part of it. It was probably drawn up in the course of the discussions to make quite clear to the Cabinet a point on which they were much more interested than in the details of the Continental settlement.
3. Not given.

With respect to the latter point they do not desire to retain any of these Colonies for their mere commercial value – too happy if by their restoration they can give other States an additional motive to cultivate the arts of peace. The only objects to which they desire to adhere are those which affect essentially the engagement and security of their own dominion.

And first as to the Danish Colonies enumerated in the Margin.[4] If they could be the means of promoting the interest of the common cause in the North of Europe, Great Britain long since offered to restore them. A treaty of peace has recently been signed with Denmark by which all their possessions (with the exception of Heligoland) are surrendered, Denmark ceding Norway to Sweden, in satisfaction of the engagements of Russia, and joining her arms to those of the Allies.

The next class to be adverted to is the Dutch Colonies as enumerated in the Margin.[5]

In the East Indies, Great Britain shall restore to France, the different settlements and factories in possession of that Crown as well on the coast of Coromandel and Orisca, as on that of Malabar, as also on Bengal at the commencement of the year 1792–3, and the Government of France engages to erect no fortifications in any part of the said settlements or factories, nor to maintain any military force therein beyond what may be deemed necessary for the purposes of police, and His Britannic Majesty engages on his part to secure to the subjects of France, without the limits of their settlements and factories, an impartial administration of justice, in all matters concerning their persons and properties and to adopt such measures as may be judged requisite to enable them to carry on commerce upon the footing of the most favoured nations.[6]

4. Not given.
5. Not given. The document stops here and is continued on a smaller sheet simply endorsed 'East Indies'.
6. A variant is given of the last sentence as follows: 'and to adopt such measures as may be judged requisite to enable the said subjects to carry on a safe and independent Trade.

38 TREATY OF UNION, CONCERT AND SUBSIDY BETWEEN AUSTRIA, GREAT BRITAIN, PRUSSIA AND RUSSIA, SIGNED AT CHAUMONT, 1 MARCH 1814

Text

In the Name of the Most Holy and Undivided Trinity.

His Majesty the King of the United Kingdom of Great Britain and Ireland, His Imperial and Royal Apostolic Majesty the Emperor of Austria, King of Hungary and Bohemia, His Majesty the Emperor of All the Russias, and His Majesty the King of Prussia, having transmitted to the French Government proposals for concluding a General Peace, and being desirous, should France refuse the Conditions therein contained, to draw closer the ties which unite them for the vigorous prosecution of a War undertaken for the salutary purpose of putting an end to the miseries of Europe, of securing its future repose, by re-establishing a just balance of Power, and being at the same time desirous, should the Almighty bless their pacific intentions, to fix the means of maintaining against every attempt the order of things which shall have been the happy consequence of their efforts, have agreed to sanction by a solemn Treaty, signed separately by each of the 4 Powers with the 3 others, this twofold engagement.

In consequence, His Majesty the King of the United Kingdom of Great Britain and Ireland has named to discuss, settle, and sign the Conditions of the present Treaty, with His Imperial and Royal Apostolic Majesty, the Right Honourable Robert Stewart, Viscount Castlereagh, one of His said Majesty's Most Honourable Privy Council, Member of Parliament, Colonel of the Londonderry Regiment of Militia, and his Principal Secretary of State for Foreign Affairs, &c., &c., &c., and His Imperial and Royal Apostolic Majesty having named, on his part, the Sieur Clement Wenceslaus Lothaire, Prince Metternich Winneburgh Ochsenhausen, Knight of the Golden Fleece, Grand Cross of the Order of St Stephen, Knight of the Russian Orders of St Andrew, of St Alexander Newsky, and of St Anne, of the First Class, Knight of the Prussian Orders of the Black and Red Eagles, Grand Cross of the Order of St Joseph of Wurtzburg, Knight of the Order of St Hubert of Bavaria, of the Golden Eagle of Wurtemburg, and of several others, his Chamberlain, Privy Councillor, Minister of State, of Conferences, and of Foreign Affairs;

The said Plenipotentiaries, after having exchanged their Full Powers, found to be in due and proper form, have agreed upon the following Articles:

ART. I. The High Contracting Parties above named solemnly engage by the present Treaty, and in the event of France refusing to accede to the Conditions of Peace now proposed, to apply all the means of their respective States to the vigorous prosecution of the War against that Power, and to employ them in perfect concert, in order to obtain for themselves and for Europe a General Peace, under the protection of which the rights and liberties of all Nations may be established and secured.

Source: Parry, Clive, *The Consolidated Treaty Series, 1648–1918* (New York: Oceana Publications, 1969–80) Vol. 63, pp. 84–95. The three Secret Articles are translated from the French by Sylvia Modelski.

This engagement shall in no respect affect the Stipulations which the several Powers have already contracted relative to the number of Troops to be kept against the Enemy; and it is understood that the Courts of England, Austria, Russia, and Prussia, engage by the present Treaty to keep in the field, each of them, 150 000 effective men, exclusive of garrisons, to be employed in active service against the common Enemy.

II. The High Contracting Parties reciprocally engage not to negotiate separately with the common Enemy, nor to sign Peace, Truce, nor Convention, but with common consent. They, moreover, engage not to lay down their Arms until the object of the War, mutually understood and agreed upon, shall have been attained.

III. In order to contribute in the most prompt and decisive manner to fulfil this great object, His Britannic Majesty engages to furnish a Subsidy of £5 000 000 for the service of the year 1814, to be divided in equal proportions amongst the 3 Powers: and His said Majesty promises moreover to arrange, before the 1st of January in each year, with Their Imperial and Royal Majesties, the further Succours to be furnished during the subsequent year, if (which God forbid) the War should so long continue.

The Subsidy above stipulated of £5 000 000 shall be paid in London, by monthly instalments, and in equal proportions, to the Ministers of the respective Powers duly authorized to receive the same.

In case Peace should be signed between the Allied Powers and France before the expiration of the year, the Subsidy, calculated upon the scale of £5 000 000, shall be paid up to the end of the month in which the Definitive Treaty shall have been signed; and His Britannic Majesty promises, in addition, to pay to Austria and to Prussia 2 months, and to Russia 4 months, over and above the stipulated Subsidy, to cover the expenses of the return of their Troops within their own Frontiers.

IV. The High Contracting Parties will be entitled respectively to accredit to the Generals commanding their Armies, Officers, who will be allowed to correspond with their Governments, for the purpose of informing them of the Military events, and of everything which relates to the operations of the Armies.

V. The High Contracting Parties, reserving to themselves to concert together, on the conclusion of a Peace with France, as to the means best adapted to guarantee to Europe, and to themselves reciprocally, the continuance of the Peace, have also determined to enter, without delay, into defensive engagements for the protection of their respective States in Europe against every attempt which France might make to infringe the order of things resulting from such Pacification.

VI. To effect this, they agree that in the event of one of the High Contracting Parties being threatened with an attack on the part of France, the others shall employ their most strenuous efforts to prevent it, by friendly interposition.

VII. In the case of these endeavours proving ineffectual, the High Contracting Parties promise to come to the immediate assistance of the Power attacked, each with a body of 60 000 men.

VIII. Such Auxiliary Corps shall respectively consist of 50 000 Infantry and 10 000 Cavalry, with a train of Artillery, and ammunition in proportion to the number of Troops: the Auxiliary Corps shall be ready to take the field in the most effective manner, for the safety of the Power attacked or threatened, within 2 months at latest after the requisition shall have been made.

IX. As the situation of the seat of War, or other circumstances, might render it difficult for Great Britain to furnish the stipulated Succours in English Troops within the term prescribed, and to maintain the same on a War establishment, His

Britannic Majesty reserves the right of furnishing his Contingent to the requiring Power in Foreign Troops in his pay, or to pay annually to that Power a sum of money, at the rate of £20 per each man for Infantry, and of £30 for Cavalry, until the stipulated Succour shall be complete.

The mode of furnishing this Succour by Great Britain shall be settled amicably, in each particular case, between His Britannic Majesty and the Power threatened or attacked, as soon as the requisition shall be made: the same principle shall be adopted with regard to the Forces which His Britannic Majesty engages to furnish by the Ist Article of the present Treaty.

X. The Auxiliary Army shall be under the orders of the Commander-in-Chief of the Army of the requiring Power; it shall be commanded by its own General, and employed in all military operations according to the rules of War. The pay of the Auxiliary Army shall be defrayed by the requiring Power; the rations and portions of provisions and forage, &c., as well as quarters, shall be furnished by the requiring Power as soon as the Auxiliary Army shall have passed its own Frontier; and that upon the same footing as the said Power maintains, or shall maintain, its own Troops in the field or in quarters.

XI. The discipline and administration of the Troops shall solely depend upon their own Commander; they shall not be separated. The trophies and booty taken from the Enemy shall belong to the Troops who take them.

XII. Whenever the amount of the stipulated Succours shall be found inadequate to the exigency of the case, the High Contracting Parties reserve to themselves to make, without loss of time, an ulterior arrangement as to the additional Succours which it may be deemed necessary to furnish.

XIII. The High Contracting Parties mutually promise, that in case they shall be reciprocally engaged in Hostilities, in consequence of furnishing the stipulated Succours, the Party requiring and the Parties called upon, and acting as Auxiliaries in the War, shall not make Peace but by common consent.

XIV. The Engagement contracted by the present Treaty, shall not prejudice those which the High Contracting Parties may have entered into with other Powers, nor prevent them from forming new engagements with other States, with a view of obtaining the same salutary result.

XV. In order to render more effectual the Defensive Engagements above stipulated, by uniting for their common defence the Powers the most exposed to a French invasion, the High Contracting Parties engage to invite those Powers to accede to the present Treaty of Defensive Alliance.

XVI. The present Treaty of Defensive Alliance having for its object to maintain the equilibrium of Europe, to secure the repose and independence of its States, and to prevent the invasions which during so many years have desolated the World, the High Contracting Parties have agreed to extend the duration of it to 20 years, to take date from the day of its Signature; and they reserve to themselves, to concert upon its ulterior prolongation, 3 years before its expiration, should circumstances require it.

XVII. The present Treaty shall be ratified, and the Ratifications exchanged within 2 months, or sooner if possible.

In witness whereof, the respective Plenipotentiaries have signed the same, and affixed thereto the Seal of their Arms.

Done at Chaumont this 1st of March, in the year of our Lord 1814.

(L.S.) CASTLEREAGH.
(L.S.) CLEMENT WENCESLAUS LOTHAIRE, PRINCE OF METTERNICH.

ADDITIONAL ARTICLE

His Britannic Majesty engages for the year 1814, to provide for the maintenance of the Russian Fleet, and its Crews, now in the Ports of England. The expense is estimated at £500 000 sterling.

In the event of Peace with France, or of the departure of the said Fleet on its return to Russia in the course of the year, His Britannic Majesty shall provide for its maintenance for 4 months, reckoning from the day of the Signature of the Peace, or of the departure of the Fleet from the Ports of England.

The present Additional Article shall have the same force and validity as if it were inserted word for word in the Treaty Patent of this day.

It shall be ratified, and the Ratifications shall be exchanged at the same time.

In witness whereof, the respective Plenipotentiaries have signed the same, and affixed to it the Seal of their Arms.

Done at Chaumont, the 1st of March in the year of our Lord 1814.

(L.S.) CASTLEREAGH.
(L.S.) CHARLES ROBERT, COMTE DE NESSELRODE.

SECRET ARTICLES

Article I.
The re-establishment of an equilibrium between the Powers and a just distribution of forces among them being the aim of the present war, their Imperial and Royal Majesties commit themselves to direct all their efforts towards the actual establishment of the following system in Europe, to wit:

Germany composed of the sovereign Princes united by a federal bond that assures and guarantees German independence.

The Swiss federation within its old boundaries, and independent, placed under the guarantee of the Great Powers of Europe, France included.

Italy divided into independent states, intermediary between the Austrian possessions in Italy and France.

Spain governed by King Ferdinand VII, within its old boundaries.

Holland, a free and independent state, under the sovereignty of the Prince of Orange, with an enlarged territory, within an established suitable frontier.

Article II.
In execution of the 15th Article of the Open Treaty of this day, the High Contracting Parties agree to invite the monarchies of Spain and Portugal, Sweden and His Royal Highness the Prince of Orange, to accede to the present Treaty of Defensive alliance, and to admit other sovereigns and states too, as the case may require.

Article III.
Considering the necessity that might exist, after the conclusion of a Definitive Treaty with France, to retain in the field, for a certain period, sufficient forces to protect the settlement which the Allies will have to make between themselves for the strengthening of the state of Europe, the High Contracting Parties are decided to concert among themselves, not only on the necessity thereof but on the magnitude and distribution of the standing army, according to the exigency of the case.

None of the High Contracting Parties shall be expected to supply forces for the objective stated above for more than one year, without its express and voluntary agreement; and England shall be free to furnish her contingent in the mode stipulated in the 9th Article.

The present separate and secret Articles shall have the same force and value as if they were inserted in the open Treaty of this day. They will be ratified and the ratifications shall be exchanged at the same time.

In witness whereof, the respective Plenipotentiaries, etc.

Done at Chaumont on the 1st March 1814.

(L.S.) CHARLES ROBERT NESSELRODE
(L.S.) PRINCE METTERNICH

39 BRITISH FOREIGN SECRETARY LORD CASTLEREAGH'S DISPATCH TO LORD LIVERPOOL, PRIME MINISTER, VIENNA, 1 JANUARY 1815

Text

Although I have had strong reason to hope that a disposition existed in the Prussian Cabinet to accommodate on the Saxon point, should a liberal offer be made them, yet there are indications which justify the utmost vigilance with respect to their ultimate policy.

The language of their entourés is very warlike, and strongly against yielding any part of Saxony, Baron Humboldt's particularly so. His reasoning yesterday in our conference, which he attends as one of the Prussian Plenipotentiaries, went every length, but that of refusing to discuss such alternatives as might be proposed. They are organising their army for the field, and, I have heard to-day, are employed in fortifying Dresden. This may be all menace to sustain their negotiation, but they may also meditate some sudden effort, in conjunction with Russia to coerce Austria and place themselves in a situation to dictate their own terms on all other points – the conduct of their employés on the left bank of the Rhine has been extremely vexatious of late towards the Prince of Orange's Government, and no attention has yet been paid here to any of their reclamations.

These indications have attracted the more seriously my attention, from a declaration incidentally made by Prince Hardenberg[1] in yesterday's conference, that should Prussia continue to consider the annexation of the whole of Saxony necessary to her re-construction, she could not, in point of expense, submit to remain in a state of provisional occupation, and that Russia and Prussia would, in such a case, consider a refusal to acknowledge, as tantamount to a declaration of war.

I took occasion to protest in the strongest terms against this principle as a most alarming and unheard-of menace; that it should be competent for one Power to invade another, and by force to compel a recognition which was founded upon no Treaty, and where no attempt had been made to disturb the possession of the invading Power in the territory to which he laid claim. That such an insinuation might operate upon a Power trembling for its existence, but must have the contrary effect upon all that were alive to their own dignity; and I added that if such a temper really prevailed, we were not deliberating in a state of independence, and it were better to break up the Congress.

This unguarded declaration was afterwards softened down, and, to a degree, explained away; but it has not failed, coupled with other expressions used in private, to create a strong sensation and alarm, that if Prussia should not ultimately yield, she will attempt, as is the practice of her Government in lesser concerns, some bold and desperate coup to deliver herself suddenly from the embarrassments of a protracted state of armament and questioned occupation.

This sort of principle, openly announced in a formal conference in the name of two great Powers avowedly ready to act, has appeared to us to call for some

Source: Webster, C. K. (ed.), *British Diplomacy 1813–1815, select documents dealing with the reconstruction of Europe* (London: G. Bell & Son, 1921) pp. 277–8.

1. Prussia's representative at the Congress.

precautionary corrective by which the other Powers may be induced to feel that, in the discharge of their functions in Congress, they are not exposed individually and in detail to the destructive effects of such a domineering dictation.

Under these circumstances I have felt it an act of imperative duty to concert with the French and Austrian Plenipotentiaries a Treaty of Defensive Alliance, confined within the strict necessity of this most extraordinary case. Without some such bond, I feel that our deliberations here are at an end; and although I flatter myself that the necessity will never arise for acting upon these engagements, yet, after what has passed, I should not consider myself justified in leaving either our common councils here, or the great interests we have at stake in other quarters, at the mercy of states promulgating such principles, without providing for them in time the best protection in my power.

I indulge the confident hope that my conduct upon this occasion may appear to the Prince Regent and his Government to have been justified by the circumstances of the case, and the exigency of the occasion.

40 DECLARATION OF THE 8 COURTS, RELATIVE TO THE UNIVERSAL ABOLITION OF THE SLAVE TRADE. ANNEX XV TO THE TREATY OF VIENNA, SIGNED AT VIENNA ON 8 FEBRUARY 1815

Introduction

The principles and intentions stated in this Declaration were reiterated in summary form in an Additional Article appended to the Definitive Treaty of Paris of 20 November 1815, to have the same force and effect 'as if it were inserted word for word in the Treaty signed this day' (*BFSP*, 1815–16, Vol. III, pp. 292–3); in a separate annex to the Declaration, also dated 8 February 1815, Portugal pledged, on her part, to abolish all slavery north of the Equator immediately, and within 8 years everywhere else, in exchange for certain trade concessions by Great Britain (see *BFSP*, Vol. III, pp. 972–4).

The issue of slavery and slave trade became a significant one in the second British cycle. The banning of slave trade at Vienna at the instigation of British public opinion was the first instrument of change at the global level. The Universal Declaration of Human Rights (1948) states in Art. 4: 'slavery and the slave trade shall be prohibited in all their forms'.

Text

The Plenipotentiaries of the Powers that have signed the Treaty of Paris of 30 May 1814, assembled in Conference:—

Having taken into consideration that the trade known under the name of *Traffic in Negroes from Africa* has been looked upon by just and enlightened men of all times as repugnant to the principles of humanity and universal morality; that the peculiar circumstances that gave birth to this trade, and the difficulty of suddenly interrupting its course, have managed to hide, up to a certain point, what was odious in its preservation, but that at last public opinion in all the civilised countries has risen to demand that it be abolished as soon as possible; but since the character and details of this commerce have become better known, and the harms of all sorts that accompany it unveiled, several of the European governments have in effect resolved to bring it to a halt, and that all the Powers that possess colonies in the different parts of the world have successively recognised, either by Legislative Acts, or by Treaties and other formal commitments, the obligation and necessity of abolishing it; that by a Separate Article of the last Treaty of Paris, Great Britain and France have pledged to unite their efforts at the Congress of Vienna to make all the Powers of Christendom declare themselves for the universal and definitive abolition of the Traffic of Negroes; that the Plenipotentiaries assembled at this Congress could not better honour their mission, fulfil their duty,

Source: *British and Foreign State Papers 1815–16* (BFSP) Vol. III, pp. 971–2.

and manifest the principles that guide their August Sovereigns, than by working towards realising this pledge, and by vowing in the name of their Sovereigns to put an end to a scourge that has devastated Africa, degraded Europe, and affected mankind for so long:– the said Plenipotentiaries have agreed to open their discussions on the means to accomplish such a salutary aim, with a solemn Declaration of the principles guiding their work.

Consequently, and duly authorised in this Act by the unanimous adhesion of their respective Courts to the principle stated in the said Separate Article of the Treaty of Paris, they declare in full view of Europe that, considering the universal abolition of the Traffic in Negroes as a measure particularly worthy of their attention, conforming to the spirit of the century, and to the generous principles of their August Sovereigns, they are moved by the sincere desire to cooperate in order to bring about the fastest and most efficacious execution of this measure, by all means at their disposal, and to act in the use of these means with all the zeal and perseverance they owe to such a great and beautiful Cause.

Only too well instructed however of their Sovereigns' sentiments not to foresee that, no matter how honourable their goal may be, they will not pursue it without just care being applied to the interests, the habits and even the prejudices of their subjects; the said Plenipotentiaries recognise, at the same time, that this general Declaration should not adversely affect the time limit that each particular Power might consider as the most convenient for the definitive abolition of the Trade in Negroes:– Consequently the determination of the date when this Trade must cease universally will be the object of Negotiation between Powers; it being well understood that no appropriate means to ensure and accelerate its progress shall be neglected; and that the reciprocal commitment pledged through the present Declaration among the Sovereigns taking part in it, shall be deemed fulfilled only when a complete success shall have crowned their united efforts.

By bringing this Declaration to the notice of Europe, and of all the civilised countries of the earth, the said Plenipotentiaries fondly hope to commit all the other Governments, and especially those that, by abolishing the Traffic in Negroes, have already expressed the same sentiments, to second them with their suffrage in a Cause whose final triumph will be one of the most beautiful monuments of the century that has embraced it and that will have gloriously accomplished it.

Vienna, the 8th February, 1815.

CASTLEREAGH.
STEWART, *Lieut.-Gen.*
WELLINGTON.
NESSELRODE.
C. LOWENHIELM.
GOMEZ LABRADOR.
PALMELLA.
SALDANHA.
LOBO.
HUMBOLDT.
METTERNICH.
TALLEYRAND.

41 *REGLEMENT* ON THE RANKING OF DIPLOMATIC AGENTS. ANNEX XVII TO THE TREATY OF VIENNA, SIGNED AT VIENNA, 19 MARCH 1815

Introduction

The Vienna Congress appointed a committee 'to establish the principles governing rank among crowned heads'. This committee proposed a three-fold classification: 1) emperors and kings; 2) grand dukes and the heads of republics; 3) dukes, princes and free cities (Minutes of meeting of the committee of 20 January 1815). The British representatives opposed this scheme and it was dropped, as was an attempt to regulate 'naval salutes', a matter of great interest to the British navy. What remained was a ranking of diplomatic representatives only.

The current rules governing this field may be found in the Convention on Diplomatic Relations adopted in 1961 by the United Nations Conference on Diplomatic Intercourse and Immunities meeting in Vienna (UN Doc. A/CONF. 20/13). The choice of the site was a tribute to the Vienna Congress *Règlement* of 1815.

Text

To prevent the embarrassments that have so often presented themselves and that might still arise between the claims of precedence among the different diplomatic representatives, the plenipotentiaries of the Great Powers signatory of the Treaty of Paris have agreed upon the following Articles, and they believe it their duty to invite those of the other crowned heads to adopt the same *Règlement*.

Art. I. Diplomatic employees are divided into 3 categories:

- That of the Ambassadors, Legates, or Nuncios.
- That of the Envoys, Ministers or others accredited to Sovereigns.
- That of the Chargé d'Affaires, accredited to the Ministers in charge of foreign affairs.

II. Only Ambassadors, Legates or Nuncios have representative character.

III. Diplomatic employees on Extraordinary Mission, as such, have no superiority in rank.

IV. Diplomatic employees shall rank themselves, within each category, according to the date of Official Notification of their arrival.

The present *Règlement* shall not introduce any innovation affecting representatives of the Pope.

V. Each State will determine its own uniform mode of reception for the diplomatic employee of each category.

VI. Bonds of kinship or matrimonial alliances between Courts bestow no precedence upon their diplomatic employees.

Source: *British and Foreign State Papers* (BFSP) 1815–16, Vol. III, pp. 179–80.

VII. In the Acts or Treaties between several Powers that admit rotation [*alternat*] in precedence, the order to be followed in the signatures shall be decided by lot drawing among the Ministers.

The present *Règlement* is inserted in the Protocol of the Plenipotentiaries of the 8 Powers signatory to the Treaty of Paris, at their sitting of 19 March 1815.

Austria	PRINCE METTERNICH.
	BARON WESSENBERG.
Spain	P. GOMEZ LABRADOR.
France	PRINCE TALLEYRAND.
	LATOUR DUPIN.
	COUNT ALEXIS DE NOAILLES.
Great Britian	CLANCARTY.
	CATHCART.
	STEWART, L. G.
Portugal	COUNT PALMELLA.
	SALDANHA.
	LOBO.
Prussia	PRINCE HARDENBERG.
	BARON HUMBOLDT.
Russia	COUNT RAZUMOFFSKY.
	COUNT STACKELBERG.
	COUNT NESSELRODE.
Sweden	COUNT LOWENHIELM.

42 TREATY OF ALLIANCE AND FRIENDSHIP BETWEEN GREAT BRITAIN, AUSTRIA, PRUSSIA AND RUSSIA (THE QUADRUPLE ALLIANCE), PARIS, 20 NOVEMBER 1815

The stipulations of the Treaty between Great Britain and Prussia, and Russia, signed at the same time, were *verbatim* the same as those of this Treaty.

Text

In the Name of the Most Holy and Undivided Trinity.

The purpose of the Alliance concluded at Vienna the 25th day of March, 1815, having been happily attained by the re-establishment in France of the order of things which the last criminal attempt of Napoleon Bonaparte had momentarily subverted; their Majesties the King of the United Kingdom of Great Britain and Ireland, the Emperor of Austria, King of Hungary and Bohemia, the Emperor of all the Russias, and the King of Prussia, considering that the repose of Europe is essentially interwoven with the confirmation of the order of things founded on the maintenance of the Royal Authority and of the Constitutional Charter, and wishing to employ all their means to prevent the general tranquillity (the object of the wishes of mankind and the constant end of their efforts) from being again disturbed; desirous moreover to draw closer the ties which unite them for the common interests of their People, have resolved to give to the principles solemnly laid down in the Treaties of Chaumont of the 1st of March, 1814, and of Vienna of the 25th of March, 1815, the application the most analogous to the present state of affairs, and to fix beforehand by a solemn Treaty the principles which they propose to follow, in order to guaranty Europe from the dangers by which she may still be menaced;

For which purpose the High Contracting Parties have named, to discuss, settle and sign the conditions of this Treaty, namely:

His Majesty the King of the United Kingdom of Great Britain and Ireland, the Right Honourable Robert Stewart, Viscount Castlereagh, Knight of the Most Noble Order of the Garter, Member of His Majesty's Most Honourable Privy Council, Member of the Parliament of the United Kingdom, Colonel of the Londonderry Regiment of Militia, and His Majesty's Principal Secretary of State for Foreign Affairs; – and the Most Illustrious and Most Noble Lord Arthur, Duke, Marquess and Earl of Wellington, Marquess of Douro, Viscount Wellington of Talavera and of Wellington, and Baron Douro, of Wellesley, one of His said Majesty's Privy Councillors, Field Marshal of his Armies, Colonel of the Royal Regiment of Horse Guards, Knight of the Most Noble Order of the Garter, Grand Cross of the Most Honourable Order of the Bath, Prince of Waterloo, Duke of Ciudad Rodrigo, and a Grandee of Spain of the First Class, Duke of Vittoria, Marquess of Torres Vedras, Earl of Vimiera in Portugal, Knight of the Most Illustrious Order of the Golden Fleece, of the Spanish Military Order of St Ferdinand, Grand Cross of the Imperial Military Order of Maria Theresa, Grand Cross of the Imperial Order of St George of Russia, Grand Cross of the Order of the Black Eagle of Prussia, Grand Cross of the Royal Portuguese Military Order of the Tower and Sword, Grand Cross of the Royal Swedish Military Order of the

Source: *British and Foreign State Papers* (BFSP) 1815–16, Vol. III, pp. 273–80.

Sword, Grand Cross of the Orders of the Elephant of Denmark, of William of The Netherlands, of the Annunciation of Sardinia, of Maximilian Joseph of Bavaria, and of several others, and Commander in Chief of the British Armies in France, and those of His Majesty The King of the Netherlands;

And His Majesty the Emperor of Austria, King of Hungary and Bohemia, the Sieur Clement Wenceslas Lothaire, Prince of Metternich-Winnebourg-Ochsenhausen, Knight of the Golden Fleece, Grand Cross of the Royal Order of St Stephen, Knight of the Orders of St Andrew, of Saint Alexander Newsky, and of St Anne of the First Class, Grand Cordon of the Legion of Honour, Knight of the Order of the Elephant, of the Supreme Order of the Annunciation, of the Black and of the Red Eagle, of the Seraphim, of St Joseph of Tuscany, of St Hubert of the Golden Eagle of Wurtemberg, of Fidelity of Baden, of St John of Jerusalem, and of several others, Chancellor of the Military Order of Marie-Theresa, Curator of the Academy of Fine Arts, Chamberlain and Privy Councillor of His Majesty the Emperor of Austria, King of Hungary and Bohemia, his Minister of State, of Conferences and for Foreign Affairs; – and the Sieur John Philip, Baron of Wessenberg, Grand Cross of the Royal Order of St Stephen, Grand Cross of the Military and Religious Orders of St Maurice and of St Lazarus, Grand Cross of the Order of the Red Eagle of Prussia, of that of the Crown of Bavaria, of St Joseph of Tuscany, and of Fidelity of Baden, Chamberlain and Privy Councillor of His Majesty the Emperor of Austria, King of Hungary and Bohemia;

Who, after having exchanged their Full Powers, found to be in good and due form, have agreed upon the following Articles:

Art. I. The High Contracting Parties reciprocally promise to maintain, in its force and vigour, the Treaty signed this day with His Most Christian Majesty, and to see that the Stipulations of the said Treaty, as well as those of the Particular Conventions which have reference thereto, shall be strictly and faithfully executed in their fullest extent.

II. The High Contracting Parties, having engaged in the War which is just terminated, for the purpose of maintaining inviolably the arrangements settled at Paris last year, for the safety and interest of Europe, have judged it advisable to renew the said engagements by the present Act, and to confirm them as mutually obligatory, – subject to the modifications contained in the Treaty signed this day with the Plenipotentiaries of His Most Christian Majesty, – and particularly those by which Napoleon Bonaparte and his Family, in pursuance of the Treaty of the 11th of April, 1814, have been for ever excluded from the Supreme Power in France, which exclusion the Contracting Powers bind themselves, by the present Act, to maintain in full vigour, and, should it be necessary, with the whole of their Forces. And as the same Revolutionary principles which upheld the last criminal usurpation, might again, under other forms, convulse France, and thereby endanger the repose of other States; under these circumstances, the High Contracting Parties, solemnly admitting it to be their duty to redouble their watchfulness for the tranquillity and interests of their People, engage, in case so unfortunate an event should again occur, to concert amongst themselves, and with His Most Christian Majesty, the measures which they may judge necessary to be pursued for the safety of their respective States, and for the general tranquillity of Europe.

III. The High Contracting Parties, in agreeing with His Most Christian Majesty that a Line of Military Positions in France should be occupied by a Corps of Allied Troops, during a certain number of years, had in view to secure, as far as lay in their power, the effect of the Stipulations contained in Articles I and II of the present Treaty; and, uniformly disposed to adopt every salutary measure calculated to secure the tranquillity of Europe by maintaining the order of things re-established in France, they argue that, in case the said Body of Troops should be attacked or menaced with an attack on the part of France, the said Powers should be again obliged to place themselves on a War Establishment against that Power, in order to maintain either of the said Stipulations, or to secure and support the great interests to which they relate, each of the High Contracting Parties shall furnish, without delay, according to the Stipulations of the Treaty of Chaumont, and especially in pursuance of the VIIth and VIIIth Articles of this Treaty, its full Contingent of 60 000 men, in addition to the Forces left in France, or such part of the said Contingent as the exigency of the case may require, should be put in motion.

IV. If, unfortunately, the Forces stipulated in the preceding Article should be found insufficient, the High Contracting Parties will concert together, without loss of time, as to the additional number of Troops to be furnished by each for the support of the Common Cause; and they engage to employ, in case of need, the whole of their Forces, in order to bring the War to a speedy and successful termination; reserving to themselves the right to prescribe, by common consent, such conditions of Peace as shall hold out to Europe a sufficient guarantee against the occurrency of a similar calamity.

V. The High Contracting Parties, having agreed to the dispositions laid down in the preceding Articles, for the purpose of securing the effect of their engagements during the period of the Temporary Occupation, declare, moreover, that even after the expiration of this measure, the said Engagements shall still remain in full force and vigour, for the purpose of carrying into effect such measures as may be deemed necessary for the maintenance of the Stipulations contained in the Articles I. and II. of the present Act.

VI. To facilitate and to secure the execution of the present Treaty, and to consolidate the connections, which at the present moment so closely unites the 4 Sovereigns for the happiness of the World, the High Contracting Parties have agreed to renew their Meetings at fixed periods, either under the immediate auspices of the Sovereigns themselves, or by their respective Ministers, for the purpose of consulting upon their common interests, and for the consideration of the measures which at each of those periods shall be considered the most salutary, for the repose and prosperity of Nations, and for the maintenance of the Peace of Europe.

VII. The present Treaty shall be ratified, and the Ratifications shall be exchanged within 2 months, or sooner, if possible.

In faith of which, the respective Plenipotentiaries have signed it, and affixed thereto the Seal of their Arms.

Done at Paris, the 20th of November, in the year of our Lord, 1815.

(L.S.) CASTLEREAGH.
(L.S.) WELLINGTON.
(L.S.) METTERNICH.
(L.S.) WESSENBERG.

43 RICHARD COBDEN'S SPEECH OF 15 JANUARY 1846, IN THE FREE TRADE HALL, MANCHESTER

Introduction

A successful textile manufacturer and Radical Member of Parliament, Cobden was, with John Bright, the leader of the Anti-Corn-Law League which was dedicated to the abolition of duties on grain imports (increasingly necessary to feed the rapidly expanding cities of the industrial north). The Free Traders, as they were known, were mostly from the North of England and religious dissenters, though Cobden himself was an exception to this rule. His campaign induced Prime Minister Robert Peel to repeal the Corn Laws in June 1846, an Act that dealt a serious blow to the Tory party from which it did not recover until the advent of Benjamin Disraeli in 1874. But for a generation after 1846 there was a period of almost unbroken Radical–Liberal government in England.

Text

I SHALL begin the few remarks which I have to offer to this meeting by proposing, contrary to my usual custom, a resolution; and it is, 'That the merchants, manufacturers, and other members of the National Anti-Corn-Law League claim no protection whatever for the manufactured products of this country, and desire to see obliterated for ever the few nominally protective duties against foreign manufactures, which still remain upon our statute books'. Gentlemen, if any of you have taken the pains to wade through the reports of the protectionist meetings, as they are called, which have been held lately, you would see that our opponents, at the end of seven years of our agitation, have found out their mistake, and are abandoning the Corn-laws; and now, like unskilful blunderers as they are, they want to take up a new position, just as we are going to achieve the victory. Then they have been telling something very like fibs, when they claimed the Corn-laws as compensation for peculiar burdens. They say now that they want merely protection in common with all other interests, and they now call themselves the advocates of protection to native industry in all its branches; and, by way of making the appeal to the less-informed portion of the community, they say that the Anti-Corn-law League are merely the advocates of free trade in corn, but that we want to preserve a monopoly in manufactures.

Now, the resolution which I have to submit to you, and which we will put to this meeting to-night – the largest by far that I ever saw in this room, and comprising men of every class and of every calling in this district – let that resolution decide, once and for ever, whether our opponents can with truth lay that to our charge henceforth. There is nothing new in this proposition, for at the very beginning of this agitation – at the meeting of the Chamber of Commerce – when that faint voice was raised in that small room in King-street in December, 1838, for the total and immediate repeal of the Corn-laws – when that ball was set

Source: Cobden, Richard, *Speeches on Questions of Public Policy*, John Bright and James E. Thorold Rogers (eds) (London: Macmillan, 1880) pp. 181–7 (excerpts).

in motion which has been accumulating in strength and velocity every since, why, the petition stated fairly that this community wanted no protection for its own industry. I will read the conclusion of that admirable petition; it is as follows:–

> Holding one of the principles of eternal justice to be the inalienable right of every man freely to exchange the result of his labour for the productions of other people, and maintaining the practice of protecting one part of the community at the expense of all other classes to be unsound and unjustifiable, your petitioners earnestly implore your honourable House to repeal all laws relating to the importation of foreign corn and other foreign articles of subsistence; and to carry out to the fullest extent, both as affects agriculture and manufactures, the true and peaceful principles of Free Trade, by removing all existing obstacles to the unrestricted employment of industry and capital.

We have passed similar resolutions at all our great aggregate meetings of delegates in London ever since that was issued.

I don't put this resolution as an argument or as an appeal to meet the appeals made in the protection societies' meetings. I believe that the men who now, in this seventh year of our discussion, can come forth before their country, and talk as those men have done – I believe that you might as well preach to the deaf adder. You cannot convince them. I doubt whether they have not been living in their shells like oysters; I doubt whether they know that such a thing is in existence as a railroad, or a penny postage, or even as an heir to the throne. They are in profound ignorance of everything, and incapable of being taught. We don't appeal to them, but to a very large portion of this community, who don't take a very prominent part in this discussion – who may be considered as important lookers-on. Many have been misled by the reiterated assertions of our opponents; and it is at this eleventh hour to convince these men, and to give them an opportunity of joining our ranks, as they will do, that I offer this proof of disinterestedness and the fairness of our proposals. I don't intend to go into an argument to convince any man here that protection to all must be protection to none. If it takes from one man's pocket, and allows him to compensate himself by taking an equivalent from another man's pocket, and if that goes on in a circle through the whole community, it is only a clumsy process of robbing all to enrich none; and simply has this effect, that it ties up the hands of industry in all directions. I need not offer one word to convince you of that. The only motive that I have to say a word is, that what I say here may convince others elsewhere – the men who meet in protection societies. But the arguments I should adduce to an intelligent audience like this, would be spoken in vain to the Members of Parliament who are now the advocates of protection. I shall meet them in less than a week in London, and there I will teach the A B C of this protection. It is of no use trying to teach children words of five syllables, when they have not got out of the alphabet. . . .

Well, there is one other quarter in which we have seen the progress of sound principles – I allude to America. We have received the American President's Message; we have had also the report of the Secretary of the Treasury, and both President Polk and Mr Secretary Walker have been taking my friend Colonel Thompson's task out of his hands, and lecturing the people of America on the subject of Free Trade. I have never read a better digest of the arguments in favour of Free Trade than that put forth by Mr Secretary Walker, and addressed to the Congress of that country. I augur from all these things that our question is making rapid progress throughout the world, and that we are coming to the consummation of our labours. We are verging now towards the session of Parliament, and I predict that the question will either receive its quietus, or that it will lead to the dissolution of this Parliament; and then the next will certainly relieve us from our burden. . . .

I believe that, owing to the scarcity everywhere – I mean in all parts of Europe – you could not, if you prayed for it, if you had your own wishing-cap on, and could make your own time and circumstances – I believe, I say, that you could never find such an opportunity for abolishing the Corn-laws totally and immediately as if it were done next week; for it so happens that the very countries from which, in ordinary times, we have been supplied, have been afflicted, like ourselves, with scarcity – that the countries of Europe are competing with us for the very small surplus existing in America. They have, in fact, anticipated us in that market, and they have left the world's markets so bare of corn, that, whatever your necessities may be, I defy you to have other than high prices of corn during the next twelve months, though the Corn-law was abolished to-morrow.

European countries are suffering as we are from the same evil. They are suffering from scarcity now, owing to their absurd legislation respecting the article of corn. Europe altogether has been corrupted by the vicious example of England in her commercial legislation. There they are, throughout the continent of Europe, with a population increasing at the rate of four or five millions a year, yet they make it their business, like ourselves, to put barriers in the way of a sufficiency of food to meet the demand of an increasing population.

I believe that if you abolish the Corn-law honestly, and adopt Free Trade in its simplicity, there will not be a tariff in Europe that will not be changed in less than five years to follow your example. . . .

Well, I have now spoken on what may be done. I have told you, too, what I should advocate; but I must say, that whatever is proposed by Sir Robert Peel, we, as Free-traders, have but one course to pursue. If he proposes a total and immediate and unconditional repeal, we shall throw up our caps for Sir Robert Peel. If he proposes anything else, then Mr Villiers will be ready, as he has been on former occasions – to move his amendment for a total and immediate repeal of the Corn-laws. We are not responsible for what Ministers may do; we are but responsible for the performance of our duty. We don't offer to do impossibilities; but we will do our utmost to carry out our principles. But, gentlemen, I tell you honestly, I think less of what this Parliament may do; I care less for their opinions, less for the intentions of the Prime Minister and the Cabinet, than what may be the opinion of a meeting like this and of the people out of doors. This question will not be carried by Ministers or by the present Parliament; it will be carried, when it is carried, by the will of the nation. We will do nothing that can remove us a hair's breadth from that rock which we have stood upon with so much safety for the last seven years. All other parties have been on a quicksand, and floated about by every wave, by every tide, and by every wind – some floating to us, others, like fragments scattered over the ocean, without rudder or compass; whilst we are upon solid ground, and no temptation, whether of parties or of Ministers, shall ever make us swerve a hair's breadth. I am anxious to hear now, at the last meeting before we go to Parliament – before we enter that arena to which all men's minds will be turned during the next week – I am anxious, not merely that we should all of us understand each other on this question, but that we should be considered as occupying as independent and isolated a position as we did at the first moment of the formation of this League. We have nothing to do with Whigs or Tories; we are stronger than either of them; and if we stick to our principles, we can, if necessary, beat both. And I hope we perfectly understand now, that we have not, in the advocacy of this great question, a single object in view but that which we have honestly avowed from the beginning. Our opponents may charge us with designs to do other things. No, gentlemen, I have never encouraged that. Some of my friends have said, 'When this work is done, you will have some influence in the country; you must do so and so'. I said then, as I say now, 'Every new political principle must have its special advocates, just as every new faith has its martyrs'. It is a mistake to suppose that this organisation can be turned to other purposes. It is a mistake to suppose that men, prominent in the advocacy of the principle of Free Trade, can with the same force and effect identify themselves with any other principle hereafter. It will be enough if the League accomplishes the triumph of the principle we have before us. I have never taken a limited view of the object or scope of this great principle. I have never advocated this question very much as a trader.

But I have been accused of looking too much to material interests. Nevertheless I can say that I have taken as large and great a view of the effects of this mighty principle as ever did any man who dreamt over it in his own study. I believe that the physical gain will be the smallest gain to humanity from the success of this principle. I look farther; I see in the Free-trade principle that which shall act on the moral world as the principle of gravitation in the universe, – drawing men together, thrusting aside the antagonism of race, and creed, and language, and uniting us in the bonds of eternal peace. I have looked even farther. I have speculated, and probably dreamt, in the dim future – ay, a thousand years hence – I have speculated on what the effect of the triumph of this principle may be. I believe that the effect will be to change the face of the world, so as to introduce a system of government entirely distinct from that which now prevails. I believe that the desire and the motive for large and mighty empires; for gigantic armies and great navies – for those materials which are used for the destruction of life and the desolation of the rewards of labour – will die away; I believe that such things will cease to be necessary, or to be used, when man becomes one family, and freely exchanges the fruits of his labour with his brother man. I believe that, if we could be allowed to reappear on this sublunary scene, we should see, at a far distant period, the governing system of this world revert to something like the municipal system; and I believe that the speculative philosopher of a thousand years hence will date the greatest revolution that ever happened in the world's history from the triumph of the principle which we have met here to advocate. I believe these things; but, whatever may have been my dreams and speculations, I have never obtruded them upon others. I have never acted upon personal or interested motives in this question; I seek no alliance with parties or favour from parties, and I will take none – but, having the feeling I have of the sacredness of the principle, I say that I can never agree to tamper with it. I, at least, will never be suspected of doing otherwise than pursuing it disinterestedly, honestly, and resolutely.

44 SPEECH ON CONSERVATIVE AND LIBERAL PRINCIPLES, GIVEN IN THE FREE TRADE HALL, MANCHESTER ON 3 APRIL 1872 BY BENJAMIN DISRAELI, LEADER OF THE OPPOSITION

Introduction

That Benjamin Disraeli, a leader of the Conservative Party, journeyed to Manchester, bastion of Liberalism, to speak in the same Free Trade Hall that Cobden had used a generation earlier (Doc. 43) is a manifestation of the changes that had occurred in Britain in the meantime. In 1846, Cobden had invoked the universal principle of free trade and offered the vision of a better world, taking for granted his country's ability to change things for the better. Now, reflecting a growing national sentiment against 'cosmopolitan ideas', Disraeli defended the monarchy, the English Constitution, and the British Empire. He dismissed those who spoke of the 'decay' and 'decline' of England's power, and instead portrayed the decline of Liberalism itself in his vivid image of the Liberal cabinet, as 'a range of exhausted volcanoes'. Two years later, the Tories were returned to power. An era of narrower vision, later characterised as one of 'splendid isolation', had begun.

Text

Gentlemen, the programme of the Conservative party is to maintain the Constitution of the country. I have not come down to Manchester to deliver an essay on the English Constitution; but when the banner of Republicanism is unfurled[1] – when the fundamental principles of our institutions are controverted – I think, perhaps, it may not be inconvenient that I should make some few practical remarks upon the character of our Constitution – upon that monarchy, limited by the co-ordinate authority of Estates of the realm, which, under the title of Queen, Lords and Commons,[2] has contributed so greatly to the prosperity of this country, and with the maintenance of which I believe that prosperity is bound up.

Gentlemen, since the settlement of that Constitution, now nearly two centuries ago, England has never experienced a revolution, though there is no country in which there has been so continuous and such considerable change. How is this? Because the wisdom of your forefathers placed the prize of supreme power without the sphere of human passions. Whatever the struggle of parties, whatever

Source: Beaconsfield, Earl of, *Selected Speeches*, T. E. Kebbel (ed.) (London, 1882) Vol. II, pp. 490–522 (excerpts).

1. In November 1871, Sir Charles Dilke, a prominent Liberal MP had spoken in Newcastle against the Monarchy. Riots in support of royalty ensued.
2. In fact, the three Estates of the Realm are the Lords Spiritual, the Lords Temporal, and the Commons.

the strife of factions, whatever the excitement and exaltation of the public mind, there has always been something in this country round which all classes and parties could rally, representing the majesty of the law, the administration of justice, and involving, at the same time, the security for every man's rights and the fountain of honour. Now, gentlemen, it is well clearly to comprehend what is meant by a country not having a revolution for two centuries. It means, for that space, the unbroken exercise and enjoyment of the ingenuity of man. It means, for that space, the continuous application of the discoveries of science to his comfort and convenience. It means the accumulation of capital, the elevation of labour, the establishment of those admirable factories which cover your district; the unwearied improvement of the cultivation of the land, which has extracted from a somewhat churlish soil harvests more exuberant than those furnished by lands nearer to the sun. It means the continuous order which is the only parent of personal liberty and political right. And you owe all these, gentlemen, to the Throne. . . .

But, gentlemen, after all, the test of political institutions is the condition of the country whose fortunes they regulate; and I do not mean to evade that test. You are the inhabitants of an island of no colossal size; which, geographically speaking, was intended by nature as the appendage of some Continental Empire – either of Gauls and Franks on the other side of the Channel, or of Teutons and Scandinavians beyond the German Sea. Such indeed, and for a long period, was your early history. You were invaded; you were pillaged and you were conquered; yet amid all these disgraces and vicissitudes there was gradually formed that English race which has brought about a very different state of affairs. Instead of being invaded, your land is proverbially the only 'inviolate land' – 'the inviolate land of the sage and free'. Instead of being plundered, you have attracted to your shores all the capital of the world. Instead of being conquered, your flag floats on many waters, and your standard waves in either zone. It may be said that these achievements are due to the race that inhabited the land, and not to its institutions. Gentlemen, in political institutions are the embodied experiences of a race. You have established a society of classes which give vigour and variety to life. But no class possesses a single exclusive privilege, and all are equal before the law. . . .

Gentlemen, I said I had not come here to make a party speech. I have addressed you upon subjects of grave, and I will venture to believe of general, interest; but to be here and altogether silent upon the present state of public affairs would not be respectful to you, and, perhaps, on the whole, would be thought incongruous. Gentlemen, I cannot pretend that our position either at home or abroad is in my opinion satisfactory. At home, at a period of immense prosperity, with a people contented and naturally loyal, we find to our surprise the most extravagant doctrines professed and the fundamental principles of our most valuable institutions impugned, and that too by persons of some authority. Gentlemen, this startling inconsistency is accounted for, in my mind, by the circumstances under which the present Administration was formed. It is the first instance in my knowledge of a British Administration being avowedly formed on a principle of violence. . . .

But, gentlemen, as time advanced it was not difficult to perceive that extravagance was being substituted for energy by the Government. The unnatural stimulus was subsiding. Their paroxysms ended in prostration. Some took refuge in melancholy, and their eminent chief alternated between a menace and a sigh. As I sat opposite the Treasury Bench the ministers reminded me of one of those marine landscapes not very unusual on the coasts of South America. You behold a range of exhausted volcanoes. Not a flame flickers on a single pallid crest. But the situation is still dangerous. There are occasional earthquakes, and ever and anon the dark rumbling of the sea.

But, gentlemen, there is one other topic on which I must touch. If the management of our domestic affairs has been founded upon a principle of violence, that certainly cannot be alleged against the management of our external relations. I know the difficulty of addressing a body of Englishmen on these topics. The very phrase 'foreign affairs' makes an Englishman convinced that I am about to treat of subjects with which he has no concern. Unhappily, the relations of England to the rest of the world, which are 'foreign affairs', are the matters which most influence his lot. Upon them depends the increase or reduction of taxation. Upon them depends the enjoyment or the embarrassment of his industry. And yet, though so momentous are the consequences of the mismanagement of our foreign relations, no one thinks of them till the mischief occurs, and then it is found how the most vital consequences have been occasioned by mere inadvertence. . . .

Gentlemen, don't suppose, because I counsel firmness and decision at the right moment, that I am of that school of statesmen who are favourable to a turbulent and aggressive diplomacy. I have resisted it during a great part of my life. I am not unaware that the relations of England to Europe have undergone a vast change during the century that has just elapsed. The relations of England to Europe are not the same as they were in the days of Lord Chatham or Frederick the Great. The Queen of England has become the Sovereign of the most powerful of Oriental States. On the other side of the globe there are now establishments belonging to her, teeming with wealth and population, which will, in due time, exercise their influence over the distribution of power. The old establishments of this country, now the United States of America, throw their lengthening shades over the Atlantic, which mix with European waters. These are vast and novel elements in the distribution of power. I acknowledge that the policy of England with respect to Europe should be a policy of reserve, but proud reserve; and in answer to those statesmen – those mistaken statesmen who have intimated the decay of the power of England and the decline of its resources, I express here my confident conviction that there never was a moment in our history when the power of England was so great and her resources so vast and inexhaustible.

And yet, gentlemen, it is not merely our fleets and armies, our powerful artillery, our accumulated capital, and our unlimited credit on which I so much depend, as upon that unbroken spirit of her people, which I believe was never prouder of the Imperial country to which they belong. Gentlemen, it is to that spirit that I above all things trust. I look upon the people of Lancashire as a fair representative of the people of England. I think the manner in which they have invited me here, locally a stranger, to receive the expression of their cordial sympathy, and only because they recognise some effort on my part to maintain the greatness of their country, is evidence of the spirit of the land. I must express to you again my deep sense of the generous manner in which you have welcomed me, and in which you have permitted me to express to you my views upon public affairs. Proud of your confidence and encouraged by your sympathy, I now deliver to you, as my last words, the cause of the Tory Party, the English Constitution, and of the British Empire.

45 AND 46 SPEECHES BY JOSEPH CHAMBERLAIN, BRITISH SECRETARY OF STATE FOR THE COLONIES, GIVEN (a) ON 31 MARCH 1897 (DOC. 45) AT THE ROYAL COLONIAL INSTITUTION AND (b) AT LEICESTER, 30 NOVEMBER 1899 (DOC. 46)

Introduction

As a youth, Joseph Chamberlain had been denied a university education because he was a Unitarian, that is, a Dissenter. Nevertheless, he proceeded to become one of the most successful men in British public life in the last quarter of the nineteenth century. He began by making his fortune as an industrialist in Birmingham. At the age of 38, he entered politics, first as mayor of that city and then as a Radical Member of Parliament. From 1895 to 1903 Chamberlain was Colonial Secretary, and a 'strong man' in the coalition government of the Conservative Lord Salisbury. In this position, he put into practice the concept of the British Empire earlier 'invented' by Disraeli (when he made Queen Victoria the Empress of India). It was Chamberlain who provided the term *Pax Britannica* (Graham, 1965, p. 111) which he uses in the first speech presented here. He held out the ideal of a 'federation of the British race', and would become the advocate of Imperial Preference, in contrast to the (by now) entrenched British policy of Free Trade.

During Chamberlain's tenure of office, Britain's world-wide interests came under severe pressure in crises such as those of Venezuela (with the United States), Fashoda (France), in the Far East (Russia) and during the Boer War (1899–1902). Britain's naval standing was about to be challenged as Germany embarked upon a programme of fleet building (initiated in 1896–9). The need to end the policy of 'splendid isolation', one way or another, became obvious to Chamberlain. To work with America was a cardinal point of his policy but not immediately attainable. Therefore he actively took steps to explore the possibility of an alliance with Germany. The November 1899 speech, given shortly after the Boer War began, and one week after Kaiser Wilhelm's visit to England, floated the idea of an Anglo–American–German alliance. In a private conversation with German Foreign Secretary Buelow, Chamberlain claimed that 'such a grouping could rule the world' (Buelow, 1930, Vol. I, p. 315), The Leicester speech itself had a bad press everywhere (Garvin, 1934, Vol. III, p. 508); some 18 months later (Doc. 47) the German option was finally abandoned, while the American one became, from then onward, ever more prominent.

Sources: Boyd, C. W. (ed.) *Mr. Chamberlain's Speeches* (London: Constable, 1914) Vol. II, pp. 1–6; *The Times* (London) 1 December 1899, p. 7 (excerpts).

Texts

(a) 45 SPEECH AT THE ROYAL COLONIAL INSTITUTE, 31 MARCH 1897

I have now the honour to propose to you the toast of 'Prosperity to the Royal Colonial Institute'. The institute was founded in 1868, almost exactly a generation ago, and I confess that I admire the faith of its promoters, who, in a time not altogether favourable to their opinions, sowed the seed of Imperial patriotism, although they must have known that few of them could live to gather the fruit and to reap the harvest. But their faith has been justified by the result of their labours, and their foresight must be recognised in the light of our present experience.

It seems to me that there are three distinct stages in our Imperial history. We began to be, and we ultimately became a great Imperial power in the eighteenth century, but, during the greater part of that time, the colonies were regarded, not only by us, but by every European power that possessed them, as possessions valuable in proportion to the pecuniary advantage which they brought to the mother country, which, under that order of ideas, was not truly a mother at all, but appeared rather in the light of a grasping and absentee landlord desiring to take from his tenants the utmost rents he could exact. The colonies were valued and maintained because it was thought that they would be a source of profit – of direct profit – to the mother country.

That was the first stage, and when we were rudely awakened by the War of Independence in America from this dream that the colonies could be held for our profit alone, the second chapter was entered upon, and public opinion seems then to have drifted to the opposite extreme; and, because the colonies were no longer a source of revenue, it seems to have been believed and argued by many people that their separation from us was only a matter of time, and that that separation should be desired and encouraged lest haply they might prove an encumbrance and a source of weakness.

It was while those views were still entertained, while the little Englanders were in their full career, that this institute was founded to protest against doctrines so injurious to our interests and so derogatory to our honour; and I rejoice that what was then, as it were, 'a voice crying in the wilderness' is now the expressed and determined will of the overwhelming majority of the British people. Partly by the efforts of this institute and similar organisations, partly by the writings of such men as Froude and Seeley, but mainly by the instinctive good sense and patriotism of the people at large, we have now reached the third stage in our history, and the true conception of our Empire.

What is that conception? As regards the self-governing colonies we no longer talk of them as dependencies. The sense of possession has given place to the sentiment of kinship. We think and speak of them as part of ourselves, as part of the British Empire, united to us, although they may be dispersed throughout the world, by ties of kindred, of religion, of history, and of language, and joined to us by the seas that formerly seemed to divide us.

But the British Empire is not confined to the self-governing colonies and the United Kingdom. It includes a much greater area, a much more numerous population in tropical climes, where no considerable European settlement is possible, and where the native population must always vastly outnumber the white inhabitants; and in these cases also the same change has come over the Imperial idea. Here also the sense of possession has given place to a different sentiment – the sense of obligation. We feel now that our rule over these territories can only be justified if we can show that it adds to the happiness and prosperity of the people, and I maintain that our rule does, and has, brought security and peace and comparative prosperity to countries that never knew these blessings before.

In carrying out this work of civilisation we are fulfilling what I believe to be our national mission, and we are finding scope for the exercise of those faculties and qualities which have made of us a great governing race. I do not say that all our methods have been beyond reproach; but I do say that in almost every instance in which the rule of the Queen has been established and the great *Pax Britannica* has been enforced, there has come with it greater security to life and property, and a material improvement in the condition of the bulk of the population. No doubt, in the first instance, when these conquests have been made, there has been bloodshed, there has been loss of life among the native populations, loss of still more precious lives among those who have been sent out to bring these countries into some kind of disciplined order, but it must be remembered that that is the condition of the mission we have to fulfil. There are, of course, among us – there always are among us, I think – a very small minority of men who are ready to be the advocates of the most detestable tyrants, provided their skin is black – men who sympathise with the sorrows of Prempeh[1] and Lobengula,[2] and who denounce as murderers those of their countrymen who have gone forth at the command of the Queen, and who have redeemed districts as large as Europe from the barbarism and the superstition in which they had been steeped for centuries. I remember a picture by Mr Selous[3] of a philanthropist – an imaginary philanthropist, I will hope – sitting cosily by his fireside and denouncing the methods by which British civilisation was promoted. This philanthropist complained of the use of Maxim guns[4] and other instruments of warfare, and asked why the impis[5] of Lobengula could not be brought before a magistrate, and fined five shillings and bound over to keep the peace.

No doubt there is a humorous exaggeration in this picture, but there is gross exaggeration in the frame of mind against which it was directed. You cannot have omelettes without breaking eggs; you cannot destroy the practices of barbarism, of slavery, of superstition, which for centuries have desolated the interior of Africa, without the use of force; but if you will fairly contrast the gain to humanity with the price which we are bound to pay for it, I think you may well rejoice in the result of such expeditions as those which have been recently conducted with such signal success in Nyassaland, Ashanti, Benin, and Nupé – expeditions which may have, and indeed have, cost valuable lives, but as to which we may rest assured that for one life lost a hundred will be gained, and the cause of civilisation and the prosperity of the people will in the long run be eminently advanced. But no doubt such a state of things, such a mission as I have described, involves heavy responsibility. In the wide dominions of the Queen the doors of

1. King of the Ashanti in West Africa who incurred British displeasure through his recalcitrance, slave trading, and human sacrifice. Soon after coming into office, Chamberlain summarily ordered his country (in today's Ghana) annexed.
2. Last King of the Ndebele in Southern Africa. His economic concessions to Cecil Rhodes only brought him the military destruction of his kingdom in 1893. He died in 1894.
3. Frederick Courteney Selous (1851–1917), famous big game hunter and explorer of South Central Africa.
4. Machine-gun, perfected in London in 1883, and invented by the American-born Sir Hiram Stevens Maxim.
5. Warriors.

the temple of Janus are never closed, and it is a gigantic task that we have undertaken when we have determined to wield the sceptre of empire. Great is the task, great is the responsibility, but great is the honour; and I am convinced that the conscience and the spirit of the country will rise to the height of its obligations, and that we shall have the strength to fulfil the mission which our history and our national character have imposed upon us.

In regard to the self-governing colonies our task is much lighter. We have undertaken, it is true, to protect them with all the strength at our command against foreign aggression, although I hope that the need for our intervention may never arise. But there remains what then will be our chief duty – that is, to give effect to that sentiment of kinship to which I have referred and which I believe is deep in the heart of every Briton. We want to promote a closer and a firmer union between all members of the great British race, and in this respect we have in recent years made great progress – so great that I think sometimes some of our friends are apt to be a little hasty, and to expect even a miracle to be accomplished. I would like to ask them to remember that time and patience are essential elements in the development of all great ideas. Let us, gentlemen, keep our ideal always before us. For my own part, I believe in the practical possibility of a federation of the British race, but I know that it will come, if it does come, not by pressure, not by anything in the nature of dictation from this country, but it will come as the realisation of a universal desire, as the expression of the dearest wish of our colonial fellow-subjects themselves.

That such a result would be desirable, would be in the interest of all of our colonies as well as of ourselves, I do not believe any sensible man will doubt. It seems to me that the tendency of the time is to throw all power into the hands of the greater empires, and the minor kingdoms – those which are non-progressive – seem to be destined to fall into a secondary and subordinate place. But, if Greater Britain remains united, no empire in the world can ever surpass it in area, in population, in wealth, or in the diversity of its resources.

Let us, then, have confidence in the future. I do not ask you to anticipate with Lord Macaulay the time when the New Zealander will come here to gaze upon the ruins of a great dead city. There are in our present condition no visible signs of decrepitude and decay. The mother country is still vigorous and fruitful, is still able to send forth troops of stalwart sons to people and to occupy the waste spaces of the earth; but yet it may well be that some of these sister nations whose love and affection we eagerly desire may in the future equal and even surpass our greatness. A trans-oceanic capital may arise across the seas, which will throw into shade the glories of London itself; but in the years that must intervene let it be our endeavour, let it be our task, to keep alight the torch of Imperial patriotism, to hold fast the affection and the confidence of our kinsmen across the seas, that so in every vicissitude of fortune the British Empire may present an unbroken front to all her foes, and may carry on even to distant ages the glorious traditions of the British flag. It is because I believe that the Royal Colonial Institute is contributing to this result that with all sincerity I propose the toast of the evening.

(b) 46 SPEECH AT LEICESTER, NOVEMBER 1899

Anglo–American Relations

I rejoice – it is perhaps natural that I should take a personal interest in the matter – in the friendly feeling, which I hope is now a permanent feeling, between two great branches of the Anglo-Saxon race. (Cheers.) I have as many friends in the United States of America almost as I have here (renewed cheers), and I can conceive of no greater disaster which could befall the two countries, or which could befall mankind, than that they should find themselves at any time in a hostile attitude the one to the other. And yet I remember well when I first visited America my surprise and astonishment at the evidence which was given by statesmen and politicians, by articles in the Press, of the constant suspicion of the objects of Great Britain, the constant doubt of her integrity, and the generally unfavourable estimate which was formed, both of our prospects and of our character. I remember on one occasion addressing a great meeting in Philadelphia, and I ventured to say to my audience that what was wanted was a new Columbus to set out from America in order to discover the United Kingdom (laughter), and that he should return to America to tell them something which they did not know of the character of the strange people who inhabit these islands. (Renewed laughter and cheers.) This ill-feeling, for it almost amounted to that, was due no doubt to many causes. It was due to the fact that the United States had never been at war with any Great Power except with Great Britain: it was due to their traditions, extending over a century; it was due to the feeling that they were insufficiently supported, that the sympathy of this country was not with them in their great civil war; it was due to the general belief that the people of this country would see with satisfaction any harm that might befall them. It appeared to me almost useless to contradict these mistaken and erroneous opinions, but what the asseverations of statesmen could not do was done by the proof of sympathy which we were able to give when the United States found itself the other day the object of something of the suspicions which so often has accompanied our own transactions, when it was engaged in what we saw at once to be a war of justice, a war against oppression, a war in favour of civilisation and of good government. (Cheers.) Our action proved to the Americans that we were indeed one people, that the same thoughts animated us, that we were guided by the same principles. The assurance, I say, that was given them during the course of the Spanish war will, I believe, never be forgotten, and has placed our relations in an admirable position. (Loud cheers.) The union – the alliance, if you please – the understanding between these two Great Nations is indeed a guarantee for the peace of the world. (Cheers.)

Great Britain and Germany

But there is something more which I think any far seeing English statesman must have long found, and that is that we should not remain permanently isolated on the continent of Europe; that I think that the moment that aspiration was formed it must have appeared evident to everybody that the natural alliance is between ourselves and the great German Empire. (Loud cheers.) We have had our differences with Germany; we have had our quarrels and contentions; we have had our misunderstandings. I do not conceal that the people of that country have been irritated and justly irritated by circumstances which we are only too glad to forget, but the root of things there has always been a force which has necessarily brought us together. What does move nations? Interest and sentiment. What interest have we which is contrary to the interest of Germany? We have had as I said, differences, but they have all been about matters so petty as regards the particular views of the case that they have not really formed occasion for anything like serious controversy. These differences have, under Lord Salisbury's wide administration of foreign affairs (cheers), been one by one greatly removed, until at the present time I cannot conceive any point which can arise in the immediate future which would bring ourselves and the Germans into antagonism of interests. (Cheers.) On the contrary I can forsee many things in the future which must be a cause of anxiety to the statesmen of Europe, but in which our interests are clearly the same as the interests of Germany, and in which that understanding of which I have spoken in the case of America might, if extended to Germany, do more good than any combination of arms in order to insure the peace of the world. (Cheers.)

A New Triple Alliance

It is not with German newspapers that we desire to have an understanding or alliance; it is with the German people; and I may point out to you that at bottom the character, the main character, of the Teutonic race differs very slightly indeed from the character of the Anglo-Saxon (cheers), and the same sentiments which bring us into close sympathy with the United States of America may also be evoked to bring us into closer sympathy and alliance with the Empire of Germany. What do we find? We find our system of justice, we find our literature, we find the very base and foundation on which our language is established the same in the two countries, and if the union between England and America is a powerful factor in the cause of reason, a new Triple Alliance between the Teutonic race and the two great branches of the Anglo-Saxon race will be a still more potent influence in the future of the world. (Cheers.) I have used the word 'alliance' sometimes in the course of what I have said, but again I desire to make it clear that to me it seems to matter little whether you have an alliance which is committed to paper or whether you have an understanding which exists in the minds of the statesmen of the respective countries. An understanding, perhaps, is better than an alliance, which may stereotype arrangements which cannot be accepted as permanent in view of the changing circumstances from day to day. An understanding, a determination to look favourably upon the motives of those with whom we desire to be on terms of friendship – a feeling of that kind, cultivated, existing, and confirmed by all these three countries will, I am certain, be to their enormous advantage, and I believe, whether they think it themselves or not, will also be to the advantage of other nations. (Cheers.)

47 MEMORANDUM BY THE MARQUESS OF SALISBURY, BRITISH PRIME MINISTER, 29 MAY 1901

Text

This is a proposal for including England within the bounds of the Triple Alliance. I understand its practical effect to be:–

1. If England were attacked by two Powers – say France and Russia – Germany, Austria, and Italy would come to her assistance.
2. Conversely, if either Austria, Germany, or Italy were attacked by France and Russia, or, if Italy were attacked by France and Spain, England must come to the rescue.

Even assuming that the Powers concerned were all despotic, and could promise anything they pleased, with a full confidence that they would be able to perform the promise, I think it is open to much question whether the bargain would be for our advantage. The liability of having to defend the German and Austrian frontiers against Russia is heavier than that of *having to defend the British Isles against France*. Even, therefore, in its most naked aspect the bargain would be a bad one for this country. Count Hatzfeldt speaks of our '*isolation*' as constituting a serious danger for us. *Have we ever felt that danger practically?* If we had succumbed in the revolutionary war, our fall would not have been due to our isolation. We had many allies, but they would not have saved us if the French Emperor had been able to command the Channel. Except during his reign we have never even been in danger; and, therefore, it is impossible for us to judge whether the 'isolation' under which we are supposed to suffer, does or does not contain in it any elements of peril. It would hardly be wise to incur novel and most onerous obligations, in order to guard against *a danger in whose existence we have no historical reason for believing*.

But though the proposed arrangement, even from this point of view, does not seem to me admissible, these are not by any means the weightiest objections that can be urged against it. The fatal circumstance is that *neither we nor the Germans are competent to make the suggested promises*. The British Government cannot undertake to declare war, for any purpose, unless it is a purpose of which the electors of this country would approve. If the Government promised to declare war for an object which did not commend itself to public opinion, the promise would be repudiated, and the Government would be turned out. I do not see how, in common honesty, we could invite other nations to rely upon our aids in a struggle, which must be formidable and probably supreme, when we have no means whatever of knowing what may be the humour of our people in circumstances which cannot be foreseen. We might, to some extent, divest ourselves of the full responsibility of such a step, *by laying our Agreement with the Triple Alliance before Parliament* as soon as it is concluded. But there are very grave objections to such a course, and I do not understand it to be recommended by the German Ambassador.

Source: Gooch, G. P. and Harold Temperley (eds), *British Documents on the Origins of the War 1898–1914* (London: HMSO, 1927) Vol. II, pp. 68–9.

The impropriety of attempting to determine by a *secret contract* the future conduct of a Representative Assembly upon an issue of peace or war would apply to German policy as much as to English, only that the German Parliament would probably pay more deference to the opinion of their Executive than would be done by the English Parliament. But a *promise of defensive alliance with England would excite bitter murmurs in every rank of German society* – if we may trust the indications of German sentiment, which we have had an opportunity of witnessing during the last two years.

It would not be safe to stake any important national interest upon the fidelity with which, in case of national exigency, either country could be trusted to fulfil the obligations of the Alliance, if the Agreement had been concluded without the assent of its Parliament.

Several times during the last sixteen years Count Hatzfeldt has tried to elicit from me, in conversation, some opinion as to the probable conduct of England, if Germany or Italy were involved in war with France. I have always replied that no English Minister could venture on such a forecast. The course of the English Government in such a crisis must depend on the view taken by public opinion in this country, and public opinion would be largely, if not exclusively, governed by the nature of the *casus belli.*

48 MEMORANDUM ON THE STATE OF BRITISH RELATIONS WITH FRANCE AND GERMANY, BY MR EYRE CROWE, A FOREIGN OFFICE OFFICIAL, 1 JANUARY 1907

Introduction

'This Memorandum by Mr Crowe is most valuable. The review of the present situation is both interesting and suggestive, and the connnected account of the diplomatic incidents of past years is most helpful as a guide to policy. The whole Memorandum contains information and reflections, which should be carefully studied.

The part of our foreign policy with which it is concerned involves the greatest issues, and requires constant attention.'

Edward Grey, Foreign Secretary, 28 January 1907

Text

. . . When the signature of the Algeciras Act brought to a close the first chapter of the conflict respecting Morocco, the Anglo–French *entente* had acquired a different significance from that which it had at the moment of its inception. Then there had been but a friendly settlement of particular outstanding differences, giving hope for future harmonious relations between two neighbouring countries that had got into the habit of looking at one another askance; now there had emerged an element of common resistance to outside dictation and aggression, a unity of special interests tending to develop into active co-operation against a third Power. It is essential to bear in mind that this new feature of the *entente* was the direct effect produced by Germany's effort to break it up, and that, failing the active or threatening hostility of Germany, such anti-German bias as the *entente* must be admitted to have at one time assumed, would certainly not exist at present, nor probably survive in the future. But whether the antagonism to Germany into which England had on this occasion been led without her wish or intention was but an ephemeral incident, or a symptomatic revelation of some deep-seated natural opposition between the policies and interests of the two countries, is a question which it clearly behoves British statesmen not to leave in any obscurity. To this point, then, inquiry must be directed.

The general character of England's foreign policy is determined by the immutable conditions of her geographical situation on the ocean flank of Europe as an island State with vast oversea colonies and dependencies, whose existence and survival as an independent community are inseparably bound up with the possession of preponderant sea power. The tremendous influence of such preponderance has been described in the classical pages of Captain Mahan. No one now disputes it. Sea power is more potent than land power, because it is as pervading as the element in which it moves and has its being. Its formidable character makes itself felt the more directly that a maritime State is, in the literal

Source: Gooch, G. P. and Harold Temperley (eds), *British Documents on the Origins of the War 1898–1914* (London: HMSO, 1928) Vol. III, pp. 397–420, passim.

sense of the word, the neighbour of every country accessible by sea. It would, therefore, be but natural that the power of a State supreme at sea should inspire universal jealousy and fear, and be ever exposed to the danger of being overthrown by a general combination of the world. Against such a combination no single nation could in the long run stand, least of all a small island kingdom not possessed of the military strength of a people trained to arms, and dependent for its food supply on oversea commerce. The danger can in practice only be averted – and history shows that it has been so averted – on condition that the national policy of the insular and naval State is so directed as to harmonize with the general desires and ideals common to all mankind, and more particularly that it is closely identified with the primary and vital interests of a majority, or as many as possible, of the other nations. Now, the first interest of all countries is the preservation of national independence. It follows that England, more than any other non-insular Power, has a direct and positive interest in the maintenance of the independence of nations, and therefore must be the natural enemy of any country threatening the independence of others, and the natural protector of the weaker communities.

Second only to the ideal of independence, nations have always cherished the right of free intercourse and trade in the world's markets, and in proportion as England champions the principle of the largest measure of general freedom of commerce, she undoubtedly strengthens her hold on the interested friendship of other nations, at least to the extent of making them feel less apprehensive of naval supremacy in the hands of a free trade England than they would in the face of a predominant protectionist Power. This is an aspect of the free trade question which is apt to be overlooked. It has been well said that every country, if it had the option, would, of course, prefer itself to hold the power of supremacy at sea, but that, this choice being excluded, it would rather see England hold that power than any other State.

History shows that the danger threatening the independence of this or that nation has generally arisen, at least in part, out of the momentary predominance of a neighbouring State at once militarily powerful, economically efficient, and ambitious to extend its frontiers or spread its influence, the danger being directly proportionate to the degree of its power and efficiency, and to the spontaneity or 'inevitableness' of its ambitions. The only check on the abuse of political predominance derived from such a position has always consisted in the opposition of an equally formidable rival, or of a combination of several countries forming leagues of defence. The equilibrium established by such a grouping of forces is technically known as the balance of power, and it has become almost an historical truism to identify England's secular policy with the maintenance of this balance by throwing her weight now in this scale and now in that, but ever on the side opposed to the political dictatorship of the strongest single State or group at a given time.

If this view of British policy is correct, the opposition into which England must inevitably be driven to any country aspiring to such a dictatorship assumes almost the form of a law of nature, as has indeed been theoretically demonstrated, and illustrated historically, by an eminent writer on English national policy.

By applying this general law to a particular case, the attempt might be made to ascertain whether, at a given time, some powerful and ambitious State is or is not in a position of natural and necessary enmity towards England; and the present position of Germany might, perhaps, be so tested. Any such investigation must take the shape of an inquiry as to whether Germany is, in fact, aiming at a political hegemony with the object of promoting purely German schemes of expansion, and establishing a German primacy in the world of international politics at the cost and to the detriment of other nations.

For purposes of foreign policy the modern German Empire may be regarded as the heir, or descendant of Prussia. Of the history of Prussia, perhaps the most remarkable feature, next to the succession of talented Sovereigns and to the energy and love of honest work characteristic of their subjects, is the process by which on the narrow foundation of the modest Margraviate of Brandenburg there was erected, in the space of a comparatively short period, the solid fabric of a European Great Power. That process was one of systematic territorial aggrandizement achieved mainly at the point of the sword, the most important and decisive conquests being deliberately embarked upon by ambitious rulers or statesmen for the avowed object of securing for Prussia the size, the cohesion, the square miles and the population necessary to elevate her to the rank and influence of a first class State. All other countries have made their conquests, many of them much larger and more bloody. There is no question now, or in this place, of weighing or discussing their relative merits or justification. Present interest lies in fixing attention on the special circumstances which have given the growth of Prussia its peculiar stamp. It has not been a case of a King's love of conquest as such, nor of the absorption of lands regarded geographically or ethnically as an integral part of the true national domain, nor of the more or less unconscious tendency of a people to expand under the influence of an exuberant vitality, for the fuller development of national life and resources. Here was rather the case of the Sovereign of a small and weak vassal State saying: 'I want my country to be independent and powerful. This it cannot be within its present frontiers and with its present population. I must have a larger territory and more inhabitants, and to this end I must organize strong military forces'.

The greatest and classic exponent in modern history of the policy of setting out deliberately to turn a small State into a big one was Frederick the Great. By his sudden seizure of Silesia in times of profound peace, and by the first partition of Poland, he practically doubled his inherited dominions. By keeping up the most efficient and powerful army of his time, and by joining England in her great effort to preserve the balance of power in face of the encroachments of France, he successfully maintained the position of his country as one of the European Great Powers. Prussian policy remained inspired by the same principles under his successors. It is hardly necessary to do more than mention the second and third partitions of Poland; the repeated attempts to annex Hanover in complicity with Napoleon; the dismemberment of Saxony, and the exchange of the Rhenish Provinces for the relinquishment of Polish lands in 1815;[1] the annexation of Schleswig-Holstein in 1864; the definite incorporation of Hanover and Electoral Hesse and other appropriations of territory in 1866; and, finally, the reconquest of Alsace-Lorraine from France in 1871. It is not, of course, pretended that all these acquisitions stand on the same footing. They have this in common – that they were all planned for the purpose of creating a big Prussia or Germany.

With the events of 1871 the spirit of Prussia passed into the new Germany. In no other country is there a conviction so deeply rooted in the very body and soul of all classes of the population that the preservation of national rights and the realization of national ideals rest absolutely on the readiness of every citizen in the last resort to stake himself and his State on their assertion and vindication. With 'blood and iron' Prussia had forged her position in the councils of the Great

1. Cf. Doc. 39.

Powers of Europe. In due course it came to pass that, with the impetus given to every branch of national activity by the newly-won unity, and more especially by the growing development of oversea trade flowing in ever-increasing volume through the now Imperial ports of the formerly 'independent' but politically insignificant Hanse Towns, the young empire found opened to its energy a whole world outside Europe, of which it had previously hardly had the opportunity to become more than dimly conscious. Sailing across the ocean in German ships, German merchants began for the first time to divine the true position of countries such as England, the United States, France, and even the Netherlands, whose political influence extends to distant seas and continents. The colonies and foreign possessions of England more especially were seen to give to that country a recognized and enviable status in a world where the name of Germany, if mentioned at all, excited no particular interest. The effect of this discovery upon the German mind was curious and instructive. Here was a vast province of human activity to which the mere title and rank of a European Great Power were not in themselves a sufficient passport. Here in a field of portentous magnitude, dwarfing altogether the proportions of European countries, others, who had been perhaps rather looked down upon as comparatively smaller folk, were at home and commanded, whilst Germany was at best received but as an honoured guest. Here was distinct inequality, with a heavy bias in favour of the maritime and colonizing Powers.

Such a state of things was not welcome to German patriotic pride. Germany had won her place as one of the leading, if not, in fact, the foremost Power on the European continent. But over and beyond the European Great Powers there seemed to stand the 'World Powers'. It was at once clear that Germany must become a 'World Power'. The evolution of this idea and its translation into practical politics followed with singular consistency the line of thought that had inspired the Prussian Kings in their efforts to make Prussia great. 'If Prussia', said Frederick the Great, 'is to count for something in the councils of Europe, she must be made a Great Power'. And the echo: 'If Germany wants to have a voice in the affairs of the larger oceanic world she must be made a "World Power".' 'I want more territory', said Prussia. 'Germany must have Colonies', says the new world-policy. And Colonies were accordingly established, in such spots as were found to be still unappropriated, or out of which others could be pushed by the vigorous assertion of a German demand for 'a place in the sun': Damaraland, Cameroons, Togoland, German East Africa, New Guinea, and groups of other islands in the Pacific. The German example, as was only natural, found ready followers, and the map of unclaimed territories was filled up with surprising rapidity. When the final reckoning was made of the actual German gain seemed, even in German eyes, somewhat meagre. A few fresh possessions were added by purchase or by international agreement – the Carolines, Samoa, Heligoland. A transaction in the old Prussian style secured Kiao-chau. On the whole, however, the 'Colonies' have proved assets of somewhat doubtful value.

Meanwhile the dream of a Colonial Empire had taken deep hold on the German imagination. Emperor, statesmen, journalists, geographers, economists, commercial and shipping houses, and the whole mass of educated and uneducated public opinion continue with one voice to declare: We *must* have real Colonies, where German emigrants can settle and spread the national ideals of the Fatherland, and we *must* have a fleet and coaling stations to keep together the Colonies which we are bound to acquire. To the question, 'Why *must*?' the ready answer is: 'A healthy and powerful State like Germany, with its 60 000 000 inhabitants, must expand, it cannot stand still, it must have territories to which its overflowing population can emigrate without giving up its nationality'. When it is objected that the world is now actually parcelled out among independent States, and that territory for colonization cannot be had except by taking it from the rightful possessor, the reply again is: 'We cannot enter into such considerations. Necessity has no law. The world belongs to the strong. A vigorous nation cannot allow its growth to be hampered by blind adherence to the *status quo*. We have no designs on other people's possessions, but where States are too feeble to put their territory to the best possible use, it is the manifest destiny of those who can and will do so to take their places'.

No one who has a knowledge of German political thought, and who enjoys the confidence of German friends speaking their minds openly and freely, can deny that these are the ideas which are proclaimed on the housetops, and that inability to sympathize with them is regarded in Germany as the mark of the prejudiced foreigner who cannot enter into the real feelings of Germans. Nor is it amiss to refer in this connection to the series of Imperial apothegms, which have from time to time served to crystallize the prevailing German sentiments, and some of which deserve quotation: 'Our future lies on the water'. 'The trident must be in our hand'. 'Germany must re-enter into her heritage of maritime dominion once unchallenged in the hands of the old Hansa'. 'No question of world politics must be settled without the consent of the German Emperor'. 'The Emperor of the Atlantic greets the Emperor of the Pacific', &c.

The significance of these individual utterances may easily be exaggerated. Taken together, their cumulative effect is to confirm the impression that Germany distinctly aims at playing on the world's political stage a much larger and much more dominant part than she finds allotted to herself under the present distribution of material power. It would be taking a narrow view of the function of political criticism to judge this theory of national self-assertion as if it were a problem of morals to be solved by the casuistical application of the principles governing private conduct in modern societies. History is apt to justify the action of States by its general results, with often but faint regard to the ethical character of the means employed. The ruthless conquests of the Roman Republic and Empire are recognized to have brought about an organization of the world's best energies, which, by the characteristic and lasting impulse it gave to the civilization of the ancients, fully compensated for the obliqueness of the conquerors' political morals. Peter the Great and Katharine II are rightly heroes in the eyes of Russia, who largely owes to their unscrupulous and crafty policies her existence as a powerful and united nation. The high-handed seizure of Silesia by Frederick the Great, the low intrigues by which the first partition of Poland was brought about, the tortuous manœuvres by which Bismarck secured Schleswig-Holstein for Prussia are forgotten or condoned in the contemplation of a powerful Germany that has brought to these and all her other territories a more enlightened government, a wider conception of national life, and a greater share in a glorious national tradition than could have been their lot in other conditions. Germans would after all be only logical if they did not hesitate to apply to their current politics the lesson conveyed in such historical judgments, and were ready to leave to posterity the burden of vindicating the employment of force for the purpose of spreading the benefits of German rule over now unwilling peoples. No modern German would plead guilty to a mere lust of conquest for the sake of conquest. But the vague and undefined schemes of Teutonic expansion ('die Ausbreitung des deutschen Volkstums') are but the expression of the deeply rooted feeling that Germany has by the strength and purity of her national purpose, the fervour of her patriotism, the depth of her religious feeling, the high standard of competency, and the perspicuous honesty of her administration, the successful pursuit of every branch of public and scientific activity, and the elevated character of her philosophy, art, and ethics, established for herself the right to assert the primacy of German national ideals. And as it is an axiom of her political faith that right, in order that it may prevail, must be backed by force, the transition is easy to the belief that the 'good German sword,' which plays so large a part in patriotic speech, is there to solve any difficulties that may be in the way of establishing the reign of those ideals in a Germanized world.

The above very fragmentary sketch has given prominence to certain general features of Germany's foreign policy, which may, with some claim to impartiality, accuracy, and clearness, be deduced from her history, from the utterances and known designs of her rulers and statesmen, and from the unmistakable manifestations of public opinion. It remains to consider whether, and to what extent, the principles so elucidated may be said, on the one hand, to govern actual present policy, and, on the other, to conflict with the vital interests of England and of other independent and vigorous States, with the free exercise of their national rights, and the fulfilment of what they, on their part, may regard as their own mission in this world.

It cannot for a moment be questioned that the mere existence and healthy activity of a powerful Germany is an undoubted blessing to the world. Germany represents in a pre-eminent degree those highest qualities and virtues of good citizenship, in the largest sense of the word, which constitutes the glory and triumph of modern civilization. The world would be unmeasurably the poorer if everything that is specifically associated with German character, German ideas, and German methods were to cease having power and influence. For England particularly, intellectual and moral kinship creates a sympathy and appreciation of what is best in the German mind, which has made her naturally predisposed to welcome, in the interest of the general progress of mankind, everything tending to strengthen that power and influence – on one condition: there must be respect for the individualities of other nations, equally valuable coadjutors, in their way, in the work of human progress, equally entitled to full elbow-room in which to contribute, in freedom, to the evolution of a higher civilization. England has, by a sound instinct, always stood for the unhampered play and interaction of national forces as most in accord with Nature's own process of development. No other State has ever gone so far and so steadily as the British Empire in the direction of giving free scope to the play of national forces in the internal organization of the divers peoples gathered under the King's sceptre. It is perhaps England's good fortune, as much as her merit, that taking this view of the manner in which the solution of the higher problems of national life must be sought, she has had but to apply the same principle to the field of external policy in order to arrive at the theory and practice governing her action as one of the international community of States.

So long, then, as Germany competes for an intellectual and moral leadership of the world in reliance on her own national advantages and energies England can but admire, applaud, and join in the race. If, on the other hand, Germany believes that greater relative preponderance of material power, wider extent of territory, inviolable frontiers, and supremacy at sea are the necessary and preliminary possessions without which any aspirations to such leadership must end in failure, then England must expect that Germany will surely seek to diminish the power of any rivals, to enhance her own by extending her dominion, to hinder the co-operation of other States, and ultimately to break up and supplant the British Empire.

Now, it is quite possible that Germany does not, nor ever will, consciously cherish any schemes of so subversive a nature. Her statesmen have openly repudiated them with indignation. Their denial may be perfectly honest, and their indignation justified. If so, they will be most unlikely to come into any kind of armed conflict with England, because, as she knows of no cause of present dispute between the two countries, so she would have difficulty in imagining where, on the hypothesis stated, any such should arise in the future. England seeks no quarrels, and will never give Germany cause for legitimate offence.

But this is not a matter in which England can safely run any risks. The assurances of German statesmen may after all be no more genuine than they were found to be on the subject of the Anglo–French *entente* and German interests in Morocco, or they may be honestly given but incapable of fulfilment. It would not be unjust to say that ambitious designs against one's neighbours are not as a rule openly proclaimed, and that therefore the absence of such proclamation, and even the profession of unlimited and universal political benevolence are not in themselves conclusive evidence for or against the existence of unpublished intentions. The aspect of German policy in the past, to which attention has already been called, would warrant a belief that a further development on the same general lines would not constitute a break with former traditions, and must be considered as at least possible. In the presence of such a possibility it may well be asked whether it would be right, or even prudent, for England to incur any sacrifices or see other, friendly, nations sacrificed merely in order to assist Germany in building up step by step the fabric of a universal preponderance, in the blind confidence that in the exercise of such preponderance Germany will confer unmixed benefits on the world at large, and promote the welfare and happiness of all other peoples without doing injury to any one. There are, as a matter of fact, weighty reasons which make it particularly difficult for England to entertain that confidence. These will have to be set out in their place. . . .

[At this point, Crowe recites the record of the 'numerous quarrels' in Anglo–German relations since 1884, each 'opened by acts of direct and unmistakable hostility to England', including those arising over Southwest Africa, Uganda, Zanzibar, South Africa, and China.]

There is no pretence to completeness in the foregoing survey of Anglo–German relations, which, in fact, gives no more than a brief reference to certain salient and typical incidents that have characterized those relations during the last twenty years. The more difficult task remains of drawing the logical conclusions. The immediate object of the present inquiry was to ascertain whether there is any real and natural ground for opposition between England and Germany. It has been shown that such opposition has, in fact, existed in an ample measure for a long period, but that it has been caused by an entirely one-sided aggressiveness, and that on the part of England the most conciliatory disposition has been coupled with never-failing readiness to purchase the resumption of friendly relations by concession after concession.

It might be deduced that the antagonism is too deeply rooted in the relative position of the two countries to allow of its being bridged over by the kind of temporary expedients to which England has so long and so patiently resorted. On this view of the case it would have to be assumed that Germany is deliberately following a policy which is essentially opposed to vital British interests, and that an armed conflict cannot in the long run be averted, except by England either sacrificing those interests, with the result that she would lose her position as an independent Great Power, or making herself too strong to give Germany the chance of succeeding in a war. This is the opinion of those who see in the whole trend of Germany's policy conclusive evidence that she is consciously aiming at the establishment of a German hegemony, at first in Europe, and eventually in the world.

After all that has been said in the preceding paragraphs, it would be idle to deny that this may be the correct interpretation of the facts. There is this further seemingly corroborative evidence that such a conception of world-policy offers perhaps the only quite consistent explanation of the tenacity with which Germany pursues the construction of a powerful navy with the avowed object of creating slowly, but surely, a weapon fit to overawe any possible enemy, however formidable at sea.

There is, however, one obvious flaw in the argument. If the German design were so far-reaching and deeply thought out as this view implies, then it ought to be clear to the meanest German understanding that its success must depend very materially on England's remaining blind to it, and being kept in good humour until the moment arrived for striking the blow fatal to her power. It would be not merely worth Germany's while, it would be her imperative duty, pending the development of her forces, to win and retain England's friendship by every means in her power. No candid critic could say that this elementary strategical rule had been even remotely followed hitherto by the German Government.

It is not unprofitable in this connection to refer to a remarkable article in one of the recent numbers of the 'Preussische Jahrbücher', written by Dr Hans Delbrück,[2] the distinguished editor of that ably conducted and influential magazine. This article discusses very candidly and dispassionately the question whether Germany could, even if she would, carry out successfully an ambitious policy of expansion which would make her follow in the footsteps of Louis XIV and of Napoleon I. The conclusion arrived at is that, unless Germany wishes to expose herself to the same overwhelming combinations which ruined the French dreams of a universal ascendancy, she must make up her mind definitely and openly to renounce all thoughts of further extending her frontiers, and substitute for the plan of territorial annexations the nobler ambition of spreading German culture by propagating German ideals in the many quarters of the globe where the German language is spoken, or at least taught and understood.

It would not do to attribute too much importance to the appearance of such an article in a country where the influence of public opinion on the conduct of the affairs of State is notoriously feeble. But this much may probably be rightly gathered from it, that the design attributed by other nations to Germany has been, and perhaps is still being, cherished in some indeterminate way by influential classes, including, perhaps, the Government itself, but that responsible statesmen must be well aware of the practical impossibility of carrying it out.

There is then, perhaps, another way of looking at the problem: It might be suggested that the great German design is in reality no more than the expression of a vague, confused, and unpractical statesmanship, not fully realizing its own drift. A charitable critic might add, by way of explanation, that the well-known qualities of mind and temperament distinguishing for good or for evil the present Ruler of Germany may not improbably be largely responsible for the erratic,

2. 'Politische Korrespondenz', *Preussische Jahrbücher*, Vol. 126, October–December 1906, pp. 187–93 (eds note).

domineering, and often frankly aggressive spirit which is recognizable at present in every branch of German public life, not merely in the region of foreign policy; and that this spirit has called forth those manifestations of discontent and alarm both at home and abroad with which the world is becoming familiar; that, in fact, Germany does not really know what she is driving at, and that all her excursions and alarums, all her underhand intrigues do not contribute to the steady working out of a well conceived and relentlessly followed system of policy, because they do not really form part of any such system. This is an hypothesis not flattering to the German Government, and it must be admitted that much might be urged against its validity. But it remains true that on this hypothesis also most of the facts of the present situation could be explained.

It is, of course, necessary to except the period of Bismarck's Chancellorship. To assume that so great a statesman was not quite clear as to the objects of his policy would be the *reductio ad absurdum* of any hypothesis. If, then, the hypothesis is to be held sound, there must be forthcoming a reasonable explanation for Bismarck's conduct towards England after 1884, and a different explanation for the continuance of German hostility after his fall in 1890. This view can be shown to be less absurd than it may at first sight appear.

Bismarck suffered from what Count Schuvaloff called *le cauchemar des coalitions*. It is beyond doubt that he particularly dreaded the hostile combination against his country of France and Russia, and that, as one certain means of counteracting that danger, he desired to bring England into the Triple Alliance, or at least to force her into independent collision with France and Russia, which would inevitably have placed her by Germany's side. He knew England's aversion to the entanglement of alliances, and to any policy of determined assertion of national rights, such as would have made her a Power to be seriously reckoned with by France and Russia. But Bismarck had also a poor opinion of the power of English Ministers to resist determined pressure. He apparently believed he could compel them to choose between Germany and a universal opposition to England. When the colonial agitation in Germany gave him an opening, he most probably determined to bring it home to England that meekness and want of determination in foreign affairs do not constitute a policy; that it was wisest, and certainly least disagreeable, for her to shape a decided course in a direction which would secure her Germany's friendship; and that in co-operation with Germany lay freedom from international troubles as well as safety, whilst a refusal to co-operate brought inglorious conflicts, and the prospect of finding Germany ranged with France and Russia for the specific purpose of damaging British interests.

Such an explanation gains plausibility from the fact that, according to Bismarck's own confession, a strictly analogous policy was followed by him before 1866 in his dealings with the minor German States. Prussia deliberately bullied and made herself disagreeable to them all, in the firm expectation that, for the sake of peace and quiet, they would follow Prussia's lead rather than Austria's. When the war of 1866 broke out Bismarck had to realize that, with the exception of a few small principalities which were practically *enclaves* in the Kingdom of Prussia, the whole of the minor German States sided with Austria. Similarly he must have begun to see towards the end of his career that his policy of browbeating England into friendship had failed, in spite of some fugitive appearance of success. But by that time the habit of bullying and offending England had almost become a tradition in the Berlin Foreign Office, and Bismarck's successors, who, there is other evidence to show, inherited very little of his political capacity and singleness of purpose, seem to have regarded the habit as a policy in itself, instead of as a method of diplomacy calculated to gain an ulterior end. Whilst the great Chancellor made

England concede demands objectionable more in the manner of presentation than in themselves, treating her somewhat in the style of Richard III wooing the Lady Ann, Bismarck's successors have apparently come to regard it as their ultimate and self-contained purpose to extract valuable concessions from England by offensive bluster and persistent nagging. Bismarck's experience having shown her to be amenable to this form of persuasion without any risk of her lasting animosity being excited.

If, merely by way of analogy and illustration, a comparison not intended to be either literally exact or disrespectful be permitted, the action of Germany towards this country since 1890 might be likened not inappropriately to that of a professional blackmailer, whose extortions are wrung from his victims by the threat of some vague and dreadful consequences in case of a refusal. To give way to the blackmailer's menaces enriches him, but it has long been proved by uniform experience that, although this may secure for the victim temporary peace, it is certain to lead to renewed molestation and higher demands after ever-shortening periods of amicable forbearance. The blackmailer's trade is generally ruined by the first resolute stand made against his exactions and the determination rather to face all risks of a possibly disagreeable situation than to continue in the path of endless concessions. But, failing such determination, it is more than probable that the relations between the two parties will grow steadily worse.

If it be possible, in this perhaps not very flattering way, to account for the German Government's persistently aggressive demeanour towards England, and the resulting state of almost perpetual friction, notwithstanding the pretence of friendship, the generally restless, explosive, and disconcerting activity of Germany in relation to all other States would find its explanation partly in the same attitude towards them and partly in the suggested want of definite political aims and purposes. A wise German statesman would recognise the limits within which any world-policy that is not to provoke a hostile combination of all the nations in arms must confine itself. He would realize that the edifice of Pan-Germanism, with its outlying bastions in the Netherlands, in the Scandinavian countries, in Switzerland, in the German provinces of Austria, and on the Adriatic, could never be built up on any other foundation than the wreckage of the liberties of Europe. A German maritime supremacy must be acknowledged to be incompatible with the existence of the British Empire, and even if that Empire disappeared, the union of the greatest military with the greatest naval Power in one State would compel the world to combine for the riddance of such an incubus. The acquisition of colonies fit for German settlement in South America cannot be reconciled with the Monroe doctrine, which is a fundamental principle of the political faith of the United States. The creation of a German India in Asia Minor must in the end stand or fall with either a German command of the sea or a German conquest of Constantinople and the countries intervening between Germany's present south-eastern frontiers and the Bosphorus. Whilst each of these grandiose schemes seems incapable of fulfilment under anything like the present conditions of the world, it looks as if Germany were playing with them all together simultaneously, and thereby wilfully concentrating in her own path all the obstacles and oppositions of a world set at defiance. That she should do this helps to prove how little of logical and consistent design and of unrelenting purpose lies behind the impetuous mobility, the bewildering surprises, and the heedless disregard of the susceptibilities of other people that have been so characteristic of recent manifestations of German policy.

If it be considered necessary to formulate and accept a theory that will fit all the ascertained facts of German foreign policy, the choice must lie between the two hypotheses here presented:–

Either Germany is definitely aiming at a general political hegemony and maritime ascendancy, threatening the independence of her neighbours and ultimately the existence of England;

Or Germany, free from any such clear-cut ambition, and thinking for the present merely of using her legitimate position and influence as one of the leading Powers in the council of nations, is seeking to promote her foreign commerce, spread the benefits of German culture, extend the scope of her national energies, and create fresh German interests all over the world wherever and whenever a peaceful opportunity offers, leaving it to an uncertain future to decide whether the occurrence of great changes in the world may not some day assign to Germany a larger share of direct political action over regions not now a part of her dominions, without that violation of the established rights of other countries which would be involved in any such action under existing political conditions.

In either case Germany would clearly be wise to build as powerful a navy as she can afford.

The above alternatives seem to exhaust the possibilities of explaining the given facts. The choice offered is a narrow one, nor easy to make with any close approach to certainty. It will, however, be seen, on reflection, that there is no actual necessity for a British Government to determine definitely which of the two theories of German policy it will accept. For it is clear that the second scheme (of semi-independent evolution, not entirely unaided by statecraft) may at any stage merge into the first, or conscious-design scheme. Moreover, if ever the evolution scheme should come to be realized, the position thereby accruing to Germany would obviously constitute as formidable a menace to the rest of the world as would be presented by any deliberate conquest of a similar position by 'malice aforethought'.

It appears, then, that the element of danger present as a visible factor in one case, also enters, though under some disguise, into the second; and against such danger, whether actual or contingent, the same general line of conduct seems prescribed. It should not be difficult briefly to indicate that line in such a way as to command the assent of all persons competent to form a judgment in this matter.

So long as England remains faithful to the general principle of the preservation of the balance of power, her interests would not be served by Germany being reduced to the rank of a weak Power, as this might easily lead to a Franco–Russian predominance equally, if not more, formidable to the British Empire. There are no existing German rights, territorial or other, which this country could wish to see diminished. Therefore, so long as Germany's action does not overstep the line of legitimate protection of existing rights she can always count upon the sympathy and good-will, and even the moral support, of England. . . .

6 The United States Accede to Global Leadership

Percipient as Eyre Crowe's analysis of 1907 was in defining the problem of German political hegemony it failed to address the question of succession. For it was not enough to oppose German ambitions, justified or unjustified; an alternative scheme of world order and alternative leadership had also to be offered. It was not enough to assume that Britain would continue for ever in the role it had played in the two cycles just past (to use our present terminology).

Writing in 1939 what to this day remains one of the best introductions to the study of International Relations, E. H. Carr was more explicit on this crucial question. He knew that the conditions that had secured the lead status for Britain in the nineteenth century no longer existed, but he was also aware that contemporary Englishmen 'sometimes console themselves with the dream that British supremacy, instead of passing altogether away, will be transmuted into the higher and more affective form of an ascendancy of the English-speaking peoples' (Carr, 1939, p. 298). This harked back to the early years of the century when many prominent leaders in both countries spoke of an Anglo–Saxon alliance and when the Washington Naval Treaty of 1922, allowing the United States and Britain the same ratio in battleships, was a 'more or less conscious bid by Great Britain for an equal partnership with the United States in the management of the world' (Carr, 1939, p. 299).

We know now that this idea did not assume permanent institutional form between 1900 and 1945, not even that of a formal treaty of alliance. Confident of its own strength and self-reliant, the United States forged ahead in the world arena on its own terms, strongly under President Theodore Roosevelt, and strikingly under President Woodrow Wilson.

LEADERSHIP OFFERED, AND DECLINED

Wilson's policies have been called unrealistic, or utopian, in retrospect. But a look at his vision does not justify a simple dismissal. Foremost in his mind, as recounted by an early chronicler (Baker, 1922–3, Vol. I, p. 18) was the need to erect a contrast with what he saw as 'the German idea' of 'the state seeking only its own safety and its own welfare'. The President did recognise that his nation was a powerful state, but he also perceived its role in the light of the Biblical precept (Mark 10:44): 'Whoever of you will be the chiefest shall be the servant of all'. He saw the United States committed 'not to its own aggrandizement, but to the service of the world'.

As the clouds of war were gathering over Europe, the President concluded his 1914 Independence Day speech in Philadelphia with these words:

> my dream is this: that as the years go on and the world knows more and more of America, it will turn to America for those moral inspirations which lie at the base of all freedom, that it will never fear America unless it finds itself engaged in some enterprise inconsistent with the rights of humanity, that America will come to that day when all shall know she puts human rights above all other rights, and that her flag is . . . the flag of humanity . . . America has lifted the light that will shine unto all generations and guide the feet of mankind to the goal of justice, liberty, and peace (*The New York Times*, 5 July 1914, p. 3).

Three years later Woodrow Wilson took the United States into the First World War. His message to Congress recommending belligerency war (Doc. 49) was cast in the same terms of moral leadership he had used earlier. He defined unrestricted submarine warfare, initiated by Germany weeks earlier, as a threat to the freedom of the seas (echoes of Grotius) and a 'challenge to all mankind'. He proclaimed the war to be an opportunity to 'make the world safe for democracy' now that upon the overthrow of the Tsar by the February Revolution the Triple Entente (with Britain and France) had lost its autocratic element. Germany, too, could be expected to shed its government.

Walter Lippmann, who at the time had reason to know what Colonel House and other Presidential advisers were thinking, believed that the real cause for war was that 'the cutting of the Atlantic communications meant the starvation of Britain and, therefore, the conquest of Western Europe by imperial Germany', a situation that 'would have made the world unsafe' for the Americas and would allow Germany 'to gain the mastery of the Atlantic Ocean'. We might notice that such reasoning closely paralleled the way in which British security was thought threatened by French mastery of the Low Countries and the narrow seas in 1793. Lippmann later expressed regret that this 'simple and self-evident American interest was not candidly made explicit' (1943, pp. 33–7).

In a historic message to Congress of January 1918, President Wilson defined the aims of the First World War in the form of Fourteen Points (Doc. 50). Of these, six were chiefly Wilson's own contributions, and constituted a statement of general principles of international relations concerning: freedom of the seas, freedom of trade, arms control, national self-determination, and the need for a 'general association of nations'. In their rhetorical flourish, these Points recall President Lincoln's Gettysburg address and the Declaration of Independence.

The eight other Points dealt with territorial questions in Europe and the drafting of them had been mostly the work of think-tank dubbed 'The Inquiry' and organised in New York by Colonel House; a leading member of 'The Inquiry' was Walter Lippmann (Steel, 1981, Chapter 11). The 14 Points gained popular acclaim, and served as the basis on which the German High Command asked for the armistice in October; they cut less ice with the allied governments at Versailles.

The 14 Principles remain persuasive to this day except for the first, about 'open covenants, openly arrived at' that some thought were incompatible with any real diplomatic negotiation. What needs to be remembered though is the context in which they were announced. That is, the furore then enveloping the allied camp over the 'secret treaties', those sordid deals entered by the Entente governments in the first two years of the war and revealed to the world when the Bolsheviks seized power in Russia the previous November. This threw confusion into Wilson's ethical conception of the purposes for which the war was then being fought. Hence his implicit denunciation of these arrangements and an attempt to sketch out a more positive vision for the future: a clear case of exercise of the leadership function of agenda-setting.

The call for the formation of the Communist International drafted by Trotsky (the same man who revealed the secret treaties) issued from Moscow in January 1919 (Doc. 51), was another case of agenda-setting, the crystallisation of a future challenge. As Germany appeared to be collapsing, the Bolsheviks were setting out to capture the left wing of the international socialist movement. Their programme, a call for the destruction of the 'capitalist world system' remains in its essentials to this day.

The League of Nations stemmed from the fourteenth of Wilson's principles and it saw implementation in the Peace Treaties. When the Senate was debating their ratification, the League became a focus of opposition, and Senator Lodge summarised his objections in the form of several 'Reservations' (Doc. 52). Wilson refused to budge at all on objections concerning the League and urged his supporters to vote against ratification that would include them. A re-reading of these reservations makes it plain that in the light of the practice of international organisations since that time, they were not at all unreasonable and did no more than define the practice that governments observed in defence of what they saw as their national interests. The League was hardly the magical key to security that Wilson might have imagined it to become.

But the rejection of the League was more than just a repudiation of Wilson's agenda on his home turf. It meant a refusal to assume the role of global leadership that Wilson had so firmly, if not always skilfully, staked out. Much water would flow under the bridges of the Potomac before that part would once again be taken up.

As we look back on this experience, some things stand out: the initial attempt at leadership failed, despite a promising start and some favourable conditions, without any one clear or simple cause. Was excess moralising, as E. H. Carr would have it, one of those reasons? Maybe it was; maybe it was no more than the failure of the first try, made when the time was not quite ripe for a decision of such immense weight and calibre.

LEADERSHIP MEDIATED, AND ASSUMED

While the strategic situation that brought America into the First World War repeated itself quite closely in 1940–1, all concerned were slow to learn from this history. The fall of France in May–June 1940 put Britain in jeopardy in just the same way that submarine warfare had endangered her in early 1917. The American reaction in 1940 was shaped again primarily in relation to Britain and in the context of a close personal rapport between President Roosevelt and Prime Minister Churchill.

The relationship began in the opening days of the Second World War by Roosevelt, who initiated a correspondence with Churchill, then First Lord of the Admiralty, on the ground that they both had occupied similar positions in the First World War (Roosevelt as Under Secretary of the Navy); they came to refer to each other as 'Former Naval Person' (Doc. 53). The letters assume a critical momentum in May of 1940 when in the wake of the defeats in France Churchill formulated his first request for a 'loan' of destroyers (Doc. 53 (b) and (c)) that came ultimately to be exchanged for certain British bases, in a 'pawn-broking' that for some recalled the Nonsuch treaty of 1585 between Elizabeth I and the Dutch (Doc. 12) Military staff conversations were begun.

The most telling item of this voluminous correspondence is Churchill's letter of 7 December, 1940, just after Roosevelt' reelection, masterfully reviewing the strategic situation and requesting a wide spectrum of American measures not as 'aid' but rather as 'the minimum action necessary to the achievement of our common purpose' (Doc. 53(d)).

The early draft of that letter (the Lothian draft, in Kimball (ed.), 1984, Vol. I, pp. 89–95) came close to basing that request upon a vision of a future world order built upon an Anglo–American supremacy. It included the following:

> I see no other prospect of a lasting peace or of a reasonably liberal world order after the war than the United States and Britain, at any rate for a number of years, should between them possess unquestionable air and sea supremacy. Peace comes from power behind law and government and not from disarmament and anarchy. Power in the hands of those two great liberal nations . . . offers the only stable prospect of peace . . . If we win victory we shall have to assume major responsibilities for a new world order.

But in its final form, as sent by Churchill, the letter omitted this passage and appealed, more generally, to the mutual interests of the two democracies and 'the kind of civilization they stand for' in the preservation of the 'bastions of sea power of the Atlantic and Indian Oceans' in 'faithful and friendly hands'. Naval matters featured prominently in this wide-ranging survey as Britain was fighting alone not only the German but also the Italian, and prospectively also the Japanese navies, and as the ratio of battleships was resting on 'a smaller margin than is satisfactory'.

The American response was prompt and generous and set in motion a fundamental redefinition of strategy. The President's message to Congress, a month later (Doc. 55) committed the nation 'to full support of all those . . . who are resisting aggression and are thereby keeping war away from our Hemisphere'. 'Our most useful and immediate role is to act as an arsenal for them as well as for ourselves'. The vision of the future was founded upon the Four Freedoms: freedom of speech and of religion and from want and fear: a fine statement of the four functional requisites of a free society.

The Four Freedoms were in part a response to the 'new order' of the Axis Powers that in the Tripartite Pact signed in Berlin the previous September asked that 'all nations of the world be given each its own proper place' in a world in which Germany and Italy would be accorded leadership in Europe, and Japan, in 'Greater East Asia' (Doc. 54). Replied the President in his message to Congress: 'The world order which we seek is the cooperation of free countries, working together in a friendly, civilized society'.

The evolution of war aims reached a plateau with the publication of the Atlantic Charter in August (Doc. 56), one of the results of the first face-to-face meeting between Roosevelt and Churchill. Less specific than Wilson's 14 Points in respect of territorial questions, it was a declaration of principles more akin to the Four Freedoms, three of which it in effect incorporated. Its issue was aimed largely for public consumption but as the war went on it assumed new roles, as when six months later it became the foundation charter for the coalition that suddenly crystallised around the United States in the days after Pearl Harbor and that was named the United Nations during the First Washington conference (cf. Table 6.1). Noteworthy about this later declaration (Doc. 56(b)) is the order of the states signing it (as arranged by FDR: Sherwood, 1950, pp. 447ff): the United States first, Britain second (but without the dominions and India), the USSR third, China fourth, and all others in alphabetical order. The Declaration also makes it plain that religious freedom (inadvertently omitted from the Atlantic Charter) is also included.

On a more operational basis US war aims were defined in a report, dated 11 September 1941 and prepared for the President by the Chiefs of Staff, General Marshall and Admiral Stark, in the opinion of Robert

Table 6.1 Summits 1941–5

Conference	*Date*	*Participants*	*Doc. No.*
Atlantic	August 9–12 1941	Roosevelt Churchill	56(a)
First Washington	December 22– January 14 1842	Roosevelt Churchill	56(b)
Second Washington	June 18–27 1942	Roosevelt Churchill	
Casablanca	January 14–23 1943	Roosevelt Churchill	
Third Washington	May 12–25 1943	Roosevelt Churchill	
First Quebec	August 14–24 1943	Roosevelt Churchill	57
Cairo (2 phases)	November 22–6 December 2–7 1943	Roosevelt Churchill	
Teheran	November 28– December 2, 1943	Roosevelt Churchill Stalin	58
Second Quebec	September 11–16 1944	Roosevelt Churchill	
Malta	January 30– February 2 1945	Roosevelt Churchill	
Yalta	February 4–11 1945	Roosevelt Churchill Stalin	59
Potsdam	July 17– August 2 1945	Truman Churchill/ Attlee Stalin	60

Sherwood (1950, p. 410) 'one of the most remarkable documents of American history, for it set down a basic strategy of a global war before this country was involved in it'. That strategy received initial formulation during formal staff conferences held with the British in Washington, when the Lend-Lease bill was moving through Congress (January–March 1941) whose product (the ABC-1 plan) laid down major strategic and administrative principles, including priority to the European theatre, and joint planning and operations (McNeill, 1953, pp. 7–13).

Marshall and Stark laid down major national objectives as follows:

> preservation of the territorial, economic and ideological integrity of the United States and of the remainder of the Western Hemisphere; prevention of the disruption of the British Empire; prevention of the further extension of Japanese territorial dominion; eventual establishment in Europe and Asia of balances of power which will most nearly ensure political stability in those regions and the future security of the United States, and, so far as practicable, the establishment of regimes favourable to economic freedom and individual liberty.

> These national policies can be effectuated in their entirety only through military victories outside this hemisphere, either by the armed forces of the United States, by the armed forces of friendly Powers, or by both (Sherwood, 1950, pp. 410–11).

COALITION POLITICS

The strategic direction of the Second World War on the part of the United Nations had all the components we observed in the Napoleonic wars: the global maritime contest, prominent and critical in 1940–1 (as in Docs 53(b)–(d)) but basically resolved in a decisive fashion with the Battle of Midway in mid-1942; an economic blockade, by now perfected by the British in particular; and aid, taking the form of Lend-Lease and made available to all allies (an elaboration of the system of subsidies maintained by the British in the earlier global contest).

Coalition coordination, too, was given a significant boost. Once the United States had entered the war, a regular practice of meetings at the highest level was instituted (as recorded in Table 6.1) with the result that in 1941–5 Roosevelt and Churchill spent on the average about one month a year in each other's company. Close contact between the political leaders was supplemented by intense interaction between the 'combined staffs' (such as the combined chiefs of staff in Washington), and by 'unified commands' in the field, overseeing the implementation of joint decisions. By October 1943 Churchill would write to Roosevelt of the 'intimacy and friendship which have been established between us and between our high staffs' (Kimball, 1984, Vol. II, p. 565) intimacy that would likely be disrupted if Russian military representatives were to be admitted to sit in on meetings of the combined staffs.

One instance of the closeness and strength of Anglo–American relations was the Quebec agreement on atomic cooperation (Doc. 57). It set out to deal with the most secret and possibly most far-reaching of the projects undertaken by the allies and it stipulated that 'we shall never use this agency against each other'; nor would they use it 'against 3rd parties' without each others' consent. The cooperative action would be directed by another 'combined staff', the Combined Policy Committee that included a Canadian representative. That was the committee that in July 1945 received notification of the British government's concurrence to the use of the nuclear weapon against Japan (FRUS, Berlin, 1960, Vol. I, pp. 941–2) and that also discussed ways in which the news would be broken to the Soviets at the forthcoming Postdam conference.

High-level Second World War strategy took shape in successive meetings between Roosevelt and Churchill. In these meetings, as through the rest of the war, the United States had the advantages of deep pockets and big battalions, but the British position had its strengths too: Churchill's relationship with Roosevelt, the fact that Britain had started, and borne the burdens of the common fight earlier, having significant and experienced forces deployed when the Americans were still mobilising, and access to significant information, including the ULTRA project for decoding German communications, and finally the fact that in most of the operational theatres including Europe, the Middle East, and Southeast Asia, Britain's experience much antedated that of her allies. The relationship was therefore not entirely unequal, but as time went on it became more so, especially as the additional weight of the Soviet Union began to be felt in the scales.

In 1940–1 the chips of global power were reckoned principally in battleships, as may be seen, for example, in Churchill's letter of 7 December 1940 (Doc. 54(d)). But as the global–naval conflict was being resolved in favour of the allies, and the fighting on land began in earnest, then army divisions became the counters of power, albeit mostly in a regional context. As the great war-lords met for the first time with Joseph Stalin in Teheran towards the end of 1943, their opening plenary session was an occasion for revealing their relative strengths (Doc. 57). Stalin could boast of 330 Soviet divisions arrayed on his Western front against some 260 under German command; by comparison the planned allied landing in France would deploy no more than 35. Even allowing for the fact that American and British divisions were significantly larger than the Soviet units, the numbers could not but impress.

But even though Soviet power now loomed increasingly larger in the European theatre of operations, and might also prove useful in the Far East, at the global level their position remained circumscribed and limited by the resources and opportunities available to the United States for exercising leadership.

No one was more conscious of this fact than Stalin himself, drawing, as through Lend-Lease, on the industrial might of the United States. Raising a toast to President Roosevelt at the Yalta conference he praised him as a man who had:

> perhaps a broader concept of national interest, and even though his country was not directly imperilled had been the chief forger of the instruments which had led to the mobilisation of war against Hitler (FRUS, Yalta, 1955, p. 798).

Addressing Harry Hopkins, an emissary of President Truman a few months later Stalin declared:

> whether the United States wished it or not it was a world power and would have to accept world-wide interests. Not only this war but the previous war had shown that without United States intervention Germany could not have been defeated . . . In fact the United States had more reason to be a world power

> than any other state. For this reason he fully recognised the right of the United States as a world power to participate in the Polish question. (FRUS, Potsdam, 1960, Vol. II, p. 39).

The most immediate recognition of American leadership occurred in procedural arrangements that seemed to be so much taken for granted that no record of their discussion seems to have survived (cf. FRUS, Teheran, 1961, p. 539). But in each of the Three Power summits the President of the United States served as presiding officer (no chairman was needed for bilateral meetings such as those between Roosevelt and Churchill). In every official photograph of the meeting the President occupies centre place.

SHAPE OF THE POST-WAR WORLD

If the United States position as *primus inter pares* was evident in the diplomatic practice of 1941–5, no such clarity existed about the shape of the emerging world order.

In the prevailing view, the world would be kept at peace, for maybe some 50 years, by an alliance of the Big Three powers who were about to win the great war. FDR's conception was that of the Four Policemen (those listed first in the United Nations Declaration (Doc. 56(b)), a close group of four powerful states prepared to deal decisively with any emerging threat to peace, as he explained to Stalin at Teheran (Doc. 58(b)) at the end of 1943.

In his *U.S. Foreign Policy* that came out in April of that year and soon sold nearly half-a-million copies, Walter Lippmann advocated basically such an alliance except that he was less sanguine about China's capacity to act in that role and saw the Anglo–American relationship, in an 'Atlantic Community' as an especially close one. For Lippmann 'the will of the most powerful states to remain allied is the only possible creator of a general international order' (1943, p. 166).

The idea found closest organisational expression in the Security Council of the UN Organisation plans for which had, by October 1944, been formulated at Dumbarton Oaks. A significant part of the discussion at Yalta the following February was therefore directed to the question of the rights and duties of the Big Powers (especially Doc. 60(a)). Stalin was the most adamant of all in declaring that the 'Three Great Powers' had the 'unanimous right to preserve the peace of the world', while Churchill was the most vocal in defending the rights of smaller states. It took some time to bring Stalin around to the view that the small states should have an opportunity at least to voice their opinions in the Security Council, even against the wishes of the big. He laughed off the suggestion that the Great

Powers might be accused of wanting to 'rule the world' (Doc. 60(b)). At a subsequent meeting the Big Three proceeded to decide which countries would be allowed to join the newly forming Organisation.

By the time of Potsdam (July–August 1945), the Big Three had been diluted to the Five Foreign Ministers who were charged with drawing up the peace settlements. Fractures in the winning coalition were there for all to see, on a great many issues, not the least among them the Polish question previously encountered at Vienna (Doc. 39) that reappeared at Teheran and Yalta. We have no space to cover any of these; suffice it to say that the unity of the Big Three on which so much store had been put began to show cracks the moment victory was in sight. Just as in Vienna in 1815 – or for that matter a century earlier still, in the circumstances surrounding the peace of Utrecht – divisions surfaced right away and the elaborate provisions for post-war coordination of policy (as in the Quadruple Alliance of 1815, Doc. 42) soon fell apart. The coalition fractured because the cement holding it together – the German threat – was no more. What did remain and continued to function were the general international institutions, in particular those in charge of the international economic order (such as the International Monetary Fund and the World Bank), that grew out of American, or Anglo–American, initiatives (Doc. 59).

This break-up of the war-time alliance was not surprising. Lippmann feared it, but thought that it would be avoided through wise and moderate policies on both sides. Stalin, too, knew, as he said at Yalta, that 'the difficult task came after the war when diverse interests tended to divide allies'. But that was not the real point. The certain result of the decisive ending of the twentieth-century period of global warfare was that the United States and the Soviet Union would be left as the two major global powers, and the relationship between them would, more likely than not, be marked by severe tensions. But when the discords did emerge, within sight of victory, was Lippmann right in giving such wide currency to the term 'cold war'? Or was he perhaps overdramatising a situation of unavoidable, but possibly necessary or even salutary, competition?

The post-war world, and the 'special relationship' that embodied and smoothed over the 'Great Succession', did not become an 'Anglo–American supremacy', as some had wished or anticipated (what Winston Churchill might have had in mind as late as his 'Iron Curtain' speech of 1946). But the cooptative process that Britain helped engineer (in a manner strikingly recalling the earlier Anglo–Dutch arrangements in which Churchill's ancestor Marlborough had played so prominent a part) did earn it considerable influence, and remained for long an asset to British foreign policy, strengthening it above and beyond what it could otherwise have aimed for.

The world's major relationship of tension in global politics has been that between the United States and the Soviet Union, with the former being, broadly speaking, the leading element, and the latter the main centre of the opposition. It has been developing generally in a similar way to that in which world powers, and challengers, had taken their stands in earlier cycles. The issues may have clarified and surfaced somewhat earlier, but their real character was hardly different.

That the 'Big Four' (Roosevelt's 'Four Policemen') and the alliance of the Three were unrealistic conceptions, and that the United States necessarily had to stand alone in its role of global leadership became unambiguous when the testing and use of atomic weapons in ending the war against Japan made clear their unique responsibility (Doc. 62).

The last act of the 'Great Succession' opened when the British Government (in two diplomatic notes delivered on 21 February 1947) announced that it was under the necessity of reducing or liquidating its commitments in several parts of the world, including Greece and Turkey. President Truman responded, in a message to Congress, with the so-called Truman Doctrine (12 March 1947). 'Great responsibilities have been placed upon us', he declared, because 'the free peoples of the world look to us for support in maintaining freedom . . . If we falter in our leadership, we may endanger the peace of the world, and we shall surely endanger the peace of this nation'.

The succession process was completed three months later when the idea of a programme for European recovery was publicly launched by Secretary of State Marshall in a commencement address at Harvard University (Doc. 63). By that time, the United States' global role in organising the peace (and not just fighting the war) was ready to be acknowledged, both by Americans and by the world at large.

Documents

49 PRESIDENT WOODROW WILSON'S WAR MESSAGE TO CONGRESS, 2 APRIL 1917

Text

I HAVE CALLED THE CONGRESS into extraordinary session because there are serious, very serious, choices of policy to be made immediately, which it was neither right not constitutionally permissible that I should assume the responsibility of making.

On the 3rd of February last, I officially laid before you the extraordinary announcement of the Imperial German government that on and after the 1st day of February it was its purpose to put aside all restraints of law or of humanity and use its submarines to sink every vessel that sought to approach either the ports of Great Britain and Ireland or the western coasts of Europe or any of the ports controlled by the enemies of Germany within the Mediterranean.

That had seemed to be the object of the German submarine warfare earlier in the war, but since April of last year the Imperial government had somewhat restrained the commanders of its undersea craft in conformity with its promise then given to us that passenger boats should not be sunk and that due warning would be given to all other vessels which its submarines might seek to destroy, when no resistance was offered or escape attempted, and care taken that their crews were given at least a fair chance to save their lives in their open boats. The precautions taken were meager and haphazard enough, as was proved in distressing instance after instance in the progress of the cruel and unmanly business, but a certain degree of restraint was observed.

The new policy has swept every restriction aside. Vessels of every kind, whatever their flag, their character, their cargo, their destination, their errand, have been ruthlessly sent to the bottom without warning and without thought of help or mercy for those on board, the vessels of friendly neutrals along with those of belligerents. Even hospital ships and ships carrying relief to the sorely bereaved and stricken people of Belgium, though the latter were provided with safe conduct through the proscribed areas by the German government itself and were distinguished by unmistakable marks of identity, have been sunk with the same reckless lack of compassion or of principle.

I was for a little while unable to believe that such things would in fact be done by any government that had hitherto subscribed to the humane practices of civilized nations. International law had its origin in the attempt to set up some law which would be respected and observed upon the seas, where no nation had right of dominion and where lay the free highways of the world. By painful stage after stage has that law been built up, with meager enough results, indeed, after all was accomplished that could be accomplished, but always with a clear view, at least, of what the heart and conscience of mankind demanded.

This minimum of right the German government has swept aside under the plea of retaliation and necessity and because it had no weapons which it could use at

Source: *Congressional Record*, Senate, Vol. 55, Part I, pp. 102–4.

sea except these which it is impossible to employ as it is employing them without throwing to the winds all scruples of humanity or of respect for the understandings that were supposed to underlie the intercourse of the world. I am not now thinking of the loss of property involved, immense and serious as that is, but only of the wanton and wholesale destruction of the lives of noncombatants, men, women, and children, engaged in pursuits which have always, even in the darkest periods of modern history, been deemed innocent and legitimate. Property can be paid for; the lives of peaceful and innocent people cannot be.

The present German submarine warfare against commerce is a warfare against mankind. It is a war against all nations. American ships have been sunk. American lives taken in ways which it has stirred us very deeply to learn of; but the ships of people of other neutral and friendly nations have been sunk and overwhelmed in the waters in the same way. There has been no discrimination. The challenge is to all mankind.

Each nation must decide for itself how it will meet it. The choice we make for ourselves must be made with a moderation of counsel and a temperateness of judgment befitting our character and our motives as a nation. We must put excited feeling away. Our motive will not be revenge or the victorious assertion of the physical might of the nation, but only the vindication of right, of human right, of which we are only a single champion.

When I addressed the Congress on the 26th of February last, I thought that it would suffice to assert our neutral rights with arms, our right to use the seas against unlawful interference, our right to keep our people safe against unlawful violence. But armed neutrality, it now appears, is impracticable. Because submarines are in effect outlaws when used as the German submarines have been used against merchant shipping, it is impossible to defend ships against their attacks as the law of nations has assumed that merchantmen would defend themselves against privateers or cruisers, visible craft giving chase upon the open sea.

It is common prudence in such circumstances, grim necessity indeed, to endeavor to destroy them before they have shown their own intention. They must be dealt with upon sight, if dealt with at all. The German government denies the right of neutrals to use arms at all within the areas of the sea which it has proscribed, even in the defense of rights which no modern publicist has ever before questioned their right to defend. The intimation is conveyed that the armed guards which we have placed on our merchant ships will be treated as beyond the pale of law and subject to be dealt with as pirates would be.

Armed neutrality is ineffectual enough at best; in such circumstances and in the face of such pretensions it is worse than ineffectual: it is likely only to produce what it was meant to prevent; it is practically certain to draw us into the war without either the rights or the effectiveness of belligerents. There is one choice we cannot make, we are incapable of making: we will not choose the path of submission and suffer the most sacred rights of our nation and our people to be ignored or violated. The wrongs against which we now array ourselves are no common wrongs; they cut to the very roots of human life.

With a profound sense of the solemn and even tragical character of the step I am taking and of the grave responsibilities which it involves, but in unhesitating obedience to what I deem my constitutional duty, I advise that the Congress declare the recent course of the Imperial German government to be in fact nothing less than war against the government and people of the United States; that it formally accept the status of belligerent which has thus been thrust upon it; and that it take immediate steps, not only to put the country in a more thorough state of defense but also to exert all its power and employ all its resources to bring the government of the German Empire to terms and end the war.

What this will involve is clear. It will involve the utmost practicable cooperation in counsel and action with the governments now at war with Germany and, as incident to that, the extension to those governments of the most liberal financial credits, in order that our resources may so far as possible be added to theirs. It will involve the organization and mobilization of all the material resources of the country to supply the materials of war and serve the incidental needs of the nation in the most abundant and yet the most economical and efficient way possible. It will involve the immediate full equipment of the Navy in all respects but particularly in supplying it with the best means of dealing with the enemy's submarines. It will involve the immediate addition to the armed forces of the United States already provided for by law in case of war at least 500 000 men, who should, in my opinion, be chosen upon the principle of universal liability to service, and also the authorization of subsequent additional increments of equal force so soon as they may be needed and can be handled in training.

It will involve also, of course, the granting of adequate credits to the government, sustained, I hope, so far as they can equitably be sustained by the present generation, by well-conceived taxation. I say sustained so far as may be equitable by taxation because it seems to me that it would be most unwise to base the credits which will now be necessary entirely on money borrowed. It is our duty, I most respectfully urge, to protect our people so far as we may against the very serious hardships and evils which would be likely to arise out of the inflation which would be produced by vast loans.

In carrying out the measures by which these things are to be accomplished, we should keep constantly in mind the wisdom of interfering as little as possible in our own preparation and in the equipment of our own military forces with the duty – for it will be a very practical duty – of supplying the nations already at war with Germany with the materials which they can obtain only from us or by our assistance. They are in the field and we should help them in every way to be effective there.

I shall take the liberty of suggesting, through the several executive departments of the government, for the consideration of your committees, measures for the accomplishment of the several objects I have mentioned. I hope that it will be your pleasure to deal with them as having been framed after very careful thought by the branch of the government upon which the responsibility of conducting the war and safeguarding the nation will most directly fall.

While we do these things, these deeply momentous things, let us be very clear, and make very clear to all the world, what our motives and our objects are. My own thought has not been driven from its habitual and normal course by the unhappy events of the last two months, and I do not believe that the thought of the nation has been altered or clouded by them. I have exactly the same things in mind now that I had in mind when I addressed the Senate on the 22nd of January last; the same that I had in mind when I addressed the Congress on the 3rd of February and on the 26th of February.

Our object now, as then, is to vindicate the principles of peace and justice in the life of the world as against selfish and autocratic power and to set up among the really free and self-governed peoples of the world such a concert of purpose and of action as will henceforth ensure the observance of those principles. Neutrality is no longer feasible or desirable where the peace of the world is involved and the freedom of its peoples, and the menace to that peace and freedom lies in the existence of autocratic governments backed by organized force which is controlled wholly by their will, not by the will of their people. We have seen the last of neutrality in such circumstances. We are at the beginning of an age in which it will be insisted that the same standards of conduct and of responsibility for wrong done shall be observed among nations and their governments that are observed among the individual citizens of civilized states.

We have no quarrel with the German people. We have no feeling toward them but one of sympathy and friendship. It was not upon their impulse that their government acted in entering this war. It was not with their previous knowledge or approval. It was a war determined upon in the old, unhappy days when peoples were nowhere consulted by their rulers and wars were provoked and waged in the interest of dynasties or of little groups of ambitious men who were accustomed to use their fellowmen as pawns and tools.

Self-governed nations do not fill their neighbor states with spies or set the course of intrigue to bring about some critical posture of affairs which will give them an opportunity to strike and make conquest. Such designs can be successfully worked out only under cover and where no one has the right to ask questions. Cunningly contrived plans of deception or aggression, carried, it may be, from generation to generation, can be worked out and kept from the light only within the privacy of courts or behind the carefully guarded confidences of a narrow and privileged class. They are happily impossible where public opinion commands and insists upon full information concerning all the nation's affairs.

A steadfast concert for peace can never be maintained except by a partnership of democratic nations. No autocratic government could be trusted to keep faith within it or observe its covenants. It must be a league of honor, a partnership of opinion. Intrigue would eat its vitals away; the plottings of inner circles who could plan what they would and render account to no one would be a corruption seated at its very heart. Only free peoples can hold their purpose and their honor steady to a common end and prefer the interests of mankind to any narrow interest of their own.

Does not every American feel that assurance has been added to our hope for the future peace of the world by the wonderful and heartening things that have been happening within the last few weeks in Russia? Russia was known by those who knew it best to have been always in fact democratic at heart, in all the vital habits of her thought, in all the intimate relationships of her people that spoke their natural instinct, their habitual attitude toward life. The autocracy that crowned the summit of her political structure, long as it had stood and terrible as was the reality of its power, was not in fact Russian in origin, character, or purpose; and now it has been shaken off and the great, generous Russian people have been added in all their naive majesty and might to the forces that are fighting for freedom in the world, for justice, and for peace. Here is a fit partner for a League of Honor.

One of the things that has served to convince us that the Prussian autocracy was not and could never be our friend is that from the very outset of the present war it has filled our unsuspecting communities and even our offices of government with spies and set criminal intrigues everywhere afoot against our national unity of counsel, our peace within and without, our industries and our commerce. Indeed, it is now evident that its spies were here even before the war began; and it is unhappily not a matter of conjecture but a fact proved in our courts of justice that the intrigues which have more than once come perilously near to disturbing the peace and dislocating the industries of the country have been carried on at the instigation, with the support, and even under the personal direction of official agents of the Imperial government accredited to the government of the United States.

Even in checking these things and trying to extirpate them, we have sought to put the most generous interpretation possible upon them because we knew that their source lay, not in any hostile feeling of purpose of the German people toward us (who were no doubt as ignorant of them as we ourselves were) but only in the selfish designs of a government that did what it pleased and told its people nothing. But they have played their part in serving to convince us at last that that government entertains no real friendship for us and means to act against our peace and security at its conveniences. That it means to stir up enemies against us at our very doors the intercepted note to the German minister at Mexico City is eloquent evidence.

We are accepting this challenge of hostile purpose because we know that in such a government, following such methods, we can never have a friend; and that in the presence of its organized power, always lying in wait to accomplish we know not what purpose, there can be no assured security for the democratic governments of the world. We are now about to accept gage of battle with this natural foe to liberty and shall, if necessary, spend the whole force of the nation to check and nullify its pretensions and its power. We are glad, now that we see the facts with no veil of false pretense about them, to fight thus for the ultimate peace of the world and for the liberation of its peoples, the German peoples included: for the rights of nations great and small and the privilege of men everywhere to choose their way of life and of obedience.

The world must be made safe for democracy. Its peace must be planted upon the tested foundations of political liberty. We have no selfish ends to serve. We desire no conquest, no dominion. We seek no indemnities for ourselves, no material compensation for the sacrifices we shall freely make. We are but one of the champions of the rights of mankind. We shall be satisfied when those rights have been made as secure as the faith and the freedom of nations can make them.

Just because we fight without rancor and without selfish object, seeking nothing for ourselves but what we shall wish to share with all free peoples, we shall, I feel confident, conduct our operations as belligerents without passion and ourselves observe with proud punctilio the principles of right and of fair play we profess to be fighting for.

I have said nothing of the governments allied with the Imperial government of Germany because they have not made war upon us or challenged us to defend our right and our honor. The Austro–Hungarian government has, indeed, avowed its unequalified endorsement and acceptance of the reckless and lawless submarine warfare adopted now without disguise by the Imperial German government, and it has therefore not been possible for this government to receive Count Tarnowski, the ambassador recently accredited to this government by the Imperial and Royal government of Austria–Hungary; but that government has not actually engaged in warfare against citizens of the United States on the seas, and I take the liberty, for the present at least, of postponing a discussion of our relations with the authorities at Vienna. We enter this war only where we are clearly forced into it because there are no other means of defending our rights.

It will be all the easier for us to conduct ourselves as belligerents in a high spirit of right and fairness because we act without animus, not in enmity toward a people or with the desire to bring any injury or disadvantage upon them, but only in armed opposition to an irresponsible government which has thrown aside all considerations of humanity and of right and is running amuck. We are, let me say again, the sincere friends of the German people, and shall desire nothing so much as the early reestablishment of intimate relations of mutual advantage between us – however hard it may be for them, for the time being, to believe that this is spoken from our hearts.

We have borne with their present government through all these bitter months because of that friendship – exercising a patience and forbearance which would otherwise have been impossible. We shall, happily, still have an opportunity to prove that friendship in our daily attitude and actions towards the millions of men and women of German birth and native sympathy who live among us and share our life, and we shall be proud to prove it toward all who are in fact loyal to their neighbors and to the government in the hour of test. They are, most of them, as true and loyal Americans as if they had never known any other fealty or allegiance. They will be prompt to stand with us in rebuking and restraining the few who may be of a different mind and purpose. If there should be disloyalty, it will be dealt with with a firm hand of stern repression; but, if it lifts its head at all, it will lift it only here and there and without countenance except from a lawless and malignant few.

It is a distressing and oppressive duty, gentlemen of the Congress, which I have performed in thus addressing you. There are, it may be, many months of fiery trial and sacrifice ahead of us. It is a fearful thing to lead this great peaceful people into war, into the most terrible and disastrous of all wars, civilization itself seeming to be in the balance. But the right is more precious than peace, and we shall fight for the things which we have always carried nearest our hearts – for democracy, for the right of those who submit to authority to have a voice in their own governments, for the rights and liberties of small nations, for a universal dominion of right by such a concert of free peoples as shall bring peace and safety to all nations and make the world itself at last free.

To such a task we can dedicate our lives and our fortunes, everything that we are and everything that we have, with the pride of those who know that the day has come when America is privileged to spend her blood and her might for the principles that gave her birth and happiness and the peace which she has treasured. God helping her, she can do no other.

50 PRESIDENT WILSON'S MESSAGES FOR WORLD PEACE: FOURTEEN POINTS (TO JOINT SESSION OF CONGRESS 8 JANUARY 1918) FOUR POINTS (MOUNT VERNON, 4 JULY 1918)

Introduction

The Fourteen Points became the agenda for the peace settlements that followed the First World War. In marked contrast with the spirit of the Vienna Congress, where the principal issues were territorial adjustments between rival empires, and where people were 'bartered about . . . as if they were mere chattels', Wilson's programme was based on two new principles: self-determination and international organisation. The first demanded that government must rest upon the consent of the governed and the principle of nationality; it was implemented by Points 6–13. The second new idea, spelled out in Point 14, soon came to assume the form of the League of Nations. The message of the Fourteen Points was reiterated many times by Wilson on various occasions throughout 1918, for example at Mount Vernon in July, in his Four Points. By the end of that year, the new principles were seen to have gained 'about universal acceptance . . . especially by the liberal and labour groups of the allied nations' (Baker, 1922–3, Vol. I, p. 19).

Texts

President Wilson's Fourteen Points

We entered this war because violations of right had occurred which touched us to the quick and made the life of our own people impossible unless they were corrected and the world secured once for all against their recurrence. What we demand in this war, therefore, is nothing peculiar to ourselves. It is that the world be made fit and safe to live in; and particularly that it be made safe for every peace-loving nation which, like our own, wishes to live its own life, determine its own institutions, be assured of justice and fair dealing by the other peoples of the world as against force and selfish aggression. All the peoples of the world are in effect partners in this interest, and for our own part we see very clearly that unless justice be done to others it will not be done to us. The programme of the world's peace, therefore, is our programme; and that programme, the only possible programme, as we see it, is this:

I. Open covenants of peace, openly arrived at, after which there shall be no private international understandings of any kind but diplomacy shall proceed always frankly and in the public view.

II. Absolute freedom of navigation upon the seas, outside territorial waters, alike in peace and in war, except as the seas may be closed in whole or in part by international action for the enforcement of international covenants.

Source: *Congressional Record*, Senate, Vol. 56, Part II, p. 11172.

III. The removal, so far as possible, of all economic barriers and the establishment of an equality of trade conditions among all the nations consenting to the peace and associating themselves for its maintenance.

IV. Adequate guarantees given and taken that national armaments will be reduced to the lowest point consistent with domestic safety.

V. A free, open-minded, and absolutely impartial adjustment of all colonial claims, based upon a strict observance of the principle that in determining all such questions of sovereignty the interests of the populations concerned must have equal weight with the equitable claims of the government whose title is to be determined.

VI. The evacuation of all Russian territory and such a settlement of all questions affecting Russia as will secure the best and freest coöperation of the other nations of the world in obtaining for her an unhampered and unembarrassed opportunity for the independent determination of her own political development and national policy and assure her of a sincere welcome into the society of free nations under institutions of her own choosing; and, more than a welcome, assistance also of every kind that she may need and may herself desire. The treatment accorded Russia by her sister nations in the months to come will be the acid test of their good will, of their comprehension of her needs as distinguished from their own interests, and of their intelligent and unselfish sympathy.

VII. Belgium, the whole world will agree, must be evacuated and restored, without any attempt to limit the sovereignty which she enjoys in common with all other free nations. No other single act will serve as this will serve to restore confidence among the nations in the laws which they have themselves set and determined for the government of their relations with one another. Without this healing act the whole structure and validity of international law is forever impaired.

VIII. All French territory should be freed and the invaded portions restored, and the wrong done to France by Prussia in 1871 in the matter of Alsace–Lorraine, which has unsettled the peace of the world for nearly fifty years, should be righted, in order that peace may once more be made secure in the interest of all.

IX. A readjustment of the frontiers of Italy should be effected along clearly recognizable lines of nationality.

X. The peoples of Austria–Hungary, whose place among the nations we wish to see safeguarded and assured, should be accorded the freest opportunity of autonomous development.

XI. Rumania, Serbia, and Montenegro should be evacuated; occupied territories restored; Serbia accorded free and secure access to the sea; and the relations of the several Balkan states to one another determined by friendly counsel along historically established lines of allegiance and nationality; and international guarantees of the political and economic independence and territorial integrity of the several Balkan states should be entered into.

XII. The Turkish portions of the present Ottoman Empire should be assured a secure sovereignty, but the other nationalities which are now under Turkish rule should be assured an undoubted security of life and absolutely unmolested opportunity of autonomous development, and the Dardanelles should be permanently opened as a free passage to the ships and commerce of all nations under international guarantees.

XIII. An independent Polish state should be erected which should include the territories inhabited by indisputably Polish populations, which should be assured a free and secure access to the sea, and whose political and economic independence and territorial integrity should be guaranteed by international covenant.

XIV. A general association of nations must be formed under specific covenants for the purpose of affording mutual guarantees of political independence and territorial integrity to great and small states alike.

In regard to these essential rectifications of wrong and assertions of right we feel ourselves to be intimate partners of all the governments and peoples associated together against the Imperialists. We cannot be separated in interest or divided in purpose. We stand together until the end.

* * *

We have spoken now, surely, in terms too concrete to admit of any further doubt or question. An evident principle runs through the whole programme I have outlined. It is the principle of justice to all peoples and nationalities, and their right to live on equal terms of liberty and safety with one another, whether they be strong or weak. Unless this principle be made its foundation no part of the structure of international justice can stand. The people of the United States could act upon no other principle; and to the vindication of this principle they are ready to devote their lives, their honor, and everything that they possess. The moral climax of this the culminating and final war for human liberty has come, and they are ready to put their own strength, their own highest purpose, their own integrity and devotion to the test.

President Wilson's Four Points
From His Address at Mount Vernon, 4 July 1918

I. The destruction of every arbitrary power anywhere that can separately, secretly, and of its single choice disturb the peace of the world; or, if it cannot be presently destroyed, at the least its reduction to virtual impotence.

II. The settlement of every question, whether of territory, of sovereignty, of economic arrangement, or of political relationship upon the basis of the free acceptance of that settlement by the people immediately concerned, and not upon the basis of the material interest or advantage of any other nation or people which may desire a different settlement for the sake of its own exterior influence or mastery.

III. The consent of all nations to be governed in their conduct toward each other by the same principles of honor and of respect for the common law of civilized society that govern the individual citizens of all modern States in their relations with one another; to the end that all promises and covenants may be sacredly observed, no private plots or conspiracies hatched, no selfish injuries wrought with impunity, and a mutual trust established upon the handsome foundation of a mutual respect for right.

IV. The establishment of an organization of peace which shall make it certain that the combined power of free nations will check every invasion of right and serve to make peace and justice the more secure by affording a definite tribunal of opinion to which all must submit and by which every international readjustment that cannot be amicably agreed upon by the peoples directly concerned shall be sanctioned. These great objects can be put into a single sentence. What we seek is the reign of law, based upon the consent of the governed and sustained by the organized opinion of mankind.

51 INVITATION TO THE FIRST CONGRESS OF THE COMMUNIST INTERNATIONAL, 24 JANUARY 1919

Introduction

The Second (Socialist) International that emerged in the closing decades of the nineteenth century was strongly influenced by the German Socialist Party, but the outbreak of the global war in 1914 destroyed that influence and caused the split that gave V. I. Lenin the opportunity to assert the leadership of the radical wing (Modelski, 1987, p. 190).

The foundation of a new international to replace the Second had been included in Lenin's April 1917 'theses' submitted to the central committee of the Bolshevik party, and the conference which followed resolved on 29 April 1917 that, 'It is the task of our party, acting in a country where the revolution has started earlier than in other countries, to take the initiative in creating a third international'.

The decision to convene an international conference of socialist parties and groups opposed to the Second International with the object of establishing the new and revolutionary international was taken hurriedly, coinciding with the opening of the Versailles Peace Conference, whose first plenary session was held on 18 January 1919 and when it also became known that an attempt to re-form the Second International was to be made. Hopes of wide representation were not entertained, since Russia was at the time virtually cut off from Europe, and the difficulties of communication and travel were very great. The Bolshevik leaders resorted to transmission by radio for this as for other communications to the outside world.

The invitation was drafted by Trotsky, and approved by a small committee which included Lenin and Chicherin, at that time Commissar for Foreign Affairs; it was first published in *Pravda* on 24 January, 1919. The lack of precision in the names of the parties and organisations to which it was addressed reflects both the confused state of labour organisations at the end of the First World War, and the ignorance of the Bolshevik leaders about developments in other countries. The signatories were all in Moscow.

Source: Degras, Jane (ed.), *The Communist International 1919–1943: Documents*, Vol. I (1919–1922) (London: Oxford University Press, 1956) pp. 1–5. Reprinted by permission.

Text

The undersigned parties and organizations consider it urgently necessary to convene the first congress of a new revolutionary international. During the war and the revolution it became conclusively clear not only that the old socialist and social-democratic parties, and with them the Second International, had become completely bankrupt, not only that the half-way elements of the old social-democracy (the so called 'centre') are incapable of positive revolutionary action, but that the outlines of a real revolutionary international are already clearly defined. The gigantic pace of the world revolution, constantly presenting new problems, the danger that this revolution may be throttled by the alliance of capitalist States, which are banding together against the revolution under the hypocritical banner of the 'League of Nations', the attempts of the social-traitors' parties to get together and, having 'amnestied' each other, to help their governments and their bourgeoisie to deceive the working classes once more; finally, the extraordinarily rich revolutionary experience already gained and the internationalization of the entire revolutionary movement, compel us to take the initiative in placing on the order of the day the convening of an international congress of revolutionary proletarian parties.

I. Aims and Tactics

In our opinion the new international should be based on the recognition of the following propositions, put forward here as a platform and worked out on the basis of the programme of the Spartakusbund in Germany and of the Communist Party (Bolsheviks) in Russia:

1. The present epoch is the epoch of the disintegration and collapse of the entire capitalist world system, which will drag the whole of European civilization down with it if capitalism with its insoluble contradictions is not destroyed.
2. The task of the proletariat now is to seize State power immediately. The seizure of State power means the destruction of the State apparatus of the bourgeoisie and the organization of a new proletarian apparatus of power.
3. This new apparatus of power should embody the dictatorship of the working class (and in some places also of the rural semi-proletariat, the village poor), that is, it should be the instrument for the systematic suppression of the exploiting classes and for their expropriation. Not false bourgeois democracy – that hypocritical form of the rule of the financial oligarchy – with its purely formal equality, but proletarian democracy, which gives the working masses the opportunity to make a reality of their freedom; not parliamentarianism, but self-government of these masses by their elected organs; not capitalist bureaucracy, but organs of administration created by the masses themselves, with the masses really taking part in the government of the country and in socialist construction – this should be the type of the proletarian State. Its concrete form is given in the regime of the Soviets or of similar organs.
4. The dictatorship of the proletariat must be the lever for the immediate expropriation of capital and for the abolition of private property in the means of production and their transformation into national property. The nationalization of large-scale industry (nationalization being understood as the abolition of private ownership and transference to the ownership of the proletarian State, to come under the socialist management of the working class) and of its organizing centres, the banks; confiscation of the estates of the large landowners and nationalization of capitalist agricultural production; monopoly of wholesale trade, nationalization

of large houses in towns and on large estates; introduction of workers' management and centralization of economic functions in the hands of agencies of the proletarian dictatorship – these are the essential problems of the day.

5. In order to safeguard the socialist revolution, to defend it against internal and external enemies, to give aid to other national sections of the fighting proletariat, etc., it is essential to disarm the bourgeoisie and their agents completely, and to arm the proletariat.

6. The world situation today demands the closest possible contact between the different sections of the revolutionary proletariat and a complete union of the countries where the socialist revolution has already triumphed.

7. The basic methods of struggle are mass actions of the proletariat right up to open armed conflict with the political power of capital.

2. *Attitude to 'Socialist' Parties*

8. The old 'International' has broken down into three main groups: the avowed social-chauvinists, who throughout the imperialist war of 1914 to 1918 supported their own bourgeoisie and turned the working class into executioners of the international revolution; the 'centre', whose theoretical leader is Kautsky, consisting of those elements who are always vacillating, incapable of a firm line of conduct, and at times outright treacherous; finally there is the left revolutionary wing.

9. Towards the social-chauvinists, who everywhere at critical moments come out in arms against the proletarian revolution, no other attitude but unrelenting struggle is possible. As to the 'centre' – the tactics of splitting off the revolutionary elements, and unsparing criticism and exposure of the leaders. Organizational separation from the centrists is at a certain stage of development absolutely essential.

10. On the other hand, it is necessary to form a bloc with those elements in the revolutionary workers' movement who, although they did not formerly belong to socialist parties, now stand by and large for the proletarian dictatorship in the form of Soviet power. Chief among these are the syndicalist elements in the workers' movement.

11. Finally it is necessary to draw in all those proletarian groups and organizations which, although they have not openly attached themselves to the left revolutionary tendency, nevertheless appear to be moving in this direction.

12. In concrete terms, we propose that representatives of the following parties, groups, and trends shall take part in the congress (full membership of the Third International shall be open to those parties which stand completely on its platform):

1. The Spartakusbund (Communist Party of Germany)
2. The Communist Party (Bolsheviks) of Russia
3. The Communist Party of Germany–Austria
4. The Communist Party of Hungary
5. The Communist Party of Poland
6. The Communist Party of Finland
7. The Communist Party of Estonia
8. The Communist Party of Latvia
9. The Communist Party of Lithuania
10. The Communist Party of White Russia
11. The Communist Party of Ukraine
12. The revolutionary elements in the Czech Social-Democratic Party

13. The 'narrow' Bulgarian Social-Democratic Party (Tesniaki)
14. The Rumanian Social-Democratic Party
15. The left wing of the Serbian Social-Democratic Party
16. The left Social-Democratic Party of Sweden
17. The Norwegian Social-Democratic Party
18. The 'Klassenkampen' group in Denmark
19. The Communist Party of Holland
20. The revolutionary elements in the Belgian Labour Party

21 and 22. The groups and organizations within the French socialist and syndicalist movement which by and large support Loriot

23. The left social-democrats of Switzerland
24. The Italian Socialist Party
25. The left elements in the Spanish Socialist Party
26. The left elements in the Portuguese Socialist Party
27. The left elements in the British Socialist Party (in particular the group represented by Maclean)
28. The Socialist Labour Party (England)
29. The I W W (England)
30. The I W of Great Britain
31. The revolutionary elements among the Shop Stewards (Great Britain)
32. The revolutionary elements in the Irish workers' organizations
33. The Socialist Workers' Party of America
34. The left elements in the American Socialist Party (in particular the group represented by Debs and the League for Socialist Propaganda)
35. The I W W (America)
36. The I W W (Australia)
37. The Workers' International Industrial Union (America)
38. Socialist groups in Tokyo and Yokohama (represented by comrade Katayama)
39. The Socialist Youth International (represented by comrade Münzenberg)

3. *The Question of Organization and the Name of the Party*

13. The basis of the Third International is already provided by the existence, in various parts of Europe, of groups and organizations of likeminded comrades which have a common platform and by and large use the same tactical methods. Chief among these are the Spartakists in Germany and the communist parties in many other countries.

14. The congress must establish a common fighting organ for the purpose of maintaining permanent co-ordination and systematic leadership of the movement, a centre of the communist international, subordinating the interests of the movement in each country to the common interest of the international revolution. The actual form to be taken by the organization, representation on it, etc., will be worked out by the congress.

15. The congress must assume the name of 'The first congress of the Communist International', and the individual parties shall become its sections. Marx and Engels had already found the name 'social-democrat' theoretically incorrect. The shameful collapse of the social-democratic 'International' also makes a break on this point necessary. Finally, the kernel of the great movement is already formed by a number of parties which have taken this name. In view of the above, we propose to all fraternal parties and organizations to discuss the

question of the convening of the international communist congress. With fraternal greetings.

The Central Committee of the Russian Communist Party (LENIN, TROTSKY)
The foreign bureau of the Communist Workers' Party of Poland (KARSKI)
The foreign bureau of the Communist Party of Hungary (RUDNIANSKY)
The foreign bureau of the Communist Party of German-Austria (DUDA)
The Russian bureau of the Central Committee of the Latvian Communist Party (ROZIN)
The Central Committee of the Communist Party of Finland (SIROLA)
The Executive Committee of the Balkan Revolutionary Social-Democratic Federation (RAKOVSKY)
For the Socialist Workers' Party of America (REINSTEIN)

52 RESERVATIONS PRESENTED TO THE UNITED STATES SENATE ON 6 NOVEMBER 1919 BY SENATOR HENRY CABOT LODGE, CHAIRMAN OF THE FOREIGN RELATIONS COMMITTEE

Text

The Committee proposes four reservations to be made a part of the resolution of ratification when it is offered. The Committee reserves, of course, the right to offer other reservations if they shall so determine. The four reservations now presented are as follows:

1. The United States reserves to itself the unconditional right to withdraw from the league of nations upon the notice provided in article 1 of the said treaty of peace with Germany.

The provision in the league covenant for withdrawal declares that any member may withdraw provided it has fulfilled all its international obligations and all its obligations under the covenant. There has been much dispute as to who would decide if the question of the fulfillment of obligations was raised, and it is very generally thought that this question would be settled by the council of the league of nations. The best that can be said about it is that the question of decision is clouded with doubt. On such a point as this there must be no doubt. The United States, which has never broken an international obligation, can not permit all its existing treaties to be reviewed and its conduct and honor questioned by other nations. The same may be said in regard to the fulfillment of the obligations to the league. It must be made perfectly clear that the United States alone is to determine as to the fulfillment of its obligations, and its right of withdrawal must therefore be unconditional as provided in the reservation.

2. The United States declines to assume, under the provisions of article 10, or under any other article, any obligation to preserve the territorial integrity or political independence of any other country or to interfere in controversies between other nations, members of the league or not, or to employ the military or naval forces of the United States in such controversies, or to adopt economic measures, for the protection of any other country, whether a member of the league or not, against external aggression or for the purpose of coercing any other country, or for the purpose of intervention in the internal conflicts or other controversies which may arise in any other country, and no mandate shall be accepted by the United States under article 22, Part I, of the treaty of peace with Germany except by action of the Congress of the United States.

This reservation is intended to meet the most vital objection to the league covenant as it stands. Under no circumstances must there be any legal or moral obligation upon the United States to enter into war or to send its Army and Navy abroad or without the unfettered action of Congress to impose economic boycotts on other countries. Under the Constitution of the United States the Congress alone has the power to declare war, and all bills to raise revenue or affecting the revenue in any way must originate in the House of Representatives, be passed by

Source: Lodge, Henry Cabot, *The Senate and the League of Nations* (New York, London: Scribners, 1925) pp. 172–7.

the Senate, and receive the signature of the President. These constitutional rights of Congress must not be impaired by any agreements such as are presented in this treaty, nor can any opportunity of charging the United States with bad faith be permitted. No American soldiers or sailors must be sent to fight in other lands at the bidding of a league of nations. American lives must not be sacrificed except by the will and command of the American people acting through their constitutional representatives in Congress.

This reservation also covers the subject of mandates. According to the provisions of the covenant of the league the acceptance of a mandate by any member is voluntary, but as to who shall have authority to refuse or to accept a mandate for any country the covenant of the league is silent. The decision as to accepting a mandate must rest exclusively within the control of the Congress of the United States as the reservation provides and must not be delegated, even by inference, to any personal agent or to any delegate or commissioner.

3. The United States reserves to itself exclusively the right to decide what questions are within its domestic jurisdiction, and declares that all domestic and political questions relating to its affairs, including immigration, coastwise traffic, the tariff, commerce, and all other domestic questions, are solely within the jurisdiction of the United States and are not under this treaty submitted in any way either to arbitration or to the consideration of the council or of the assembly of the league of nations, or to the decision or recommendation of any other power.

This reservation speaks for itself. It is not necessary to follow out here all tortuous windings, which to those who have followed them through the labyrinth disclose the fact that the league under certain conditions will have power to pass upon and decide questions of immigration and tariff, as well as the others mentioned in the reservation. It is believed by the committee that this reservation relieves the United States from any dangers or any obligations in this direction.

The fourth and last reservation is as follows:

4. The United States declines to submit for arbitration or inquiry by the assembly or the council of the league of nations provided for in said treaty of peace any questions which in the judgment of the United States depend upon or relate to its long-established policy, commonly known as the Monroe doctrine; said doctrine is to be interpreted by the United States alone, and is hereby declared to be wholly outside the jurisdiction of said league of nations and entirely unaffected by any provision contained in the said treaty of peace with Germany.

The purpose of this reservation is clear. It is intended to preserve the Monroe doctrine from any interference or interpretation by foreign powers. As the Monroe doctrine has protected the United States, so, it is believed by the Committee, will this reservation protect the Monroe doctrine from the destruction with which it is threatened by article 21 in the covenant of the league and leave it, where it has always been, within the sole and complete control of the United States.

This covenant of the league of nations is an alliance and not a league, as is amply shown by the provisions of the treaty with Germany which vests all essential power in five great nations. Those same nations, the principal allied and associated powers, also dominate the league through the council.

The Committee believe that the league as it stands will breed wars instead of securing peace. They also believe that the covenant of the league demands sacrifices of American independence and sovereignty which would in no way promote the world's peace but which are fraught with the gravest dangers to the future safety and well being of the United States. The amendments and reservations alike are governed by a single purpose and that is to guard American rights and American sovereignty, the invasion of which would stimulate breaches of faith, encourage conflicts, and generate wars. The United States can serve the cause of peace best, as she has served it in the past, and do more to secure liberty and civilization throughout the world by proceeding along the paths she has always followed and by not permitting herself to be fettered by the dictates of other nations or immersed and entangled in all the broils and conflicts of Europe.

We have heard it frequently said that the United States 'must' do this and do that in regard to this league of nations and the terms of the German peace. There is no 'must' about it. 'Must' is not a word to be used by foreign nations or domestic officials to the American people or their representatives. Equally unfitting is the attempt to frighten the unthinking by suggesting that if the Senate adopts amendments or reservations the United States may be excluded from the league. That is the one thing that certainly will not happen. The other nations know well that there is no threat of retaliation possible with the United States because we have asked nothing for ourselves and have received nothing. We seek no guarantees, no territory, no commercial benefits or advantages. The other nations will take us on our own terms, for without us their league is a wreck and all their gains from a victorious peace are imperiled. We exact nothing selfish for ourselves, but we insist that we shall be the judges, and the only judges, as to the preservation of our rights, our sovereignty, our safety, and our independence.

At this moment the United States is free from any entanglements or obligations which legally or in the name of honor would compel her to do anything contrary to the dictates of conscience or to the freedom and in the interests of the American people. This is the hour when we can say precisely what we will do and exactly what we will not do, and no man can ever question our good faith if we speak now. When we are once caught in the meshes of a treaty of alliance or a league of nations composed of 26 other powers our freedom of action is gone. To preserve American independence and American sovereignty and thereby best serve the welfare of mankind the Committee propose these amendments and reservations.

53 ROOSEVELT–CHURCHILL CORRESPONDENCE (1939–40)

Texts

(a) *Roosevelt to Churchill*

September 11, 1939

My dear Churchill:

It is because you and I occupied similar positions in the World War[1] that I want you to know how glad I am that you are back again in the Admiralty. Your problems are, I realize, complicated by new factors but the essential is not very different. What I want you and the Prime Minister[2] to know is that I shall at all times welcome it if you will keep me in touch personally with anything you want me to know about. You can always send sealed letters through your pouch or my pouch.

I am glad you did the Marlboro [*sic*] volumes[3] before this thing started – and I much enjoyed reading them.

Sources: Loewenheim, Francis L., Harold D. Langley, Manfred Jonas (eds), *Roosevelt and Churchill: their secret wartime correspondence* (New York: Saturday Review Press/E.P. Dutton, 1975) pp. (a) 89, (b) 94–5, (c) 108–9; Kimball, Warren F. (ed.), *Roosevelt and Churchill: the complete correspondence* (Princeton: Princeton University Press, 1984) Vol. I, pp. (d) 102–9 (underlining omitted).

1. Roosevelt served as Assistant Secretary of the Navy from 1913 to 1920, Churchill as First Lord of the Admiralty from 1911 to 1915.
2. Neville Chamberlain became Prime Minister of Great Britain on 28 May 1937.
3. The fourth and final volume of Churchill's *Marlborough – His Life and Times* had appeared in 1938.

(b) *Churchill to Roosevelt*

May 15, 1940

Although I have changed my office,[4] I am sure you would not wish me to discontinue our intimate, private correspondence. As you are no doubt aware, the scene has darkened swiftly.[5] The enemy have a marked preponderance in the air,[6] and their new technique is making a deep impression upon the French.[7] I think myself the battle on land has only just begun, and I should like to see tanks engaged. Up to the present, Hitler is working with specialised units in tanks and air. The small countries are simply smashed up, one by one, like matchwood. We must expect, though it is not yet certain, that Mussolini will hurry in to share the loot of civilization. We expect to be attacked here ourselves, both from the air and by parachute and airborne troops in the near future, and are getting ready for them. If necessary, we shall continue the war alone and we are not afraid of that. But I trust you realise, Mr. President, that the voice and force of the United States may count for nothing if they are withheld too long. You may have a completely subjugated, Nazified Europe established with astounding swiftness, and the weight may be more than we can bear. All I ask now is that you should proclaim nonbelligerency, which would mean that you would help us with everything short of actually engaging armed forces. Immediate needs are: first of all, the loan of forty or fifty of your older destroyers to bridge the gap between what we have now and the large new construction we put in hand at the beginning of the war. This time next year we shall have plenty. But if in the interval Italy comes in against us with another one hundred submarines, we may be strained to the breaking point. Secondly, we want several hundred of the latest types of aircraft, of which you are now getting delivery. These can be repaid by those now being constructed in the United States for us. Thirdly, anti-aircraft equipment and ammunition, of which again there will be plenty next year, if we are alive to see it. Fourthly, the fact that our ore supply is being compromised from Sweden, from North America, and perhaps from northern Spain makes it necessary to purchase steel in the United States. This also applies to other materials. We shall go on paying dollars for as long as we can, but I should like to feel reasonably sure that when we can pay no more, you will give us the stuff all the same. Fifthly, we have many reports of possible German parachute or airborne descents in Ireland. The visit of a United States squadron to Irish ports, which might well be prolonged, would be invaluable. Sixthly, I am looking to you to keep that Japanese dog quiet in the Pacific, using Singapore in any way convenient. The details of the material which we have in mind will be communicated to you separately.

4. Churchill had succeeded Neville Chamberlain as Prime Minister on 10 May.
5. The long-planned German attack on France, the Low Countries, and Luxembourg had begun early on the morning of 10 May.
6. On 14 May the German air force had carried out a terror raid, the first of its kind in the west, on Rotterdam, killing nearly 900 people and rendering nearly 80 000 homeless. The following morning the Dutch military forces capitulated.
7. On 14 May French Premier Paul Reynaud had pleaded with the British government to send ten more fighter squadrons; he repeated his appeal the following morning.

(c) *Roosevelt to Churchill*

August 13, 1940

It is my belief that it may be possible to furnish to the British Government as immediate assistance at least fifty destroyers, the motor torpedo boats heretofore referred to, and, insofar as airplanes are concerned, five planes each of the categories mentioned, the latter to be furnished for war-testing purposes. Such assistance, as I am sure you will understand, would only be furnished if the American people and the Congress frankly recognized that in return therefor the national defense and security of the United States would be enhanced. For that reason it would be necessary, in the event that it proves possible to release the matériel above mentioned, that the British Government find itself able and willing to take the following steps:

1. Assurance on the part of the Prime Minister that in the event that the waters of Great Britain become untenable for British ships of war, the latter would not be turned over to the Germans or sunk but would be sent to other parts of the Empire for continued defense of the Empire.
2. An agreement on the part of Great Britain that the British Government would authorize the use of Newfoundlands, Bermuda, the Bahamas, Jamaica, St. Lucia, Trinidad, and British Guiana as naval and air bases by the United States in the event of an attack on the American hemisphere by any non-American nation; and in the meantime the United States to have the right to establish such bases and to use them for training and exercise purposes with the understanding that the land necessary for the above could be acquired by the United States through purchase or through ninety-nine-year lease.

With the agreement suggested in point 2 above, I feel confident that specific details need not be considered at this time and that such questions as the exact locations of the land which the United States might desire to purchase or lease could be readily determined upon subsequently through friendly negotiation between the two Governments . . .

(d) *Churchill to Roosevelt*

London
December 7th, 1940. [Dated Dec. 8 in PREM 3/486/1.]

My Dear Mr. President,

As we reach the end of this year I feel that you will expect me to lay before you the prospects for 1941. I do so strongly and confidently because it seems to me that the vast majority of American citizens have recorded their conviction that the safety of the United States as well as the future of our two democracies and the kind of civilisation for which they stand are bound up with the survival and independence of the British Commonwealth of Nations. Only thus can those bastions of sea-power, upon which the control of the Atlantic and the Indian Oceans depends, be preserved in faithful and friendly hands. The control of the Pacific by the United States Navy and of the Atlantic by the British Navy is indispensable to the security of the trade routes of both our countries and the surest means to preventing the war from reaching the shores of the United States.

2. There is another aspect. It takes between three and four years to convert the industries of a modern state to war purposes. Saturation point is reached when the maximum industrial effort that can be spared from civilian needs has been applied to war production. Germany certainly reached this point by the end of 1939. We in the British Empire are now only about half-way through the second year. The United States, I should suppose, was by no means so far advanced as we. Moreover, I understand that immense programmes of naval, military and air defence are now on foot in the United States, to complete which certainly two years are needed. It is our British duty in the common interest as also for our own survival to hold the front and grapple with Nazi power until the preparations of the United States are complete. Victory may come before the next two years are out; but we have no right to count upon it to the extent of relaxing any effort that is humanly possible. Therefore I submit with very great respect for your good and friendly consideration that there is a solid identity of interest between the British Empire and the United States while these conditions last. It is upon this footing that I venture to address you.

3. The form which this war has taken and seems likely to hold does not enable us to match the immense armies of Germany in any theatre where their main power can be brought to bear. We can however by the use of sea power and air power meet the German armies in the regions where only comparatively small forces can be brought into action. We must do our best to prevent German domination of Europe spreading into Africa and into Southern Asia. We have also to maintain in constant readiness in this Island armies strong enough to make the problem of an overseas invasion insoluble. For these purposes we are forming as fast as possible, as you are already aware, between fifty and sixty divisions. Even if the United States was our ally instead of our friend and indispensable partner we should not ask for a large American expeditionary army. Shipping, not men, is the limiting factor and the power to transport munitions and supplies claims priority over the movement by sea of large numbers of soldiers.

4. The first half of 1940 was a period of disaster for the Allies and for the Empire. The last five months have witnessed a strong and perhaps unexpected recovery by Great Britain; fighting alone but with invaluable aid in munitions and in destroyers placed at our disposal by the great Republic of which you are for the third time chosen Chief.

5. The danger of Great Britain being destroyed by a swift overwhelming blow

has for the time being very greatly receded. In its place there is a long, gradually maturing danger, less sudden and less spectacular but equally deadly. This mortal danger is the steady and increasing diminution of sea tonnage. We can endure the shattering of our dwellings and the slaughter of our civilian population by indiscriminate air attacks and we hope to parry these increasingly as our science develops and to repay them upon military objectives in Germany as our Air Force more nearly approaches the strength of the enemy. The decision for 1941 lies upon the seas; unless we can establish our ability to feed this Island, to import munitions of all kinds which we need, unless we can move our armies to the various theatres where Hitler and his confederate Mussolini must be met, and maintain them there and do all this with the assurance of being able to carry it on till the spirit of the continental dictators is broken, we may fall by the way and the time needed by the United States to complete her defensive preparations may not be forthcoming. It is therefore in shipping and in the power to transport across the oceans, particularly the Atlantic Ocean, that in 1941 the crunch of the whole war will be found. If on the other hand we are able to move the necessary tonnage to and fro across the salt water indefinitely, it may well be that the application of superior air power to the German homeland and the rising anger of the German and other Nazi-gripped populations will bring the agony of civilization to a merciful and glorious end. But do not let us underrate the task.

6. Our shipping losses, the figures for which in recent months are appended, have been on a scale almost comparable to that of the worst years of the last war. In the 5 weeks ending November 3rd the losses reached a total of 420 300 tons. Our estimation of the annual tonnage which ought to be imported in order to maintain our war effort at full strength is 43 000 000 tons; the tonnage entering in September was only at the rate of 37 000 000 tons and in October at 38 000 000 tons. Were the diminution to continue at this rate it would be fatal, unless indeed immensely greater replenishment than anything at present in sight could be achieved in time. Although we are doing all we can to meet this situation by new methods, the difficulty of limiting the losses is obviously much greater than in the last war. We lack the assistance of the French Navy, the Italian Navy and the Japanese Navy, and above all the United States Navy, which was of such vital help to us during the culminating years. The enemy commands the ports all around the northern and western coast of France. He is increasingly basing his submarines, flying boats and combat planes on these ports and on the islands off the French coast. We lack the use of ports or territory in Eire in which to organise our coastal patrols by air and sea. In fact, we have now only one effective passage of entry to the British Isles namely, the northern approach, against which the enemy is increasingly concentrating, reaching ever farther out by the U-boat action and long distance bombing. In addition, there have for some months been merchant ship raiders both in the Atlantic and in the Indian Oceans. And now we have powerful warship raiders to contend with as well. We need ships both to hunt down and to escort. Large as are our resources and preparations we do not possess enough.

7. The next six or seven months bring the relative battleship strength in home waters to a smaller margin than is satisfactory. The *Bismarck* and the *Tirpitz* will certainly be in service in January. We have already the *King George V* and hope to have the *Prince of Wales* at the same time. These modern ships are of course far better armoured, especially against air attack, than vessels like the *Rodney* and *Nelson* designed twenty years ago. We have recently had to use the *Rodney* on trans-Atlantic escort and at any time when numbers are so small, a mine or a torpedo may alter decisively the strength of the line of battle. We get relief in

June when the *Duke of York* will be ready and will be still better off at the end of 1941 when the *Anson* also will have joined. But these two first class, modern, thirty-five thousand ton, fifteen inch gun German battleships force us to maintain a concentration never previously necessary in this war.

8. We hope that the two Italian *Littorios* will be out of action for a while and anyway they are not so dangerous as if they were manned by the Germans. Perhaps they might be! We are indebted to you for your help about the *Richelieu* and the *Jean Bart* and I daresay that will be all right. But, Mr. President, as no one will see more clearly than you, we have during these months to consider for the first time in this war, a fleet action in which the enemy will have two ships at least as good [as] our two best and only two modern ones. It will be impossible to reduce our strength in the Mediterranean because of the attitude of Turkey and indeed the whole position in the Eastern basin depends upon our having a strong fleet there. The older un-modernized battleships will have to go for convoy. Thus even in the battleship class we are at full extension.

9. There is a second field of danger: the Vichy Government may either by joining Hitler's new order in Europe or through some manoeuvre such as forcing us to attack an expedition despatched by sea against free French Colonies, find an excuse for ranging with the Axis Powers the very considerable undamaged naval forces still under its control. If the French Navy were to join the Axis, the control of West Africa would pass immediately into their hands with the gravest consequence to our communications between the northern and southern Atlantic, and also affect Dakar and of course thereafter South America.

10. A third sphere of danger is in the Far East. Here it seems clear that the Japanese are thrusting Southward through Indo China to Saigon and other naval and air bases, thus bringing them within a comparatively short distance of Singapore and the Dutch East Indies. It is reported that the Japanese are preparing five good divisions for possible use as an overseas expeditionary force. We have to-day no forces in the Far East capable of dealing with this situation should it develop.

11. In the face of these dangers, we must try to use the year 1941 to build up such a supply of weapons, particularly aircraft, both by increased output at home in spite of bombardment, and through ocean-borne supplies, as will lay the foundation of victory. In view of the difficulty and magnitude of this task, as outlined by all the facts I have set forth to which many others could be added, I feel entitled, nay bound, to lay before you the various ways in which the United States could give supreme and decisive help to what is, in certain aspects, the common cause.

12. The prime need is to check or limit the loss of tonnage on the Atlantic approaches to our Islands. This may be achieved both by increasing the naval forces which cope with attacks, and by adding to the number of merchant ships on which we depend. For the first purpose there would seem to be the following alternatives:

(1) The reassertion by the United States of the doctrine of the freedom of the seas from illegal and barbarous warfare in accordance with the decisions reached after the late Great War, and as freely accepted and defined by Germany in 1935. From this, the United States ships should be free to trade with countries against which there is not an effective legal blockade.

(2) It would, I suggest, follow that protection should be given to this lawful trading by United States forces i.e. escorting battleships, cruisers, destroyers and air flotillas. Protection would be immediately more effective if you were able to

obtain bases in Eire for the duration of the war. I think it is improbable that such protection would provoke a declaration of war by Germany upon the United States though probably sea incidents of a dangerous character would from time to time occur. Hitler has shown himself inclined to avoid the Kaiser's mistake. He does not wish to be drawn into war with the United States until he has gravely undermined the power of Great Britain. His maxim is 'one at a time'. The policy I have ventured to outline, or something like it, would constitute a decisive act of constructive non-belligerency by the United States, and more than any other measure would make certain that British resistance could be effectively prolonged for the desired period and victory gained.

(3) Failing the above, the gift, loan or supply of a large number of American vessels of war, above all destroyers already in the Atlantic, is indispensable to the maintenance of the Atlantic route. Further, could not United States naval forces extend their sea control over the American side of the Atlantic, so as to prevent molestation by enemy vessels of the approaches to the new line of naval and air bases which the United States is establishing in British islands in the Western Hemisphere. The strength of the United States naval forces is such that the assistance in the Atlantic that they could afford us, as described above, would not jeopardise control over the Pacific.

(4) We should also then need the good offices of the United States and the whole influence of its Government continually exerted, to procure for Great Britain the necessary facilities upon the southern and western shores of Eire for our flotillas, and still more important, for our aircraft, working westward into the Atlantic. If it were proclaimed an American interest that the resistance of Great Britain should be prolonged and the Atlantic route kept open for the important armaments now being prepared for Great Britain in North America, the Irish in the United States might be willing to point out to the Government of Eire the dangers which its present policy is creating for the United States itself.

His Majesty's Government would of course take the most effective steps beforehand to protect Ireland if Irish action exposed it to a German attack. It is not possible for us to compel the people of Northern Ireland against their will to leave the United Kingdom and join Southern Ireland. But I do not doubt that if the Government of Eire would show its solidarity with the democracies of the English speaking world at this crisis a Council of Defence of all Ireland could be set up out of which the unity of the island would probably in some form or other emerge after the war.

13. The object of the foregoing measures is to reduce to manageable proportions the present destructive losses at sea. In addition it is indispensable that the merchant tonnage available for supplying Great Britain and for the waging of the war by Great Britain with all vigour, should be substantially increased beyond the one and a quarter million tons per annum which is the utmost we can now build. The convoy system, the detours, the zig-zags, the great distances from which we now have to bring our imports, and the congestion of our western harbours, have reduced by about one third the value of our existing tonnage. To ensure final victory, not less than three million tons of additional merchant ship-building capacity will be required. Only the United States can supply this need. Looking to the future it would seem that production on a scale comparable with that of the Hog Island scheme of the last war ought to be faced for 1942. In the meanwhile, we ask that in 1941 the United States should make available to us every ton of merchant shipping, surplus to its own requirements, which it possesses or controls and should find some means of putting into our

'hands' a large proportion of the merchant shipping now under construction for the National Maritime Board.

14. Moreover we look to the industrial energy of the Republic for a reinforcement of our domestic capacity to manufacture combat aircraft. Without that reinforcement reaching us in a substantial measure, we shall not achieve the massive preponderance in the air on which we must rely to loosen and disintegrate the German grip on Europe. The development of the Air Forces of the Empire provides for a total of nearly 7000 combat aircraft in the fighting squadrons by the spring of 1942, backed by about an equal number in the training units. But it is abundantly clear that this programme will not suffice to give us the weighty superiority which will force open the doors of victory. In order to achieve such superiority it is plain that we shall need the greatest production of aircraft which United States of America are capable of sending us. It is our anxious hope that in the teeth of continuing bombardment we shall realize the greater part of production which we have planned in this country. But not even with the addition to our squadrons of all the aircraft which under present arrangements, we may derive from the planned output in the United States can we hope to achieve the necessary ascendancy. May I invite you then, Mr. President, to give earnest consideration to an immediate order on joint account for a further 2000 combat aircraft a month? Of these aircraft I would submit that the highest possible proportion should be heavy bombers, the weapon on which above all others we depend to shatter the foundations of German military power. I am aware of the formidable task that this would impose upon the industrial organisation of the United States. Yet, in our heavy need, we call with confidence to the most resourceful and ingenious technicians in the world. We ask for an unexampled effort believing that it can be made.

15. You have also received information about the needs of our armies. In the munitions sphere, in spite of enemy bombing, we are making steady progress. Without your continued assistance in the supply of machine tools and in the further release from stock of certain articles we could not hope to equip as many as 50 divisions in 1941. I am grateful for the arrangements already practically completed for your aid in the equipment of the army which we have already planned and for the provision of American-type weapons for an additional 10 divisions in time for the campaign of 1942. But when the tide of dictatorship begins to recede many countries, trying to regain their freedom, may be asking for arms, and there is no source to which they can look except to the factories of the United States. I must therefore also urge the importance of expanding to the utmost American productive capacity for small arms, artillery and tanks.

16. I am arranging to present you with a complete programme of munitions of all kinds which we seek to obtain from you, the greater part of which is of course already agreed. An important economy of time and effort will be produced if the types selected for the United States Services should, whenever possible, conform to those which have proved their merit under actual conditions of war. In this way reserves of guns and ammunition and of aeroplanes become inter-changeable and are by that very fact augmented. This is however a sphere so highly technical that I do not enlarge upon it.

17. Last of all I come to the question of finance. The more rapid and abundant the flow of munitions and ships which you are able to send us, the sooner will our dollar credits be exhausted. They are already as you know very heavily drawn upon by payments we have made to date. Indeed as you know orders already placed or under negotiation, including expenditure settled or pending for creating munitions factories in the United States, many times exceed

the total exchange resources remaining at the disposal of Great Britain. The moment approaches when we shall no longer be able to pay cash for shipping and other supplies. While we will do our utmost and shrink from no proper sacrifice to make payments across the exchange, I believe that you will agree that it would be wrong in principle, and mutually disadvantageous in effect if, at the height of this struggle, Great Britain were to be divested of all saleable assets so that after victory was won with our blood, civilisation saved and time gained for the United States to be fully armed against all eventualities, we should stand stripped to the bone. Such a course would not be in the moral or economic interests of either of our countries. We here would be unable after the war to purchase the large balance of imports from the United States over and above the volume of our exports which is agreeable to your tariffs and domestic economy. Not only should we in Great Britain suffer cruel privations but widespread unemployment in the United States would follow the curtailment of American exporting power.

18. Moreover I do not believe the Government and people of the United States would find it in accordance with the principles which guide them, to confine the help which they have so generously promised only to such munitions of war and commodities as could be immediately paid for. You may be assured that we shall prove ourselves ready to suffer and sacrifice to the utmost for the Cause, and that we glory in being its champion. The rest we leave with confidence to you and to your people, being sure that ways and means will be found which future generations on both sides of the Atlantic will approve and admire.

19. If, as I believe, you are convinced, Mr President, that the defeat of the Nazi and Fascist tyranny is a matter of high consequence to the people of the United States and to the Western Hemisphere, you will regard this letter not as an appeal for aid, but as a statement of the minimum action necessary to the achievement of our common purpose.

I remain, Yours very sincerely, Winston S. Churchill.

54 TRIPARTITE PACT SIGNED AT BERLIN BY THE AXIS POWERS, 27 SEPTEMBER 1940

Signatories Ribbentrop (Germany)
Ciano (Italy)
Kurusu (Japan)

Text

The Governments of Germany, Italy and Japan, considering it as a condition precedent of any lasting peace that all nations of the world be given each its own proper place, have decided to stand by and co-operate with one another in regard to their efforts in Greater East Asia and the regions of Europe respectively wherein it is their prime purpose to establish and maintain a new order of things calculated to promote the mutual prosperity and welfare of the peoples concerned.

Furthermore, it is the desire of the three Governments to extend co-operation to such nations in other spheres of the world as may be inclined to put forth endeavours along lines similar to their own, in order that their ultimate aspirations for world peace may thus be realised.

Accordingly, the Governments of Germany, Italy and Japan have agreed as follows:–

I. Japan recognises and respects the leadership of Germany and Italy in the establishment of a new order in Europe.

II. Germany and Italy recognise and respect the leadership of Japan in the establishment of a new order in Greater East Asia.

III. Germany, Italy and Japan agree to co-operate in their efforts on the aforesaid lines. They further undertake to assist one another with all political, economic and military means when one of the three contracting Powers is attacked by a Power at present not involved in the European war or in the Chinese–Japanese conflict.

IV. With a view to implementing the present pact, joint technical commissions, the members of which are to be appointed by the respective Governments of Germany, Italy, and Japan, will meet without delay.

V. Germany, Italy and Japan affirm that the aforesaid terms do not in any way affect the political status which exists at present as between each of the three contracting parties and Soviet Russia.

VI. The present pact shall come into effect immediately upon signature and shall remain in force ten years from the date of its coming into force. At the proper time before the expiration of the said term the high contracting parties shall at the request of any one of them enter into negotiations for its renewal.[1]

Source: HMSO (1942) Cmd 6388. (Translation.)

1. The German Government have announced the following accessions to the Tripartite Pact of Berlin: Hungary (20 November 1940), Roumania (23 November 1940), Slovakia (24 November 1940), Bulgaria (1 March 1941), Croatia (1 June 1941). Yugoslavia, which signed the pact on 25 March 1941, refused later to ratify.

55 FRANKLIN D. ROOSEVELT'S 'FOUR FREEDOMS' MESSAGE TO CONGRESS, 6 JANUARY 1941

Text

JUST AS OUR NATIONAL POLICY in internal affairs has been based upon a decent respect for the rights and dignity of all our fellow-men within our gates, so our national policy in foreign affairs has been based on a decent respect for the rights and dignity of all nations, large and small. And the justice of morality must and will win in the end.

Our national policy is this:

First, by an impressive expression of the public will and without regard to partisanship, we are committed to all-inclusive national defense.

Second, by an impressive expression of the public will and without regard to partisanship, we are committed to full support of all those resolute people, everywhere, who are resisting aggression and are thereby keeping war away from our Hemisphere. By this support, we express our determination that the domestic cause shall prevail, and we strengthen the defense and security of our own nation.

Third, by an impressive expression of the public will and without regard to partisanship, we are committed to the proposition that principles of morality and considerations for our own security will never permit us to acquiesce in a peace dictated by aggressors and sponsored by appeasers. We know that enduring peace cannot be bought at the cost of other people's freedom.

In the recent national election there was no substantial difference between the two great parties in respect to that national policy. No issue was fought out on this line before the American electorate. Today it is abundantly evident that American citizens everywhere are demanding and supporting speedy and complete action in recognition of obvious danger. Therefore, the immediate need is a swift and driving increase in our armament production.

Leaders of industry and labor have responded to our summons. Goals of speed have been set. In some cases these goals are being reached ahead of time; in some cases we are on schedule; in other cases there are slight but not serious delays; and in some cases – and I am sorry to say very important cases – we are all concerned by the slowness of the accomplishment of our plans. The Army and Navy, however, have made substantial progress during the past year. Actual experience is improving and speeding up our methods of production with every passing day. And today's best is not good enough for tomorrow.

I am not satisfied with the progress thus far made. The men in charge of the program represent the best in training, ability and patriotism. They are not satisfied with the progress thus far made. None of us will be satisfied until the job is done.

No matter whether the original goal was set too high or too low, our objective is quicker and better results.

To give two illustrations:

We are behind schedule in turning out finished airplanes; we are working day and night to solve the innumerable problems and to catch up.

We are ahead of schedule in building warships; but we are working to get even further ahead of schedule.

Source: *Congressional Record*, House, Vol. 87, Part I, pp. 44–47.

To change a whole nation from a basis of peacetime production of implements of peace to a basis of wartime production of implements of war is no small task. And the greatest difficulty comes at the beginning of the program, when new tools and plant facilities and new assembly lines and shipways must first be constructed before the actual matériel begins to flow steadily and speedily from them.

The Congress, of course, must rightly keep itself informed at all times of the progress of the program. However, there is certain information, as the Congress itself will readily recognize, which, in the interests of our own security and those of the nations we are supporting, must of needs be kept in confidence.

New circumstances are constantly begetting new needs for our safety. I shall ask this Congress for greatly increased new appropriations and authorizations to carry what we have begun. I also ask this Congress for authority and for funds sufficient to manufacture additional munitions and war supplies of many kinds to be turned over to those nations which are now in actual war with aggressor nations.

Our most useful and immediate role is to act as an arsenal for them as well as for ourselves. They do not need manpower. They do need billions of dollars' worth of the weapons of defense.

The time is near when they will not be able to pay for them in ready cash. We cannot, and will not, tell them they must surrender merely because of present inability to pay for the weapons which we know they must have. I do not recommend that we make them a loan of dollars with which to pay for these weapons – a loan to be repaid in dollars. I recommend that we make it possible for those nations to continue to obtain war materials in the United States, fitting their orders into our own program. Nearly all of their matériel would, if the time ever came, be useful for our own defense.

Taking counsel of expert military and naval authorities, considering what is best for our own security, we are free to decide how much should be kept here and how much should be sent abroad to our friends who, by their determined and heroic resistance, are giving us time in which to make ready our own defense. For what we send abroad we shall be repaid, within a reasonable time following the close of hostilities, in similar materials or, at our option, in other goods of many kinds which they can produce and which we need.

Let us say to the democracies, 'We Americans are vitally concerned in your defense of freedom. We are putting forth our energies, our resources, and our organizing powers to give you the strength to regain and maintain a free world. We shall send you, in ever increasing numbers, ships, planes, tanks, guns. This is our purpose and our pledge'.

In fulfillment of this purpose we will not be intimidated by the threats of dictators that they will regard as a breach of international law and as an act of war our aid to the democracies which dare to resist their aggression. Such aid is not an act of war, even if a dictator should unilaterally proclaim it so to be. When the dictators are ready to make war upon us, they will not wait for an act of war on our part. They did not wait for Norway or Belgium or the Netherlands to commit an act of war. Their only interest is in a new one-way international law, which lacks mutuality in its observance and, therefore, becomes an instrument of oppression.

The happiness of future generations of Americans may well depend upon how effective and how immediate we can make our aid felt. No one can tell the exact character of the emergency situations that we may be called upon to meet. The nation's life is in danger. We must all prepare to make the sacrifices that the emergency – as serious as war itself – demands. Whatever stands in the way of speed and efficiency in defense preparations must give way to the national need.

A free nation has the right to expect full cooperation from all groups. A free nation has the right to look to the leaders of business, of labor, and of agriculture to take the lead in stimulating effort, not among other groups but within their own groups.

The best way of dealing with the few slackers or troublemakers in our midst is, first, to shame them by patriotic example; and if that fails, to use the sovereignty of government to save government.

As men do not live by bread alone, they do not fight by armaments alone. Those who man our defenses and those behind them who build our defenses must have the stamina and courage which come from an unshakable belief in the manner of life which they are defending. The mighty action which we are calling for cannot be based on a disregard of all things worth fighting for.

The nation takes great satisfaction and much strength from the things which have been done to make its people conscious of their individual stake in the preservation of democratic life in America. Those things have toughened the fiber of our people, have renewed their faith and strengthened their devotion to the institutions we make ready to protect.

Certainly this is no time to stop thinking about the social and economic problems which are the root cause of the social revolution which is today a supreme factor in the world. There is nothing mysterious about the foundations of a healthy and strong democracy. The basic things expected by our people of their political and economic systems are simple. They are: Equality of opportunity for youth and for others; jobs for those who can work; security for those who need it; the ending of special privilege for the few; the preservation of civil liberties for all; the enjoyment of the fruits of scientific progress in a wider and constantly rising standard of living. These are the simple and basic things that must never be lost sight of in the turmoil and unbelievable complexity of our modern world. The inner and abiding strength of our economic and political system is dependent upon the degree to which they fulfill these expectations.

Many subjects connected with our social economy call for immediate improvement. As examples:

We should bring more citizens under the coverage of old-age pensions and unemployment insurance.

We should widen the opportunities for adequate medical care.

We should plan a better system by which persons deserving or needing gainful employment may obtain it.

I have called for personal sacrifice. I am assured of the willingness of almost all Americans to respond to that call. A part of the sacrifice means the payment of more money in taxes. In my budget message I recommend that a greater portion of this great defense program be paid for from taxation than we are paying today. No person should try, or be allowed, to get rich out of this program; and the principle of tax payments in accordance with ability to pay should be constantly before our eyes to guide our legislation. If the Congress maintains these principles, the voters, putting patriotism ahead of pocketbooks, will give you their applause.

In the future days, which we seek to make secure, we look forward to a world founded upon four essential human freedoms.

The first is freedom of speech and expression everywhere in the world.

The second is freedom of every person to worship God in his own way everywhere in the world.

The third is freedom from want, which, translated into world terms, means economic understandings which will secure to every nation a healthy peacetime life for its inhabitants everywhere in the world.

The fourth is freedom from fear – which, translated into world terms, means a worldwide reduction of armaments to such a point and in such a thorough fashion that no nation will be in a position to commit an act of physical aggression against any neighbor — anywhere in the world.

That is no vision of a distant millennium. It is a definite basis for a kind of world attainable in our own time and generation. That kind of world is the very antithesis of the so-called new order of tyranny which the dictators seek to create with the crash of a bomb.

To that new order we oppose the greater conception – the moral order. A good society is able to face schemes of world domination and foreign revolutions alike without fear.

Since the beginning of our American history, we have been engaged in change – in a perpetual peaceful revolution – a revolution which goes on steadily, quietly adjusting itself to changing conditions – without the concentration camp or the quicklime in the ditch. The world order which we seek is the cooperation of free countries, working together in a friendly, civilized society.

This nation has placed its destiny in the hands and hearts of its millions of free men and women, and its faith in freedom under the guidance of God. Freedom means the supremacy of human rights everywhere. Our support goes to those who struggle to gain those rights or keep them. Our strength is in our unity of purpose. To that high concept there can be no end save victory.

56 THE ATLANTIC CHARTER, 14 AUGUST 1941

Introduction

The origin of the Charter lies in a message from President Roosevelt to Prime Minister Churchill expressing concern over 'rumours' that the British Government had begun to assume commitments to 'trades or deals' that reminded the President of the 'serious trouble' that arose over 'secret treaties' in the course of the First World War (Gilbert, 1986, Vol. VI, pp. 1161–4). The statement drawn up by the two leaders made it plain that the two countries sought no territorial aggrandisement, and reaffirmed Wilson's principles of self-determination and cooperation. The Charter was the 'platform' on which the United Nations coalition 'ran' in the Second World War.

Text

The President of the United States and the Prime Minister, Mr Churchill, representing His Majesty's Government in the United Kingdom, have met at sea.

They have been accompanied by officials of their two governments, including high ranking officers of their military, naval and air services.

The whole problem of the supply of munitions of war, as provided by the Lease-Land Act, for the armed forces of the United States and for those countries actively engaged in resisting aggression has been further examined.

Lord Beaverbrook, the Minister of Supply of the British Government, has joined in these conferences. He is going to proceed to Washington to discuss further details with appropriate officials of the United States Government. These conferences will also cover the supply problems of the Soviet Union.

The President and the Prime Minister have had several conferences. They have considered the dangers to world civilization arising from the policies of military domination by conquest upon which the Hitlerite government of Germany and other governments associated therewith have embarked, and have made clear the steps which their countries are respectively taking for their safety in the face of these dangers.

They have agreed upon the following joint declaration:

The President of the United States of America and the Prime Minister, Mr Churchill, representing His Majesty's Government in the United Kingdom, being met together, deem it right to make known certain common principles in the national policies of their respective countries on which they base their hopes for a better future for the world.

FIRST, their countries seek no aggrandizement, territorial or other;

SECOND, they desire to see no territorial changes that do not accord with the freely expressed wishes of the peoples concerned;

THIRD, they respect the right of all peoples to choose the form of government under which they will live; and they wish to see sovereign rights and self-government restored to those who have been forcibly deprived of them;

Source: *The New York Times*, 15 August 1941, p. 1.

FOURTH, they will endeavor, with due respect for their existing obligations, to further the enjoyment by all States, great or small, victor or vanquished, of access, on equal terms, to the trade and to the raw materials of the world which are needed for their economic prosperity;

FIFTH, they desire to bring about the fullest collaboration between all nations in the economic field with the object of securing, for all, improved labor standards, economic adjustment and social security;

SIXTH, after the final destruction of the Nazi tyranny, they hope to see established a peace which will afford to all nations the means of dwelling in safety within their own boundaries, and which will afford assurance that all the men in all the lands may live out their lives in freedom from fear and want;

SEVENTH, such a peace should enable all men to traverse the high seas and oceans without hindrance;

EIGHTH, they believe that all of the nations of the world, for realistic as well as spiritual reasons, must come to the abandonment of the use of force. Since no future peace can be maintained if land, sea or air armaments continue to be employed by nations which threaten, or may threaten, aggression outside of their frontiers, they believe, pending the establishment of a wider and permanent system of general security, that the disarmament of such nations is essential. They will likewise aid and encourage all other practicable measures which will lighten for peace-loving peoples the crushing burden of armaments.

FRANKLIN D. ROOSEVELT.
WINSTON S. CHURCHILL.

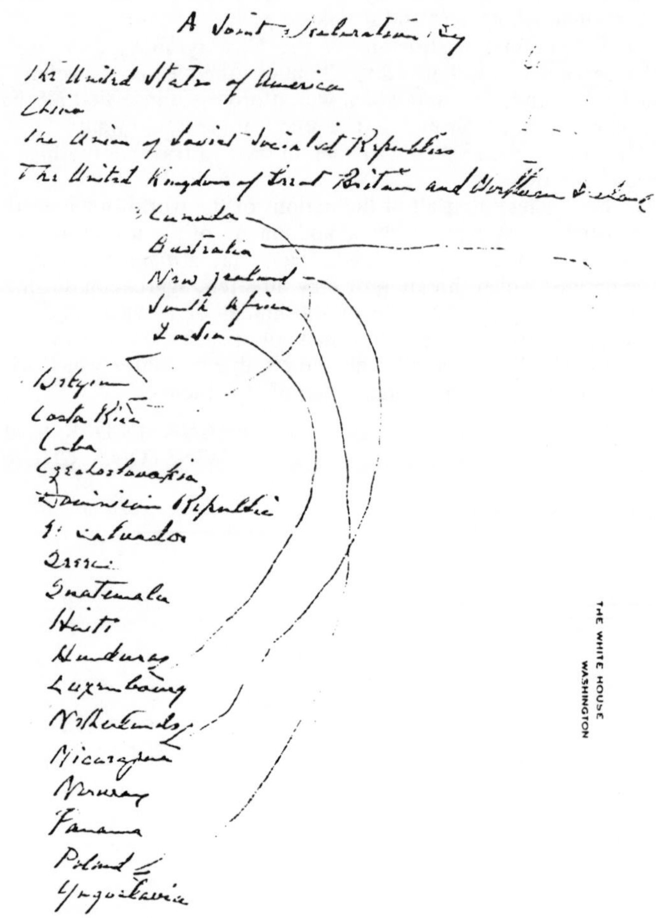

Figure 6.1 Roosevelt's regrouping of the order in which the signatories to the United Nations Declaration were to be listed (Doc. 56) (Franklin D. Roosevelt Library).

APPENDIX

Joint Declaration by United Nations issued at Washington, 1 January 1942

The Governments signatory hereto:

Having subscribed to a common programme of purposes and principles embodied in the Joint Declaration of the President of the United States of America and the Prime Minister of the United Kingdom of Great Britain and Northern Ireland, dated 14th August, 1941, known as the Atlantic Charter.

Being convinced that complete victory over their enemies is essential to defend life, liberty, independence, and religious freedom, and to preserve human rights and justice in their own lands as well as in other lands, and that they are now engaged in a common struggle against savage and brutal forces seeking to subjugate the world, DECLARE:

(1) Each Government pledges itself to employ its full resources, military or economic, against those members of the Tripartite Pact and its adherents with which such Government is at war;

(2) Each Government pledges itself to co-operate with the Governments signatory hereto, and not to make a separate armistice or peace with the enemies.

The foregoing declaration may be adhered to by other nations[1] which are, or which may be, rendering material assistance and contributions in the struggle for victory over Hitlerism.

The United States of American, by Franklin D. Roosevelt.
The United Kingdom of Great Britain and Northern Ireland, by Winston S. Churchill.
On behalf of the Government of the Union of Soviet Socialist Republics, Maxim Litvinov, Ambassador.
National Government of the Republic of China, Tse-Vung Soong, Minister for Foreign Affairs.
The Commonwealth of Australia, by R. G. Casey.
The Kingdom of Belgium, by Cte. R. v. Straten.
Canada, by Leighton McCarthy.
The Republic of Costa Rica, by Luis Fernández.
The Republic of Cuba, by Aurelio F. Concheso.
Czechoslovak Republic, by V. S. Hurban.
The Dominican Republic, by J. M. Troncoso.
The Republic of El Salvador, by C. A. Alfaro.
The Kingdom of Greece, by Cimon G. Diamantopoulos.
The Republic of Guatemala, by Enrique Lopez-Herrarte.
La Républic d'Haiti, par Fernand Dennis.
The Republic of Honduras, by Julián R. Cáceres.
India, by Girja Shankar Bajpai.
The Grand Duchy of Luxemburg, by Hugues le Gallais.
The Kingdom of the Netherlands, by A. Loudon.
Signed on behalf of the Government of the Dominion of New Zealand, by Frank Langstone.

1. Mexico adhered to the Declaration by United Nations on 5 June and the Commonwealth of the Philippines on 10 June 1942.

The Republic of Nicaragua, by Léon De Bayle.
The Kingdom of Norway, by W. Munthe Morgenstierne.
The Republic of Panamá, by Jaén Guardia.
The Republic of Poland, by Jan Ciechanowski.
The Union of South Africa, by Ralph W. Close.
The Kingdom of Yugoslavia, by Constantin A. Fotitch.

57 THE QUEBEC AGREEMENT ON ATOMIC ENERGY COOPERATION, AUGUST 1943

Introduction

It was the British who first conceived of an atomic bomb project. As early as 1939, refugee German scientists had alerted British scientists and officials to the implications of nuclear fission research. The Frisch–Peierls memorandum of March 1940 was the first, anywhere, to foretell with scientific conviction the practical possibility of making a bomb. By April 1940, research with the object of producing a fission weapon had been launched in earnest by the 'Maud' Committee in Britain. Although not formally at war, but eager to take advantage of a substantial British head start, the United States asked to participate. The British were anxious to maintain their independence, and rejected the American request.

In 1943 the situation was reversed, with the British bogged down through lack of resources. By this time the United States' Manhattan Project had progressed to the point where no outside help was needed, and sharing was considered undesirable for security reasons. But Prime Minister Churchill continued to petition for British collaboration on the American project and finally won his battle at the Quebec Conference (see Gowing, 1964, pp. 164–77, and passim).

The operation of this agreement was drastically curtailed by the McMahon Act of 1946 but it remains in Force.

Text

THE CITADEL, QUEBEC

Articles of Agreement

governing collaboration between the authorities of the USA and the UK in the matter of Tube Alloys[1]

Whereas it is vital to our common safety in the present War to bring the Tube Alloys project to fruition at the earliest moment; and whereas this may be more speedily achieved if all available British and American brains and resources are pooled; and whereas owing to war conditions it would be an improvident use of war resources to duplicate plants on a large scale on both sides of the Atlantic and therefore a far greater expense has fallen upon the United States;

It is agreed between us

First, that we will never use this agency against each other.

Secondly, that we will not use it against third parties without each other's consent.

Source: *United States Treaties and other International Agreements*, Vol. V. Part I, p. 1114.

1. Atomic energy research and development.

Thirdly, that we will not either of us communicate any information about Tube Alloys to third parties except by mutual consent.

Fourthly, that in view of the heavy burden of production falling upon the United States as the result of a wise division of war effort, the British Government recognize that any post-war advantages of an industrial or commercial character shall be dealt with as between the United States and Great Britain on terms to be specified by the President of the United States to the Prime Minister of Great Britain. The Prime Minister expressly disclaims any interest in these industrial and commercial aspects beyond what may be considered by the President of the United States to be fair and just and in harmony with the economic welfare of the world.

And Fifthly, that the following arrangements shall be made to ensure full and effective collaboration between the two countries in bringing the project to fruition:

(a) There shall be set up in Washington a Combined Policy Committee composed of:

THE SECRETARY OF WAR	(United States)
Dr VANNEVAR BUSH	(United States)
Dr JAMES B. CONANT	(United States)
Field-Marshal Sir JOHN DILL, G.C.B., C.M.G., D.S.O.	(United Kingdom)
Colonel the Right Hon. J. J. LLEWELLIN, C.B.E., M.C., M.P.	(United Kingdom)
The Honourable C. D. HOWE	(Canada)

The functions of this Committee, subject to the control of the respective Governments, will be:

(1) To agree from time to time upon the programme of work to be carried out in the two countries.
(2) To keep all sections of the project under constant review.
(3) To allocate materials, apparatus and plant, in limited supply, in accordance with the requirements of the programme agreed by the Committee.
(4) To settle any questions which may arise on the interpretation or application of this Agreement.

(b) There shall be complete interchange of information and ideas on all sections of the project between members of the Policy Committee and their immediate technical advisers.

(c) In the field of scientific research and development there shall be full and effective interchange of information and ideas between those in the two countries engaged in the same sections of the field.

(d) In the field of design, construction and operation of large-scale plants, interchange of information and ideas shall be regulated by such *ad hoc* arrangements as may, in each section of the field, appear to be necessary or desirable if the project is to be brought to fruition at the earliest moment. Such *ad hoc* arrangements shall be subject to the approval of the Policy Committee.

Approved

August 19 1943

FRANKLIN D. ROOSEVELT
WINSTON S. CHURCHILL

58 THE TEHERAN CONFERENCE, 27 NOVEMBER–DECEMBER 1943

(a) *First Plenary meeting, 29 November*
(b) *Roosevelt–Stalin meeting, 29 November*

Texts

(a) *First Plenary Meeting, 28 November 1943, 4 p.m., Conference Room, Soviet Embassy*

Present

United States	*United Kingdom*	*Soviet Union*
President Roosevelt	Prime Minister Churchill	Marshal Stalin
Mr Hopkins	Foreign Secretary Eden	Foreign Commissar Molotov
Admiral Leahy	Field Marshal Dill	Marshal Voroshilov
Admiral King	General Brooke	Mr Pavlov
Major General Deane	Admiral of the Fleet Cunningham	Mr Berezhkov
Captain Royal	Air Chief Marshal Portal	
Mr Bohlen	Lieutenant General Ismay	
	Major Birse	

Bohlen Minutes

SECRET

THE PRESIDENT said as the youngest of the three present he ventured to welcome his elders.[1] He said he wished to welcome the new members to the family circle and tell them that meetings of this character were conducted as between friends with complete frankness on all sides with nothing that was said to be made public. He added that he was confident that this meeting would be successful and that our three great nations would not only work in close cooperation for the prosecution of the war but would also remain in close touch for generations to come.

THE PRIME MINISTER then pointed out that this was the greatest concentration of power that the world had ever seen. In our hands here is the possible certainty of shortening the war, the much greater certainty of victories, but the absolute certainty that we held the happy future of mankind. He added that he prayed that we might be worthy of this God-given opportunity.

Source: Foreign Relations of the United States: Diplomatic Papers, *The Conference at Cairo and Tehran, 1943*, (Washington, D.C.: USGPO, 1961) pp. 487–97; 529–33.

1. According to Churchill (1952, p. 347), he (Churchill) and Stalin had agreed beforehand that Roosevelt should preside at this first conference of the three Heads of Government, and Roosevelt consented to do so. See also Sherwood, 1950, p. 778. No official record of this agreement has been found.

Seated on the portico of the Soviet Embassy on 29 November:
Marshall Stalin, President Roosevelt, Prime Minister Churchill
Standing, left to right:
Harry Hopkins, Vyacheslav Molotov, Averell Harriman, Sir Clark Kerr, Anthony Eden (Doc. 58) (US National Archives)

Figure 6.2 The Teheran Conference, November–December 1943

MARSHAL STALIN welcomed the representatives of Great Britain and the United States. He then said that history had given to us here a great opportunity and it was up to the representatives here to use wisely the power which their respective peoples had given to them and to take full advantage of this fraternal meeting.

THE PRESIDENT then gave a general survey of the war as a whole and the needs of the war from the American point of view. Before turning to the war in the Pacific, THE PRESIDENT said he desired to emphasize that the United States shared equally with the Soviet Union and Great Britain the desire to hasten in every way possible the day of victory. He then said that the United States was more directly affected by the war in the Pacific and that the United States forces were bearing the chief burden in that theater with, of course, help from Australian and British forces in that area; the greater part of the U S naval establishment was in the Pacific and over a million men were being maintained there. He pointed out as evidence of the immense distances in the Pacific that one supply ship operating from the United States could only make three round trips a year. The allied strategy in the Pacific was based on the doctrine of attrition which was proving successful. We were sinking more Japanese tonnage than the Japanese were able to replace. He said that the allies were moving forward through the southern islands and now through the islands to the east of Japan. On the north little more could be done due to the distance between the Aleutian and Kurile islands. On the west our one great objective was to keep China in the war, and for this purpose an expedition was in preparation to attack through North Burma and from Yun[n]an province. In this operation Anglo-British [*Anglo-American*] forces would operate in North Burma and Chinese forces from Yun[n]an. The entire operation would be under the command of Lord Louis Mountbatten. In addition, amphibious operations were planned south of Burma to attack the important Japanese bases and lines of communication in the vicinity of Bangkok. The President pointed out that although these operations extended over vast expanses of territory the number of ships and men allocated for the purpose were being held down to a minimum. He summed up the aims of these operations as follows: (1) to open the road to China and supply that country in order to keep it in the war, and (2), by opening the road to China and through increased use of transport planes to put ourselves in position to bomb Japan proper.

THE PRESIDENT then said he would turn to the most important theater of the war – Europe. He said he wished to emphasize that for over one year and a half in the last two or three conferences which he had had with the Prime Minister all military plans had revolved around the question of relieving the German pressure on the Soviet front; that largely because of the difficulties of sea transport it had not been possible until Quebec to set a date for the cross-channel operations. He pointed out that the English channel was a disagreeable body of water and it was unsafe for military operations prior to the month of May, and that the plan adopted at Quebec involved an immense expedition and had been set at that time for May 1, 1944.

THE PRIME MINISTER interposed and remarked that the British had every reason to be thankful that the English channel was such a disagreeable body of water.

THE PRESIDENT then said that one of the questions to be considered here was what use could be made of allied forces in the Mediterranean in such a way as to bring the maximum aid to the Soviet armies on the Eastern front. He added that some of these possibilities might involve a delay of one, two or three months in the large cross-channel operation and that before making any decision as to future operations in the Mediterranean he and the Prime Minister had desired to ascertain the views of Marshal Stalin on this point. He pointed out that among the possible points of future operation in the Mediterranean were Italy, the Adriatic and Aegean Seas and Turkey. In conclusion THE PRESIDENT emphasized the fact that in his opinion the large cross-channel operation should not be delayed by secondary operations.

MARSHAL STALIN stated that in regard to the Pacific war the Soviet Government welcomed the successes of the Anglo–American forces against the Japanese; that up to the present to their regret they had not been able to join the effort of the Soviet Union to that of the United States and England against the Japanese because the Soviet armies were too deeply engaged in the west. He added that the Soviet forces in Siberia were sufficient for defensive purposes but would have to be increased three-fold before they would be adequate for offensive operations. Once Germany was finally defeated, it would then be possible to send the necessary reinforcements to Siberia and then we shall be able by our common front to beat Japan. MARSHAL STALIN then gave a brief review of military developments in the Soviet–German front since the the German offensive in July. He said that the Soviet High Command had been preparing an offensive of its own but that the Germans had stolen the march on them and attacked first. Following the failure of the German offensive, the Soviet forces had passed over to the attack, and he admitted that the successes which they had achieved this summer and autumn had far exceeded their expectations as they had found the German army much weaker than they had expected. He said that at the present time there were 210 German Divisions facing the Soviet armies with six more in the process of transfer from the west. To this should be added 50 non-German Divisions (10 Hungarian, 20 Finnish, 16 to 18 Rumanian), making a total of 260 Divisions facing the Soviet armies with six more on the way. In reply to the President's question, MARSHAL STALIN stated that the normal battle strength of a German front line Division was from 8000 to 9000 but that if Auxiliary corps, supply, etc. forces were added the total strength of each Division was around 12 000. He said that last year the Soviet armies had faced 240 Axis Divisions of which 179 were German, whereas this year they faced 260 of which 210 were German with six more on the way. He said that the Soviet Union had had 330 Divisions at the start of the summer campaign and that it was this numerical superiority over the Germans which permitted the offensive operations to develop so successively [*successfully*?]. He added, however, that the numerical superiority was gradually being evened up. He said one of the great difficulties encountered by the Soviet Armies in advancing was the question of supply since the Germans destroyed literally everything in their retreat. He mentioned that although the initiative on the front as a whole remained in Soviet hands, the offensive because of weather conditions had slowed down in those sectors. In fact, in the sector south and southwest of Kiev the German counteroffensive had recaptured the town of Zhitomir and would probably recapture Korosten in the near future. He said the Germans were using for this counter-attack three old and five new tank Divisions and twenty to twenty-three motorized infantry Divisions in an attempt to retake Kiev.

MARSHAL STALIN then turned to the allied operations in Italy. He said that from their point of view the great value of the Italian campaign was the freeing of the Mediterranean to allied shipping but that they did not consider that Italy was a suitable place from which to attempt to attack Germany proper; that the Alps constituted an almost insuperable barrier as the famous Russian General Suvorov had discovered in his time.[2] He added that in the opinion of the Soviet military leaders, Hitler was endeavoring to retain as many allied Divisions as possible in Italy where no decision could be reached, and that the best method in the Soviet opinion was getting at the heart of Germany with an attack through northern or northwestern France and even through southern France. He admitted that this would be a very difficult operation since the Germans would fight like devils to prevent it. MARSHAL STALIN went on to say that it would be helpful if Turkey would enter the war and open the way to the Balkans, but even so the Balkans were far from the heart of Germany, and while with Turkish participation operations there would be useful, northern France was still the best.

THE PRIME MINISTER stated that the United States and Great Britain had long agreed as to the necessity of the cross-channel operation and that at the present time this operation, which is known as OVERLORD, was absorbing most of our combined resources and efforts. He added that it would take a long statement of facts and figures to explain why, to our disappointment, it would be impossible to undertake this operation in 1943 but that we were determined to carry it out in the late spring or early summer of 1944. He went on to say that the operations in North Africa and Italy had been clearly recognized by both the President and himself as secondary in character but that it was the best that could be done in 1943. He said that the forces which were now in process of execution [*accumulation*?] for the OVERLORD operation involved an initial assault of 16 British and 19 U S Divisions, a total of 35. He pointed out that the strength of the individual British and American Divisions was considerably stronger than a German Division. He said it was contemplated to put one million men on the continent of Europe in May, June and July.

MARSHAL STALIN remarked at this point that he had not meant to convey the impression that he considered the North Africa or Italian operations as secondary or belittle their significance since they were of very real value.

THE PRIME MINISTER thanked the Marshal for his courtesy by repeating that neither he nor the President had ever considered the operations in the Mediterranean [as anything more than a stepping-stone?] for the main cross-channel operation. He said that when the 16 British Divisions earmarked for OVERLORD had landed in France, they would be maintained by reinforcements, but that no additional British Divisions could be sent to Europe since, taking into consideration the British forces in the Middle East, India and the size of the Royal Air Force which was not idle, this would utilize all British manpower which was based on a population of only 46 million. He added that it was the United States which would send in a steady stream of necessary reinforcements for the development of OVERLORD. He added, however, that the summer of 1944 was a long way off and that following the capture of Rome, which was hoped would take place in January, 1944, it would be six months before OVERLORD would begin. He and the President had repeatedly asked themselves what could be done with forces in the Mediterranean area during this period to bring the greatest pressure to bear on the enemy and help relieve the Soviet front. He said he did not wish to have any allied forces to remain idle during this period. He admitted that some of the operations which had been discussed might involve a delay of some two months in OVERLORD. He added, however, that they are all ready to withdraw seven of the best British Divisions from the Italian theater in preparation

2. In the autumn of 1799 a Russian army under Field Marshal Alexander Suvorov suffered a disastrous defeat in attempting to cross the Swiss Alps from south to north.

for OVERLORD, but emphasized that the great difficulty lay in the shortage of landing craft and that this constituted a great bottleneck of all allied operations.

Reverting to the Italian theater, THE PRIME MINISTER said that the weather had been exceptionally bad in Italy and that General Alexander, who under General Eisenhower was in command of the 15th Army Group in Italy, believed that in taking Rome there was an excellent opportunity of destroying or at least mauling 10 to 15 German Divisions. There was no plan for going into the broad part of Italy subsequent to the taking of Rome, and once the great airfields in the vicinity of that city had been captured and the Pisa–Rimini line had been reached, the allied forces would be free for other operations, possibly in southern France, or an enterprise across the Adriatic.

He said that the operations of the Partisans in Yugoslavia, which had been greater and better than those of Mihailovic, opened up the prospects to the allies to send additional help to Yugoslavia, but there was no plan to send a large army to the Balkans, although through commandos and small expeditions something might be done in that area.

THE PRIME MINISTER then said that he had come to one of the largest questions we had before us, namely, the question of Turkey's entrance into the war which we should urge upon that country in the strongest possible terms. If Turkey would enter the war it would open up the Aegean sea and assure an uninterrupted supply route to Russia into the Black Sea. He mentioned that only 4 Arctic convoys to the North Russian Ports could be considered with OVERLORD. He then inquired, how shall we persuade Turkey to enter the war and in what manner? Should she provide the allies with bases or should she attack Bulgaria and declare war on Germany, or should she move forward or stay on the defensive on the fortified lines in Thrace. He added that Bulgaria owed a debt of gratitude to Russia for her liberation from Turkish rule.

MARSHAL STALIN interposed to remark that this liberation had taken place a long time ago.[3]

THE PRIME MINISTER said that Turkey's entrance into the war would undoubtedly have an effect from Rumania from whom peace feelers had already been received, and also from Hungary and might well start a landslide among the satellite States. He added that the Soviet Government had special feelings and special knowledge on these questions and he would welcome their views. THE PRIME MINISTER concluded by inquiring whether any of the possible operations in the Mediterranean were of sufficient interest to the Soviet Union if these operations involved a two or three months delay in OVERLORD. He said that he and the President could not make any decision until they knew the Soviet views on the subject and therefore had drawn up no definite plans.

THE PRESIDENT then said that he had thought of a possible operation at the head of the Adriatic to make a junction with the Partisans under Tito and then to operate northeast into Rumania in conjunction with the Soviet advance from the region of Odessa.

THE PRIME MINISTER remarked that if we take Rome and smash up the German armies there we will have a choice of moving west or, as the President says, east in the Mediterranean, and suggested that a sub-committee be appointed to work out the details of the various possibilities.

MARSHAL STALIN inquired if the 35 Divisions which he understood were earmarked for OVERLORD would be affected in any way by the continuation of the operations in Italy.

3. The reference is to Russian action in 1877–8.

THE PRIME MINISTER replied that they would not, since entirely separate Divisions were being used in the Italian Theater. THE PRIME MINISTER, in reply to Marshal Stalin's questions as to the relationship of the operations which he had outlined, explained that after the taking of Rome there would be available some 20 to 23 British, American, French and Polish Divisions which would be available for operations in the Mediterranean without in any way affecting the preparations for OVERLORD. He repeated that this force could either move west, or as the President suggested, to the eastern part of the Mediterranean. He said that since shipping was already allocated, any movements of effectives between OVERLORD and the Mediterranean would be very limited. He added that while the OVERLORD involved an initial assault of 35 Divisions, of which 16 would be British, the development of the operation envisioned by July 50 or 60 Allied Divisions on the continent, but repeated that the additional Divisions would come from the United States and not Great Britain. He added that the total strength of an American or British Division, including auxiliary forces, amounted to 40 000 men. He also stated that although the British and American air forces were very large and undertaking great operations, it was expected that the United States air force would be doubled or tripled within the next six months. He proposed to make available to Marshal Stalin the exact schedule of movements of supplies from the United States to Great Britain which already involved one million tons of stores.

MARSHAL STALIN then inquired if Turkey entered the war would some Anglo–American forces be allocated to that area.

THE PRIME MINISTER replied that two or three Divisions, British or British controlled, were available for the capture of the islands of the Aegean, and that as an immediate aid to Turkey it was proposed to send 20 squadrons of fighters and several anti-aircraft regiments, adding that the preparation[s] to send these forces to Turkey were already far advanced.

MARSHAL STALIN replied that in his opinion he questioned the wisdom of dispersing allied forces of [*for*?] the various operations mentioned such as Turkey, the Adriatic and Southern France since there would be no direct connection between these scattered forces. He said he thought it would be better to take OVERLORD as the basis for all 1944 operations; that after the capture of Rome the troops thus relieved might be sent to Southern France, and in conjunction with forces operating from Corsica might eventually meet in France the main force of OVERLORD from the north. These would be in the nature of diversionary operations to assist OVERLORD. Marshal Stalin said that he favored the operations in Southern France particularly as he thought Turkey would not enter the war. He repeated that he was convinced that Turkey would not enter the war.

THE PRESIDENT remarked that there would be 8 or 9 French Divisions, which included native Divisions, available for an operation against southern France.

MARSHAL STALIN remarked that in an operation against southern France the transportation difficulties would be greatly facilitated.

THE PRIME MINISTER said he agreed with Marshal Stalin in regard to the inadvisability of scattering our forces. He pointed out that the squadrons destined for Turkey and the Divisions for the seizure of the Aegean islands were now being used for defense of Egypt and that their use would not distract in any way from OVERLORD or the operations in Italy.

MARSHAL STALIN remarked that these operations would be worth while only if Turkey entered the war which he again repeated he did not believe would happen.

THE PRIME MINISTER replied that he had in mind the six months which would elapse after the expected capture of Rome before the beginning of OVERLORD, and that both he and the President were most anxious that their troops should not remain idle since if they were fighting, the British and American governments would not be exposed to the criticism that they were letting the Soviet Union bear the brunt of the war.

MARSHAL STALIN replied that in his opinion OVERLORD represented a very large operation and that it would be facilitated and, in fact, would be certain of success if the invasion of southern France was undertaken some two months before OVERLORD. This would divert German troops from the northern part of France and assure the success of OVERLORD. He said that as an extreme measure he would be inclined to leave 10 Divisions in Italy and postpone the capture of Rome in order to launch the attack in southern France two months in advance of OVERLORD.

THE PRIME MINISTER replied that he was sure Marshal Stalin would permit him to develop arguments to demonstrate why it was necessary for the allied forces to capture Rome, otherwise it would have the appearance of a great allied defeat in Italy. He pointed out that the allied forces would be no stronger before the capture of Rome than after, and in fact without the fighter cover which would be possible only from the north Italian fields it would be impossible to invade northern France. In reply to Marshal Stalin's questions regarding Corsica, the PRIME MINISTER pointed out that there were no adequate airfields on the island.

THE PRESIDENT said that he thought the question [of] relative timing was very important and that he personally felt that nothing should be done to delay the carrying out of OVERLORD which might be necessary if any operations in the eastern Mediterranean were undertaken. He proposed, therefore, that the staffs work out tomorrow morning a plan of operations for striking at southern France.

MARSHAL STALIN pointed out that the Russian experience had shown that an attack from one direction was not effective and that the Soviet armies now launched an offensive from two sides at once which forced the enemy to move his reserve back and forth. He added that he thought such a two way operation in France would be very successful.

THE PRIME MINISTER stated that he personally did not disagree with what the Marshal had said and that he did not think he had said anything here which could possibly affect adversely an operation in southern France, but he added it would be difficult for him to leave idle the British forces in the eastern Mediterranean which numbered some 20 Divisions, British controlled, which could not be used outside of that area, merely for the purpose of avoiding any insignificant delay in OVERLORD. He said that if such was the decision they would, of course, agree, but they could not wholeheartedly agree to postpone operations in the Mediterranean. He added, of course, that if Turkey does not enter the war that is the end of that, but that he personally favored some flexibility in the exact date of OVERLORD. He proposed that the matter be considered overnight and have the staffs examine the various possibilities in the morning.

MARSHAL STALIN stated that as they had not expected to discuss technical military questions he had no military staff but that Marshal Voroshilov would do his best.

THE PRIME MINISTER stated it would not [*now*?] be necessary to consider how far we could meet Turkey's request in the event that she agreed to enter the war.

MARSHAL STALIN replied that Turkey was an ally of Great Britain and at the same time had relations of friendship with the United States and the Soviet Union who as friends could ask Turkey and indeed bring pressure to bear on her to carry out her obligations as an ally of Great Britain. He said that all Neutrals considered Belligerents to be fools and it was up to the countries represented here to show that the Neutrals were the ones that were fools and that we must prove to Turkey that if they stay out of the war on the winning side that they were indeed the fools.

THE PRIME MINISTER said he thought it would be an act of supreme unwisdom if the Turks were to refuse an invitation from Russia to join the war on the winning side. He added that Christmas in England was a poor season for Turkeys. When the joke had been explained to Marshal Stalin he said he regretted that he was not an Englishman.

THE PRESIDENT then stated that should he meet the President of Turkey he would, of course, do everything possible to persuade him to enter the war, but that if he were in the Turkish President's place he would demand such a price in planes, tanks and equipment that to grant the request would indefinitely postpone OVERLORD.

MARSHAL STALIN repeated his doubt as to Turkey's intention and said that they had in fact already replied to the suggestion that they enter the war. Although many considered this reply favorable, he personally thought it was negative in character.

THE PRIME MINISTER remarked that in his opinion the Turks were crazy.

MARSHAL STALIN said there were some people who apparently preferred to remain crazy.

The meeting adjourned until 4 P.M., November 29, 1943.

(b) *Roosevelt–Stalin Meeting, 29 November 1943, 2:45 p.m., Roosevelt's Quarters, Soviet Embassy*

Present[1]

United States	*Soviet Union*
President Roosevelt	Marshal Stalin
Mr Bohlen	Mr Berezhkov

Bohlen Minutes

SECRET

THE PRESIDENT . . . said he had a great many . . . matters relating to the future of the world which he would like to talk over informally with the Marshal and obtain his view on them. He said that he hoped to discuss some of them before they both left Tehran. He said that he was willing to discuss any subject military or political which the Marshal desired.

MARSHAL STALIN replied there was nothing to prevent them from discussing anything they wished.

THE PRESIDENT then said the question of a post war organization to preserve peace had not been fully explained and dealt with and he would like to discuss with the Marshal the prospect of some organization based on the United Nations.

THE PRESIDENT then outlined the following general plan:

(1) There would be a large organization composed of some 35 members of the United Nations which would meet periodically at different places, discuss and make recommendations to a smaller body.

MARSHAL STALIN inquired whether this organization was to be world-wide or European, to which the President replied, world-wide.

THE PRESIDENT continued that there would be set up an executive committee composed of the Soviet Union, the United States, United Kingdom and China, together with two additional European states, one South American, one Near East, one Far Eastern country, and one British Dominion. He mentioned that Mr. Churchill did not like this proposal for the reason that the British Empire only had two votes. This Executive Committee would deal with all non-military questions such as agriculture, food, health, and economic questions, as well as the setting up of an International Committee. This Committee would likewise meet in various places.

MARSHAL STALIN inquired whether this body would have the right to make decisions binding on the nations of the world.

THE PRESIDENT replied, yes and no. It could make recommendations for settling disputes with the hope that the nations concerned would be guided thereby, but that, for example, he did not believe the Congress of the United States would accept as binding a decision of such a body. THE PRESIDENT

1. The listing of those present is based on the Bohlen minutes. As regards those present for the United States, Elliott Roosevelt mentions his father and himself but not Bohlen. As regards those present for the Soviet Union, Elliott Roosevelt and a log mention Stalin, Molotov, and Pavlov but not Berezhkov; and Churchill (1952, p. 363) mentions Stalin and Molotov.

then turned to the third organization which he termed 'The Four Policemen', namely, the Soviet Union, United States, Great Britain, and China. This organization would have the power to deal immediately with any threat to the peace and any sudden emergency which requires this action. He went on to say that in 1935, when Italy attacked Ethiopia, the only machinery in existence was the League of Nations. He personally had begged France to close the Suez Canal, but they instead referred it to the League which disputed the question and in the end did nothing. The result was that the Italian Armies went through the Suez Canal and destroyed Ethiopia. THE PRESIDENT pointed out that had the machinery of the Four Policemen, which he had in mind, been in existence, it would have been possible to close the Suez Canal. THE PRESIDENT then summarized briefly the idea that he had in mind.

MARSHAL STALIN said that he did not think that the small nations of Europe would like the organization composed of the Four Policemen. He said, for example, that a European state would probably resent China having the right to apply certain machinery to it. And in any event, he did not think China would be very powerful at the end of the war. He suggested as a possible alternative, the creation of a European or a Far Eastern Committee and a European or a Worldwide organization. He said that in the European Commission there would be the United States, Great Britain, the Soviet Union and possibly one other European state.

THE PRESIDENT said that the idea just expressed by Marshall Stalin was somewhat similar to Mr Churchill's idea of a Regional Committee, one for Europe, one for the Far East, and one for the Americas. Mr Churchill had also suggested that the United States be a member of the European Commission, but he doubted if the United States Congress would agree to the United States' participation in an exclusively European Committee which might be able to force the dispatch of American troops to Europe.

THE PRESIDENT added that it would take a terrible crisis such as at present before Congress would ever agree to that step.

MARSHAL STALIN pointed out that the world organization suggested by the President, and in particular the Four Policemen, might also require the sending of American troops to Europe.

THE PRESIDENT pointed out that he had only envisaged the sending of American planes and ships to Europe, and that England and the Soviet Union would have to handle the land armies in the event of any future threat to the peace. He went on to say that if the Japanese had not attacked the United States he doubted very much if it would have been possible to send any American forces to Europe. THE PRESIDENT added that he saw two methods of dealing with possible threats to the peace. In one case if the threat arose from a revolution or developments in a small country, it might be possible to apply the quarantine method, closing the frontiers of the countries in question and imposing embargoes. In the second case, if the threat was more serious, the four powers, acting as policemen, would send an ultimatum to the nation in question and if refused, [it] would result in the immediate bombardment and possible invasion of that country.

MARSHAL STALIN said that yesterday he had discussed the question of safeguarding against Germany with Mr Churchill and found him optimistic on the subject in that Mr Churchill believed that Germany would not rise again. He, Stalin, personally thought that unless prevented, Germany would completely recovery [*recover*] within 15 to 20 years, and that therefore we must have something more serious than the type of organization proposed by the President. He pointed out that the first German aggression had occurred in 1870 and then 42

[*44*] years later in the 1st World War, whereas only 21 years elapsed between the end of the last war and the beginning of the present. He added that he did not believe the period between the revival of German strength would be any longer in the future and therefore he did not consider the organizations outlined by the President were enough.

He went on to say that what was needed was the control of certain strong physical points either within Germany along German borders, or even farther away, to insure that Germany would not embark on another course of aggression. He mentioned specifically Dakar as one of those points. He added that the same method should be applied in the case of Japan and that the islands in the vicinity of Japan should remain under strong control to prevent Japan's embarking on a course of aggression.

He stated that any commission or body which was set up to preserve peace should have the right to not only make decisions but to occupy such strong points against Germany and Japan.

THE PRESIDENT said that he agreed 100% with Marshal Stalin.

MARSHAL STALIN then stated he still was dubious about the question of Chinese participation.

THE PRESIDENT replied that he had insisted on the participation of China in the 4 Power Declaration at Moscow not because he did not realize the weakness of China at present, but he was thinking farther into the future and that after all China was a nation of 400 million people, and it was better to have them as friends rather than as a potential source of trouble.

THE PRESIDENT, reverting to Marshal Stalin's statements as to the ease of converting factories, said that a strong and effective world organization of the 4 Powers could move swiftly when the first signs arose of the beginning of the conversion of such factories for warlike purposes.

MARSHAL STALIN replied that the Germans had shown great ability to conceal such beginnings.

THE PRESIDENT accepted Marshal Stalin's remark. He again expressed his agreement with Marshal Stalin that strategic positions in the world should be at the disposal of some world organization to prevent a revival of German and Japanese aggression.

59 ADDRESS BY UNITED STATES TREASURY SECRETARY HENRY MORGENTHAU, JR AT THE CLOSING PLENARY SESSION OF THE UNITED NATIONS MONETARY AND FINANCIAL CONFERENCE HELD AT BRETTON WOODS, 22 JULY 1944

Introduction

The Bretton Woods agreements fulfilled the promise of 'the fullest cooperation between all nations in the economic field' made in the fifth point of the Atlantic Charter (Doc. 56). They went much further than the post-First World War financial arrangements which had been strongly criticised at the time by many, including the economist John Maynard Keynes, for being inadequate. In the 1944 negotiations, the prime movers were Harry Dexter White, a member of the US Treasury in charge of international financial problems, and Keynes, temporarily on the staff of the British Treasury (see Gardner, 1956, pp. 111ff.).

Text

I am gratified to announce that the Conference at Bretton Woods has successfully completed the task before it.

It was, as we knew when we began, a difficult task, involving complicated technical problems. We came here to work out methods which would do away with the economic evils – the competitive currency devaluation and destructive impediments to trade – which preceded the present war. We have succeeded in that effort.

The actual details of an international monetary and financial agreement may seem mysterious to the general public. Yet at the heart of it lie the most elementary bread and butter realities of daily life. What we have done here in Bretton Woods is to devise machinery by which men and women everywhere can freely exchange, on a fair and stable basis, the goods which they produce through their labor. And we have taken the initial steps through which the Nations of the world will be able to help one another in economic development to their mutual advantage and for the enrichment of all.

The representatives of the 44 nations faced differences of opinion frankly, and reached an agreement which is rooted in genuine understanding. None of the nations represented here has altogether had its own way. We have had to yield to one another not in respect to principles or essentials but in respect to methods and procedural details. The fact that we have done so, and that we have done it in a continuing spirit of good will and mutual trust, is, I believe, one of the hopeful and heartening portents of our times. Here is a sign blazoned upon the horizon, written large upon the threshold of the future – a sign for men in battle, for men at work in mines and mills, and in the fields, and a sign for women whose hearts have been burdened and anxious lest the cancer of war assail yet another

Source: *Proceedings and documents of the United Nations Monetary and Financial Conference, Bretton Woods, New Hampshire, July 1–22, 1944, Washington, D.C.: USGPO, 1948*, Vol. 1, pp. 1116–20.

generation – a sign that the peoples of the earth are learning how to join hands and work in unity.

There is a curious notion that the protection of national interests and the development of international cooperation are conflicting philosophies – that somehow or other men of different nations cannot work together without sacrificing the interests of their particular nations. There has been talk of this sort – and from people who ought to know better – concerning the international cooperative nature of the undertaking just completed at Bretton Woods. I am perfectly certain that no delegation to this Conference has lost sight for a moment of the particular national interests it was sent here to represent. The American Delegation which I have had the honor of leading, has at all times been conscious of its primary obligation – the protection of American interests. And the other representatives here have been no less loyal or devoted to the welfare of their own people.

Yet none of us has found any incompatibility between devotion to our own countries and joint action. Indeed, we have found on the contrary that the only genuine safeguard for our national interests lies in international cooperation. We have come to recognize that the wisest and most effective way to protect our national interests is through international cooperation – that is to say, through united effort for the attainment of common goals. This has been the great lesson taught by the war and is, I think, the great lesson of contemporary life – that the peoples of the earth are inseparably linked to one another by a deep, underlying community of purpose. This community of purpose is no less real and vital in peace than in war, and cooperation is no less essential to its fulfillment.

To seek the achievement of our aims separately through the planless, senseless rivalry that divided us in the past, or through the outright economic aggression which turned neighbors into enemies, would be to invite ruin again upon us all. Worse, it would be once more to start our steps irretraceably down the steep, disastrous road to war. That sort of extreme nationalism belongs to an era that is dead. Today the only enlightened form of national self-interest lies in international accord. At Bretton Woods we have taken practical steps toward putting this lesson into practice in the monetary and economic field.

I take it as an axiom that after this war is ended no people – and therefore no government of the people – will again tolerate prolonged and widespread unemployment. A revival of international trade is indispensable if full employment is to be achieved in a peaceful world and with standards of living which will permit the realization of men's reasonable hopes.

What are the fundamental conditions under which commerce among the nations can once more flourish?

First, there must be a reasonably stable standard of international exchange to which all countries can adhere without sacrificing the freedom of action necessary to meet their internal economic problems.

This is the alternative to the desperate tactics of the past – competitive currency depreciation, excessive tariff barriers, uneconomic barter deals, multiple currency practices and unnecessary exchange restrictions – by which governments vainly sought to maintain employment and uphold living standards. In the final analysis, these tactics only succeeded in contributing to world-wide depression and even war. The International Fund agreed upon at Bretton Woods will help remedy this situation.

Second, long-term financial aid must be made available at reasonable rates to those countries whose industry and agriculture have been destroyed by the ruthless torch of an invader or by the heroic scorched-earth policy of their defenders.

Long-term funds must be made available also to promote sound industry and increase industrial and agricultural production in nations whose economic potentialities have not yet been developed. It is essential to us all that these nations play their full part in the exchange of goods throughout the world.

They must be enabled to produce and to sell if they are to be able to purchase and consume. The Bank for International Reconstruction and Development is designed to meet this need.

Objections to this Bank have been raised by some bankers and a few economists. The institutions proposed by the Bretton Woods Conference would indeed limit the control which certain private bankers have in the past exercised over international finance. It would by no means restrict the investment sphere in which bankers could engage. On the contrary, it would greatly expand this sphere by enlarging the volume of international investment and would act as an enormously effective stabilizer and guarantor of loans which they might make. The chief purpose of the Bank for International Reconstruction and Development is to guarantee private loans made through the usual investment channels. It would make loans only when these could not be floated through the normal channels at reasonable rates. The effect would be to provide capital for those who need it at lower interest rates than in the past and to drive only the usurious money lenders from the temple of international finance. For my own part I cannot look upon this outcome with any sense of dismay.

Capital, like any other commodity, should be free from monopoly control, and available upon reasonable terms to those who will put it to use for the general welfare.

The Delegates and Technical Staffs at Bretton Woods have completed their portion of the job. They sat down together, talked as friends and perfected plans to cope with the international monetary and financial problems which all their countries face. These proposals now must be submitted to the Legislatures and the peoples of the participating nations. They will pass upon what has been accomplished here.

The result will be of vital importance to every one in every country. In the last analysis, it will help determine whether or not people have jobs and the amount of money they are to find in their weekly pay envelopes. More important still, it concerns the kind of world in which our children are to grow to maturity. It concerns the opportunities which will await millions of young men when at last they can take off their uniforms and come home and roll up their sleeves and go to work.

This monetary agreement is but one step, of course, in the broad program of international action necessary for the shaping of a free future. But it is an indispensable step and a vital test of our intentions.

Incidentally, tonight we had a dramatic demonstration of these intentions. Tonight the Soviet Government informed me, through Mr Stepanov, Chairman of its Delegation here in Bretton Woods, that it has authorized an increase in its subscription to the International Bank for Reconstruction and Development to $1 200 000 000. This was done after a subscription of $900 000 000 had been agreed upon unanimously by the Conference. By this action, the Union of Soviet Socialist Republics is voluntarily taking a greatly increased responsibility for the success of this Bank in the post-war world. This is an indication of the true spirit of international cooperation demonstrated throughout this Conference.[1]

We are at the crossroads, and we must go one way or the other. The Conference at Bretton Woods has erected a signpost – a signpost pointing down a highway broad enough for all men to walk in step and side by side. If they will set out together, there is nothing on earth that need stop them.

1. In the event, the USSR declined to join the two institutions.

60 THE YALTA CONFERENCE, 4–11 FEBRUARY 1945

(a) *Tripartite dinner, 4 February*
(b) *Third Plenary meeting, 6 February*

Texts

(a) *Tripartite Dinner Meeting, 4 February 1945, 8:30 p.m., Livadia Palace*[1]

Present

United States	*United Kingdom*	*Soviet Union*
President Roosevelt	Prime Minister Churchill	Marshal Stalin
Secretary Stettinius	Foreign Secretary Eden	Foreign Commissar Molotov
Mr Byrnes[2]	Sir Archibald Clark Kerr	Mr Vyshinsky
Mr Harriman	Major Birse	Mr Gromyko
Mr Bohlen		Mr Pavlov

Bohlen Minutes

TOP SECRET

Subject: Voice of Smaller Powers in Postwar Peace Organization.

Before dinner and during the greater part of the dinner the conversation was general and personal in character. Marshal Stalin, the President and the Prime Minister appeared to be in very good humour throughout the dinner. No political or military subjects of any importance were discussed until the last half hour of the dinner when indirectly the subject of the responsibility and rights of the big powers as against those of the small powers came up.

MARSHAL STALIN made it quite plain on a number of occasions that he felt that the three Great Powers which had borne the brunt of the war and had liberated from German domination the small powers should have the unanimous right to preserve the peace of the world. He said that he could serve no other interest than that of the Soviet state and people but that in the international arena the Soviet Union was prepared to pay its share in the preservation of peace. He said that it was ridiculous to believe that Albania would have an equal voice with the three Great Powers who had won the war and were present at this dinner. He said some of the liberated countries seemed to believe that the Great Powers had been forced to shed their blood in order to liberate them and that they were now scolding these Great Powers for failure to take into consideration the rights of these small powers.

MARSHAL STALIN said that he was prepared in concert with the United States and Great Britain to protect the rights of the small powers but that he

Sources: The 4 February meeting is reproduced from Foreign Relations of the United States: Diplomatic Papers, *The Conferences at Malta and Yalta*: Washington, D.C. USGPO, 1955) pp. 589–91. The 6 February sitting is taken from: Beitzell, Robert (ed.), *Tehran Yalta Potsdam: the Soviet Protocols* (Academic International, 1970) pp 74–84.

1. The President acted as host.
2. Listed in a log, and by Stettinius, as being among those present, but not so listed by Bohlen.

would never agree to having any action of any the Great Powers submitted to the judgment of the small powers.

THE PRESIDENT said he agreed that the Great Powers bore the greater responsibility and that the peace should be written by the Three Powers represented at this table.

THE PRIME MINISTER said that there was no question of the small powers dictating to the big powers but that the great nations of the world should discharge their moral responsibility and leadership and should exercise their power with moderation and great respect for the rights of the smaller nations. (Mr Vyshinski said to Mr Bohlen that they would never agree to the right of the small powers to judge the acts of the Great Powers, and in reply to an observation by Mr Bohlen concerning the opinion of American people he replied that the American people should learn to obey their leaders. Mr Bohlen said that if Mr Vyshinski would visit the United States he would like to see him undertake to tell that to the American people. Mr Vyshinski replied that he would be glad to do so.)

Following a toast by the Prime Minister to the proletariat masses of the world, there was considerable discussion about the rights of people to govern themselves in relation to their leaders.

THE PRIME MINISTER said that although he was constantly being 'beaten up' as a reactionary, he was the only representative present who could be thrown out at any time by the universal suffrage of his own people and that personally he gloried in that danger.

MARSHAL STALIN ironically remarked that the Prime Minister seemed to fear these elections, to which the PRIME MINISTER replied that he not only did not fear them but that he was proud of the right of the British people to change their government at any time they saw fit. He added that he felt that the three nations represented here were moving toward the same goal by different methods.

THE PRIME MINISTER, referring to the rights of the small nations, gave a quotation which said: 'The eagle should permit the small birds to sing and care not wherefor they sang'.

After Marshal Stalin and the President had departed the Prime Minister discussed with Mr Eden and Mr Stettinius further the voting question in the Security Council. THE PRIME MINISTER said that he was inclined to the Russian view on voting procedure because he felt that everything depended on the unity of the three Great Powers and that without that the world would be subjected to inestimable catastrophe; anything that deserved [*preserved*?] that unity would have his vote. MR EDEN took vigorous exception to the Prime Minister and pointed out that there would be no attraction or reason for the small nations to join an organization based on that principle and that he personally believed it would find no support among the English public. THE PRIME MINISTER said that he did not agree in the slightest with Mr Eden because he was thinking of the realities of the international situation.

In reply to an inquiry of the Prime Minister in regard to the American proposal to the solution of the voting question, MR BOHLEN remarked that the American proposal reminded him of the story of the Southern planter who had given a bottle of whiskey to a Negro as a present. The next day he asked the Negro how he had liked the whiskey, to which the Negro replied that it was perfect. The planter asked what he meant, and the Negro said if it had been any better it would not have been given to him, and if it had been any worse he could not have drunk it.

Soon thereafter the Prime Minister and Mr Eden took their departure, obviously in disagreement on the voting procedure on the Security Council of the Dumbarton Oaks organization.

(b) *Third Sitting at Livadia Palace*

6 February 1945

[. . .] *Roosevelt* declared that a discussion of the question of an international security organisation could be started that day. Roosevelt believed it was their task to ensure peace for at least 50 years. In view of the fact that neither he, Roosevelt, nor Marshal Stalin, nor Churchill, had been present at Dumbarton Oaks, it would be a good idea for Stettinius to report on the question.

Stettinius said that an agreement had been reached at Dumbarton Oaks to leave certain questions for further examination and future solution. Of those questions the principal one was that of the voting procedure to be applied in the Security Council. At Dumbarton Oaks, the three delegations had had a throrough discussion of that question. Since then it had been subjected to continued and intensive study on the part of each of the three Governments.

On December 5, 1944, the President had sent Marshal Stalin and Prime Minister Churchill a proposal to have the question decided by setting forth Section C of Chapter VI of the proposals, adopted at Dumbarton Oaks, in the following manner:

C. Voting

1. Each member of the Security Council shall have one vote.
2. Decisions of the Security Council on procedural matters shall be made by an affirmative vote of seven members.
3. Decisions of the Security Council on all other matters shall be made by an affirmative vote of seven members including the concurring votes of the permanent members: provided that in decisions under Section A of Chapter VIII and under the second phrase of the first paragraph of Section C, Chapter VIII, a party to a dispute shall abstain from voting.

The text which he, Stettinius, had just read out, contained minor drafting amendments made in accordance with the Soviet and British remarks on the initial text proposed by the President.

The American proposal was in complete accord with the special responsibility of the Great Powers for the maintenance of universal peace. In effect, the American proposal demanded unqualified unanimity of the permanent members of the Council on all key issues relating to the maintenance of peace, including economic and military enforcement measures.

At the same time, the American proposal recognised the desirability of a direct declaration on the part of the permanent members that the pacific settlement of any dispute that might arise was a matter of general concern, a matter on which the sovereign states which were not permanent members had the right to set forth their views without any limitations whatsoever. Unless such freedom of discussion was ensured in the Council, the establishment of a world organisation, which they all wanted, might be seriously hampered or even made altogether impossible. Without the right of free and full discussion of such matters in the Council, an international security organisation, even if established, would differ greatly from what had been originally intended.

The document which the American delegation had presented to the two other delegations set forth the text of the provisions which he, Stettinius, had read out and a special list of decisions of the Council which, according to the American proposal, would demand unqualified unanimity, and a separate list of matters (in the sphere of disputes and their pacific settlement) on which a party to the dispute must abstain from voting.

From the standpoint of the Government of the United States, there were two important elements in the question of voting procedure.

The first was that for the maintenance of universal peace, which he, Stettinius, had mentioned, unanimity of the permanent members was needed.

The second was that for the people of the United States it was of exceptional importance that fair treatment for all the members of the Organisation be provided for.

The task was to reconcile those two main elements. The proposals made by the President to Marshal Stalin and Prime Minister Churchill on December 5, 1944, provided a reasonable and just solution and combined the two elements satisfactorily.

Roosevelt declared that in his opinion it would be well to have Stettinius list the types of decisions which were to be adopted in the Security Council on the unanimity principle.

Stettinius said that, according to the formula proposed by the President, the following decisions would require an affirmative vote of seven members of the Security Council, including the votes of all the permanent members:

(I)—Recommendations to the General Assembly on:

1. Admission of new members;
2. Suspension of a member;
3. Expulsion of a member;
4. Election of the Secretary-General.

(II) Restoration of the rights and privileges of a suspended member.

(III) Elimination of a threat to the peace and suppression of breaches of the peace, including the following questions:

1. Is the peace endangered as a result of non-settlement of a dispute between the parties by means of their own choice or in accordance with the recommendations of the Security Council?
2. Is there a threat to the peace or breach of the peace from any other action on the part of one or another country?
3. What are the measures to be taken by the Council for the maintenance or restoration of the peace and how are these measures to be implemented?
4. Should not the implementation of enforcement measures be entrusted to a regional body?

(IV) Approval of special agreement or agreements on the provision of armed forces and facilities.

(V) Formulation of plans for a general system of arms regulation and presentation of such plans to the member states.

(VI) Decision on the question whether the nature and activity of a regional body or regional measures for the maintenance of peace and security are compatible with the aims and purposes of the world organisation.

An affirmative vote of seven members of the Security Council, including the votes of all the permanent members, provided, however, that a member of the Council abstained from voting on any decision relating to a dispute to which he was a party, should be required for the following decisions relating to the pacific settlement of a dispute:

(I) Is the dispute or situation brought to the notice of the Council of such a nature that its continuance may endanger the peace?

(II) Should the Council call upon the sides to settle or adjust the dispute or situation by means of their own choice?

(III) Should the Council give recommendations to the sides in respect of the methods and procedures of settlement?

(IV) Should the legal aspects of the matter before the Council be referred to the International Court of Justice for an advisory opinion?

(V) In the event there is a regional body for the specific settlement of local disputes, should the body be requested to deal with the disputes?

Roosevelt believed the question could be discussed and settled. Big and small nations had one and the same purpose, namely, the preservation of peace, and procedural issues should not hamper the attainment of that aim.

Stalin asked what was new in the proposals set forth by Stettinius as compared with what the President had communicated in his message of December 5.

Roosevelt replied that those proposals were similar, with only minor drafting amendments.

Stalin asked what drafting amendments had been made.

Stettinius set forth these drafting amendments.

Molotov declared that the Soviet delegation also attached great importance to the questions raised and would like to study Stettinius's proposal. That was why he proposed that the discussion of the question be postponed until the next day's sitting.

Churchill remarked that he agreed with that. There should be no undue haste in the study of such an important matter. Its discussion could be postponed until the next day. He had not been quite satisfied with the initial proposals worked out at Dumbarton Oaks, because he had not been quite sure that those proposals had taken full account of the real position of the three Great Powers. After studying the President's new proposals, Churchill's doubts had disappeared, at any rate, as far as the British Commonwealth of Nations and the British Empire were concerned. That also applied to the independent dominions of the British Crown.

Churchill recognised that the question of whether the peace would be built on sound foundations depended on the friendship and co-operation of the three Great Powers; however, the Allies would be putting themselves in a false position and would be unfair to their intentions, if they did not provide for the possibility of the small states freely expressing their claims. Otherwise it would appear that the three chief Powers claimed to rule the world. As it was what they actually wanted was to serve the world and safeguard it from the horrors that had hit most of the nations in the current war. That was why the three Great Powers should show a readiness to submit to the interest of the common cause.

He, Churchill, was naturally thinking primarily of the effect the new situation would have on the future of the British Commonwealth of Nations. He would like to give a concrete example, an example which was a difficult one for Britain–Hong Kong. If the President's proposal was adopted, and China requested the return of Hong Kong, Great Britain would have the right to express her point of view and defend it; however, Great Britain would not be able to take part in voting on the questions set out at the end of the American document. For her part, China would have the right fully to express her view on the question of Hong Kong, and the Security Council would have to decide on the issue, without the British Government taking part in the voting.

Stalin asked whether Egypt was to be a member of the Assembly.

Churchill replied that Egypt would be a member of the Assembly but not of the Council.

Stalin declared that he would like to take another example, that of the Suez Canal, which was situated on the territory of Egypt.

Churchill asked that his example be examined first. Assuming that the British Government could not agree to the examination of one of the questions dealt with in Paragraph 3, because it considered that the question infringed the sovereignty of the British Empire. In that case, the British Government would be assured of success, because, in accordance with Paragraph 3, every permanent member would have the right to veto the actions of the Security Council. On the other hand, it would be unfair for China not to have the possibility of expressing her view on the substance of the case.

The same applied to Egypt. In the event Egypt raised a question against the British pertaining to the Suez Canal, he, Churchill, would allow the discussion of the question without any apprehension, because British interests were ensured by Paragraph 3, which provided for the right of veto. He also believed that if Argentina made a claim against the United States, the United States would submit to the established procedure of examination, but the United States would have the right to object and veto any decision by the Security Council. It could apply the Monroe Doctrine.

Roosevelt said that in the Tehran Declaration the three Powers had announced their readiness to accept responsibility for the establishment of a peace that would receive the approval of the peoples of the world.

Churchill stated that for the reasons which he had set forth the British Government did not object to the adoption of the U.S. proposals. Churchill believed it would be undesirable to create the impression that the three Powers wanted to dominate the world, without letting the other countries express their opinion.

Stalin declared that he would first of all ask that the Soviet delegation be handed the document which Stettinius had read out, because it was hard to study the proposals it contained by ear. To him, Stalin, it seemed that the said document was a commentary on the President's proposals.

Referring to the interpretation of the American proposals made at the sitting, Stalin said it seemed to him the Dumbarton Oaks decisions had aimed to ensure various countries not only the right to voice their opinion. That right was not worth much. No one denied it. The matter was much more serious. If any nation raised a question of great importance to it, it would do so not only to have the opportunity to set out its view, but to obtain a decision on it. None of those present would dispute the right of nations to speak in the Assembly. But that was not the heart of the matter. Churchill apparently believed that if China raised the question of Hong Kong, her only desire would be to speak out. That was not so. China would demand a decision. In much the same way, if Egypt raised the question of a return of the Suez Canal she would not be content with voicing her opinion on the matter. Egypt would demand a solution of the question. That was why the question was not just of ensuring the possibility of voicing one's opinions, but of much more important things.

Churchill expressed the apprehension that there might be an impression that the three Great Powers wanted to dominate the world. But who was contemplating such domination? Was it the United States? No, it was not thinking of that. [*The President laughed and made an eloquent gesture.*] Was it Britain? No, once again. [*Churchill laughed and made an eloquent gesture.*] Thus, two Great Powers were beyond suspicion. That left the third – the USSR. So it was the USSR that was striving for world domination? [*General laughter.*] Or could it be China that was striving for world domination? [*General laughter.*] It was clear that the talk of striving for world domination was pointless. His friend Churchill could not name a single Power that wanted to dominate the world.

Churchill interposed that he himself did not, of course, believe in the striving for world domination on the part of any of the three Allies. But the position of those Allies was so powerful that others might think so, unless the appropriate preventive measures were taken.

Stalin, continuing his speech, declared that so far two Great Powers had adopted the charter of an international security organisation, which, in the opinion of Churchill, would protect them from being charged with a desire to rule the world. The third Power had not yet given its consent to the charter. However, he would study the proposals formulated by Stettinius, and would possibly see the point more clearly. He believed, however, that the Allies were faced with much more serious problems than the right of nations to express their opinion or the question of the three chief Powers striving for world domination.

Churchill said there was no reason to fear anything undesirable even in the event of the American proposals being adopted. Indeed, so long as they were all alive, there was nothing to fear. They would not allow any dangerous divergences between them. They would not permit another aggression against anyone of their countries. But 10 years or possibly less might pass, and they would be gone. There would be a new generation which had not gone through what they had, and which would possibly view many questions in a different light. What would happen then? They seemed to be setting themselves the task of ensuring peace for at least another 50 years. Or was that the impression he, Stalin, had got because of his naïveté?

The unity of the three Powers was the most important requisite for the preservation of a lasting peace. If such unity was preserved, there was no need to fear the German danger. Thought should, therefore, be given to how best to ensure a united front between the three Powers, to which France and China should be added. That was why the question of the future charter of an international security organisation acquired such importance. It was necessary to create as many obstacles as possible to any divergence between the three chief Powers in future. A charter should be framed that would make it as difficult as possible for conflicts to arise between them. That was the main task.

On the more concrete question of the voting in the Security Council, Stalin asked the conference to excuse him for not having had the time to study the Dumbarton Oaks documents in every detail. He had been very busy with some other matters and hoped to have the indulgence of the British and American delegations.

Roosevelt and *Churchill* indicated by gestures and exclamations that they were well aware of what Stalin had been doing.

Stalin, continuing, said that, as far as he understood, all conflicts which might be brought up for examination by the Security Council fell into two categories. The first included disputes whose settlement demanded the application of economic, political, military or other kinds of sanctions. The second category included disputes which might be settled by peaceful means, without the application of sanctions. Stalin asked whether his understanding was correct.

Roosevelt and *Churchill* replied that it was correct.

Stalin then declared that, as far as he had understood it, there was to be freedom of discussion in the examination of conflicts of the first category, but the unanimity of the permanent members of the Council was required in the adoption of a decision. In that case, all the permanent members of the Council should take part in the voting, i.e., the Power which was party to a dispute would not be asked to leave. As for conflicts of the second category which were to be settled by peaceful means, another procedure was proposed in that case: the Power which was a party to a dispute (including permanent members of the Council) should not take part in the voting. Stalin asked whether his understanding of the provision was correct.

Roosevelt and *Churchill* again confirmed that Stalin had a fully correct understanding of the provision.

Stalin, concluding, said the Soviet Union was being accused of putting too much emphasis on the question of the voting in the Security Council. The Soviet Union was being reproached for making too much ado on the point. Indeed, the Soviet Union did pay great attention to the voting procedure, because the Soviet Union was most of all interested in the decisions to be adopted by the Security Council. After all, the decisions would be adopted by a vote. Discussions could go on for a hundred years, without deciding anything. But it was the decisions that mattered for the Soviet Union. And not only for it.

He, Stalin, asked those present to return for a moment to the examples given at the sitting. If China demanded the return of Hong Kong or Egypt the return of the Suez Canal, the question would be up for a vote in the Assembly and in the Security Council. Stalin could assure his friend Churchill that China and Egypt would not be alone in that. They would have their friends in an international organisation. That had a direct bearing on the question of voting.

Churchill stated that if the said countries demanded the satisfaction of their claims, Great Britain would say 'no'. The authority of an international organisation could not be used against the three great Powers.

Stalin asked whether that was in fact the case.

Eden replied that countries might talk and argue but no decision could be adopted without the consent of the three chief Powers.

Stalin asked once again whether that was actually the case.

Churchill and *Roosevelt* replied in the affirmative.

Stettinius declared that no economic sanctions could be applied by the Security Council without the unanimity of the permanent members.

Molotov asked whether the same applied to recommendations.

Churchill replied that that applied only to those recommendations which were mentioned in the five points formulated at the end of the American document. The international security organisation did not exclude diplomatic relations between the great and the small countries. Diplomatic procedures would continue to exist. It would be wrong to exaggerate the power or to abuse it or to raise questions that could divide the three chief Powers.

Stalin said there was another danger. His colleagues surely remembered that during the Russo–Finnish war the British and the French had roused the League of Nations against the Russians, isolated the Soviet Union and expelled it from the League of Nations, by mobilising everyone against the USSR. A repetition of such things in future must be precluded.

Eden declared that that could not happen if the American proposals were adopted.

Churchill confirmed that in the said case that kind of danger would be ruled out.

Molotov said that was the first time the Soviet side heard of that.

Roosevelt declared that there could be no recurrence of a case similar to the one mentioned by Marshal Stalin, because the expulsion of a member required the consent of all the permanent members.

Stalin pointed out that even if the adoption of the American proposals made it impossible to expel a member, there still remained the possibility of mobilising public opinion against any one member.

Churchill said he could allow a case when a broad campaign was started against a member, but then diplomacy would be operating at the same time. Churchill did not think that the President would want to come out against Britain or support any action against her. He was confident that Roosevelt would want to stop such attacks. Churchill was also confident that Marshal Stalin would not want to come out against Britain, without having a talk with Britain beforehand. He, Churchill, was confident that a way to settle disputes could always be found. At any rate, he could vouch for himself.

Stalin declared that he, too, could vouch for himself; [*half in jest*] perhaps Maisky over there would start attacking Britain?

Roosevelt noted that the unity of the Great Powers was one of their aims. He, Roosevelt, believed that the American proposals promoted the attainment of that aim. If any contradictions should unfortunately arise between the Great Powers, they would be known to all the world, despite any voting procedure. At any rate, it was impossible to eliminate the discussion of contradictions in the Assembly. The American Government believed that by allowing freedom of discussion in the Council, the Great Powers would demonstrate to the world the confidence they had in each other.

Stalin replied that that was correct and proposed that the discussion of the question be continued the next day.

61 The POTSDAM CONFERENCE, 16 JULY–2 AUGUST 1945

(*First Plenary Meeting, 17 July*)

Text

Churchill: Who is to be chairman at our Conference?

Stalin: I propose President Truman of the United States.

Churchill: The British delegation supports this proposal.

Truman: I accept the chairmanship of this Conference. Let me put before you some of the questions that have accumulated by the time of our meeting and that require urgent examination. We can then discuss the procedure of the Conference.

Churchill: We shall have the right to add to the agenda.

Truman: One of the most acute problems at present is to set up some kind of mechanism for arranging peace talks. Without it, Europe's economic development will continue to the detriment of the cause of the Allies and the whole world.

The experience of the Versailles Conference after the First World War showed that a peace conference can have very many flaws unless it is prepared beforehand by the victor Powers. A peace conference without the preliminary preparations takes place in a tense atmosphere of contending sides, which inevitably delays the working out of its decisions.

That is why I propose, considering the experience of the Versailles Conference, that we should here and now set up a special Council of Foreign Ministers, consisting of the Ministers of Great Britain, the USSR, the United States, France and China, that is, the permanent members of the Security Council of the United Nations set up at the San Francisco Conference. This Council of Foreign Ministers for preparing a peace conference should meet as soon as possible after our meeting. It is in this spirit and on these lines that I have drawn up a draft for the setting up of a Council of Foreign Ministers for preparing a peace conference which I now put before you.

Churchill: I propose that we refer the matter for consideration to our Foreign Ministers, who will report to us at our next sitting.

Stalin: I agree, but I am not quite clear about the participation of China's Foreign Minister in the Council. After all, this is a question of European problems, isn't it? How appropriate is the participation of China's representative?

Truman: We can discuss this question after the Foreign Ministers report to us.

Stalin: All right.

Truman: About a Control Council for Germany. This Council should start its work as soon as possible, in accordance with the agreement reached. With that end in view I submit for your consideration a draft containing the principles which, in our opinion, should govern the work of this Control Council.

Churchill: I have had no chance to read this document, but I shall read it with full attention and respect, and it then could be discussed. This question is so broad that it should not be referred to the Foreign Ministers, but we should study and discuss it ourselves, and then, if need be, refer it to the Ministers.

Truman: We could discuss this matter tomorrow.

Source: Beitzell, Robert (ed.), *Tehran Yalta Potsdam: the Soviet Protocols* (Academic International, 1970) pp. 141–52.

Seated:
Prime Minister Attlee (who replaced Churchill in mid-conference following the Labour Party's victory in the British General Election of 1945), President Truman, Marshall Stalin.
Standing, left to right:
US Fleet Admiral Leahy, British Foreign Secretary Bevin, Secretary of State Byrnes, Foreign Minister Molotov (Doc. 61) (US National Archives)

Figure 6.3 The Potsdam Conference, July–August 1945

Stalin: Indeed, we could discuss the question tomorrow. The Ministers could acquaint themselves with it beforehand; that would be advisable, because we ourselves will be studying the question at the same time.

Churchill: Our Ministers already have enough to do on the first document. Tomorrow we could refer this second question to them as well, couldn't we?

Stalin: Good, let's do that tomorrow.

Truman reads the content of a memorandum which says that under the decisions of the Yalta Declaration on Liberated Europe the three Powers undertook certain obligations in respect of the liberated peoples of Europe and Germany's former satellites. These decisions provided for an agreed policy of the three Powers and their joint action in the solution of the political and economic problems of liberated Europe in accordance with democratic principles.

Since the Yalta Conference, the obligations undertaken by us in the Declaration on Liberated Europe remain unfulfilled. In the opinion of the US Government, continued failure to fulfil these obligations will be regarded all over the world as indicating lack of unity between the three Great Powers and will undermine confidence in the sincerity and unity of purpose among the United Nations. That is why the US Government proposes that the fulfilment of the obligations of this Declaration should be fully co-ordinated at this Conference.

The three great Allied states must agree to the need for an immediate reorganisation of the present Governments of Rumania and Bulgaria in strict conformity with Paragraph 3, Point 'c' of the Declaration on Liberated Europe. Consultations must be held immediately to work out the procedure necessary for the reorganisation of these Governments so that they include representatives of all important democratic groups. After these Governments are reorganised, there may be diplomatic recognition of them on the part of the Allied Powers and conclusion of corresponding treaties.

In conformity with the obligations of the three Powers, set forth in Paragraph 3, Point 'd' of the Declaration on Liberated Europe, the Governments of the three Powers must discuss how best to help the work of the provisional Governments in holding free and fair elections. Such help will be required in Rumania, Bulgaria, and, possibly, in other countries too.

One of the most important tasks facing us is to determine our attitude to Italy. In view of the fact that Italy recently declared war on Japan, I hope that the Conference will deem it possible to agree to support Italy's application to become a member of the United Nations. The Foreign Ministers could work out an appropriate statement on this matter on behalf of the United Nations Governments.

Is it necessary to read the whole of this document? Do we have the time?

Churchill: Mr President, these are very important problems and we must have time to discuss them. The point is that our positions on these issues differ. We were attacked by Italy at the most critical moment, when she stabbed France in the back. We had been fighting Italy in Africa for two years, before America entered the war, and we suffered great losses. We even had to risk the forces of the United Kingdom, and to reduce our defences in the United Kingdom in order to send troops to Africa. We had big naval battles in the Mediterranean. We have the best of intentions in respect of Italy, and we have proved this by letting them keep their ships.

Stalin: That is very good, but today we must confine ourselves to drawing up an agenda with the additional points. When the agenda is drawn up any question can be discussed on its merits.

Truman: I fully agree.

Churchill: I am very grateful to the President for having opened this discussion, thereby making a big contribution to our work, but I think that we must have time to discuss these questions. This is the first time I see them. I am not saying that I cannot agree with these proposals, but there must be time to discuss them. I propose that the President should complete making his proposals, if he has any more, so that afterwards we could draw up the agenda.

Stalin: Good.

Truman: The aim of the three Governments in respect of Italy is to promote her political independence and economic rehabilitation and to ensure the Italian people the right to choose their form of government.

The present position of Italy, as a co-belligerent and as a Power that had surrendered unconditionally, is anomalous and hampers every attempt both of the Allies and of Italy herself to improve her economic and political position. This anomaly can be finally eliminated only through the conclusion of a peace treaty with Italy. The drafting of such a treaty should be one of the first tasks set before the Council of Foreign Ministers.

At the same time, an improvement of Italy's internal situation can be achieved by creating an atmosphere in which Italy's contribution to the defeat of Germany will be recognised. That is why it is recommended that the brief terms of Italy's surrender, and the comprehensive terms of Italy's surrender should be annulled and replaced by the Italian Government's obligations flowing from the new situation in Italy.

These obligations must stipulate that the Italian Government refrains from hostile action against any member of the United Nations; the Italian Government must not have any naval or air forces and equipment, except those that will be established by the Allies, and will observe all the instructions of the Allies; pending the conclusion of a peace treaty, control over Italy should be exercised as the need arises; simultaneously, there must be a decision on how long the Allied armed forces are to remain on the territory of Italy; finally, a fair settlement of territorial disputes must be ensured.

Because I was unexpectedly elected Chairman of this Conference, I was unable to express my feelings at once. I am very glad to meet you, Generalissimo, and you, Mr Prime Minister. I am well aware that I am now substituting for a man whom it is impossible to substitute, the late President Roosevelt. I am glad to serve, even if partially, the memory which you preserve of President Roosevelt. I want to consolidate the friendship which existed between you.

The matters which I have put before you are, of course, highly important. But this does not exclude the placing of additional questions on the agenda.

Churchill: Do you have anything to say, Generalissimo, in reply to Mr President, or will you allow me to do so?

Stalin: Please do.

Churchill: On behalf of the British delegation I should like to voice our sincere gratitude to the President of the United States for having accepted the chairmanship of this Conference, and I thank him for having expressed the views of the great republic which he represents and of which he is the head, and wish to tell him: I am sure the Generalissimo will agree with me that we welcome him very sincerely and it is our desire to tell him at this important moment that we shall have the same warm feelings for him that we had for President Roosevelt. He has come at a historic moment, and it is our desire that the present tasks and the aims for which we had fought should be attained now, in peacetime. We have respect not only for the American people but also for their President personally, and I hope this feeling of respect will grow and serve to improve our relations.

Stalin: Let me say on behalf of the Russian delegation that we fully share the sentiments expressed by Mr Churchill.

Churchill: I think we should now pass on to the ordinary items of the agenda and elaborate some kind of programme for our work to see whether we are able to cope with this agenda ourselves, or whether we should refer a part of the items to the Foreign Ministers. I do not think we should lay down the whole of the agenda at once, but can confine ourselves to an agenda for each day. For instance, we should like to add the Polish question.

Stalin: Still it would be well for all the three delegations to set forth all the questions they consider necessary to put on the agenda. The Russians have questions on the division of the German navy and others. On the question of the navy the President and I had an exchange of letters and had reached an understanding.

The second question is that of reparations.

Then we should discuss the question of trust territories.

Churchill: Do you mean the territories in Europe or all over the world?

Stalin: We shall discuss that. I do not know exactly what these territories are but the Russians would like to take part in the administration of trust territories.

We should like to raise as a separate question the resumption of diplomatic relations with Germany's former satellites.

It is also necessary to examine the question of the regime in Spain. We Russians consider that the present Franco regime in Spain was imposed on the Spanish people by Germany and Italy. It is fraught with grave danger for the freedom-loving United Nations. We think it would be good to create conditions for the Spanish people to establish a regime of their choice.

Churchill: We are still discussing the items to be put on the agenda. I agree that the question of Spain should be put on the agenda.

Stalin: I was merely explaining the idea behind the question.

Then we should also raise the question of Tangiers.

Churchill: Mr Eden has told me that if we got to the Tangiers question we could reach only a temporary agreement because of the absence of the French.

Stalin: Still it is interesting to know the opinion of the three Great Powers on this matter.

Then there should be a discussion of the question of Syria and the Lebanon. It is also necessary to discuss the Polish question with a view to solving the questions which arise from the fact that the Government of National Unity has been formed in Poland and the consequent necessity to disband the émigré Polish Government.

Churchill: I consider it necessary to discuss the Polish question. The discussion of this question which took place after the Crimea Conference undoubtedly resulted in a satisfactory solution of the Polish question. I quite agree to have the question examined as also the corollary question of the disbandment of the Polish Government in London.

Stalin: That's right, that's right.

Churchill: I hope that the Generalissimo and the President will understand that we have the London Polish Government which had been the basis for the maintenance of the Polish Army which fought against Germany. This produces a number of secondary questions connected with the disbandment of the Polish Government in London. I think that our aims are similar, but we certainly have a more difficult task than the other two Powers. In connection with the disbandment of the Polish Government we cannot fail to provide for the soldiers. But we must solve these question in the spirit and in the light of the Yalta Conference. In connection with the Polish question we attach very great importance, in Poland's interests, to the matter of elections, which should be an expression of the Polish people's sincere desire.

Stalin: For the time being, the Russian delegation has no more questions for the agenda.

Churchill: We have already presented our agenda to you. If you will allow me, Mr President, I should like to make a proposal concerning the procedure to be followed at the Conference. I propose that the three Foreign Ministers should meet today or tomorrow morning to select the questions which could best be discussed by us here tomorrow. We could follow the same procedure for the subsequent days of the Conference. The Ministers could draw up a better agenda by selecting three, four or five items. They could meet tomorrow morning and draw up an agenda for us.

Stalin: I have no objections.

Truman: Agreed.

Churchill: I think we have a general outline of our task and an idea of the volume of our work. I think the Foreign Ministers should now make their choice and put it before us, and then we can start working.

Stalin: I agree. What shall we do today? Shall we continue our sitting until the Ministers let us have five or six questions? I think we could discuss the setting up of the Council of Foreign Ministers as a preparatory institution for the coming peace conference.

Truman: All right.

Churchill: All right.

Stalin: We should discuss the question of the participation of China's representative in the Council of Foreign Ministers, if the idea is that the Council will deal with European questions.

Truman: China will be one of the permanent members of the Security Council set up at San Francisco.

Stalin: Is the decision of the Crimea Conference, under which the Foreign Ministers are to meet periodically to examine various questions, to be dropped?

Truman: We propose to set up the Council of Foreign Ministers for a definite purpose: to work out the terms of a peace treaty and to prepare a peace conference.

Stalin: It was established at the Crimea Conference that the Foreign Ministers are to meet every three or four months to discuss separate questions. This seems to be no longer necessary, doesn't it? In that case, the European Advisory Commission seems to be no longer necessary either? That is how I see it, and I should like to know whether or not I am taking the correct view.

Truman: The Council of Foreign Ministers is being set up only for a definite purpose – to work out the terms of the peace treaty.

Stalin: I have no objection to setting up the Council of Foreign Ministers, but then the meetings of Ministers laid down by the decision of the Crimea Conference are apparently called off and one should think that the European Advisory Commission is also no longer necessary. Both these institutions will be replaced by the Council of Foreign Ministers.

Churchill: The three Foreign Ministers, as we laid down at the Crimea Conference, were to meet every three or four months in order to give us advice on a number of important questions relating to Europe. I think if we add the representative of China to the Council of Foreign Ministers of the three Great Powers, this will only complicate matters, because the Council is to discuss questions relating to European countries. When we discuss the peace treaty relating to the whole world, and not only to Europe, the representative of China can be invited. Our three Ministers will be able to do their work more fruitfully and with greater ease. The participation of China's representative in the day-to-day activity of the Council would merely complicate its work. It is very easy to create organisations on paper, but if they produce nothing in reality, I think they are superfluous. In fact, are we not able to solve the question of the future administration of Germany without the participation of China? Let us confine ourselves to the three Ministers in the Council of Foreign Ministers.

Truman: I propose that we should postpone the discussion of the question of terminating the periodic meetings of the Ministers as laid down by the decision of the Yalta Conference. We are now discussing the setting up of a Council of Ministers to draft a peace treaty, and this is quite a different matter. I should like to submit to you the US draft on the Council of Foreign Ministers setting forth the principles of its organisation.

This draft calls for a Council of Foreign Ministers consisting of the Ministers of Foreign Affairs of the USSR, the United States, Great Britain, China and France. The Council is to meet periodically, and its first meeting is to take place on such and such a date.

Each of the Foreign Ministers is to be accompanied by a high-ranking deputy duly authorised and able to work independently in the absence of the Foreign Minister. He should also be accompanied by a limited staff of technical advisers. A joint secretariat is also to be set up.

The Council is to be empowered to draw up, with the aim of submitting to the Governments of the United Nations, peace treaties with Italy, Rumania, Bulgaria and Hungary. The Council is also to propose ways of settling territorial questions remaining open since the end of the war in Europe. The Council is to prepare comprehensive terms for a peace treaty with Germany which are to be accepted by the future Government of Germany, when a German Government suitable for that purpose is set up.

When the Council of Foreign Ministers deals with matters having a direct bearing on a state not represented on the Council, that state is to be invited to attend the Council meetings to take part in discussing the given question. That does not mean that invariable rules are being laid down for the work of the Council. The Council shall lay down a procedure in conformity with a given problem. In some cases the Council may be convened for preliminary discussion with the participation of other interested states; in other cases it may be desirable to convene the Council before inviting interested sides.

Stalin: Will it be a Council preparing questions for the future international peace conference?

Truman: Yes.

Churchill: The peace conference which will end the war.

Stalin: In Europe the war is over. The Council will determine and suggest the date for the convocation of a peace conference.

Truman: We think the conference should not be called before we are duly prepared for it.

Churchill: It seems to me there is no difficulty in concerting the aim we are striving for. We must set up a Council of Foreign Ministers to draft a peace treaty. But this Council should not substitute the organisations which already exist and deal with day-to-day matters – the regular meetings of the three Ministers and the European Advisory Commission, in which France is also taking part. The Council of Foreign Ministers is a broader organisation. There one can establish to what extent the European Advisory Commission and the regular meetings of the Ministers may deal with the questions of the peace treaty.

Stalin: Who in that case is to be subordinate to whom?

Churchill: The Council of Foreign Ministers is to exist parallel to the Security Council, in which China is also taking part, and parallel to the regular meetings of Foreign Ministers and the European Advisory Commission. Until victory over Japan, China will find it hard to take part in discussing European questions. We cannot benefit in any way from China's taking part in discussing European questions at present. Europe has always been a great volcano, and its problems should be regarded as being highly important. It is possible that at the time when the peace conference will be convened we shall have better news from the Far East and we could then invite China too.

I propose that in principle the peace treaty should be drafted by the five principal Powers, but as for Europe, its problems should be discussed only by the four Powers which have a direct interest in these matters. In this way we shall not disrupt the work of the European Advisory Commission and the regular meetings of Foreign Ministers. Both these organisations will be able to continue their work simultaneously.

Stalin: Perhaps we should refer this question to the Ministers for discussion?

Truman: I agree and do not object to China being excluded from the Council of Foreign Ministers.

Churchill: I think it would be possible to arrange things in such a way that some members would not take part in all the sittings, although they would enjoy full rights, as all the other members, but they would attend the sittings only when there was an examination of questions they were interested in.

Truman: As I see it, this question should be referred to the Foreign Ministers for discussion.

Stalin: Yes, that's right.

Truman: Can we discuss anything more today?

Stalin: Since all the questions are to be discussed by the Foreign Ministers, we have nothing else to do today.

Churchill: I propose that the Foreign Ministers should examine the question of whether there should be four or five members. But that this Council should deal exclusively with preparations for the peace treaty first for Europe and then for the whole world.

Stalin: A peace treaty or a peace conference?

Churchill: The Council will prepare a plan which it will put before the Heads of Government for examination.

Stalin: Let the Foreign Ministers discuss how necessary it is to keep alive the European Advisory Commission in Europe and how necessary it is for the regular meetings of the three Ministers, established in accordance with the Yalta decision, to continue their functions. Let the Ministers also discuss these questions.

Churchill: That depends on the situation in Europe and on what headway these organisations make in their work. I propose that the three Foreign Ministers should continue their regular meetings and that the European Advisory Commission should also continue its work.

Truman: We must specify the concrete questions for discussion at tomorrow's sitting.

Churchill: We should want to have something definite in the bag every night as we return home.

Truman: I should like the Foreign Ministers to give us something definite for discussion every day.

Stalin: I agree.

Truman: I also propose that we should start our sittings at four o'clock instead of five.

Stalin: Four? Well, all right.

Churchill: We submit to the Chairman.

Truman: If that is accepted, let us postpone the examination of questions until 4.00 p.m. tomorrow.

Stalin: Yes, let's do that. There is only one other question: why does Mr Churchill deny the Russians their share of the German navy?

Churchill: I have no objections. But since you have asked me this question, here is my answer: this navy should be either sunk or divided.

Stalin: Do you want it sunk or divided?

Churchill: All means of war are terrible things.

Stalin: The navy should be divided. If Mr Churchill prefers to sink the navy, he is free to sink his share of it; I have no intention of sinking mine.

Churchill: At present, nearly the whole of the German navy is in our hands.

Stalin: That's the whole point. That's the whole point. That is why we need to decide the question.

Truman: Tomorrow the sitting is at 4 o'clock.

62 STATEMENT BY PRESIDENT TRUMAN ANNOUNCING THE USE OF THE A-BOMB AT HIROSHIMA, 6 AUGUST 1945

Introduction

At the Potsdam Conference, President Truman had informed Marshal Stalin that the United States had developed a new weapon of great destructive power, but Stalin showed no special interest. All he said was that he was glad to hear this and hoped 'we would make "good use of it against the Japanese" ' (FRUS, 1960, Berlin, Vol. II, p. 378).

The present statement was drafted before the President left Germany, and Secretary of War Stimson was authorised to release it in Washington when the bomb was delivered. On 6 August, while returning from the Potsdam conference aboard USS *Augusta*, the President was handed a message from Secretary Stimson informing him that the bomb had been dropped at 7.15 p.m. on 5 August.

This is how the world at large first heard about nuclear weapons. Projects for their construction had been vigorously pursued throughout the Second World War, but their existence was wrapped in deepest secrecy. As the programme approached completion, discussions were held in the United States and Britain (prominently involving the Nobel scientist Niels Bohr) about disclosing the secret, because, as British Minister Sir John Anderson argued, the 'plans for world security which do not take account [of nuclear weapons] must be quite unreal . . . the future of the world will in fact depend whether [they are] used for the benefit or destruction of mankind (Gowing, 1964, p. 352).

But, meeting at Hyde Park on 19 September 1944, President Roosevelt and Prime Minister Churchill rejected the suggestion that 'the world should be informed regarding tube alloys [the bomb] with a view to an international agreement regarding its control and use' (Gowing, 1964, p. 447), and decided that a 'bomb' 'might perhaps, after mature consideration, be used against the Japanese'. But the last paragraph of Truman's statement here reproduced did launch the international negotiations on this subject that began with the Acheson–Lilienthal report of March 1946 and have continued to this day.

Source: *Public Papers of the Presidents of the United States: Harry S. Truman, April 12–December 31 1945* (Washington, D.C.: USGPO, 1961), Item 93, pp. 197–200.

Text

SIXTEEN HOURS AGO an American airplane dropped one bomb on Hiroshima, an important Japanese Army base. That bomb had more power than 20 000 tons of TNT. It had more than two thousand times the blast power of the British 'Grand Slam' which is the largest bomb ever yet used in the history of warfare.

The Japanese began the war from the air at Pearl Harbor. They have been repaid many fold. And the end is not yet. With this bomb we have now added a new and revolutionary increase in destruction to supplement the growing power of our armed forces. In their present form these bombs are now in production and even more powerful forms are in development.

It is an atomic bomb. It is a harnessing of the basic power of the universe. The force from which the sun draws its power has been loosed against those who brought war to the Far East.

Before 1939, it was the accepted belief of scientists that it was theoretically possible to release atomic energy. But no one knew any practical method of doing it. By 1942, however, we knew that the Germans were working feverishly to find a way to add atomic energy to the other engines of war with which they hoped to enslave the world. But they failed. We may be grateful to Providence that the Germans got the V-1's and V-2's late and in limited quantities and even more grateful that they did not get the atomic bomb at all.

The battle of the laboratories held fateful risks for us as well as the battles of the air, land and sea, and we have now won the battle of the laboratories as we have won the other battles.

Beginning in 1940, before Pearl Harbor, scientific knowledge useful in war was pooled between the United States and Great Britain, and many priceless helps to our victories have come from that arrangement. Under that general policy the research on the atomic bomb was begun. With American and British scientists working together we entered the race of discovery against the Germans.

The United States had available the large number of scientists of distinction in the many needed areas of knowledge. It had the tremendous industrial and financial resources necessary for the project and they could be devoted to it without undue impairment of other vital war work. In the United States the laboratory work and the production plants, on which a substantial start had already been made, would be out of reach of enemy bombing, while at that time Britain was exposed to constant air attack and was still threatened with the possibility of invasion. For these reasons Prime Minister Churchill and President Roosevelt agreed that it was wise to carry on the project here. We now have two great plants and many lesser works devoted to the production of atomic power. Employment during peak construction numbered 125 000 and over 65 000 individuals are even now engaged in operating the plants. Many have worked there for two and a half years. Few know what they have been producing. They see great quantities of material going in and they see nothing coming out of these plants, for the physical size of the explosive charge is exceedingly small. We have spent two billion dollars on the greatest scientific gamble in history – and won.

But the greatest marvel is not the size of the enterprise, its secrecy, nor its cost, but the achievement of scientific brains in putting together infinitely complex pieces of knowledge held by many men in different fields of science into a workable plan. And hardly less marvelous has been the capacity of industry to design, and of labor to operate, the machines and methods to do things never done before so that the brain child of many minds came forth in physical shape and performed as it was supposed to do. Both science and industry worked under the direction of the United States Army, which achieved a unique success in managing so diverse a problem in the advancement of knowledge in an amazingly short time. It is doubtful if such another combination could be got together in the world. What has been done is the greatest achievement of organised science in history. It was done under high pressure and without failure.

We are now prepared to obliterate more rapidly and completely every productive enterprise the Japanese have above grounds in any city. We shall destroy their docks, their factories, and their communications. Let there be no mistake; we shall completely destroy Japan's power to make war.

It was to spare the Japanese people from utter destruction that the ultimatum of July 26 was issued at Potsdam. Their leaders promptly rejected that ultimatum. If they do not now accept our terms they may expect a rain of ruin from the air, the like of which has never been seen on this earth. Behind this air attack will follow sea and land forces in such numbers and power as they have not yet seen and with the fighting skill of which they are already well aware.

The Secretary of War, who has kept in personal touch with all phases of the project, will immediately make public a statement giving further details.

His statement will give facts concerning the sites at Oak Ridge near Knoxville, Tennessee, and at Richland near Pasco, Washington, and an installation near Santa Fe, New Mexico. Although the workers at the sites have been making materials to be used in producing the greatest destructive force in history they have not themselves been in danger beyond that of many other occupations, for the utmost care has been taken of their safety.

The fact that we can release atomic energy ushers in a new era in man's understanding of nature's forces. Atomic energy may in the future supplement the power than now comes from coal, oil, and falling water, but at present it cannot be produced on a basis to compete with them commercially. Before that comes there must be a long period of intensive research.

It has never been the habit of the scientists of this country or the policy of this Government to withhold from the world scientific knowledge. Normally, therefore, everything about the work with atomic energy would be made public.

But under present circumstances it is not intended to divulge the technical processes of production or all the military applications, pending further examination of possible methods of protecting us and the rest of the world from the danger of sudden destruction.

I shall recommend that the Congress of the United States consider promptly the establishment of an appropriate commission to control the production and use of atomic power within the United States. I shall give further consideration and make further recommendations to the Congress as to how atomic power can become a powerful and forceful influence towards the maintenance of world peace.

63 ADDRESS BY UNITED STATES SECRETARY OF STATE GEORGE C. MARSHALL, URGING A PROGRAMME FOR EUROPEAN RECOVERY. GIVEN AT HARVARD UNIVERSITY, 5 JUNE 1947

Text

I need not tell you, gentlemen, that the world situation is very serious. That must be apparent to all intelligent people. I think one difficulty is that the problem is one of such enormous complexity that the very mass of facts presented to the public by press and radio make it exceedingly difficult for the man in the street to reach a clear appraisement of the situation. Furthermore, the people of this country are distant from the troubled areas of the earth and it is hard for them to comprehend the plight and consequent reactions of the long-suffering peoples, and the effect of those reactions on their governments in connection with our efforts to promote peace in the world.

In considering the requirements for the rehabilitation of Europe, the physical loss of life, the visible destruction of cities, factories, mines and railroads was correctly estimated, but it has become obvious during recent months that this visible destruction was probably less serious than the dislocation of the entire fabric of European economy. For the past ten years conditions have been highly abnormal.

The feverish preparation for war and the more feverish maintenance of the war effort engulfed all aspects of national economies. Machinery has fallen into disrepair or is entirely obsolete. Under the arbitrary and destructive Nazi rule, virtually every possible enterprise was geared into the German war machine. Long-standing commercial ties, private institutions, banks, insurance companies and shipping companies disappeared, through loss of capital, absorption through nationalisation or by simple destruction.

Economic System Not Working

In many countries, confidence in the local currency has been severely shaken. The breakdown of the business structure of Europe during the war was complete. Recovery has been seriously retarded by the fact that two years after the close of hostilities a peace settlement with Germany and Austria has not been agreed upon. But even given a more prompt solution of these difficult problems, the rehabilitation of the economic structure of Europe quite evidently will require a much longer time and greater effort than had been foreseen.

There is a phase of this matter which is both interesting and serious. The farmer has always produced the foodstuffs to exchange with the city dweller for the other necessities of life. This division of labor is the basis of modern civilization. At the present time it is threatened with breakdown. The town and city industries are not producing adequate goods to exchange with the food-producing farmer. Raw materials and fuel are in short supply. Machinery is lacking or worn out.

The farmer or the peasant cannot find the goods for sale which he desires to purchase. So the sale of his farm produce for money which he cannot use seems to him an unprofitable transaction. He, therefore, has withdrawn many fields from

Source: *The New York Times*, 6 June 1947.

crop cultivation and is using them for grazing. He feeds more grain to stock and finds for himself and his family an ample supply of food, however short he may be on clothing and the other ordinary gadgets of civilization. Meanwhile, people in the cities are short of food and fuel. So the governments are forced to use their foreign money and credits to procure these necessities abroad. This process exhausts funds which are urgently needed for reconstruction. Thus a very serious situation is rapidly developing which bodes no good for the world. The modern system of the division of labor upon which the exchange of products is based is in danger of breaking down.

The truth of the matter is that Europe's requirements for the next three or four years of foreign food and other essential products – principally from America – are so much greater than her present ability to pay that she must have substantial additional help, or face economic, social and political deterioration of a very grave character.

The remedy lies in breaking the vicious circle and restoring the confidence of the European people in the economic future of their own countries and of Europe as a whole. The manufacturer and the farmer throughout wide areas must be able and willing to exchange their products for currencies, the continuing value of which is not open to question.

Aside from the demoralizing effect on the world at large and the possibilities of disturbances arising as a result of the desperation of the people concerned, the consequences to the economy of the United States should be apparent to all. It is logical that the United States should do whatever it is able to do to assist in the return of normal economic health in the world, without which there can be no political stability and no assured peace.

Our policy is directed not against any country or doctrine but against hunger, poverty, desperation and chaos. Its purpose should be the revival of a working economy in the world so as to permit the emergence of political and social conditions in which free institutions can exist. Such assistance, I am convinced, must not be on a piecemeal basis as various crises develop. Any assistance that this Government may render in the future should provide a cure rather than a mere palliative.

Any government that is willing to assist in the task of recovery will find full cooperation, I am sure, on the part of the United States Government. Any government which maneuvers to block the recovery of other countries cannot expect help from us. Furthermore, governments, political parties or groups which seek to perpetuate human misery in order to profit therefrom politically or otherwise will encounter the opposition of the United States.

European Agreement Needed

It is already evident that, before the United States Government can proceed much further in its efforts to alleviate the situation and help start the European world on its way to recovery, there must be some agreement among the countries of Europe as to the requirements of the situation and the part those countries themselves will take in order to give proper effect to whatever action might be undertaken by this Government. It would be neither fitting nor efficacious for this Government to undertake to draw up unilaterally a program designed to place Europe on its feet economically. This is the business of the Europeans. The initiative, I think, must come from Europe. The role of this country should consist of friendly aid in the drafting of a European program and of later support of such a program so far as it may be practical for us to do so. The program should be a joint one, agreed to by a number if not all European nations.

An essential part of any successful action on the part of the United States is an understanding on the part of the people of America of the character of the problem and the remedies to be applied. Political passion and prejudice should have no part. With foresight, and a willingness on the part of our people to face up to the vast responsibility which history has clearly placed upon our country, the difficulties I have outlined can and will be overcome.

Notes and References

Introduction

1. Collections of treaties are among the standard sources for the study of world politics, important instances coming to mind being Dumont (1726–31), Rymer (1732), Martens (1803), and Parry (1969–80). In his introduction to Fred Israel's four volumes of *Major Peace Treaties of Modern History 1648–1967* (1967), Arnold Toynbee described peace treaties as the 'main sources' of the 'essential knowledge' of the history of modern international relations. Our own selection starts in earnest in 1494 (rather than 1648), and encompasses also political documentation that includes other treaties besides peace treaties, as well as speeches, messages, and legislative acts. In contrast with the Israel collection, the present work emphasises global politics and global problems rather than nation-states and territorial (prominently European) issues.

2 Portugal Starts a Global System

1. Among the presents sent from Africa was the first giraffe ever seen in China.
2. One *li* = approximately one-third of a mile.
3. He also signed a treaty of alliance with Maximilian, then ruling in the Netherlands.
4. Being a key participant, *inter alia*, in the wars of Italy (1494–1516), which, while regional in scope, were a precondition of Portuguese success at the global level. Notable moments of these wars included the League of Venice (1495) to counter the French invasion of Italy, and the League of Cambrai (1508) directed specifically against Venice.

4 The Cooptation of Britain

1. In one of his rare quips, soon after the landing, Calvinist William asked Anglican bishop Gilbert Burnet (who accompanied him as Royal Chaplain): 'Well, Doctor, what do you think of predestination now?' (Macaulay, 1914, p. 1128; Carswell, 1969, p. 184).
2. Heneage Finch, later 1st Earl of Nottingham, a signatory of both the Treaties of Westminster (Doc. 19) and Whitehall (Doc. 23).
3. At the time of writing this memorandum Leibniz was in the employ of the Archbishop Elector of Mainz. After 1676 he served the Dukes of Braunschweig–Luneberg, including the one who in 1714 succeeded to the British throne as George I. For another discussion of the memorandum, see Mahan, 1957, pp. 92; 124–5.
4. The Latin term *arbiter* includes the meaning of judge, umpire, and even master of the sea. The expression *arbiter mundi* was first used by Seneca with reference to Jupiter, and in the medieval period it carried religious connotations. (We have this information from Drs P. W. A. T. van der Laan and J. J. V. de Vet.) The Dutch, as a nation, were seen by their opponents as setting themselves up as 'arbiter and judge' over others (see introduction to Doc. 19 below.)
5. Leibniz argued that *dominium maris* confers an *arbitrium rerum* that in a French draft he described as 'la direction universelle des affaires et l'arbitrage entre tous les princes et toutes les républiques'.
6. Leibniz reached Paris in late March 1672 but never saw, or directly communicated with, Louis XIV or any of his ministers.

Bibliography

ALMEIDA, FORTUNATO DE (1922–9) História de Portugal, Coimbra: Imprensa da Universidade, Vol. 6.

ANONYMOUS (n.d.) *Armadas da India*, The British Library, MS: Additionals 20902.

Archives Parlementaires de 1787 à 1860 (1898, 1900), Paris: Tome 53, 58, Ière serie.

BAKER, RAY STANNARD (1922–3) *Woodrow Wilson and World Settlement*, New York: Doubleday, Page, 3 Vols.

BEACONSFIELD, EARL OF (1882) *Selected Speeches*, T. E. Kebbel (ed.), London: Longmans Green, 2 Vols.

BEAZLEY, C. RAYMOND (1894) 'The colonial empire of the Portuguese to the death of Albuquerque', London: *Transactions of the Royal Historical Society*, n.s., Vol. VIII.

BEITZELL, ROBERT (ed.) (1970) *Tehran Yalta Potsdam: the Soviet Protocols*, Hattiesburg, Miss.: Academic International.

BFSP: see British and Foreign State Papers.

BLAIR, EMMA HELEN and JAMES ALEXANDER ROBERTSON (1903–9) *The Philippine Islands*, Cleveland: A. H. Clark, Vol. I.

BOORSTIN, DANIEL J. (1983) *The Discoverers*, New York: Random House.

BOURNE, KENNETH (1970) *The Foreign Policy of Victorian England 1830–1902*, Oxford: Clarendon Press.

BOXER, C. R. (1969) *The Portuguese Seaborne Empire, 1415–1825*, New York: Alfred Knopf.

BOYD, C. W. (ed.) (1914) *Mr. Chamberlain's Speeches*, London: Constable, Vol. II.

BRANDT, REV. GERARD (1720–3) *The History of the Reformation and other Ecclesiastical Transactions in and about the Low-Countries*, London: Timothy Childe, Vols II and III.

BRAUDEL, FERNAND (1984) *The Perspective of the World*, London: Collins.

BRISSOT, JACQUES-PIERRE (n.d.) *Mémoires*, Paris: C. Perroud.

British and Foreign State Papers (BFSP), London, various years.

BRUCKER, GENE (1977) *The Civic World of Early Renaissance Florence*, Princeton: Princeton University Press.

BULHÃO PATO, RAIMUNDO DE (ed.) (1898) *Cartas de Affonso de Albuquerque seguidas de documentos que as elucidam*, Lisboa: Academia das Sciencias, Vol. 2.

BUELOW, BERNHARD FUERST VON (1930) *Denkwuerdigkeiten*, Berlin: Ullstein, Vol. I.

CARR, E. H. (1939) *The Twenty Years' Crisis 1919–1939: an Introduction to the Study of International Relations*, London: Macmillan.

CARSWELL, JOHN (1969) *The Descent on England*, New York: John Day.

CESSI, ROBERTO and PAOLO SAMBIN (eds) (1943) 'Diarii Veneziani del secolo Decimosesto: Delphini, Petri (Pietro Dolfin), Pars IV', in *Annalium Venetorum* (Annali Veneti), Venice: Istituto Veneto di Scienze Lettere ed Arti.

CHANDLER, DAVID G. (1979) *Dictionary of the Napoleonic Wars*, London: Arms and Armour Press.

CHURCHILL, WINSTON S. (1952) *The Second World War* (Vol. V, 'Closing the Ring'), London: Cassell.

——— (1974) *His Complete Speeches, 1897–1963*, Robert R. James (ed.), New York, Chelsea House Publishers: Vol. VII (1943–9).

CHYS, JACOBUS ANNE VAN DER (1857) *Geschiedenis der Stichting van de Vereenigde O.I. Compagnie en der maatregelen van de Nederlandsche regering betreffende de vaart op Oost-Indie, wellke aan deze Stichting voorafgingen*, Leiden: P. Engels.

CLARK, GEORGE NORMAN (1923) *The Dutch Alliance and the War against French Trade, 1688–1697*, Manchester: The University Press.

CLÉMENT, PIERRE (ed.) (1863) *Lettres, Instructions et Mémoires de Colbert*, Paris: Imprimerie Impériale, Vol. II(2).

COBBETT, WILLIAM (1809 . . .) *Parliamentary History of England from the Norman Conquest in 1066 to the Year 1803* and *Parliamentary Debates, 1803–*, London: Hansard, various Vols.

COBDEN, RICHARD (1880) *Speeches on Questions of Public Policy*, John Bright and James F. Thorold Rogers (eds), London: Macmillan.

COLE, CHARLES W. (1964) *Colbert and a Century of French Mercantilism*, Hamden, Conn.: Archon Books, 2 Vols.

CORTESÃO, JAIME, in Damião Peres (ed.) (1932) *História de Portugal: edição monumental*, Barcelos: Portucalense Editora, Vol. IV.

COSTIN, W. C. and J. STEVEN WATSON (1952) *The Law and Working of the Constitution: Documents 1660–1914*, London: A & C. Black, Vol. I (1660–1783).

COURT, PIETER DE LA (1702) *The True Interest of Holland*, London, Boxer.

DARU, PIERRE-ANTOINE (1840) *Histoire de Venise*, Brussels: Société Typographique Belge, A. Wahlen, Vol. 3.

DAVENPORT, FRANCES GARDINER (1917) *European Treaties bearing on the History of the United States and its Dependencies to 1648*, Washington, D.C.: Carnegie, Vol. 1.

DEGRAS, JANE (ed.) (1956) *The Communist International, 1919–1943: Documents*, London: Oxford University Press, Vol. I, 1919–22.

DELLA ROBBIA, LUCA DI SIMONE (1843) 'Vita di Bartolomeo Valori', Florence: *Archivio Storico Italiano*, Tome 4 (Part 1).

DIFFIE, BAILEY W. and GEORGE D. WINIUS (1977) *Foundations of the Portuguese Empire: 1415–1580*, Minneapolis: University of Minnesota Press.

DORT, SYNOD OF (1619) *Judgement*, London: John Bill.

DUYVENDAK, J. J. L. (1949) *China's Discovery of Africa*, London: A. Probsthain.

DUMONT, JEAN (1726–31) *Corps Universel Diplomatique du Droit des Gens*, Amsterdam: P. Brunel, R. et G. Wetstein, etc., Vol. 5.

FIRTH, SIR CHARLES HARDING and ROBERT SANGSTER RAIT (1911) *Acts and Ordinances of the Interregnum 1642–1660*, London: HMSO, Vol. II (1649–60).

FOREIGN RELATIONS OF THE UNITED STATES (FRUS): DIPLOMATIC PAPERS (1955) *The Conferences at Malta and Yalta 1945*, Washington, D.C.: USGPO.

——— (1960) *The Conference of Berlin 1945 (Potsdam)*, Washington, D.C.: USGPO, 2 Vols.

——— (1961) *The Conferences at Cairo and Tehran, 1943*, Washington, D.C.: USGPO.

FRANKLYN, JULIAN (1960) *Shield and Crest*, London: MacGibbon & Kee.

FRASER, ANTONIA (1979) *Royal Charles: Charles II and the Restoration*, New York: Alfred Knopf.

FRUS (1955, 1960, 1961) See Foreign Relations of the United States: Diplomatic Papers.

GARDNER, RICHARD N. (1956) *Sterling–Dollar Diplomacy*, Oxford: Clarendon.

GARVIN, J. L. (1934) *The Life of Joseph Chamberlain*, London: Macmillan, Vol. III.

GILBERT, MARTIN (1986) *Winston S. Churchill, Finest Hour 1939–1941*, London: Heinemann, Vol. VI.

GODINHO, VITORINO MAGALHÃES (1943–56) *Documentos sobre a expansão portuguesa*, Lisboa: Editorial Gleba, Vol. I 1943; Vol. II 1945; Edicoes Cosmos, Vol. III 1956. (Vol. I: navigation in fourteenth century; Ceuta, Canaries, Azores; Vol. II: Morocco, Tangier, African exploration to 1445; Vol. III: Piracy and commerce; Cadamosto; Alcacer–Segue; Cape Verde Islands to 1462; Western voyages.)

——— (1982) *Os Descobrimentos e a economia mundial*, Lisbon: Editorial Presenca, 4 Vols, 2nd edn.

GOIS, DAMIÃO DE (1949) *Cronica do Felicissimo Rei D. Manuel*, Coimbra: Imprensa da Universidade, new edn.

GOOCH, G. P. and HAROLD TEMPERLEY (eds) (1927, 1928) *British Documents on the Origins of the War, 1898–1914*, London: HMSO, Vols II and III.

GOWING, MARGARET (1964) *Britain and Atomic Energy, 1939–1945*, London: Macmillan.

GRAHAM, GERALD S. (1965) *The Politics of Naval Supremacy*, Cambridge: Cambridge University Press.

GREENLEE, WILLIAM BROOKS (1938) *The Voyage of Pedro Alvares Cabral to Brazil and India*, London: The Hakluyt Society, 2nd series, no. 81.

GROTIUS, HUGO (1916) *Mare Liberum*, James Brown Scott (ed.), English translation by Ralph Van Deman Magoffin, in *The Freedom of the Seas or the Right which belongs to the Dutch to take Part in the East Indian Trade, a Dissertation by Hugo Grotius*, New York: Oxford University Press.

GULICK, EDWARD VOSE (1955) *Europe's Classical Balance of Power*, New York: Norton.

HARLOW, VINCENT T. (1952, 1964) *The Founding of the Second British Empire 1763–1793*, London: Oxford University Press, 2 Vols.

HAZLITT, WILLIAM CAREW (1915) *The Venetian Republic*, London: A. & C. Black, Vol. I.

HOLK, L. E. VAN and C. G. ROELOFSEN (eds) (1983) *Grotius Reader*, The Hague: T.M.C. Asser Institute.

HOWARTH, DAVID (1982) *The Voyage of the Armada: the Spanish Story*, New York: Penguin Books.

ISRAEL, FRED L. (1967) *Major Peace Treaties of Modern History 1648–1967*, New York: Chelsea House, 4 Vols.

ISRAEL, JONATHAN I. (1982) *The Dutch Republic and the Hispanic World 1606–1661*, Oxford: Clarendon.

JENKINSON, CHARLES (ed.) (1785) *A Collection of all the Treaties of Peace, Alliance and Commerce between Great Britain and other Powers, from the Treaty signed at Munster in 1648, to the Treaties signed at Paris in 1783*, London: J. Debrett.

KENNAN, GEORGE F. (1967) *Memoirs 1925–1950*, Boston: Little, Brown & Co.

KIMBALL, WARREN F. (ed.) (1984) *Roosevelt and Churchill: the complete correspondence*, Princeton: Princeton University Press, Vols I and II.

LANE, FREDERIC, C. (1973) *Venice: A Maritime Republic*, Baltimore: Johns Hopkins.

LINCOLN, W. BRUCE (1968) *Documents in World History 1945–1967*, San Francisco: Chandler.

LIPPMANN, WALTER (1943) *U.S. Foreign Policy: Shield of the Republic*, Boston: Little, Brown & Co.

LODGE, HENRY CABOT (1925) *The Senate and the League of Nations*, New York, London: Scribners.

LOEWENHEIM, FRANCIS L., HAROLD D. LANGLEY and MANFRED JONAS (eds) (1975) *Roosevelt and Churchill: their secret wartime correspondence*, New York: Saturday Review Press/E. P. Dutton.

LOPES DE MENDONÇA, HENRIQUE (1892) *Estudos sobre os navios portuguezes dos séculos XV e XVI*, Lisboa: Typographia da Academia Real das Sciencias.

LOUIS, WILLIAM ROGER and HEDLEY BULL (eds) (1986) *The Special Relationship: Anglo–American relations since 1945*, New York: Oxford University Press.

MACAULAY, LORD (1914) *The History of England from the Accession of James II*, London: Macmillan, 6 Vols.

MAHAN, ALFRED T. (1957) *The Influence of Sea Power upon History 1660–1783*, New York: Hill & Wang.

MATTINGLY, GARRETT (1955) *Renaissance Diplomacy*, Baltimore: Penguin Books.

MCNEILL, WILLIAM H. (1953) *America, Britain, & Russia: Their Co-operation and Conflict 1941–1946*, London: Oxford University Press.

MITFORD, NANCY (1966) *The Sun King*, London: Michael Joseph.

MODELSKI, GEORGE (1987) *Long Cycles in World Politics*, London: Macmillan; Seattle: University of Washington Press.

——— and WILLIAM R. THOMPSON (1988) *Seapower in Global Politics, 1494–1993*, London: Macmillan; Seattle: University of Washington Press.

MOTLEY, JAMES LOTHROP (1856) *The Rise of the Dutch Republic*, London: Routledge.

——— (1895) *History of the United Netherlands*, New York: Harper, 2 Vols.

MURATORI, L. A. (ed.) (1733) *Rerum Italicarum Scriptores*, Vol. 22: 'Vite de' Dogi di Marino Sanuto', Milan: Typographia Societatis Palatinae.

MILLER, JOHN (1983) *The Glorious Revolution*, London: Longman.

NAPIER, HENRY EDWARD (1847) *Florentine History*, London: E. Moxon, Vol. 3.

NAPOLÉON 1er (1861–3) *Correspondence*, Paris: Plon, Dumaine, Vols 8, 10, 13.

NORWICH, JOHN JULIUS (1982) *A History of Venice*, New York: Penguin Books.

OLIVEIRA MARQUES, A. H. DE (1976) *History of Portugal*, New York: Columbia University Press, 2 Vols.

PANIKKAR, K. M. (1929) *Malabar and the Portuguese*, Bombay: D. B. Taraporevala.

PARRY, CLIVE (1969–80) *The Consolidated Treaty Series, 1648–1918*, New York: Oceana Publications.

PERES, DAMIÃO (ed.) (1932) *História de Portugal*, Barcelos: Portucalense Editoria, Vol. 4 (of 8).

——— (1947) *Regimento das Cazas das Indias e Mina*, Coimbra: Instituto de Estudios Historicos, Universidade de Coimbra.

PETRIE, CHARLES (1940) *Joseph Chamberlain*, London: Duckworth.

POSTHUMUS, N. W. (1964) *Inquiry into the History of Prices in Holland*, Leiden: E. J. Brill, Vol. I.

PRESCOTT, WILLIAM H. (1854) *History of the Reign of Ferdinand and Isabella*, London: Routledge, 2 Vols.

PRESTAGE, EDGAR (1929) *Afonso de Albuquerque*, Watford: Voss and Michael.

——— (1933) *The Portuguese Pioneers*, London: A. & C. Black.

PRESTWICH, MENNA (ed.) (1985) *International Calvinism, 1541–1715*, Oxford: Clarendon.

PRIULI, GIROLAMO (1934) *Diarii*, L. A. Muratori (ed.), Bologna: N. Zanichelli, Vol. II, Tome 34, Part III.

RANKE, LEOPOLD VON (1915) *History of the Latin and Teutonic Nations (1494 to 1514)*, London: G. Bell and Sons.

RANUM, OREST and PATRICIA (1972) *The Century of Louis XIV*, New York: Walker.

RAPKIN, DAVID (1987) 'World leadership', in G. Modelski (ed.), *Exploring long cycles*, Boulder, Col.: Lynne Rienner.

RAVENSTEIN, E. G. (ed.) (1898) *A Journal of the First Voyage of Vasco da Gama, 1497–99*, New York: Burt Franklin Publications, originally published by the Hakluyt Society, No. 99.

Reale Commissione per la publicazione dei documenti financiari delle Republica di Venezia (1912) *Bilanci Generali*, Venice: 2nd series, Vol. I, Tome 1.

ROMANIN, SAMUELE (1913) *Storia Documentata di Venezia*, Venice: Guisto Fuga, Vol. IV.

RYMER, THOMAS (1732) *Foedera*, London: J. Tonson, Vol. 11.

ROWEN, HERBERT H. (ed.) (1972) *The Low Countries in Early Modern Times*, New York: Walker.

SANUDO, MARINO (1969) *Diarii*, Bologna: Forni, Vols III and IV.

SARGENT, RALPH M. (1935) *At the Court of Queen Elizabeth: The Life and Lyrics of Sir Edward Dyer*, London: Oxford University Press.

SHERWOOD, ROBERT E. (1950) *Roosevelt and Hopkins: An Intimate History*, New York: Harper.

SOTTAS, JULES (1938) *Les Messageries Maritimes de Venise aux XIVe & XVe Siècles*, Paris: Société d'éditions geographiques, maritimes et coloniales.

STEEL, RONALD (1981) *Walter Lippmann and the American Century*, New York: Vintage Books.

SWIFT, JONATHAN (1951) *Political Tracts: 1711–13*, Herbert Davis (ed.), Princeton: Princeton University Press.

TACITUS, CORNELIUS (1971) *The Annals of Imperial Rome*, translated by Michael Grant, Dorset Press.

TEMPLE, SIR WILLIAM (1754) *The Works of Sir William Temple*, London: J. Clarke, T. Wotton, D. Brown, etc., Vol. III.

THATCHER, JOHN BOYD (1903) *Christopher Columbus*, New York and London: The Knickerbocker Press, 2 Vols.

THIRIET, FREDDY (1959) *Régestes des déliberations du Sénat de Venise concernant la Romanie*, Paris: Mouton, Tome 2, 1400–1430.

THOMPSON, WILLIAM R. and GARY ZUK (1986) 'World Power and the Strategic Trap of Territorial Commitments' *International Studies Quarterly*, Vol. 30(3), September, pp. 249–68.

TOYNBEE, ARNOLD (1967) 'Anarchy by Treaty, 1648–1967: a Commentary on the Documentary Record', in Fred L. Israel (ed.), *Major Peace Treaties of Modern History, 1648–1967*, New York: Chelsea House, 4 Vols.

TREVELYAN, GEORGE MACAULAY (1929) *History of England*, London: Longmans Green.

——— (1932) *Bolingbroke's Defence of the Treaty of Utrecht*, Cambridge: Cambridge University Press.

WEBER, MAX (1958) *The Protestant Ethic and the Spirit of Capitalism*, translated by Talcott Parsons, New York: Scribners.

WEBSTER, C. K. (ed.) (1921) *British Diplomacy, 1813–1815: select documents dealing with the reconstruction of Europe*, London: G. Bell and Son.

———(1969) *The Congress of Vienna 1814–1815*, London: Thames and Hudson.

WEINSTEIN, Donald (1960) *Ambassador from Venice: Pietro Pasqualigo in Lisbon, 1501*, Minneapolis: University of Minnesota Press.

WIENER, JOEL H. (ed.) (1972) *Great Britain: Foreign Policy and the Span of Empire 1689–1971, a Documentary History*, New York: Chelsea House, Vols. 1 and 3.

WILSON, CHARLES (1970) *Queen Elizabeth and the Revolt of the Netherlands*, London: Macmillan.

WOLF, JOHN B. (1951) *The Emergence of the Great Powers, 1685–1715*, New York: Harper & Row.

Index of Names